Diatessarica
PART X, SECTION II

THE FOURFOLD GOSPEL
THE BEGINNING

THE FOURFOLD GOSPEL

SECTION II
THE BEGINNING

BY

EDWIN A. ABBOTT

Honorary Fellow of St John's College, Cambridge
Fellow of the British Academy

"*The beginning of the gospel of Jesus Christ.*"
St Mark i. 1
"*In the beginning was the Word.*"
St John i. 1

WIPF & STOCK · Eugene, Oregon

Wipf and Stock Publishers
199 W 8th Ave, Suite 3
Eugene, OR 97401

The Fourfold Gospel; Section II
The Beginning
By Abbott, Edwin A.
Softcover ISBN-13: 978-1-6667-0096-1
Hardcover ISBN-13: 978-1-6667-0097-8
eBook ISBN-13: 978-1-6667-0098-5
Publication date 2/9/2021
Previously published by Cambridge University Press, 1914

This edition is a scanned facsimile of the original edition published in 1914.

PREFACE

THIS first volume of comment on the Fourfold Gospel must necessarily seem disproportionately large compared with the small number of the Synoptic verses covered by it. The reason is, that Mark's first chapter introduces a number of terms that must be discussed, each as it presents itself for the first time, and then not again. Should the work reach its proposed conclusion it would include about four Parts, as follows :—

Part I. The Beginning, that is to say, the antecedents, acts, and words, of John the Baptist, and the relations between John and Jesus up to the time when Jesus, as Mark says, came into Galilee "after John had been delivered up."

Part II. The Proclamation of the New Kingdom —the Kingdom of the Son—and the conflict between the Old and the New.

Part III. The Law of the New Kingdom—Victory through Defeat.

Part IV. The Defeat and the Victory.

The work is based on three convictions, strengthened by each additional year of study :—

(1) Each Gospel should be considered as a collection of traditions varying in date, source, authority,

historical accuracy, and spiritual insight. (2) All the Evangelists had great difficulties to contend with in ascertaining facts, and Mark, though the earliest, was the least capable of contending with these difficulties, owing to his ignorance of almost all the acts of the Lord except those in Galilee, and (probably) owing to circumstances that prevented him from completing or revising his Gospel. (3) The Fourth Evangelist, though a poet, is never consciously a writer of fiction. He sometimes records what is not true, but never what he knows to be untrue. He is a seer of the things in heaven, but one who begins by seeing the things on earth. We learn from his Gospel that angels must ascend before they descend, and that we cannot worship Jesus as Son of God until we have loved Him as Son of Man.

To the friends mentioned in the Prefaces of previous volumes of Diatessarica, Mr W. S. Aldis, Mr H. Candler, and the Rev. J. Hunter Smith, my thanks are again due for help in revising my proofs.

EDWIN A. ABBOTT.

Wellside, Well Walk
Hampstead, N W
1 Jan 1914

CONTENTS[1]

	PAGE
INTRODUCTION . .	xi

CHAPTER I

THE BEGINNING OF THE GOSPEL

§ 1	The subject for discussion	1
§ 2	"The beginning," in Mark	4
§ 3	Later aspects of "the beginning"	6
§ 4	What preceded "the beginning"?	8
§ 5	"Gospel" not mentioned by Luke and John	9
§ 6	Why does John prefer "word" and "life" to "gospel" in speaking of "the beginning"?	11
§ 7	The connection between "life" and "light"	15
§ 8	The Baptist is not "the light" but a witness to it	16
§ 9	The "light" is a Person, to be "received" by "believing"	18
§ 10	"Grace" through "Jesus Christ" . .	22
§ 11	"Declaring God" as distinct from "preaching the gospel"	25

CHAPTER II

JOHN BAPTIZING THE PEOPLE

§ 1	John the Baptist, (1) "preaching," (2) "bearing witness"	32
§ 2	"As it is written in Isaiah the prophet"	33
§ 3	"This was he that they said"	35
§ 4	"My messenger" .	36
§ 5	"Are we to expect another?"	37
§ 6	"The voice of one crying"	40
§ 7	Is "in the wilderness" to be taken with "crying" or with "prepare ye"? . . .	42

---

[1] For References and Abbreviations, see Introductory Volume, p. xiii foll.

CONTENTS

	PAGE
§ 8 "Preaching" or "making proclamation"	45
§ 9 Baptism	46
§ 10 In the Fourth Gospel, "baptizing" is subordinated to "bearing-witness"	50
§ 11 The baptism of John, continued by the disciples of Jesus	53
§ 12 Repentance	56
§ 13 "[With a view] to remission of sins"	59
§ 14 "Remission" and "washing"	62
§ 15 John's conditions for baptism	64
§ 16 Where did John baptize the people?	67
§ 17 John's clothing and food, passed over in the Third and the Fourth Gospel	68

CHAPTER III
JOHN PREACHING OR PROPHESYING

§ 1 John's first utterance	72
§ 2 "There cometh" and "behind me"	74
§ 3 "He that is mightier than I"	77
§ 4 "The latchet of whose shoes I am not sufficient to stoop-down and loose"	79
§ 5 "I [for my part] have baptized you with water, but he will baptize you with the Holy Spirit—and with fire"	81
§ 6 Baptism with blood	83
§ 7 "The Lamb of God"	85
§ 8 In what sense might the Baptist speak of Jesus as "the Lamb of God"?	88

CHAPTER IV
THE BAPTISM OF JESUS

§ 1 The "coming" of Jesus, when was it?	93
§ 2 The "coming" of Jesus, whither was it?	100
§ 3 "From Nazareth," "of Nazareth," "Nazarene," "Nazoraean"	102
§ 4 The place where Jesus was baptized	107
§ 5 "Ascending from the water," and "praying"	110
§ 6 The opening of the heavens	112
§ 7 "And straightway...he saw"	114
§ 8 The descent of the Spirit	117
§ 9 The Dove	120
§ 10 The voice from heaven	123
§ 11 The Baptist's interpretation of the voice	129
§ 12 The Johannine interpretation of the voice and the vision	131
§ 13 "The Son of Man"	133

CONTENTS

CHAPTER V

THE TEMPTATION

		PAGE
§ 1	"Tempting" in the Four Gospels	144
§ 2	Jesus, "driven forth" or "led up" or "led"	148
§ 3	"Into," or "in," "the wilderness"	154
§ 4	What happened during the "forty days"?	156
§ 5	"He was with the wild-beasts," in Mark	158
§ 6	The Johannine equivalent of Mark	164
§ 7	"And the angels began-to-minister (or, were-ministering) unto him"	173
§ 8	Matthew's version, and Luke's omission, of the "ministering" of the "angels"	176
§ 9	John, on this "ministering" of the "angels"	178
§ 10	"An angel hath spoken to him," in John	180
§ 11	"Angels," at the tomb of Jesus, in John	190
§ 12	"Temptation," implied in John	194

CHAPTER VI

JOURNEYING INTO GALILEE

§ 1	Mark's account	204
§ 2	Matthew's account	206
§ 3	Luke's account	207
§ 4	John's account of a first visit to Galilee	211
§ 5	John's account of a second visit to Galilee	215
§ 6	What happened in the Synoptic visit to Galilee?	216
§ 7	What happened in the first Johannine visit to Galilee?	219
§ 8	What happened in the second Johannine visit to Galilee?	227

CHAPTER VII

JESUS BEGINNING TO "PREACH"

§ 1	Christ's first words—in Mark and Matthew	234
§ 2	Christ's first words—in Luke	238
§ 3	Objections to the Lucan account of Christ's first words	241
§ 4	John on "appointed-time"	243
§ 5	John on "kingdom," "repentance," and "gospel"	245
§ 6	Christ's first words—in John	247
§ 7	The Dialogue with Nathanael	251

CONTENTS

		PAGE
§ 8	Which of these accounts is the closest to history?	253
§ 9	Why is not the gospel, or "good-tidings," called "the good-tidings of peace" by Mark, as by Isaiah?	259
§ 10	"I came not to send peace but a sword" . .	264
§ 11	"Peace," in Mark and Matthew .	267
§ 12	"Peace," at the beginning of Luke but not at the end	273
§ 13	"Peace," at the end of John, promised . . .	280
§ 14	"Peace" and "the Paraclete" .	283
§ 15	"Peace," in John, how imparted . .	289
§ 16	The Johannine "peace" and the Epictetian "peace"	293
§ 17	The last Johannine mention of "peace" . .	297
§ 18	Conclusion .	304

APPENDIX I

Nazarene and Nazoraean .   309

APPENDIX II

The Disciple that was " known unto the high priest "   351

APPENDIX III

The Interpretation of Early Christian Poetry[1] .   372

---

[1] This Appendix aims at illustrating from the Odes of Solomon the transition of Jewish poetic thought as it passed from Judaism into Christianity, and it is incorporated in this volume because many of the illustrations in it appeared to have an important bearing on the study of the Four Gospels both singly and conjointly For a detailed Table of its Contents, see p. 308.

INTRODUCTION

THOSE who have read the Introductory Volume that forms the first section of The Fourfold Gospel will be prepared to find in the following pages, on the one hand much less than a commentary on the Four Gospels, but on the other hand somewhat more than detached comments on those small portions of the narrative of the life of Christ which all the Four Gospels have in common.

The reasons for entitling it The Fourfold Gospel, having been stated in the Introductory Volume, will not be repeated here. Another title of the book might have been—and indeed was for many years in my manuscript—*Johannine Interventions*. Ultimately, this was rejected as being too technical, and also as suggesting that the Evangelist did not write a continuous gospel of his own, but merely wrote as an intervener, supplementing, rearranging, correcting, and patching, the writings of others John did much more than intervene. He composed a work that from first to last breathes artistic as well as spiritual unity. Yet the mention of the discarded title may usefully emphasize the fact that among the aspects in which the author of the Fourth Gospel will be regarded in the following pages, one will be that of an Intervener.

To the question "In behalf of what or whom does John intervene?" the Introductory Volume has given *prima facie* grounds for replying "In behalf of Mark, in order to explain harsh or obscure Marcan expressions altered or omitted by Luke (and sometimes by Matthew also)."

This work will deal with such expressions. Taking them in their Marcan order, we shall append to each, and explain, its corresponding Johannine intervention, if there is one If there is not, we shall note our failure to find it.

INTRODUCTION

For example, when we come to the saying of the Baptist about Jesus "There cometh *after* (or, *behind*) *me*," and find that Luke omits "*after* (or, *behind*) *me*," we shall look for a Johannine intervention. Finding that John does intervene—repeating "after me" more than once—we shall try to understand, in the first place, what John says, and in the second place, why John says it—in other words, 1st, the Johannine meaning, 2nd, the Johannine motive.

In this particular case both the meaning and the motive are fairly clear As regards the meaning, John repeats "after me" along with "before me" in such a way as to call the reader's attention to the double meaning of the prepositions, namely, order of time and order of dignity.

As regards the motive, we shall probably approximate to a correct sense of it if we imagine John as thinking aloud while the rolls of the Three Gospels lie open before him, and as saying "Luke omits 'behind me' because he thinks it implies that the Lord was the Baptist's inferior, but if the Lord from heaven followed 'behind' the Baptist for a time on earth, that is not a thing for His disciples to be ashamed of as though it denied that the Lord was 'before' the Baptist in nature and in eternal pre-existence. Mark's phrase, therefore, ought not to be passed over but rather to be set forth more fully so as to explain its meaning."

In this attempt to enter into the mind and purpose of the Fourth Evangelist we shall have to take into account other circumstances besides the rapidly growing authority of the Three Synoptic Gospels—circumstances of time and circumstances of place. Time, for the Christian Church, moved (so to speak) at a quickened pace toward the end of the first century. During the generation that followed the fall of Jerusalem, when the nations of the Empire began to flow into, and sometimes almost to overflow, the Churches founded by Jewish Apostles, a single decad might bring about for Christians in some parts of the Empire such changes of thought

INTRODUCTION

as a whole century could not have produced a little later on—new thoughts about the Coming of the Lord, and about His Person, and about the Kingdom of which He was to be the Ruler.

In different cities, as well as in different decads, different and varying influences would be at work. An Evangelist's course would have been comparatively simple if the Church had been battling with nothing more than Jewish conservatism, imperial suspicion, and philosophic contempt. These were persistent and calculable forces. So, too, was the opposition of ordinary paganism, or orthodox idolatry, the established worship of the gods of the several nations of the Empire. But, besides these, there was superstition in widely varying forms, sometimes satisfying itself with heathen mysteries, but occasionally deserting the camp of heathendom and creeping into the Church of Christ as supplying new kinds of secret rites, new methods of initiation, and perhaps more potent charms and incantations. Writing near Ephesus, a home of magic, midway between East and West, the author of the Fourth Gospel must be supposed to have taken cognisance of all these influences, and they may well make it difficult for us to follow all the ramifications of his allusive thought.

In our method of procedure there will also be this difficulty, that in passing consecutively from Marcan phrase to Marcan phrase, and comparing each with its Johannine equivalent, we may find it hard to retain consecutiveness of thought, or, at all events, of Johannine thought. The first words in Mark are "*The beginning* of the gospel of Jesus Christ." The first words in John are "In *the beginning.*" But what follows "the beginning" in John is very different from what follows "the beginning" in Mark. There is a consequent danger that our comment may occasionally break itself up into small fragments dealing with isolated verbalisms and not clearly bringing out a continuous line of thought.

INTRODUCTION

This danger we shall endeavour to avoid, partly by prefixing to each group of phrases a summary of the contextual thought, and partly by allowing ourselves great latitude in the Johannine comment. True, we shall regard the Evangelist as having the Three Synoptic Gospels open before him. But we also think of him as contemplating the changed and changing condition of the Churches of Christ, keeping his eyes open to those "other circumstances" above mentioned which demanded from him a Gospel that should be, not a mere patching, or enlarging, of Mark, but a new and spiritual exposition of Christ's Gospel, so new as almost to amount to a new manifestation of His Spirit. He will be regarded as looking forward in his Gospel rather than backward—forward to the needs of Christ's Church rather than backward to the exact record of His acts and words in Galilee and Judaea.

These Johannine comments will be given as far as possible without footnotes or disquisitions on special points interesting in themselves but liable to call off attention from the subject in hand. Yet now and then there may occur an instance of Mark-John parallelism which absolutely requires discussion before we can proceed, and for the discussion of which we cannot refer to any previous Part of Diatessarica. Take, for example, the first Marcan mention of Nazareth, "there came Jesus *from* (or, *of*) *Nazareth.*" The parallel Matthew and Luke omit the word. John, therefore, according to our rule, is bound to intervene, and we have to note the intervention.

In this case—one of special importance because the terms Nazarene, Nazoraean, and Nazareth, are curiously varied by the Synoptists, and eminent modern students are doubtful as to their origin—we cannot possibly pass over the fact that John, alone of the Evangelists, connects his first mention of "Nazareth" with an objection to it raised by Nathanael. Also John, alone of the Evangelists, includes "the Nazoraean" in the title written by Pilate on the Cross. That is especially

INTRODUCTION

noteworthy because John tells us that the chief priests wished to have a part of the title modified, and that Pilate refused, saying "What I have written, I have written."

This raises a number of questions: "Did John regard Pilate as the mere instrument of Providence in writing the whole of this title? Did he believe that there was some mystical meaning in "*Nazoraean*" as well as in "King of the Jews[1]"? Did he share Matthew's belief that Christ's residence in Nazareth was ordained as a fulfilment of the prophecy "He shall be called a *Nazoraean*"? If so, what "prophecy" did he suppose to have contained these words? And what was the meaning of "*Nazoraean*" in the "prophecy"? To give some brief answer to these questions at once—when Nazareth first came before us—seemed necessary. Yet to give it briefly without an Appendix to support it was impossible[2].

The reader will notice that, in the brief outline of the four proposed parts of The Fourfold Gospel given in the Preface, the New Kingdom is mentioned twice. That accords with the prominence given to "the Kingdom of God" by the Synoptists. But it does not accord with the nomenclature of the Fourth Gospel, which nowhere mentions "the Kingdom of God" or Christ's "Kingdom," except in two brief passages, where Jesus tells Nicodemus and Pilate, severally, that, in effect, they do not understand what "the Kingdom" means[3]. The Fourth Gospel presents God to us not as King but as

---

[1] The Synoptists all have here "The King of the Jews," but not "the Nazoraean"

[2] Appendix I deals with Nazareth Appendix II, on "the disciple" that was (R.V.) "known unto the high priest," bears on the antecedents of the reputed author of the Fourth Gospel

Appendix III, on the interpretation of early Christian poetry, following the line of investigation indicated in *Light on the Gospel from an Ancient Poet*, attempts to shew the importance of keeping in view Hebrew and Jewish (as distinct from Greek) thought and language, in the interpretation of Christian poetry that may be of a very early date.

[3] Jn iii 3—5, xviii. 36.

INTRODUCTION

Father. Nor does it define the Father as being "in heaven" To be with the Father is to be in heaven. "Heaven" is rarely mentioned in the Fourth Gospel except in connection with "the bread from heaven" or "the Son from heaven"; and after the conclusion of the doctrine of "the bread from heaven" Jesus does not mention "heaven" any more[1]. We are to be one with the Father, or in the Father through the Son, or we are to live through the Son as the Son lives through the Father. Place is nowhere mentioned by Jesus in this Gospel except as being "prepared" by Himself[2]. Place is nothing, personality is everything.

And is there not a great deal to be said historically for this view as correctly representing Christ's teaching, not indeed in its words but in its thought? Did not Jesus *always* mean —though He may have seldom said so in express words— that the pure in heart see God, that heaven is the regenerate conscience; that the way to receive the Father is to receive the Son; and that the way to receive the Son is to receive those whom the Son loves as His brethren and whom He bids us love with the love with which He loved us? This will appear to be the case (I think) as we proceed with our comparison of the Three Gospels with the Fourth; and the Synoptic doctrine of receiving little children and becoming as little children will appear to be radically the same as the Johannine doctrine of being begotten from above by receiving the Son.

At the same time it cannot be denied that the local as well as the temporal environment of the Evangelist probably modified the form of the Johannine Gospel. Tradition says that the Gospel originated from Ephesus, the first of the

---

[1] "Heaven" is mentioned by Jesus in vi 32—58, about eight times, and not afterwards. In Jn iii 13 the words "*who is in heaven*" (*Joh Gr* 2275) are rejected by W. H.

[2] "Place" is nowhere mentioned by Jesus exc Jn xiv 2—3 (twice) "I go to prepare a place for you"

INTRODUCTION

Seven Churches addressed in Revelation. Ephesus (according to the Acts) was the place where many people "practised magical arts," and where certain Jews attempted to cast out evil spirits with the words "I adjure you by Jesus whom Paul preacheth[1]" Plutarch says that "magicians" recommended, to "those possessed by demons," the use of "Ephesian writings (*or*, letters)[2]" They were to be repeated by the sufferers, word for word, and name for name, when the paroxysm attacked them. These two lines of independent evidence point to the conclusion that in the Church of Ephesus, more than in others, there would be a tendency to turn the moral and spiritual doctrines of Jesus into magical prescriptions or charm-doctrines that would deliver those who used them, not from sin but from bodily pains and superstitious fears

In such a city, more than in any other, it might be thought expedient to publish a Gospel of Jesus Christ that might omit every one of His acts of exorcism and also every reference to such acts proceeding either from friends or from enemies or from the neutral and undecided multitude

In such a city also, it might be deemed more than usually necessary to anticipate, and if possible to check, a tendency to convert God's attributes, or characters, or gifts, into angels, principalities, or powers, intervening between God and men This tendency would be natural for polytheists, who had but yesterday regarded God as "the Father of *gods* and men," and who came to-day into a Church where the old "*gods*" disappeared. Giving up their old "*gods*," they might crave some substitutes to bridge the gulf of which they were conscious between them and the One solitary God of the Hebrews, whom they were now expected to worship, but whom they could not worship rightly as God the Father because they failed to love Him as their real Father, not first

---

[1] Acts xix 13—19
[2] See *Enc Bibl* col 1304, quoting Plutarch *Symp.* vii 5. 4

INTRODUCTION

loving Christ as His real Son Not realising the divinity of the Love revealed in Christ, and the divine nature of the loving unity between Father and Son and between God and regenerate Man, they substituted for this one real and spiritual link a number of unreal quasi-spiritual or quasi-intellectual links that put God far off from them instead of drawing them nearer to Him. It is against such a tendency—nominally a bridging over, but really a rending asunder—that Paul records his protest in behalf of "love" as the only true union : " I am persuaded that neither death nor life, nor angels nor principalities, nor things present nor things to come, nor powers, nor height, nor depth, nor any other created thing, shall be able to separate us from the love of God which is in Christ Jesus our Lord[1]."

Bearing the probability of this tendency in mind we can hardly fail to learn something from a comparison of the Prologue of the Fourth Gospel with the first chapter of Irenaeus' Treatise against Heresies. Both of them mention Beginning (Arché), and Word (Logos), and Life (Zoe), and Man (Anthropos), and Only begotten (Monogenēs), and Grace (Charis), and Truth (Aletheia), and Fulness (Pleroma). But the Gospel concentrates all these thoughts on the revelation of God, who is mentioned almost at once : " In the beginning was the Word, and the Word was with *God*." Also, without at first mentioning the word "Father," the Prologue leads us to the thought of the divine Fatherhood by describing men as receiving authority to become God's "children," and as being "begotten from God."

The heretics on the other hand (according to Irenaeus) did not mention God at first, but began by maintaining that

---

[1] Rom viii 38—9 Comp. Eph iii 17—19 "that ye, being rooted and grounded *in love*, may be strong to apprehend, with all the saints, what is the breadth and length and height and depth, and to know *the love of Christ* which passeth knowledge, that ye may be filled unto all the fulness of God."

INTRODUCTION

"there is in the invisible and ineffable heights above a perfect *aeon*, being-before [all]" This (he says) "they call Proarché (Fore-beginning) and Propator (Fore-father) and Bythos (Depth)" Thence they deduced a group of aeons or emanations, making some thirty in all.

It will be observed that the term "Father"—which is absent from the first section of the Johannine Prologue—occurs here in the term "Fore-father." Later on, it occurs as "Father" simply. But much of the beauty of the thought of fatherhood disappears when we are given to understand apparently that "Fore-father" is the higher appellation; and it almost entirely evaporates when we learn that the highest appellation is Depth

Obviously the Gnostic heretics borrowed much from the Fourth Gospel But they did not borrow from it the first of their aeons, that is, Bythos, or Depth, for the Fourth Gospel does not mention this. Did they derive this from the language in the Epistle to the Romans about "angels and principalities" and "powers" and "height and *depth*"? Hardly, for in the first place the Pauline *Bathos* is not quite the same as the Gnostic *Bythos*[1], and in the next place the Pauline language is against the Gnostic erection of such an abstraction as the Depth into the position of the First of divine Beings. It seems reasonable, however, to say that the similarity is not accidental, and that Gnostic talk about a divine unfathomable Depth—even before Gnosticism had taken definite shape—was already in the air when Paul wrote to the Romans from Ephesus, and still more afterwards when the Ephesian Epistle connected "the breadth and length and height and *depth*" with "the love of Christ which passeth knowledge."

---

[1] The Gnostic word is βυθός, the Pauline is βάθος Elsewhere βάθος is used in a good sense being connected expressly or by implication with God (Rom xi 33, 1 Cor ii. 10, Eph iii 18). Rev ii. 24 mentions "the deep-things (βαθέα) [not of God but] of Satan."

INTRODUCTION

If this was the case, and if even such early documents as the Epistles to the Romans and to the Ephesians contain hints that "height and depth," even though divine, must not be made into divine beings or regarded as objects of intellectual apprehension, much more easily may we suppose hints or warnings of this kind to underlie the Fourth Gospel. Perhaps, by contrast, they may help to explain what has been called by some the egotism attributed to Jesus in it. This, it has been said, is not historical. And indeed it is true that nothing can be found in the Synoptic Gospels resembling such expressions as "I am the true bread," "I am the good shepherd," "I am the light of the world," "I am the way, the truth, and the life."

But the Fourth Evangelist knew that the concentration implied by him in this repeated "I," was implied by the Synoptists in the claims put forward for "the Son of Man" Only "the Son of Man" was not a title that brought home to Greek readers all that Jesus meant by it. Even for Jews it had complex associations. But it was still more obscure for Gentiles, especially when they began to connect the term with one aspect of it, and that a narrow one—the thought of the Son as the Judge seated on the clouds of heaven Thus narrowed, the term did not express the claims of the personality of Jesus, the One Lord, upon the loyalty and love of His followers on earth. Gnostics, or those who were preparing the way for Gnosticism, were dissipating that personality, and substituting for it a multitude of aeons, principalities, or powers. Ebionites, or those who were preparing the way for Ebionitism, were narrowing down the personality to that of a Son of David, a king or prophet-king of Israel, superior to all preceding kings of Israel and Judah, and indeed to all the kings of the earth—but still, of the earth

For instructing or warning both these classes, whether rudimentary Gnostics or rudimentary Ebionites, it might seem to the Evangelist expedient that Jesus should be presented as a Person who continually said "*I*" and "*me*[1]", as one whose first precept to His disciples was "*Come*"—meaning "Come and see where I abide", and whose last prayer for them to the Father was that the love wherewith the Father loved Him should be in them, "*and I in them*"—a Son indeed, but a Son who could say "He that hath seen me hath seen the Father[2]."

This doctrine, this combination of authority with obedience, of lordship with sonship, of outward littleness with inward greatness, and of the perfectly human with the perfectly divine, was implied in the Marcan doctrine identifying the reception of the "little child" with the reception of Jesus, and the reception of Jesus with the reception of God—"Whosoever receiveth me receiveth not me but him that sent me." But it needed to be illustrated and inculcated, so as to shew that "receiving" did not mean receiving as a mere guest, or as a mere temporary tenant, but as a part of one's own self, and yet as an indwelling Spirit that controlled one's own self. To explain this, or rather to insinuate the feeling of it into us, the Evangelist accumulates metaphor on metaphor—sometimes in his own person, sometimes through the language of Jesus, whether in dialogue or in prolonged discourse—metaphors of purifying, of feeding, of enlightening, of healing, generating, and life-giving

All these point to one truth—that God cannot be rightly worshipped by legal or prescribed rule, or by visible and material guidance, but only in the Spirit of His Son, who lived and died visibly for mankind once that He might live invisibly in mankind for ever. That Jesus did not actually use all these metaphors is probable, if not certain. But that is quite consistent with the belief that He meant all that they

---

[1] See *Joh Voc.* 1713 shewing that "I" (nom) occurs in Jn nearly twice as often as in the three Synoptists taken all together.
[2] Jn 1 39, xvii 26, xiv 9

INTRODUCTION

mean, and a great deal more that neither they nor any metaphor can express

This lengthy Introduction would have been needless if the author could have felt sure that his readers were familiar with the Jewish canon "Whosoever translates a verse of scripture according to its outward form is a liar." Let us try to realise how much this canon may explain in an Evangelist striving to express the thoughts of Jesus in a form adapted for Greeks, at a time when the words of Jesus had begun to assume, for Christians, the authority of Oracles (*Logia*) or Scripture.

The instance given in the canon is from Exodus "*they saw the God of Israel*" Whoever translates that literally is said to be "a liar," for "they could not possibly *see God*[1]." Now the New Scripture, according to Matthew, says that "the clean in heart" shall "*see God.*" Luke omits this. John begins his Gospel with the admission that "*no man hath seen God*[2]" But the same sentence adds that Christ has "declared" Him. And John proceeds to shew how Christ not only declared Him in doctrine but also made His disciples "*clean*[3]," so that they *might* "*see God*", and, later on, how He said to Philip "He that hath *seen me* hath *seen the Father*[4]." Thus we are taught, first, negatively, that a materialistic theophany is impossible, and then, positively, that an "interpretation" or "declaration" is possible, but not one that comes through the understanding, or from a priest. It must be through the heart and from the Son. Philip, without knowing it, has already "seen the Father" because he has "seen the Son" who has made him "clean in heart."

Even those who feel unable to believe that Jesus uttered these words to Philip may be able to believe that Jesus,

---

[1] See *Son of Man* **3374** A (6) quoting Exod xxiv 10.
[2] Jn i 18
[3] Jn xiii 10, xv 3. On "declaring" see p 25, n 3.
[4] Jn xiv 9.

though expressing the deed in different words, did the deed implied by the words. That is to say, He cleansed the hearts of the disciples so that they saw in Him, and loved in Him, the fulness of the grace and truth of God, thus being led to the love of the Father in heaven through the love of the Son on earth. It is this characteristic—this dealing with spiritual *fact*—that often gives the Fourth Gospel a peculiar value It often intervenes where the Three Gospels differ in words, as though it said, "I cannot tell you the *words* of Christ, but I can tell you His *mind*, as it was revealed to the Disciple whom He loved."

But perhaps "I can tell you the *mind* of Christ" is not the right expression. It is too weak. For "mind" is weaker than "love" And it is too strong. For did the Evangelist really think that he was able to "tell" so deep a mystery—or even to "tell" it in the form in which it was "revealed" to the beloved Disciple? Perhaps it would be better to regard him as conscious that he could not tell it, but that he could prepare his readers to receive it—"the mystery of God, namely, Christ[1]." If his readers had asked him for a definite answer to the question "Who is your Lord?" he would perhaps have replied to them—although the Lord was all the while enthroned in his heart—"Indeed, I cannot tell[2]."

---

[1] Coloss ii 2
[2] Comp *Gitanjali* § 102 "I boasted among men that I had known you They see your pictures in all works of mine They come and ask me, 'Who is he?' I know not how to answer them I say, '*Indeed, I cannot tell*' They blame me and they go away in scorn. And you sit there smiling"

CHAPTER I

THE BEGINNING OF THE GOSPEL

§ 1. *The subject for discussion*

IN the following discussion of Mark's opening words the first difficulty is to perceive that there is anything to discuss The phrase is Pauline. "*In the beginning of the gospel,*" says Paul to the Philippians, "when I departed from Macedonia, no church had fellowship with me in the matter of giving and receiving but ye only, for even in Thessalonica ye sent once and again unto my need[1]." Here "*the gospel*" means "the preaching of *the gospel in Europe,*" and "*the beginning of the gospel*" means the time when Paul was beginning to preach it in Europe—first in Philippi, then in Thessalonica, and then, when he "departed from Macedonia," in Athens and Corinth. The Apostle of the West speaks of the beginning of the gospel in the West as a general might say—to officers who had recently fought under his command against a special enemy—"in the beginning of *the campaign.*" It does not mean "when I began to preach the gospel, that is, in Damascus," and still less "when the Apostles began to preach."

The meaning is not quite so obvious in Clement's Epistle to the Corinthians: "Take up again the Epistle of the blessed Apostle Paul. What was the first thing he wrote to you *in the beginning of the gospel?* He...gave-you-charge-in-the-epistle .. about himself and Cephas and Apollos[2]." This "Epistle," the

---

[1] Philipp. iv. 15, comp 1 5
[2] Clem Rom § 47 (on which see Lightfoot) referring to 1 Cor. 1 10. "Gave-you-charge-in-the-epistle" is intended to express ἐπέστειλεν ὑμῖν so as to retain its similarity to ἐπιστολή.

first Epistle to the Corinthians, was not sent till several months had elapsed after "the beginning of the gospel" in Corinth. Nevertheless Clement almost certainly speaks of it as belonging to the period of "the beginning of the gospel in Corinth," or, perhaps, "in the West." Some modern commentators however take it as meaning "in the beginning of *the evangelical teaching contained in the Epistle*", and this at all events indicates possibilities of various interpretations of "the beginning of the gospel" in early times[1].

The extract from Clement may be illustrated by two earlier extracts (1) "Let us hasten back to the goal of peace which has been *handed down from the beginning* to us, and let us look stedfastly unto the Father and Maker of the whole world," (2) "Let us unfold the records of things *from the beginning*. Why was our father, Abraham, blessed[2]?" In the first of these extracts it seems at first as though the meaning is "*from the beginning*, [*the pure fountain head of the gospel*]" as it existed before it was falsified by heretics, just as Polycarp says to the Philippians "Therefore abandoning...*false doctrines* let us return to the word that was delivered to us *from the beginning*[3]."

But comparing Clement's reference in the first extract to "the Father and Maker of the whole world" with the reference in the second extract to "Abraham," we perceive that Clement may not be speaking, in either, of the "beginning" of the New Testament gospel, but of the beginning of God's revelation to mankind, first, through the Creation, as "Father and Maker of the whole world," and then as the God through whom "our father Abraham was blessed."

If that is the meaning, Clement was cautioning the Corinthians against a tendency, manifested clearly in the second

---

[1] Comp. Polyc. *Philipp.* § 11 "qui estis *in principio* epistulae eius," calling the Philippian Church Paul's "Epistle [of commendation] *in the beginning*," that is, "*in the beginning* of the gospel of the West."

[2] Clem. Rom. §§ 19, 31.

[3] Polyc *Philipp.* § 7. Comp. Jude 3 "the faith that was once for all delivered to the saints."

THE BEGINNING OF THE GOSPEL

century, to divide the New Testament from the Old and to represent the Creation as the work of an inferior God. In such a view the Old Testament and the Law would be regarded as a blank or failure. The real Creation, the real Beginning, would be looked for in the Gospel. The Pauline Epistles hardly ever use the word "beginning," but when they do, they use language orthodox in itself, but capable of being perverted (with very slight changes) to heterodox ends. Christ is called "*the beginning*", the Thessalonians are "chosen from *the beginning*", and "if any man is in Christ he is a new creation, the old things are passed away, behold, they are become new[1]." In the Acts, "*the beginning*" is the name given by Peter to the first Christian Pentecost when—as he reminds his fellow Apostles—the Holy Spirit fell on them "*in the beginning*" Here he uses the same phrase as that with which John begins his Gospel· "*In the beginning* was the Word[2]." Barnabas also, quoting Isaiah's reprobation of "the sabbaths" of Judah, represents God as saying "Having caused all [the ancient] things to cease, I will make the beginning of an eighth day, *the beginning of another world*[3]."

Other passages might be quoted, from Justin Martyr and Tertullian, to shew that it had become necessary in many Churches[4] during the second century, for Christians, believing in an eternal Father revealed through an eternal Son in an eternal Spirit, to strengthen themselves and others against the notion that there was a discontinuity, or return to chaos, instead of a continuous preparation and progress, from the beginning of the Creation The sense of this necessity is

---

[1] Col 1. 18, 2 Thess ii 13, 2 Cor. v. 17. "Beginning" does not occur elsewhere in the Pauline Epistles except in the above-quoted Philipp iv. 15.

[2] Acts xi. 15 ἐν ἀρχῇ.

[3] Barn xv 8 ἄλλου κόσμου ἀρχήν.

[4] "In many Churches" Not perhaps in all. It is remarkable that Hermas uses the word "beginning" but once *Sim* ix 11 9, and that without doctrinal significance, whereas Clement, Barnabas, and Ignatius, in comparatively small space, use it frequently

THE BEGINNING OF THE GOSPEL

indicated in the use of the phrase "from the beginning" no less than ten times in the Johannine Epistles. Doubtless, Mark was quite innocent of any intention to raise discussions of this kind, but his words could hardly fail to raise them. And the object of the following discussion is to shew that the thought of "the beginning," thus raised by Mark, explains some things in Matthew, and more in Luke, but most of all in John, whose Prologue appears to include in its objects that of helping the faithful to stand fast in the creed of a divine continuity: "As it was in the beginning is now and ever shall be."

§ 2. *"The beginning," in Mark*

Mark's opening words are "The beginning of the gospel of Jesus Christ[1], God's Son[2]." This is printed in our Revised Version as a separate sentence. If that interpretation were correct the words would be a title. In that case they would resemble the LXX version of what are almost the opening words of the Books of the Prophets, Hosea being placed first by the LXX, "The beginning of the word of the Lord in Hosea[3]." But Irenaeus and Origen run Mark's sentence on, "The beginning...even as it is written in Isaiah the prophet...." Thus punctuated, the words might mean that the beginning was in accordance with prophecy, or with the prophetic spirit, of which John was the last representative. Or the sentence might be continued still further, thus: "The beginning of the gospel...was (*or*, came-to-pass) John, he that was baptizing...," or possibly "[As] the beginning of the gospel...there came-[to-pass] John...[4]."

---

[1] "Christ," see App. I § 4

[2] "God's Son" is omitted by some authorities.

[3] Hos. 1. 1—2 (LXX) "The word of the Lord that came-to-pass unto Hosea. *The beginning of the word of the Lord in Hosea* (Heb. *When the Lord spake at the first in Hosea*)"

[4] Mk 1. 4 ἐγένετο Ἰωάνης ὁ βαπτίζων ἐν τῇ ἐρήμῳ κηρύσσων is parall to Mt. iii. 1 παραγίνεται Ἰ. ὁ βαπτιστὴς κηρύσσων ἐν τῇ ἐρήμῳ. Luke has

THE BEGINNING OF THE GOSPEL

Origen against Celsus quotes Mark as "shewing that 'the beginning of the gospel' *depends on Jewish Scriptures*[1]." But elsewhere he implies that as "Moses" might personify "the law," so John the Baptist might personify "the beginning of the gospel," either as being "the whole of the Old Testament of which John is the type," or else as being "the conclusions of the Old represented by John for the sake of the connection of the Old with the New[2]." This is somewhat subtle. And Origen's context shews that plain people took Mark as meaning substantially that "the beginning of the gospel" *was* "John." For Origen goes on to ask certain heretics, "How can *John be the beginning of the gospel* if they suppose that he belongs to a different God?" Cramer also prints an ancient scholium (on the first verse in Mark) which, besides quoting Origen by name as to the error in "Isaiah," begins thus, "John, therefore, the last of the prophets, *Mark declares to be the beginning of the gospel*."

Early patristic interpretation, if it were undoubting and unanimous on a point of this kind, ought to carry great weight, and none the less because it may seem abrupt and harsh to us in modern times. But Origen's language indicates the existence of doubt. And there is cause for it. Perhaps Mark merely meant "The book I am now writing is entitled *The Gospel of Jesus Christ*, and this is the beginning of it." Perhaps his intention was to describe, first, the prophecies about John, and then John himself as baptizing and "preaching" repentance, but *not a "gospel"—only the preparation for a gospel*. The "gospel," perhaps, seemed to Mark to be reserved for Jesus, and not to be mentioned till He mentions it later on, "Repent ye and believe in the gospel[3]."

(III 2) ἐγένετο ῥῆμα θεοῦ ἐπὶ Ἰωάνην...ἐν τῇ ἐρήμῳ   John has (1 6) ἐγένετο ἄνθρωπος...ὄνομα αὐτῷ Ἰωάνης.   [1] Origen *Cels.* II 4.
[2] *Comm. Joann.* I 14 ἤτοι πᾶσά ἐστιν ἡ παλαιὰ διαθήκη, τύπου αὐτῆς ὄντος Ἰωάννου, ἢ διὰ τὴν συναφὴν τῆς καινῆς πρὸς τὴν παλαιὰν τὰ τέλη τῆς παλαιᾶς διὰ Ἰωάννου παριστάμενα   [3] Mk 1. 15.

THE BEGINNING OF THE GOSPEL

§ 3. *Later aspects of "the beginning"*

In view of the obscurity of Mark's "beginning" we may reasonably suppose that later evangelists would take up the thought, if not the word. Apart from Mark, "the beginning" would have an interest for Christians in many ways. They would think with reverence of it when they thought of the birth of their religion. But they would also very soon be forced to think of it apologetically or controversially, when they had to answer antagonists, who scoffingly asked them, "What was your God doing for mankind before your religion 'began,' before 'the beginning' of your 'gospel'?"

If "gospel" means the good tidings uttered by Jesus with His own lips, then according to Matthew it did not "begin" till after the Baptist was delivered over to Herod; for Matthew says "from that time *began Jesus to preach*[1]." But the parallel Mark and Luke do not use the word "*began.*"

Luke elsewhere says that Jesus "was, *when-beginning*, about thirty years old," but mentions no definite "beginning" of preaching at that time[2]. Later on, when Jesus came to Nazareth, and entered the synagogue and read there, from Isaiah, the words "the Spirit of the Lord is upon me because he hath anointed me to *preach-the-gospel* to the poor...," Luke adds that when He had closed the book, He "*began* to say unto them, This day hath this scripture *been fulfilled in your ears*[3]." But Luke has previously said that Jesus had "taught in their synagogues being glorified by all[4]." Unless, therefore, we suppose that the previous "teaching" did not expressly claim to fulfil Isaiah's "preach-the-gospel," we cannot conclude that Luke meant the "gospel" to have "begun" from that

---

[1] Mt. iv. 17 The parall. Mk i 14—15 mentions a "coming" into Galilee and "preaching," but not a beginning. The parall. Lk iv 14—15 differs altogether.   [2] Lk. iii 23

[3] Lk. iv 18—21. On ἄρχομαι (Mk (26), Mt (13), Lk. (31), Jn (1)) see *Joh. Voc.* **1674** *a*.   [4] Lk. iv 15

THE BEGINNING OF THE GOSPEL

utterance in the synagogue of Nazareth. " Began," in "*began to say*," seems (as often) to mean " entered on a discourse of some little duration."

Other passages in Luke and the Acts reflect various views of "the beginning." If the gospel was supposed to date from the time of the fulfilment of the promise of the Holy Spirit, and from the consequent apostolic preaching of the gospel, then it might be said to "*begin* from Jerusalem[1]." But if it was supposed to date from the time of the descent of the Holy Spirit on Jesus, then we are taken back to what might be called "the baptism of John" as in the Petrine description of the "going in and going out of the Lord Jesus among us, *beginning from the baptism of John*[2]." The latter view is taken again by Peter in the words "*beginning from Galilee, after the baptism which John preached*[3]," but the former again by Peter when he says "the Holy Spirit fell on them, *even as on us at the beginning*[4]." But neither "beginning from Jerusalem" nor "beginning from Galilee" meets the question that might be put to Christians, "What was your God doing for men *before* 'the beginning of the gospel'?" It is expressed by Celsus thus, "After so vast a space of time, then, did God bethink Himself of making men's life righteous, while neglecting it before[5]?" To this Origen replies that there never was a time when God did not desire to do this, and that He always made this His care; and he implies that this was God's object in "setting the bounds of the nations," and in making Israel His chosen people[6]. This is a kind of answer. It is a doctrine of divine development. It does not indeed pretend to answer the unanswerable question, "Why did not God make man unassailably perfect

---

[1] Lk. xxiv 47   [2] Acts i. 21—2   [3] Acts x 37.
[4] Acts xi. 15   [5] Origen *Cels*. iv. 7.
[6] Origen *Cels* iv. 8, quoting Deut xxxii. 8—9 (LXX), but not Acts xvii. 26 (which R.V. places in margin of Deut). If Origen had quoted Acts xvii 26 foll., some critics might have replied criticizing Acts xvii. 30 " God, *overlooking* the times of ignorance."

7

from the beginning?" but it is a reasonable answer for those who can believe that there are spheres of thought, where—knowledge of the ordinary kind being impossible, and action being necessary—it is reasonable, as well as expedient and honest, to act in accordance with faith.

§ 4. *What preceded "the beginning"?*

Do the Synoptists contain any suggestion of such an "answer" as the one quoted above, given by Origen to Celsus? Mark can hardly be said to do so except so far as he implies it in the words "Isaiah the prophet," which indicate that the coming of John ("the beginning") was "prophesied," and therefore expressly foreordained. Matthew goes further. For he begins his Gospel with the mention of two great names of Christ's ancestors—"the book of the generation of Jesus Christ, the son of *David*, the son of *Abraham*"—both of which, but especially that of Abraham, imply what may be called, in Origen's words, God's "desire" and "care" to "make men righteous" "The son of Abraham" or "the seed of Abraham" is specially connected with God's "promise," *i.e.* good-tidings or gospel[1], and Matthew proceeds consistently to trace the genealogy of Jesus from Abraham Luke chooses another way of indicating God's "desire" or "care" above mentioned. He connects it with the sending of John the Baptist. The Baptist's birth, he says, was the subject of God's special promise, made through the angel Gabriel, that he should "go before his face in the spirit and power of Elijah...to make ready for the Lord a people prepared[2]."

There is nothing in Luke's Gospel that indicates any definite intention to carry the "beginning" further back But in his genealogy of Jesus there appears an indefinite suggestion of

---

[1] See also Clem Rom. §§ 19, 31 (quoted above, p. 2) on the Creation, and on Abraham in connection with the "beginning"
[2] Lk. 1 17.

something of the kind. For whereas Matthew carried it back to Abraham, Luke gives, as its close, "the son of Enos, the son of Seth, the son of Adam, the son of God[1]." As every human being can claim a genealogy with the same termination, this is meaningless on the surface. But it may convey a latent reminder of some truth liable to be obscured by the doctrine of the supernatural birth The author of this genealogy may have meant "Although Jesus was not the son of Joseph yet He was the Son of Mary after the flesh, and therefore ultimately Son of Adam after the flesh, not a mere phantom as some heretics say, but literally Son of the fallen Adam, or Man, whom He was destined to redeem in His own person."

Regarded in this way, "son of Adam" might be intended by the genealogist to illustrate Christ's self-appellation "Son of Man." But what are we to say in defence of the last words of all—"son of God"? If "son of God" is to be interpreted in the same way as "son of Adam" or "son of Seth," we should be driven to say that "son of" means "*begotten by*," and that Adam was "*begotten by God*." Was that Luke's intention, or, at all events, the intention of the genealogist? If it was, then "the beginning of the gospel," so far as Luke's genealogy went, would take us back to the creation of man— and to a tradition in which the "creating" was regarded as a "begetting."

§ 5   "*Gospel*" *not mentioned by Luke and John*

From the foregoing quotations it appears that "the beginning of the gospel" was a phrase capable of several interpretations, and liable to one serious objection on the part of those who confused "*gospel*" with "*salvation*," and who protested against what they supposed to be the Christian

---

[1] Lk. iii. 38.

doctrine—that God did not begin to "save" men till the days of Jesus.

One way of avoiding this confusion was to avoid the word "gospel" altogether. Luke and John do avoid it. They may have been influenced, in part, by the fact that the Greek *euangelion*, or "good-message," sometimes meant the reward bestowed on a messenger bringing tidings of unexpected good-luck. But there was also before them this consideration, that "the gospel," having come to be used in contrast with "the law," might be regarded externally and materially, as a book, or collection of doctrines. Taken thus, no "gospel" could be called, *in itself*, a blessing or thing of goodness. It would not be a blessing except so far as it proceeded from spirit to spirit, influencing the recipient for good. This latter consideration may explain why Luke allows himself freely to use the verb "*evangelize*," or "bring-a-good-message," though he never uses the noun "*evangel*." John abstains from the verb as well as from the noun.

In this abstinence, John may have been (and probably was) influenced by an additional motive that would not have influenced Luke. The word *ev-angel* implies an *angel*, or "*messenger*," of good news. Luke's Gospel deals largely with "*angels*." John's Gospel does not. Like the Epistle to the Hebrews, which begins by exalting the Son above angels, so the Fourth Gospel represents one of the earliest utterances of Jesus as declaring that "angels" are dependent on the Son of Man: "Ye shall see the heaven opened and the angels of God ascending and descending on the Son of Man[1]." And elsewhere this Gospel subordinates them[2]. How could it be right, then, that He who was the Way, the Truth, and the Life, should speak in the character of a "messenger," or "angel,"

---

[1] Jn 1. 51.
[2] See *Son* **3135** *a* "Angels in this gospel are thrown quite into the background."

THE BEGINNING OF THE GOSPEL

"*evangelizing*"? Surely it was better that He should speak as the Son, having, and imparting, "words of eternal life[1]."

Yet of course John was alive to the prevalence and convenience of such phrases as that attributed by Mark to Jesus, "Believe in *the gospel*[2]." Nor could he be so ignorant of human nature as to suppose that he could have exterminated the compendious expression, even if he had desired to do so Such extermination was not in his line. He seldom or never contradicts Synoptic expressions. But he paraphrases them. Or rather he goes to the root of what they mean (or ought to mean) and sets that before his readers in such a form that they may accept it at once for its own sake as true, and may subsequently find that it illustrates some truth that had escaped them in the earlier Gospels.

§ 6 *Why does John prefer "word" and "life" to "gospel" in speaking of "the beginning"?*

What John says about "the beginning" at the outset of his Gospel may profitably be regarded in a twofold aspect as, on the one hand, answering minor questions arising out of Mark, but, on the other, teaching a doctrine important for its own sake, that of divine development

To John—regarding "gospel" as a popular but somewhat coarse and inadequate word to express the revelation of the grace and truth of God—it could not but seem that Christians were derogating from the divine nature when they spoke of the dawn or rising of the Son of Righteousness on men as though it came on them altogether unexpectedly and (so to speak) as a detached, causeless, and arbitrary thing. We may

---

[1] Jn vi 68. In John, "words," ῥήματα, are described as (xv. 7, xvii. 8) "abiding in," and "given to," the disciples

[2] I am indebted to a friend for an interesting instance of εὐαγγέλιον used in a good sense, taken from Deissmann's *Light from the Ancient East*, p 370, quoting a calendar inscription of Priene about 9 B C, referring to the birthday of the Emperor Augustus · ἦρξεν δὲ τῶν (?) κόσμων (?) (?τῷ κόσμῳ) τῶν δι' αὐτὸν εὐαγγελίων ἡ γενέθλιος τοῦ θεοῦ.

illustrate the Evangelist's feeling perhaps by reference to a Jewish tradition which describes new-created Man as in despair when he saw the sun go down for the first time, and thought himself abandoned to darkness for ever. If at that moment Gabriel had appeared to Adam saying "Fear not, the sun will rise tomorrow," that would have been a "gospel." But it would have been a poor "gospel" compared with the imparting of the knowledge that the regular rising of the sun was a part of the will and the word of the Lord in the beginning. Some thought of this kind, some latent sense of contrast between "gospel," which he does *not* mention, and "logos," which he substitutes for it, may help us to a better understanding of the whole of John's Prologue. Every word in it is simple and intelligible; every clause is brief and direct; and the connection between clause and clause, corresponding to the connection between stage and stage of divine development, is so arranged that language, style, and thought, all combine to make the reader feel, even when he is on the point of reading of the incarnation of the Logos, "There is nothing sudden here. There is no thought of 'good luck' or unexpected 'good news.' All is prepared for. All is in accordance with the nature of the Logos, that is to say, with the continuous Harmony, and eternal Pre-ordinance of God."

Greek thought is combined with Hebrew and Jewish poetry in this Prologue. The Greek word *logos* is felt as a controlling influence in almost every sentence. But we can also feel the poetic spirit that made Peter write to the Gentile Churches about "the lamb foreknown before the foundation of the world," which is described in Revelation as "the lamb that hath been slain from the foundation of the world," and which corresponds to the language of the Jewish Targumist who says "And Abraham lifted up his eyes, and saw, and behold, a certain ram, which had been created between the evenings of the foundation of the world[1]"

---

[1] 1 Pet. i. 20, Rev xiii. 8, Jer Targ on Gen. xxii. 13.

THE BEGINNING OF THE GOSPEL

From Jewish influence also proceeds that combination of the negative with the positive, so prominent in the Prologue as to force itself on our notice—even in the Fourth Gospel where such a combination is much more common than in the Three[1]. Negatively, the Evangelist declines to speak of *evangel*, positively, he prefers to speak of *logos* and to follow out the path of orderly sequence suggested by the word From the negative aspect arise negations and limitations that seem at first uncalled for. *Nothing* was made apart from the Logos. The darkness did *not* overcome the light. John the Baptist was *not* "the light," but only a witness to the light The Logos was "God," John was a "man" The Logos "*was* [absolutely]," John "came-into-being." The Logos (it is assumed) was Word in the Greek sense—that is, either word, or reason, or thought, or discourse, or other things implying manifestation of thought in orderly and harmonious arrangement, John (so it is implied in the Prologue and expressed by his own confession afterwards) in comparison with this "Word," was a mere "voice" or "sound."

Doubtless, the Prologue also contains allusions to Philonian doctrine and to Philonian negations of Incarnation. According to Philo, there are three kinds of life, 1st, the life that has to do with God, 2nd, that which has to do with "*becoming*" (that is to say, *genesis*, as distinct from God, who IS, and who may be called THE BEING), 3rd, the life that lies between these two, a blend of both Roughly, the three may be called, the spiritual, the animal, and the human. As to the first, Philo says "*It did not [ever] come down to us or enter into the prison of a body*[2]."

---

[1] Concerning negation as a Johannine characteristic see *Joh Gr* Index In the first 25 verses of the several Gospels, if we omit Mt.'s genealogy, οὐ occurs roughly as follows. Mk (2), Mt (1. 17—11 17) (1), Lk. (4), Jn (9). It also occurs in Jn 1 26, 27, 31, 33, 47.

[2] Philo 1 479 *lit* "Now as for the life that has to do with God (τὸ μὲν οὖν πρὸς θεὸν) it descended not to us nor came into the necessities of a body (οὐ κατέβη πρὸς ἡμᾶς, οὐδὲ ἦλθεν εἰς τὰς σώματος ἀνάγκας)"

Contradicting this assertion about the highest "life," the Johannine Prologue leads us through rapidly successive stages to the conclusion that the Logos itself, the Sphere of Life, "became flesh"—a very strong way of affirming that the highest "life" *has* "come down to us and entered into the prison of a body"—or, at all events, into the limitations or constraining necessities that a body implies. It also declares that this first "life," the life that IS, has influenced the third life, which is in the debateable region between BEING and *becoming*.

This highest kind of "life" the Prologue describes as "that which has come into being in the Logos, or Word," apparently meaning, by "Word," the creative Order or Harmony of the Universe, acting in the divine Concord, and in the Spirit of God. To call this a "gospel," or "good-tidings," might (as we have seen) imply unexpectedness. To call it a "promise" would be to limit its action to the future. But this concordant Word was never unexpected and never limited in time or space. It was always present as well as always infinite, being itself God: "In the beginning was the Logos, and the Logos was with (*lit.* toward) God, and the Logos was God...All things came-into-being through him (*or*, it), and apart from him (*or*, it) there came-into-being not one single thing. That which hath-come-into-being in him (*or*, it) was life[1]" That is to say, everything, inanimate as well as animate, so far as it obeys the Law or Logos of its being—praising the Lord, as the Psalmist says, by "fulfilling His word[2]"—was, in some sense, "life."

This conception of life as a present spiritual possession is not inconsistent, as will be seen later on, with the doctrine of a "raising up at the last day." For the Messiah Himself will

---

[1] Jn i. 1—4. For the reasons for the rendering given above, see *Joh Gr*, textual Index.

[2] Ps cxlviii 8

be expressly declared to be "the raising up" or "resurrection[1]." And it is also assumed that He is the Omega, or End, as well as the Alpha, or Beginning, of spiritual Creation[2].

§ 7. *The connection between "life" and "light"*

From "life" we are to pass to "light," or rather to "the light of men." What is the link between the two? In order to answer this question, looking for some analogy in the opening words of Genesis about "the beginning," we shall find that there is no mention of "life" there, before the *fiat*, "Let there be light." But there is a mention of the Spirit of God that "moved (*or*, brooded) upon the face of the waters"; and this "moving" or "brooding" of "the Spirit of God" implies the motion of a life-giving Being which the Jerusalem Targum calls "the Spirit of mercies (*or*, of love)." What the Evangelist says is, that for "*men*"—that is, for creatures endowed with *logos*, and akin to the Word—the "life" is "light." For "dragons," and "deeps," and "stormy wind" fulfilling God's "word[3]," life, such as it is, is not light. But, for men, "life," in the sense of true life, opens their eyes to the goodness and beauty and truth of the Logos, who is in them, and in whom they are, so that the Logos is *their* "*light*[4]"

---

[1] This is stated very significantly (Jn xi. 24—5) in reply to Martha—when she utters the phrase "in the last day" in a popular, temporal, and unspiritual sense.

[2] This will appear later on, when we discuss the Synoptic views of "the end," or its Lucan equivalent (see *Son* 3349 foll), and also Matthew's (xix. 28) resort to the Greek notion of παλιγγενεσία, against which, in a Stoical sense, when connected with ἐκπύρωσις, Philo (ii 497, 508) protests John also protests tacitly against it by recurring to "in the last day"—not used by the Synoptists—a form of the old Hebrew hopeful phrase (Gesen 31 *a*) "in the sequel of the days [of trial]"

[3] Ps. cxlviii 7—8.

[4] Comp. *Gitanjali* §§ 3—4 "The light of thy music illumines the world The life breath of thy music runs from sky to sky....My heart longs to join in thy song, but vainly struggles for a voice....Life of my life, I shall ever try to keep my body pure, knowing that thy living touch

In the first Genesis, there is no mention of human beings in connection with the first mention of "light"; and, as for "life," it is mentioned for the first time in connection with "the moving creature that hath-life," which "the waters" are to "bring forth abundantly[1]." But in this second Genesis a higher conception is introduced, both of life and of light. Along with it, however, comes a conception of a consequent complication, antithesis, or even conflict, in which there looms a suggestion—suggested but at once contradicted—that the light might possibly be "overcome" by some hostile element:— "And the light shineth in the darkness, and the darkness overcame it not[2]" Perhaps there is also a suggestion of the victory of light, or the subordination of darkness, the latter being made a foil to the former, as though the meaning were : "The light shines all the more in the darkness; and the darkness never succeeded in overcoming it."

§ 8 *The Baptist is not "the light" but a witness to it*

Then comes a brief and parenthetical negation, adapted for those who were disposed to misunderstand the Marcan tradition about "John" as "the beginning of the gospel." "John" was neither the Word, nor the Life, nor the Light. John was a mere "man," one of those about whom it has been said above "The life was the light of men." He was "sent from God," it is true—but not as "the light," only to "bear witness concerning the light." The Logos "*was*." John "*came-into-being*." If therefore John is to be thought of as a beginning, it must be only as a witness, not preceding the Light but preceding other "men" in the recognition of it :—" There *came-into-being* a *man*, sent from God ; his name [was] John ;

---

is upon all my limbs   I shall ever try to keep all untruths out from my thoughts, knowing that thou art that truth which has kindled the light of reason in my mind ..."
[1] Gen. 1. 20.   [2] Jn 1. 5.

THE BEGINNING OF THE GOSPEL

this [man] came for *witness*, that he *might bear-witness* concerning the light, that all might believe through that [light][1]. He (*emph.*) was not the light, but [only came] that he might *bear-witness* concerning the light[2]."

It is not said that John "preached" (or "proclaimed," or "heralded") concerning the Light. The Synoptists alone use the Greek word thus rendered. And it is appropriate for the announcement of the approach of a mortal king, newly crowned, or newly coming into any region of his kingdom. But if the "king" is God, who has always been King and has always been visiting every region of His Kingdom, though most men have not known it, then it is better to speak of His prophets and seers as "testifying," or "bearing witness," to that which they have known of Him, that others may believe.

This "bearing witness" did not begin from John, or from the most ancient of the prophets, but from the coming of the light into the conscience. It came to Adam, Abel, Enoch, Noah and Abraham. But it came also to Cain, to the evil as well as to the good, to those who received it not, as well as to those who received it. After saying, therefore, that "John came to bear witness to the light," it is added, "There was [from the beginning] the true light, which, coming [continually] into the [whole] world, enlightens every human being. In the world it was (*or*, he was) [from the beginning], and the world came-into-being through it (*or*, through him) and the world recognised him not. He came unto his own, and they that were his own received him not[3]."

The writer keeps us in doubt about the gender of the pronoun referring to the Light till the last clause, which describes men's failure to recognise the Light as a failure to recognise "*him*". This may mean, either that the great non-recognition came to pass at the Incarnation, or else that, from the beginning, men failed to recognise the humanity of the Word and Light which was continuously appealing to them.

---

[1] *Joh. Gr.* **2303**—4.   [2] Jn i. 6—8.   [3] Jn i 9—11.

THE BEGINNING OF THE GOSPEL

§ 9. *The "light" is a Person, to be "received" by "believing"*

Thus the Word, being also the Life and the Light, is found to be, not a mere promise or gospel, but a person. And this person is to be "recognised" and "received." But with what kind of "recognition" and "reception"? Clearly there is to be something of loyalty in it, something of passion, something of that enthusiasm with which Amasai devoted himself to David when "the spirit fell upon him," and he exclaimed "Thine are we, David, and on thy side, thou son of Jesse Peace, peace, be unto thee, and peace be to thine helpers, for thy God helpeth thee[1]."

For such a passionate loyalty in his subjects or followers every great king or leader of men makes some kind of return by binding himself to them, as well as them to himself and to one another, in a spirit of unity and self-sacrifice, which gives "life" to the whole community, whatever it may be—to a country and to each citizen in it, to an army and every soldier in it. The return of "life" thus made by Jehovah, the King of Israel, to those who "received" Him into their hearts by "cleaving" to Him, even when rather literalised in expression, suggested a spiritual meaning to spiritual Israelites, as in the words, "Love the Lord thy God, obey his voice, and cleave unto him, for *he is thy life,*" and also in the Psalms, "The Lord is *the portion of mine inheritance and of my cup,*" and in the Lord's saying to Abraham, "*I am...thy exceeding great reward*[2]." The development of this Hebrew thought, the thought of the regeneration of Man by taking the life of God into himself, so as to be born into God's family—is expressed in many different metaphors throughout

---

[1] 1 Chr xii 18

[2] Deut. xxx. 20, Ps xvi 5, Gen. xv. 1 The meaning is obscured by the context in Deuteronomy, and hence not fully brought out by Philo and still less by the Talmudists But no spiritual Jew would take "life" to be identical with Deut *ib* "length of days"

THE BEGINNING OF THE GOSPEL

this Gospel, and it comes before us for the first time here: "He came to his own [kingdom] and his own [people] took him not into [their hearts]. But as many as did [thus] take him [into their hearts], unto them he gave authority to become children of God[1]."

It is natural to ask why the Evangelist says "children," and not "sons," of God; for the phrase is not found in the Bible and perhaps not in Jewish tradition[2]. Origen quotes the Johannine passage, together with two from Paul, after others that mention "sons" in Deuteronomy, Isaiah, and Malachi, to prove that "the stability and unmovableness of the [true] sonship was not to be seen of old[3]." But he does not point out that the Johannine word for "children" implies (in certain contexts and possibly here) a participation in the parental nature, and a dependence on the parental love, that are not implied by the word "sons[4]." A "son" may be of alien blood, made legally a son by what Paul frequently calls "son-adoption"; but the word "child-adoption" does not appear to exist in Greek[5].

Another reason for preferring the phrase "children of

---

[1] Jn i 11—12

[2] *Hor Hebr* and Wetstein (and Schottgen, except Sohar) allege no Jewish parallel

[3] *De Orat* § 22, quoting Deut xxxii 20, Is. i. 2, Mal i 6, Gal iv 1—2, Rom viii 15, Jn i 12.

[4] Comp Jn viii 39 "If ye are [real] *children* (τέκνα) of Abraham, then ye are [in virtue of your child-nature] doing the deeds of Abraham" (see *Joh Gr* 2078—9); Eph v 1—2 "Be ye therefore *imitators of God*, as beloved *children*, and *walk in love, even as Christ also loved you*"; 1 Jn iii. 2 (RV) "Beloved, now are we *children of God*, and it is not yet made manifest what we shall be We know that, if he [*marg*. it] shall be manifested, *we shall be like him*," that is to say, the likeness of the "children" to the parental nature, though it may be changed and developed by growth, will still remain

[5] Υἱοθεσία (Rom viii 15, 23 &c), though non-existent in the Indices of the Berlin Urkunde (vols 1—iv), seems to have been common in ancient Rhodian and Ægean inscriptions (Boeckh, 2513, 2524, 2539) Steph. *Thes* gives no instance of τεκνοθεσία.

God" to "sons of God" may perhaps be reasonably inferred from the comment of Ammonius on the Johannine context: "'*As many as received him*'—that is to say, slaves or free, Greeks or barbarians, unlearned or learned, *women or men*[1]." Though everyone would of course admit that the expression "sons of God" includes women, there is a manifestly greater fitness in the phrase "children of God" to express this inclusion. But the principal reason for this preference, from the Johannine point of view, is probably this, that "children," better than "sons," expresses, or attempts to express, what the Fourth Evangelist felt to be Christ's own inexpressible conception of the passionate love and longing of the Father in heaven for His "little-ones" on earth, helpless without His help, and yet, too often, refusing to be helped[2].

To this we must return hereafter when we discuss the Marcan doctrine of Christ and His little ones whom He receives in His arms and blesses[3]. For the present, confining ourselves to the illustration of the Johannine Prologue, we may say that, in the view of the Fourth Evangelist, the term "sons of God" might seem to be an Old Testament expression,

---

[1] See Cramer on Jn i. 9 foll

[2] This may be illustrated by Paul's language to the wilful Corinthians (1 Cor. iv. 14) and Galatians (iv 19), the "children" whom he has "begotten," or with whom he is "in travail" once again The latter he calls (W H.) τεκνία, a word that occurs nowhere else in N T. except 1 Jn about seven times, and Jn xiii 33, where Jesus says to His disciples "Little-children, yet a short [time] am I with you," meaning that they are helpless babes unless He is with them, and that He can be with them now on earth only a few minutes longer

[3] Mk x. 13, Mt. xix 13, Lk xviii 15 καὶ τὰ βρέφη, where the Lucan "babes" has given Origen much to say. Βρέφος occurs in only one passage of the Apostolic Fathers (Hermas, *Sim.* ix 29) and one passage of the early Apologists (Tatian § 30), and the two passages use the word in opposite aspects. On the connection between "babe" or "little one" and "lamb" see *Son* **3440** *b*, **3443** *a—b*. See also below (p 88 foll.). Clem. Alex. 69, in a discourse on regeneration and "the nurslings (τρόφιμοι) of God," introduces God as crying to them "Come hither, come hither, my own νεολαία"—that is, the young of both sexes

hardened by use, so to speak, into various meanings, suitable for the Law and the Prophets, but not for the new and higher revelation—not at least here, where the doctrine of a new birth, or bringing forth, is being introduced. The writer is preparing the way for the Marcan title "Jesus Christ," in connection with "Son of God," by leading us to reflect on the spiritual meaning of divine sonship What does it mean when we say that this or that man is "a son of God"? It means that he has become a "child," or "one brought forth," in a new way. The new way is connected with "belief," thus:—"Unto them he gave authority to become children of God, unto them [I say] *that believe in*[*to*] *his name*, who, not from the blood [of the Passover or of Circumcision] nor from desire of flesh or desire of husband, but from God were begotten[1]"

"*Believe*" has been used absolutely in this Gospel above, where it was said that John the Baptist came "that he might bear witness about the light that all might *believe* through that [light]." What is meant now by the fuller expression "*believe in*[*to*] *his name*," following that previous statement? Origen suggests that it is the first and rudimentary stage of that new "belief" for which the Baptist was to prepare the way. If that is so, it would seem to be a kind of half-official half-personal "belief," to be merged ultimately in a belief that is wholly personal[2]. But in any case this mention of believing in "*the name*" of the Logos, as the condition for receiving "authority" to become one of "the *children of God*," who are "*begotten from God*," appears to be the conclusion of the process of bridging over the interval of thought between (1) the "beginning" and (2) "Jesus Christ the Son of God," so that "the Word" and "the Son"—the latter, under the name of the Only-begotten or Monogenēs—will now appear in the same sentence: "And *the Word* became flesh, and

---

[1] Jn 1. 12—13. On "not from *blood*," lit. *bloods*, s *Joh. Gr.* **2268**—9
[2] See *Joh Voc.* **1483**—7.

THE BEGINNING OF THE GOSPEL

tabernacled among (*lit.* in) us—and we beheld his glory, glory as of *Monogenēs*, [coming] from the Father—full of grace and truth[1]."

The "glory" here is not that of the Transfiguration, literally interpreted, nor is it that kind of "glory" which we can behold by the conventional "looking up." Rather we may say, with a modern poet, that we must look down and "cannot reach down" deep enough to the depth of His glory which consists in His suffering with those whom He loves[2]

§ 10. "*Grace*" *through* "*Jesus Christ*"

We have seen that, after the mention of the "glory as of the Only-begotten," there came the first mention of "grace." "The grace of our Lord Jesus Christ" is a beautiful expression, of which the beauty grows upon us the more we think about it. In the Prologue, "Grace" seems to supplement the colder word "Logos" or "Word," without introducing that thought of unexpectedness which we found in "Gospel." The connection seems to be this "When the Word became flesh, then, being from the first full of grace, He became incarnate graciousness or kindness." "Grace" seems most appropriately introduced a little before the first mention of "Jesus Christ."

It is difficult to define "grace"—a word frequently mentioned in Philo and still more frequently (in proportion to space) in the Odes of Solomon[3]. It may be described—though roughly and inadequately—as free and self-originated kindness bestowed without thought of payment or hire or

---

[1] Jn i. 14.
[2] Compare *Gitanjali* §§ 10—11 "Here is thy footstool and there rest thy feet where live the poorest, and lowliest, and lost. When I try to bow to thee, my obeisance cannot reach down to the depth where thy feet rest among the poorest, and lowliest, and lost. Pride can never approach to where thou walkest in the clothes of the humble among the poorest, and lowliest, and lost....Our master himself has joyfully taken upon him the bonds of creation, he is bound with us all for ever"
[3] *Light* 3724.

return of any kind. It implies naturalness as well as goodness, and, in that aspect, it is the antithesis of "hypocrisy." Mark and Matthew nowhere use the word. Luke (except in the phrase " have thank(s) ") uses it only once concerning the public life of Jesus · "they wondered at the words of *grace* which proceeded out of his mouth[1]" It is not clear whether, by "the words of grace," Luke means the prophecy of Isaiah as read by Jesus, or the words of Jesus applying the prophecy to Himself, or a confused mixture of the two. Grace, or graciousness, attracts all that recognise it. But at Nazareth, the hearers, instead of being attracted, are repelled In such a context, the Lucan phrase seems to tell us nothing and to lead to nothing.

In John, "grace" is mentioned for the first time along with "truth." " Grace and truth " may correspond to "*kindness* (R.V *mercy*) and *truth*" in Genesis[2]. If so, John substitutes *charis* "grace," for what is usually and inadequately rendered "mercy." Though John does not here mention Abraham, he almost certainly has Abraham in his mind, as being the Patriarch whom Philo regards as "the inheritor of divine things[3]," and whom Paul regards as the archetype of those who are saved by "grace," and by faith in the Promise.

At this point in the Prologue the Baptist is introduced again parenthetically to bear witness, not now to the Light as

---

[1] In the Lucan Introduction, it occurs about Jesus in Lk 11 40 "and the child grew and the *grace* of God was upon him," and Lk 11 52 "And Jesus advanced in wisdom and stature and *favour* (or, *grace*) with God and men." The " words of *grace*" (Lk. iv. 22) refer to (iv 21) " He began to say unto them, To-day hath this scripture"—Is lxi 1—2 which Jesus has just read in the synagogue—"been fulfilled in your ears " For "grace" meaning "thank(s)" see Lk. vi. 32—4, xvii 9

[2] Gen xxiv 27, which contains (*Son* 3553 *c*) the first Biblical mention of "truth." But there may be a primary reference to the Psalm of the Bridegroom (Ps xlv 2—4) "*grace*...ride on...because of *truth*." See p 25, n 2.

[3] Comp Philo 1 473 " Now it is my purpose to inquire who is the heir of divine things (ὁ τῶν θείων πραγμάτων κληρονόμος)," just before quoting Gen xv. 1

being Light, but to the priority of the incarnate Word or Light as compared with himself ("he was before me[1]"). Then, after the parenthesis, the Evangelist returns to the subject of "grace," preparing us to perceive its exact meaning, not by defining it, but by placing it in antithesis with Law

Not that grace is against all law. For "grace" goes with "truth"; and the highest truth implies correspondence to a harmonious system which we call Law. But the Evangelist has in view the imperfect Law of Moses, following the Promise of grace and truth to Abraham—and following, not as fulfilling that Promise, but only as preparing the way for that fulfilment To make this clear, he introduces the name of Moses as the representative of the imperfect law, and thus, at last, he brings us, by antithesis, to the name Jesus, and the title Christ, as belonging to the representative of grace: "Because from his fulness we all received, and grace succeeding grace[2], because [though] the law [of God from Sinai] was given through Moses, the grace [of God] and the truth [of God] came-into-being through Jesus Christ[3]"

Does this imply that no "grace" and no "truth" for men "came-into-being" till "the word of God came unto John in the fifteenth year of Tiberius Caesar[4]"? Assuredly not. They came into being for Abraham But according to our Evangelist they came into being for Abraham through Christ, who says concerning him, "Abraham rejoiced that he might see my day, and he saw it and was glad[5]." The author of the Fourth Gospel doubtless shared Paul's belief that "Christ"

---

[1] Jn i 15 [2] See *Joh Gr* **2284—7.**
[3] Jn i 16—17. The antithesis between Law and Grace, and the attitude of the world, "waiting" to "give itself up" to gracious love, may be illustrated from *Gitanjali* § 17 "They come with their laws and their codes to bind me fast; but I evade them ever, for I am only waiting for love to give myself up at last into his hands"
[4] Lk iii 1—2.
[5] Jn viii. 56.

was with Israel in the wilderness[1], and, if so, surely with Abraham their progenitor. We must therefore regard the Johannine expression as condensed: "The Law of God was given through Moses, but the grace of God and the truth of God, before the Law, and under the Law, and apart from the Law, and also after the Law had been fulfilled, came into being through the eternal Word or Son who, in due course, became flesh as Jesus Christ[2]."

§ 11. *"Declaring God" as distinct from "preaching the gospel"*

The Prologue ends with a negation limiting our expectations of the truth about God to be expected from the senses, and with an affirmation enlarging our expectations of the truth about God to be expected from the Only-begotten: "No man hath seen God at any time. Monogenēs, God, he that is in (*lit.* into) the bosom of the Father—he declared [him][3]" The negation sets itself not only against vulgar

---

[1] 1 Cor. x. 4 "They drank of a spiritual rock that followed them, and the rock was Christ"

[2] It is possible that in this threefold mention of "*grace*" (Jn 1. 14, 16, 17) (which John never mentions again) as an introduction to the name "*Christ*" or "*Anointed*," John may have in view the Psalm of the Royal Bridegroom, Ps xlv. 2, 7 "Thou art fairer than the sons of man, *grace* is poured out in thy lips," "God hath *anointed* thee with the oil of gladness above thy fellows"—a passage quoted in Heb. 1. 9 as predicting the bringing of the Son into the world. But an adequate motive may be found in the feeling that "the grace of our Lord Jesus Christ" ought to receive a prominent position in any document that professed to give the essence of Christ's teaching. The undoubted allusions to the Bridegroom in the early part of the Fourth Gospel will come before us later on when we consider the Synoptic doctrine of the Children of the Bridechamber. These, and the Jewish traditions about (*Son of Man*, Index) "the Bridegroom of the Beginning" and "the Bridegroom of the Law," favour the view that Jn 1. 14—17 does allude to the Psalm of the Bridegroom

[3] Jn 1. 18 μονογενὴς θεὸς ὁ ὢν εἰς τὸν κόλπον τοῦ πατρὸς ἐκεῖνος ἐξηγήσατο. Ἐξηγέομαι, *lit.* "take the lead," means, among other things, "dictate"

THE BEGINNING OF THE GOSPEL

Pagan notions of mysteries, and magic incantations professing to make God visible, but also against materialistic Jewish conceptions of the glory of God based on literal acceptations of Old Testament lightnings and thunders and pillars of cloud and fire. This negation needs little comment.

Not so the affirmation. For this suggests the answer to a question that would probably occur to every thoughtful student of religious writings, if he approached the Prologue for the first time and read it through attentively, having also some notion of the contents of the whole of the Gospel to which it is prefixed, and of the Epistle that expresses the Gospel's results. Would he not say "'Life,' 'light,' 'glory,' 'grace,' 'truth'—so far, so good, but where is 'love'?"

The Prologue gives, in effect, this answer: "Love is everywhere in this book; not mentioned till toward the end, but embodied in the incarnate Word and declared or interpreted to the sons of man by the Only-begotten Son of God I said at first that 'the Word was toward God,' meaning 'in converse with God'—converse not of face with face but of spirit with spirit Now I express another aspect of the same truth by 'Only-begotten' (meaning the Son in unique unity of will with the Father) and 'God' (meaning that 'the Only-begotten' is one with God in nature as well as in will) and 'into the bosom of the Father' (meaning not only that He is Himself eternally in the bosom of the Father, but also that He, as

---

a charm, or incantation, or the names of gods, as when Ægeus says to Medea (l 745) "*dictate* the gods [by whom I shall swear]" Hence it might be used about priests, diviners, magicians, or seers, who "teach authoritatively" what is clean or unclean, or "declare" the meaning of a dream or vision. Ἐξηγητής, thrice found in LXX, means "*diviner*" twice.

John probably uses "declare" or "interpret" in a kind of understatement Later on, he will represent Jesus as saying to Philip, "He that hath seen me hath seen the Father." But here—writing for those who were prone to mysteries, incantations, and initiations, seeking after visible gods with strange names, with the aid of "diviners" or "interpreters"—he says, in effect, "You cannot see God in that way. The true God is the Father, and 'the Only-begotten' is His 'interpreter'."

THE BEGINNING OF THE GOSPEL

being incarnate on earth for us, is perpetually ascending from earth to heaven, *up to*, and *into*, the bosom of the Father, and taking us thither with Himself).

"'Love' is not, and must not be, mentioned here. For, if mentioned, it would be misunderstood, being taken for something less than it is—for ordinary love. The love brought into the world by Christ was love of a new kind, not to be known except by knowing Him. And none could know Him except by loving Him, and by being 'in His bosom' as He was 'in the bosom of the Father.'

"It is for this reason that the author of this Gospel will not be called 'John the son of Zebedee' True, the son of Zebedee was in some sense the begetter of it. But he himself would not have wished that it should be called by his name, or indeed by any '*proper name*,' that is, 'name of one's own[1].'

"To have 'John' for 'a proper name,' shall be reserved for the 'man sent from God, whose name was John,' and who, though he prepared the way for the baptism from above, was himself 'from the earth' and 'spake from the earth[2].' But the author of this Gospel shall have no 'name.' It is enough for him, and more than enough, to be called 'the disciple whom Jesus loved,' and, in that unnamed character, to attempt to shew, through the story of His life, how God's 'Only-begotten' became also [God's] Declarer, so that His disciples, seeing Him, saw the Father."

---

[1] The thought of one's "proper name," as being a defining or "enclosing" thing, may be illustrated from *Gitanjali* § 29 "He whom I enclose with my name is weeping in this dungeon I am ever busy building this wall all around, and as this wall goes up into the sky day by day I lose sight of my true being in its dark shadow. I take pride in this great wall, and I plaster it with dust and sand lest a least hole should be left in this name; and for all the care I take I lose sight of my true being."

[2] Jn iii. 31, comp. iii. 11—12, on which see *Son* **3387**. John the Baptist "spake from the earth" when he sent the message recorded in Mt. xi 3, Lk. vii. 19.

Some may feel that the introduction of "Only-begotten," Monogenēs—almost in the character of a new god—does not help, but rather hinders, their appreciation of the simple statement that "the Word became flesh." But we have to remember that the Evangelist was writing, in great measure, for educated people. And, to educated people at the end of the first century, the term Monogenēs would convey a very distinct meaning, connected with the preceding context, and spiritually valuable as a protest against error in high places of philosophy.

"Do you not know"—we might be asked by some intelligent reader of the Fourth Gospel in the second century—"that Plato in his Timaeus had long ago introduced Monogenēs to the Greeks, and that Cicero, in his translation of the Timaeus, had passed on the term to the Romans? Cicero says '*In order that this world* (mundus) *might be as like as possible to a living-creature complete in itself* (animanti absoluto) —*in this respect, [namely] that it was alone and one*—therefore God procreated this world singular and *only-begotten* (singularem Deus hunc mundum atque unigenam procreavit)[1].' Plato's Timaeus, besides calling the Cosmos 'a living creature,' says that '*the Maker would not make worlds* (cosmoi) *two or infinite in number; but on the contrary this only-begotten heaven, having-come-into-being, both exists and will exist*[2].' You see that Plato takes 'cosmos' and 'heaven' to mean much the same thing, and to be a '*living-creature.*' Later on, he suggests that our '*kinship with heaven*' lies in the top of our body, the head, as being nearest to the heaven[3]. And he concludes the Timaeus thus · '*Having received mortal and immortal living-beings, and having been therewith fully-filled, this cosmos, thus [equipped]—a visible living-creature, including*

---

[1] Cicero, *Timaeus De Universo* § 4.
[2] Plato, *Timaeus* § 6 (p 31 B) ἀλλ' εἶς ὅδε μονογενὴς οὐρανὸς γεγονὼς ἔστι τε καὶ ἔτ' ἔσται.
[3] *Timaeus* § 43 (p. 90 A).

[*all*] *the* [*things that are*] *visible—hath become* [*the*] *Image of the Maker, God perceptible, Greatest, and Best, both Most Beautiful and Most Perfect, One* [*only*] *Heaven, this Only-begotten,* [*always*] *BEING*[1].'

"Now all this—or at all events, this, as it was interpreted by many later writers—was entirely contrary to the belief of the Evangelist. He rejected the notions of some, that the Cosmos was a living-creature; and that the heavenly bodies had a divine nature superior to that of Man; and that ascension to the Father meant ascending to any perceptible upper sphere. For the beloved Disciple held fast to the Divinity of Love and Goodness, and, in comparison with a good man, the stars seemed to him as naught. Yet many in his days, Jews as well as Gentiles—and some even of the Christians—were carried away by various versions, or perversions, or fragments, of Plato's doctrine. Among these was Philo[2], who describes God as '*begetting* [the things that make up] the Whole,' and as making the Logos a Mediator, 'standing midway' between the Maker and the made, so that the Logos says to men '*I stood between the Lord and you*[3], being neither *unbegotten* (as God) nor *begotten* (as you are)[4].'

---

[1] *Timaeus* § 44 (p 92 C) θνητὰ γὰρ καὶ ἀθάνατα ζῷα λαβὼν καὶ ξυμπληρωθεὶς ὅδε ὁ κόσμος οὕτω, ζῷον ὁρατὸν τὰ ὁρατὰ περιέχον, εἰκὼν τοῦ ποιητοῦ, θεὸς αἰσθητός, μέγιστος καὶ ἄριστος κάλλιστός τε καὶ τελεώτατος γέγονεν, εἷς οὐρανὸς ὅδε μονογενὴς ὤν. The bald translation given above, and the capital letters of BEING, are intended to shew (1) the identification of "heaven" and "cosmos," (2) the emphasis on ὤν, the final word in the treatise

[2] Philo i. 501—2 τῷ δὲ ἀρχαγγέλῳ καὶ πρεσβυτάτῳ λόγῳ δωρεὰν ἐξαίρετον ἔδωκεν ὁ τὰ ὅλα γεννήσας πατήρ, ἵνα μεθόριος στὰς τὸ γενόμενον διακρίνῃ τοῦ πεποιηκότος...οὔτε ἀγέννητος ὡς ὁ θεὸς ὤν, οὔτε γεννητὸς ὡς ὑμεῖς

[3] These are the words of Moses in Deut v. 5

[4] This is compatible with the assertion "I was uniquely begotten," but "unigena" (or "unigenitus") does not occur in Mangey's Index to Philo, nor does Drummond give μονογενής among the many titles of the Logos. In i. 501, Philo seems to use γεννήσας as meaning, or including, ποιήσας, and it is in this point that he differs from the Fourth Gospel

"Here Philo seems to confuse '*create*' with '*beget*.' And many others, among those for whose sake largely the Evangelist wrote, were led astray by their interpretations of Plato, and, in particular, of the Timaeus[1]. And therefore to Plato, and to his Timaeus, the Evangelist here makes allusion, repeating Plato's title of Monogenēs but applying it to the spiritually and eternally begotten Son, who offers to the sons of men the power of being spiritually begotten again, so as to be like Himself—a thing quite different from physical begetting, or physical creation. Moreover the Evangelist refers yet once again to the Timaeus at the conclusion of his prologue where he says that 'no man hath seen God at any time' but that 'Monogenēs hath declared Him.' For the Timaeus says '*It is a hard matter to find out the Maker and Father of this All-that-is*[2] [*around us*]; *and after having found Him out, it is impossible to tell Him forth into the* [*ears and hearts of*] *all*[3].'

---

[1] Plutarch (*De Defect. Orac.* § 23, ii 422—3) in a dialogue on the passage in the Timaeus, has ἐν οἷς γε μάχεται [Πλάτων] τοῖς ἀπείρους κόσμους ὑποτιθεμένοις, αὐτῷ δὴ φησι δοκεῖν ἕνα τοῦτον εἶναι μονογενῆ τῷ θεῷ καὶ ἀγαπητὸν... This adds "*beloved* by God" to "*only-begotten*" as an epithet of the cosmos. The context censures Plato for giving cause for misinterpretations of this doctrine of a single cosmos. Another Dialogue of Plutarch gives μονογενής as an epithet to Persephone (*De Facie in Orbe Lunae* § 28, ii. 943) ἡ δὲ Φερσεφόνη πρᾴως καὶ χρόνῳ πολλῷ [λύει] τὸν νοῦν ἀπὸ τῆς ψυχῆς, καὶ διὰ τοῦτο μονογενὴς κέκληται· μόνον γὰρ γίνεται τὸ βέλτιστον τοῦ ἀνθρώπου διακρινόμενον [ὑπ'] αὐτῆς. There is manifestly some play on "*only*," but its exact nature is not clear to me. The passage is of some importance as an indication of the frequency of discussions about μονογενής in, and before, Plutarch's time.

[2] "Of this All-that-is," τοῦδε τοῦ παντός.

[3] This is quoted by Celsus (from Timaeus p. 28 C). Origen (*Cels.* vii. 42) accepts the words as "noble and admirable," but adds that, because of this very difficulty and impossibility, "the Word was made flesh," in order that "the Word might be able to make its way into all (εἰς πάντας δυνατὸς ᾖ φθάνειν ὁ Λόγος)—[that very Word] which Plato says it is impossible, even for him who has found it, to convey-by-speech into [the hearts of] all (εἰς πάντας ἀδύνατον λέγειν)."

Elsewhere Origen points out that κόσμος has two meanings, (1) the universe, (2) human beings. In the former sense he seems ready to go

THE BEGINNING OF THE GOSPEL

"To this our Evangelist replies, in effect, that although it is impossible to '*declare*' Him, or '*tell Him forth*,' to all, or indeed to any human being, by the force of mere words, yet the incarnate Son, 'full of grace and truth,' being that Monogenēs or Only-begotten after whom Plato was groping and feeling his way—was assuredly able to '*declare*' God, the Father, to those who received the Spirit of the Son into their hearts[1]"

---

a long way with Plato in the exaltation of the κόσμος. See Origen on Gen. i 16—18 (Lomm viii 45—7), on Mt xviii 7 (*Comm Matth* xiii 20), and *Comm. Joann.* i 24, vi 38 Also Clement of Alexandria, quoting the Timaeus about the difficulty of finding "the Maker and Father of this All-that-is," says (701) that Plato, by calling God "Father" of it, "not only shewed that the Cosmos came-into-being (οὐ μόνον γενητόν τε ἔδειξε τὸν κόσμον) but also signifies that it has come-into-being from Him as a son (ἐξ αὐτοῦ γεγονέναι σημαίνει, καθάπερ υἱόν) and that He is called the Father of it (αὐτοῦ) inasmuch as it came-into-being from [Him] alone (ὡς ἂν ἐκ μόνου γενομένου) and became substance from [a state of] not-being (ἐκ μὴ ὄντος ὑποστάντος)" Is this an attempt to explain Plato's μονογενής, applied to κόσμος, as though it meant "*coming-into-being from the Alone*, or, *from God alone*"? See above, p 30, n 1, on the reason for calling Persephone μονογενής.

[1] Μονογενής (Heb יְחִיד, Gesen 402 *b*) occurs in Midrash (Levy iii 51 *b*) as a Hebraized noun (but not in Aram or Syr) meaning "only (son)." In this sense יְחִיד, but LXX ἀγαπητός, is thrice applied to Isaac (Gen xxii 2, 12 (comp. Heb xi 17 τὸν μονογενῆ), 16) as being the "*unique*" son of the Promise "My *only one*" in Ps. xxii 20, xxxv 17, LXX μονογενής, means "my [*very*] *life*," as being a *unique* irreplaceable possession In Jer Targ I and II (on Gen xxii 10) the angels call Abraham and Isaac "these *unique* [*ones*]" In *Pesachim* 118 *a*, God says "I am *unique* in my world, and Abraham *unique* in his," and in *Ps Sol* xviii 4 the seed of Abraham says "Thy chastening is upon us as [upon] a son, firstborn, *only-begotten* (μονογενῆ)" A contrast is drawn between God's "only-begotten" and "the world" in *Ezr Apoc* vi 58—9 (ed. Box) "But we, thy people, whom thou hast called thy firstborn, thy *only-begotten* (unigenitum)...if *the world* has indeed been created for our sakes, why do we not enter into possession of our *world*?"

The Johannine Gospel answers this question as to the relation between the "only-begotten" and "the world" by referring the reader to the Incarnation. It denies both the Greek view, that the "only-begotten" is identical with the world, and also the Jewish view, that the "only-begotten" is Israel after the flesh.

CHAPTER II

JOHN BAPTIZING THE PEOPLE

§ 1. *John the Baptist,* (1) "*preaching,*"
(2) "*bearing witness*"

THE Synoptists describe the Baptist as "preaching," John describes him as "bearing witness." This difference pervades the two streams of narrative. The Synoptists take an interest, so to speak, in the Prophet for his own sake. John does not.

For example, Mark (followed by Matthew) describes the Baptist's ascetic diet and clothing; Luke, too, though omitting this description, records the rules of conduct laid down by the Baptist for what may be called the inferior laity—the publicans, soldiers, and common people generally—who said to the Prophet "What shall we do?" John omits both the Marcan and the Lucan details, but dwells on the mission of the Baptist to "bear-witness," and on the "witness" when borne[1].

The reader will infer from these facts that in this chapter,—as in others that deal with details about John the Baptist—we must not expect the rule of Johannine Intervention to be observed. The Marcan mention of the Baptist's "leathern girdle" and "locusts and wild honey," omitted by Luke, must not be expected to be restored, or to have an equivalent in its place, in the Fourth Gospel.

---

[1] John uses μαρτυρέω five times, and μαρτυρία twice, about the Baptist in his first chapter, besides many instances in other contexts Mark never uses μαρτυρέω at all, Matthew and Luke use it each only once. Μαρτυρία is used by Synoptists only as to false witness against Jesus on His trial.

§ 2   "*As it is written in Isaiah the prophet*"

Mark says "The beginning of the gospel (*lit* good-message) ..even *as it is written* (lit *it has been written*) in Isaiah the prophet, Behold I send my messenger...The voice of one crying aloud in the wilderness, .there-was (*or*, came) John who was baptizing in the wilderness.. [1]"

On this we may imagine a Christian writer, perhaps a disciple of John, at the end of the first century, making the following comment :—

"'*Behold I send...*' is not in Isaiah but in Malachi. Moreover, '*good-message*,' closely followed by '*my messenger,*' would lead some to suppose that the '*good-message,*' or 'gospel,' was wholly delivered by the '*messenger*,' i.e. by John the Baptist   Also the phrase '*as it is written*,' though fit for quoting scripture that applies to all time (as when the Lord Jesus says '*It is written*, thou shalt not live by bread alone') would not be so fit concerning the mere sending of a messenger on a certain occasion, even though it were a great occasion.

"Isaiah spoke first of 'the voice' and afterwards of 'the word of our God'   The Baptist did not compare himself with 'the word of our God' which 'shall stand for ever[2].' What he meant was that he himself was only a voice : ' I am the voice of one crying ..make straight the way of the Lord,' as said Isaiah the prophet[3].

"Luke retains '*as it is written*,' and writes out three or four verses of the prophecy, '*As it is written in the book of the words of Isaiah the prophet ..and all flesh shall see the salvation of God*[4].' Matthew does not do this. He inserts 'saying' in

---

[1] Mk 1 1—4, quoting Mal. iii. 1 and Is xl. 3

[2] Is xl 3—8 "*The voice* of one crying...*the word* of our God shall stand for ever"   [3] Jn 1 23

[4] Lk. iii 4—6   Jn uses the Synoptic "has been written" twice (viii. 17, xx. 31), but mostly he uses the participle, "that which has been written," or the noun "writing" (*i e* "scripture"), probably to denote permanence (as in x 35 "the scripture cannot be broken")

a doubtful connection, and in such a way that we are perhaps to infer that the Baptist said the whole of what follows: 'Repent ye, for the kingdom of the heavens hath drawn near. *For this is he* (or, *He*) *that was said, through Isaiah the prophet*, saying, The voice of one crying...[1].'

"Now the point of importance for us is, not that 'Isaiah' said this, or 'Malachi' that, but that the Spirit of prophecy prophesied about the Messiah in all the prophets from the first to the last, so that the last of them, namely the Baptist, was able to say concerning the Lord Jesus ' *This was He that I, the Lord's prophet, said*,' or, ' *This was He that they, the Lord's prophets, said*,' meaning, ' *This was He concerning whom we all prophesied*.'"

Such a meaning might be extracted from the tradition in the Fourth Gospel without altering a letter of it: " *This was he that they* [i.e. the prophets] *said*[2]." Somewhat similarly the Gospel of the Hebrews represents the Holy Spirit as saying to Jesus at His baptism, "My son, *in all the prophets* I was expecting thee[3]."

---

[1] Mt iii. 3 οὗτος γάρ ἐστιν ὁ ῥηθεὶς διὰ 'Ησαίου .λέγοντος I have found no instance of ὁ ῥηθείς applied to persons in the Greek Bible. In Gk, the genitive λέγοντος makes it clear that Isaiah is the person "saying" But in Heb and Syr, "saying," or "who said," may refer to "he," i.e. the Baptist, or to "Isaiah" Palest. has "This is he that *said*, in Isaiah the prophet" (with v r " *was said*"). "Saying" is omitted by Syr. (Walton) and *b*.

The obscurity of Matthew is increased by other considerations, *e.g.* the fact that "this is he" may mean "I am he," for which see p 41.

[2] Jn i. 15.

[3] See *Joh. Gr* **1927** *c* quoting from *The Gospel of the Hebrews* (as quoted by Jerome on Is xi. 2) "Fili mi, in omnibus Prophetis expectabam te" Also, on Is. liii 1 "Who hath believed our report? and to whom hath the arm of the Lord been revealed?" Jerome says, "After the words of the Father announcing to the world the future coming of His Son *the chorus of the Prophets answered* that they had done their duty and (as far as in them lay) had announced His arm and power to all."

§ 3. "*This was he that they said*"

If the unique expression in Matthew is thus connected with the obscure and uncouth and almost unique expression in John, it becomes lawful to infer that neither Evangelist resorts to such strange language out of mere eccentricity. Both perhaps are endeavouring to interpret some ambiguous Greek tradition capable of meaning (1) "This was he that they said," (2) "This was he that I said," and—with a very slight change indeed—(3) "This was he that said."

Of these three interpretations, Mark and Matthew adopt the first, identifying "they" with "the prophets," represented by "Isaiah." But the Fourth Evangelist appears to adopt the second. The scene that he sees before Christ's baptism differs from that presented by any of the Synoptists. Not one of the Three, not even Luke, tells us that God had said to the Baptist, in effect, "Not only is the Messiah at hand, but I appoint unto thee a sign by which thou shalt know Him." But the Fourth Evangelist does this. The expectant position of the Baptist in the Fourth Gospel is somewhat like the expectant position of Samuel after the Lord had said to him "I have provided me a king[1]" When David passes before him, the prophet hears a voice saying "Arise, anoint him, for *this is he*." Instead of "This *is* he," the Evangelist puts into the mouth of the Baptist "This *was* he." By this is meant, first, "This *was from the beginning* the foreordained Messiah," and secondly, "This *was* the Messiah, *even during the time when He was close to me, as my disciple, and I knew Him not*, because the Spirit had not yet descended upon Him."

Thus the last and greatest of the prophets, to whom it was given to be the first to see and to proclaim to the world the Baptizer with the Holy Spirit, simultaneously magnifies the greatness of this Bringer of the Spirit and

---

[1] 1 S xvi 1

confesses his own comparative littleness, by avowing that he did not recognise Him at first even when present, though he had proclaimed His future coming. This confession is expressed in language that is ampler—as is often the case with an inspired prophet—than the conception of the prophet himself. The Baptist, in his own understanding, may have meant no more than this, "Even while He was following behind me as a disciple, He was all the time *essentially before me*, being *my Chief*, though I knew Him not." But the words are capable of meaning "He *was, even from the beginning of things*, my Chief and my Lord[1]"

§ 4. "*My messenger*"

Mark has "Even as it is written in Isaiah the prophet, *Behold, I send my messenger before thy face, who shall prepare thy way*. The voice of one crying...[2]." Matthew and Luke omit, here, the italicised words; but, later on, they represent Jesus as saying to the multitudes, concerning the Baptist, that he is "a prophet," and "more than a prophet," for "this is he of whom it is written, *Behold, I send my messenger before thy face, who shall prepare thy way before thee*[3]."

These words are from Malachi, where they are connected with the Purification of the Temple, thus "*Behold, I send my messenger, and he shall prepare the way before my face*, and *the Lord*, whom ye seek, shall suddenly come to his temple, and *the messenger of the covenant*, whom ye delight in, behold, he *cometh*, saith the Lord of hosts. But who may abide the day of his coming?...For he is like a refiner's fire...and he shall sit as a refiner and purifier of silver...[4]." The persons indicated by the twice repeated "messenger" (or "angel") are not clear. Still less clear are they in the text as quoted by

---

[1] On "before me," see *Joh Gr* ad loc.
[2] Mk 1. 2.
[3] Mt xi. 9—10, Lk. vii. 26—7.   [4] Mal. iii. 1—3.

Clement of Rome, "The Lord shall suddenly come to His Temple, *and* the Holy One whom ye expect," where the Greek "*and*" is rendered "*even*" in Lightfoot's translation[1].

Avoiding the Marcan quotation of Malachi, the Johannine writer appears to have described, in his record of an early purification of the Temple, what he regards as its fulfilment.—the Lord "*suddenly coming*" to the Temple, and "purifying" it, at least for the time. Also, if any early difficulties arose in connection with Mark's reference to John the Baptist as a "messenger" or "angel," the writer avoids these by avoiding the term in connection with the Baptist, whom he prefers to describe as "*a man sent from God*," and afterwards as saying "Ye yourselves bear me witness that I said, I (*emph.*) am not the Christ, but that I am [*one*] *sent* before him[2]." When did the Baptist say this? Nowhere in these exact words, but in similar words, thus, "*He that sent me* [*on a mission*] *to baptize in water*—he said unto me, 'On whomsoever thou shalt see...' and I have borne witness that this [same] is the Son of God[3]"

§ 5 "*Are we to expect another?*"

But there are other difficulties in Matthew and Luke not so easily met, arising out of the quotation from Malachi. For

---

[1] Clem Rom § 23 See *Light* 3731 *t*, 3763 *c* &c Rashi takes "the Lord" (in Malachi III 1) as "the God of judgment" (comp Mal II. 17 "where is the God of judgment?") and "the messenger," first-mentioned, as being apparently the same as that mentioned second, namely, the Messenger of the Covenant Origen (*Comm Joann* II. 24—5) maintained that the Baptist was an "angel" Pseudo-Jerome on Mk says "The voice of the Holy Spirit through Malachi sounds forth to the Father concerning the Son who is His Face," *i e*, apparently, "I, the Spirit, send my messenger, John, before thy Son, O Father, to prepare thy way" These facts indicate the difficulties that would arise out of Mark's text for Christians in the first century

[2] Jn I. 6, III. 28

[3] Jn I. 33—4. On the difference between "send" and "send on a mission," see *Joh. Voc.* 1723 *g*

they, later on, represent the messenger-prophet as saying to Him whose way he came to prepare, "Art thou he that is to come? Or are we to expect another[1]?" And, in reply to the two disciples of the Baptist who bring this message, Jesus says, in effect, that although the Baptist is not inferior to any "among those born of women," yet the little one "in the kingdom of God is greater than he[2]" The Baptist's faith at that time would seem to have been shaken. Matthew and Luke say that Jesus dismissed the two messengers with the words "Go, tell John the things ye hear and see...and blessed is he whosoever shall not stumble in me." Are these words intended to suggest a rebuke for stumbling or a help against stumbling? Are we to infer that this "blessing" finally rested on the Baptist, who was confirmed in faith by the Lord's warning, so that in the end he did not finally "stumble"?

The Fourth Gospel seems to point to this inference, though only indirectly. It shews that from first to last the Prophet was always devoted to the Bridegroom But he is the "friend," not one of the Family of the Bridegroom. Perhaps therefore we are intended to regard the Prophet as among the class of those "born of women," as Matthew and Luke say. This class is described in the Fourth Gospel as those begotten "from blood, or from the desire of the flesh, or from the will of the husband," and is contrasted with those who "were begotten from God[3]" These last are born of the Spirit, and the Evangelist says that the Spirit was not given till Jesus was glorified. Although therefore John saw the Spirit descending on Jesus, he did not himself receive it. Yet he rejoiced in it, and in the Messiah who received it.

---

[1] "Expect," comp. Clem. Rom. § 23 (above quoted) "the Holy One whom ye expect"

[2] Mt xi. 11, Lk. vii. 28, on "the little one" (*lit* "more little") see *Son* 3523*a* foll

[3] Jn i. 13.

JOHN BAPTIZING THE PEOPLE

Matthew and Luke mention disciples of the Baptist (Luke says "two") coming from him to Jesus with the message, "Art thou he that is to come?" The Fourth Gospel says that—in quite different circumstances—two disciples of the Baptist were, in effect, sent by him to Jesus as being "the Lamb of God[1]." This, like the miraculous Draught of Fishes, is one of several instances where the Fourth Gospel supplements Luke, without contradicting him. The two disciples, in Luke, were to report what things "they heard and saw." The two disciples, in the Fourth Gospel also, were invited to "come" that they might "see," and they "came" and "saw." The former saw miracles of healing. The latter saw Jesus Himself and where He "abode." That is, they received a partial revelation of the Father[2], and thus these two disciples became the beginnings of the Church of Christ.

This does not imply a denial that, later on, "two" disciples of the Baptist came as Luke relates. But it places before us another and earlier aspect of the Baptist and "two" of his disciples which Luke has not related. Afterwards, indeed, the Fourth Gospel admits that some of the disciples of the Baptist were jealous of the Lord Jesus. But the prophet himself says to them "He that hath the Bride is the Bridegroom," and declares that he, as being the Bridegroom's friend, "rejoiceth with [great] joy by reason of the Bridegroom's voice." Then he adds—and these are the Prophet's last words—"This my joy therefore is fulfilled. He must increase, but I must decrease[3]."

Such is the description in the Fourth Gospel of the prophet whom the Three call "messenger." That he did deliver a message, and was a "messenger," is clearly stated, but in such a way as to avoid difficulties arising out of the word

---

[1] Jn i 35 foll.
[2] Comp. Clem. Alex. 956 "Behold ($\theta\epsilon\hat{\omega}$) the mysteries of love, and then shalt thou receive-the-sacred-sight ($\epsilon\pi o\pi\tau\epsilon\acute{u}\sigma\epsilon\iota\varsigma$) of the bosom of the Father, whom the Only-begotten Son, God, alone declared"
[3] Jn iii 25—30 (see *Joh Gr* pref. p viii).

"messenger" as used by Malachi. And that the messenger was merely for the season and not for all time is implied in the words uttered later on by Jesus concerning him, "He was the torch that burns away and shines," that is to say, shines by burning away, and not like the sun, the light of the world which is a constant source of light[1].

§ 6 "*The voice of one crying*"

In Mark, this quotation from Isaiah is introduced without any clear connection. The reader might take the words in this among other ways "The beginning of the gospel.. [was] the voice of one crying." Matthew has "For this is he that was *spoken of* through Isaiah the prophet, *saying*, The *voice* of one crying...[2]." Luke says that "the word (*or*, utterance) of God came-to-pass on John...and he came...proclaiming.. as it is written in the book of the *words* of Isaiah the prophet, The *voice* of one ..[3]."

Isaiah tells us how the "crying" comes to pass. Israel was returning from captivity in Babylon and journeying through the wilderness to Jerusalem; and God commanded the prophets and rulers of Israel to comfort His people and prepare the way of the Lord in that wilderness: "Comfort ye, comfort ye my people . and cry ye unto her that her warfare is accomplished, that her iniquity is pardoned, [and] that she hath received of the Lord's hand double for all her sins —*The voice of one that crieth, Prepare ye in the wilderness the way of the Lord*...[4]." Whose is "the voice of one that crieth"? It does not appear to be the voice of any one prophet. For Isaiah continues thus, "The voice of one saying *Cry*. And one said, What shall I cry?" That is

---

[1] Jn v 35. See *Joh. Gr* 2275 *b*
[2] Mt iii. 3. See above, p. 34, n 1.
[3] Lk. iii. 2—4, "word (*or*, utterance)"=$\dot{\rho}\hat{\eta}\mu\alpha$, "words"=$\lambda\acute{o}\gamma o\iota$
[4] Is xl. 1—3

to say, the prophet answers the appeal, and asks what he is to prophesy. This seems to shew that (as Rashi says) "the voice of one that crieth" is the Voice of the Holy Spirit of Prophecy calling on the prophets to "cry." Hence if the prophecy were strictly applied in the Gospels, "the voice" would not be exactly that of the Baptist, but rather that of the Holy Spirit possessing the Baptist, and, through him, bidding the teachers and rulers of Israel to comfort Israel and prepare the way of the Lord[1].

There is a recognised distinction in Hebrew (resembling the distinction in Greek) between "word" and "voice" The "voice of the Lord God" may come through thunder, or through angels, or through the leaves of the trees in Paradise[2]. When Moses heard "*the word*" from Sinai, it is said that Israel heard it not, "but belike they heard *the voice*[3]." Philo makes the same distinction. Ignatius says that if his friends permit him to be a martyr, he is "*a word of God*," but if they will not, "I shall be *a [mere] voice* again[4]." The Fourth Gospel represents the Baptist as saying "*I am a voice,*" somewhat in the sense in which Ignatius said it And Matthew himself shews us how some such tradition may have arisen. For in Hebrew, as well as in Greek, a man sometimes speaks of himself as "*this man,*" meaning "I, even this man who stands before you", and the words last quoted from Matthew might be rendered thus : "Repent ye, for the kingdom of the heavens hath drawn near, *For this man* [*who stands before you*, i.e *I*]

---

[1] Rashi says that in Is xl. 3—6 the Voice is the Holy Spirit, or the Voice from the Holy and Blessed, and he paraphrases "one said" as "My spirit said to Him" Comp Is. vi 8 where God says "Whom shall I send, and who will go for us?" and the prophet replies "Here am I, send me."

[2] Gen. iii 8 "they heard *the voice of the Lord God* walking"

[3] See *Numb. r.* (on Numb vii 89, Wu p 392) referring to Exod. xxix 42 "*you...thee*"

[4] Ign. *Rom* § 2. On Philo i. 624—5 s *Son* **3628** *d*

JOHN BAPTIZING THE PEOPLE

is he that was spoken of by Isaiah the prophet, saying, *The Voice...*[1]*."*

Also Luke represents "the people" as expecting, and reasoning in their hearts "whether perchance he [*i.e.* the Baptist] were the Christ." The Fourth Gospel goes further and says that the Baptist was asked "Who art thou?" and he—knowing that they meant, though they did not say, "Art thou the Christ?"—confessed, and denied not, and confessed, "I am not the Christ." Then, in answer to further questioning, he said "I am the voice of one crying...." Thus the Fourth Gospel appears to carry on the traditions of the Three, explaining what was obscure in Mark and Matthew, but explaining it somewhat differently from Luke, and in such a way as to lead the reader—while he is being taught about the Baptist and the Voice—to think about these as severally inferior to Jesus and to the Word.

§ 7. *Is "in the wilderness" to be taken with "crying" or with "prepare ye"?*

All the Synoptists agree in quoting, after a mention of "Isaiah the prophet," the words "The voice of one crying *in the wilderness*, Make ye ready the way of the Lord, make his paths straight[2]." This agrees almost exactly with the LXX except that they substitute "his paths" for LXX "the paths of our God." In the Hebrew, which differs, there is a parallelism between "*in the wilderness*" and "*in the desert*"; and this suggests that both phrases should be connected with imperatives ("*prepare ye in the wilderness...make straight in the desert*")[3]. The Revised Version (text) adopts this connection

---

[1] Mt. iii 2—3. On "*this man*" meaning "*I*," s *Son* **3068** (1).

[2] Mk i 3, Mt iii 3, Lk. iii 4 Jn i 23 has "the voice of one crying in the wilderness Make ye straight the way of the Lord—as said Isaiah the prophet." In Greek as in English we might punctuate after crying ("crying, In the wilderness make ye .") But it would be harsh.

[3] Is. xl. 3 (R V. *txt*) "that crieth, *Prepare ye in the wilderness* (*marg.* that crieth in the wilderness, Prepare ye) the way of the Lord, make

in Isaiah, but does not even suggest it as an alternative in the Gospels. Why is this?

Probably it is, in part, because Mark and Matthew in their several contexts describe the Baptist as "baptizing *in the wilderness*" and "preaching *in the wilderness*," evidently taking this to be a fulfilment of the prophecy about "one crying *in the wilderness*[1]." Luke on the other hand, instead of saying that the Baptist "preached in the wilderness," implies that *he did not preach till he came out of it*[2]. It is therefore quite possible (though not probable) that Luke took "in the wilderness" with "prepare ye."

The truth is that no parallel can be drawn between any literal "wilderness" in which the Baptist can have preached (whether it was "the wilderness" of Judaea or any other) and that pathless "wilderness" in Isaiah through which Jehovah bade the rulers of Israel prepare a path for the Lord, which should also be a path for His people. But "wilderness" might be regarded metaphorically. The Fourth Gospel, while retaining the ambiguous form of the unpunctuated quotation ("crying in the wilderness prepare ye") does not follow any of the Synoptists in making any independent mention of a literal "wilderness." Also it condenses the Hebrew parallels "prepare ye" (or "make ye ready"), "make ye straight," into a form of the latter, used by Joshua when saying to Israel

---

straight in the desert a high way for our God." The LXX drops the parallel "in the desert," and does not express literally "high way for our God."

[1] Mk i 4, Mt iii. 1 But Matthew adds "of Judaea," on which see *Hor Heb.* ad loc contrasting the metrical standards of "Jerusalem" with those of "the wilderness"

[2] Lk i 80 "was in the desert places ($\tau\alpha\hat{\iota}s$ $\dot{\epsilon}\rho\dot{\eta}\mu o\iota s$) till...," iii 2—3 "The word of God came on John...*in the wilderness*, and he came into all [the] circle of the Jordan" On the other hand, Mt iii 5 says that "all the circle of the Jordan" came out to the Baptist Early confusion appears to have existed as to the meaning of "wilderness," "circle" &c. Luke himself (vii. 24) agrees with Mt xi. 7, that Jesus said, about the Baptist, to the multitudes, "What went ye out *into the wilderness* to behold?"

"*straighten* ye your heart unto the Lord," and by Philo describing Abraham as among those who "*straighten* (or, *keep straight*) the safe *way* to God," namely, through faith[1].

As to the scene of the Baptist's preaching and baptizing, it will be seen, later on, that the Fourth Gospel says it was "Bethany, beyond Jordan." "*Beyond Jordan*" might express a spiritual aspect of "*the wilderness*," as being a place where Israel is away from its home, journeying from captivity in Egypt, or from captivity in Babylon, toward the Promised Land or toward the New Jerusalem[2]. The phrase also suggests the coming victory of Jesus. For whereas Moses merely looked across the Jordan, the first Jesus passed through it and led Israel through it into the Promised Land, and that is what the second Jesus, in His baptism, is regarded as now beginning to do.

In this aspect, as announcing the revelation of a glorious conqueror, we may note the contrast between Luke and John in dealing with the Isaiah quotation. Luke gives much space to it, as describing the long line of the redeemed of Israel, whose return from captivity across the desert is smoothed by the removal of "valley" and "mountain," "crooked" and "rough" places. But he omits "and the glory of the Lord shall be revealed[3]." The Fourth Gospel has previously emphasized the "glory, as of the Only begotten"; and it now utilises the quotation from Isaiah mainly for the purpose of representing the Baptist as contrasting himself, the mere "voice"—calling on Israel to "make straight the way of the

---

[1] Εὐθύνατε See Josh xxiv 23, Philo ii 39, and Sir ii. 2, 6 "straighten thy heart...thy ways" It is implied that "straightening the way in one's heart" is "straightening the way of the Lord in one's heart" Comp. Zech 1 3 "Return unto me.. and I will return unto you."

[2] "Wilderness" means the wilderness of Sinai in Jn iii. 14, vi. 31, 49. Its meaning in Jn xi. 54 "near the wilderness," and the reason for the insertion of the phrase, are matters for discussion

[3] Lk. iii. 3—6, quoting from Is. xl. 3—5

JOHN BAPTIZING THE PEOPLE

Lord"—with "the mightier one," about whom the Baptist goes on to say "But that he should be made manifest to Israel, for this cause came I baptizing with water[1]."

§ 8. *"Preaching" or "making proclamation"*

The Synoptists all use here—and all for the first time—the verb "proclaim-as-a-herald," commonly rendered "preach" in the Gospels, Matthew, perhaps regarding the Baptist as a herald announcing the approach of a king, thus, "*proclaiming*. . repent, *for the kingdom of the heavens hath drawn near*"; but Mark and Luke say "*proclaiming* a baptism of repentance unto remission of sins," without any mention of "kingdom[2]"

The Fourth Gospel neither here nor elsewhere ever makes mention of "heralding" or "preaching," either about the Baptist or about Jesus Relatively to Jesus, the Baptist is not a herald, he is the Voice compared with the Word, or the Bridegroom's friend compared with the Bridegroom. And, relatively to God, Jesus is not a herald, He is the Son compared with the Father Not that the Fourth Gospel denies that there is a divine Kingdom with edicts to be heralded or proclaimed, but it insists that the King cannot be "seen," and it implies that His edicts cannot be heard so as to be understood except through the "declaration" of the Son "No man hath seen God at any time, the only begotten Son (*or*, God only begotten) that is in the bosom of the Father, he hath declared him"

This affords an adequate reason for the Johannine avoidance of the word "proclaim-as-a-herald" all through the Gospel, and particularly here in connection with the testimony of the Baptist. It is rather as "a crier," and as "crying aloud"—than

---

[1] Jn 1. 14, 23, 31.
[2] Mt iii 1, Mk i. 4, Lk iii. 3. Comp Justin Martyr *Tryph* § 49 "The spirit of God that had been in Elijah came-before Christ's first manifestation, *as a herald*, in John, who, on the river Jordan, tarrying (*lit* sitting, a Hebraism) *cried* (ἐβόα) I indeed baptize you. "

JOHN BAPTIZING THE PEOPLE

as a "herald"—that the Baptist is brought before us in the Fourth Gospel. "John beareth witness concerning him, and *crieth-aloud*," it says, using the word employed by Theodotion concerning the appeal of Wisdom in Proverbs, "Doth not Wisdom *cry* (Theod. *cry aloud*), and understanding put forth her voice?. .Unto you, O men, do I call, and my voice is to the sons of man[1]." Both in Proverbs and here there is a suggestion that those who are addressed are hard of hearing. "To cry-aloud" is not so inconsistent as "to herald" would have been with the Baptist's subsequent protest that he is no person, but, as it were, a mere utterance, "I [am a mere] voice."

§ 9 *Baptism*

" We now approach one of the most obscure of all the obscure subjects in the New Testament, the nature of the baptism introduced by John the Baptist. It will be found that Mark has two brief phrases—one about "*baptizing*," the other about "*baptism.*" Of these, Matthew selects a version of the former, Luke selects the latter

Mk 1. 4	Mt iii 1-2	Lk. iii. 2-3
There-came[2] John *the baptizer* (or, *he that was baptizing*) in the wilderness, proclaiming a *baptism* of repentance [with a view] to remission of sins.	There-cometh-forward[3] John the *Baptist*, proclaiming in the wilderness of Judaea, saying, Repent ye, for the Kingdom of the heavens hath drawn near.	There-came[2] the word of God on John the son of Zacharias in the wilderness, and he went[4] proclaiming a *baptism* of repentance [with a view] to remission of sins

---

[1] Jn 1. 15 "crieth-aloud (κέκραγεν)," Prov. viii 1 (Heb) "crieth," Theod κεκράξεται.

[2] " There-came," in Mk 1 4, Lk iii. 2, ἐγένετο.

[3] " There-cometh-forward," in Mt iii. 1, παραγίνεται

[4] "Went," ἦλθεν The word is translated thus so as to be distinguished from ἐγένετο, " came," which is applied by Luke to "the word of God" on John, but by Mark to " John " Luke says "went into all the surrounding-country of the Jordan."

Here we must carefully note that Matthew, when he says that "John the Baptist" began to preach, may not mean that John began to baptize at the same time. Mark ("the baptizer," or "he that was baptizing") may mean this And Luke apparently means this. But Matthew may be using "John the Baptist" simply as the Prophet's name, known to everyone, derived from his subsequent practice.

The Baptist's teaching may well have passed through various phases. He was at first (so the Fourth Gospel says, and Matthew confirms it) regarded favourably by some of the Pharisees, who were "willing for a season to rejoice in his light[1]." At that time he may not have inculcated baptism. For was it likely that Pharisees would favour a prophet inculcating such an innovation? Some interval is required to explain the alienation of the Pharisees, and also the awakening of the suspicions and fears of Herod Antipas For Josephus tells us that the Tetrarch put John to death, not because of any women's plottings (of which the historian makes no mention) but because John gathered round him such multitudes of restless and excited people as to give grounds for apprehending a revolution[2]. Even after his death, the prophet had such a hold on the people that the Pharisees themselves dared not publicly deny—when Jesus challenged them publicly —that John's baptism was from heaven. So say the Synoptic Gospels Josephus adds that the common people deemed the defeat of Herod Antipas by the Arabians to be a divine judgment on him for murdering the Prophet[3]. Outside Palestine, Apollos the Alexandrian and certain Christians in Ephesus are found to be Christians indeed, but "knowing *only the baptism of John*[4]." From all this it seems probable that

---

[1] Jn v 35. This is confirmed by Mt. iii 7.

[2] On the possibility of a connection between John's teaching and the "remission" of debts, see *Joh Voc* **1690** *b* (i)—(vii) quoted below (p 59, n 2)

[3] Joseph *Ant.* xviii. 5 2   [4] Acts xviii 25.

47

John's public life lasted for a period to be measured by years rather than by months. During those years he may have received a series of revelations resulting in corresponding prophecies or doctrines, very few of which have come down to us because they have been merged in, or superseded by, the doctrine of Christ.

Matthew may have believed that the Prophet did not begin to baptize till after he had for some time preached "repentance." At all events he makes no mention of *"baptizing"* till he says (as does Mark also) that people came to John and *"began to be* (or, *were being*) *baptized* by him in the river Jordan confessing their sins[1]." There is reason, however, for thinking that Matthew, at this point—and especially in omitting the words "[*with a view*] *to remission of sins*"—may have been influenced by doctrinal inferences and interpretations. For near the end of his Gospel, he, and he alone, inserts the phrase thus, "This is my blood...which is being shed for many [*with a view*] *to remission of sins*[2]." Perhaps, therefore, he considered that the clause about remission, being in its place there, must be out of place here, arguing thus: "'Repentance' cannot bring 'remission of sins.' 'Repentance' could only prepare the heart to believe in Jesus and to receive 'remission of sins' later on from His blood." The Marcan tradition, 'baptism of repentance with a view to remission of sins,' might lead people to suppose that John the Baptist taught his disciples to hope that, when they emerged from the water after confession of sins, their sins would have been then and there remitted, and that they were saved. That was not true. It will be better to make it clear that the Baptist was, in effect, a herald saying 'Repent ye, for the King of Israel is at hand ready to bring salvation,' or, in other words, 'Repent ye, for the kingdom of the heavens hath drawn near.'"

---

[1] Mt. iii 6, Mk i 5.
[2] Mt. xxvi. 28. The parall. Mk xiv 24 omits the italicised words

But there is this defect in Matthew, that, having thus departed from Mark by omitting "baptism," he proceeds—just as though he had inserted it—to say, with Mark, that the people "began-to-be baptized[1]" Yet Matthew has not told us either that the Baptist enjoined baptism, or that he taught anything about its nature. Mark and Luke also, though to a less extent, are obscurely reticent No one would guess from the Synoptists—at least, no Gentile—that, although "baptisms" for purification[2] were habitual among the Jews, a "baptism of repentance"—a baptism for Jews, to be performed once for all—was an entirely new thing among them. For proselytes, indeed, baptism appears to have been at an early date[3] regularly used after circumcision, as part of their introduction into the Covenant; but for Jews it was unheard of in any such sense

Perhaps Mark and Matthew relied on the name and the title, "John the Baptizer, or the Baptist," which they had previously mentioned when introducing the prophet: "In those days there cometh-forth John the Baptist[4]" They may have assumed that the last of the prophets would not have been called by this title unless his baptism had been of a special nature With still more reason would Luke, after giving us his account of the miraculous birth of John for a divine purpose, assume that we knew his "baptism" to be of a special and divine nature. But he nowhere says so.

As for Matthew, he does not even say distinctly whether the Baptist insisted on baptism or merely recommended it, nor whether he enjoined it on all, or only on those whom the Jews

---

[1] Mt iii 6, Mk i 5

[2] Comp Mk vii 4 on "baptizing (v.r sprinkling)" of men, and "immersions ($\beta\alpha\pi\tau\iota\sigma\mu o\grave{u}s$) of cups," and Heb. vi 2 "teaching of baptisms ($\beta\alpha\pi\tau\iota\sigma\mu\hat{\omega}\nu$)" (comp ib. ix 10)

[3] See Schurer II. ii 319 foll. On Exod. xii 44 "when thou hast circumcised him," Jer. Targ. I has (Walton) "circumcides eum et *lavabis eum.*"

[4] Mt iii 1, comp Mk i 4

called "sinners", nor what the baptized were to gain by baptism. Later on, where the Three agree in representing the Baptist as saying that his baptism was merely with "water," Matthew alone adds "*to repentance*[1]," apparently meaning that "repentance" is to be the result or concomitant of the baptism, not the condition for being baptized. Thus he again differs from Mark and Luke.

§ 10. *In the Fourth Gospel, "baptizing" is subordinated to "bearing-witness"*

The Fourth Gospel neither introduces John as "the Baptist," nor ever calls him by that title. Nor is John's baptizing brought before us formally and directly in any statement of the Evangelist's It comes only, as it were, incidentally and dramatically in a question put by the Pharisees to John, "*Why baptizest thou, then*, if thou art not the Christ, nor yet Elijah, nor yet the Prophet[2]?" This opens our eyes at once to the enormous importance attached by the Pharisees to this prophetically introduced rite of baptism Only one of these three great—we may almost say supernatural—Persons would (in their opinion) have the right to introduce it. It is clearly seen to be (in their eyes) something entirely different from the immersions and sprinklings enjoined by the Law for the removal of Levitical "uncleanness."

But the reply of the Baptist also opens our eyes to the extraordinarily little importance that he himself attached to it, in itself and for its own sake "I baptize with water; in the midst of you there standeth..." We expect the sentence to be completed with an antithetical mention of some one greater than himself who will introduce some higher kind of baptism. But it stops short of this. It mentions the nearness of the

---

[1] Mk i 8, Mt iii 11, Lk. iii 16.
[2] Jn i 25 On "the prophet," see *From Letter* **829**, *Joh. Gr.* **1940, 1965.**

great unrecognised Person, but no higher baptism at present[1]. "On the morrow" (but why is it delayed till "the morrow"?) the Baptist adds that his own baptizing was simply for the sake of this Person, "that he should be made manifest to Israel, for this cause came I baptizing with water." But still he mentions no higher baptism. The next sentence, however, "bears witness" to a vision: "And John bare witness saying, I have beheld the Spirit descending as a dove .," in connection with which it is said "He that sent me to baptize with water, he said unto me, Upon whomsoever thou shalt see the Spirit descending and abiding upon him, the same is he that baptizeth with the Holy Spirit"

The impression produced by all these Johannine statements or dramatic questions and suggestions is that the Baptist's rite, though a stupendous innovation in the eyes of the Pharisees, was a very small and rudimentary thing as compared with that for which it prepared the way—the descent of the Spirit and baptism with the Spirit. The baptism of John was nothing more than a witness to the need of a baptism by One greater than John, and the right name for John, spiritually regarded, was not the Baptist, but the Witness Accordingly it is in this character that he is introduced—immediately after the mention of the light as not being overcome by the darkness—"There came a man, sent from God, whose name was John The same came for witness, that he might bear witness of the light", and this is the character that he sustains throughout the Fourth Gospel.

We shall have to return hereafter to the Baptist's preaching about baptism when we compare the Synoptic with the Johannine version of it. For the present, we are simply comparing the Synoptic introduction of John as "the Baptist," or as "preaching a baptism of repentance," with the Johannine

---

[1] Jn i. 26—7 "in the midst of you standeth one whom ye know not, one coming behind (*or*, after) me, the latchet of whose shoe I am not worthy to unloose."

introduction of John as the Witness in the first place, and as the Baptizer in the second. Those who look at the matter historically may say, "If John preached and baptized for a period to be measured by years, it would seem probable that he preached repentance and baptism—a baptism, perhaps, like that mentioned in Ezekiel[1]—for some time before he proclaimed the advent of the Baptizer with the Holy Spirit. *As it turned out in the end*, no doubt, the more important part played by John was that of a Witness to Christ; but his contemporaries were right in calling him '*the Baptist*' For it was as *the Baptizer* that he took hold of the hearts of his countrymen. Moreover it was his baptism, and no other, that passed into the use of the disciples of Christ themselves, as long as 'the Spirit was not yet [given] because Jesus was not yet glorified[2].' Even in these days, perhaps, multitudes of Christians owe many of their thoughts, both right and wrong, about Christian baptism, to the practice and the doctrine originated by John the Baptist"

There is much that deserves consideration in these remarks The Johannine Gospel may have deviated from history in subordinating too much the early sanguine Prophet, the national Reformer and would-be Regenerator, to the later disillusioned Prophet, who felt that it was not given to him by any immersions in water, even when accompanied by confessions of sins, to clear Israel from their defilements and to cause them to return to the Lord. In his later days the Baptist may have been taught to look to a disciple—and may at last have looked face to face on a disciple—who could do what he himself could not do, by calling down the Spirit of the clean heart and the new life. This disciple indeed would be a veritable Lamb of God taking away the sins of the world.

The two disciples of the Baptist who are said in the Fourth Gospel to have actually heard him say of Jesus

---

[1] Ezek. xxxvi. 25 foll   [2] Jn vii. 39.

"Behold, the Lamb of God!" might be excused if this final utterance of their Master, speaking as a Witness, swallowed up much of their Master's previous doctrine in which he spoke as the Baptizer. The Fourth Gospel is written in the name of one of those two disciples[1], and we must allow for consequent bias, or, let us rather say, preference of aspect.

Nevertheless, taken as a whole, the Fourth Gospel seems a most valuable supplement to the Three in setting before us the probabilities of different phases of the Baptist's doctrine about baptism, and of the effect it would be likely to produce, both upon the multitudes who accepted it and on the Pharisees by whom it was rejected. And even as regards the Johannine view of the predominant and absorbing part played by Jesus in the Baptist's teaching there is this to be said, that it has a kind of precedent in the Old Testament account of Elijah, anointing Elisha as his successor, and promising him "a double portion" of his own "spirit" if he could behold his ascension to heaven. Although the Fourth Gospel makes John say "I *am not* Elijah," it also asserts that he was *asked whether he was* Elijah. And thus the Fourth agrees with the Three in indicating that John would be almost forced, by what others thought, to think of himself in connection with Elijah, and consequently in connection with Elijah's successor, and with the "Spirit" poured out on the two prophets. This thought might justify, as historical, the Johannine emphasis laid on the personal relations between John and Jesus, and the readiness of John to accept in Jesus a successor more powerful than himself

§ 11. *The baptism of John, continued by the disciples of Jesus*

Something ought to be added, though the subject can be only touched on here, on what the Fourth Gospel suggests—but the Three do not suggest—the transition of baptism from

---

[1] For the proof of this, see *Son* **3460** *a—g*.

John to the disciples of Jesus. The Fourth Evangelist says that Jesus "*was tarrying with his disciples and was baptizing*," at a time when John also was baptizing not far off. He adds that a question arose on the part of John's disciples with a Jew about purifying. Yet after saying "Jesus...was baptizing," he subsequently says "*yet Jesus himself baptized not*[1]." Why not have said, from the first—"Jesus was tarrying with his disciples and *they* were baptizing"? Apparently because the Evangelist wished to exhibit in a striking manner the origin, as well as *the fallacy, of the notion that Jesus ever baptized with water*, for, before making this correction, he represents some jealous Jews as coming to the Baptist and saying, "Rabbi, he that was with thee beyond Jordan and to whom thou hast borne witness, behold, *the same baptizeth*, and all men come unto him." Thus, as it were, the Evangelist takes us into his confidence, and says, "You see how natural this way of speaking was, yes, and still is. I used it myself, a few sentences back, and shewed how the Jews took it to be literally true. But the exact truth is, as I am now explaining to you, that *Jesus never baptized with water*"

Perhaps He did not. And indeed, if He did at first, and then left off, it would be difficult to explain when and why He left off On the other hand, if He never baptized, what are we to say about Nathanael and Philip and the rest of the Twelve (excluding Andrew and Peter and the two sons of Zebedee who were presumably baptized by John)? Were Philip and Nathanael never baptized with water? Or were they exceptionally baptized by Jesus before He gave up the practice? Or were they baptized, at the command of Jesus, by some disciple previously baptized by John the Baptist, such as Andrew? These questions we cannot answer But we can say, "They are brought before us by the Fourth Evangelist and left by him unanswered in such a way as to

---

[1] Jn iii. 22 foll , iv. 2.

suggest that the answer does not greatly matter. All deficiencies would be supplied when Jesus ascended to the Father, and the Spirit or Paraclete came down."

The same suggestion applies to other questions about the forms of baptism practised by John and by the disciples of Jesus, at the time when both kinds of baptism were going on simultaneously Were they identical or different? If they were identical at that time, as they probably were at first, perhaps we may find evidence to shew by what steps one form might pass into the other. Supposing, for example, that the original form was "I baptize thee into repentance" or "into the name of repentance," or "I baptize thee into the NAME," we might shew how this might pass into the shorter Christian formula as we find it in the Acts, and into the longer formula which we find near the end of Matthew's Gospel[1].

A word may be added in answer to the question "If the Fourth Evangelist has accurately described the attitude of John the Baptist to Jesus, ought he not consistently to tell us that John became a disciple of Jesus, instead of continuing to baptize and to labour as though the Messiah had not really appeared? Surely the Baptist would not have continued to make disciples of his own?"

The Fourth Gospel seems to reply that the Baptist did *not* "make disciples of his own"—not at least in the narrow sense implied in the question asked above—after he had recognised Jesus as the Messiah No doubt he continued to "baptize." But that did not constitute a claim of superiority. For the disciples of Jesus themselves "baptized" Rather we may say that non-baptizing pointed to such a superiority, for

---

[1] See *Son* **3534** *d* on Mk ix 41 "*in the name*" as perhaps pointing to an original "in the NAME," *i e* "in God's Name," and comp. **3218** *a* In baptism, "in the name" was sometimes used of the character in which a person was baptized, *e g* (*Hor Heb* ii 57) "If an Israelite. . find a Gentile infant, and baptizeth him *in the name of a proselyte*,—behold, he is a proselyte." The different uses of the phrase might cause confusion.

it is expressly said that Jesus Himself—as though above the level of the baptizers—"did *not* baptize." When therefore we read that "*John's disciples*" complained to John about the popularity of Jesus, and that Jesus was "making more disciples and baptizing [more] than John"—as though John were continuing to "make disciples"—we must read this in the light of the context, which expressly declares that Jesus did *not* "baptize," and implies that John no longer regarded himself as independent of Jesus. To those who still called themselves John's "disciples" the Prophet protested that Jesus was the Bridegroom, while he was only the Bridegroom's friend. Why should not the Bridegroom's "friend," as well as the Bridegroom's "disciples," baptize into the NAME those souls in Israel that were moved to turn toward the Lord and to enter into His Kingdom?

All these questions come before us indirectly now in the short and (in appearance) casual expressions quoted above from the Fourth Gospel. But the whole subject will be brought before us directly in the Dialogue between Jesus and Nicodemus, where Jesus develops the doctrine of the New Birth, to which we shall have to refer when we discuss the Synoptic doctrines of becoming a little one, and taking up the cross. For the present we may repeat our conclusion that the Fourth Evangelist desires to subordinate all questions about outward forms of baptism to the doctrine of the inward and spiritual regeneration.

§ 12. *Repentance*

Matthew, by writing, "*Repent ye*" instead of "baptism of repentance," has put into the mouth of the Baptist the same exhortation as the prophets of old addressed to Israel[1] But

---

[1] It occurs repeatedly (Mandelk p 1152) in Isaiah, Jeremiah, Ezekiel, Joel, Zechariah, and Malachi, and is rendered by R V "return" (or "turn") But A V has "*repent*" in Ezek xiv 6, xviii 30 (as also in 1 K. viii 47 where R.V has "turn again")

it meant "*return ye*," not "be ye sorry" or "change your minds" "Return ye" is the Syriac rendering (as also Delitzsch's Hebrew rendering) of the Greek here; and the same Hebrew occurs in the words "*Return ye* unto me and *I will return* unto you, saith the Lord of hosts[1]," and "*Return*, ye sons that turn-away[2]." This "*returning*" may be expressed in various ways. For example, the Targum has "*Return ye to my law*," where Isaiah has "*Wash you*," and Rashi says, on that passage, that the prophet's ten admonitions signifying "*returning* (or *penitence*)" correspond to the reading of ten passages of scripture on the Day of Atonement, the beginning of the New Year, when God, as King, judges the whole world[3].

"Return ye," in Zechariah, is addressed to those that have "turned away." "Wash you," in Isaiah, is addressed to those that are defiled In the same passage Isaiah says "thy silver is become dross" and "thy wine is mixed with water" How the dross is to be removed from the silver the prophet proceeds to shew, saying, "I will purge away thy dross"—

---

[1] Zech 1. 3, Mal iii 7
[2] Jerem. iii 14, 22, comp Ezek. xiv 6, xviii. 30.
[3] Is. i. 16—18. Also see Ezek xxxvi 25—6 "I will sprinkle clean water (comp. Heb. x 22) upon you and ye shall be clean a new heart also will I give you, and a new spirit will I put within you" These words were connected by the Jews with the water of purification sprinkled on Israel at the beginning of the New Year It was said that whereas the priests do it in this world, the Lord Himself will do it in the next, and a commentary on the Song of Songs (1 2) quotes Ezekiel to illustrate the different aspects of the Law, which both cleanses and nourishes man, being likened in Scripture to milk, honey, and wine, as well as to water (*Pesikt* Wu p 49, Cant. Wu p 19, and see Rashi, and *Megill* 30 *a*, and *Joma* 85 *b* which contains Akiba's comment on the words of Ezekiel). Jerome regards Ezekiel as referring to Christian baptism. Akiba and others take the "clean water" in Ezekiel as referring to the water that contained "the ashes of the heifer," about which the Epistle to the Hebrews says (ix 13—14) "If . the ashes of a heifer. sanctify unto the cleanness of the flesh, how much more shall the blood of Christ, who through the Eternal Spirit offered himself without blemish unto God, cleanse your conscience from dead works to serve the living God !"

that is, by fire[1]. But he does not shew how the "wine mixed with water" is to become pure wine again The Fourth Gospel seems to suggest some kind of separation—or rather of keeping separate—by which the water of the Law "given through Moses" is to be kept by itself, placed in separate vessels "after the Jews' manner of purifying," while the water of "grace and truth," which "came through Jesus Christ," is to be "drawn," fresh from the Fountain, and to be brought to the Bridegroom of the Feast, who will pronounce it "the good wine[2]."

Whether this be the case or not with respect to the sign at Cana, it is certainly true of many other parts of the Fourth Gospel, and must be constantly borne in mind, that the Evangelist, while consistently avoiding the Greek words "repent" and "repentance[3]," nevertheless leads us to the Hebrew conception in its purest form by a kind of dramatic representation. For, by itself, the mere Hebrew word "return" is not enough to express the return to Light and Life. Malachi himself shews the possibility of a very narrow view of this "returning" by putting into God's mouth these words: "But ye say, 'Wherein shall we *return*?' Will a man rob God? Yet ye rob me. But ye say, 'Wherein have we robbed thee?' In tithes and offerings[4]." This reminds us indeed of the doctrine of Jesus, but only by contrast. The Pharisees laid stress on tithe-paying, but they did not "return" in the true and spiritual sense. In the Fourth Gospel, the converting or turning of the first two converts is described as an act of literal departure, in which they leave their former Master and "followed Jesus," and Jesus *turned* and beheld them "following. In answer to their question "Rabbi, where abidest thou?" He says, "Come, and ye shall see." They came and abode with

---

[1] Is 1 22—5   [2] Jn 11. 6 foll., 1 17   [3] See *Son* **3564** *a*.
[4] Mal. 111. 7—8. The preceding context however lays stress on the duty of kindness toward the widow, the fatherless, and others

Him It is not added that they "were turned," in response to the "turning" of Jesus. But it is implied in that they turned others to Jesus, each bringing to Him a brother as disciple[1].

The picture seems to correspond to the twofold turning in Zechariah and Malachi. For when the two brethren "follow" the Lord, the Lord "turns" to them, and takes them to Himself. There may be nothing deliberately scenical or typical in this picture of the first conversion, or "turning to the Lord," that resulted from the testimony of John the Baptist. But at all events it illustrates the way in which the Fourth Gospel sets itself against the notion that the process of "repentance" through which man's soul is to pass into unity with the Father in heaven is an unmixed sorrow. And it is instructive to note how there goes hand in hand, along with this turning of the soul to Jesus, a thought, in each of the two converts, for the soul of his brother.

§ 13. "[*With a view*] *to remission of sins*"

Matthew, as has been said above, omits these words here, but inserts them in his account of the Lord's Supper. Mark (who is followed by Luke) does not definitely say that the Baptist uses these words, but merely that this was the object of his baptism, and he never mentions the full phrase "*remission of sins*" again. Luke mentions it five times in the Acts, and thrice in his Gospel[2]. He also represents Jesus as reading from Isaiah—but according to a confused version of the LXX—"...He hath sent me to proclaim *remission* to captives,. to send away [free] them that are oppressed, in *remission* (*i.e.* in freedom)[3]"; and Jesus says "To-day hath

---

[1] See *Son* **3374** *c*, **3626** *a*

[2] On *aphesis*, "remission," see *Joh Voc.* **1690** *a* foll (where, however, in quoting Joseph. *Ant.* III 12 3 "the name [of Jubilee] denotes *Aphesis*," there is an error. It should have been "*freedom*," ἐλευθερία)

[3] Lk IV 18 (on which see *Son*, Index) quoting Is lxi 1

this scripture been fulfilled in your ears." The Fourth Gospel nowhere mentions "*remission.*" Nor does it mention "*remitting*" sins, till after the Resurrection[1]. Nor does it represent Jesus as publicly mentioning "sin" till the words, "I go away, and ye shall seek me and shall die in your sin[2]."

Thus the first public mention of "sin" in the Fourth Gospel is connected with failing to "follow" the Light. For Jesus has just said "I am the light of the world. He that followeth me shall not walk in the darkness but shall have the light of life" This prepares the way for the doctrine that bondage and "sin" and "death" assail every soul that will not obey the voice of the Light when it calls to the soul and says "Be free." Jesus says, in the same passage, "the truth shall make you free[3]."

This aspect of sin—as a failure, a more or less obstinate and self-willed failure, to "follow" the Light—illustrates the difficult Johannine doctrine, "whosesoever sins ye retain they are retained." The Pharisees were sinful. They shut their eyes to the light and said they saw. Jesus warned them, saying, "For judgment have I come into this world, that they that see not may see, and that they that see may become blind." Then, when they mockingly asked Him whether they, too, were "blind," He said, "If ye were blind, ye would have no sin, but now ye say, We see: *your sin remaineth.*" In those last words He "retained" their sin[4].

Just before this, the man born blind—having been cast out from the synagogue by Christ's enemies for protesting against those who said about Him "We know that this man is a sinner"—had received from Jesus Himself the revelation that He was the lawful centre of belief; and "he said, Lord, I believe, and he worshipped him." " He worshipped" means

---

[1] Jn xx. 23

[2] Jn viii 21. Jesus has however previously and privately mentioned the verb "sin" in v. 14 " No longer *sin* "

[3] Jn viii. 12, 32.   [4] Jn ix 39—41.

that the eyes of the man's soul were opened. It means that he saw the Father through the Son, that he was henceforth "free," in a state of "grace"—in other words, to speak Synoptically, that "his sins were forgiven." Jesus does not say to him in express words "thy sins are forgiven thee"; but he virtually says the same thing about him, when he includes him among those about whom he says, "For judgment have I come into this world, that they that see not may see."

There is a contrast. The sins of the blind man are forgiven because he longs for the light. The sins of the Pharisees are retained because they closed their eyes against the light, or rather, perhaps, because they persisted in shutting it out, preferring a light of their own. The light and the glory of God, when they dawn upon us, ought to make pale and ineffectual the light and the glory of men. But the Pharisees preferred the latter: "They loved the glory of men more than the glory of God[1]." And for this cause "judgment" fell upon them.

It is the fact—fundamentally recognised, I believe, in the Fourth Gospel, but in any case the fact—that every man, so far as he breathes the Spirit of Christ, goes about the world "judging" in this Johannine way. That is to say, in a greater or less degree, and by no means always consciously, he makes some feel that their sins are "remitted" and others that their sins are "retained"—processes by no means the less real because they are not accompanied with a definite "absolvo" or "damno."

---

[1] Jn xii 39—43 "For this cause they could not believe, for that Isaiah said again, He hath blinded their eyes...more than the glory of God." The passage suggests, without defining, the indefinable borderland between the condition in which we *will not* "believe" and that in which we *can not* "believe."

JOHN BAPTIZING THE PEOPLE

§ 14. *"Remission" and "washing"*

Josephus—in words that are perhaps best explained as not being his own but supplied to him by one or more persons whose traditions he gives in a confused form—writing about the "immersion" or "immersing" inculcated by the Baptist, says, " He commanded the Jews, while exercising virtue, both in righteousness toward one another and in piety toward God, to assemble together, practising (*lit.* using) immersion; for subject to these conditions [he said], even the [act of] immersing [oneself] would appear acceptable to Him, that is to say, if they practised it not with a view to begging off [the punishment of] certain [slight] errors, but with a view to purity of the body—on the understanding that the soul had been previously purified[1]."

In the Fourth Gospel, the doctrine of "remitting," though not mentioned, is, by implication, connected with "washing" by the following links The Lord's Prayer says "*Remit* to us our *debts* as also we have remitted to our *debtors.*" What are the debts? Paul replies "*Owe* no man anything save *to love one another*; for *he that loveth his neighbour* hath fulfilled the

---

[1] Joseph *Ant* xviii 5 2. The Latin version and Whiston's take βαπτισμῷ συνιέναι together, as meaning "come to baptism" But Steph. *Thes* gives no instance of συνιέναι thus used with dative If the text is correct, χρωμένοις here—as certainly in the next sentence—appears to mean "practising" and to be connected with "immersion" Βάπτισις hardly exists (Steph *Thes*) except here Josephus seems to mean "There was no superstition in this, for John thought that even what one might ridicule as mere 'dipping' might be acceptable to God, if accompanied by moral preparation"

Josephus has expressed himself in such a way as to explain how it was that some early writers regarded John as a Hemerobaptist, that is to say, one who inculcated daily baptism "To meet together practising immersion" suggests that the act was a part of daily worship.

His contemptuous remark about "begging off" and "[slight] errors," ἁμαρτάδων (sometimes used to mean physical failure), may illustrate the dislike that others might feel for the use of ἄφεσις, as a mere "letting off" of punishment.

law"—where "the law" means "*the law of Christ* fulfilling the law of Moses," as is shewn by his words elsewhere, "Bear ye one another's burdens and so fulfil *the law of Christ*[1]."

In the picture of Christ washing the feet of the disciples, the Fourth Gospel puts all this into a metaphor, in which the infirmities and errors and lapses manifested by us in our daily walk through life are likened to the dust on the feet of the traveller. Concerning the true disciple, Jesus says, "He that is bathed needeth not save to wash his feet[2]." All (it is implied), even the best, need this daily washing. At the close of the scene, Jesus says, "If I...have washed your feet, ye also owe [as a debt] to wash one another's feet[3]." This is almost the only use of the word "*owe*" in this Gospel[4] It means that we "*owe*" *the debt of* "*love*" to God and to man, and that, although we may approximate, we can never quite attain, to the full payment of it. An unkind nurse, with a child walking in a miry lane, might exact punishment for each spot caused by a slight carelessness. We ask God our Nursing Father to be kind, and daily to wash away such spots from us, as we also endeavour to wash them from our brethren. This is no *aphesis* in the sense of "*letting off*," but it is an *aphesis* in the sense of "putting away sin," and it suggests, in a very helpful way, the twofold mystery of that mercy, or kindness, or forgivingness, which is "twice blest," because the forgiver, while "restoring" others "in a spirit of gentleness[5]," is found to be also at the same time restoring, refreshing, and strengthening his own soul.

---

[1] Rom. xiii. 8, Gal. vi. 2. On this, and on "Metaphors expressing sin," see *Son* **3495** *a—e*

[2] Jn xiii 10. On the reading, see *Joh. Gr.* **2659** *e*, to which add Clem. Alex 116 πάντα μὲν οὖν ἀπολουόμεθα τὰ ἁμαρτήματα, οὐκέτι δέ ἐσμεν παρὰ πόδας κακοί (Clark "no longer *entangled in evil*," but really "no longer *evil except as to the feet*"), see Steph *Thes* vi. 202 and comp Jas. iii 2 "in many things we all stumble (πταίομεν)."

[3] Jn xiii 14.   [4] It occurs also in Jn xix. 7.

[5] Gal vi 1 "Restore such a one in *a spirit of gentleness*."

§ 15. *John's conditions for baptism*

Mark says that all the country of Judaea, and all the people of Jerusalem, "began to be baptized" or "were being baptized" by John, "confessing their sins," and Matthew (adding "the [people of the] circle of the Jordan") agrees with Mark as to "confessing their sins[1]." But Luke omits this mention of "confession."

In fact, however, though Luke omits the word, he inserts a great deal that implies it, supplying what is missing in Mark. For Mark does not say whether the confession was of a general or particular kind, nor whether it was accompanied by anything but mere words. But Luke says that the multitudes asked the Baptist "What must we do?" And the Baptist replied—besides other things addressed to the rich who had "two coats"—that the publicans were not to extort and the soldiers not to do violence. This leads us to suppose that if we had the exhortations of the Baptist fully before us—extending over many months, or perhaps years, before the arrival of Jesus—we should find that the publicans, like Zacchaeus, "confessed" that they had "extorted," and promised to "restore fourfold," and that some of the avaricious (who were the men with "two coats") promised, like Zacchaeus, to give "the half" of their goods to "the poor."

Moreover, Matthew and Luke agree in saying that the Baptist said to certain persons—whom Matthew calls "many of the Pharisees and Sadducees," but Luke "multitudes[2]"—that they must "produce fruit worthy of [their] repentance." The same passage has these words, "Think not to say in yourselves, 'We have Abraham as our father,' for I say unto

---

[1] Mk i 5, Mt iii 6.

[2] Possibly there may have been some confusion arising from a Hebrew gospel in which "*the many*" might be confused with "*the great people*," who formed the Sanhedrin, where the chief priests belonged to the Sadducean party Comp. *Erub.* 75 *b* "R. Joseph said 'I confused *rabbîm* with *rabbi*,'" i e. "many" with "rabbi"

you that God is able from these stones to raise up children to Abraham[1]" Some have thought that "stones" meant those with the "stony heart" mentioned by Ezekiel, to whom the Lord promised to give "one heart and a new spirit[2]." But in any case the Baptist, by using such words, makes us think of God as creating sons of Abraham out of "stones," as He created Adam out of "dust." And how, we ask, would He do this except by breathing His Spirit into the stones, as He breathed it into the dust of Adam? Thus we are prepared for the doctrine of a new birth.

The Fourth Gospel contains, later on, a discussion between the Jews and Jesus about Abraham. In this, Jesus denies that they are Abraham's children because they do not the works of Abraham, and denies that God is their Father because they do not love Him, the Son of the Father. The reference to Abraham's works certainly includes a reference to Abraham's kindness, hospitality, and—to use the Philonian term—"*philanthropy*[3]." There, Jesus makes regeneration, and sonship to God, depend, in effect, upon "love" According to Matthew and Luke, the Baptist, though not teaching this, prepares the way for Him who was to teach it.

About all these matters of the Baptist's teaching, and about the conditions he imposed for admitting men to baptism, the Fourth Gospel is silent. It confines itself to the "witness" of the Baptist. Apparently it passes over all his early teaching[4]

---

[1] Mt. iii 7—10, Lk iii 7—9 (with "begin" instead of "think")

[2] Ezek. xi 19, xxxvi. 26 Jerome on Mt iii 9 quotes Ezek. and takes it as signifying the inclusion of the Gentiles

[3] Jn viii 39, 41—2 On Abraham's φιλανθρωπία see *Joh. Gr.* **1935**, and Philo ii 16, 30 where the preceding context (ii 13) mentions God's φιλανθρωπία. The Gospel, and Philo, both imply that one cannot be a "child of Abraham" without loving man.

[4] Comp Jn i 15 "This was he that *I said* (or, *they said*)" These are the Baptist's first words, and, according to the former rendering, they may mean "*For years I have been saying* and this, though I knew it not till to-day, was the Person about whom I was saying it ."

and baptizing, so as not to begin till he had made so great a name that the rulers sent from Jerusalem to question him as to his mission and authority. In that interview, it happens, by accident, that the Evangelist does mention "confessing" in connection with the Baptist, but it has nothing to do with men's "confession" of their sins to him; it introduces his "confession" to the deputation from Jerusalem, thus. "And he *confessed*, and denied not, and he *confessed*, I am not the Christ[1]."

The Johannine non-intervention as to this "confessing" of "sins" is but one of many instances where John agrees with Luke in omitting some detail about the Baptist inserted by Mark and Matthew. As such, it does not require further comment. But it should be noted, in passing, (1) that the confession of sins was a prominent part of the Jewish service on the Day of Atonement, (2) that part of this service was a purification with "clean water" (as mentioned above, p. 57, n. 3) connected by the Jews with a prophecy of Ezekiel about "a new heart" and "a new spirit," (3) that this purification coincided with the beginning of the New Year, so that it might well have been in the Baptist's mind when he called on Israel to enter on a new stage of spiritual life in turning to Jehovah.

As to the forms of words in which the candidates for baptism made confession, and the Baptist admitted them to baptism or baptized them, we have absolutely no definite knowledge. But we know that the Mishna recording the High Priest's confession of sins on the Day of Atonement, represents him as twice addressing God in the words "Alas, O NAME, thy people, the house of Israel, has sinned[2]." If the Baptist baptized "(*lit.*) into the NAME," and if some form of words including this term passed from him to Christ's

---

[1] Jn 1 20 On the repetition through negation, and on the twofold "*confessed*," see *Joh. Gr* **2598, 2607**.

[2] See *Joma* 35 *b*, repeated in 41 *b*, 66 *a*, and comp Dalman *Words* pp. 182—3 on the habitual use of "the Name" for the Tetragrammaton.

disciples, before the Resurrection, it becomes easy to understand how the form would become naturally and rightly interpreted as "the name of Jesus," or "the name of the Son," or "the name of the Father as revealed by the Son through His Spirit," or "the name of the Father, the Son, and the Holy Spirit[1]" Also it becomes easy to understand Paul's saying to the Corinthians, "I thank God that I baptized none of you save Crispus and Gaius, lest any should say that ye were baptized into *my own name*[2]." Without some hypothesis of a mention of THE NAME, and on the hypothesis of some definite name such as "Father," or "Son," or "Jesus," the words are difficult. For, if Paul, when baptizing "Crispus" for example, said, "I baptize thee *into the name of Jesus*," how could anyone say "Paul baptized Crispus into his own name"?

§ 16. *Where did John baptize the people?*

Mark and Matthew say that the people of Jerusalem and Judaea (Matthew adding "and all the surrounding-country of the Jordan") "*made-their-way-forth* to John and were baptized by him in the river Jordan", and Luke, using the same verb of motion, reports what John said "to the multitudes that *made-their-way-forth* to be baptized by him," but does not mention "the Jordan," or any other neighbourhood as the place of the baptizing[3]. Luke's parallel mention of Jordan—almost the only mention in his Gospel—is in a sentence that reverses the words peculiar to Matthew quoted above. For whereas Matthew says that (what we may call) "*the circle of the Jordan*" *came to John*, Luke says that *John* "*came to all [the] circle of the Jordan*[4]."

---

[1] See *Son* (Index "Name") "To the name," "into the name," and "in the name," have so many meanings in Hebrew and Greek (not to speak of Latin) that the baptismal form might easily assume different shades of meaning.   [2] 1 Cor. 1 14—15.

[3] "Make-one's-way-forth" is ἐκπορεύομαι in Mk i 5, Mt iii 5, Lk iii 7.

[4] Lk iii. 3 ἦλθεν εἰς πᾶσαν περίχωρον τοῦ Ἰορδάνου The other instance in Lk. is iv. 1 ὑπέστρεψεν ἀπὸ τοῦ Ἰορδάνου.

We cannot expect the Fourth Evangelist to intervene in a direct way here. From his point of view, what does it matter, such a mere detail as this? It refers to the Baptist in his relation to the people, not to the Baptist in his relation to Jesus; and the Fourth Evangelist is not interested in John the Baptist at all except in the latter relation, that is to say, so far as the Baptist "bears witness to the Light." Consequently there is no Johannine intervention at this point to tell us where *the people* were baptized. But there will be when he comes to clear up later obscurities of the Synoptists, and to tell us where "John was baptizing" on the day before he "seeth Jesus coming to him."

Later on, too, the Fourth Gospel will shew us indirectly that Mark and Matthew are probably wrong here, and Luke is right. John moved about from place to place. Matthew had grasped the facts but the facts reversed. It was not that "all the circle of the Jordan came to John," but that John "came to all the circle of the Jordan," presumably choosing places where there was "much water." At one time, the Fourth Evangelist will tell us, it was "Ænon near to Salim[1]." But, before that, it was "Bethany beyond Jordan where John was [at the time] baptizing[2]." And it was there that the Baptist testified most conspicuously to Jesus. Probably, too, though the Evangelist does not describe the baptism of Jesus by John, he intends us to assume that, as Bethany on the West of Jordan was the scene of His anointing, so Bethany on the East was the scene of His baptism.

§ 17. *John's clothing and food, passed over in the Third and the Fourth Gospel*

Mark and Matthew describe the Baptist as having "a leathern girdle about his loins[3]." This is said of no other man in the Bible except Elijah. Mark also says that he was "clothed with the hairs of a camel." This might seem to

---

[1] Jn iii. 23 [2] Jn i. 28. [3] Mk i. 6, Mt iii. 4

mean "with the hairy skin of a camel," which would be hardly possible owing to its size and weight. Matthew, however, says "clothing made from the hairs of a camel." Now the Jews used clothing made for the rich from the soft wool of a camel. Sackcloth—not necessarily made from the hairs of a camel[1]—they always called by its name of "sackcloth." If the Baptist wore a "mantle of hair," *i.e.* a sheepskin or goat-skin, such as is mentioned as the usual clothing of a prophet in Zechariah[2], early tradition may have applied to him the passage that describes Elijah as wearing a "leathern girdle," and as being "*a lord* (or, *owner*) *of hair*" Some take this as meaning "*long-haired*" Others take it as "*wearing a garment of hairy, or untrimmed, skin*[3]." Perhaps Mark's tradition arose out of an original statement that the Baptist, like Elijah, was "*a lord of hair,*" supplemented by an addition intended to make it clear that it was not the hair of the prophet himself. Matthew adopted Mark's version with a slight change

Luke simply says "The word of God came-[to-pass] on John ..in the wilderness."

If this instance of Lucan parallelism with Mark-Matthew tradition about the Baptist could fairly be considered by itself apart from other instances, we might argue that they were two different interpretations of a Hebrew original saying that *the Spirit of God* "*clothed*—or *clothed itself with—John in the wilderness,*" that is, "came mightily upon him," as is said sometimes in Scripture[4]. Mark and Matthew might take this as describing the manner in which John, under the influence of the Spirit, actually and literally clothed himself, and might add details to make the meaning clear. Luke

---

[1] See *Hor Heb* on Mk 1 6, and Levy iv. 200 *a*

[2] Zech xiii 4 "a mantle of hair" The phrase occurs also in Gen xxv. 25 about Esau Comp. Heb xi 37.

[3] 2 K 1 8 Gesen 972 *a* takes the phrase thus The LXX regularly renders "mantle," when connected with Elijah, by "sheepskin"

[4] Judg vi 34, 1 Chr xii 18, 2 Chr xxiv. 20.

might take it metaphorically and spiritually. Similarly Luke says expressly, in the Introduction to his Gospel, that John the son of Zacharias was to be (not Elijah, nor even like Elijah, but) one going before the face of the Lord "in the spirit and power of Elijah[1]." But another explanation may be found in the fact that Luke omits many passages in Mark where Elijah is mentioned[2].

The Fourth Evangelist, though for the most part disagreeing with Luke where Luke diverges from Mark, agrees with Luke in rejecting those passages which might seem to encourage the belief that the Baptist was literally Elijah. But he goes further He denies the truth of such a belief This he does dramatically, through the Baptist himself, at the outset of the Baptist's testimony, in the words "They asked him, What then? *Art thou Elijah?* And he saith, *I am not.*"

As regards the food of the Baptist, namely, that it was "locusts and wild honey," Mark appears to have inserted this detail to shew how the Baptist was supported in the wilderness by the hand as it were of God, without the hand of man, somewhat like Elijah by the brook Cherith[3].

Mark places these details just after the words "and they were baptized by him...confessing their sins," and just before the words "And he preached saying, There cometh he that is stronger than I." Matthew, perhaps thinking that the

---

[1] Lk. i. 17   [2] *E.g.* Mk ix 11—13, xv 35—6.

[3] "Locusts" were a regular article of food for the poor, so that there is nothing improbable in this detail. It is worth noting, however, that (1) the usual Hebrew word for "locust" in Hebrew, *'arbeh*, resembles words from *arb*, meaning "*raven*," "*wilderness*," "*sweet*"; (2) there was much discussion among Jews as to the "ravens" that supplied Elijah (see *Cholin* 5 *a*, and *Gen r* Wu. p. 147 (on Gen. viii. 7) &c.). Some maintained that Elijah's "ravens" were men Jewish disciples of the Baptist might say about his food in the *arabah*, playing on the word and on Elijah's "ravens," that the "honey" was God's gift, like the "honey from the rock" in the Psalms, and that what were "*ravens*" in Elijah's case were "*locusts*" in the case of John

account of the Baptist's clothing and diet did not come suitably just before his announcement of the Saviour, places the details before the baptizing, altering Mark's order. And, to many, Mark's mention of the "leathern girdle" and the rest might well seem out of place and out of proportion. But if we understand that the clothing and the food of the prophet John in the desert seemed to Mark the appointed outward signs of his being Elijah, coming as a herald to the Messiah, then we shall agree that he did not place them unfitly from his point of view, meaning: "Thus came John with the outward signs of being Elijah, the herald of the Lord, and then he began to proclaim as a herald, saying, 'There cometh he that is mightier than I....'"

The rule of *Johannine non-intervention in matters affecting John the Baptist,* where Luke omits what Mark inserts, has been stated and illustrated above somewhat fully, in order to dispense with the necessity of restating the rule hereafter. In future instances the rule will simply be referred to.

CHAPTER III

JOHN PREACHING OR PROPHESYING

IN this Chapter the prominent difference between Mark and the other Synoptists is not of the kind that will usually come before us, where Mark expresses harshly or obscurely something that is altered or omitted by Luke. On the contrary it is an instance of Marcan omission. But here, as elsewhere when we use the term "omission," we must not commit ourselves to the view that Mark omitted what he knew to exist but regarded as outside the scope of his Gospel, or outside the scope of his subject for the time being. It is possible—or at all events we must for the present regard it as possible—that Mark knew nothing about the words omitted, which relate to the nature of the future baptism. Mark speaks merely of "baptizing *with the Holy Spirit*" Matthew and Luke add "*and with fire.*" John does not adopt this addition. Part of the object of this Chapter is to shew why he does not add this, and why he adds something else.

---

§ 1 *John's first utterance*

According to Mark, the Baptist "was-preaching (*or*, began-to-preach) saying, *There-cometh* he that is mightier than I...," so that his first public utterance was "There-cometh[1]" But according to Matthew and Luke, his first public utterance was "*Ye offspring of vipers*[2]."

---

[1] Mk 1 7 [2] Mt iii 7, Lk. iii 7

This can be explained on the hypothesis that Mark writes with a view to brevity and edification, omitting all the Baptist's utterances except those that bore witness to Jesus ; whereas Matthew and Luke write at greater length telling the reader more about circumstance and fact. And the fact seems to have been (according to Matthew-Luke) that the Baptist did not utter the Marcan saying about "coming" till he had rebuked the "offspring of vipers," who approached him for baptism—whom Matthew calls " many of the Pharisees and Sadducees," but Luke "the multitudes." These men were presumably hypocrites. If so, it is probable that they did not come to be baptized until the new baptism had become fashionable, or, at least, notorious. To acquire such notoriety it must have been going on for some time. It would seem, then, a legitimate inference that the Baptist did not begin to utter his testimony to Jesus till he had experienced some sense of failure. He had begun to baptize unto repentance. At first, those whom he attracted were for the most part the devout and earnest. But presently he became the fashion and multitudes flocked to him. Among these were some that were lukewarm or insincere. At last came some, men of high position, who were mere " vipers " Then, and not till then (it might be inferred) the Baptist began to preach the advent of a Mightier One " I and my baptism cannot deal with this evil: there cometh a Mightier One, bringing with Him a more searching baptism , He must deal with it."

The Fourth Evangelist, with even more than his usual sense of dramatic fitness or natural development, meets any controversial questioning as to the Baptist's first utterance, by bringing him on the stage, as it were, with a reference to what *he had said before he was brought on the stage*: " John beareth-witness of him, and crieth, saying, *This was he that I said—* he that cometh behind me is become before me...[1]." Thus

---

[1] Jn 1. 15 (see above, p 35 foll).

he suggests to the reader of the Three the reflection that, although the mention of the Coming One as the Baptizer with the Spirit may have been late in the Baptist's teaching, yet the mention of the Coming One in a general way may have been very much earlier and may have been very often repeated.

§ 2. *"There cometh" and "behind me"*

The Marcan tradition about the Baptist's first word, "*there-cometh*," must be compared with the Matthew-Luke tradition that the Baptist, on the point of death, sent two disciples to Jesus with the question, " Art thou *he-that-cometh*, or are-we-to-expect another[1]?" Both there, and in the Entry into Jerusalem, "*he-that-cometh*" is a title of the Deliverer[2]. The "coming" is regarded, not as mere *futurity*, but as *divinely decreed futurity*. It represents *future righteous judgment of God*, according to the words in the Psalms "*for he cometh, for he cometh, to judge the earth*[3]." The title, though popular in Galilee at the time, seems to have been a transient one In the Epistle to the Hebrews, "*He that cometh* will come" is a misquotation of Habakkuk's "coming it will come," that is, "it will surely come[4]"; and I have not been able to find any late Jewish or Aramaic use of "*he-that-cometh*" in this sense[5]. But it is easily intelligible that, during a period of intense Messianic expectation—when "*the age that is to come*" often meant the Messianic age—"*he that is to come*" would mean

---

[1] Mt. xi 3, Lk vii 19 (lit.) "Art thou the coming-one (ὁ ἐρχόμενος)?"

[2] See *Joh. Voc* **1633** Ὁ ἐρχόμενος is in all the Gospels But Mt. xxi 9 has also "son of David," Lk xix 38 "King," Jn xii 13 "King of Israel," Mk xi 10 adds "Blessed is the coming kingdom of our father David."

[3] Ps xcvi. 13.

[4] Heb x. 37 quoting Hab ii 3

[5] On Mt xi 3, *Hor. Heb*, Wetstein, and Schottgen, give no instances Nor does Dalman's *Words* (Index ἐρχόμενος) give any.

the Messiah in popular parlance[1]. When that disappointing period had passed away—carrying with it recollections of many Messianic Pretenders—Jewish tradition might naturally drop the title that pointed to a coming Person ("*he that is to come*"), though they retained the title that pointed to a coming Age ("*the age that is to come*").

To return to the Marcan tradition "*There-cometh* he that is mightier than I". There is no difficulty in regarding these words, if taken by themselves, as a prediction of a Messiah in popular talk, which we may illustrate from the Woman of Samaria's talk, "I know that Messiah *cometh*[2]." But the next words, "after me," or "behind me," introduce an ambiguity. For though, in that position, they are still compatible with the hypothesis that "*there-cometh*" refers to the Messiah, they are also compatible with the hypothesis that "*there-cometh*" is to be taken with "after me," or "behind me"— "there *cometh after* (or, *behind*) *me* he that is mightier than I." In that case, "*cometh*" loses its technical Messianic meaning by being combined with "after" so as to mean "followeth as a disciple," or "followeth in point of time."

This arrangement has actually been adopted by Matthew, who has "*He that cometh after* (or, *behind*) *me* is mightier than I" Luke, on the other hand, retains the possibility of a Messianic use of "*coming*," but he sacrifices "*after* (or, *behind*) *me*"—"I baptize you with water, but there cometh he that is mightier than I." Luke's reason for doing this— namely, the ambiguity of the Mark-Matthew phrase "*after* (or, *behind*) me"—is shewn by his substitution of a different and unambiguous Greek preposition in the Acts, where he represents Paul as repeating the words of the Baptist in such a form as to shew that he took the meaning to be, not

---

[1] Levy (1 184 a, 197) gives several instances of "May it *come* on me if" This he interprets as meaning "May *misfortune* befall me if"—a form of oath Perhaps it would be better to say "May *retribution*, or *judgment*, fall on me." [2] Jn iv 25

"*behind* me," but "*after* me [*in point of time*]," thus, "And as John was fulfilling his course, he said, What suppose ye that I am? I am not [he]"—meaning, "I am not the Coming One, or the Redeemer"; and then, "But behold, there cometh one *after me* [*in point of time*], the shoe of whose feet I am not worthy to unloose[1]."

Passing to the Fourth Evangelist, we have to ask whether he, too, when introducing John the Baptist on the stage, reproduces any of these phrases about "coming" and "behind me." It has been shewn in the Introductory Volume[2] that he represents the Baptist as repeating, and playing on, the double meaning of "behind me," in such a way as to shew that to be temporarily "behind," in the character of a disciple, was not incompatible with an essential and permanent superiority. But we have now to add that the Evangelist *does this thrice in connection with "coming*[3]." And, before all these clauses, he introduces the word "*coming*" in his contrast between the "man" (John) and the Light, thus: "He (emph.) [*i.e.* John] was not the light...There-was the light, the true [light]—which lighteth every man—*coming* [*continually*] into the world[4]."

These repetitions and plays on words point to a mystical meaning, namely, that the Messiah or Redeemer of man is to be regarded, not in the popular Galilaean aspect—as "*He that is to come* in *the age that is to come*," or "*He that is to come* as the Son of David and to reign over His prosperous people for a thousand years or more*"—but as the Benefactor, who has been "coming" to men's help from the beginning—and whose business it is (so to speak) thus to "come." In this aspect of "coming," the Word of God is not only the present

---

[1] Acts xiii 25 "after," μετὰ, not ὀπίσω
[2] *Fourfold Gospel, Introduction*, p 2 foll
[3] Jn 1 15 ὁ ὀπίσω μου ἐρχόμενος ἔμπροσθέν μου γέγονεν, 1. 27 ὀπίσω μου ἐρχόμενος, 1. 30 ὀπίσω μου ἔρχεται ἀνήρ
[4] Jn 1. 8—9 (*Joh Gr.* 2508).

Life and Light of men, it also quickens and illuminates their glance into the future. The Johannine Revelation tells us that God is the BEING and the WAS and the COMING[1]. The Johannine Prologue, partly through the confessions of John the Baptist, but still more through the declarations of the Evangelist himself, gives suggestions of the same doctrine about the Logos.—In the beginning WAS the Logos; the true Light WAS, but it was also continually COMING, its name is Monogenēs, the BEING in the bosom of the Father. All these are statements of the Evangelist. But they are confirmed by sayings of the Baptist about the incarnate Logos—sayings that, although they might only imply precedence, are capable of being taken as pointing to an eternal pre-existence: "He was before me," "He was my First (*or*, Chief)[2]" Modern critics, perhaps, hardly make sufficient allowance for the latitude that might be given by Jews of a mystical or spiritual turn to such words as those of Micah, who represents God as saying "There shall come forth unto me one that is to be ruler in Israel, *whose goings forth are from of old, from everlasting*"—where the Targum has "There shall come forth...*the Messiah* to be ruler...[3]."

§ 3 "*He that is mightier than I*"

The Greek word "mighty" (elsewhere often rendered "strong") frequently refers to the "might" or "strength" of this world, as when Israel says, concerning the Canaanites, "They are *stronger* than we," and Paul, "God hath chosen the weak things of the world that he might put to shame *the strong things*", and Zechariah, "Not by might, *nor by strength*, but by my spirit, saith the Lord of hosts[4]." In the Three Gospels,

---

[1] Rev. i. 4, 8.   [2] See *Joh. Gr* **2665**—7.
[3] Mic. v. 2. See *Enoch* xlviii 2—6 (ed Charles) and editor's note *ad loc.*
[4] Numb xiii. 31 (comp. Deut iv 38, vii. 1), 1 Cor. i. 25—7, Zech iv 6, all using ἰσχυρός or ἰσχύς.

Jesus only once mentions "*the strong one.*" Then it refers to Satan. There Luke adds a mention about "a stronger than he," that is to say, God[1] But Epictetus declares that no good and free man will "follow the *stronger*," i.e. the tyrant of the hour[2].

The Fourth Gospel never mentions either "strength" or "strong." It implies "strength" indeed—not, however, the strength that drives, but the strength that draws—as when Jesus says, "I, if I am lifted up from the earth, will *draw* all men unto me[3]." "Drawing" implies the strength of the King, whereas "driving" would imply the strength of the Despot. The "drawing" of Jesus is the same as that with which the Lord "drew" Israel, saying "I drew them with cords of a man, with bands of love." There the love is that of the Father[4] In the Song of Songs the love is that of the Bridegroom, to whom the Bride says "Draw me, we will run after thee[5]."

Though the Fourth Gospel does not represent the Baptist as saying that Jesus is "strong," or "stronger" than himself, it represents him, later on, as declaring that Jesus is the Bridegroom, whereas he himself is only the Bridegroom's friend. That later utterance of the Baptist may throw light on his use, here—in the climax constituted by the third repetition of " after me "—of that Greek word for "man" which mostly means "mighty man" or "husband"· "After me cometh *a man*[6]." In the LXX, this word very often represents forms of the Hebrew "*mighty*" or "*mighty-man*" Knowing this, the Fourth Evangelist might consider that the Greek word for "man" in the

---

[1] Mk iii. 27, Mt. xii 29, Lk xi 21—2
[2] Epictet ii. 13, 22—3, quoted in *Joh Gr.* **2799** *a*.
[3] Jn xii. 32.   [4] Hos xi 4.
[5] Cant. i 4   Part of the Targ is " Draw us to the foot of Mount Sinai and grant unto us thy Law " See *Son* **3583** (ix) *c* "on Sinai, where the espousals took place "
[6] Jn i 30.

noblest sense, better than the Greek word for "strong," expressed the Baptist's meaning[1].

§ 4. "*The latchet of whose shoes I am not sufficient to stoop-down and loose*[2]"

Luke omits a word, "stoop-down," inserted by Mark. But it is a detail in the expressions of John the Baptist that does not bear on his relations with Jesus and is therefore not one of the instances where the Fourth Gospel can be expected to intervene.

Some of the variations of this tradition, including Mark's "stooping-down," may be explained by the fact that the only "loosing of the shoe-latchet" mentioned in the Law is not a menial act but an act expressive of contempt for the person whose shoe-latchet is loosed. In order to indicate that the act is here that of a menial, Mark may have inserted "stooping-down", but it is expressed more clearly by the paraphrase "I am not worthy" in the Acts and the Fourth Gospel[3].

---

[1] The Greek ἀνήρ, in LXX, corresponds to the Heb. or Aram. for "*mighty*," "*mighty-man* (vir)" &c. about 40 times. In Prov. xxiv. 5, "*man* (vir)" is rendered by LXX κρείσσων.

[2] The following variations should be noted:
Mk. i. 7 "the latchet of whose shoes I am not sufficient (ἱκανὸς) to stoop-down (κύψας) and loose"
Mt. iii. 11 "whose shoes I am not sufficient to carry (βαστάσαι)"
Lk. iii. 16 "the latchet of whose shoes I am not sufficient to loose" (omitting "stoop-down")
Jn. i. 27 "the latchet of whose shoe I am not worthy (ἄξιος) to loose"
Acts xiii. 25 (Paul is speaking) "But when John was fulfilling the course [of his prophecy], he said (*or*, used to say, ἔλεγεν) What do ye suppose me to be? I am not [he]. But behold there cometh after me (μετ' ἐμέ) one of whom I am not worthy to loose (lit.) the shoe of the feet."

Ἱκανός might mean "sufficiently strong". It is not such good Greek as ἄξιος in the sense of "worthy". Ὑπολύω (not λύω) is the correct Greek for loosing the shoe-latchet in the ordinary way, and it is the word used in Deut. xxv. 9, 10. But there the man "whose shoe-latchet is loosed" is a title of contempt.

[3] The Heb. given by Delitzsch for ἄξιος in Jn. i. 27 (which is also the

Matthew appears to have substituted some other tradition, which he supposed to be of similar meaning and to be free from the appearance of conflicting with the Law. But this, too, is obscure. Horae Hebraicae illustrates it from Jewish rules as to what services may be performed by Jewish (not Gentile) servants for masters taking a bath[1]. But perhaps the origin of the phrase is entirely different. It may have been some early Galilaean contrast between two methods of preaching the gospel, with allusion to Isaiah's saying (quoted by Paul) concerning the " beautiful feet" of the preachers[2]. Luke alone—and he only in the Mission of the Seventy—has preserved a tradition of *prohibition*, which might mean that the Missionary *is not to* "*carry*" cumbersome things, including "shoes with thongs," which perhaps we might here call "*boots*[3]." The parallel Mark, and Mark alone, has preserved a tradition of *positive precept*, that the Missionary *is to be shod with* "*sandals*," i.e. to wear light or festive shoes[4].

Space forbids discussion of these verbal details. But the mention of them gives us a profitable glimpse into submerged regions of early Galilaean allusive expression, the past existence of which we are bound to keep always in mind though we may be seldom able to detect its present effect with certainty in any particular case.

---

regular Heb for ἄξιος in LXX) somewhat resembles the Heb given by Delitzsch for κύψας in Mk i 7 (which is also occasionally the Heb for κύπτω in LXX) Possibly Mark may be combining two renderings of one word. The margin of a Hebrew Gospel perhaps gave the Heb. "worthy" *instead of* the Heb "sufficient," and the former was erroneously incorporated in the text as "stooping-down" *along with* "sufficient."

[1] Comp *Mechilt.* Wu p 236 (on Exod. xxi. 2) "He shall not wash thy feet, nor take off thy sandals, nor carry things to the bath house." Add *Gen r.* on Gen xvi 6 "*dealt hardly*, i e. made Hagar carry her sandals to the bath"

[2] See Origen on Rom. x 14 foll (Lomm vii. 214) quoting Is lii 7 and Mt. x 10, but not the parall. Mark, nor Luke on the Seventy.

[3] Lk x. 4   In the Precepts to the Twelve, Lk ix 3 does not mention ὑποδήματα

[4] Mk vi 9   On σανδάλιον and ὑπόδημα see *Corrections* 390 (ii) (ε) a

JOHN PREACHING OR PROPHESYING

§ 5. "*I* [*for my part*] *have baptized you with water, but he will baptize you with the Holy Spirit—and with fire*"

In Mark, the words "with the Holy Spirit" terminate the Baptist's preaching[1]. The Prophet says, in effect, to those who have received his baptism, "I for my part have now done for you the work I was sent to do. But it is by its nature incomplete. I was sent merely to baptize with water. He that comes after me will baptize you *with the Holy Spirit* That is my gospel, or good-tidings, to you."

But in Matthew, as also in Luke, the last words of the Baptist are, "*the chaff he will burn up with unquenchable fire*[2]." These do not seem exactly "gospel" or "*good-tidings.*" Yet Luke adds: "With many other exhortations therefore *preached-he-good-tidings* unto the people[3]"

Matthew and Luke also differ from Mark in this respect, that they represent the Baptist as saying, not "*I have baptized you*," but "*I am baptizing you.*" In Matthew, these words are uttered as part of a continuous utterance to those who are called "offspring of vipers", and Matthew (alone) inserts "unto repentance" after "baptize," as though to emphasize their wickedness. But Luke makes a break, after the warning to the "offspring of vipers," and introduces a new audience thus. "And when the people were expecting, and all were reasoning in their hearts about John lest by chance he might be the Christ, John made answer saying to all, 'I for-my-part....'"

This distinction of audiences—Matthew's being the "offspring of vipers," while Luke's is "the people"—may make a difference in the interpretation of the words that they both add after "*He will baptize you with the Holy Spirit*"

---

[1] Mk i. 8   But Mt iii. 11—12, Lk. iii 16—17 add "and with fire, whose fan is in his hand. .the chaff he will burn up with unquenchable fire"

[2] Mt. iii 12, Lk. iii 17   [3] Lk iii 18

—namely, "*and with fire*, whose fan is in his hand, and he will thoroughly cleanse his threshing floor, and gather the wheat into his garner, but the chaff he will burn up with unquenchable fire[1]"

In Matthew, the fire would seem to be the fire of retributive destruction—as though the Baptist said "the Messiah will baptize you with the Spirit if you accept Him, and with the fire of destruction if you reject Him." But in Luke, the fire may be regarded as cleansing souls, just as, in the Law, fire is appointed to cleanse metals, so that Luke may mean "with the Spirit and with its cleansing fire." In the context, both of Matthew and of Luke, the Spirit seems to be regarded as a winnowing wind that does what is best (so to speak) both for the wheat and for the chaff. The fire, cleansing the pure metal from the dross, may perhaps be regarded as "doing what is best" in the same way. The announcement of this purifying, this "doing of what is best" for the good and the bad, may be called "good tidings[2]." But the introduction of the thought of this twofold influence takes off the reader's attention from the bright and joyous character of the gospel of Christ for which the Baptist prepared the way. And, since it is also ambiguous—Matthew apparently regarding it as a threat addressed to an "offspring of vipers," but Luke rather as a declaration of God's righteous will addressed to "the people"—we cannot be surprised if the Fourth Evangelist not only omits all mention of baptism with fire, but also suggests in the context, and emphasizes afterwards, other kinds of purification, and, in particular, purification with blood.

---

[1] Mt. iii. 12, Lk. iii. 17 (almost identical).

[2] Comp. Epict. ii. 6, 11 foll. about the duty of the ear of wheat to pray that it may be "parched," that is, ripened.

JOHN PREACHING OR PROPHESYING

§ 6. *Baptism with blood*

The two prophets, Ezekiel and John the son of Zacharias, had some experiences or characteristics in common, shared by no other prophet. Ezekiel, alone among the ancient prophets, saw—what John also saw—"the heavens opened[1]." Ezekiel also alone spoke of a bestowal of new life on the "dry bones" of Israel, by means of "wind," "breath," or "spirit[2]." And, in Ezekiel, the new life follows a promise of a "sprinkling with clean water" as well as the promise of "a new heart" and "a new spirit[3]." These two predictions resemble the Baptist's prediction of "baptizing with the Spirit."

But further, Ezekiel goes on to say, in the name of Jehovah, "Neither will I hide my face any more from them, *because I [shall] have poured out my Spirit upon the house of Israel*, saith the Lord God[4]." The perfect ("*have* poured out") in itself creates a difficulty. And in Ezekiel, elsewhere, this "pouring out" on the part of Jehovah, mentioned in about a dozen other passages, always refers to God's fury or wrath. Here, accordingly, the LXX takes "spirit" to mean "the wrath of my spirit," and adopts the rendering "*poured out my wrath*[5]." Jewish tradition, however, interprets this as one of four passages where "pour out" is used in a good sense[6]. Two of

---

[1] Ezek. i. 1.   [2] Ezek. xxxvii. 1 foll.

[3] See *Son* **3544** *b*, where it was shewn that "sprinkle" meant "throw in a volume", but there should have been added the references to Ezek. xxxix. 29 &c. which follow above.

[4] Ezek. xxxix. 29 "I [shall] have poured out," is an attempt to express, by the English equivalent of "effudero," what Jerome more exactly expresses by "effuderim" (which he distinguishes from Joel ii. 28 "effundam").

[5] The LXX means "I have exhausted my wrath and will henceforth be propitious."

[6] Gesen. 1049 *b* gives these four passages, and no others, as mentioning the "pouring out" of Jehovah's "spirit." *Echa* (Wu p. 108, rep. p. 140, on Lam. ii. 4) quotes the four instances of "pouring out" in a good sense, and also four instances in a bad sense, *e.g.* Lam. ii. 4 "he poured out his fury like fire."

these, quoted from Joel by Peter in the Acts of the Apostles, are applied by him to the first Pentecostal outpouring of the Spirit on the Church[1]. In Joel, the "pouring out" is to be "upon all flesh," and it is added "also upon the servants and the handmaids will I pour out my spirit." R. Tanchuma quotes this universal outpouring of the Spirit "in the age to come" as a contrast to the giving of the Spirit to this or that prophet or ruler in the present age; and another tradition connects Joel's prophecy with the saying of Isaiah, quoted in John, that "all men" shall hereafter "be God's disciples[2]."

The instance of "pouring out the spirit" in Zechariah is not of the same kind as the other three. "I will *pour out* upon the house of David, and upon the inhabitants of Jerusalem, *the spirit of grace and supplication*, and they shall look unto me (*or*, him) whom they have pierced[3]." But still the thought is present of a purifying spirit coming *in a flood* upon those who lift up their hearts in prayer, and the words—when combined with the contextual "they shall look unto him whom they pierced," and when interpreted in a mystical Christian sense—prepare the reader for the thought of a baptism with the blood of the crucified Saviour.

The stress laid by John, not only in his Gospel, on the "*water*" issuing with the "*blood*" from the side of the crucified Jesus, after He had "delivered up his Spirit," but also in his Epistle, on the threefold witness of "the *spirit*" and "the *water*" and "the *blood*," must be considered along with his express quotation from Zechariah about looking unto Him "whom

---

[1] Acts ii. 17—18 quoting Joel ii 28—29.

[2] *Numb r* (on Numb. xi 16, Wu. p 413), *Deut. r.* (on Deut. xxiv 9, Wu p 83) quoting Ezek xxxvi. 26 "a heart of stone," Joel ii. 28, and Is liv 13 (quoted in Jn vi. 45) It may be noted that Luke, who in the Acts quotes Joel's prophecy about "*all flesh*," quotes also in his Gospel (in connection with John the Baptist's prediction of the new baptism) words in the context of Isaiah that are not quoted by Mk-Mt, namely, "and *all flesh* shall see it together" (Lk (as LXX) "and *all flesh* shall see the salvation of God"). [3] Zech xii. 10.

they pierced[1]." John does not, it is true, expressly quote the words "pour out...the *spirit*," as well as the words "look unto him whom they pierced" But it is practically certain that he must have interpreted the former in the same mystical way as the latter, and that he regarded the whole of Zechariah's prophecy as applying to the crucified Saviour, who became "a fountain" for the cleansing of "sin," and for the regeneration of believers with a birth "from above[2]."

§ 7. "*The Lamb of God*"

Both before and after the Johannine mention of "baptizing with the Holy Spirit," the Fourth Gospel places a declaration of the Baptist about Jesus that He is "the Lamb of God that taketh away the sin of the world[3]." (1) What precisely does the Evangelist mean by this? (2) What does he suppose the Baptist to have meant by it? And (3) what is a historian to say about it if asked, "Did the Baptist actually use these words?"

The Evangelist's purpose is probably to enlarge our notions of purification or baptism—and, in particular, to lift us out of the ruts of controversial dogmas about baptism in fire as distinct from baptism in water—by suggesting to us other metaphors of purification. The Logos (says Origen) when regarded as "drink," is "to some men, water, to others, wine, to others again, blood", and, when regarded as baptism, "the same Logos is baptism of water, and of spirit, and of fire, but, to some also, of blood[4]." According to this

---

[1] Jn xix 34—7, 1 Jn v 6—8, Zech xii 10

[2] Comp Zech xiii 1 "In that day there shall be a fountain opened .. for sin." Rev 1 7 "every eye shall see him, and *they that pierced him*, and all the tribes of the earth *shall mourn* over him," combines the "piercing" with the "mourning" of Zech xii. 10—14

[3] Jn i 29, 36, shortened, in the second instance, to "the Lamb of God"

[4] Origen *Comm Joann* vi 26 (Lomm i 243) Prof Flinders Petrie (*Religion of the Egyptians*, 1912, p 13) quoting from the Hermetic

view, the Baptist's twofold testimony to Jesus as "the Lamb of God" would seem intended by the Evangelist to prepare us for the thought of "the blood of the Lamb"; and it is akin to the symbolism of the closely-following Feast at Cana, where the "six waterpots of stone after the Jews' manner of purifying" are to be contrasted with the "water become wine", and that same "wine" is to be regarded as a type of the "blood" which is to flow, along with "water," from the Crucified Saviour.

Also, by this twofold exclamation of the Baptist—which sounds like a confession suddenly extorted by a spiritual presence—our minds are suddenly arrested and half-turned, and then (on reflection) turned right round, to the thought of a Person, mysteriously pure, purifying, innocent, and gentle—gentle to everything except to the tyranny of sin. We forget the Baptist's reproaches of the "offspring of vipers," and his threatenings of "fire", and we concentrate our thoughts on Him whom he calls, first, "the Lamb of God that taketh away the sin of the world," and then "the Lamb of God" without any mention of "sin." The first utterance suggests

---

treatise *About the Common Mind* (before 332 B C) says "In that is the rule of Fate, Agathodaimon, the First-born God, Life owing to Energy, Power, and Aeon, and Logos often used of human reason, the strongest phrase being 'Unto this Logos pay thy adoration and thy worship'" In the treatise on the Cup, or rather Font, the Logos doctrine begins to develop thus 'With Logos not with hands did the Demiourgos make the universal Cosmos' Conversion is the prominent motive of the treatise The great Crater or Font full of Mind had been sent from God for men, 'Baptize thyself with this Font's baptism, thou that hast faith that thou canst ascend to Him who hath sent down the Font, . as many as understood the tidings, and immersed themselves in Mind, became partakers in the Gnosis' With this we must connect the baptism of the ascetics described about 10 A D, where the initiate was 'made a partaker of the waters of purification'" There is much food for thought in the phrase "Cup, or rather Font," especially when we bear in mind that the word for "cup" is κρατήρ, "mixing-bowl," called (Steph *Thes* iv 1927) κρατὴρ Ἀγαθοῦ Δαίμονος, of which the primary meaning would refer to drinking, not to washing

the Lamb of the Passover, or of the Daily Offering, purifying the sinful, the second suggests that those who are purified are now sinless, "purchased" by the blood of the Lamb, so that, as Revelation says, they "follow the Lamb whithersoever he goeth[1]." And the very next sentence in the Gospel mentions disciples "following[2]."

But secondly, what does John suppose the Baptist to have meant by it? Can we suppose that, in the Evangelist's opinion, these truths about the Lamb of God, which were not made known to the Apostles till after the Lord's Resurrection, were revealed to the Baptist already? More probably he believed that the Baptist, as being a prophet and the greatest of the prophets, was led to use language that was not only true for himself as he understood it, but also more amply true for those that were to come. This is what we might infer from many prophecies in the Old Testament and from what is said about them in the New. The Epistle of St Peter recognises that the ancient prophets "sought and searched diligently[3]," but implies that they did not find fully. And this Gospel distinctly recognises (as also do the Synoptic Gospels) that the Baptist did not "find fully." He was "of the earth", Jesus was "from the heaven and above all[4]." That being so, we have now to attempt an answer to the third question before us, namely, as to the meaning that could have been attached by the Baptist himself to these words, since he could not have meant all that we Christians mean by them.

---

[1] Rev. xiv. 4 "These," it is said, "were purchased from among men," and Rev v 9 describes them as "purchased" with the "blood" of the Lamb

[2] Jn 1 37 "the two disciples heard him speak, and they *followed* Jesus"

[3] 1 Pet 1 10   [4] Jn iii 31

§ 8. *In what sense might the Baptist speak of Jesus as "the Lamb of God"?*

Some help for modern readers toward answering this difficult question might be derived from the remarks of Clement of Alexandria about the babes or lambs of God in general, and about Jesus as the Babe or Lamb of God in particular[1]. We must also think of the Aramaic "youngling," in Hebrew, "lamb", and of the Hebrew use of "suckling" to mean a "pupil", and of the passage in Isaiah where Aquila and Theodotion support, in effect, the testimony of the LXX describing the Suffering Servant of God as a "suckling," apparently despised for his youth as well as for his humble presence[2]. A Targum on the birth of Moses in Exodus says that Pharaoh had a dream in which "a lamb"—that is, Moses—is seen in one scale of a balance, outweighing the whole of the land of Egypt which is placed in the other[3]. These verbal usages, and these associations, may help us to understand how the Baptist—without any definite allusion, and perhaps without any allusion at all, to the Lamb of the Passover or the Lamb of the Daily Sacrifice[4]—might burst out into a rapturous expression of admiration and devotion for his own pupil "Not my pupil, but God's, God's own 'suckling,' a very Lamb of God!"

Toward such a homage the last of the Prophets, being himself of a comparatively austere and stern disposition,

---

[1] Clem. Alex. 104—112 (see "Babe of God" in *Light* **3705, 3817** *a—i*)

[2] See *Son* **3519** *e—f* (quoting Jerome on Is liii 2 (R V) "a tender plant")

[3] Exod. i. 13 (Jer. Targ.)

[4] That is to say, though there are both these allusions, they are not made by the Baptist. The Baptist uttered the words, the Evangelist found in them the allusions. Of course, whenever a pious Jew used the word "lamb" in a metaphorical sense, he might connect it *distantly* with the sacrificial "lamb" But that is a different thing from connecting it *directly* with the thought of the Lamb of the Passover.

might be all the more moved by a sense of contrast, and by a recognition of a new and strange and divinely attractive power in this Little One, who taught, or seemed to teach, a new doctrine, or rather to convey a new power, by which the "lambs" were to prevail over the wolves, and the "little ones" over those whom this world called great

The homage cannot be understood unless we make an effort to apprehend the possibility of a combination of babe-like purity and God-like power, which might absolutely constrain the Baptist to make an exclamation of this kind, somewhat as (we may suppose) the sons of Heth were forced, by the recognition of a prince-like and noble nature, to say to Abraham "Hear us, my lord, thou art *a prince of God among us*[1]"

Against this view there may be quoted the words of the Baptist himself, "*And I knew him not*, but he that sent me to baptize with water, he said unto me, *Upon whomsoever thou shalt see the Spirit descending, and abiding upon him*, the same is he that baptizeth with the Holy Spirit[2]." This may be urged as shewing that the Baptist's belief was not based on the innate beauty and divineness of the character of Jesus, but on a sign, such as that which the Pharisees were always demanding, "a sign from heaven."

But there are "signs" and "signs" Such an argument ignores the difference between a sign that is moral or spiritual and one that is non-moral or non-spiritual If a magician promises to make me see him stop, with his uplifted hand,

---

[1] Gen xxiii 6, LXX "a king *from God*," Targ "great in the presence of the Lord" Comp Exod ii 2 (about Moses) the babe was "good [to look on]," Acts vii. 20 "goodly *to God*" Josephus *Ant* ii 9 7 "*divine* in form." The Jews said that one of the names of Moses was "*Tob-iah*," *i e.* "the Good One *of the Lord*" See Wu (on Lev i 1) and *Pesikt* p 243 Jewish traditions on Eccles iv 13—14 (Wu. *ad loc*) say that the "poor and wise youth" may be either (1) the principle of goodness that enters into man from his thirteenth year, or (2) "Abraham *the prince of God*."   [2] Jn i 33

the motion of the earth—or, to speak popularly, the motion of the sun—and if he does it and then says to me, " Is not this a great thing!" I am obliged to say "Yes." But I may add, "Yet it is not spiritually great, and, in comparison with spiritual goodness, it is a very small thing." On the other hand, to have one's eyes opened so as to be enabled to discern the Spirit of Goodness descending, is great in a different way, great in a spiritual region, and with a greatness above all kinds of material greatness And if this influx of spiritual vision came on John the Baptist during intercourse with Jesus of Nazareth, is it not a reasonable as well as a spiritual supposition that the vision was connected with that intercourse as effect with cause? Perhaps it would not be too bold to say that John would never have seen "the Spirit descending" on Jesus, if he had not first been disposed to exclaim, even before the descent, " I have need to be baptized by thee," and perhaps even, " Behold, the Lamb of God "

It is probable that John, who was like Ezekiel in "seeing the heaven opened," followed him also in his ways of thought so far at least as this, that he often dwelt in meditation on that "likeness as the appearance of a man" which Ezekiel saw above the Chariot on high[1] If so, he would not find so great a difficulty as some modern thinkers find in seeing a connection—a "natural" connection, in the sense of divine "nature"—between God in heaven and Man on earth. On this point we may take a hint from the early Christian poet Nonnus, who, when describing Christ, "walking," as "seen" by John the Baptist, paraphrases the text in such a way as to convey an allusion to Ezekiel's chariot :—

> Having seen Christ walking on the earth as a traveller on foot,
> The uplifted Charioteer of the Chariot that goeth on high[2]

---

[1] Ezek. 1 26.
[2] See Nonnus on Jn 1 36 and *Son* **3583**(xii) *f,* comp **3040** *d* On περιπατῶν "walking" (amid the Churches), see *Notes* **2998** (xxviii) *f*

This poetic paraphrase is, if one may so say, in all probability historically correct. That is to say, it represents the historical fact so far as this, that the mystic John the Baptist perceived in Jesus a fulfilment of his dreams and visions of the revival of Israel, as predicted by Ezekiel. There was to be the descent of a divine power along with "the appearance of a man". There was to be the divine gift of a new heart, a new spirit, a cleansing with water from above, a new life in the dry bones of Israel[1]. Not only the prospect of all this, but also the actual presence of a part of it, he realised in Jesus, from whom he personally felt a flow of spiritual life coming forth to himself, somewhat as Peter felt when he exclaimed, "Lord, to whom shall we go? Thou hast words of eternal life." According to Matthew, the Baptist said to Jesus, "I have need to be baptized by thee." According to the Fourth Gospel, the Baptist said about Jesus, "Behold, the Lamb of God."

By the laws of evidence—laws which men who know them are bound morally as well as logically to observe—we are not justified in accepting either the Matthaean or the Johannine tradition in its exact words, as having an authority equal to that of a saying of Christ supported by the threefold Synoptic testimony. But we are justified in accepting both as being neither inventions, nor gross and absurd exaggerations, nor mere anachronisms, but honest and reasonable attempts to hand down, in a reasonable though somewhat idealised form, the Christian traditions, accepted at the time, about the attitude of John the Baptist toward Jesus of Nazareth[2]. From a spiritual point of view, these early Christian traditions may well be regarded, even by the keenest and most ardent lovers of scientific and historical research, as

---

[1] Ezek xxxvi 25—7, xxxvii 1—14

[2] For a sketch of the difficulties attending the tasks of the several Evangelists, see *Son* 3374 A

being no overstatement but perhaps rather an understatement of the truth[1].

---

[1] A word should perhaps have been added about the Baptist's probable attitude to the sacrifices in the Temple. If he held Essene views he would not—if we may believe Josephus (*Ant* xviii. 1, quoted in *Son* **3584** *b*)—participate in those sacrifices. But he might have a very high and pure conception of what the spiritual sacrifice ought to be (comp. Ps xl 8 "to do thy will, O my God"). Hence he might conceivably use language like that which the Fourth Gospel imputes to him concerning Jesus as fulfilling that ideal. John the Baptist is clearly regarded by the Fourth Evangelist as not accompanying Jesus to Jerusalem on the occasion when He attempted to purify the Temple. What is the Evangelist's view of this absence? Is the Baptist to be regarded as holding aloof (1) in accordance with his general Essene habit, or (2) for some special reason? If the latter, may we suppose that he regarded Jesus as running unwarranted risks, endangering both Himself and the success of His mission by opposing the rulers of the Jews in a region where they reigned supreme? Did he, in a word, regard his disciple and successor, Jesus, as being like the "lamb" in Jeremiah (xi 19 (LXX) ἀρνίον) or in Isaiah (liii. 17 (LXX) ἀμνός)? See *Son* **3519** *f*, and *Notes* **2998** (xxxii) *b—d*.

The multitude of possible meanings and allusions attachable to the Baptist's words "the lamb of God" diminishes the probability of any one particular meaning or allusion. But it also increases the probability that *some* one or more of these meanings and allusions must be accepted, and thus strengthens the conclusion that some title of this kind was actually given by John the Baptist to Jesus, and that it is not a fiction of the Fourth Evangelist.

CHAPTER IV

THE BAPTISM OF JESUS

THE Fourth Gospel does not describe "The Baptism of Jesus." "On what ground, then," it may be asked, "can a Chapter be claimed for it in a treatise entitled The Fourfold Gospel?" On this ground, that the Fourth Gospel assumes the Baptism, alludes to the Synoptic traditions about it, adds traditions of its own about it, and subsequently enlarges on baptism with water and the Spirit in such a way as to shew that it has in view wrong deductions, as well as right deductions, that might be drawn from it.

On the terrestrial baptism of Jesus in the Jordan, and on the momentary "opening" of the sky above the Jordan, the Fourth Gospel says nothing; but (if one may so express it) on the celestial act corresponding to that terrestrial phenomenon, and on the future consequences of that act, it says a great deal In no Chapter more remarkably than in this will it be found that the study of what the Fourth Evangelist pointedly omits is almost as important as the study of what he inserts to explain his omissions.

---

§ 1 *The "coming" of Jesus, when was it?*

When did Jesus "come"? Mark—in a clause placed immediately after the Baptist's final words "I baptized you with water, but he will baptize you with the Holy Spirit"—answers the question thus. "And it came to pass *in those days* came Jesus" "*In those days*"—meaning in Scripture

THE BAPTISM OF JESUS

almost always evil days when applied to the past[1]—is used as follows about Moses, with the Hebraic "and it came to pass," as in Mark: "*And it came to pass in those days*, when Moses was grown up, that he came forth unto his brethren and looked on their burdens[2]" It would therefore be a fit phrase for introducing the advent of Jesus when He came forth to look upon the burdens of His fellow men and to bring them from evil days of servitude into an aeon, or age, of freedom.

Why, then, does not Matthew use it? Perhaps because he has already used it about John the Baptist—"*In those days* arriveth John the Baptist preaching .[3]" Perhaps Matthew regards the evil days as being ended with the coming of John. He introduces the coming of Jesus immediately after the Baptist's doctrine, thus, "...'he shall burn with fire unquenchable.' *Then* arriveth Jesus...[4]"

Luke uses "*in these* (or *those*) *days*" in connection with the conception and birth of Jesus[5], but not about His "coming."

---

[1] Gen vi 4 "There were giants *in those days*" is the first instance

[2] Exod ii 11 The LXX has "in those many days," partly influenced, perhaps, by a following sentence (Exod ii 23), "And it came to pass *in those many days* that the king of Egypt died, and the children of Israel sighed" There are many other instances in the Bible where "many days" is used, as the Jews said, not because the days were *really* "many," but because they were *really* weary, and *seemed* "many" See *Lev r* (on Lev xv 25) where Wü p 126 quotes, by error, Exod ii 11 "Es war nach vielen Tagen" It should be Exod ii. 23

Moses "went forth" again (Exod ii. 13) "on the second day," and the Midrash calls attention to this, as if it had a mystical meaning. See below on Jn 1 29—35 "*On the morrow* he [*i e* John] seeth Jesus coming unto him ...*Again on the morrow* John .looked upon Jesus as he walked."

[3] Mt iii 1 "arriveth (παραγίνεται)."

[4] Mt iii 12—13 "arriveth (παραγίνεται)" "*Then*" is a characteristic adverb in Matthew, and therefore nothing symbolical can be inferred from it in his Gospel, though it is often symbolically interpreted in the Midrash (see *Exod r* on Exod xv 1)

[5] Lk i. 39, ii 1 Lk iv 2 "in those [forty] days" stands on a different footing from the Hebraic phrase

THE BAPTISM OF JESUS

The Baptist's "coming" he dates with precise reference to the reign of Tiberius Caesar[1]. But, in contrast, he does not date the "coming" of Jesus, or definitely describe Him anywhere as "coming." Indeed he seems to avoid such a mention in connection with the Messiah and to reserve it for His forerunner. It is the Baptist whom he brings on the stage as "*coming*" into the circle of the Jordan "in the fifteenth year of Tiberius Caesar." And it is to the Baptist alone that Luke immediately afterwards directs our thoughts:—to his proclamation of the baptism of repentance, his warnings to the multitudes, his precepts to various classes of disciples, his indirect disavowal of any claim to be the Christ, and his avowal of his own inferiority to a future baptizer with the Holy Spirit and fire, concluding with the statement that, after he had "preached good tidings with many other exhortations" to the people, "Herod the tetrarch...shut up John in prison[2]"

Not till these last words have removed the Baptist from the scene (and almost altogether from Luke's Gospel), does Luke now go back to Jesus whom his last mention left at Nazareth, as a boy of twelve years old, "advancing...in favour with God and men[3]." And even now Luke tells us nothing about what Jesus had been doing during this long interval; nor at what time, nor whence, nor whither Jesus now came, when He presented Himself to John for baptism; nor what, if anything, John said to Jesus, or about Jesus, after His arrival, or still later, after the baptism had been accomplished. Even if we regard Luke's last sentence about John's being "shut up" as a parenthetical anticipation, still the introduction of "Jesus" as already "*having been baptized*" is strangely abrupt if we read the sentences rapidly together, thus ·— "...he shut up John in prison. Now it came to pass, when all the people had been baptized, that, *Jesus also having been*

---

[1] Lk iii 1—3   [2] Lk iii 1—20   [3] Lk ii 52

THE BAPTISM OF JESUS

baptized, and being in the act of praying, the heaven was opened." How natural for Luke's readers to say, "But you have not told us when or where Jesus was 'baptized,' or even that He was 'baptized' at all, why do you omit all these things?"

An answer to these questions is suggested, in part by Luke's own Introduction, but in part also by the following parallel in the two earlier Gospels which Luke had before him:—

Mk i 9	Mt iii. 13
came Jesus from Nazareth of Galilee *and was baptized* . by John	arriveth Jesus from Galilee toward John *to be baptized* by him.

Matthew implies an interval, or at all events the possibility of one, between the "arrival" and the "baptism" Jesus "arrived" (we may reasonably infer from the context) not alone, but with other postulants for baptism. These postulants the Prophet must have tested in some way before baptizing them. To test such a multitude—some of whom he rejected, as being "offspring of vipers[1]"—must have taken time For a time, then, Jesus may have been a disciple of John, either in one and the same place, or following "behind him" from place to place, in the circle of the Jordan True, Matthew tells us that John said to Jesus "I have need to be baptized by thee," but Matthew gives us no grounds for supposing that John said this to Jesus in view of any previous acquaintance or connection between them.

This is Matthew's position, and it presents no difficulty. But how different is the position of Luke! For Luke has distinctly told us in his Introduction that there had been between the mother of John and the mother of Jesus a very close connection before the birth of either child. Had the two mothers never met again? Had the two children never

---

[1] Mt iii 7, Lk iii. 7

THE BAPTISM OF JESUS

met, since the day when Elisabeth called Mary "the mother of my Lord[1]"? Even if the two children had never met, had they never heard of one another? Had the son of Elisabeth never heard of that Son of Mary whom his mother called her "Lord"? In any case, when they did meet at last in the circle of the Jordan, what did they say to one another? All these questions about the meeting of the two grown-up children so imperatively demanded an answer from Luke, if he described their meeting, that he may very well have decided—since he could not answer them—not to describe their meeting at all.

In the Fourth Gospel the time of the "coming" is signified by nothing but the phrase "*on the morrow.*" This appears to have a mystical meaning, as referring to the six days of the spiritual Genesis, that is to say, the Creation of the Church.— "*On the morrow he* [i.e. *John*] *seeth Jesus coming unto him* and saith, Behold, the Lamb of God, which taketh away the sin of the world!" Origen and the Diatessaron appear to be right in regarding these words as uttered by John at the moment of Christ's coming to him *to be baptized*[2]. On the preceding day Jesus had been "behind" John, as a disciple, "in the midst of" the crowd, unrecognised by the Pharisees, but already so far recognised by John that he could say of Him "In the midst of you standeth one whom ye know not, one coming behind me, the latchet of whose shoe I am not worthy to loose." But now, when the Prophet "*sees*" the Logos—"the light that lighteth every human being, [*continually*] *coming* into the world"—"*coming*" to him, and no longer "behind" him, he himself receives enlightening, and his eyes are opened to enable him to discern the Spirit descending. And immediately afterwards, the baptism having

---

[1] Lk 1 43
[2] Origen *Comm. Joann* vi. 30 (on Jn 1. 29) οἱονεὶ γὰρ ἐν ἑξῆς φωτισμῷ appears to refer to the baptism technically called "enlightening [that follows] next-day," see below

now taken place, John exclaims, "I have beheld the Spirit descending as a dove out of heaven and it abode on him[1]" According to Origen, a progress in revelation is implied by "*on the morrow*," as compared with the preceding day; and he says—perhaps playing on the double meaning of "enlightening[2]," technically used for "baptism"—"Jesus cometh as it were in enlightening [that follows] next-day," being now "not only *recognised* as standing 'in the midst even of those who knew [Him] not,' but by this time also *seen*...." This use of "on the morrow" here to introduce a new period of progressive creation would accord well with its meaning elsewhere in the context[3].

Reviewing the facts, and asking whether the Fourth Gospel has anything that spiritually corresponds to the Marcan phrase "*in those days*" in connection with the "coming" of Jesus—in accordance with its Jewish traditional meaning, that is, "days of darkness and trouble"—we may reply that the Johannine day before "the morrow" is metaphorically a day of darkness, or at all events of twilight before the dawn. It is the day of the Priests and Levites and Pharisees; the day of those who, under the conventional tyranny of names— "the Christ," "Elijah," "the Prophet"—dispute the authority of the Spirit, the day in which the Deliverer "stands in the

---

[1] Jn 1 32 It may be asked, "Where is the Temptation to come, so as to fit in with this arrangement?" The Diatessaron places it between Jn 1 34 and Jn 1 35, in other words, between two episodes which are severally introduced with the phrase (1 29) "*On the morrow*," and (1 35) "*on the morrow again*" The omission may be illustrated by the omission in Chronicles (noted in the Introductory Volume, pp 79—80) of the rebellion of Absalom &c after the phrase "*after these things*."

[2] See *Son* 3407 (vii) *a*. One reason why Greeks might avoid the use of "the baptized" (substituting "enlightened") might be that "baptized" was regularly used for people "*immersed* [*in pleasure*]," "*soaked* [*in wine*]" &c, see Steph *Thes*

[3] See *Joh Voc* 1717 *h* and *Son* 3583 (xii) *d* on the Hexaemeron of the Creation of the Church which is implied by the context, and by the use of ἐπαύριον in Jn 1 29, 35, 43

midst of" the people who "do not know" Him; a day in which the darkness is striving to overcome the dawning Light of the World, and the Prophet himself, though recognising the approach of a Master, has not yet received the sign that is to announce the future Baptizer of Israel "The morrow" changes all this The eyes of the Prophet are opened, and "he seeth" Jesus, the Light of the World, "coming" to him. This is the first day of the new Genesis, on which the new Enlightenment or Baptism is to begin, and it corresponds to the day when "God saw the light that it was good[1]."

In all this, the contrast between the Johannine Gospel and Luke—both in those respects in which Luke differs from Mark and Matthew and in others—is very striking. Both Mark and Matthew describe the "coming" of Jesus to John or connect it closely with John, Luke mentions no "coming" of Jesus at all, the Fourth Gospel says that the occasion on which John "saw" Jesus "coming" was the one on which he hailed Him as "The Lamb of God which taketh away the sin of the world."

Then—as if to say to the readers of Luke, "This was not the result of any previous acquaintance between John and Jesus or between Elisabeth and Mary"—it adds immediately the following words of John, "*And I knew him not.*" We are not to suppose that the Fourth Gospel hereby denies the historical truth of Luke's narrative about Elisabeth and Mary, but rather that it makes a spiritual protest against wrong inferences from it: "Some say that John the son of Elisabeth '*knew*' Jesus the son of Mary to be his Lord, even from

---

[1] This is not the place to discuss the stages of the Creation of the Church in the Hexaemeron of the Fourth Gospel, but we may contrast it, perhaps, with the seven days in Ezek iii 16—17 (on which see Origen) regarded typically as needful for the "watchman's training." During that time the prophet Ezekiel does nothing; but Jesus builds up the Church.

childhood. That was not a prophet's '*knowing*.' The '*knowing*' of Jesus by John—such 'knowing' as might enable John to bear witness to Him that all men might believe—did not come, and could not come, till the Spirit descended and said to John, as in old days to Samuel anointing David, 'This is he'."

To the question, therefore, "When was the 'coming' of Jesus?" Mark and Matthew convey vague answers, Luke gives no answer at all, and the Fourth Gospel says, in effect, "The 'coming' was not into this place or that, nor into the bodily presence of this person or that, but into the hearts of men, represented by John the Baptist, who was the 'man sent from God,' the appointed witness, that all might believe in the Light. And He, the Light, came into the heart of John '*on the morrow*'—after the time of darkness during which the Lord had been 'standing in the midst' of men and John himself had not known Him. The 'morrow' was like the morrow after the darkness that was on the face of the deep; on that 'morrow,' and on this, God said 'Let there be light'."

§ 2. *The "coming" of Jesus, whither was it?*

Luke's omission of the "coming" may be in part explained by some early obscurity indicated in the slight verbal deviation of Matthew from Mark —

Mk i. 9	Mt iii 13
.came Jesus from Nazareth of Galilee and was baptized (*lit*) into the Jordan by John	arriveth Jesus from Galilee to (*or*, near) the Jordan toward John to be baptized by him.

The expression "baptized *into* the Jordan" might be defended, as vernacular Greek, from a passage in Plutarch, quoting a vulgar Greek charm that says to a sufferer, "Baptize thyself *into* the sea[1]." But such a use is non-existent in the

---

[1] Plut *Mor.* 166 A "call the old witch, and baptize thyself *into* the sea"

THE BAPTISM OF JESUS

Greek Testament. And it is difficult to believe that Mark would use "baptized *into* Jordan" here, after having used "baptized *in* Jordan" in the preceding context

The Jew in Origen's Celsus speaks of Jesus as "being bathed *by the side of John*," where one MS has "*Jordan*" for "*John*[1]"; and Origen previously refers to extracts taken by Celsus from "the gospel of Matthew—*but perhaps, too, from the rest of the gospels*—about the dove that alighted on the Saviour when He was being baptized (lit.) *from the side of John*[2]." Here two MSS omit "*from the side of John*" and one has "*by the side of John*," and the Editor says "What if the right reading is *by the side of Jordan*?" In N T., "baptize *into*" is used only in connection with a spiritual element (sometimes represented by a person) *into* which, or whom, one passes by baptism, *e.g.* "baptized into *repentance*," "into *Christ Jesus*," "into *Christ's death*," "into *the name of Paul*," "into *John's baptism*," "into *Moses*," "into *Christ*," "into *the name of the Lord Jesus*."

These facts—and perhaps we may add the variations of the MSS in Mark as to the order of the words—make it doubtful whether the extant text of Mark is free from error—the original having perhaps been "came and was baptized *into the baptism of John*," or "*into John*," or "came *to the baptism of John*" This would agree with Matthew's version, "came... toward John to be baptized by him."

The Fourth Gospel appears at first sight to agree with Matthew in saying that Jesus "came" to John. But the contexts differ. Matthew seems to imply a journeying ("arriveth") to John. The Fourth Gospel may mean that Jesus, who had been on a certain day "standing" among John's disciples, "came" to John "on the morrow" to be baptized[3]

---

[1] *From Letter* **1039** *a*, quoting *Cels* 1 41 παρὰ τῷ Ἰωάννῃ
[2] Origen *Cels* 1 40 παρὰ τοῦ Ἰ
[3] Jn 1 26—9

It is true that a place—about which we shall speak presently—is mentioned in the Johannine context "*These things were done in Bethany beyond Jordan*, where John was baptizing. On the morrow he [*i.e.* John] seeth Jesus coming unto him...." But "*these things were done*" is vague We are not told that Jesus "*came*" to Bethany. John moved from place to place baptizing. As we do not know how long Jesus had been with him, we can only infer, as probable, that there had been a "coming" of Jesus to Bethany; but we know, as a certainty, that there had been a "coming" of Jesus to John. The Fourth Gospel prefers to regard the "coming" as connected with persons, not with places. It first described the non-incarnate Light as "coming into the world"—that is, to the inhabited world, to enlighten it. Then (in the Baptist's words) the incarnate Light or Word is twice mentioned as "coming behind" His forerunner. Now at last He is "*seen coming to*" that forerunner through whose "seeing" He is to be "seen" by mankind.

§ 3. "*From Nazareth*," "*of Nazareth*," "*Nazarene*," "*Nazoraean*." (*See also Appendix I.*)

There is an ambiguity in Mark's tradition about Christ's "coming":—

Mk i. 9	Mt iii. 13
And it came to pass in those days there came Jesus *from Nazareth*[1] of Galilee .	Then arriveth Jesus *from Galilee*.

It may be illustrated by:—

Mk xv. 43	Mt. xxvii. 57	Lk xxiii. 50—52
There came Joseph *from Arimathaea*[2].	There came a rich man *from Arimathaea*, named Joseph	A man named Joseph [*a man*] *from Arimathaea* approached Pilate

---

[1] "Jesus from, *i e* of, Nazareth" occurs elsewhere in Mt. xxi 11, Jn i 45, Acts x 38, but always with the article before ἀπό

[2] W. H. marg places the article before ἀπό.

The Revised Version, in the first of these two Marcan passages, has "*from* Nazareth," and, in the second, "*of* Arimathaea." Probably the distinction is correct But it is justified only by inference, not by any distinction in the Marcan Greek[1]. As to Joseph, the Lucan parallel shews that Luke took "*from* Arimathaea" to mean "*a man from*, or, *of*, Arimathaea," and the circumstances shew that Luke was right. As to Jesus, the parallel Matthew shews that Matthew took the meaning to be "*journeying from* Galilee." For "Jesus *from* Galilee" meaning "Jesus *of* Galilee" is unheard of in the Gospels. Perhaps Matthew omitted "from Nazareth" because of its ambiguity. But if this was Matthew's motive it is not certain that he was right. It is possible, though not probable, that Mark meant "there came Jesus *of Nazareth of Galilee*," where "*Nazareth of Galilee*" would be used like "*Bethlehem of Judaea.*"

The only other Synoptic instance of "*from Nazareth*" occurs in Matthew's description (peculiar to himself) of the crowd shouting round Jesus as He rides into Jerusalem, "This is the prophet, Jesus, *the* [*man*] *from Nazareth* of Galilee[2]," where the other three Gospels mention "king," or "kingdom"

Luke nowhere uses the phrase "*from Nazareth*," though he mentions "Nazareth" almost as often as the other three Evangelists taken together[3]. The reason is probably this, that he is anxious to emphasize the fact that Jesus was born not in Nazareth but in Bethlehem His parents indeed— such is Luke's view—lived in Nazareth, and Jesus would naturally have been born in Nazareth. But, by a providential interposition, He was born in Bethlehem, so that He might

---

[1] That is, the text of W H., which has no article before ἀπό

[2] Mt xxi. 11, a short insertion peculiar to Matthew.

[3] Mt (3), Mk (1), Jn (2), but Lk. five times, of which four are in the Introduction

have been described with strict accuracy as "Jesus *from Bethlehem*," not "Jesus *from Nazareth*"

Matthew, though agreeing with Luke as to facts—namely, birth at Bethlehem, but domicile at Nazareth — takes an exactly opposite view of providential interposition. Jesus, he says, was born in Bethlehem of Judaea, the home of His parents, and would have been domiciled there in the natural course of things. But when His parents, after fleeing with the babe to Egypt, "returned" to the land of Israel, Joseph was afraid to go to Judaea, and, being "warned [by God] in a dream, he withdrew into the parts of Galilee, and came and dwelt in a city called Nazareth, that it might be fulfilled which was spoken by the prophets [saying] that 'He shall be called a Nazoraean[1].'"

These two opposite views are brought before the reader of Mark here, when Mark for the first time mentions "*Jesus from Nazareth*," without any parallel mention of it in Matthew or Luke, and where the question arises "Does this imply that Jesus was born at Nazareth, or merely domiciled there?"

We have now to ask how John intervenes. He does it, as often, dramatically, in a dialogue. The dialogue mentions "*from Nazareth*" *in two Greek forms*, 1st, "*from*," *meaning domicile*, 2nd, "*from*" *or* "*out of*," *meaning extraction*[2]. The dialogue is between Philip and Nathanael. Philip says to Nathanael "Him have we found who has been portrayed by Moses in the Law, and by the Prophets—Jesus, son of Joseph, the [man] *from* (i.e. *domiciled at*) *Nazareth*[3]." The preceding verse uses the two Greek prepositions about Philip, thus: "Now Philip was *from* [i e *domiciled at*] Bethsaida, [but] *out of*

---

[1] Mt ii 22—3

[2] "From" meaning domicile, ἀπό "from," or "out of," meaning extraction, ἐκ See *Joh Gr* **2289**—**93** "'Ἀπό and ἐκ describing domicile or birth-place"

[3] Jn 1. 45 ἔγραψεν See *Son* **3493** *n* "γράφω with a personal object regularly means 'draw'" "From" is here ἀπό.

[i.e *a native of*] the city of Andrew and Peter [Capernaum][1]."
Thus the reader has been prepared to render "*from Nazareth*,"
in Philip's utterance, "*domiciled at Nazareth*." But Nathanael
has not been thus prepared, and he consequently confuses the
two. He substitutes "*out of*," that is, "*native of*," in his reply:
"*Out of* Nazareth can any good thing be[2]?"

Philip does not retort on Nathanael "You have confused
domicile with *extraction*." He simply says, "Come and see."
Nathanael comes, and sees, and believes. No mention is made
of his confusion of one word with another and consequent error
in inference. No explanation is given, such as, "Jesus might
have been *domiciled at* Nazareth, though *born at* Bethlehem."
Thus the Evangelist, by what he does not say, and by what he
does say, achieves two objects. He makes us say to ourselves,
"There *was* an answer to Nathanael's objection, although
neither he nor Philip saw it." At the same time we are led
to imitate the faith of Nathanael and Philip and to say to
ourselves concerning the conflicting accounts of Matthew and
Luke, "There may be similar answers to objections of our
own arising out of these accounts, although we at present
cannot see the answers."

Space forbids detailed discussion of the Johannine motive
in illustrating the Mark-Matthew phrase "Jesus from Nazareth," but a word may be added in answer to the question
"Does the Fourth Evangelist favour the Matthaean or the
Lucan view of what has been called above 'the providential
interposition'?" The answer should probably be, "He
favours both." But it cannot be justified here, for it depends

---

[1] Jn 1 44 "from" ἀπό, "out of" ἐκ. If Philip had known Andrew in
early life, that would explain why Jesus went to call him, after Andrew
and Peter had become His disciples. According to Clem. Alex. 522
(*Son* 3377 a), it was to Philip that Jesus said "follow me," and "leave the
dead to bury their own dead."

[2] "Out of," ἐκ. See *Son* 3375, suggesting, as the right reading, "Can
Good, i.e. Redemption, spring from Nazareth?"

THE BAPTISM OF JESUS

on the meaning of the word "Nazoraean" and its relation to "Nazareth"—one of the most difficult of New Testament questions from the earliest time, and now perhaps more difficult than ever, because we know more definitely the insignificance of Nazareth—a place nowhere mentioned in the Talmuds or Josephus—and because of etymological difficulties arising from the forms Nazoraean and Nazarene in the New Testament, and other forms preserved by Epiphanius.

The question is discussed in Appendix I. But an outline of the answer is this. While accepting Luke's view that Jesus was providentially born at Bethlehem, John also accepted Matthew's view that Jesus was providentially domiciled at some obscure village called *Nassara, Natzara,* or *Nazara,* "*in order that*" He should be called by the common people "*Natzoraean.*" "*Natzoraean*" was primarily derived from the name *Nêtzer,* the Branch, or Rod, of Jesse, given in Isaiah to the Messiah on whom "the Spirit of the Lord" was to "rest[1]." This title, apparently used with allusion to David as being the youngest son of the aged Jesse[2], symbolized rejuvenescence for decaying Israel, and was sometimes used by the populace like "the Son of David," to denote the Messiah as the Healer, Lifegiver, and Restorer of Liberty to Israelites.

When the Roman soldiers—presumably neither knowing nor caring what "*the Nazoraean*" meant but only using it as the title given by the Galilaeans to their ringleader—tell Jesus that they seek "Jesus *the Nazoraean*," John represents Jesus as replying "I am he." Also John and John alone,

---

[1] Is xi 1—10 To this there appears an allusion in Philo ii 437 καθάπερ γὰρ ὑποτμηθέντων στελεχῶν (comp Is x 33—4 "lop the boughs .. cut down the thickets") ..νέα ἔρνη βλαστάνουσιν (Is xi. 1) Mangey's Index to Philo gives only four quotations from Isaiah, but one of them occurs (ii 435, Is. liv. 1) a little above.

[2] Comp. 1 S xvii 12 (R V) "an old man ..stricken [in years]," and see Appendix I, p 315 foll

inserts "*the Nazoraean*" (as well as "the King of the Jews") in the title written by Pilate (presumably as God's instrument) on the Cross. These facts suggest that John may possibly have had in view some allusion to the "providential" domicile in Nazareth when he makes the learned Nathanael pass suddenly from his objection to "from Nazareth" into a rapturous acceptance of Jesus as "King of Israel"—as if he said to himself—playing on the word, after the manner of Jews—"Say not 'from *Nazara*,' but rather '*Nêtzer*,' for He is the Branch of Jesse, on whom rests the Spirit of the Lord, He is the Son of God, the King of Israel." If this is the Johannine thought, then it is not an accidental coincidence that the first mention of "Nazareth" in the Fourth Gospel is followed shortly by a mention of "King of Israel," and the last mention of "Nazoraean," in the same Gospel, is connected with "King of the Jews[1]."

§ 4. *The place where Jesus was baptized*

The place where John was at first baptizing has been discussed above. The place where Jesus was baptized may have been different. Mark—or at all events Mark's present text—says that Jesus was baptized "in" (literally, "into") the Jordan[2]. Matthew says that Jesus came to the Jordan to be baptized. Both imply that it was some place on the bank of the Jordan. Luke is curiously indirect. In the two passages which contain his only mentions of the Jordan, he tell us that (1) "John came into all *the circle of the*

---

[1] In Appendix I, attention has been called to passages in the *Aboth* where a birthplace-name is substituted for the usual "*ben*," "son of." It may be added that "man of (*vir*)" is also sometimes substituted (or added), e.g. I. 3 "Antigonus *a man of* (vir) *Soco*." In some instances the meaning is disputed and the text is doubtful, but in this the text does not vary; and there is a play on the personal name "Soco" in 1 Chr iv. 18, see *Lev. r.* (on Lev 1 1, Wu p 3) and *Megill* 13 a, where two different reasons are given for applying "Soco" to Moses.

[2] But there is some doubt about the text, see above, p 101.

Jordan," (2) "Jesus turned back *from the Jordan*[1]." But as to the meeting between Jesus and John, and the place of it, and the place where Jesus was subsequently baptized, he tells us nothing. Both places might have been either on the bank, or at some distance from the bank, in "the circle of the Jordan."

The Fourth Evangelist, after relating John's predictions concerning the Messiah, says "These things were done in Bethany beyond Jordan, where John was baptizing. On the morrow he seeth Jesus coming unto him." If (as was shewn above to be probable) this "coming" was "coming" to baptism, which immediately took place, we may infer that the Johannine writer desired to suggest that Jesus was baptized in Bethany. But he does no more than suggest it. Perhaps, toward the end of the first century (as in Origen's time) there were on the Jordan more places than one that claimed to be the exact place, and the Evangelist did not desire to arbitrate between them. Similarly, he avoids other details of the baptism, saying, for example (through John the Baptist) that the Spirit was to descend, and did descend, but not that it descended at the moment of the baptism—which indeed he refrains from describing.

Why then does the Fourth Evangelist mention any place at all in connection with John's baptizing? And is there any reason why, if he mentions any place at all, he should mention this place in particular, "Bethany beyond Jordan"?

It is characteristic of this Gospel that things at the beginning prepare the way for things at the end. There is a hexaemeron, and a Passover, both at the beginning and at the end. The water and the wine at Cana prepare the way for the water and blood from the Cross. We have seen in the last section that "Nazareth" and "King of Israel," in the story of Nathanael's conversion, perhaps prepare the way for Pilate's inscription "Jesus the Nazoraean, the King of the Jews" So

---

[1] Lk iii 3, iv 1

THE BAPTISM OF JESUS

here, perhaps, the anointing of Jesus from heaven in Bethany beyond Jordan, when He began His Gospel, and the anointing of Jesus on earth in Bethany this side of the Jordan, when He was on the point of closing His Gospel, may have appeared to the Fourth Evangelist to present a correspondence worthy of record

There may have been another reason "Beyond Jordan" was a symbolic phrase. True, it was ambiguous. Luke—perhaps because it was ambiguous—never uses it[1]. But it might well seem a pity to omit all mention of the fact that Jesus, at this stage of the Gospel, was in the position of His first namesake, Joshua, or Jesus, "beyond Jordan," preparing to cross over to war and conquest. Another reason for using the phrase might be that Isaiah mentions "*beyond Jordan, Galilee of the nations*" in connection with the people who "saw a great light," and that this is quoted by Matthew as referring to the coming of Jesus when He "came and dwelt in Capernaum which is by the sea[2]." To Matthew's interpretation of Isaiah the careful historian, Luke, might object that Capernaum was not "beyond Jordan"—which, for an Israelite, naturally meant the East of Jordan. This objection the Fourth Gospel perhaps has in mind, and at all events certainly meets, by substituting for "Capernaum" Bethany, to the East of Jordan, as the place where "John was baptizing" on the day before "*he seeth Jesus coming unto him*"—Jesus, the "*great light*[3]"

---

[1] On Luke's non-use of "beyond Jordan" see *Joh Voc.* **1813** *b*, comp. **1714** *b*

[2] Mt iv 13 foll., quoting Is ix 1—2

[3] Jn i. 28—9 No one has ascertained the existence of a town called "Bethany" beyond Jordan It might mean "the place of fountains," or "the place of a boat." There are various readings, such as "Bethabarah," and "Betharabah" Origen would like to amend "Bethany," but testifies indirectly to Bethany as being the original reading

I have been informed by a friend that it has been identified by Colonel Conder (*P E F.Q S* 1877, pages 184—7) with "the well known

THE BAPTISM OF JESUS

§ 5. *"Ascending from the water," and "praying"*

Just before the vision of the opening of the heavens and of the descent of the Spirit, Mark apparently, and Matthew certainly, speak about Jesus as "ascending from the water," and as seeing the vision. But Mark might possibly mean John, not Jesus. Luke mentions, not "*ascending*" but "*praying*," thus, "when Jesus *was praying* the heaven was opened[1]." Also Justin Martyr, Irenaeus, and other very early authorities, state, or imply, that a "fire," or "light," was kindled on the Jordan when Jesus rose up from the water[2]. Perhaps the parallelism between "*ascending*" and "*praying*," and these legends about "light" and "fire," may be due, in part, to some Hebrew traditions derived from the various meanings of a Hebrew verb meaning "*lift up*," "*light* [*a candle*]," "*burn*," and of its noun-forms meaning "*ascension*," "*whole-burnt-offering*[3]."

But the recently-discovered Odes of Solomon suggest another explanation arising from the use of "soul" for "self[4]" sometimes in Hebrew, and much more frequently in Syriac, so that "lifting up *the soul*" (that is, in prayer) might be taken to mean "lifting up *himself*" (that is, in bodily action) "emerging" (as Justin says) from the waters of the Jordan[5]. Thus the Odes say "I spread out my hands in *the ascension of my soul*," and "I rested on *the Spirit of the Lord and it*

---

district of Batanea, which has left traces of its name to the present day in the district called Ard el Bethânieh 'beyond Jordan'." Ps. lxviii. 22 "*from Bashan*.. from the depths of the sea," might be supposed to refer to the passage of the Jordan, but Targ and Jewish traditions, e g *Gittin* 57 *b*, take "*Ba-shan*" as implying a deliverance from the "teeth' of "wild beasts"

[1] Mk i 10, Mt. iii 16, Lk iii. 21
[2] See *From Letter* **557—9, 583—5, 620** foll.
[3] See *From Letter* on Mk i 10 &c
[4] On "soul" meaning "self" see Gesen. 660 *a*. In Hebrew, it would mean the real self, but not the bodily self
[5] *Tryph.* § 88 quoted in *From Letter* **557**.

THE BAPTISM OF JESUS

lifted-me-on-high to the high place[1]." The Biblical Hebrew Psalms thrice mention the "*lifting up*" of "*the soul*" to God, and the Targum in each case adds "*in prayer*", but the Syriac has "*I lift up my soul,*" without "in prayer" This, but for the context, would mean, in Syriac, "*I lift up myself*[2]."

Ezekiel is said to have been "lifted up," and "carried," that is, by the Spirit[3] So also was Jesus, in the Temptation. Paul was caught up into the third heaven[4]. In Revelation, the Seer hears a voice saying, "Come up hither," and immediately he is "in the Spirit" and sees a vision[5]. The Fourth Gospel does not say that there was any "lifting up" or "praying," but it says that the descent of the Spirit was foretold by God to John the Baptist, as the sign by which he was to recognise Him who was to baptize with the Spirit. The words "On whomsoever *thou shalt see*[6]," imply that others would *not* "see," so that the sight was of the nature of a "vision," and, as being a "vision," might imply "lifting up in the Spirit"

This part of Luke's narrative shews signs of being drawn from Hebrew[7]. In Hebrew, "soul" would have its usual meaning. But Luke might think it well to paraphrase it as "*praying,*" just as the Targumist of the Psalms thought it well to add "*in prayer.*" This Luke might do for clearness, in order to indicate that (in his view) what followed was not a vision produced by the "lifting up of the soul," but the sight

---

[1] *Odes of Solomon* xxxv 8, xxxvi. 1 foll quoted in *Light* **3922** *s*
[2] Ps. xxv 1, lxxxvi. 4, cxliii 8
[3] *Light* **3986**.   [4] 2 Cor. xii. 2
[5] Rev iv. 1—2   [6] Jn i 33.
[7] Because of the constr (Lk iii 21) with ἐν τῷ See *Introd.* p 112 and *Son* **3333** *e* The temporal ἐν τῷ, referring to the past and meaning *when*, must be distinguished from ἐν τῷ referring to the present and meaning "*in the midst of,*" "*in the act of,*" as in *Ox. Pap* iv. 743 (B.C. 2) ἐν τῷ δέ με περισπᾶσθαι (lit.) "*in the midst of my being distracted* at the time I was unable to meet Apollonius," ed. "*owing to my worries.*" I hope to deal with the Lucan use of ἐν τῷ in Section III of this work

of something in a bodily form, simultaneous with "praying." The Fourth Gospel on the other hand makes it clear that what followed was a vision

§ 6 *The opening of the heavens*

Mark says that Jesus (or, less probably, John) " saw the heavens *in-the-act-of-being-rent* (or, *cloven*) "; Matthew and Luke, that "the heaven *was opened*[1]." It is probable that "*rent*" was the original, and was corrected into "*opened*," as being the more common word in such cases. "Rend the heavens" occurs in Scripture nowhere but in Isaiah "O that thou wouldst rend the heavens[2]." This the Targum explains as alluding to the descent of fire at the prayer of Elijah. But other Jewish traditions explain it as referring to the giving of the Law at Sinai, as though the Prophet said, "O that thou

---

[1] Mk i. 10, Mt iii 16 "heavens" (pl), Lk iii 21.

[2] Is lxiv 1   The LXX has "open (ἀνοίγω)" (like Mt -Lk) but Aq , Symm , and Theod have "tear (ῥήγνυμι)"   This passage is the only one where the LXX renders the Heb. by ἀνοίγω, whereas it has διαῤῥήγνυμι more than forty times

See *From Letter* **568** quoting *Test XII Patr Levi* 18 (ed Sinker) "The heavens shall be opened...and the glory of the Highest shall be uttered on Him, and a spirit of understanding and sanctification (*or*, consecration) shall rest upon Him in the water." But note that *ib*, ed. Charles, adds that "*in the water*" is "a Christian addition found in all versions and in all MSS but *e* of the Greek"   Also add *Test XII Patr Jud* 24 (ed. Charles) "And the heavens shall be opened unto him, to pour out the spirit, even the blessing of the Holy Father , and He shall pour out the spirit of grace upon you ; and ye shall be unto Him sons in truth," but A "And the heavens shall be opened unto him, and the blessings of the Holy Father will be poured down upon him. And He will pour down upon us the spirit of grace   And ye shall be His true children by adoption "   Israel, being baptized in the Red Sea on its way to Sinai where the heaven was opened so as to send down the Law to the Chosen People, might be regarded as prefiguring a baptism of Israel's Messiah , but no actual baptism is mentioned in either of these two passages   In both, ἀνοίγω, not σχίζω, describes the "opening" of the heavens

THE BAPTISM OF JESUS

wouldst come down to men again, as thou didst in the giving of the Law at Sinai, giving us the Law anew!"

Isaiah's prophecy goes on to mention "fire[1]," and "adversaries," in such a context as to suggest that the "rending" of the heavens is for the moment merely, to allow the descent of the lightnings of God's chastisement. In the Gospel, the context speaks of "a dove," and conveys the thought of peace and divine favour. But still the question arises, "Are we to regard this "rending, or cleaving, of the heavens" as temporary, like that in the Book of Wisdom, which, when describing "things that pass away like a shadow," likens them to "the light air *being rent*, or *cloven*, by the force of the whirring of a bird's wings[2]?" The same word is used there as in Mark. Moreover Justin Martyr, the Sibylline Oracles, and others[3]—though they speak of the dove as "alighting," and one writer adds "from the lower-air[4]"—make no mention of the heaven being "rent" or "cloven[5]."

The Fourth Gospel, a little later on, speaks of "the heaven" as being destined hereafter to be "seen" as "*set-open*," i.e. permanently open. This is so expressed as not to contradict the belief that there *had before* been a vision of "rending." It represents Jesus as making promises, first to Nathanael, "Thou shalt see greater things than these," and

---

[1] Is lxiv 2 "As when fire kindleth the brushwood and the fire causeth the waters to boil, to make thy name known to thy adversaries." Comp. Lk ix. 54 where James and John (formerly disciples of John the Baptist) say "Lord, wilt thou that we bid fire to come down from heaven and consume them?"

[2] Wisd v 11 πνεῦμα...σχιζόμενον

[3] *From Letter* **643** foll.

[4] Comp. Deut iv. 17 "any winged fowl that flieth *in the heaven*," where the Targums have "*in the lower air of the firmament of the heaven*." It is a Jew in Origen's *Celsus* that speaks of "the lower-air" (*From Letter* **644**)

[5] Comp *Odes of Solomon* xxiv 1 where (*Light* **3999** (ii) 5) the right translation seems to be "The Dove *flew down on* the head of our Lord Messiah, because He was her head"

THE BAPTISM OF JESUS

then to his companions, "Ye shall see *the heaven set-open*, and the angels of God ascending and descending upon the Son of Man[1]." The disciples are apparently supposed to have heard of the preceding "rending" or "opening" of the heavens, not indeed described in this Gospel, but perhaps implied in God's promise to the Baptist, "thou shalt see the Spirit descending." These words might well be assumed to mean that for him, as for Ezekiel, the "heavens" would be "opened" that he might see "visions of God." This being so, Christ's words would appear to mean, "John saw the heavens opened for a moment, but ye shall see them opened so as not to be shut again[2], and opened to allow, not only descent from heaven to man, but also ascent from man to heaven."

§ 7. "*And straightway...he saw*"

The words "straightway" and "saw" bear on the question, "Are the writers recording what follows as a vision or as a fact?" The passage is one of a very few where Mark's frequently used "*straightway*" is also used by Matthew, Mark having "*and straightway* going up," and Matthew "*straightway* went up[3]." "*And straightway*," in the LXX, thrice represents the Hebrew "*and behold*"; and, in the present narrative, Matthew has "*behold*, the heavens were opened," whereas Mark has "he beheld the heavens being...[4]."

The Hebrew "*and behold*," *without a finite verb, is used in narrative* for the first time thus, "And God saw all that he

---

[1] Jn i 50—1 "set-open (ἀνεῳγότα)"

[2] Jn i 51 ἀνεῳγότα τε "open" (not "opened")—as we distinguish in English between "the door is *open*," and "the door is *opened*." This use of the word is condemned by Phrynichus, and much discussed by grammarians. It does not occur in LXX exc Tob. ii 10. In different contexts (1 Cor xvi. 9, 2 Cor ii 12) Paul speaks of a "door *open* (ἀνέῳγεν)," and a "door *opened* (ἀνεῳγμένη)." On the whole passage, see *Son* **3138**.

[3] Mk i 10, Mt iii 16 εὐθύς (not εὐθέως which Mark never uses).

[4] Mk i. 10 εἶδεν, rendered here "*he beheld*" to shew its similarity to Mt iii. 16 ἰδού, "*behold*." On εὐθύς, Heb. "*behold*," see *Corrections* **455** *a*

THE BAPTISM OF JESUS

had made, *and behold, good,* exceedingly¹," where Symmachus inserts "*was*" before "good." The next instance is about Noah's dove, "*And behold,* in her mouth, an olive leaf," where the LXX omits "behold" and has "*had* an olive leaf²." The next is about the Word of the Lord coming to Abraham, "*And behold,* the Word of Jehovah to him, saying," where the LXX has "*And straightway* the Voice of the Lord *came-to-pass* to him, [the Lord] saying...³." In the account of the ram that was Isaac's substitute, "And Abraham lifted up his eyes, and looked, and *behold,* a ram behind [him]. ," Symmachus has "and *there appeared* a ram⁴." These facts may explain why, in parallel passages in the Three Gospels, (1) "*behold,*" (2) "*immediately,*" and (3) "*there appeared*" or "*there came,*" are so frequently used as equivalents⁵. In all such cases "*behold*" appears to have been the original, which was differently paraphrased by the different Evangelists

In the passage under consideration, according to Hebrew precedent, "*and behold*" would occur without a verb, thus, "*And behold,* [*there were in a vision*] the heavens being-rent-asunder, and the Spirit descending, and a Voice from the

---

¹ Gen 1 31 Symm inserts "*was*" (καὶ ἦν καλά) but it is not in the Hebrew

² Gen viii 11 These instances are taken from Mandelkern p 337 In Gen viii 13 (where the Heb adds a verb) "he looked, and *behold* the face of the ground was dried," LXX has merely one verb, "*he beheld that* (ἴδεν ὅτι)"

³ *Gesen.* 244 *a* In Gen xv 4 καὶ εὐθὺς φωνὴ Κυρίου ἐγένετο πρὸς αὐτὸν λέγων, the masc participle seems to be used because "the Voice" implies "the Lord." [In Gen xv 3, which is omitted as being speech not narrative, LXX renders "behold" by ὁ δέ]

⁴ Gen xxii 13 This instance is not in Strong's Concordance nor in Gesen 244 *a*

⁵ See *Corrections* **352** for five passages where Mark appears to have paraphrased "*and behold*" while Matthew and Luke agree in retaining it In one of these Mark (xiv 43) has his favourite phrase "*and straight-way*" See also *ib* **454** foll for passages where Matthew's exclamatory "*behold*" is parallel to Mark's verbal "*behold*" Mark never uses the Hebraic "*and behold*"

THE BAPTISM OF JESUS

heavens...[1]." Mark seems to have taken "*behold!*" as "*beheld*" but also to have paraphrased it as "*immediately*[2]." So he has "*immediately...beheld*" And he includes in this "beholding" the "Spirit" as well as "the heavens." But when he comes to the "Voice," perceiving that this could not have been "*beheld*," he leaves it in the nominative ("and [there was] [ἐγένετο] a voice")—very harshly and unexpectedly[3].

Matthew improves on this. He has, correctly, "*and behold.*" But he paraphrases the abrupt Hebrew nominative without verb, by saying "the heavens were opened" Then he follows Mark in applying "*beheld*" to "the Spirit descending as a dove" Lastly, he inserts "*behold!*" a second time before "Voice," so as to shew that the meaning is "*and behold, [there was]* a Voice saying," adding the nominative participle ' saying" to make the construction still more clear.

Luke, on the other hand, perceiving that the three marvels —the opening of the "heavens," the descent of the Spirit, and the Voice—are all on the same level as respects truth and reality, sees a defect in Mark and Matthew, who place them on a different level. For about the Spirit they say merely "he *saw the Spirit.*" But then, changing the construction, they go on to say "And [*there was*] *a voice,*" or "And behold [*there was*] *a voice,*" as though the latter were more real than the former Therefore Luke not only applies to all these three revelations the words "it came to pass that" (so as to place them on an equality) but also adds about the Holy Spirit that it descended "in a bodily form[4]."

---

[1] Comp Mk 1 11 W H καὶ φωνὴ [ἐγένετο] ἐκ τῶν οὐρανῶν.

[2] On Mark's habit of combining two Greek renderings of one Hebrew original (called "conflation") see *Clue* 145 foll ; and on his tendency to follow the style of the LXX in Genesis, see 353 *a*, 455 *a*, 456 (11) *a*

[3] This assumes that W H. [ἐγένετο] is not a part of the text

[4] The constructions in the Three Gospels are severally, Mk 1 10—11 εἶδεν σχιζομένους τοὺς οὐρανοὺς καὶ τὸ πνεῦμα. .καταβαῖνον. καὶ φωνὴ

THE BAPTISM OF JESUS

The Fourth Gospel does not relate these three events, but merely represents John as testifying to one of them, namely, the descent of the Spirit, thus, "*I have beheld the Spirit descending as a dove out of heaven*, and it abode upon him. And I knew him not, but he that sent me to baptize in water—he said unto me, 'Upon whomsoever thou shalt see the Spirit descending and abiding upon him, *this is* he that baptizeth in the Holy Spirit.' And I have seen and have borne witness that *this is* the Son of God[1]." This does not deny the vision of the opening of the heavens, nor a Voice from heaven, but it withdraws the attention from these things and fixes it on the descent of the Spirit, as being witnessed by John, and on this as being a sign promised beforehand by the Word of God speaking to John

The Diatessaron gives the Voice from heaven as "*This is* my beloved Son," with Matthew; not "*Thou art* my beloved Son," with Mark and Luke. The Fourth Gospel avoids choosing between the two by giving neither. But it leads us to the conclusion that "*This is*" represents the more important aspect, namely, the promise of God to John, and the testimony of John that the promise had been fulfilled. The Synoptic Gospels do not shew, as the Fourth Gospel does, that the descent of the Spirit was not seen by anyone except the Baptist, whose office it was to testify to it.

§ 8 *The descent of the Spirit*

Mark says "The Spirit, as a dove, coming-down *into* him"; Matthew, "the Spirit of God, coming-down, as if [it were] a dove, coming *upon* (or, *toward*) him"; Luke, "[that]

[ἐγένετο] , Mt iii 16—17 καὶ ἰδοὺ ἠνεῴχθησαν (marg +αὐτῷ) οἱ οὐρανοὶ καὶ εἶδεν πνεῦμα θεοῦ καταβαῖνον καὶ ἰδοὺ φωνὴ .λέγουσα..., Lk. iii 21—2 ἐγένετο δὲ ἀνεῳχθῆναι τὸν οὐρανὸν καὶ καταβῆναι τὸ πνεῦμα τὸ ἅγιον. . καὶ φωνὴν .γενέσθαι . Luke alone describes the Spirit here as "the Holy Spirit"

[1] Jn i. 32—4

THE BAPTISM OF JESUS

the Holy Spirit came-down in a bodily form[1] as a dove *upon* (or, *toward*) him[2]." These differences may be illustrated by the "coming" of the Spirit "into" Ezekiel, where the Hebrew, Aramaic, and Syriac have "*into*," but the Greek has "*upon*[3]."

Mark appears to mean that the Spirit did not merely *alight upon* Jesus as a bird on a branch, but passed into Him, as a bird into its nest. This need not mean that the Spirit was "seen" in the form of a dove; but it must include the meaning that the Spirit was in some way perceived by John to be not merely alighting "upon" Jesus or coming-down "upon" Him, but also "*abiding*." But here a difficulty arises. It could be seen *entering* "*into*" Him, but it could not be seen *abiding* "*in*" Him.

The Fourth Gospel meets the difficulty by subordinating "as a dove" and sacrificing "*entering into*." But it compensates by emphasizing the "*abiding*." This is repeated twice. First the Baptist says "I have beheld the Spirit coming down as a dove from heaven, and it *abode upon* him." Then God's prediction of this descent is added. God had before said to him, "On whomsoever thou shalt see the Spirit coming down and *abiding upon* him, this is he that is [to be] baptizing in the Holy Spirit[4]."

Here it is to be noted that "*as a dove*" does not occur in the divine prediction, but only in the Prophet's account of the

---

[1] "A bodily form" may have been suggested by some Aramaic version of Mark's tradition, namely, that the Spirit passed "*into*" Jesus. "*Into*," or "*into the midst of*," might be represented by "*in the body of*," see Gesen 156 *a* on Job xxx. 5, "The *midst* (Aram.) of men," where the word for "*midst*" is identical—except for vowel pointing—with a word rendered σῶμα in Nehem. ix. 26, Ezek. xxiii. 35.

[2] Mk i 10 "*into* (εἰς)," Mt iii 16, Lk. iii 22 "*upon* (or, *toward*) (ἐπί with accus.)." For the rendering of εἰς τινα after ἔρχομαι as "come *to* (or, *on*) a person," neither Thayer nor Swete (*ad loc*) gives any instance in the correct text of N T (*From Letter* 680 *a*); Lk xv. 17 is not one.

[3] Ezek. ii 2, iii 24 ἦλθεν ἐπί. In Ezek xxxvii. 10, the LXX agrees with Heb and Aram. and Syr (εἰσῆλθεν εἰς). The Heb might mean "in me" or "into me." [4] Jn i 32, 33.

vision that fulfilled it. The context indirectly implies a contradiction of the notion that the dove was "in a bodily form." For we can hardly suppose that it was continually seen, even by John, "in a bodily form as a dove," and "*abiding on*" Jesus.

The descent "as a dove" is perhaps intended to be distinguished from the descent of an eagle suddenly descending on its prey. And the "abiding" indicates that the dove has found her nest The Baptist perceives in Jesus the continual abiding of the Spirit. How he perceived this we are not told. But he might know it, not by any outward brightness on the face of Jesus like that on the face of Moses—which, according to the Biblical narrative, was seen by all, and which endured only for a season and at intervals—but by an inward and spiritual grace and permanent glory discernible by the Prophet in virtue of his prophetic insight.

It has been noted above that Luke, alone of the Synoptists, describes the descent as being, not that of " the Spirit," or " the Spirit of God," but that of " the Holy Spirit." On the other hand the Fourth Evangelist appears to emphasize the fact that it is "the Spirit" and *not* "the Holy Spirit" by repeating the two phrases in the same sentence uttered by God ("thou shalt see *the Spirit* .baptizing in *the Holy Spirit*"). Perhaps he implies that the Baptist, not being "from above," could not see "the Spirit" in the form indicated by "the Holy Spirit," "the Paraclete," whom the Father would send in the name of the Son, but "whom the world cannot receive, for it beholdeth him not[1]", but that he could see "the Spirit" so far as the Spirit could be manifested to one of the Prophets who, like himself, were "of the earth," though sent to prepare the way for Him that "cometh from above[2]."

---

[1] Jn xiv 26, 16—17
[2] Jn iii 31   In Jn, "Holy Spirit" occurs only in i. 33, xiv. 26, xx 22 See *Son* 3622 *b*

THE BAPTISM OF JESUS

§ 9. *The Dove*

For Greeks and Romans, the Dove, as a symbol, meant Love and Peace. For Jews it was more complex. Often it meant Love and Fear. The fear of the Enemy along with the Love of the Lord is suggested in the words "Oh that I had wings like a dove!" and there Israel is the Dove chased by powers of evil, and sighing that she might "fly away" to her Lord and "be at rest[1]." Similarly one of the Odes of Solomon says, "The Dove flew down on the head of our Lord Messiah because He was her head[2]." That seems to regard the Dove as the Bride. But another Ode says, "As the wings of doves over their nestlings...so are the wings of the Spirit over my heart[3]." That suggests the thought of the Dove as the Mother of the saints.

These passages indicate how the Dove, meaning the spiritual Israel, might be regarded as the emblem both of the spiritual Bride and also of the spiritual Mother. A well-known passage in the Talmud represents "a Voice from Heaven" as "sighing *like a dove*," and saying, "Alas, that I have destroyed my house, burned my temple, and made my people exiles among the Gentiles[4]!" Presumably this is the Voice of the Holy Spirit, regarded as that of God—the Mother[5], or (as He is called in the Law) the Nursing Father, of Israel.

Another aspect of the Dove is suggested by the scriptural

---

[1] Ps lv 6

[2] *Light* **3999** (ii) 5, quoting Ode xxiv 1 from Codex N.

[3] *Odes of Solomon* xxviii 1—2, see Light **3793** *c*. Comp Jerome on Is xi 2 quoting the *Gospel of the Nazarenes* in which the Holy Spirit, descending on Jesus, said, "*My Son*, in all the prophets I have been expecting thee." This implies the utterance of the Dove, the Mother, but in a new sense—as the Mother in heaven, corresponding to the Father and the Son in heaven.

[4] *Berach* 3 *a*

[5] "God the Mother." Comp Clem Alex 956 (*Quis Div* § 37) τὸ μὲν ἄρρητον αὐτοῦ Πατήρ, τὸ δὲ ἡμῖν συμπαθὲς γέγονε Μήτηρ

THE BAPTISM OF JESUS

narrative of the Creation. There the Spirit that "hovered" or "brooded" upon the face of the waters seems likened to a bird. In Jewish traditions, it was likened by some to "a dove[1]." Whether the Baptist had, or had not, this image in view, it was probably in the mind of the Fourth Evangelist, who, as has been frequently said above, regards the beginning of the Gospel as corresponding to the beginning of Creation.

Again, another tradition connects itself with the Dove of Noah. "When," it asks, "did the Dove bring light into the world? In the days of Noah." The meaning is that the Dove, which is the type of Israel, brought the olive leaf, which represents the Law of Light and Peace, when all the world was under the waters of sin and darkness[2]. Thus the Dove, Israel on earth, may be regarded as doing below what is done above by the Dove, the Mother of Israel in heaven—which Mother might be identified with the Spirit that is by the side of God, the divine Wisdom, described in Scripture as His "delight" above, and as finding "delight" in "the habitable earth" and in "the sons of man[3]."

It might seem that the Baptist, if he was of the same temper as his two disciples James and John—who wished to call down fire from heaven on those who repelled Jesus—would be prepared to see the "hovering" of the Spirit rather in the vision of an eagle, as described in Deuteronomy[4], than in

---

[1] Gen. i 2, Deut xxxii 11 (Gesen. 934 *a*) the only instances of the Heb "hover" or "brood." Comp. J *Chag* ii and *Chag.* 15 *a* and *Gen. r.* (on Gen. i. 2, Wu p. 10) all referring to the same traditional utterance of Ben Zoma. His inference is condemned by R. Jehoshua, but not (apparently) his assumption that the action of a bird is contemplated. *Gen r ib* has "this bird" instead of "dove." *Gen r ib* gives another tradition "The Spirit of God is the Spirit of King Messiah."

[2] *Cant r* on Cant. iv 1, Wu p. 103

[3] Prov. viii 22, 30, 31 In *Pesikt* Wu p. 59 foll, Cant. ii 12 "the voice of the turtle-dove" is explained as referring to Moses, Joshua, Cyrus, Messiah, each of whom is the herald of Spring.

[4] See Deut. xxxii 9—11 "For the Lord's portion. As an eagle. he bare them on his pinions"

that of a dove, traditionally connected with the opening words of Genesis. But this argument, though plausible, would ignore the basis of all the Baptist's prophesying, namely, the thought of a new and regenerate Israel. The Deuteronomic "eagle" does not imply regeneration. It is the guardian of Israel in "the waste howling wilderness." It lifts them up above perils. But it does not make Israel anew. What the Baptist contemplates is a new era, the beginning, the spring, of a new spiritual Year, of which the Dove would be the fit harbinger.

Philo speaks of the Deluge in language that would harmonize with such a thought. It is, he says, " a purification of sublunary things, the earth having washed itself clean and risen-to-light as it was belike when first created[1]." This implies a kind of baptism. Also the Odes of Solomon, after saying that the Dove "flew down upon the Messiah," and that she sang over Him and her voice was heard, goes on to speak of the Deluge, apparently saying that the end and the object of the destruction was a new life[2].

Philo also bears witness to the existence of very early traditions that connect the purification of the earth by the Deluge with Spirit as well as with water. The Scripture, it is true, says simply that "God made a *wind* to pass over the earth, and the waters assuaged[3]." But the Hebrew for "wind" is the same as the Hebrew for "spirit" in the sentence "the *Spirit* of God moved on the face of the waters." In both sentences the Jerusalem Targum has "*the spirit* of kindnesses, or mercies" (presumably meaning "spirit," not "wind"). Philo, while admitting that "some say it means *wind*" (in the story of the Deluge), adds that he does not understand how wind could have this effect. He calls it "a

---

[1] Philo ii 144
[2] *Odes of Solomon* xxiv 1, 6 (*Light* **3781** *g*, **3793** *a*).
[3] Gen. viii. 1

spirit of divine power[1]." According to the Midrash on Genesis, the first mention of "the *spirit* (or, *wind*)," as "hovering," points to the second similar use of it, "God brought a *spirit* (or, *wind*) over the earth." That is to say, in both cases God said, "How long shall the world lie in darkness? Let light break forth[2]."

These facts shew that Jews, from the first century onwards, connected the Spirit of God on the waters at the Creation with the thought of a Dove in one way, and the Spirit of God on the waters of the Deluge with the thought of a Dove in another way—different it is true but agreeing in representing the Dove as the sign of life and light emerging from the waters of death and darkness, after the world had been as it were "buried" in baptism and had begun to rise to a new and purified existence In both these aspects, the thought of the Dove, as accompanying the Messiah who was to baptize with the Spirit, would be appropriate to John the baptizer with water[3].

§ 10. *The voice from heaven*

The Fourth Gospel gives no version of a "voice" of God "from heaven" concerning Jesus as being "beloved Son." But it mentions—what the Three do not mention—an utterance of God to the Baptist about Jesus · "Upon whomsoever thou shalt see...this is *he that baptizeth in the Holy*

---

[1] Philo *ad loc* "spiritum divinitatis," "vix vento sed invisibili virtute divina." Josephus omits "wind" altogether in giving the substance of Gen viii 1 Perhaps he agreed with Philo negatively (that "wind" could not have the power attributed to it) but either dissented from Philo's positive and theological inferences or thought it inexpedient to submit them to Gentile criticism.

[2] *Gen r* on Gen 1 2, Wu p 9

[3] My discussion of "the dove" in *From Letter* (**685—724**), published in 1903, did not take sufficient cognisance of the parallelism between the Creation and the Deluge, and the Jewish poetic traditions about both ; nor could it include the passages in the *Odes of Solomon* published in 1909.

THE BAPTISM OF JESUS

Spirit," and it adds that John afterwards refers to the fulfilment of God's utterance as follows " And I have seen and have borne witness that this is *the Son of God* (or, *the Elect of God*)[1]." Let us note the sequence, or rather the apparent want of sequence. God promised the Baptist that the descent of the Spirit should designate the future Baptizer. The Spirit descends. The Baptist exclaims, not, " I have seen *the future Baptizer*," but " I have seen *the Son* (or, *the Elect*) *of God.*" How can we explain this? Does the Prophet assume that " *he that baptizeth in the Holy Spirit*" must be identical with " *the Son* (or, *the Elect*) *of God*"[2]?

Taking "baptize with the Holy Spirit" as a metaphor expressive of the most searching purification, we may say that we are on the search for some original tradition that might be expressed in three forms " *son*," " *elect*," " *purifier*[3]." Hence a *primâ facie* case appears for an original Aramaic *bar*, meaning " *son* " in Aramaic, but in Hebrew "*pure*," " *clean*," and also " *winnowed wheat*," being derived from a Hebrew word meaning " purge out " or ' purify " The case is strengthened by the fact that in the second Psalm, applied by

---

[1] Jn 1 33—4 (SS "elect" for "son")

[2] Comp Mk ix 7, Mt xvii 5 "*beloved* son," Lk ix 35 "*elect* (or, *chosen*) (ἐκλελεγμένος) son " In *From Letter* 786—816, an attempt was made to explain the variation of "*elect*" and "*beloved*," but only in a particular case, and the parallelism between "one baptizing " and "elect" (or "son") was not considered at all

[3] It is important to remember by what widely differing words the thought of " purification " may be expressed For example, there is the word "lye," used in melting metals The Hebrew for this—identical in consonants with the Aramaic *bar*, "son"—occurs only (Gesen. 141 *a*) in Is. 1 25 " as with *lye*, I will purge away thy dross " But it is only one of many kindred Hebrew forms signifying *purification by selection*, e g by winnowing corn, refining metal &c Jerome, in his commentary on Is 1 25, calls attention to these differences of metaphor " But also in the Gospel," he says, "*the same sense is given under a different metaphor* (Mt iii. 12, Lk iii. 17) 'whose winnowing-fan is in his hand, and he will cleanse his threshing-floor, and he will purify the wheat " (so Jerome), "and gather the corn into barns, but the chaff he will burn-up in fire unquenchable' "

THE BAPTISM OF JESUS

all early Christians (and by what Rashi calls "our Rabbis") to the Messiah, there occurs the word "*bar*" in a passage rendered, by R.V. text, "kiss *the son*," but, in R.V. margin, "lay hold of *instruction*" or "worship *in purity*." Here "instruction" is the rendering of the LXX, as also of the Targum, but "*purity*" is that of the later and more accurate Greek translators. Thus "*son*" and "*purifying*" are connected, as alternatives of a very early date indeed, in the interpretation of one of the most frequently quoted Messianic Psalms

But this same Psalm has the word "*son*," in unmistakable Hebrew (*ben*, not *bar*), thus, "Thou art *my Son*, this day have I begotten thee." And this is the utterance of the Voice from heaven in Luke according to some very early authorities[1]. This leads us to ask whether these very early authorities may not be right. Luke, if his text is correctly given by Codex D, may have followed a Hebrew Gospel, which gave the Voice in Hebrew, as a quotation from the second Psalm. Luke may have rendered the Hebrew exactly into Greek. Mark and Matthew may have followed an Aramaic paraphrase

Such a paraphrase—freer and fuller than that of Mark-Matthew, supposing Mark-Matthew to contain a paraphrase—is actually extant in the Aramaic Targum on the second Psalm. It avoids—possibly as being anthropomorphic—the words "I have begotten thee," as follows. "Beloved, even as son to father, [even so] art thou pure unto me, even as on the day on which I had created thee." This introduces into the Hebrew the words "*beloved*" and "*thou art pure unto me.*" The tradition followed by Mark and Matthew (supposing it to be a paraphrase) introduces "*beloved*" and "*in thee I am well pleased.*" Between these two paraphrases, as

---

[1] *E g* Justin Martyr and Codex D See *Son* **3333** *f*, comparing Mk xv 34, where Codex D gives the quotation from the Psalms "Eli, Eli &c" in Hebrew instead of Aramaic

THE BAPTISM OF JESUS

paraphrases, there is this difference, that the Jewish Targum avoids "begotten," and gives quite a new context to "day," while the Christian Gospels (except Luke in Codex D) avoid "begotten this day"—in both cases, perhaps, for doctrinal reasons.

We must now return from "This is my Son" to the above-quoted "kiss the Son" in the same Psalm, where "Son" is *bar*. This is one of two Scriptural passages where *bar* means "*son*." Jewish tradition, commenting on both, endeavoured to shew that in both the word meant also "*pure*," and especially that purified and winnowed "*wheat*" which made up the bread of the Law[1]. In the context of the Synoptic passage now under consideration, Matthew and Luke describe the Messiah with His winnowing fan, and with His fire, purifying and gathering the wheat—and this in close connection with ' baptizing with fire[2]."

Very similar is the substance of a Jewish parable on the "kiss" in the second Psalm It personifies the Straw, the Stubble and the Chaff "The world was made for me," says each of the three. The Wheat replies, " Wait till you come to the threshing-floor." The parable proceeds "Then came the Master of the House and winnowed the chaff to the winds, and cast the straw down for litter, and burned up the stubble, but the wheat he stored up, and whoever saw it threw it kisses (Ps. ii. 12, taken as 'kiss the pure [wheat]')[3]."

These traditions reveal a connection between Jewish

---

[1] See *Lev r* on Lev x. 9 (Wu p 83) quoting Prov xxxi. 2 "what, my son," that is, "the commandments and warnings of the Law, which are named *bar* 'pure,' as in Ps ii 12 because all its words are '*pure*'" (iep *Numb. r.* on Numb vi 2 (Wu p. 214)) See also *Gen r* on Gen xxxvi. 43 (Wu p 407) On *bar* "son," see Gesen. pp 135 and 141

[2] Mt iii. 12, Lk iii 17, immediately following the words "shall baptize in the Holy Spirit and fire"

[3] *Gen r* (on Gen. xxxvi 43) Wu p. 407, rep. *Cant r* (on *Cant.* vii 3) Wu p 168 Both quote Mal iv 1 on the fire, and Is xli. 16 on the winnowing wind

THE BAPTISM OF JESUS

thoughts of Messiah (1) as the Son, (2) as the Elect, or Pure, of God, (3) as the Purifier[1] For the Jews, the second Psalm was a Psalm of war. The Son was to have "the Gentiles" for His " inheritance," and to " break them in pieces with a rod of iron," if they did not accept their appointed Sovereign. " Kiss the pure [wheat] " meant " Accept the purifying Law and the chastising reign of the Messiah."

This War Psalm of the Jews appears in the Acts as the War Psalm of the Christians, the first utterance of Christian Psalmody There, of course, the old phrases assume a new meaning. The Targum said that " kiss the Son, or the Pure," meant "receive the Law." The LXX said that it meant " lay hold of *instruction*," using a word (*paideia*, familiar to us in *pedagogue*) that called up thoughts of " boy-training " and hence of the " little-boy (*paidion*) " who, in our Gospels—under the name of " little-child "—is often the centre of our Lord's doctrine. The influence of the War Psalm, and in particular of the phrases " thou art my *son* " and " lay-hold-of *paideia*[2],"

---

[1] Such a connection, so far as it concerned "sonship" and "purifying," would be facilitated in Greek by the LXX of Ps. ii. 12 "lay hold of *instruction* (παιδείαν)," i e. etymologically "boy-training," or "child-training" On παιδεία Philo and Clement of Alexandria are diffuse see *Light* **3769** *c*, and **3974—5** (quoting Clem Alex on "the child-training of that Little Child," i e of Christ on the Cross) But in the Psalm, the Messiah is Himself training or chastising, not being trained

[2] See *Light* **3769** *c*, quoting Philo i 544—5 The only two LXX instances of παῖς representing Heb "son" are Prov iv 1 "Hear, [my] sons (παῖδες), the *instruction* (παιδείαν) of a father" (which may be explained as a play on words) and *ib* xx 7 "a just man blessed are his sons (παῖδας) after him" (where I cannot explain the use of παῖδας for υἱούς)

Philo (i. 369) describes Jacob as "reputable in the sight of (Prov iv 3) both the Parents" (the Mother being Παιδεία) Being "trained" as an athlete, Jacob received the name of Israel, i e. Seeing God Comp Ps xviii 26 "with the *pure* thou wilt shew thyself *pure*," Targ "cum Jacobo qui fuit *purus* coram te, elegisti filios ejus de cunctis populis, segregastique ," where, as often, the Targ paraphrase of the Heb "*pure*" includes a mention of "selecting"—"pure," or "purified," being taken to mean "refined," or "chastened," so as to become "elect"

is apparent in the early Petrine speeches in the Acts where Jesus is repeatedly called *pais*[1], or "boy" (probably not "servant") in connection with His resurrection and with His defeat of "the kings of the earth" by means of the Cross.

In accordance with these thoughts Clement of Alexandria says that the "*child-training* of the *Little-Child*" extended "to all the *children, guiding-as-children* us His babes," and he connects this "child-training" with the "spreading out of the hands" on the Cross. The Cross is connected both by him and by Origen with the Psalmist's "*rod of iron*," with which the Child is to "*break the nations in pieces*" according to the Hebrew original, but to "*shepherd them*" according to the LXX[2].

---

[1] Παῖς occurs in Acts iii. 13, 26, iv 25, 27, 30 (and not again till xx 12 "they brought the *boy* living") In all these passages there is an echo of the War Psalm, and παῖς means "Jesus" in all except iv 25 (where context is doubtful).

[2] See *Light* **3974—5** on Clement, and add Origen on Ps ii. 9, where he tries to reconcile the "*shepherding*" with the sternness of the context, and concludes by saying that Jesus is "a shepherd shepherding with an iron rod, and (Jn x 11) 'a *good shepherd*'," and that the iron rod is the cross, for, "though the substance of it is wood, the strength of it is iron" Ποιμαίνειν, "to shepherd," occurs thrice in Rev (ii 27, xii. 5, xix 15) quoting Ps ii. 9 (LXX) "shepherd with the iron rod" and once (Rev vii. 17) of "the Lamb that is in the midst of the throne" shepherding the Saints

Gesen 949 *b* prefers the LXX, supported by Syr. and Vulg. ("reges"), to the Heb supported by the Targum But (1) "break" (not "shepherd") seems favoured by the parall. "dash in pieces", (2) "break" is similarly applied in Job xxxiv 24 (Gesen. by error xxxiv 34) "he *breaketh-in-pieces* mighty men and setteth others in their stead," and Jerem xv. 12 "can one break iron, iron out of the north", (3) the Heb for ποιμαίνω is very much more common than the Heb here used for "break in pieces" and is very similar to the latter and likely to have been corruptly substituted for the latter, (4) ποιμαίνω is 4 times erroneously substituted by the LXX for other words (besides in Ps ii 9)

§ 11   *The Baptist's interpretation of the voice*

There is no probability that John the Baptist would have been influenced by the LXX. If therefore the Voice about the " Son " at the baptism of Jesus seemed to him akin to the utterance about the " Son " in the second Psalm, we must infer that he regarded Jesus as destined to " break in pieces " " the nations " either in a literal or in a spiritual sense. The literal sense—taking " kings of the earth " and " rulers " and " judges of the earth," to refer to Herod Antipas and his Jewish party, and to the chief priests, as well as to Pontius Pilate[1]—would seem the more probable. It would accord with the Baptist's subsequent imprisonment by Antipas, with his message to Jesus, interpreted as an appeal to Jesus to release him from prison, and with the account of the Baptist given by Josephus. It would also harmonize with the tone of James and John, the Baptist's former disciples, beseeching their new Master, Jesus, to let them call down fire on a Samaritan village

Taking this view of the promised Son, as coming with " a rod of iron," the Baptist's preaching would naturally contain a large, if not a predominant, element of warning or threatening, and the " baptism with the Spirit " would be for the evil as well as for the good, destroying the former by the same means that refined and purified the latter.

But when we speak of " the Baptist's preaching," what do we mean? It may have lasted for some years. It must certainly have lasted for many months. Is it likely that it remained the same from the beginning to the end? The Baptist says in the Fourth Gospel, concerning Jesus, " And I *knew him not.*" However we may interpret " *knew him*," can we suppose that when at last the Baptist really " *knew him*," his teaching was not affected by the " *knowing* " ? Most Christians will feel assured that it must have been affected,

---

[1] Comp Acts iv 25 foll.

THE BAPTISM OF JESUS

and affected profoundly. The former confidence of the Baptist in the Lion of the tribe of Judah may have been combined later on with a new hope in the Lamb of God, and the fusion may well have been incomplete At one time "The Lamb of God" might be uttered with conviction. At another, when the Lion of Judah seemed needed, the question could not be kept back, "Art thou he that is to come, or do we look for another?"

Modern students of the New Testament have perhaps not sufficiently considered the effect that would be produced upon John the Baptist (according to Johannine narrative) by Jesus as Worker of "signs." According to the Synoptists, John was shut up in prison before Jesus performed any "mighty works", but according to the Fourth Gospel, Jesus had performed them in abundance before the Baptist's imprisonment and while Prophet and Messiah were co-operating. What would be the result? We have to place ourselves among men unaccustomed to distinguish (so-called) "miracle" from "miracle." Acts of healing, stupendous, but still natural, they would place on the same level as actions that no man could now by any possibility call "natural." Would they not consequently acclaim Jesus as a Prophet for whom all things were possible, and before whom, if He but willed it, the bars of Herod's prison would fall to the ground and the imprisoned prophet would be released? Would not the Baptist share this belief? And when the belief was not fulfilled, when the bars did not fall, might he not consequently pass from his old faith in Jesus, to disappointment in Jesus, though perhaps ultimately to new faith in Jesus of a higher kind?

If there was indeed, as seems certain, some variation in the Baptist's teaching at various times, we must be on our guard against inferring too much from the silence of Mark, who gives to the Prophet's words rather less than twice the space he devotes to his food and clothing. Both Matthew and Luke, in their enlargements, testify that it

THE BAPTISM OF JESUS

contained a note of warning or threatening, and their view is in itself probable and confirmed by such scanty evidence as exists. But, even if the Baptist interpreted the Voice about the Son, or Baptizer, largely in this sinister sense, it does not follow that the Fourth Evangelist regarded it as the right interpretation. If John the Baptist interpreted the Voice in one way, and the Evangelist regarded Jesus as interpreting it in another, we can understand better why the Fourth Gospel does not record it as definite words "coming from heaven," but only as a "saying" of God communicated to the Prophet according to prophetic precedent.

§ 12. *The Johannine interpretation of the voice and the vision*

We pass to the question of the highest interpretation of the heavenly voice and vision, as distinct from the lower interpretation of it likely to have been adopted by a Prophet who, great though he was, was not equal to the typical "little one," or "lesser one," who was "in the Kingdom of God[1]."

This is a subject of the very greatest importance If this very beginning of the Gospel, this opening of the heavens, this descent of the Spirit, this voice of God, conveyed a different meaning to the Last of the Prophets from that which it conveyed to the Firstborn of the Kingdom, then we must expect to find in the doctrine of Jesus, from the first, a gentle negative protest, increasing in its strength, against the old teaching and in favour of the new.

The view of the Messiah so far as it was derived from the second Psalm, might be expressed, for example, in the words of Revelation "She [*i.e.* Zion, the Church, the Mother of the faithful] was delivered of a son, a male-child, who is destined to shepherd all the nations with an iron rod, and her child was snatched up to God and to his throne[2]." Nothing here

---

[1] See *Son* 3523 foll.
[2] Rev. xii 5 ἔτεκεν υἱόν, ἄρσεν is strange, and cannot well be explained

THE BAPTISM OF JESUS

about the life, the sufferings, the death and the resurrection of the "son"! Nothing to indicate that He was the "firstborn among many brethren"! Nothing to suggest that in His Ascension, He was not "snatched up" so as to leave His brethren desolate, but went away from them, for the purpose, and (as it were) on the condition, of coming to them again continually in His Spirit, or Paraclete, so that He might be continually descending to answer their prayers, and ascending with their prayers that the prayers might be answered!

Against such a negative and unsatisfying conception it is reasonable to expect that Jesus Himself would directly or indirectly protest. That He did so indirectly we know from the Synoptic account of His doctrine about kings, and rulers, and from His answers to the question " Who is the greatest ? " And inquiring whether in the Fourth Gospel there is any suggestion of such a protest in connection with the "opening of the heavens" and with the mention of a Son, we call to mind that Jesus alluded to that part of the Synoptic narrative which described the opening of the heavens, promising His disciples that they also should hereafter behold them opened, and that, too, permanently, so as to see through them "the angels of God," and these, not merely "descending" but also "ascending" Here there are two things that might naturally take the reader by surprise " Ye shall see the heaven opened and the angels of God ascending and descending on the Son of Man." Would not the angels "descend" before they "ascend"? And should we not expect "the Son of God" rather than "the Son of Man"?

This unexpected "Son of Man" is all the more strange because Nathanael has just acclaimed Jesus with the latter title, " Rabbi, thou art *the Son of God*." He has also said,

---

by Jerem xx. 15 (lit.) "a son [yes] a man-child" (in the mouth of a messenger) Perhaps it is to suggest force, "a man [from the cradle]." Comp however Lk. ii 23 ἄρσεν, which represents in Exod. xiii 2 "firstborn (LXX πρωτότοκον πρωτογενές)."

"Thou art King of Israel" The reply of Jesus seems to mean "You do not quite understand at present what 'Son of God' means, or what 'King of Israel' means Before you can know what is meant by 'Son of God' you must know more of what is meant by 'son of man' And before you can know 'the King of Israel' you must know what a true 'King' is The 'King' ministers to His subjects. The angels or messengers of God minister to 'the son of man'." Thus Jesus seems to be setting Himself against a worldly interpretation of the Voice proclaiming Him God's Son. The new King was not to subdue "the kings of the earth" with an earthly "rod of iron[1]."

But this is negative. It is more difficult to explain what is positive in this doctrine. In particular, what is meant by "the Son of Man" on whom "the angels of God" are to "ascend and descend"?

§ 13. *"The Son of Man"*

For a full discussion of the meaning of "the Son of Man" in the Gospels the reader is referred to the treatise thus entitled in this series There, attention was called to Balaam's doctrine "God is not a man (*vir*) that he should lie, nor *a son of man* (filius hominis) *that he should repent*," and the belief was expressed that Jesus, embodying the conception of the "son of man" in His own person, might teach a doctrine antithetical or at all events supplementary to that of Balaam "God *is* Man that He should pity, and the Son of Man that

---

[1] In the Fourth Gospel, "king" is almost exclusively used by those who misunderstand Jesus (vi 15, xviii 33—9, xix 3—21) In Jn xii 13, the multitude welcomes Jesus as "king," in the fulfilment of prophecy (Jn xii 15, Zech ix 9), but it is probably implied that they do not understand what the term means, as thus applied, any more than the multitude understands it when they sought (vi 15) "to take him by force to make him a king"

THE BAPTISM OF JESUS

He should love[1]." But the last word in this expression was not well chosen. Instead of "*love*," it would have been better—as the question is about changing one's mind and "repenting" of the "evil" that one proposed to inflict—to have said "*forgive*." And to this we shall have to recur later on, when Mark, with startling abruptness, brings the title Son of Man before us for the first time in the words "But that ye may know that *the Son of Man hath authority upon earth to forgive sins*." But for the present the question is how to explain the Johannine introduction of the Son of Man in connection with "the angels of God ascending and descending."

The Bible nowhere mentions such an ascent and descent of angels except in the narrative of Jacob's dream about the ladder that reached to heaven[2]. In the Biblical text there, the Son of Man finds no place. Nor is it easy for modern readers to see how Jacob could be regarded as the type of an ideal Son of Man on whom angels might descend. But the Jerusalem Targum shews that Jews could thus regard him. It describes the angels as descending to look on "*Jacob the pious whose likeness is in the throne of glory*." Another tradition says "They ascended and beheld the *express-image* above, they descended and beheld the *express-image* below," where the editor explains that there is an allusion to the vision

---

[1] See *Son* 3119. The Midrash on Numb. xxiii 19 *ad loc* and elsewhere calls attention to instances (*e.g.* Exod. xxxii 14) where God *does* "*repent* concerning the evil" that He proposed to bring on sinners, but maintains that He does not "repent" concerning the good that He has promised. The word here used for "repent" (*nhm*) implies a change of mind (1) to, or (2) from, sorrow or anger (Gesen 636—7). In the second sense it means "*comfort*" or "*soothe*" "*Me-nahem*," the Comforter, is given as a name of the Messiah in *Jer. Berach* ii 4 (3) in a long story about the destruction and the rebuilding of the Temple, ending with a quotation from Isaiah (x 34, xi. 1) about the "fall" of "Lebanon" (where the context speaks of a "lopping of boughs") and the "rod out of the stem of Jesse"

[2] Gen xxviii. 10 foll.

of Ezekiel mentioning "man" in various connections with the "throne" in heaven[1].

According to Philo, the "ladder"—so far as human nature is concerned—is the soul, of which the basis is the bodily sense and the top is the mind, and through which the *logoi* of God pass unceasingly up and down[2].

In a different tone and style, the Midrash on "Let us make man" introduces a saying endorsed by several Rabbis that, after "God saw all that he had made," we should read—instead of *"and behold [it was] very good"*—*"and behold MAN good*[3]." And this quaint fancy immediately follows a still more quaint interpretation of a passage in the Psalms personifying some of the relations between God and Man. "Surely his salvation is nigh them that fear him, that *glory* may *tabernacle* in our land. *Kindness* (R.V. mercy) and *truth* are met together, *righteousness* and *peace* have kissed each other. *Truth* springeth out of the earth and *righteousness* hath looked down from heaven[4]." In the Bereshith, these attributes of God are regarded as angels, contending against one another, some supporting, some attacking, the proposal to create such a being as "man," or "the son of man[5]." Against such wild and dangerous personifications there comes as it were an

---

[1] Gen. xxviii 11—12, Ezek. i 5, 10, 26, *Chullin* 91 *b* (transl Goldschmidt). See Levy i 394—5 quoting passages that distinguish between "the likeness of the express-image" and "the express-image itself," but giving a different text of *Chullin* 91 *b* distinguishing between "the likeness" and "the likeness of the express image"

[2] See *Son* **3378** quoting Philo i. 641—3. From what Jesus says about the "angels" of "the little ones," we may infer that He regarded the "angels" as associated with prayers from man and answers from God. See *Son* **3159** *b* quoting Ephrem on Mt. xviii 10, and Sir xxxv 17 *a*—*c* Heb "The crying of the poor..will not remove till God shall visit."

[3] Reading *m-a-d* i e "*very*," as *a-d-m* i e "*adam*" or "*man*"

[4] Ps lxxxv 9—11, see *Gen r.* on Gen 1 26 (Wu p 32).

[5] The same context quotes Ps viii 4 "What is man that thou art mindful of him, and the son of man that thou visitest him?" as being uttered by angels pouring contempt on man.

admonition in the doctrine of Jesus that "the angels of God" wait on "the son of man"—consistently with what is said in the Johannine Prologue where the Psalmist's words—"*glory*" and "*tabernacle*" and "*kindness*"—are connected with the Word from whose "fulness we all received":—"The Word... tabernacled among us—and we beheld his *glory*...full of *grace* and *truth*...from his fulness we all received¹."

The Lucan story of the song of the angels at Christ's birth describes angels as descending to sing to the shepherds, concerning the Babe in the cradle, "*Glory* to God in the highest, and on earth *peace* among men in whom he is well pleased²." They may be said to "descend on the Son of Man" on that occasion, waiting on Him as it were, at the moment of His entrance into this material world. But the Lucan angels are not Johannine angels. The former are beautiful figures, helping us from outside with heaven-sent help. The latter are inseparable from humanity, being perhaps describable as the thoughts of God helpfully identifying themselves with the purified personalities of men. The Fourth Gospel, instead of "peace, *among men in whom God is well pleased*," leads us to think of "peace, *in the Man in whom God is well pleased*," peace in the incarnate Logos, "from whose fulness we all received." It is a part of His being. Not that the gift of "peace" is to come at first. "Peace" is Christ's gift at parting³. The angels ascend before they descend. At first, the "glory" that issues from the Son must be that of "grace and truth" whereby He draws disciples to Himself

---

¹ Jn i 14, 16. "Kindness" in the Psalm corresponds, much more closely than "mercy" would, to "grace" in the Gospel (see *Son* **3553** c)

² Lk ii 14

³ Jn xiv 27—8 "*Peace* I leave with you ye have heard how I said to you, I go away," xvi 33 "These things I have spoken unto you that in me ye may have *peace*," followed by the threefold post-resurrectional utterance xx 19, 21, 26, "*Peace* be unto you," are the only mentions of "*peace*" in the Fourth Gospel. Note also the frequent N T salutation, "grace and peace"—"grace" first, "peace" afterwards

and promises, through Himself, to convey to heaven their aspirations after truth and kindness and righteousness, and, through Himself, to bring them down fulfilled for them on earth. Then, and not till then, can they have "peace"

The more closely we examine this utterance to Nathanael, the more exactly will it seem to summarise the gospel of Jesus But it also summarises the gospel of Ezekiel. It turns our thoughts away from the Psalmist heralding the approach of the Son with "the rod of iron" to that Prophet for whom the "heavens were opened," revealing a "throne" on "wheels," drawn by four living creatures, all, so to speak, imbued in some sort by the appearance of a "man," and with the "appearance of a man" seated above the throne itself, and the whole of this moving system—this Chariot as the Jews called it—instinct with a "spirit" that inspires its motion Fresh from this vision of "the appearance of a man" above, the prophet is himself addressed as "son of man" below, and is made to feel that by this title, though often used elsewhere contemptuously, he himself is encouraged to claim kinship with God. At the same time he is bidden to exercise his human privilege of "standing,' without which, if he remains grovelling as a beast, he cannot hear God—" Stand upon thy feet and I will speak with thee[1]"

Then the Spirit enters into Ezekiel, as also it entered into Jesus, and the prophet receives his message. It is not indeed

---

[1] Ezek ii 1, on which see Jerome "*Jacens sermonem Dei audire non poterat* Sed audit cum Moyse (Deut v 31) Tu vero hic *sta mecum* Quod et Daniel (x 11) accidisse sibi commemorat" Comp Gen iii 18 (Targ Jer I and sim Jer II) " Adam answered, I pray.. that we be not accounted as the cattle to eat the herb of the face of the field ; let us *stand up* and labour with the labour of the hands .and thus let there be distinction, before thee, between the children of men and the offspring of cattle" See *Son* **3117** " The Man on the throne in heaven addresses the prophet as 'son of man' on earth, as much as to say, 'Thou, made in my image, art destined to be superior to the Beasts on earth, as I am superior to them in heaven , and thou art to go as my messenger to deliver Israel from the Beasts'"

a message of good-tidings, but it is intended to prepare for good-tidings, and, such as it is, it is the prophet's food[1], given to him before the Spirit lifts him up and carries him away[2]. Somewhat similarly "the Spirit," as we shall see, carries Jesus into the wilderness[3], where He proclaims that man "lives" "not by bread alone" but by "the word of God," and the angels are described as "ministering" to Him[4]

In the Synoptists, the subsequent mentions of the Spirit in a positive aspect are overshadowed by the frequent mentions of "unclean spirits," and by the prominence given to sin against the Holy Spirit. They also give prominence to "angels." They do not make us feel (so keenly as the Fourth Gospel does) the new atmosphere that must have come into the world if indeed "the Spirit" that fills the Universe with God's goodness came down into the man, Jesus, and not only came down into Him but also abode on Him, already touching, as it were, those whom He called and whom He helped, even before the time had come that it should pass into their spirits, after His resurrection But the Fourth Evangelist does make us feel this. The Dialogue with Nicodemus (on the new birth in "water and the Spirit") and the Dialogue with the Samaritan woman (on worshipping God "in spirit," because "God is Spirit") though they do not pretend to expound Christ's thoughts in Christ's words, appear to be nearer to the expression of the kernel of His doctrine than the isolated Marcan traditions about Spirit in a good sense or "spirits" in a bad sense.

And so, too, as regards "the angels of God," the Fourth Gospel seems here to express Christ's actual doctrine, in its

---

[1] Ezek. iii. 1 "Son of man, eat that thou findest"
[2] Ezek. iii. 12 "Then the spirit lifted me up."
[3] See below, p. 148 foll for the "carrying" of Jesus by the Spirit, variously expressed by the Synoptists
[4] See below, pp. 146 foll., 173 foll., where Luke is shewn to omit mention of the "angels"

spiritual essence, more correctly than do those Synoptic passages which, perhaps by misunderstanding[1], represent "angels" instead of "saints," as co-assessors in the judgment of the world. Among the Jews themselves it is probable that many different classes of angels were recognised—participating, some more, some less, in human personality and human attributes. The Fourth Evangelist appears to regard them as ministers of salvation inseparable from the Son of Man, and as ascending from earth before they descend from heaven, and perhaps best (though only approximately) described as men's real, purified, and spiritualised selves

Reserving further comment on the title "Son of Man" until it comes before us in its Marcan order as the title of Him who had "authority on earth to forgive sins," we conclude at present that in the Fourth Gospel it represents the unity between God and Man symbolized by the opening of the heavens and the ascent and descent of the angels of God. In the context in which it is introduced, it seems to shew a deliberate anthropomorphic suggestion as opposed to what we might call the theomorphic exclamation of Nathanael " Thou art the Son of God."

It has been shewn elsewhere, in the traditions about Jesse, called the Man, and about David, the Rod of Jesse, that a Talmudist played on the saying in the Song of Moses, "the Lord is *a Man*[2]" The Song adds—"of War" And that addition suits the tone of the warlike interpretation of the Second Psalm But if Jesus interpreted that Psalm, and all the warlike Psalms, in a spiritual sense as denoting a warfare against evil and a "breaking in pieces" of the powers of Sin, then He may well have read a new meaning into "Man of War" For Him it would signify "The Man who creates Peace

---

[1] See *Son* Index "angels," and especially **3220—33**
[2] Exod. xv. 3, see Appendix I, p 316

out of War," "the Man who conquers sin by forgiveness." Contradicting Balaam, He would say "God *is* like 'the son of man,' and most of all like him when the son of man bears the sins of others in pity—not the pity of contempt, but that divine pity which is breathed by love, hope and faith—and, by this pitying, forgives."

CHAPTER V

THE TEMPTATION

ONE object of this Chapter is to shew what there is in the Fourth Gospel corresponding to "temptation" in the Three But another object, and perhaps a more important one, is to ascertain in what way, if in any, John intervenes, as regards a Mark-Matthew tradition, omitted by Luke, that "angels ministered" to Jesus during or after the Temptation, and also to examine the Johannine attitude toward "angels," as compared with that of the Synoptists severally.

As regards "temptation," I have met with a protest which, if it were well founded, would render it superfluous to enter into a detailed examination of the Synoptic narrative. "John," it is said, "recognised that the Synoptists described a veritable temptation, as of the sons of men But the Johannine eternal Son could not be 'tempted.' The whole Synoptic narrative, to him, was impossible. He could not modify and spiritualise and transform it *more suo*. He could not insert a particle of the story in any form It is not worth while therefore, in a study of the Fourfold Gospel, to go into any details about the additions of Matthew and Luke to Mark, or even about the omissions of two or three Marcan words by Matthew and Luke."

There is some truth at the bottom of this protest. Some hasty readers of the Synoptic narrative, passing by the second and the third temptations as being out of the range of human experience, and fastening on the first, might carry away from it, as their sole inference, that Jesus was tempted by hunger to turn stones into bread—which might be called "a veritable temptation, as of the sons of men." But would Mark be responsible for that—Mark, who nowhere at this point mentions either "hunger" or "bread"? It would be truer, surely, to say that Mark specified no temptation at all, whereas Matthew and Luke specified three, one of which appeals—or appears at first sight to appeal—to man's animal nature. And, if that is so, we might reasonably expect to find John, in the course of his Gospel, helping the perplexed readers of the earlier Gospels to understand that which Mark left in obscurity, and which Matthew and Luke amplified in such a manner as to leave the way open for false inferences.

Here are some of the questions that the latest of the Evangelists might be expected to answer. "In what sense did Christ feel 'hunger' or 'thirst'? What was His 'meat' or 'bread'? Did He ever ask any human being to give Him meat or drink? If He did—under what circumstances, and with what result? Again, Mark says that Jesus was 'with the wild-beasts.' Is it possible that Jesus discerned, around Himself, 'wild-beasts,' 'serpents,' 'scorpions,' 'dogs,' 'bulls of Bashan'—such as the Psalmist speaks of—besetting His path, even before that path led Him to the Cross where they gathered round Him in His last moments?"

This last question reminds us of many poetic commonplaces about the "untameable" nature of "the tongue," and about "the keen tooth" of calumny, ingratitude, and treachery. In particular, it suggests reflections as to the effect on Christ's mind produced by the defection, and even hostility, of former disciples, culminating in Iscariot's betrayal. How far could a Son of God go in feeling these human stings and wounds without ceasing to be divine? How far could He be free from them, and above them, without ceasing to be human? Epictetus maintained that the true Man, being one with God in will, was, in effect, the true king, above all suffering and trouble. Is that the Johannine view?

THE TEMPTATION

An opposite view is set before us—by a weak sovereign to whom Shakespeare has given immortality—of a king after a different fashion. This "king" is above all needs and pains because he is protected from them He does not need "bread" because he has plenty of bread. He feels no want because all his wants are supplied. Take his "bread" away, let "wants" press in upon him, and he ceases to be "a king":—

> I live with bread, like you...,
> Feel want, taste grief, need friends. Subjected thus,
> How can you say to me, I am a king?[1]

Does this represent—we will not say the Synoptic view—but an inferential view that might be drawn from the Synoptic narrative by materialistic minds?

One more question The Epistle to the Hebrews emphasizes the similarity between our temptations and those of Jesus as follows "It behoved him in all things to be made like unto his brethren ...For wherein he himself hath suffered, having been tempted, he is able to succour them that are [from time to time] being-tempted," and again, "We have not a high priest that cannot suffer-with our infirmities, but one that hath been tempted in all things according to [the] likeness [of our temptations]—apart from sin[2]." But where, in the three Temptations of Matthew and Luke, do we find any clear indication that Jesus "suffered with our infirmities," unless it be an "infirmity" to feel hunger? And what is the "likeness" between the temptations of ordinary men and the temptation recorded about Jesus as conveyed in the words "Cast thyself down"? No doubt, that temptation may be called "typical" and may be said to "include a likeness" to ordinary temptations. But is the "likeness" clear to a plain man?

---

[1] *Richard II*, iii. 2 175—7
[2] Heb. ii. 17—18; iv. 15 συνπαθῆσαι ταῖς ἀσθενείαις ἡμῶν In N.T, συνπαθεῖν occurs only here and *ib* x. 34 τοῖς δεσμίοις συνεπαθήσατε (R.V.

THE TEMPTATION

It seems to me that the Fourth Evangelist, taking a wide as well as a deep view of the trials and temptations that beset the noblest natures, perceived that the Synoptic narrative, even in its fullest form, omitted the temptations of the heart, and especially those depressing pangs—weakening if not quickly suppressed—which might momentarily arise in the heart of the Redeemer of Mankind, when saddened and troubled by the sorrows, the weaknesses, and the sins, of those whom He came to redeem. For the present we cannot enter into this question. When the discussion of the Marcan doctrine of the "compassion" of Jesus comes before us in its order, there will be an opportunity of considering whether that doctrine does not indirectly give us no less insight (or, perhaps, more insight) into the temptations of Jesus than is to be derived from the Matthew-Luke narrative of the threefold formal Temptation in the Wilderness. Meantime we may do well to keep before us the possibility that John, while accepting that narrative, may have been deliberately attempting to supplement it by adding a threefold "trouble" that befell the Saviour—first, at the grave of Lazarus whom He rescued from death, secondly, at the coming of the Gentile world which He was to rescue from sin, and thirdly, at the "going forth" of Judas Iscariot whom He was not able to rescue[1].

§ 1. "*Tempting*" *in the Four Gospels*

The Fourth Gospel does not agree with the Three in the use of the words "tempt" and "temptation." "Temptation" it never mentions. "Tempt" it uses once, but only in a good

---

had compassion on) and συμπαθής only in 1 Pet iii 8 (R V) "compassionate (*marg Gr* sympathetic)." See *Son* **3185**, on "suffering" and "sympathy," and **3189** *k*, to which add Origen (on Ezek xvi 5—8) συμπάσχει ὁ θεὸς τῷ ἐλεῆσαι οὐ γὰρ ἄσπλαγχνος ὁ θεός

[1] Jn xi 33, xii 27, xiii 21, on which see the Introductory Volume, pp 159—62, and *Son* **3476**.

THE TEMPTATION

sense—of Jesus "tempting" Philip (as God "tempted" Abraham) that is to say "trying" him, in order to make him "tried," or approved[1]

"Tempt," in the Synoptists, is always used in a bad sense —of Satan or the enemies of Jesus "tempting" Him that He may fall On one occasion they connect it with the seeking of a sign from Jesus[2] It is to be "a sign from heaven." This "tempting" is placed by Mark and Matthew immediately after the Feeding of the Four Thousand, but by Luke—who omits that miracle—immediately after an act of exorcism, which causes "some" to declare that Jesus casts out devils by Beelzebub, but "others" to "seek a sign from heaven," as though to shew that Christ's power was from God above and not from Satan below

John represents Christ's adversaries as twice asking Him for a "sign." "What sign shewest thou unto us," say the Jews to Jesus purifying the Temple, "seeing that thou doest these things[3]?" And again, after the Feeding of the Five Thousand, they say "What then doest thou as a sign?. .Our fathers ate the manna in the wilderness, even as it is written, He gave them bread from heaven to eat[4]." In neither passage is the "sign" expressly demanded "from heaven"; but in the second one Jesus inserts "from heaven" in His

---

[1] Jn vi 5—6 "Whence are we to buy bread that these may eat? And this he said, *trying* him [*i e.* Philip] " Philip (in the Fourth Gospel) is the only one of the first six converts whom Jesus calls with the words "Follow me" He is the disciple to whom the Greeks come saying (*ib* xii 21) "Sir, we would see Jesus" When he says to Jesus (*ib* xiv 8) "shew us the Father," Jesus replies "Have I been so long time with *you* [*all*], and *dost thou* not know me, Philip?" According to Clement of Alexandria, Philip was the disciple who was bidden to "leave the dead to bury their own dead" See *Son* 3377 *a* It is through Philip that Christ says to the world "He that hath seen me hath seen the Father"

[2] Mk viii 11, Mt xvi 1, Lk xi 16

[3] Jn ii. 18

[4] Jn vi 30—31 "*Thou*" is emphatic —"Moses brought bread *from heaven*, what canst *thou* do in the same way as a sign *from heaven*?"

A. B 10

THE TEMPTATION

reply: "Moses gave you not the bread *from heaven*, but my Father giveth you the true bread *from heaven*." Jesus implies that the manna from the visible heaven was not "from heaven," in the "true" or spiritual sense, and He clearly regards the Jews as demanding a sign from the visible heaven. This makes it probable that, in the Temple also, the demand was for a sign from the visible heaven, where no magician (it was thought) had power to work signs. But in neither passage does John describe this demand of the Jews as an act of "tempting."

It might seem, therefore, that the Synoptic account of Christ's Temptation ought to be excluded from this treatise on the Fourfold Gospel. But such an exclusion would be contrary to our rule of including everything in Mark that has been altered or omitted by Luke. The Marcan narrative, though little more than a sentence, contains two statements omitted by Luke. The first is, that Jesus "was with the wild beasts." The second is, that "the angels were ministering to him[1]." If the Fourth Gospel has nothing to say on these two points the plan of our work requires us to note the omission, and either to explain why John would not intervene in these two cases, or to confess that the rule of Johannine Intervention is broken. We know of course that John nowhere uses the *word* "wild-beasts", but, as we have repeatedly found, difference in word must not prevent us from searching for correspondence in *thought*

As to "angels," we have seen above that John seems to regard them as ascending and descending on the Son of Man like human aspirations that go up to the divine throne to return as divine ministrations. This is a very different kind of "angel" from the one described by Luke in his Introduction as "Gabriel[2]" Here, we find Mark inserting, and Luke

---

[1] Mk 1. 13
[2] Lk. 1. 19, 26. Not elsewhere in N T In O.T only in Dan viii. 16, ix 21. See *Gen. r* on Gen. xviii 1—2 "Resh Lakish said that the Jews

omitting, a tradition about "angels" as "ministering" to Jesus while He "was with the wild-beasts." The plan of our work obliges us to ask, What was Luke's motive here? But while attempting to ascertain this particular point, we shall also ask the same question about other passages in the Gospels making mention, or omitting mention, of angels, and especially any that mention them as ministering to, or attending on, Christ.

"Wild-beasts" then, and "angels," will be the two main subjects of this chapter. But they will have to be discussed in their context, that is to say, as features of a narrative about "temptation." And we ought also to bear in mind that Mark in his next chapter represents Jesus as abruptly calling Himself the Son of Man[1]. Are we to suppose that Mark's brief tradition about the "tempting" of Jesus is based on a thought of "the son of man," described in the Eighth Psalm as being "a little lower than the angels"? This view is at all events suggested by the connection of thoughts in the Epistle to the Hebrews For it quotes the Psalm at great length, applying to Jesus the words "*son of man*" and "a little lower than *the angels*." It concludes by saying that the phase of existence implied for the Son of Man in "a little lower than the angels" was ordained in order that He might be "*tempted*" for the sake, not of angels but of men: "For in that he himself hath suffered, being *tempted*, he is able to succour them that are *tempted*[2]."

This indication of the possibilities of poetical allusion, in these brief phrases peculiar to Mark, gives importance to other contextual phrases, which he shares with Matthew or Luke, and makes it desirable to examine the whole of Mark's account of the Temptation, clause by clause.

---

brought with them from Babylon the names of the angels, *e g*. Michael, Raphael, and Gabriel"

[1] Mk ii. 10. The only preceding Marcan mentions of υἱός are Mk i. 1 [υἱὸς θεοῦ], 1 11 ὁ υἱός μου ὁ ἀγαπητός.   [2] Heb. ii 5—18.

THE TEMPTATION

§ 2 *Jesus, "driven forth" or "led up" or "led"*

Mk i 12 (R V)	Mt iv. 1 (R.V.)	Lk iv 1 (R V)
And straightway the Spirit driveth him forth into the wilderness	Then was Jesus led up of the Spirit into the wilderness.	And Jesus, full of the Holy Spirit, returned from the Jordan and was led by (*or*, in) the Spirit in the wilderness

Mark (R V "*driveth forth*") here uses a word that he habitually uses elsewhere to mean "*casting out*" and mostly applies to the exorcism of evil spirits When applied to persons in LXX it regularly implies violence, and Philo, on the "casting out" of Adam from Paradise, has a long comment on the word as meaning permanent exile[1]. It is difficult to understand Mark's use of this word unless it was an attempt to render some very strong original expression about the force of the divine impulse, such as that in Ezekiel, " The Spirit lifted me up and took me away…and the hand of the Lord was strong upon me[2]"

---

[1] Philo i 138—9 on Gen iii 24 Some might quote Mt ix 38 (Lk x. 2) to shew that ἐκβάλλω may mean simply "send forth" But Origen's comment (*Comm. Matth* xv 12, Lomm iii 351) and the paraphrase in Clem Alex 319, shew that it means much more than that As a rule, in LXX it represents Heb "expello," but even in the five instances where it represents (Trommius) Heb " exire facio," *e g* 2 Chr. xxiii 14 &c, it implies violence or constraint, or the casting out of something that is unclean

[2] Ezek iii 12—14 Comp Lk iv 1 (SS) "and the Holy Spirit *took him and sent him forth into* the wilderness," and the quotations (Burk.) (1) "*And then* the Spirit sent him forth that he might be tempted" (omitting "wilderness"), (2) "*Immediately* the Holy Spirit took [and] *led him out into a desert* "

There appears to be here a combination of Luke with Mark, making a distinction between Christ's (1) "*return* [to Nazareth]" and (2) "*being sent forth* to the wilderness" So, too, the Diatessaron —"(Lk) And Jesus *returned* from the Jordan full of the Holy Spirit (Mk) And immediately the Spirit *took him out* into the wilderness " On ὑποστρέφω, always "return" in Luke, see below, p. 150, n 3

Matthew uses the word regularly employed to denote the "*bringing up*" of Israel out of the land of Egypt, where the upward motion is partly metaphorical, meaning ascent from degrading bondage, but partly literal, since Israel is regarded as being "*led up*" first to Sinai, after the baptism in the Red Sea, and then, ultimately, to Jerusalem[1]. Apart from the Acts (where it is often passively used, of putting out to sea, as also once in Luke) it is not used in N.T. except about Jesus as being "brought up" (1) "to Jerusalem," (2) to a place unnamed, whence "the kingdoms of the world" are seen, (3) "from the dead[2]" We must therefore suppose that Matthew means something by preferring "bring up" to "bring" or "lead." Since He was "brought up" out of the valley of the Jordan, the upward motion or ascent would be literal for Jesus, as well as typical of the ascent of Israel from Egypt. It is possible that Matthew regarded the Spirit as bringing Jesus "up" in the air (like Ezekiel) and transporting Him into the desert But such "transporting" seems not to come till afterwards Here Matthew is more probably thinking of "the wilderness" of Sinai as having Sinai for its centre; so that the going up of Jesus was like that of Israel, or, more particularly, of Moses, led up by God through the baptism of the Red Sea to the wilderness, where he ascended Mount Horeb. It was natural to regard Jesus as the type of Israel, "brought up" into "the wilderness" of Sinai, to be tempted as Israel was tempted, but not to fall

Later on, we shall find the parallel Luke using this rare word to describe the "leading up" of Jesus to a special temptation, where Matthew speaks of "a mountain[3]." But in the parallel to the present passage Luke omits "up" and uses, instead, a rare form that is not used elsewhere in the Greek

---

[1] Ἀνάγω of Israel brought from Egypt, Gen 1 24 (comp Exod xxxiii 12 "bring up this people"), Lev. xi 45 &c

[2] Lk ii 22, iv 5, Rom x. 7, Heb. xiii 20

[3] Lk iv 5 ἀναγαγών, Mt iv 8 παραλαμβάνει

THE TEMPTATION

Testament, Old or New, except in the sense of being led to bonds or death[1]. The thought is apparently similar to that which is expressed in Paul's saying "Behold, I go, *bound in the spirit*, unto Jerusalem, not knowing the things that shall befall me there, save that *the Holy Spirit testifieth unto me* in every city saying that bonds and afflictions abide me[2]." But, instead of "*bound in the spirit*," Luke says "Jesus, *full of the Holy Spirit*, returned [home][3] from the Jordan, and [afterwards] was led *in the Spirit* [like one going to bonds or death] in the wilderness."

It seems that there were early differences of opinion about this "leading" or "leading up." And this is confirmed by Luke's later use of the word in this story. It describes the "leading up" of Jesus, *not into the scene of the Temptation as a whole, and not to a mountain, but into some place—not mentioned—where one of the three special temptations was encountered;* and here the parallel Matthew explains that it was "an exceeding high mountain":—

Mt. iv. 8	Lk iv 5
Again the devil taketh him with [himself] *to an exceeding high mountain* and sheweth him all the kingdoms of the world	And *having led him up* he shewed him *all the kingdoms of the inhabited-world in a moment of time.*

Why does Luke omit "to an exceeding high mountain"? And why does he insert "in a moment of time"? Apparently for the following reason He does not believe in the existence

---

[1] Lk iv 1 ἤγετο Comp Lk xxiii 32 "there were also being led (ἤγοντο) others, malefactors,. .to be put to death," and comp. 1 Cor. xii 2. In LXX ἤγοντο occurs 5 times (Nahum ii 7, 2 Macc. i 19, 3 Macc iv 5, 4 Macc x 1, xi. 13) and always meaning "led" to bonds or death.

[2] Acts xx 22—3.

[3] "Returned [home]" or "returned to the place whence one came" is always the meaning of ὑποστρέφω in Luke, who uses it about 20 times No other Evangelist uses it It implies an interval between the baptism and the temptation This would emphasize the deliberate obedience of Jesus to the prompting of the Holy Spirit that "filled" Him

of a material "mountain" to which Jesus was transported in order that He might look round toward the four quarters of the world and see them all. The vision was "in a moment," and the place was nowhere except in thought or in the world of visions Somewhat similarly Jerome and Rashi explain, as spiritual not as local, Ezekiel's transportation, "He [*i.e.* God] put forth the form of a hand, and took me by a lock of mine head ; and the spirit lifted me up between the earth and the heaven, and brought me in the visions of God to Jerusalem[1]."

We have now mentioned two instances of "*bringing up*," expressed or implied by Matthew and Luke, in two of the three temptations which they record , whereas Mark merely says that the Spirit "driveth forth" Jesus "*into* the wilderness" —adding afterwards "and he was *in* the wilderness forty days being tempted by Satan," but not specifying any particular temptation. Before discussing the difference between "*in*" and "*into*" the wilderness (Mark having both "*into*" and "*in*," while Matthew has "*into*" alone, and Luke has "*in*" alone) we must point out that the temptation placed third by Luke, but second by Matthew, also implies "bringing up" or at all events placing on high, as follows —

Mt iv. 5	Lk. iv. 9
Then the devil taketh him with [himself] into the holy city and caused him to stand on the pinnacle (so R V) of the temple	But he led (*or*, brought) him to Jerusalem and caused him to stand on the pinnacle (so R.V) of the temple

---

[1] Ezek viii. 3. Origen, *ad loc*, speaks of it as a spectacle of sins, taking the "northern world (κόσμος)" allegorically, but adding, in a material sense, "There are also other worlds in the earth," for which statement he quotes Clement of Alexandria Origen also quotes (*Comm. Joann.* ii 6, Lomm i 113) "the Gospel according to the Hebrews, where the Saviour Himself says, 'My mother, the Holy Spirit, took me just now by one of my hairs and carried me off to the great mount Tabor'" (quoted again by Origen, *Comm Jerem* xv. 4, and partially by Jerome ("modo me tulit Mater mea, Spiritus Sanctus") on Is xl 11)

THE TEMPTATION

Here the exact agreement of Matthew and Luke shews that they must have followed a Greek verbal tradition, but there is this difficulty, that the word rendered "pinnacle" is not alleged to occur elsewhere in LXX or in Greek literature in that sense[1]. It means "*wing*," *not in a literal sense, but when applied to anything that is like a wing*, e.g. fin, shoulder-blade, corner of a garment. But a pinnacle cannot be said to be "*like a wing*." In LXX, however, it is used of the wings of the cherubim[2]. And the question arises whether the tradition followed by Matthew and Luke originally contained some mention of "wing" literally, which has been confused with "wing" taken metaphorically, i.e. "extremity" or "corner" as applied to the building of the Temple. This view is favoured by the following expansion of the metaphor of "eagles' wings" in the Targum of Exodus, if we remember that "*eagle*," in Greek, is a regular architectural term meaning "*the pediment of a temple*" —

Hebrew	Jer. Targ I.
Ye have seen...how I bare you *on eagles' wings* and brought you unto myself[3]	Ye have seen how I bare you upon the clouds *as upon eagles' wings from Pelusin, to take you to the place of the Sanctuary*, there to solemnize the Pascha, and in the same night brought you back to Pelusin, and from thence have brought you nigh to [receive] the doctrine of my Law

---

[1] Steph *Thes* (πτερύγιον) gives only Lk iv 9 and (in brackets) Joseph *Ant* xv 11 5. The latter does not contain the word. Clement of Alexandria (Euseb ii. 1. 5, comp. ii. 23 3) and Hegesippus (*ib.* 12) use it about the martyrdom of James, apparently borrowing it from the Gospels ("cast from the pinnacle," "made him stand on the pinnacle of the temple")   [2] 1 K vi. 24, and see Ezek. xxviii 16 (Field)

[3] Exod xix 4   *Mechilt*—on Exod xii 37 "journeyed from Rameses to Succoth, about six hundred thousand men .."—says that they made the journey "*in a single moment*, to prove the truth of Exod. xix 4 'on eagles' wings'." This shews how Luke's (iv 5) "*in a moment of time*" might be introduced as a paraphrase

THE TEMPTATION

Here the LXX and the Targums, including Onkelos, insert "as" after "bare you" and before "eagles' wings" But the Hebrew has no "as." Hence, if the Hebrew was translated literally into Greek, and if the Greek "eagle" was taken to mean "the pediment of the Temple," the meaning of "wing" might be taken in an architectural sense as "extremity" The plural ("eagles' wings") ought certainly to have prevented such an error But Deuteronomy repeats the same metaphor with "eagle" in the singular[1]; so that a writer convinced that "a journey to the sanctuary" was meant would need but a slight alteration of the text to adapt it to his conviction.

The reader will note that, except as to the words "caused him to stand on the pinnacle of the temple," Matthew and Luke differ in their contexts (Matthew "Then the devil taketh him with himself into the holy city," Luke "But he led (*or*, brought) him to Jerusalem") This, and the different order in which Matthew and Luke arrange the second and the third temptations, favour the view that the two Evangelists —while amplifying and smoothing Mark's harsh tradition about the "casting out" of Jesus by the Spirit—resorted to scriptural precedents or to early Christian modifications of such precedents, for the purpose of expressing the means by which a prophet, subjected by the permission of God to temptation, might be transported from place to place by the Tempter

Precedents for spiritual transportation of individuals in Scripture were almost, if not entirely, confined to Ezekiel. There was also, however, in Exodus, the above-quoted beautiful description of the transportation of Israel (of whom Christ was the representative) as "borne on eagles' wings" through the wilderness—explained by tradition as being borne "to the place of the Sanctuary" It seems

---

[1] Deut xxxii 11

antecedently probable that Evangelists in search of such precedents would use this tradition. In its Hebrew form, it might represent an actual temptation in which the Messiah, while being carried aloft as on an eagle's wing by the Holy One of Israel, was tempted to cast Himself down, for a sign to unbelievers. An easy corruption in the Greek rendering might convert this into a temptation to cast Himself down from "the wing of the pediment [*lit.* eagle] of the Holy [Place]," *i.e* the roof of the Temple[1].

§ 3. "*Into*," or "*in*," "*the wilderness*"[2]

The interpretation of "into (*or,* in) the wilderness" will depend, in part on the preposition, "in" or "into," but in part on the nature of "the wilderness." Are we to regard Jesus as being "led *into the wilderness of Arabia*," or "led *into the wilderness of Judaea*"? And again, was He "led on, *in* the wilderness" to some definite spot, perhaps some mountain, where the temptation took place? Or did the temptation take place in the wilderness itself while He was journeying in it? In the former case, the wilderness would certainly seem to be that of Arabia, and the definite spot Mount Sinai. And even in the latter case, the wilderness of Arabia rather than that of Judaea would seem to be more suitable for a prolonged journeying of forty days.

Mark, after saying that John was "baptizing in the wilderness," now says that the Spirit "casteth out" Jesus "into the wilderness." The parallel Matthew calls "the wilderness" in the first case "the wilderness of Judaea," but, in the second, "the wilderness" simply. The inference is, that Matthew regarded Mark's repetition of the same term as misleading,

---

[1] Wetstein on Mt. iv 4 quotes Eustathius as saying that the names "eagle (ἀετός)" and "wing (πτερόν)" are given (as well as ἀέτωμα) to certain parts of a temple, and gives passages shewing that the "wing" was a comparatively "low" part of the building

[2] Mk i 12, Mt iv 1 "into," Lk. iv 1 "in"

"the wilderness" being, in the first case, that of Judaea, but in the second (as it almost always is in the Pentateuch) that of Arabia. Luke gives us no definite assistance. But he has previously said "The word of God came on John ..in *the wilderness*," quoting from Isaiah, "The voice of one crying in *the wilderness*"; and later on he represents Jesus as saying "What went ye out into *the wilderness* to behold[1]?" In the first and third of these cases he means the wilderness of Judaea. This may be regarded as stretching into the wilderness of Arabia, which bordered on it—a fact of which we are reminded in the story of Elijah's journey to Mount Horeb[2].

This, then, is probably in Luke's mind, when he says that Jesus "was led [onward] in the Spirit in the wilderness forty days being tempted by the devil[3]." Paul makes a similar journey immediately after his conversion, and he definitely mentions "Arabia." Paul also gives his readers to understand that he "conferred not with flesh and blood" but went to "Arabia[4]." And to what spot, if any, in Arabia? We may well suppose that it was to that sacred mountain whence the Law had been first given to Moses, and where Elijah had heard the still small voice, and this view is confirmed by his reference to Sinai in the same Epistle "These are two covenants, one from Mount Sinai, bearing children unto

---

[1] Lk iii 2, 4, vii 24 The only other Lucan instance of ἡ ἔρημος is Lk xv 4, of a flock left in "the wilderness," *i e* in the open pasture-land, where the parall Mt xviii 12 has "on the mountains"

[2] Beersheba was on the border line Comp 1 K xix 3—8 "He [*i.e* Elijah] arose and went for his life, and came to *Beersheba, which belongeth to Judah*, and left his servant there But he himself went a day's journey *into the wilderness* . and he arose and did eat and drink and went in the strength of that meat forty days and forty nights unto Horeb, the mount of God"

[3] Lk iv 1

[4] Gal i 15—17 "When it was the good pleasure of God . to reveal his Son in me immediately I conferred not with flesh and blood; neither went I up to Jerusalem to them that were apostles before me; but I went away into *Arabia*"

bondage, which is Hagar Now this Hagar is Mount Sinai in Arabia, and answereth to the Jerusalem that now is, for she is in bondage with her children. But the Jerusalem that is above is free, which is our mother[1]" It was natural in any case that the Apostle should feel a prompting of his spirit to think out the relation between the Law and the Gospel, in the very place where the Law was first given, but it would be all the more natural if Paul believed that Jesus, too, like Moses, and like Elijah, had journeyed to the same mountain.

The conclusion appears to be that "the wilderness" is regarded by the Synoptists as, in effect, that of Arabia, but it remains quite uncertain, as will be seen later on, whether the temptation is to be taken as occurring during forty days, while Jesus was being led onward from place to place *in* the wilderness, or at the end of the forty days. In the former case, Jesus might be regarded as the type of Israel, tempted for forty years while wandering in the desert—only with this difference that Jesus triumphed over temptation while Israel succumbed In the latter case, and especially if "fasting" is introduced—of which Mark makes no mention—our thoughts are led toward Moses fasting for forty days *on* Mount Horeb, and toward Elijah fasting for forty days *on his way to* Mount Horeb.

§ 4 *What happened during the "forty days"?*

According to Mark, what happened during the forty days was (to speak precisely) merely this, that Jesus was "being tempted" by Satan Mark adds, in one continuous sentence, "and he was with the wild-beasts, and the angels were ministering to him", and this might naturally mean that the "wild-beasts" were present and the "angels" were

---

[1] Gal iv 24—6 Elsewhere (Rom xi 2—4) Paul refers to the dialogue between God and Elijah on Mount Sinai, as leading to the inference (*ib* 5) "Even so, then, at this present time also, there is a remnant according to the election of grace"

THE TEMPTATION

"ministering," throughout the forty days But it is not certain. Mark tells us nothing of the nature of the "tempting." He omits "fasting" (or "not eating")[1].

Matthew says "When he had fasted forty days and forty nights, he afterwards hungered" What happened during the forty days was simply the "fasting." Not till this fasting is over does any tempting begin "And the Tempter came and said unto him. .[2]."

According to Luke, what happened during the forty days was that Jesus was "led-on in the wilderness, being tempted by the devil," apparently meaning that He was "led-on," either like Elijah or like Israel[3]. Luke does not use the word "fast," but he says "And he ate nothing," defining the time by the phrase "in those days[4]" And he adds "when they were completed he became-hungry." This agrees with Matthew, in sense, though not in word, as to the abstinence from food Possibly Luke regards Jesus as being, like Elijah, supplied with food from God sufficing for the forty days. So Moses, on Horeb, is regarded by Philo.

These are the three different answers given by the three Synoptists to the question, "What happened during the 'forty days'?" The result leaves us uncertain as to almost every

---

[1] Mk 1 13

[2] Mt iv 3 'Ο πειράζων occurs, in N T , only here and 1 Thess iii 5 No illustrative instance of the absol use of "the Tempter," for Satan, is alleged by *Hor Heb*, Schottgen, or Wetstein

[3] Comp Numb xiv 34 "After the number of the days even *forty days—for every day a year*, shall ye bear your iniquities, even *forty years*" See also Ezek iv 6 "thou shalt bear the iniquity of the house of Judah *forty days, each day for a year*. " The "forty days" of Moses were not spent in journeying, but on Mount Horeb "Horeb," however, is almost identical in Heb with some words meaning "desert" (Gesen 352 *a*)

[4] "Fast" does not occur in the Pentateuch, but a fuller form of Luke's phrase occurs in Exod xxxiv. 28 "he [*i e* Moses] did neither eat bread nor drink water" On this Philo (1 115, ii 146) says that Moses was receiving spiritual food, and so does Jewish tradition "Fast," therefore, might well seem an inappropriate word

point except that Jesus was "tempted" by Satan. Even as to that, we do not know whether the temptation is to be regarded as taking place during the "forty days" (as seems probable), or "afterwards," at the end of the "forty days"

§ 5. "*He was with the wild-beasts*," *in Mark*

A brief comparison of this Marcan passage[1] with the parallels in Matthew and Luke, which omit "*wild-beasts*" but mention "*fasting*" (or "*not eating*"), suggested that a Hebrew original meaning "*wild-beasts*" had been confused by Matthew and Luke with a very similar word meaning "*fasting*." In support of this view other reasons may be added, some of which may throw light on the fact that whereas Matthew and Luke represent Jesus as being tempted to create bread, John—in his nearest approach to a recognition that Jesus could crave anything—describes Him as asking for water, and as exclaiming "I thirst[2]."

Against this hypothesis of a confusion between "wild-beasts" and "fasting" may be urged the extreme rarity of the Hebrew word for the former. It does not mean beasts of an ordinary kind but beasts of the desert—and especially of a dry waterless desert—such as serpents, asps, scorpions, which in Greek, as well as in Hebrew, might be called "wild-beasts[3]."

---

[1] See *Clue* **192**. "The most appropriate Hebrew for 'wild-beasts' in a 'wilderness'—associated with mention of Satan and suggestive of Christ's words about 'the power of the enemy'—is a word rendered by the Septuagint once 'wild-beasts,' once 'apparitions,' and once 'demons.' The word is very rare (ציים) and closely resembles one that is very common (צום). The latter means 'fast'."

[2] Jn iv 6—7 "Jesus being wearied out...saith unto her, Give me to drink," xix 28 "I thirst." Contrast iv 32 "I have meat to eat that ye know not of."

[3] See Justin Martyr *Apol* § 60 on the "poisonous (ἰοβόλα) *wild-beasts* (θηρία)—[namely], vipers, and asps, and every kind of serpent" that met the Israelites in the wilderness, and comp *Tryph.* § 112 "Moses [in setting up the brazen serpent] was not trying to persuade the people to

But it may be replied that these are precisely the "beasts" that Mark's original might contemplate. It is true that they are called ambiguously in the Psalms, "*they-that-dwell-in-the-dry-desert,*" and it is predicted that "they shall bow before" Solomon[1]. But Jewish poetry claimed for Solomon power over devils; and the Midrash on the promise to Noah "the fear of you shall be...upon every beast of the earth" declared that the "dominion" over the beasts (as distinct from "fear") did not return till Solomon[2]. It was natural therefore that Jewish traditions about the Messiah should describe these "inhabitants-of-the-dry-desert" as bowing before the second and greater Son of David

We have seen above that the "wilderness" first mentioned by Mark is called by Matthew "the wilderness of Judaea," which bordered on Arabia Now a Psalm entitled "A Psalm of David when he was in the wilderness of Judah" opens with the words "O God, thou art my God...my soul thirsteth for thee, my flesh longeth for thee in *a land of drought* and weariness where no water is[3]." The word here used for "*drought*" is etymologically connected with the word for "*beasts-in-the-dry-desert,*" which we are considering; and "*land of drought*" is a very frequent phrase Jeremiah describes Israel as being led "*through a land of drought* and of the shadow of death,*"* and Isaiah speaks of the Messiah as growing up "like a root out of *a land of drought*[4]" Also a Rabbi—while commenting on Jacob's dream, in which the Lord was revealed at the top of a ladder whereon angels were ascending and descending—quotes the words "My soul

---

place their hopes on a *wild-beast* (θηρίον)—[that same] through which the transgression and disobedience originated."

[1] Ps lxxii 9, LXX "Aethiopians," Rashi "turmas principum," quoting Numb xxiv 24 The reading varies, some taking it as "devils," some as "princes" (Taig ὕπαρχοι) Gesen 850*b* conjectures "adversaries"

[2] *Gen. r.* on Gen ix 2, quoting 1 K iv 24

[3] Ps lxiii 1   [4] Jerem ii. 6, Is. liii. 2.

thirsteth for thee," apparently implying that the "thirst," or aspiration, of Jacob ascended and brought down a descending blessing. Another Rabbi supports this view in a homely metaphor, "As those sponges which draw water into themselves[1]"

Thus the Messiah, typified by Jacob, may be regarded as triumphing over temptation in "*the land of drought*" by thirsting after God. On the other hand the Psalmist says that Israel "went on still to rebel against the Most High *in the drought*." Here Symmachus renders "*in drought*" by "*in thirst*[2]." This shews how naturally the thought of "*tempting in a wilderness*" might suggest to a Jew the thought of "*tempting by means of thirst*" As a fact, Israel was tempted both by thirst and by hunger ("pined with hunger and with drouth") but "*in the land of drouth*" the temptation of "*drouth*" would be the more prominent of the two.

Joshua ben Levi on "the Psalm of David in the wilderness of Judah," quoting Deuteronomy on "the great and terrible wilderness, [the] serpent, burning (*lit* seraph), and scorpion, and thirsty-ground where there was no water," said "Serpent points to Babel, Seraph to Media, Scorpion to Greece, Thirsty-ground where no water is to Rome (*lit.* Edom) The Serpent has a banner, the Seraph has a banner, and the Scorpion has a banner, but the Thirsty-ground where no water is has no banner[3]." In the context, the Rabbi apparently personifies Rome as Revelation does. He seems to mean that Rome was more insidiously dangerous than the other Empires While tolerating Judaism (as long as it did not disturb the

---

[1] *Gen r* on Gen xxviii 13, quoting Ps lxiii 1

[2] Ps lxxviii 17 Compare the two following instances of "drouth" in Milton *P Regained* i 325 "pined with hunger and with *drouth*" (i e *thirst*) and *ib* iii. 274 "and inaccessible the Arabian *drouth*" (i e *desert*)

[3] See *Tehill* on Ps lxiii 1 (Wu p 340) quoting Deut viii 15 The Heb. for "thirsty-ground" (Gesen 855 *a*) somewhat resembles the Heb for "fast," but is never confused with it In Amos viii 11, the reading of Trommius (i 993 *a*), $\lambda\iota\mu\acute{o}\nu$ ($\ddot{v}\delta\alpha\tau\sigma s$), is an error for $\delta\acute{\iota}\psi\alpha\nu$ ($\ddot{v}\delta\alpha\tau\sigma s$).

Empire) she corrupted the Chosen People by diffusing a love of servile quietude and a thirst for material pleasures. "This sinful woman (*Frevlerin*)" he says, "has no banner."

The same passage of Deuteronomy is quoted by Philo in connection with the serpents in the wilderness, and the Serpent of brass, and the supply of water from the Rock, to shew how like is to be cured by like in both cases. The bite of the Serpent that is below is to be healed by Temperance, the Serpent that is from above. The thirst for the water that is below is to be satisfied by thirsting for, and drinking, the water that is from above[1].

In concluding these observations on the Marcan tradition, "He was with the wild-beasts," we must take some notice of the ambiguity of the word "serpents" in other passages of the Gospels. In Luke, Jesus speaks about giving to the Seventy authority "to tread upon serpents and scorpions and over all the power of the enemy." The Mark-Appendix has "they shall take up serpents" after "they shall cast out devils." The latter passage indicates a belief that power over serpents or wild-beasts in the literal sense, went hand in hand with power over serpents or wild-beasts in a spiritual sense. But the former (Luke) seems to take "serpents" merely in a spiritual sense, whether called "wild-beasts" under the domination of their superior, "the Wild-Beast," or "serpents" under "the Serpent[2]." Also, the Matthew-Luke account of the Temptation, though nowhere mentioning "serpents," or "wild-beasts," introduces a quotation from a Psalm which suggests a picture of the Messiah carried on the arms of angels in the air above a multitude of wild-beasts or serpents on the earth below[3].

---

[1] Philo i 80—2, on which see *Son* **3391** foll.

[2] Lk x 19, Mk xvi. 17—18.

[3] Mt. iv 6, Lk. iv 10—11, quoting Ps. xci 11—12 "He shall give his angels...against a stone." After this follows "Thou shalt tread on the lion and the adder...."

On the whole, it appears a reasonable conclusion, apart from the possibility of a verbal confusion between "*wild-beasts*" and "fasting," that Matthew and Luke have omitted the former because of its obscurity. This may be illustrated by the Pauline saying about "fighting-with-wild-beasts" at Ephesus, which some have taken literally as meaning "fighting with beasts in the amphitheatre"—though no Roman citizen was liable to this[1]. Tertullian illustrates the saying by quoting "We were weighed down exceedingly, beyond our power, insomuch that we despaired even of life[2]." This shews that he regarded "fighting-with-wild-beasts" as a metaphor denoting an extreme form of trial.

On this point the language of Ignatius, on his way to martyrdom in Rome, is very instructive. To the Smyrnaeans he says, literally—and almost as if it had become a proverb for Christian martyrs—" In the presence of wild-beasts—in the presence of God[3]." But to the Romans he uses the Pauline verb, "From Syria even to Rome I *fight-with-wild-beasts* by night and by day, being bound amidst ten leopards, even a company of soldiers[4], who only wax worse when they are kindly treated. Howbeit through their wrong doings I become more completely a disciple, '*yet am I not hereby justified*'. May I have joy of the *wild-beasts* that have been prepared for me.[5]" Here we have the verb "*fight-with-wild-beasts*" used metaphorically and yet with allusion to the

---

[1] 1 Cor. xv. 32.

[2] Tertull. *De Resurrect.* 48, quoting 2 Cor. i. 8. His words ("illas scilicet bestias Asiaticae pressurae") indicate that he assumes the "beasts" to be metaphorical.

[3] Ign. *Smyrn.* § 4.

[4] "Even soldiers" Lightfoot says "This looks like a gloss at first sight, but it is found in all the copies. It is added somewhat awkwardly in explanation by Ignatius, as his obscure metaphor might otherwise have been misunderstood." If it was added by the Martyr's amanuensis, or at some very early date, by another hand, it would illustrate the attitude of some Christians toward the obscure "wild-beasts" in Mark.

[5] Ign. *Rom.* § 5.

THE TEMPTATION

literal fulfilment that is in prospect, indicated by the noun "*wild-beast*." And it should be noted that while he anticipates with joy the onslaught of the literal wild-beasts of the arena, he feels bitterly the contact, night and day, with the human wild-beasts, who became all the more bestial for kind treatment.

This may illustrate the nature of the "wild-beasts" by which the Son of Man may be supposed to have been tempted. They were not only the "demons" or ministers of Satan that He exorcised from the possessed; they were also the demons that He could not exorcise. They were the serpents and scorpions in the hearts of those who declared that He cast out devils by Beelzebub, and who exulted over His disciples when they could not cast out a devil from a poor demoniac child, making Jesus Himself exclaim, "O faithless and perverse generation, how long shall I be with you, how long shall I bear you[1]!" Such also were the "wild-beasts" that collected round the Cross—whom early Christians would regard as fulfilling the Psalmist's predictions about "lions" and "dogs" and "bulls of Bashan"—exulting over the Crucified. It was not about such creatures as those that Ignatius could have said "In the presence of the wild-beasts —in the presence of God!" On the contrary, the more Jesus loved mankind, the more He must have shrunk from the presence of such perversions of humanity, trophies of Satan, almost as if He were forced to say "In the presence of such wild-beasts—in the absence of God! *Eli, Eli, lama sabachthani*[2]!"

---

[1] See *Son* **3518** *d* on Mk ix 19.

[2] If the Temptation could be regarded as a prophetic summary of Christ's Progress through what Bunyan calls "the wilderness of this world," then we might perhaps illustrate the Marcan emphasis on "wild-beasts" by the Johannine emphasis on "the wolf," which, though but once mentioned in the Fourth Gospel, is an essential feature of the Parable of the Good Shepherd, and could not be removed without a serious misrepresentation of the object of Christ's whole life. The repeated attempts, or desires, to kill Jesus—of which the Synoptists say

THE TEMPTATION

Having dealt with the Marcan tradition and with its omission by Matthew and Luke, we have now to ask whether John appears to make any attempt to express its spiritual meaning.

§ 6. *The Johannine equivalent of Mark*

We have seen above that John differs from the Synoptists fundamentally as to the use of the word "*tempt*," since he uses it only in a good sense whereas they use it in a bad one Also the Synoptic accounts of the "temptation" have left us in doubt as to the nature of "the wilderness" in which it took place and the period of its duration, though all mention "forty days" Further, though they agree that Satan or the devil was the tempter, it is only Matthew and Luke that represent Satan as addressing words of temptation to Jesus. In Mark, we are left free to believe that Jesus was tempted by Satan, with the permission of God, as Job was, without direct utterance of Satan to the person tempted. In Chronicles, where "*Satan*" is said to have "*moved* David," the parallel Samuel says "*The anger of the Lord* was kindled against Israel and *he moved* David[1]." Elsewhere the Scripture speaks of God Himself as "*tempting*" Israel, and uses the same Hebrew word as when it charges Israel with "*tempting*" God[2]. In such cases our English Versions mostly vary their

---

something, but comparatively little—are part of the trial of the Good Shepherd who is always contending against "the wolf" and ready to do what the "hireling" will not do—to "lay down his life for the sheep" Of this metaphor Mark (vi. 34, xiv 27) and Matthew (ix 36, xxvi 31) give but slight suggestions, and the parallel Luke gives none at all (see *Son* 3278, 3425 *c*, 3440 *b*, 3548). But if we may accept the Marcan "wildbeasts" in the Temptation as including a reference to the assaults of "the wolf" upon "the sheep," then we may say that Mark does in an obscure and indirect way include a latent reference to Jesus as the Shepherd of Israel, which the other Synoptists have omitted but which John has amplified and emphasized

[1] 1 Chr xxi 1, 2 S. xxiv 1
[2] Gen xxii 1, Exod. xv 25, xx 20, &c. See Gesen 650 *a*

THE TEMPTATION

rendering, and describe Israel as "*tempting*," but God as "*proving*." There is, however, one notable exception. Our Authorised Version describes God as "*tempting*" Abraham. But the Revised has "*proved*." Symmachus, taking the word as identical with a similar one meaning "*uplift as a banner*," renders it "*glorified*[1]"

This resembles the Johannine paraphrases of the Synoptic traditions about the "crucifying" or "killing" of Jesus For these John substitutes "*glorifying*" or "*lifting up*." It would therefore not be surprising if, instead of speaking of Jesus as being "*tempted*," John were to say "*glorified*" or "*lifted up*." In referring to the Temptation, this would result in the phrase "*lifted up in the wilderness*." Such a phrase we find applied to the Brazen Serpent and connected with Jesus in a saying that follows the doctrine about regeneration from above with water and the Spirit "As Moses *lifted up the serpent in the wilderness*, even so must the Son of Man be *lifted up*, that whosoever believeth may in him have eternal life[2]"

John seems to be here glancing at the Marcan narrative which says that Jesus was "*tempted in the wilderness*" immediately after His baptism[3]. He treats this, not as a historical fact about Jesus, but as a spiritual law of general application, that after the baptism there must be a "lifting up in the wilderness[4]." But when this law is exemplified in the

---

[1] Gen xxii 1 on which see Field, quoting Ps iv 6

[2] Jn iii 14

[3] See above, p 148, comp p. 150, n 3, where it is shewn that the parallel Luke does not imply "immediately."

[4] Comp Pseudo-Jerome on Mk i 12—13 "Tunc Spiritus nos expellit in desertum quadragenario numero tentandos a Satana, ut patientia nobis probationem, probatio autem spem, spes vero charitatem generet Cum non sit nobis colluctatio adversus carnem et sanguinem, sed adversus principatus, et reliqua Et tunc bestiae pacatae erunt nobiscum, cum in arca animae nostrae, munda cum immundis animalibus mansuescimus, et cum leonibus sicut Daniel cubamus, cum spiritus non sit adversus carnem et sanguinem, nec caro concupiscat adversus spiritum"

THE TEMPTATION

Word or Son, it means a lifting up on the Cross, as on a banner, a lifting up, for sinners, of the Son of Man—made like unto sinners, and indeed, as Paul says, "made sin," for the sinful sons of man. The essence of the Marcan saying that Jesus "was *with* the wild-beasts (*or*, serpents)" is expressed by saying that He became, in outward form, one of themselves, the Serpent of Brass, identified with that which was most sinful in themselves, in order that He, the Serpent, or Seraph (so Origen implied) of celestial fire, might heal those bitten by the serpents of the fires of earth[1].

For details of the connection—at first sight so abrupt—between the Johannine doctrine of the serpent and regeneration by water and the Spirit, the reader is referred to a previous treatise[2]. Here it will be well to add something about John's way of regarding the wilderness as a land of "thirst" and of "wild-beasts," attaching to both words all the associations that Scripture attaches to the cravings that made Israel murmur against the Lord, and to the serpents and scorpions that attacked Israel as a chastisement. We may regard him —or rather some early and sympathetic disciple of his—as soliloquising thus·

"Matthew and Luke seem not to have perceived that Mark's tradition had Deuteronomy in view, where it is said to Israel, 'The Lord thy God hath led thee these forty years in the wilderness, that he might humble thee, to *tempt* (or, *prove*) thee,' and again, 'He led thee through the great and terrible wilderness, serpent, burning (*lit* seraph), and scorpion, and thirsty-ground where there was no water[3]'

---

[1] See *Son* **3396** foll "on 'fiery [serpent]' or 'seraph,'" where, however, the suggestion (**3397**) that Jerome is "probably following Origen" is an error See Jerome's *Letters* xviii and lxi expressly condemning Origen's view

[2] *Son* **3391** foll, "'Water' and 'the serpent,' how connected"

[3] Deut viii 2, 15, quoted above, p 160, where a Rabbi finds an allusion to the four empires of the world

THE TEMPTATION

"That the temptation was in some sense a 'lifting up' Matthew and Luke have perceived. But they have taken it as only a lifting up on the Temple, or on a high mountain. Also they have spoken of the Lord as looking down on the principalities and powers of this world. But what are the powers of this evil world except the wild-beasts, or serpents, or scorpions, mentioned in the Law and in the Psalms, above which the Messiah is lifted up? These they do not mention. But Mark mentions them when he speaks of 'wild-beasts'

"Also Matthew and Luke represent the first temptation as being to create bread. But the Law places first 'the thirsty ground where there was no water,' and then the water from the rock, and not till afterwards the manna[1]. Elsewhere, the Three Gospels speak of the Lord as giving bread to men, but they do not speak of Him as giving water. Yet all temptation may be best described as thirst, the thirst for the pleasures of the flesh. And the antidote to this is not to be found in any negative Law that says, in effect, 'Thou shalt *not* drink this, or that.' The only antidote is the fountain of the living water, the Holy Spirit, in man's own heart, making man athirst to do good—good service to the Father in heaven and to the brethren on earth[2].

"Philo speaks of the serpents of pleasure, and of the brazen Serpent of Temperance. But the disciples of Christ say that their brazen Serpent is Christ Himself, their Love, their Passion[3]. Their thirst for His love, being daily satisfied,

---

[1] Deut. viii. 15—16

[2] Comp Sir xxiv. 21 "They that eat me [*i e* Wisdom] shall yet be hungry, and they that drink me shall yet be thirsty"

[3] Comp Ign *Rom* § 7 ζῶν [γὰρ] γράφω ὑμῖν ἐρῶν τοῦ ἀποθανεῖν· ὁ ἐμὸς ἔρως ἐσταύρωται, καὶ οὐκ ἔστιν ἐν ἐμοὶ πῦρ φιλόυλον. Origen (see *Light* 3681 *a* "though perhaps wrongly") and other Greek authorities take ἔρως as meaning the personified Passion of Love, and as being applied to Christ somewhat as ἀγάπη is applied to God. Lightfoot *ad loc* objects, as "fatal," that "it would tear the clause out of the context"

and yet daily increased, by the living water of His Spirit, should make them do good, not because they control their evil impulses, but because they have no impulse that is not good.

"How then can the two truths be expressed, the one, the truth concerning the Lord, as being the type of Israel, tempted in the land of thirst, the other, the truth about that which satisfies the righteous and spiritual thirst of the soul?

"First, in the first of the Lord's signs, it is shewn that the Lord superseded the purifications of the Law, and the water-pots of the Jews, by the new wine of the Gospel. He did not neglect the former He filled up the water-pots from the water of the well. But the water in them is not said to have become wine Then He caused that same water—or else perhaps the water direct from the well—to be brought to the table of the Bridegroom's Feast. And now, in the presence of the Bridegroom, it became wine[1]

"Secondly, it is shewn that although the Lord felt thirst after the flesh, He was not really 'tempted' by thirst after the flesh Meeting a woman of Samaria, at noon[2], and when He was 'tired out' with travel, He said 'Give me to drink.' At once, she refused. Yet Jesus, in His thirst and weariness, converted her to belief Afterwards He converted the Samaritan village But meantime, to the disciples who had come bringing Him food, He said that He had food of which they knew not,

---

I now think that Origen is right This explanation of ἔρως suits the preceding ἐρῶν "I *passionately-desire* to die, *my Passionate Desire* is crucified [and I am crucified with Him in anticipation]; there is no longer in me the fire that clings to matter.." This is abrupt, but not (I think) "fatal" dislocation If Christ is called Eros, Desire, the name at once calls up to Greeks the familiar "*bite*" of Desire, and helps us to understand the obscure type of the Brazen Serpent. See *Son* **3397** and **3397** *a*, on Origen's prayer "May the divine word *bite* us ! May it burn up our souls !", and on Philo's definition of the business of the Serpent, Temperance, " to *bite*, wound, and destroy passion "

[1] See *Joh Gr* **2281—3**.

[2] Jn iv 6 "about the sixth hour," comp Ps xci 6 (LXX) "the midday demon"

THE TEMPTATION

namely, the doing of the will of the Father. Might He not then have said to the woman of Samaria 'I have water to drink that ye know not of'? He *did* say this to her afterwards, in effect—teaching her the doctrine of the living water. But at the beginning He said, 'Give me to drink,' making the thirst of the flesh subordinate to the thirst to do the Father's will by converting the souls of the Samaritans.

"Thirdly, in the end of all the temptations, when He was uttering His last words on the Cross, 'Jesus, knowing that all things were now finished, that the scriptures might be accomplished, saith, *I thirst*' Now here Mark and Matthew say that Jesus cried aloud a saying from the Psalms 'Eli, Eli (that is, my God, my God) why hast thou forsaken me?' Luke omits this, partly, perhaps, because, if it were taken by itself, and not as the first verse of a Psalm beginning with sorrow and ending with joy, it might be misunderstood as though the Son believed that He had been 'forsaken' by the Father in some manner not consonant with divine justice or righteousness[1]

"Yet, if it may be said that the face of the Father is hidden from those who sin, then it may be also said that He who placed Himself with sinners—in order to feel the burdens that they feel, and to take them upon Himself—might perhaps also be constrained, for the time, to see that which sinners see, so that He saw the Father, for the moment, as if forsaking Him, and all the more earnestly desired to enter into His presence and to rest in His bosom as a babe on the mother's breast. And this is expressed by the Psalmist in the words that address God calling Him 'Eli' and saying, "O God (Elohim), Eli (*i.e.* my God) art thou...my soul thirsteth for thee, my flesh longeth for thee, in a land of drought and faintness where no water is[2].' This was the temptation, or

---

[1] See Mk xv. 34, Mt. xxvii 46, quoting the first words of Ps. xxii, which ends with *ib.* 21—31 "thou hast answered me he hath done it"
[2] Ps lxiii 1 Targ has "O God, my strength art thou"

THE TEMPTATION

the chief part of it, that befell Israel in the wilderness. Only the thirst of Israel was after the flesh But the thirst of Jesus —though it was also bodily thirst—was thirst after the Spirit, thirsting for the presence of the God of heaven at the moment of passing out of the wilderness of this world

"But as to this thirst the Three differ from one another in the following matter·

Mk xv. 36	Mt. xxvii. 48	Lk. xxiii. 36
And one ran, and filling a sponge full of vinegar gave him to drink.	And one of them ran and took a sponge, and filled it with vinegar and gave him to drink.	And the soldiers also mocked him, offering him vinegar.

"Here Luke is right in saying that those who offered the 'vinegar' were 'the soldiers.' It was indeed the ordinary drink of soldiers, so that they had brought it to the place where they were on guard. But whereas Luke places this act some time before the Lord's last words and regards it as an act of mockery, Mark appears to be right in placing it later on, perhaps as an offering of kindness. To Luke it may have seemed that kindness could not be intended because it was a fulfilment of the Psalmist's words, and the Psalm speaks of 'gall' given 'for meat,' and then adds 'In my thirst they gave me vinegar to drink[1].' Luke does not quote this from the Psalms, nor does he mention the word 'scripture' here; nor does Mark or Matthew, but certainly 'Scripture' was thereby 'fulfilled,' and the words of the Psalm certainly imply mockery.

"Yet it does not seem that the vinegar was in this last moment offered in mockery, even if it was offered thus before In the Three Gospels it is said that, when Jesus cried out for the last time, the centurion said 'Truly this man was God's son, or, righteous[2].' If the centurion expressed what the other

---

[1] Ps lxix 21
[2] Mk xv. 39, Mt xxvii. 54 (om "man"), Lk xxiii 47. Somewhat

THE TEMPTATION

soldiers felt, it would seem that at that time their hearts had been turned toward the Lord And when did they begin to be turned? If the vinegar was offered in answer to His own request—(for 'I thirst' was truly a request)—and this, too, when they were on the point of calling Him 'Son of God' or 'righteous,' then it would seem that already they had begun to be friendly. They may have mocked before, but they could not well be mocking now.

"But some may say—as perhaps Luke said—'If the vinegar was not offered in mockery, then there was no fulfilment of Scripture,' and they may ask 'Does it not seem needful that the Scripture should have been hereby fulfilled?' It does And this is shewn expressly, in the words, '*Jesus, knowing that all things were now finished, that the scripture might be accomplished, saith, I thirst*[1].' But it is not to be supposed that the Lord's purpose, in saying, '*I thirst*,' was merely this—that the Roman soldiers, like machines, should be moved to fulfil a prophecy about 'vinegar,' and that afterwards His disciples should go about the world, saying, 'See, Jesus is the Lord, because He fulfilled a number of prophecies, ending with a prophecy about *vinegar*'

"Assuredly we are not to suppose this. Much rather we are to suppose that along with the fulfilment of the letter of the prophecy, there was a fulfilment, and that an unexpected one, in the Spirit. Of somewhat the same kind was the fulfilment of the words 'They shall look unto him whom they pierced[2].' One of the soldiers pierced the Lord's side with

---

similarly (Jn 1 49—51) when Nathanael called Jesus "Son of God," Jesus, in reply, spoke of Himself as "Son of Man" But in the Synoptic passages the same speaker is recorded as speaking differently.

[1] Jn xix 28 See *Joh Gr.* **2115** "Our conclusion is, then, that according to Johannine *grammar* the ἵνα clause depends on τετέλεσται, but, according to Johannine *suggestion and intention*, the ἵνα clause is to be repeated so as to depend on λέγει "

[2] Jn xix 37, quoting Zech. xii 10, "unto (εἰς)," Heb. "unto me" with v.r. "unto him " LXX has πρὸς μέ. .

his spear and straightway there came out blood and water. The man by no means did this out of mere cruelty and still less to fulfil prophecy. He did it, in the way of a soldier's duty, to make sure that the Lord Jesus had died on the Cross. Yet from this act, which some would call a matter of chance, there came forth what the Prophet Zechariah calls a fountain for sin and uncleanness in Israel[1], so that the Gentile world being cleansed in this blood and water might 'look unto him whom they pierced.'

"Let us go back to the saying of Jesus to the Samaritan woman. To her He said nearly the same thing as to the Roman soldiers, namely, 'Give me to drink.' By those words He led the way to the conversion of Samaria and prepared the Samaritans to receive from Him the gift of the living water. And so here, when He said 'I thirst,' the words were so shaped as to mean, in effect, 'Give me to drink, and I will give you to drink.' And so it came to pass. For straightway He gave them the fountain of blood and water.

"I do not deny that the words 'I thirst' are far from seeming superhuman or divine. The Greeks might say that they do not seem worthy even of one whom they would call 'a hero.' But the tradition is that He uttered them 'in order that the Scripture might be fulfilled' Does this mean merely that He might fulfil that single passage in the Scripture which spoke of 'vinegar'? Does it not rather mean that the whole of Scripture regards the Father in heaven as continually saying to each son of man on earth 'My son, give me thine heart[2],' so that He Himself, the Giver of all good, the Eternal Love, may be said to be, in some sense, thirsting for our love, to gain which He sent His Son to live and to die for men, expressing the divine thirst upon the Cross?

"Regarded in this light, the saying 'I thirst,' followed by 'It is finished,' is not unworthy to be the last utterance of the

---

[1] Zech xiii 1   [2] Prov xxiii 26

THE TEMPTATION

Son of God, incarnate as the Son of Man. Nor does it seem the less worthy because it condescends (so to speak) to thoughts of unspiritual souls. To the Roman soldiers, 'thirst for the presence of God' would have been an unintelligible form of words, but bodily thirst was a thing that they could understand and compassionate. 'This mad Nazoraean whom we have been mocking,' they might say, 'is after all, not so much up in the air that he cannot feel what we feel. He thirsts, like one of us, let us do something for him.'

"If the Lord Jesus succeeded thus in converting mockery into pity, it was a victory not unworthy of Him. In some copies of Luke's Gospel, the Lord is said to have added, concerning the Roman soldiers, "Father, forgive them, for they know not what they do[1].' To those who consider the meaning of 'forgiveness,' and how it depends upon a change of heart, it may seem that the Lord Jesus, by turning the hearts of the soldiers from mockery to compassion, prepared the way for the forgiveness of their sins by crying 'I thirst,' no less than if He had said 'I pray for these men that they may be forgiven'."

§ 7. *"And the angels began-to-minister (or, were-ministering) unto him"*

Luke altogether omits this. And there is a slight difference between Mark and Matthew. Matthew omits the article before "angels" and adds "come" in the past tense, to "minister" in the imperfect tense —

Mk i. 13	Mt iv. 11
And the angels began-to-minister (*or*, were ministering) unto him.	And behold, angels came-near and began-to-minister unto him[2]

---

[1] Lk. xxiii. 34 Placed by W. H. in double brackets.

[2] Mt iv 11 προσῆλθον καὶ διηκόνουν shews that Matthew distinguishes the past "came" from the imperfect "began-to-minister" It also makes "were ministering" an impossible rendering Perhaps Matthew desired

THE TEMPTATION

This ministration of angels to the Son of Man occurring at the outset of His public work on earth, recalls the words "But when he again bringeth-in the Firstborn into the world, he saith, 'And let all *the angels of God* worship him[1].'" But what are these "angels of God"? There is some doubt whether the quotation is from the Psalms "Worship him all ye *gods* (LXX *His* (i e. *God's*) *angels*)," or from a very corrupt LXX version of Deuteronomy "Rejoice, *O ye nations*, [with] his people"; but in either case the Greek "*angels of God*" might mean "*gods of the nations*" so that the summons is addressed to "false gods" to worship the true one[2]. Hence it is possible that Mark here might mean, or might be regarded by Luke as possibly meaning, that angels of evil, being subdued by Christ, came over to His side, as it were, and served Him. Clement of Alexandria has preserved an old tradition about Mark's angels to the following obscure effect: "Having overcome these [*i e.* the beasts] and their ruler, He is now 'ministered to' by angels, as being now a manifest King. For he that has *overcome angels in the flesh* is *naturally now served by angels*[3]"

---

to remove the Marcan ambiguity as regards "ministering" But why does Matthew omit "the"? See below, n 3 "The angels" would naturally mean "the angels of God" "Angels" might mean "evil angels."

[1] Heb. 1 6.

[2] Ps. xcvii 7, "Elohim," Targ "the nations that serve idols," Syr "his angels", Deut. xxxii 43 (LXX) "(1) Rejoice, ye heavens, with him; and (2) let the sons of God worship him ; (3) rejoice, ye nations, with his people , and (4) let all the angels of God find-strength in him."

Comp Jer. *Aboda Zara* iv. 7 "Enfin, dit R Nahman au nom de R Mena, un jour l'idole viendra s'agenouiller devant l'Éternel, puis disparaîtra de la terre, selon les mots (Ps xcvii. 7) tous les faux dieux se prosterneront devant Lui"

[3] Clem. Alex. 988, *Excerpt. Theod* lxxxv. 1. In such a context, it seems probable that *ib* lxxxvi 3, which classes the "angels" in 1 Pet 1. 12 ("angels desire to look into") with (Mt xxv 11) the "foolish virgins," does not take "angels" as "the holy angels." Who are the angels that are "overcome"? Are they the "wild-beasts," regarded as "angels of Satan"?

THE TEMPTATION

To what occasion does the Epistle to the Hebrews refer the summons to the "angels" to "worship"? The words "when he again bringeth-in the Firstborn into the world" are ambiguous, and make the answer doubtful[1] Some might regard the Marcan "angels" as having recognised Christ at His Baptism and as immediately following Him into the wilderness where they began to "minister" to Him. Accepting that as one of the occasions, we may say that angels might minister to Christ at His Birth, Baptism, Resurrection, Ascension, and Second Advent. The same ambiguity attaches itself to the words "*appeared to angels*" in a Pastoral Epistle: "He who was manifested in the flesh, was justified in the Spirit, *appeared to angels*, was preached among the nations, was believed on in the world, was received up in glory[2]." Perhaps the least unsatisfactory explanation of this brief and early creed would be that "was preached among the nations" is a corruption for "was preached among the Gentiles in Sheol[3]." In that case, "appeared to angels" might refer to Christ's Resurrection, which might be presumed by some to have been witnessed by "angels" before they announced it

---

[1] Ambiguity is created by "again" and "Firstborn" "Again" may mean (1) "on the other hand," or (2) "back again"; "Firstborn" may mean, not Jesus born at Bethlehem, but Jesus (Rom. 1. 4) "defined" as Firstborn "by the resurrection of the dead" See Chrysostom's comment

[2] 1 Tim iii 16 The explanation of Chrysostom is not satisfactory. He appears to quote without acknowledgment (if it is a quotation) a passage about the "mystery" of "angels seeing Christ *along with us*" from Clem Alex (see Clem Alex Fragm 7th book of Hypotyposeis, ed Stahlin, vol iii. p 200) Stahlin does not refer to Chrysostom The text of Clement is perhaps corrupt.

[3] Against this, among several objections, is this, that we should have expected, not "*was preached*," but, as in 1 Pet iii 19, "*he preached*" If "was received up in glory" could mean (as has been suggested by a friend) "was lifted up in glory among the Churches of the Gentiles," the order would be explicable But that meaning does not seem to me probable.

THE TEMPTATION

to the women. Then followed belief "in the world" (earth above Sheol) and then that "receiving up in glory" which we call the Ascension.

§ 8. *Matthew's version, and Luke's omission, of the "ministering" of the "angels"*

Between Mark and Matthew, as has been pointed out above, there is probably a difference as to the time of the ministration. But Mark differs also from Matthew and Luke in that he makes no mention of any departure of Satan or of any end of the temptation.—

Mk i 13 (probably)	Mt iv 11 (probably)	Lk. iv. 13
And the angels were [all the while] ministering unto him.	Then the devil leaveth him[1], and behold, angels approached, and began-to-minister unto him.	And having completed every temptation, the devil departed from him[1] until a season.

If we may introduce Luke as thinking aloud, his probable reasons for amending Matthew might be expressed thus· "It is not seemly to describe the devil as 'letting go' or 'dismissing' the Lord Jesus, which Matthew's word might mean Moreover, since it sometimes means 'sending away for ever[2]' it might convey a wrong meaning, for the Lord was tempted afterwards shortly before He suffered It will therefore be better to say that the devil 'departed,' or was 'caused to depart,' from the Lord Jesus, using the language of Paul who 'besought the Lord thrice' that 'an angel of Satan' might 'depart' from him[3]. That 'angel of Satan'

---

[1] "Leaveth," ἀφίησιν, might mean "leaves alone" or "dismisses" "Departed," ἀπέστη, might mean "withdrew" from something opposite in nature as in Lk xiii 27, Ps vi. 8 ("*depart* from me, all ye workers of iniquity") Comp 2 Cor xii. 8 "I besought the Lord thrice that it [*i.e.* the angel of Satan, above mentioned] might *depart* from me." The latter is the more appropriate word here

[2] *E g.*, when applied to the divorce of wives, and in some other cases.

[3] 2 Cor xii. 8

THE TEMPTATION

did not 'depart' from the Apostle. But on this occasion Satan 'departed' from the Lord Jesus, because the Lord had fulfilled the whole of the temptation appointed for the time. And this can be made plain by adding 'having completed [according to the will of God]¹ every temptation'

"Also"—Luke might say—"'*until a season*' will prepare my readers for the temptation before the Passion. At that time, Mark and Matthew agree that He said 'Pray that ye enter not into temptation.' But I add a tradition that He said to the chief priests 'This is your hour, and the [appointed] power² of darkness', and some traditions say that, during the temptation before the Passion, 'There appeared unto him an angel from heaven strengthening him³.' Whether this be so or not it seems to me that Mark is wrong in saying here that 'the angels were ministering to him,' namely, supplying the

---

¹ Συντελέσας "having completely-finished." The word occurs, in the Gospels, only here and Mk xiii 4 (of the divine completion of all things predicted) and Lk iv 2 (of the divinely ordained "forty days" of temptation). Elsewhere in N T (thrice) it refers to a sacred number of days (Acts xxi 27) or to God's accomplishments (Rom ix. 28, Heb. viii 8, quotations). And so here, "having completely-finished [according to the will of God]."

² Lk. xxii 53 "[appointed] power," ἐξουσία. The word mostly means "authority," or "lawful power." Here it means the temporary and apparent reign of Satan, permitted (so far as outward acts go) for the fulfilment of God's will. Comp Jn xiv 30 "the prince of the world cometh," where the "coming" is regarded not only as future but also as permitted by the Father.

³ Lk xxii. 43 ἐνισχύων αὐτόν. The word occurs in N.T. elsewhere only in Acts ix 19 "and having taken food he *received-strength* (ἐνισχύθη)." In LXX it is freq., and is once used with "angels," namely, Deut xxxii. 43 "let all the angels of God (?) *strengthen* (or, *find strength in*) him (αὐτῷ v.r. αὐτούς)," on which see p 174, n. 2. Steph *Thes* gives no instance (exc. Theophr fr 1 65 (error for 63), "this, in each thing, is strong (τοῦτ' ἐνισχύειν ἑκάστῳ)") of ἐνισχύω with dative. But see the corrupt Hos. x. 11.

The rare use of ἐνισχύω in N T, and its occurrence with ἄγγελος in (1) a certainly corrupt version of Deut xxxii 43 and (2) a possibly corrupt version of Lk xxii. 43, suggest that the latter (2) was derived from the former (1).

THE TEMPTATION

Lord with food during the forty days. For, if so, how could He have fasted? Mark, it is true, is silent about the fasting. But Moses fasted—or rather, to be exact, he ate nothing—on Mount Horeb, and Elijah on the way to it, and both for 'forty days.' So that Mark seems to have omitted the fasting through error. Or perhaps he thought that 'fasting' implies 'afflicting one's soul,' and that Jesus did not thus 'fast' And that is true, so that 'ate nothing' would be more exact than 'fasted[1]' But perhaps he omitted it only through extreme brevity, assuming that his readers would take it for granted And for the same reasons he may have omitted all mention of the departure of Satan which—as I have said—was only for a time."

§ 9. *John, on this "ministering" of the "angels"*

On the special point in question, namely, the difference between Mark—who says that the angels were ministering to Jesus—and Luke—who says, in effect, that the angels did not minister now but, perhaps, at a later "season"—John appears to intervene by placing, almost immediately after the baptism of Jesus, and as His first utterance to the disciples collectively, that sentence which we have already frequently quoted and must frequently quote hereafter, being a key-sentence in the Johannine Gospel, "Ye shall see the heaven opened [for ever], and the angels of God ascending and descending on the Son of Man[2]" Also, as regards the objection raised above against Mark, "The angels could not have been ministering to Jesus during the forty days in the wilderness, for, if so, He would not have fasted," John indirectly suggests an answer elsewhere by saying, in effect, that Jesus did *not* "fast." He must have had food all the while. For He was doing the will of the Father, and He

---

[1] See § 4 above.
[2] Jn i. 51, on which see *Son* **3133—40, 3374** foll

Himself said to the disciples, when they offered Him food, "I have meat to eat that ye know not of,...my meat is to do the will of him that sent me[1]."

As to the first of these utterances we have been led to the conclusion that the angels ascending are the aspirations and prayers of men, and the angels descending are the blessings of God sent down as answers. Somewhat similarly Philo—having in view (as John has) the "ascending and descending angels" on the "ladder" in Jacob's dream, calls the "angels" the "*words*" sent down to be the physicians to the souls of men[2]. But in Philo the Word itself, the Logos, is the name given to the Sphere, or Place, in which the *logoi* or "words" have their motion. In the Gospel, the "angels" ascend and descend, not upon a "ladder," nor in a "place," but upon a Person, the Son of Man, that is to say the incarnate Word—a conception alien from Philo's thought.

In the second of these utterances ("My meat is to do the will of him that sent me") John seems to be correcting a defect in Luke, who does not shew, so clearly as Matthew does, the meaning of Christ's doctrine concerning bread. For in Luke's story of the Temptation Jesus says to Satan "It is written that man shall not live on bread alone"—not adding what man does live on. But Matthew adds "but upon every word that proceedeth out of the mouth of God[3]." And again, in the Lord's Prayer, Luke places the prayer for "bread" after "Thy kingdom come" without any intervening clause, but Matthew inserts "*Thy will be done, as in heaven, so upon earth*," thereby suggesting that there is some connection between *the "giving" of "bread" by God from heaven* to man, and *the "doing" of God's "will" by man on earth* for

---

[1] Jn iv 32, 34
[2] "Physicians (ἰατρεύουσι)," Philo i. 631 Comp *ib* i 122, God gives food from Himself but "healing" through "angels" and "*words* (*logoi*)" And note that "Raphael" means "God's *Healer*"
[3] Mt iv 4, Lk iv 4, quoting Deut viii 3

God. And this John expresses in the words "*My meat is to do the will* of him that sent me."

Thus far concerning John's treatment of the tradition in Mark (omitted by Matthew and Luke) about the ministering of angels to Christ after His baptism, and about the manner in which John regards angels and their ministering. But as we have touched on other passages in the Gospels and the Epistles where angels are mentioned in connection with Jesus, it will be well here to note, at this stage, the two instances where John elsewhere mentions angels or refers to them.

§ 10. "*An angel hath spoken to him,*" *in John*

The Johannine instance of "angel" just discussed occurs in a saying of Jesus. Putting aside—as an interpolated though almost necessary explanation of the text—the words about "the angel of the Lord" who "went down at certain seasons into the pool" of Bethesda[1], we may say that the only other Johannine instances are two, one where some of "the multitude" say that "an angel hath spoken" to Jesus, and another where Mary Magdalene "beholdeth two angels in white" in the tomb of Jesus[2]. For the present we deal with the "angel" that is said to have "spoken."

It is *not* called an "angel" by the Evangelist, but a voice, "There came therefore a *voice* out of heaven." And Jesus Himself confirms this language by immediately saying to the multitude "This *voice* hath not come for my sake but for your sakes." The larger part of the people seem to have believed that it was neither a voice nor an angel: "*The multitude therefore that stood by and heard it, said that it had thundered;* others said, An angel hath spoken to him." The voice is uttered in answer to the Son's prayer, "Father, glorify thy

---

[1] See R.V marg of Jn v 2—3, giving the interpolation in full, and, as alternative names, Bethsaida, and Bethzatha.

[2] Jn xii. 29, xx 12

THE TEMPTATION

name!" It is uttered in the first person, "I have both glorified it and will glorify it again" Presumably these words were heard by the Disciple whom Jesus loved (in whose name the Gospel is written) and by other Disciples, but not by the multitude. The multitude heard a *kôl*, that is, in Hebrew, "voice" But *kôl* also means "thunder," and especially miraculous thunder *Bath Kol*, Daughter of Voice, was a recognised term, in the first century, for a miraculous "voice from heaven," a kind of substitute for that "word of the Lord" which came to Prophets in old days. This then is what "the multitude" thought they heard, and some of them called it "thunder," others the voice of an "angel[1]."

These varieties of expression bring us face to face with questions about Jewish beliefs in the first century concerning angels, and about John's exact attitude toward them—questions important for several reasons. They bear on the evidence for Christ's Resurrection, which all the Evangelists connect in some way with angels, though Luke calls them "men (*viri*)[2]" They also bear on modern thought and modern practice among Christians. May we or may we not regard the holy angel Michael, for example, as, in some sense, a Person? If so, may we look to him as in any sense a mediator, or a transmitter of our prayers, and as deserving of our worship, or adoration, in some form lower altogether than that due to God, but still a real form[3]?

Apart from the book of Daniel, which mentions Michael and Gabriel, the Hebrew Scripture appears to accept no personal angels. Resh Lakish said that the names of angels, such as Michael, Raphael, and Gabriel, were brought back by

---

[1] See "Bath Kol, or Voices from Heaven in Jewish Tradition," in *From Letter* 725—85

[2] Lk. xxiv. 4, see below, p. 191

[3] See *Jer Berach* ix 1 (Schwab p. 156) "Rabbi Judan...said that, if evil comes on men, they must not invoke Michael or Gabriel, but God who will grant the prayer, as it is written (Joel ii. 32)...."

Israel from Babylon[1]. The Scripture frequently mentions what is called by modern Hebraists "the theophanic angel[2]." But no "proper name" is either given, or suggested, to that. And there is very little to suggest that this or that angel in Scripture has individuality or a special character

In Genesis, for example, "*three men*" are described as appearing to Abraham They are addressed by him as "my lord" Afterwards they are described as "*the men*" and it is ominously said that they "looked toward Sodom." But a little later we read "*the two angels* came to Sodom[3]." In the whole of this mysterious story, no names are mentioned in Scripture But Jewish commentators say that Michael, Gabriel, and Raphael are signified They also explain, somewhat obscurely, why these celestial beings are called "*men*" to Abraham but "*angels*" to Lot. Abraham is of nobler nature than Lot. To the former therefore come the Three, including the central Figure who represents the Shechinah and who deigns His presence; and the Three, as "men," hold converse with the man, Abraham[4]. To Lot come only two, and these not as "men" to a man, but as angels of wrath to the dwellers in a sinful city. Apparently the change from "*three men*" to "*two angels*" is to be explained as follows The central "*man*," if he were named, would be called Michael; Michael represents the Shechinah, bringing the promise to Abraham. When the whole of the

---

[1] *Gen. r* on Gen xviii 1 (Wü p 225), xix 1 (Wü p 237) on both of which see Rashi

[2] Gesen. 521 *b*, giving as the first instances (1) Gen xxi 17 "the angel of Elohim," (2) *ib* xvi 7, 9, 10, 11 "the angel of Jehovah"

[3] Gen xviii. 1 foll "And the Lord appeared unto him...and he lifted up his eyes. .and lo, *three men* stood over against him...and he said My lord," *ib*. 16 "And *the men* rose up from thence and looked toward Sodom and Abraham went with them...And the Lord said...," *ib*. 33 "And *the Lord went his way*, as soon as he had finished communing with Abraham, and Abraham returned to his place (xix. 1) And *the two angels* came to Sodom at even. ."

[4] See *Gen r*, Rashi, and Philo on Gen. xviii. 1 foll and xix. 1 foll

THE TEMPTATION

mission to Abraham has been discharged (including the disclosure of the doom of Sodom which elicits Abraham's intercession) Michael, that is, the Shechinah, disappears from the Sacred Triad ("*and the Lord went his way*") Then "*the two angels,*" passing on to their several tasks, Raphael to rescue Lot, Gabriel to smite the City of Sin, "came to Sodom" in the fatal "even" That appears to be the view taken by Jewish tradition.

The Midrash on "the two angels" says "The doctrine is, One angel cannot perform two missions, and two angels cannot perform one mission." But why not? The doctrine would be explicable if an "angel" were nothing more than a movement of material creation, adapted to a special occasion and then passing away, as when the Lord "maketh winds his *angels* [and] a flaming fire his ministers[1]." But the angels sent to Abraham and to Lot appear to be of a higher order This is expressly stated by the two Jerusalem Targums which —while quoting the Rabbinical doctrine about one angel for one mission—describe these three angels, severally, as "*ministering angels*" and "*high angels*[2]" It is a reasonable inference

---

[1] Ps civ 4 where R V marg has "his angels winds" *Tehill.* ad loc. and other treatises state, as R Jochanan's view, that the message-bringing angels were made of wind, and the ministering angels were made of fire. In the former case it is suggested that "one sent," or "apostle," would be a more exact word than "angel" to represent the meaning Ps civ. 4 is referred to very frequently in the Midrash, *e g* on Gen. iii 24, where it is said that the "turnings" of the "sword" implied that they became now men, now women, now winds, now angels *Exod r* on Exod. xii 1—2 (Wu p 107) says that the angels [of fire] renew themselves daily by going back into the fire-stream whence they issued The thought of *personal* angels, with names, such as Michael, Gabriel &c, does not belong to O.T. (apart from Daniel)

[2] On Gen xviii 1, Targ. Jer I "Behold three angels in the resemblance of men were standing before him, [angels] who had been sent from the necessity of three things, because it is not possible for *a ministering angel* to be sent for more than one purpose at a time"; Jer. II "The three were sent for three things, because it is not possible that one of *the high angels* should be sent for more things than one"

from these facts, and from the language of Philo about angels, that in the first century, among orthodox Jews themselves, apart from the views of Sadducees, there would be considerable differences of usage, even where there was no definite difference of dogma.

For example, some Jews, accepting Daniel's Michael, might draw the line there. Michael, they might say, meant "Who is like God?" That is to say, "There is none like God[1]." Such a name was uniquely fit for the collective champion-name of Israel, the champion of Monotheism The Johannine Revelation, accepting this name and no other, abounds in mentions of angels in various contexts. The seven churches have seven "angels" The "seven stars" in the right hand of the Living One are these seven angels. There is an angel for each trumpet and for each phial of woe, besides warlike angels of all kinds, each for its special errand, conforming to the Jewish canon "One angel, one mission" But not one of these angels is named. One of them indeed is worshipped, at least incipiently, but the incipient attempt is immediately checked, and the Seer is twice told, "See thou do it not. I am a fellow-servant with thee and with thy brethren that hold the testimony of Jesus, worship God[2]."

Passing to the Gospels, we find that Luke alone mentions

---

[1] See *Son* **3385** *b*, on "Michael," quoting *Numb. r.* (on Numb. II 31, Wu p 20) which explains the origin of the name *Mi-cha-el*, by combining Exod xv. 11 and Deut xxxiii 26, and also quoting Rashi, on Exod xxxiii 14 "My *presence* (lit *face*) shall *go* [*with thee*]," as saying "Juxta Targum ejus [erit explicatio] non mittam amplius angelum, *ego ipse ibo*" But it might have been added that "Targum" means "The Targum of Onkelos," which has "My Shechinah shall go" The Jerusalem Targum has "*wrath*" instead of "*presence*" and interprets "go" as "go away" — "Await until the (lit) *expression of the countenance of my wrath* shall have *gone away*, and afterwards I will give thee rest" (and sim in *ib* 15 "If thy *wrath* go not *from us*"). This illustrates the remarkable diversity of Jewish language about "angels" and about their equivalents.

[2] Rev xix 10, rep. xxii. 8—9.

THE TEMPTATION

an angel by name, and the name is not Michael but Gabriel. To exclude Gabriel from a narrative of angelic visitation would of course have been illogical for any orthodox Christian writer in the first century, since Christians accepted Daniel as Scripture, and Daniel mentioned Gabriel. No Christian could censure Luke, or the author of the traditions followed by Luke, for representing the promise of the birth, first of John the Baptist, and then of Jesus, as having been made, severally, to Zacharias and to Mary, by Gabriel[1]. And "Gabriel" may have seemed more fit than "Michael," since the latter, in Daniel (as well as in Revelation) was associated with warfare, while Gabriel was the Enlightener and the Bearer of Promise[2].

Yet many first-century Christians might feel that it was unwise to encourage in the Church traditions that seemed lightly to introduce, according to the precedent in Daniel, a named and personal angel, where "the angel of the Lord," or "the angel of the Lord Jesus," or "the Spirit of Jesus," or "the Lord Jesus," seemed likely to be nearer to the truth. The multiplicity of angels in the book of Enoch and early Jewish apocrypha, and the language about them used by Paul, Peter, and the Epistle to the Hebrews, shew that the tendency—condemned above by R. Judan[3]—to "invoke Michael and Gabriel," might easily include Uriel, the Light of God, and a multitude of other divine attributes converted into persons.

These details may seem out of place in a treatise on the Fourfold Gospel. And so they would be, if we were discussing merely the words of the Four Gospels. But we are also comparing their thoughts, their tendencies, and (what we may call) their anti-tendencies. And through these details we

---

[1] Lk i. 19, 26

[2] Dan. viii. 16, ix 21 Jerome says that the man that says to Gabriel "Make this man understand" is called Michael by the Jews (*Son* **3374** *c*)

[3] See above, p 181, n. 3.

THE TEMPTATION

may perceive an "anti-tendency," on the subject of angels, in the doctrine of the Fourth Gospel at its outset. It teaches us two definitely distinct truths, in the promise of Jesus (recently and frequently quoted above) that we shall see the angels of God ascending and descending upon the Son of Man[1]. One truth is that the motion of the angels depends on the Son of Man. The other truth is that the angels ascend as well as descend, and apparently ascend before they descend. They are the higher thoughts and wishes of the human soul, drawn up from earth to heaven by the Spirit of the Son of Man as clouds of aspiration and prayer, and coming down from heaven to earth by the same Spirit transmuted into showers of blessing.

In the Johannine narrative of the Voice from Heaven, it appears at first sight as though the Son of Man Himself were aspiring or praying on His own account. But looking more closely we see it is not on His own account. We are on the point of beholding a great crisis or judgment—a judgment of "this world[2]" The Pharisees themselves have just said about Jesus, "The world is gone after him[3]" Jesus says, "Now shall the prince of this world be cast out." Between these two utterances we are to imagine the Gentile "world," represented by "certain Greeks"—timidly and gradually, and, as it were through intercessors—drawing near to the Intercessor Himself[4] The Intercessor recognises the condition that attends His intercession· "The hour is come that the Son of Man should be glorified" And "to be glorified" means to die—that His death may bring forth the fruit of life for others: "Except a grain of wheat fall into the earth

---

[1] Jn i. 51

[2] Comp. Jn xii 31 "Now is the *judgment* of this world, now shall the prince of this world be cast out."

[3] Jn xii 19

[4] Jn xii. 21—2 " they came to Philip...saying, Sir, we would see Jesus ; Philip cometh and telleth Andrew ; Andrew cometh, and Philip, and they tell Jesus "

THE TEMPTATION

and die, it abideth by itself, alone; but if it die, it beareth much fruit[1]"

---

[1] Jn xii 23—4 "fruit" This is not the place to discuss the extent to which the Johannine narrative at this point may be regarded as historical That must be deferred till we come to Mark-Matthew's miracle, and Luke's parable, of the Fig-tree But it may be said here that the word "*fruit*" suggests a clue to the interpretation of all the four Gospels Christ's thoughts were bent on the Vine or Fig-tree of Israel "The Lord shewed me," says Jeremiah (xxiv 1) "and behold, two baskets of figs, set before the temple of the Lord" One of these contained good figs, and represented those who were to be redeemed of Israel But Amos, who saw a similar vision of (Am. viii 1 foll) "summer fruit," discerned nothing except that "the end is come"

Jesus was at this time coming to the Fig-tree of Israel to seek fruit from the tree Or, as the parable of the Vineyard (Mk xii 1 foll, Mt xxi 33 foll, Lk xx 9 foll) puts it, He was the heir, seeking its fruits from the rebellious Vinedressers. The Vineyard (say the Synoptists) was to be taken from its present vinedressers and to be "given to others" According to John, this future giving to others was as it were enacted by Christ's reception of (Jn xii 20 foll) "Greeks." Jesus first recognised them as the promise of the "fruit" that was to spring from the "dying" of "the grain of wheat", then He heard a Voice from heaven proclaiming that God would "glorify" His "name" both in the dying and in the bearing of fruit

Those who urge that the narrative of the Fourth Gospel is "not historical" must surely admit that it is closer to history than the Mark-Matthew parallel narrative of the Withering of the Fig-tree Perhaps Luke is right in saying that the Coming of the Lord to seek fruit from the Fig-tree was one of Christ's parables But on the other hand Luke may have softened down into a mere parable a vision of Jesus, imparted by Him to His disciples If Paul (Acts xxii 17—21), while he prayed in the temple, "fell into a trance," and "saw" the Lord bidding him "go far hence unto the Gentiles," why should not Jesus have had a vision, and uttered a prayer, in such circumstances as to make bystanders regard Him, in various ways, as receiving an answer from above, like the Jewish Bath Kol—a common phenomenon in the belief of Jews of the first century? At all events John appears to be very far from spinning a fiction of his own He may possibly be recording a vision of the beloved Disciple. But the facts suggest that he is recording a vision seen by Jesus, upon which Mark has based a portentous miracle omitted (or paraphrased) by Luke The conception of a Prophet's vision of the Harvest may be illustrated by Jn iv 35 "Lift up your eyes and look on the fields" (see *Joh Gr.* **2230** (ii)—(iii)) interpreted spiritually

It is in the moment of this balancing of these two visions —the vision of "death" for Himself and the vision of "fruit" for others—that there comes upon the Lord Jesus "a trouble" of the "soul," and a thought-cloud, which just rises up, only to be dispelled by the Spirit · "What shall I say? Father, save me from this hour? [Nay] but for this cause came I, unto this hour"—and then the prayer, "Father, glorify thy name." And as His prayer goes up, the answer comes down "I have both glorified it and will glorify it again[1]." By telling us that the multitude thought, some that this voice was "thunder," others that it was the voice of an "angel," the Evangelist suggests to us the conclusion that the theory of an "angel" was not much more spiritual or adequate than the theory of "thunder." It was the Father Himself who spoke. In the case of other pious sons of man, the disciples whom the Lord called His "little ones," it might be adequately said that their prayers went up and the answers came down as angels on the Son of Man. But it could not be adequately said concerning the prayer of the Son of Man Himself. No "voice of an angel" could reply to Him No "angel" could strengthen Him To suppose such a thing was a popular delusion

But it may be urged that Matthew himself represents Jesus as at all events contemplating the possibility of being strengthened by angels, in the words · "Or thinkest thou that I am not able to beseech my Father, and he will place by my side at this moment more than twelve legions of angels—how then could the scriptures be fulfilled...[2]?" This passage, though peculiar to Matthew, will come before us again in the discussion of the Fourfold Gospel on Christ's arrest. But here we may note that Matthew's own context, and the parallels in the other three Gospels, prove that we have here a case of Johannine intervention For in this passage a saying of

---

[1] Jn xii 27–8   [2] Mt xxvi. 53–4

THE TEMPTATION

Christ about "*fulfilment*" has been (1) obscurely expressed by Mark, (2) repeated in two versions—the first of which is given above, the second in the note below—by Matthew, (3) omitted by Luke, (4) repeated in quite a different context by John[1]

In due course it will be shewn that Matthew's first version given above was probably one of two attempts to explain some obscure sentence containing the words " took" and " *but on the other hand that it might be fulfilled*" It regarded the thought as being as follows, " Ye took me not before, [*and ye should not take me now, thanks to my Father's legions of angels, were it not that I knew my hour to have arrived*], but [*I ask for no legions and I surrender myself*] that the scriptures might be fulfilled " Thus, reserving "ye took me not" for the second utterance (" in that hour Jesus said ") Matthew enlarged, in

---

[1] Compare —

Mk xiv 49	Mt xxvi 55—6	Lk xxii. 53	Jn xviii 8—9
I was daily with you ..and ye took me not But (ἀλλὰ) [ ]—*that the scriptures might be fulfilled.*	I sat daily and ye took me not. But (δέ) all this is come to pass *that the scriptures of the prophets might be fulfilled*	I was daily with you .. ye stretched not forth your hands against me But (ἀλλὰ) this is your hour, and the power of darkness	Suffer these to depart—*that there might be fulfilled the word that he spake,* Those whom thou hast given me I lost not one of them.

John apparently interpreted the ἀλλά in Mark as implying a changed condition of things (*Joh Gr* 2111—2), and his paraphrastic expansion indicates that he had some thought of this kind

" Jesus said ' Ye took me not in times past, *but now*— ' Then He broke off But He completed His sentence by what He did. He meant ' But now the time has come that I should complete my sacrifice for my disciples.' And He did complete it by going forward to meet the soldiers in order that He might fulfil the scriptures, because His hour was come, and in order that He might begin the saving of the world by saving His disciples "

John probably took the Marcan "*that might be fulfilled*" as a comment of the Evangelist, regarding Jesus Himself as *acting*, but not as *mentioning* " fulfilment "

the first utterance, on the "twelve legions of angels[1]." It is doubtful whether John would have accepted these words about angels as Christ's, but if he did, he would probably have said with Origen that He uttered them "on a level with the notions of Peter," who was desirous of helping Him with the sword, "For the angels have more need of the help of the Only-begotten Son of God than He has of theirs[2]."

Concluding this investigation into the second Johannine mention of "angel," we find that the Evangelist consistently, though indirectly, subordinates the thought of angelic ministration, and leads his readers to be on their guard against it as a popular but sometimes erroneous method of expression—always erroneous if it gave to angels any individuality that would separate them from the Person of the Son of Man.

§ 11. *"Angels," at the tomb of Jesus, in John*

We now pass to the third and most difficult of the Johannine mentions of angels, the one connected with Christ's Resurrection. By "difficult," we do not refer to the fact that the Johannine narrative is difficult to reconcile with that of

---

[1] Comp Jn xviii 36 "If my kingdom were from this world, my servants would fight"

The use of ἀλλά in Mark and Luke indicates that they took all the words to be Christ's But Matthew's use of δέ, in his second version—and also his use of γέγονε (*Joh Gr* **2478** *a*)—shews that he took the clause about "fulfilment," in his second version, to be evangelistic comment In his first version, Matthew shews that the words about fulfilment are Christ's by making them interrogative ("How then could the scriptures be fulfilled?"). An explanatory gloss attached to the obscure words "But on the other hand, in order that the scriptures might be fulfilled," might run thus, in Hebrew or Greek "Now what He meant was—for He had Peter in His mind—Thinkest thou, O Peter, that I cannot pray to the Father for twelve legions of angels instead of thy single sword? But *on the other hand* [*I must not*, for, *if I did*] *How could the scriptures be fulfilled?*" This gloss, with a little smoothing, appears to have become part of Matthew's text. On "*meant*," lit "*said*," see Indices to *Son* and *Light*

[2] Origen on Mt xxvi 53 *ad loc*.

THE TEMPTATION

Mark (about "a young man...in a white robe") and that of Matthew (about "an angel") and that of Luke (about "two men[1]"). Those difficulties—which must be reserved till we deal with them in their order—extend to much that the angels say and do, but not (so far, at all events, as concerns Mark and Matthew) to the utterance of the word RISEN[2]. On the other hand the angels in John neither say "He is risen" nor make any announcement of the Resurrection. They make no statement at all. They simply ask a question "Woman, why weepest thou[3]?" We are tempted to say, "They are practically mutes." Surely this is a difficulty in the Fourth Gospel even when taken by itself, apart from the Three.

It may be asserted that the angels meant "Woman, weep not," and that they assumed that Mary would understand the inference "He is not dead, but is risen[4]." But Mary does not understand it. She does not say, "I do not believe it." She replies in such a way as to shew that it had not even entered into her mind. "Because they have taken away my Lord and I know not where they have laid him." Such an assertion is also inconsistent with what follows, where Jesus, unrecognised, repeats "Woman, why weepest thou? Whom seekest thou[5]?"

---

[1] Mk xvi. 5, Mt xxviii. 2 foll., Lk xxiv. 4. On "men" and "angels" interchanged in Genesis, see above, pp. 182—3.

[2] Mk xvi. 6 ἠγέρθη, οὐκ ἔστιν ὧδε, Mt xxviii. 6 οὐκ ἔστιν ὧδε, ἠγέρθη γάρ., Lk xxiv. 6 [[οὐκ ἔστιν ὧδε, ἀλλὰ ἠγέρθη]] The bracketed words in Luke are now known to be retained by SS. John, if he thought Luke had omitted the Marcan "risen," was bound (by the Rule of Johannine Intervention) to insert something corresponding to it. But he has not done so. The first Johannine announcement of the Resurrection is not like Lk. xxiv. 34 "*The Lord is risen indeed* and appeared unto Simon." It is (Jn xx. 18) "*I have seen the Lord*." The facts slightly favour the conclusion that John accepted the ancient Lucan tradition as a genuine part of Luke.

[3] Jn xx. 13.

[4] Comp. Mk v. 39 "*Why* make ye much ado and *weep?*" Lk. viii. 52 "*Weep not*." Both add "she is not dead but sleepeth."

[5] The risen Saviour utters, as almost His first words, a question very much like His first utterance to His first converts (Jn i. 38) "What seek ye?" See *Introductory Volume*, p. 142 foll.

THE TEMPTATION

For Mary's reply, "Tell me where thou hast laid him," shews that she is still in total darkness. What, then, is the use of it all—this repeated questioning, following the continued weeping? It seems intended to draw out from Mary the most passionate expression of her utter hopelessness and despair In contrast with the unnamed disciple, who, along with Peter, has gone into the empty tomb and has seen "the linen cloths" and "the napkin," and has "believed," Mary shews not a vestige of belief or hope. She is absorbed in the thought of Christ's dead body, and of the outrage that might be done to "him," the dead helpless creature whom "they have taken away," but who is still "Lord" to her "Tell me where thou hast laid him and I will take him away[1]."

These angels also raise this further question, "Why did not the two disciples see them on entering the tomb just before? Were they there, but invisible? Or did they come down in the interval between the departure of the disciples "unto their own home" and the "looking" of Mary "into the tomb[2]?" Lastly, after Mary has answered the question of the angels, why does she, without cause specified, turn her back upon them: "When she had thus said, she turned herself back and beholdeth Jesus standing?"

As regards this last point, the explanation of Chrysostom is, that immediately after Mary's despairing answer to the angels, Jesus suddenly appears behind Mary's back The angels recognise Him with visible amazement, and Mary, turning suddenly round to see what causes it, sees Jesus but does not recognise Him Presumably, the angels now disappear, having done their work. At all events they are not mentioned again.

---

[1] Jn xx 13—15 "*they have taken away my Lord.. away*"

[2] Jn xx. 10—12 "So the disciples went away again unto their own home But Mary was standing without at the tomb weeping so, as she wept, she stooped and looked into the tomb; and she beholdeth two angels in white sitting, one at the head, and one at the feet, where the body of Jesus had lain"

THE TEMPTATION

This explanation, as we have seen above (p 175, n. 2), probably goes back to Clement of Alexandria, and Chrysostom may not have done justice to it. To us, though it must necessarily seem farfetched, it will be of use if it protects us from assuming that the Fourth Evangelist is indulging in self-willed fiction, deviating in a wild and purposeless fashion from the Synoptists. According to this ancient view, the angels may be said to see the risen Saviour along with Mary, not to announce His rising to Mary And their presence in the tomb to Mary's eyes, but not to the eyes of the disciples who had previously entered, may be explained, on Johannine principles, by that law which regulates the ascent and descent of angels on the Son of Man Prayers are angels. But tears, too, are angels. Most of all, perhaps, are they angels when they express an aspiration that is loving as well as passionate, even when it is no more than " O, that it might have been !" As the hopeless tears of Mary the sister of Lazarus brought tears from the eyes of Jesus and prepared the way for the raising of Lazarus from the dead, so the hopeless tears of Mary Magdalene expressing by their visible fall the invisible ascent of her passionate love, brought down to aid her weakness a revelation of angels through whom came the revelation of her Lord Himself[1]. The beloved Disciple did not need this He " believed " without it. But would the world have believed without it?

To this question the Fourth Evangelist appears to give an indirect reply in the negative, "No, it would not have believed "

---

[1] What are we to suppose as to the attitude of Peter, and the other disciple (who "believed"), to Mary? Did they attempt to console her and to help her to believe? When they turned away, leaving her at the sepulchre, did their hearts sorrow for her, and perhaps send up prayers for her? If they did, did John see any connection between the heart-prayers going up and the angels coming down? To many the thought of such a connection will seem ridiculous But to John (1 51) such " ascending" and " descending" might seem no more ridiculous than the law of gravitation seems to us.

THE TEMPTATION

He confirms the ancient tradition that "when Jesus was risen early on the first day of the week, he appeared first to Mary Magdalene, from whom he had cast out seven devils[1]." He did not "appear first" to the beloved Disciple. The Disciple "came" first to the Tomb. But Peter "entered" first. The Disciple was the first to "believe." But Mary was the first to "see." It was so ordained. The words of Mary to the disciples, "*I have seen* the Lord," prepared them also for "seeing," and their "seeing" prepared the way for the fulfilment of the saying "Blessed are they that have *not seen* and yet have *believed*[2]." The part played by angels in bringing about this consummation was quite subordinated to divinely human influences. No Michael, Gabriel, or Raphael intervened. Heart spoke to heart—the appeal of the human heart of loving Sorrow bringing down the response from the divine heart of loving Pity.

When we come, in due course, to the narrative of the Resurrection, an attempt will be made to compare the Johannine with the Synoptic details of the angelic manifestations at the tomb. In the present section we have been merely examining the attitude of the Fourth Gospel toward angels in the narrative of the Resurrection, with the view of comparing it with the attitude of the same Gospel toward angels elsewhere. The conclusion arrived at is, that here, as elsewhere, it subordinates angels so completely to the Son of Man as to leave them very little trace of a separate and personal nature.

§ 12. "*Temptation*," *implied in John*

The Johannine conception of "temptation," so far as it could be applied to Christ, may be in the first place illustrated negatively, by reference to the first of the three Temptations mentioned by Matthew and Luke—to turn stones into bread. Matthew says that, before this temptation came, Jesus had

---

[1] Mk [xvi. 9]   [2] Jn xx. 29

THE TEMPTATION

"fasted forty days and forty nights." Luke, avoiding the word "fasting," says that (like Moses on Mount Sinai)[1] Jesus "did eat nothing in those days." Both agree that "afterward," or "when they [*i.e.* the days] were completed," "he hungered." Then came Satan saying in effect, "If thou art Son of God, satisfy thy hunger by turning stones to bread."

John practically, though indirectly, denies this. He knew that Moses did not "fast," but, as Philo says[2], was supplied with food by God during the forty days and nights on Mount Sinai or Horeb. He knew also that Elijah did not "fast," but was similarly strengthened by divine food during his journey of forty days and nights to the same mountain. And therefore he tells us elsewhere that Jesus could not "fast." He puts it dramatically. The disciples, he says, brought Jesus food that they had "bought." But Jesus had already the food that Isaiah declares to be without price. His food, the food of the Son, was "to do the will" of the Father[3]. To say to Jesus "Satisfy thine own hunger" would have been to put Him below the level of Moses and Elijah. That this was the temptation addressed to Him we may safely deny.

It is not so safe to affirm. But we may be sure that the temptation was to do something for others, not for Himself. It may have been to bring men nearer to God in some way that was not in accordance with God's will—to attempt, perhaps, to coerce them into believing in the Father by means of signs and wonders wrought by the Son. "Hear now, ye rebels," said Moses and Aaron to their brethren, "shall we bring you forth water out of this rock?" They brought it. But the Lord reproved them. "Ye believed not in me, to sanctify me in the eyes of the children of Israel[4]." Perhaps

---

[1] Exod. xxxiv. 28   [2] See Philo ii. 146
[3] Jn iv. 8 "his disciples were gone away into the city to buy food," *ib.* 31 "Rabbi, eat," *ib.* 32 "I have meat to eat that ye know not," *ib.* 34 "my meat is to do the will of him that sent me."
[4] Numb. xx. 10—12

THE TEMPTATION

Jesus, in His vision, was tempted to repeat the error of Moses—to do for men by coercion the divine good that God Himself will not and cannot do for them without their co-operant aid. That, at least, is an intelligible temptation that might appeal even to one greater than Moses.

But it may be said "Jesus *did*, in effect, perform this very miracle for the Five Thousand." That miracle, when discussed hereafter, will be shewn to be something different from the creation of bread out of stone. In some respects, though on a much larger scale, it is like the miracle of the widow's oil and flour wrought by Elijah In the Old Testament, the widow gives, God multiplies Somewhat similarly in the New, Jesus says to the Twelve "Give ye them to eat[1]." They give—all that they have. God multiplies for the multitude, and returns to the Twelve, twelve basketsful to the Twelve. But that (John would probably say) was bread of a peculiar kind. It was not "bought" True, Jesus mentioned the word "buy" But that was only in gentle irony to Philip:— "Whence are we to buy bread—that kind of bread which the Twelve went to buy for me near Sychar[2], and which I would not eat?" The bread in that "sign" meant the bread "without money and without price," the bread that no money can "buy," the bread that man gives to man when he "draws out his soul to the hungry[3]" in pity and compassion, following, at a distance, in the footsteps of the Son of Man. After the sign, Jesus reproached some of those who had partaken of the food with following Him in the belief that the sign implied the power of the Messiah to give them "loaves and fishes" at will. Reproving their error, He told them that the moral of it

---

[1] Mk vi 37, Mt xiv 16, Lk ix 13 In the Feeding of the Four Thousand this clause is omitted, but Jesus says (Mk viii. 2, Mt xv 32) "I have compassion on the multitude "

[2] Jn iv 8 ἀγοράσωσιν On the triple use of this word in John, and on the Jewish associations with it, see *Son* **3445** *a—b*

[3] Is lviii 10

was that they were to "work," presumably in acts of kindness to their brethren like the Father's acts of kindness to His children—for "the food that abideth unto eternal life[1]"

Passing to the temptation of the pinnacle ("cast thyself down") we perceive that it might represent in a vision such an appeal as might present itself to Jesus when He cleansed the Temple, and on other occasions when He imperilled His life before His "hour" had come. The state of the Temple was what a prophet might describe as a "reproach" to the living God. The Psalmist said "The zeal of thine house hath eaten me up, and the reproaches of them that reproach thee are fallen upon me[2]" Paul expressly connects the last part of this passage with Christ's conduct. "We that are strong," he says, "ought to bear the infirmities of the weak and not to please ourselves.... Christ also pleased not himself, but as it is written, '*The reproaches of them that reproached thee are fallen upon me*'." John, in his account of the cleansing of the Temple, does not indeed say that Jesus used the Psalmist's words, but he says, in connection with it, that His disciples called to mind a part of the Psalmist's utterance. "They remembered that it was written '*The zeal of thine house shall eat me up*'" It was a noble temptation for a Son of God to rush into battle, taking up arms against an overwhelming avalanche of "reproach" directed against His Father, and attempting to destroy it by coercion, although it was not the Father's will that it should be destroyed in that way or at that time[3]

---

[1] Jn vi 26—7

[2] Ps lxix 9, of which Jn ii 17 quotes the first half, and Rom xv 1—3 the second. Whenever Israel was humiliated or desolated by idolaters so that their conquerors could say, "Where is now thy God?" the nation was said to have become "*a reproach*" Comp Ps lxxix. 4 "We are become a *reproach* to our neighbours," *ib* 12 "render to our neighbours. their *reproach* wherewith they have *reproached* thee, O Lord,"—a psalm which begins with lamentation over the "temple" as "defiled" But the Temple, defiled by its priests, was a still greater "*reproach*" than when defiled by conquerors

[3] Comp Jn vii 3—5 "His brethren therefore said unto him, Depart

THE TEMPTATION

Applying the same altruistic interpretation to the temptation to bow down to Satan for the sake of receiving "all the kingdoms of the earth," we may possibly be right in finding some allusion to it in the statement, peculiar to John, that after the Feeding of the Five Thousand, Jesus withdrew into the mountain, because He perceived that the multitude desired "to come and take him by force to make him king[1]" Not for His own sake, but for the sake of the uplifting of the ensign of righteousness, and the worship of the one true God, there might present itself (so some might think) a temptation to conquer the kings of the earth by becoming one of them, conforming to the ways of "the ruler of this (*or*, the) world[2]"

But we must go far away from Matthew's and Luke's Temptations in the wilderness if we wish to understand what John regarded as the main source of trial and trouble to Jesus. It has been touched on in the Introductory Volume, where the threefold mention of Christ's "trouble" was dealt with. But it appears also in His sense of the mystery of evil—an

---

hence, and go into Judaea, that thy disciples also may behold thy works which thou doest For no man doeth anything in secret, and himself seeketh to be known openly. If thou doest these things, manifest thyself to the world. For even his brethren did not believe on him" These words, following *ib.* vii 1 " he would not walk in Judaea, because the Jews sought to kill him," present, in a very acute form, the temptation to face peril before the time Jesus replies "My time is not yet come "

[1] Jn vi 15.
[2] John alone combines ἄρχων and κόσμος, xii 31, xiv. 30, xvi 11— probably with allusion to the Jewish title adopted into Hebrew as *Cosmocrator* (on which s. Levy, as also on "Samael," and on the Hebraized *Archôn*). The Johannine feeling against the kings of the earth (as compared with the Good Shepherd) may come before us again when we consider Mk x 42 ἄρχειν, with gen. unique in N T. (according to Moulton's Concordance) except Rom xv. 12 quoting Is. xi. 10 (but prob we should add Rev i. 5 ὁ ἄρχων τῶν βασιλέων τῆς γῆς, for ὁ ἄρχων, if noun, would be subordinate to ὁ βασιλεύς) It is doubtful whether John would have regarded the appeal of earthly royalty or dominion as constituting any kind of temptation to Jesus He despises it in the spirit of Epictetus, as well as in consistency with Synoptic doctrine about (Mk x 42) "supposed rulers "

THE TEMPTATION

evil that must not be constrained to be good—and in His consciousness of a terrible responsibility for what He repeatedly calls, in prayer to the Father, "all that thou hast given to me" He means the disciples, the little nucleus of the Church. Once, with other waverers, they, too, shew signs of wavering, and He exclaims "Do ye, too, desire to depart?" When Peter protests fidelity He replies, emphasizing His own responsibility, "*Was it not I*[1] that chose you, the Twelve? And one of you is a devil." Neither here, nor afterwards, is Jesus recorded as having made any direct attempt—except perhaps by the gift of the bread and wine, given that it might either cure or kill—to divert Judas from his treachery. And the treachery was (it is implied) the bitterest of His three "troubles." It troubled Him "in the Spirit[2]."

Christ's sense of His powerlessness to coerce makes the long Johannine account of His last discourse with the disciples, and His last prayer to the Father, much more intelligible, and much more suggestive of the nature of His final trial or (what the Synoptists would call) "temptation." His very Resurrection—so far as we read it in the Fourth Gospel, and so far as it could help the Disciples from whom He was about to be parted—depended, not on Himself alone, but on His disciples too, and on their co-operation. He could not compel them to see Him, even when He had risen, unless they loved Him.

Mary does not see Him until she weeps. When she sees Him she does not recognise Him until He calls her by her name. Afterwards, on the shore of Gennesaret, the fishermen Disciples do not recognise Him until the beloved Disciple says "It is the Lord." Before this, Judas not Iscariot has

---

[1] Jn vi 70 οὐκ ἐγώ. ἐξελεξάμην. The insertion of ἐγώ differentiates this from the ordinary "Did-I-not," where ἐγώ is omitted, as in Gen xxix. 25, Numb. xxii 37, 1 K ii 42, xxii 18, 2 K iv 28, 2 Chr xviii 17. Jesus takes the responsibility upon Himself with emphasis.

[2] See *Introduction*, pp 161—2

asked, perplexed, "Lord, what is come to pass that thou wilt manifest thyself unto us and not unto the world?" and the answer prefixes the unalterable condition "*If a man love me*[1]."

The other Judas, Judas Iscariot, loves darkness rather than light, so that he shrinks back repelled from the Light of the world. He may be said to be harmed by it—yes, even "destroyed," for it is worth noting that the same Greek word means both "I have lost" and "I have destroyed", and the Evangelist seems determined to bring before us, in its most perplexing aspect, the insoluble problem of God's responsibility for "destroying" a soul. It comes before us as follows.

In order to save the Eleven Apostles from the Roman soldiers Jesus is represented as saying "Let these go their way" It is added that He said this "that the word might be fulfilled which he spake, 'Of those whom thou hast given me *I have lost* (lit. *destroyed*) not one[2]." This seems to point back to Christ's prayer to the Father, for those whom He calls "those whom thou hast given me", concerning whom He says "I guarded them...and *not one of them was destroyed* —save-only the son of *destruction*, that the scripture might be fulfilled[3]." Do these two passages hint at a distinction between "He *was destroyed*" and "I *destroyed* him"? Are we to infer the meaning "He destroyed himself, Jesus did not destroy him"? Origen seems to say that there is such a distinction and inference[4]. But it is very doubtful. More probably the

---

[1] Jn xiv. 23   [2] Jn xviii 9 "I have lost," ἀπώλεσα.
[3] Jn xvii 12 οὐδεὶς ἐξ αὐτῶν ἀπώλετο εἰ μὴ ὁ υἱὸς τῆς ἀπωλείας, ἵνα ἡ γραφὴ πληρωθῇ
[4] See *Comm Rom* ii. 8 (Lomm vi 103—4), where, among passages about "the lost," Origen quotes Lk xv 8—10 "drachma quae perierat" (thus avoiding "perdidit" or "perdidi") and Mt xv 24 "oves perditas," on which he notes "'perditas,' *non 'quas perdiderat'*" He also says "In his omnibus nusquam Deus aliquem dicitur *perdidisse*... Et cum ipse Dominus dicit, (Jn xvii 12) 'Omnes,' inquit, 'quos dedisti mihi, servavi, et *nullus ex iis periit*' non dixit '*nullum ex iis perdidi*'" This is a strange statement in view of Jn xviii 9 "*neminem ex his perdidi*" The latter text Origen nowhere quotes

Evangelist means that Judas was never "given" to Jesus. He never belonged to that band of whom Jesus said, after the Feeding of the Five Thousand, "This is the will of him that sent me, that of *all that which he hath given me I should lose* (lit *destroy*) *nothing..* ¹." This view is confirmed by the statement—which follows soon afterwards—that Jesus "knew from the beginning...who it was that should betray him," and that He "spake of Judas" when He said "Was it not I that chose you, the twelve, and one of you is a devil²?"

Why, then, did Jesus "choose" Judas? The Evangelist seems to suggest as the answer that it was an instance of what we should call "an error of judgment" on the part of the incarnate Son, permitted by the Father. For this "error" the Son takes the sole responsibility ("Was it not I?"). It turned out to be a part of the foreordained Redemption. But it was a part, and may well have been the heaviest part, of the burdens that Jesus took, or brought, upon Himself, in bearing the sins and carrying the iniquities of mankind. And the heaviest part of this heavy burden is, that it suggests a thought—to be suppressed as soon as suggested—of an error of some kind in the Father Himself

The quotations given above may help to teach us something of the nature of Christ's deepest "temptation." It was perhaps the strain of bearing up against the superincumbent pressure of a world that seemed bent on self-destruction. God "loved the world" and gave His Son that "everyone that believed in him might not be destroyed" The Son was not sent to judge the world, He came to save it³ Yet "the ruler of the world"—if the world was represented by Judas "the son of destruction"—seemed able to snatch the world victoriously out of His hands, "the wolf" prevailing over "the good shepherd⁴."

---

¹ Jn vi 39   ² Jn vi 64, 70, 71   ³ Jn iii 16—17
⁴ See *From Letter* **960** quoting *Acts of John* § 6 where "another like Jesus," a Tempter, comes down and says to Him, "Jesus, those whom

THE TEMPTATION

"This is the judgment," says the Evangelist, "that the light hath come into the world and men loved the darkness rather than the light because their deeds were evil[1]."

When a great Reformer recognises the apparent rottenness of that which he is attempting to reform, what is he tempted to do? Moses, when Israel went wrong, was "exceedingly terrified"—not for his own sake but for Israel's—and broke the Tables of the Law[2]. Elijah, finding his reformation by the sword a failure, complained against Israel as if he were the only faithful Israelite left, and received a rebuke and a successor[3]. The last thoughts of Jesus on the night before the Crucifixion, as represented by the Fourth Gospel at much greater length than by the Three, reveal Him as not yielding to the temptations of blind optimism or faithless pessimism, but as feeling at once the weakness and the strength that awaited His disciples.

Their weakness He seems to bear as His own, with a passionate tension of affectionate anticipation like that of an anxious mother. But their strength, too, he realises, the underlying and conquering strength of the love with which—without what this world calls constraint—He has constrained them to love Him. So confident is He in the strength of this love that the prayer for the preservation of the disciples passes away at its close into an utterance of exultation, because He will be ever in the Disciples and the Disciples in Him,

---

thou hast chosen do still not believe in thee." On Isaiah xxv. 7 ("the covering . the veil") the Targum gives personifications . "And there shall be cast down in that mountain the countenance of *the ruler who is ruler over all the peoples* and the countenance of *the king that reigns over all the kingdoms.*"

[1] Jn iii. 19
[2] See *Light* **3731** *g* on the correct explanation of Heb. xii. 21
[3] 1 K xix 10--18 The elemental forces through which Elijah is rebuked are called by the Targum angels Moses on Mount Horeb is represented by some traditions as being terrified by angels of wrath. See *Notes*, *Son*, and *Light* (Indices "Angels").

through their knowledge of the name of Him who is the Eternal Love : " I made known unto them thy name, and will make it known ; that the love wherewith thou lovedst me may be in them, and I in them[1]."

[1] Jn xvii. 26.

CHAPTER VI

JOURNEYING INTO GALILEE[1]

THIS Chapter will cover comparatively little Synoptic, but much Johannine ground. It will endeavour to shew that if the Fourth Gospel is right, the Three have omitted altogether the first of two visits to Galilee, and have given a wrong impression about the second. In the second visit, Jesus journeyed to Galilee from Judaea, where He had been preaching. Mark has omitted all mention of any preaching in Judaea. Luke, in the correct text of his Gospel (which however our Revised Version has given only in the margin), just mentions it, but does no more. John, on the other hand, gives full details of Christ's acts and sayings in Judaea, while John the Baptist was still free, thus giving an entirely different impression of that second visit to Galilee which took place just before the Baptist's arrest, and which would naturally be regarded by readers of Mark as synchronizing with the beginning of Christ's public career

---

§ 1. *Mark's account*

All the Synoptists describe a journey into Galilee immediately after their descriptions of the Temptation. And, if Mark—inserting his customary "and straightway," which

---

[1] Mk 1 14 καὶ μετὰ τὸ παραδοθῆναι τὸν Ἰωάνην ἦλθεν ὁ Ἰησοῦς εἰς τὴν Γαλιλαίαν (where many but inferior authorities read δέ for καί and R V. has "now"), Mt iv. 12 ἀκούσας δὲ ὅτι Ἰωάνης παρεδόθη, ἀνεχώρησεν εἰς τὴν Γαλιλαίαν, Lk. iv. 14 καὶ ὑπέστρεψεν ὁ Ἰησοῦς ἐν τῇ δυνάμει τοῦ πνεύματος εἰς τὴν Γαλιλαίαν.

occurs no less than eleven times in his first chapter—had written "And the angels were ministering to him *And straightway* Jesus came into Galilee preaching," we might then have safely inferred that he regarded the journey as following the Temptation, if not quite immediately, at all events after no long interval. But, instead of "and straightway," Mark has, "*And after John had been delivered up.*"

This leaves us free to suppose that an interval, and even a considerable interval, elapsed between the end of the Temptation and the beginning of the journey, during which interval John was delivered up Mark may mean that Jesus remained silent till John's arrest. That event—leaving John's place vacant and his work unfinished—might seem to demand that his successor should not delay Or Mark may mean that, after John had been delivered up, Jesus—who had been hitherto preaching the gospel and baptizing in Judaea or beyond Jordan (perhaps in company with John)—now for the first time brought the gospel into Galilee. By "Mark" we designate the text of Mark's Gospel. The writer of the text, the person whom we call Mark, may have had neither of these two meanings. He may have simply noted down the tradition that came to him, and may have formed no opinion about the things that the text omitted, or the interval that the text, at this point, seemed to imply

In any case, Mark leaves us in doubt as to the length of the interval—if there was an interval. Mark also leaves us in doubt, not only as to when and where Jesus began His public work, and whence He came into Galilee, but even as to the motive of His coming Did He come to escape from Antipas who had arrested John? That would be strange, since Antipas was Tetrarch of Galilee. Did He come in order to fulfil prophecy about "Galilee of the nations"? Or did some special need of the gospel in Galilee cause Jesus to begin His preaching in that province? All these questions Mark leaves unanswered.

§ 2. *Matthew's account*

As to one of these doubtful points in Mark, the motive of Christ's journey, Matthew indirectly supplies an answer. He does not say, with Mark, "*After* John had been delivered up," but "*Having heard* that John had been delivered up[1]." Matthew also substitutes "withdrew" for Mark's "came." "Withdraw," a rare word in LXX and mostly implying fear or flight, and never used by Luke, is used once by Mark to describe Christ as withdrawing from the plots of the Herodians; and Matthew uses it not only there but also in many other passages, probably to illustrate a prophecy (which he alone quotes) about the Messiah's retiring disposition[2]. In the present passage Matthew adds "And, giving up his abode in Nazareth, he came and dwelt in Capernaum which is by the sea in the borders of Zebulun and Naphtali." The reason for adding these geographical details appears immediately in a quotation, "That it might be fulfilled which was spoken by Isaiah the prophet, saying, The land of Zebulun and the land of Naphtali, [by the] way of the sea, beyond Jordan, Galilee of the nations; the people that sat in darkness saw a great light...[3]." In other words Matthew desires to shew that Christ's coming to Galilee, and to this particular city of Galilee, when He

---

[1] Mt. iv. 12 ἀκούσας δέ. That implies "*because* John had been delivered up." See 2 K. ix 13 "(*lit.*) and (but R V then) they hasted," LXX "and *hearing it* they hasted," Esth. iv. 4 "and the queen was grieved," LXX "and *hearing it* . she was troubled" (comp Gen xxxix 18) In Josh. ix 11, where Heb. and R.V. have "*and*," A.V. has "*wherefore*," and LXX "*and having heard it.*" The paraphrases of A V. and LXX proceed from a desire to shew that the Heb. means, not merely *sequence* of facts, but also *consequence* of purpose arising from the influence of a *fact* upon a *person*. So here, Matthew means that Christ's action was taken, not merely "*after*" the Baptist's arrest, but also after it reached His ears so that it could influence His action.

[2] Mk iii 7 ἀνεχώρησεν is parall. to Mt xii 15 "withdrew from thence," which is followed by (xii. 19) a prophecy from Is. xlii. 1—3 ("...neither shall anyone hear his voice in the streets")

[3] Mt. iv. 14—16 quoting Is. ix. 1—2.

JOURNEYING INTO GALILEE

"began to preach[1]" the gospel, exactly fulfilled the prophecy of Isaiah. Nazareth was in "Galilee," but not "by the sea." Capernaum was both.

The parallel Mark does not mention this prophecy. But that may be explained by the fact that Mark often merely alludes to prophecy where Matthew quotes it[2]. And Mark here—besides the preceding mention (" came into Galilee ")—almost immediately afterwards describes Jesus as calling the fishermen to be apostles while passing along "*by the sea of Galilee*[3]" and then as "coming into Capernaum[4]."

§ 3. *Luke's account*

Luke, after saying that "the devil departed" from Jesus "until a season," proceeds, "And Jesus turned back in the power of the Spirit to Galilee. And a fame went out concerning him throughout the whole of the region round about. And he taught in their synagogues, being glorified by all. And he came to Nazareth...[5]." He does not here mention any arrival at Capernaum. Yet Jesus, in His discourse at Nazareth, which here follows, says, " Doubtless ye will say unto me... 'Whatsoever we have heard *done at Capernaum*, do also here, in thine own country'." This implies that Jesus had been first at Capernaum, and long enough to allow the fame of His doings there to penetrate to Nazareth.

Why then does Luke omit all mention of this visit to Capernaum? And why does he, after recording Christ's words about what had been "*done at Capernaum*," go on to speak about it as though he had never mentioned it before, saying

---

[1] Mt iv 17 "From that time Jesus *began to preach*" (not in the parallel Luke, but comp. Mk i 14)

[2] See *Son* **3518** *d*.

[3] "Galilee" is mentioned in this context twice by Mark (i. 14—16), thrice in the parallel Matthew (iv. 12, 15, 18), once in the parallel Luke (iv 14) Lk. v 1 "lake of Gennesaret" is parallel to Mk-Mt. "sea of Galilee"

[4] Mk i. 16, 21   [5] Lk iv 14—16.

that Jesus, after escaping from those who would have killed Him in Nazareth, "came down to *Capernaum, a city of Galilee*"? It looks as though Luke were combining, out of their right order, two traditions that would have been consistent in their right order. It will be seen, later on, that Luke, in describing this visit to Nazareth, as the scene of Christ's first proclamation of the gospel, not only places very early a visit that in many details closely resembles a visit placed by Mark and Matthew very much later, but also introduces an attempt on Christ's life made by the inhabitants of Nazareth who, a few minutes before, wondered at the words of grace that had fallen from His mouth

Here we must note that confusion might arise from the use of an ambiguous word, a favourite one with Luke, meaning "the country-round-about." In Greek it is *Perichōros*, but it is also Hebraized as *Perichōron* in the sense of neighbourhood[1]. In *Corrections*, it has been shewn that the term, though meaning "the circle" round any town as centre, was used especially to mean the circle of the Jordan round Jericho, and the "circle" round Jerusalem[2] In the first passage where Luke uses it ("John came into all [the] *Perichōros of Jordan*") Mark says that "the *Chōrā* (i e *country*) *of Judaea*, and all the Jerusalemites," came to John[3]. In Luke's second instance (now under consideration) there is no Marcan parallel. In his third, "fame went out concerning him into every place of the *Perichōros*," the parallel Mark has "the report of him came out everywhere into the whole of the *Perichōros of Galilee*[4]." In Luke's next

---

[1] Levy iv 96 *b* quoting J. Schebi ix 38 *d* "von Beth Choron bis zum Meere ist eine Stadt, ein *Gebiet (Perichōron).*" But Schwab ii 416 translates this "'De Beth-Horon jusqu'à la mer, est-il dit, on ne compte qu une province,' tout le reste y est compris à titre de voisinage περιχορόν (sic)" He adds a note, "L'éd d'Amsterdam ayant divisé ce mot en deux, les commentateurs se sont fourvoyés pour lui donner un sens"

[2] *Corrections* **335** *a*. It occurs in the Gospels, Mk (1), Mt (2), Lk (5), Jn (0)   It is not Aramaicized   [3] Mk i. 5, Lk. iii. 3.

[4] Mk i 28, Lk iv. 37 "*Every place* of the Perichōros" seems to

instance (the miracle at Naın, peculiar to Luke) the words "in the whole of Judaea *and in all the Perichōros*" might mean either "in the whole of Judaea *and especially the circle round Jerusalem*," or "in the whole of Judaea, *and also in the circle of the Jordan*[1]."

To these facts we must add the following parallels:—

Mk i 39	Mt iv 23	Lk. iv 44
And he went into their synagogues (*lit*) into (but R V. throughout) the whole of *Galilee* preaching and casting out devils	And he went about in the whole of *Galilee*, teaching in their synagogues and preaching the gospel of the kingdom, and healing all manner of disease among the people	And he was preaching in (*lit*. into) the synagogues of *Judaea*[2]

Obviously scribes and editors of Luke must have been under a strong temptation to conform Luke to Mark (and Matthew) by altering the Lucan "Judaea" into "Galilee." Yet all the most ancient MSS read "Judaea," and so does the recently discovered Syro-Sinaitic version.

The Arabic Diatessaron, it is true, like all the Versions except the Syro-Sinaitic, has, in its present text, "*Galilee*." But *the context favours the view that the reading was originally* "*Judaea*." For the Diatessaron tears this verse out of its Lucan text, placing it much earlier than the preceding Lucan

---

apply better to the circle round a great City like Jerusalem than to that round Capernaum.

[1] Lk. vii 17. Lk viii. 37 "all the multitude of the *Perichōros* of the Gerasenes" needs no comment Matthew's second instance (xiv. 35) "they sent into the whole of that *Perichōros*" is parall to Mk vi 55 "the whole of that *Chōrā* (country)"

[2] R V. retains the reading of A.V "Galilee" in its text, but adds "very many ancient authorities read Judaea" These authorities are now strengthened by the addition of SS W H, which once (1881) gave "Galilee" in the margin, now gives "Judaea" without alternative

words ("I must preach of the kingdom of God in other cities also; for because of this gospel was I sent¹"), and connecting it with a passage of John thus "(John) And this is the second sign that Jesus did when he returned from Judaea to Galilee. (Luke) *And he was preaching* (? *Now he had been preaching*) in the synagogues of *Galilee* (? *Judaea*)" As there is no pluperfect in Hebrew², the rendering "*he had been preaching*" for "he was preaching" is a very small alteration, and it would suit a parenthetic construction; while "Judaea," for "Galilee," would exactly suit the preceding mention of "Judaea." According to this view, the meaning of the Harmonist would be, in effect:—" He returned (as John tells us) from Judaea to Galilee. And here it may be well to insert (what Luke says) that he had been preaching in the synagogues of Judaea."

It may be urged that Luke uses "Judaea" here to mean Palestine He does this when he calls Herod "king of Judaea," and perhaps elsewhere³ But that is unlikely here in view of the parallel "Galilee" in Mark and Matthew. More probably the original tradition here contained an ambiguous word like *Perichōros*, which Luke—being influenced by the preceding context ("to the other cities I must needs preach") as if it implied a missionary journey over a wide area—

---

¹ Lk. iv. 44 is in *Diatess* vi 35, Lk iv 43 is in *Diatess*. vii. 6

² See *Joh Gr* 2480 Lk iv 44 ἦν κηρύσσων (not ἐκήρυσσεν) might very well mean "*he had been preaching*" In N T. the Greek pluperfect is extremely rare except with a few verbs such as δίδωμι.

³ Lk i. 5 "Herod king of Judaea" In Lk. vii. 17, SS has "in all the land of Judaea and in all the country round about them," possibly meaning "all Palestine and all the adjacent countries" The *Onomastica Sacra* regularly uses "Judaea" in this sense, calling Saul (*ib* p. 121) "rex Judaeae" (perhaps because "king of Israel" would imply "king of the ten tribes"). In 1 Esdr v 7, Ἰουδαία is parall to Ezr ii. 1 χώρα (R V "province") and in 1 Esdr v 8 "Jerusalem and *the rest of Judaea*" is parall to Ezr ii 1 "Jerusalem and *Judah*" Strabo (749, τίθεμεν ἔνιοι δὲ) appears to imply that there were different ways of classifying "Judaea."

interpreted as meaning, or including, the *Perichōros* in the South, far away from Capernaum, where Jesus then was[1]

Even if Luke had meant "Palestine," his meaning would have *included* Judaea   We are therefore justified in concluding that these Lucan divergences from Mark indicate, 1st, that Luke believed Judaea to have been influenced by Christ's early preaching in ways not mentioned by Mark, 2nd, that a source of confusion might be found in the Hebraized Greek word Perichōros.   And, since the word is Hebrew and not Aramaic, there results the inference that Luke may be borrowing the passages in which the word is used, partly or wholly, from a Hebrew Gospel   All this gives weight to the slight Lucan indications that things had been going on in Judaea, at the beginning of the gospel, concerning which Mark is silent   In other words, Luke hints at that which John, as we shall see in the next section, emphasizes and amplifies

§ 4. *John's account of a first visit to Galilee*

According to John, there were two early visits to Galilee —one, made by Jesus before the Baptist's arrest, and another some time afterwards, perhaps about the time of the arrest but certainly not in consequence of it   He leaves it open to us to suppose that these two may have been confused.

---

[1] For a similar reason, instead of Mk 1 38 εἰς τὰς ἐχομένας κωμοπόλεις, Luke (iv 43) has ταῖς ἑτέραις πόλεσιν, and, for Mark's εἰς τοῦτο γὰρ ἐξῆλθον, Luke has ὅτι ἐπὶ τοῦτο ἀπεστάλην   Mark's words might imply that Jesus "came-out [of the house]" for a short mission   Luke describes the Mission of Christ's life (" I was sent ")   The Marcan ἐξῆλθον might be interpreted Messianically   See Mt ii 6 (quoting Mic v 2), also Numb. xxiv 7 (LXX), and Is xi 1, xlii 13 &c   Comp Jn viii 42 ἐγὼ γὰρ ἐκ τοῦ θεοῦ ἐξῆλθον καὶ ἥκω   We shall return to the doctrine of "coming-forth" when we discuss Mk i. 38 in its order.   The first O T "coming-forth" describes (Gen ii. 10) the River which (Philo 1 250, 690) waters the world "with four virtues"

JOURNEYING INTO GALILEE

As to the first visit, he uses an expression that invites careful study, as indeed does the whole context, for it is one of the most remarkable among many remarkable instances of the Johannine method of teaching by allusions We are told that the journey took place " on the morrow " after the call of Peter, which had been preceded by the call of Andrew · " On the morrow *it was his desire* (or, *he resolved*) to go forth into Galilee, and he findeth Philip , and Jesus saith unto him, ' Follow me[1]." This leads us to ask, Why mention this *desire* (or *resolve*) as though to deny that He did it by constraint? And how came Jesus to "*find*" Philip? Was it by accident or as the result of search? And why is Philip the only one of the apostles in the Fourth Gospel whom Jesus is described as calling with the words " Follow me "? The other Gospels describe other apostles as being thus called. The Fourth Gospel does not deny that , but it omits that, and inserts this—the special calling of Philip to " follow." Why is this?

Towards answering these questions the Evangelist leads us a little way by adding, in effect, " *Now I ought perhaps to have told you that* Philip was domiciled at Bethsaida, though born a native of the city of Andrew and Peter[2] " " The city of Andrew and Peter" was not Bethsaida but Capernaum. This is proved by the mention of " the house of Simon and Andrew " in Mark, and by similar expressions in Matthew and Luke, where the contexts assume that Capernaum was their home[3].

---

[1] Jn 1 43   On ἠθέλησεν, see *Joh Gr* **2471**a foll

[2] Jn 1. 44   On δέ parenthetic, s *Joh Gr*. **2631** foll   On ἀπό and ἐκ, s *Joh Gr* **2289**—**90**   The former implies domicile , the latter, extraction

[3] Mk 1 29 " into *the house of Simon and Andrew* " (sim Mt. viii 14, Lk iv 38, but omitting "Andrew")   Westcott (on Jn 1 44) says " The Synoptists mention that Simon and Andrew had a house at Capernaum " It would have been well to add (1) that all the Synoptists call it "*the house*" , (2) that they nowhere mention any other house of Andrew or Peter ; and (3) that John, by speaking of "*the city* of Andrew and Peter," implies that only *one* "*city*" (i e Capernaum) could claim to be so called.

Bethsaida was, in effect, a newly constructed Greek city into which its founder Philip the Tetrarch brought a large number of inhabitants, calling it Julias after the name of the Emperor's daughter[1]. Into this Greek city Philip passed (perhaps with others taking the Tetrarch's name) but not forgotten (it would seem) by his old neighbours Andrew and Peter. Clement of Alexandria assumes that Philip was living among "the dead" when he describes a perversion of "the saying of the Lord, who says *to Philip*, Leave the dead to bury their own dead, but follow thou me[2]" Origen assumes that Philip was in some sense "lost," when Jesus went forth to rescue him "And on the fourth day *having resolved* to go-forth to Galilee, *He that 'came-forth to seek that which is lost' findeth Philip*, and saith unto him Follow me[3]."

It would seem then that Philip is regarded as being in a position somewhat like that of Abraham when the word of the Lord said unto him, "Get thee out of thy country, and from thy kindred and thy father's house" Abraham's family was tainted with idolatry and he was to go forth from it. But tradition represents him as pleading that he could not leave his father, Terah, in his old age, and nevertheless, as receiving the command to go forth And somewhat the same thing here would seem to apply to Philip[4]. His father (who

---

[1] Joseph *Ant* xviii 2. 1.
[2] Clem. Alex 522, Mt. viii. 22, comp Lk ix. 60.
[3] Origen *Comm. Joann* vi 30 θελήσας ἐξελθεῖν εἰς τὴν Γαλιλαίαν ὁ ἐξελθὼν ζητῆσαι τὸ ἀπολωλὸς εὑρίσκει Φίλιππον Comp Lk xix 10 ἦλθεν ζητῆσαι καὶ σῶσαι τὸ ἀπολωλός. Politically, Bethsaida, being just inside the tetrarchy of Philip, would not be a part of the Tetrarchy of Galilee and Peraea. But that would hardly prevent Evangelists—writing with Isaiah's prophecy in their minds about "Galilee of the Gentiles"— from regarding Bethsaida as belonging to the Galilaean "people that sat in darkness"
[4] See *Gen. r* on Gen xii 1 (Wu p 175) and Rashi It was supposed, either (1) that Terah *actually* died, or (2) that his death (Gen xi 32) is mentioned out of its chronological place, and that he is to be regarded as dead, before Abraham "goes forth."

perhaps had brought him from Capernaum to Bethsaida) was spiritually "dead," and Philip was not to wait on in the city of death in order to "bury the dead"

This view will help to explain the above-mentioned use of the word "*desire*" or "*resolve*" in connection with the first journey into Galilee. But there are other reasons also. Mark had described Jesus as being "*driven forth*" by "*the Spirit*," immediately after His baptism. Luke softens this into "*He turned back, full of the Holy Spirit, from the Jordan*." Later on, Luke says, "*He turned back in the power of the Spirit* into Galilee." But even in this softened form these expressions suggest that in both cases Jesus was under a constraining influence somewhat like that which is said to have lifted up Ezekiel in his visions. At all events there is nothing of "desire" or "resolve" in the Lucan view. But the Johannine view emphasizes, in an unusual way, the "*desire*" of Jesus to take this journey. John also gives us a reason, or rather leads us to supply the reason, as though we were bound to supply it, if we had any sense at all of what Jesus really was.

It is as though John said: "I have told my readers that Jesus was the Lamb of God that takes away sins. I have told them of the effect that His personal presence produced on Andrew and his companion; I have led them to feel what it must have been on Simon to whom He promised the name of Cephas. Now I am about to describe Him as taking a journey and as '*desiring*' to take it. Is it necessary to say what the Saviour's '*desire*' was? Is it necessary to protest against the notion that He journeyed into Galilee because the Spirit drove Him thither, or because He was to fulfil a prophecy of Isaiah about Galilee? His '*desire*,' of course, was to do the Father's will by saving the souls of men. And He, being one who knew and loved the souls of men, knew, through Andrew, the soul of Philip, once Andrew's companion and friend in Capernaum, but now in Bethsaida and surrounded by temptations arising both from his family and from the neighbourhood. Like Abraham, Philip was in danger of death, if he remained where he was; but, like Abraham, he had abundant capacity for life, if he but heard the voice of the Son of the living God, saying, 'Come forth from thy kindred and from thy father's house and follow me'."

§ 5. *John's account of a second visit to Galilee*

The second Johannine visit to Galilee is introduced as follows: "When therefore the Lord understood that the Pharisees had heard [the report] that 'Jesus is making more disciples and is baptizing more [than] John[1]'—and yet Jesus himself was not baptizing, but [only] his disciples [were baptizing in his name]—he left Judaea and departed again to Galilee." Probably the text is corrupt. We have seen above, that whereas Mark wrote "after John was delivered up," Matthew expanded this into "when Jesus *heard* that John was delivered up." The same motive has perhaps affected early editors of the Fourth Gospel's text. But in any case what the Evangelist says here makes it almost certain that (in his opinion) Jesus did not take this journey because He had heard of John's

---

[1] Jn iv 1. The text indicates corruption. See Hort's note, to which add that *e* has "convenit" for ἔγνω, and that Origen (*Comm. Joann* xiii 39, Lomm ii 73, διὰ τὸ ἐγνωκέναι τοὺς Φαρισαίους ὅτι Ἰησοῦς πλείονας μαθητὰς ποιεῖ καὶ βαπτίζει [ἢ] Ἰωάννης) indicates how variations may have arisen. The original may have simply said ὡς οὖν ἔγνωσαν οἱ Φαρισαῖοι. But it may have been argued that it was not the *knowledge* of the Pharisees, but *the Lord's hearing of this*, that prompted His action. See above (p 206, n 1) as to the frequent insertion of "hearing" in the LXX to express thoughts of this kind.

If ἢ is to be omitted after βαπτίζει the meaning must be "Jesus is making more disciples [than ever] and John is baptizing them," but this does not agree with what follows. Curet Syr has "Now when Jesus knew that the Pharisees heard that his disciples were many, and [that] he was baptizing more than John—not that Jesus [himself] was baptizing, but his disciples." SS has "Now when our Lord knew that the Pharisees heard of (? *om*) many disciples", and instead of "not that ..baptizing," it has "because not only was our Lord baptizing."

arrest. And this is made more certain by what he says a little before, speaking of Jesus as baptizing, at the same time as John, in Judaea—"*for John had not yet been cast into prison*"—and describing the apparent jealousy of some of John's disciples at the popularity of Jesus[1]

The Diatessaron places John's arrest immediately after Christ's leaving Judaea[2] This probably accords with the Johannine view For the Prophet's words—uttered a little before the account of Christ's departure—"He [*ie* Jesus] must increase, but I must decrease," seem to be intended as a kind of farewell to public life If John was arrested a few days after these words, Christ's enemies might say, "Jesus fled immediately afterwards to escape the same fate" All the more necessary it might seem to shew that there was no such motive for Christ's journey John was "*not yet*" arrested.

§ 6. *What happened in the Synoptic visit to Galilee?*

According to Mark, Jesus "came into Galilee preaching the gospel of God [3]" Deferring the consideration of the following words describing the "gospel," we pass to the parallel Matthew, which says " He withdrew to Galilee, and having given up his home at Nazareth, he came and took up his abode in Capernaum by the sea .that it might be fulfilled (Is. ix. 1—2) From that time began Jesus to preach and to say[4]." Luke says "And Jesus turned back in the power of the Spirit to Galilee, and a fame went out over the whole of the country round about concerning him, and he began-to-teach

---

[1] Jn iii 22—6.
[2] *Diatess.* § 6 It combines Jn iv 3 *a* with Lk iii 19—20, "*And* [*so*] *he left Judaea. And Herod the governor shut up John in prison*" The actual journey through Samaria and the Dialogue with the Samaritan woman are placed by the *Diatessaron* very much later (§ 21) "And while he was passing through the land of Samaria," omitting the inconvenient (Jn iv 4) ἔδει
[3] Mk i 14   [4] Mt iv 12—17

in their synagogues [1]." Luke does not say, as Mark and Matthew do, *what* Jesus taught. But he adds what was the effect of His teaching, "He began to teach in their synagogues, being glorified by all" This is somewhat disappointing. When the Son of God is recorded as coming down to earth to be the Saviour of the world, and to preach the Good Tidings of man's redemption, the reader naturally awaits with interest the first word of that Good Tidings. About most teachers, especially teachers of new truth, we should say that to be "glorified by all" was a very bad sign, indicating that they were teaching, not what was true, but what was pleasant to the multitude

Not improbably the original was ambiguous and led to various inferences. The Greek "*fame*," on the one occasion where it occurs in canonical LXX is, in Hebrew, literally, "hearing[2]." The Hebrew word occurs in Isaiah, "Lord, who hath believed *our report?*"—which is taken both by Paul and by John as meaning "*our preaching,*" although Rashi and Ibn Ezra seem to take it as meaning "*that which we have heard [and which we have seen fulfilled]*[3]." Also the verb "report" (literally "cause to be heard"), when it occurs in Isaiah "How beautiful...are the feet of him *that bringeth-tidings, that reporteth peace,*" is misrendered as a noun by LXX "*that bringeth-tidings of the report of peace*[4]." This shews how, owing to verbal ambiguities, evangelists might differ at this point as to the question whether a "*gospel*" or a "*fame*" was contemplated.

---

[1] Lk iv. 14—15. As Luke here uses ἐδίδασκεν, and iv 31 ἦν διδάσκων, and xi 1 ἐδίδαξεν, it is best to distinguish the first by rendering it "began-to-teach" The parall Mt iv 17 has ἤρξατο κηρύσσειν The word for "fame" in Lk iv 14 is φήμη [2] Prov xv. 30, LXX φήμη.

[3] Is. liii. 1 (R.V. txt "*our report,*" marg "or, *that which we have heard,*" Gesen 1035 *a* "*the report that reached us*") quoted in Jn xii 38, Rom. x 16 as LXX τῇ ἀκοῇ ἡμῶν Luke never uses this ambiguous word except in vii 1 εἰς τὰς ἀκοὰς τοῦ λαοῦ, where there can be no ambiguity

[4] Is lii 7

But, further, Luke (as we shall presently see) does not apparently believe that the time has come to say anything about the details of Christ's "gospel." These he reserves for the visit to Nazareth, which he introduces in the next verse, his intention being to shew that all through Galilee Jesus was "glorified," but in Nazareth He was rejected and assaulted — "And he began-to-teach in their synagogues [*i.e.* the synagogues of Galilee] being glorified by all. And he came to Nazareth..."

It is natural to compare this with the juxtaposition of events in Matthew —"He withdrew into Galilee, and giving up his home in Nazareth he came and took up his abode in Capernaum." It looks as though Luke, accepting this account of Christ's changes of residence, said to himself, "Yes, but this needs explanation. Why did He leave His home at Nazareth? Because, when He carried the gospel thither, His life was threatened. And why did He take up His abode in Capernaum? Because He was glorified there on account of His mighty works, so that His fellow-townsmen at Nazareth were described by Jesus Himself as disposed to say, 'Whatsoever we have heard done at Capernaum, do also here in thine own country'." So Luke infers that he must insert at this point that visit of Jesus to Nazareth, and these sayings of Jesus about a "prophet" being "without honour in his own country," which Mark and Matthew (and probably John as we shall see) place much later.

Whatever be the reasons, this at least is the fact, that, whereas Mark and Matthew connect Christ's visit to Galilee with His preaching of the "*gospel*," Luke connects it merely with a course of "*teaching*" resulting in a "glorification" of the Teacher. He does not mention the preaching of the gospel till a special visit to Nazareth, where the preaching is rejected.

§ 7 What happened in the first Johannine visit to Galilee?

According to John, what happened in Galilee must be divided into four parts, 1st, the call of Philip, presumably taking place in Bethsaida, the city in which Philip was then residing, 2nd, the conversion of Nathanael, and the promise that the disciples should see the heaven opened and the angels of God ascending and descending on the Son of Man, 3rd, the sign at Cana, 4th, the going down to Capernaum—as to which it is added "They abode there not many days. And the passover of the Jews was at hand." No mention is made of Nazareth as being visited first before the "going down" to Capernaum. We are prepared, of course, for finding no mention of "gospel." But there is also no fulfilment of prophecy except Philip's enthusiastic declaration that Jesus fulfils "the law and the prophets"—damped for the moment by Nathanael's brief objection to "Nazareth" as a Messiah's birth-place. There is no "preaching," no "teaching," no suggestion of publicity or "fame." The nearest approach to publicity is the Supper at Cana. The only "glory" is from the "sign" of the New Wine. And that only affects the small band of "his disciples," who "believed on him[1]." His brethren are mentioned as going down to Capernaum with Him. But they are not said to have "believed", and, later on, it is expressly said that they did not believe[2]

Deferring to a future section the consideration of what may be said to be implied in all this, of such a nature as to correspond to a "gospel," we may note the verbal agreement between John and Luke as to Capernaum. Matthew had said that Jesus "came and *took up his abode at Capernaum* which is by the sea," in order that the prophecy might be fulfilled concerning "Galilee of the Gentiles" and "the way

---

[1] Christ's "disciples" are mentioned for the first time in Jn ii 2 " But there had been bidden also Jesus and *his disciples* to the wedding"

[2] Jn vii 5

of the sea", Luke, who would not have agreed that Capernaum was "*by the sea*[1]," simply says, without quoting any prophecy, that when Christ's life had been attempted at Nazareth, He "*came down to Capernaum, a city of Galilee.*"

Luke's words derive additional importance from the fact that Marcion practically made them the beginning of his gospel, which was, in fact, Luke with excisions. Marcion arranged it thus:—"In the fifteenth year of the reign of Tiberius, he came down to the Galilaean city of Capernaum[2]." To do this, meant, in effect, to begin the gospel with an act of exorcism[3], and to represent Jesus as appealing to men in the character of an Exorcist and a Healer possessing miraculous powers. Capernaum was notoriously the principal scene of these "mighty works[4]" These considerations may help to explain the brief addition to Luke made by John as follows — "After this he went down to Capernaum, he and his mother and the brethren [of Jesus], and his disciples, *and there they remained not many days*[5]." The intention seems to be to subordinate what we may call "the gospel of Capernaum," or,

---

[1] On Luke's avoidance of "sea" applied to the Lake of Gennesaret, see *Joh Voc* 1811 *d*

[2] Lk iii 1 and iv 31 quoted by Tertullian *Adv Marc* iv. 7

[3] Mk i 21—8, Lk. iv 31—7

[4] Lk iv 23 "the things that we have heard done at Capernaum," and comp. Mt xi 23 In Jn iv 46, the nobleman to whom it is said "except ye see signs and wonders ye will not believe," is described as having his son sick "at Capernaum"

[5] Jn ii 12. This is John's first mention of Christ's "brethren" Origen comments on the fact that, though not present at Cana, they are described, immediately after the story of Cana, as coming down with Jesus and His mother and His disciples to Capernaum Chrysostom must be supposed to have believed (impossible though the supposition may appear) that Christ's brethren *were* present at Cana For he twice misquotes Jn ii 1 "Now the mother of Jesus was also there *and his brethren*" Also, he adds, "As therefore they invited *her and the brethren [of Jesus]*, so they invited Jesus too," i e. doing Him no special honour I have found no trace of any such reading in any other authority

at all events, to correct the impression that at this early period Jesus, as Matthew says, "took up his abode at Capernaum."

But there appears also an intention to describe Jesus as at this time separating Himself (like Abraham) from His "kindred," in order to go forth on the journeying prescribed by God. It is done, like most things in the Fourth Gospel, not by statement but by suggestion. At the Wedding in Cana, "the mother of Jesus" is said to have been "there", and Jesus and His "disciples" were "bidden." But His "brethren" are neither "there" nor "bidden." The sign at Cana was a success so far as the disciples were concerned, "and *his disciples* believed on him." But a contrast between "disciples" and "brethren" is suggested, at all events interrogatively, in the continuous text, which runs thus: "And his disciples believed on him. *After this he went down to Capernaum, he and his mother and [his] brethren and his disciples.*" Where have the "brethren" been all this time? Are we to suppose that they had "believed" before the sign at Cana? That would be, even at this point, almost impossible. And it is made quite impossible by what follows later on, "For even his brethren did not believe on him[1]."

These last words about Christ's brethren ("did not believe on him") referring to a later period, contrast with what is said about Christ's disciples now ("believed on him") and suggest a further answer to the question "What happened in this visit?" It was the introduction of a new power into the world, the power of "faith" or "belief"—not "belief" in general, but that particular kind of belief which had Jesus for

---

[1] Jn vii 5. In the Synoptists, the only instance of Christ's "mother" and "brethren" mentioned together (Mk iii 31 foll., Mt. xii. 46 foll, Lk. viii. 19 foll.) is in the narrative of their attempt to reach Jesus in the midst of His disciples, when Jesus says (Mk iii 35) "Whosoever shall do the will of God, the same is my brother and sister and mother." But comp Mk vi 3, Mt. xiii 55—6 (no parall. in Lk.) where Christ's "mother,' "brothers," and "sisters" are mentioned as a cause, or excuse, for disbelief in Him.

its object The Evangelist has already told us that the Baptist's testimony was ordained "that all might believe", that to them who believe in the incarnate Word there has been given "authority to become children of God"; and Jesus Himself has gently taught Nathanael that belief in Him must be based on something greater than admiration for what might be called Christ's powers of "second sight[1]" But no statement has yet been made that any disciple has "believed." Now the statement is made, and with such an addition as to signify that the right kind of belief has been at last attained "This did Jesus [as the] beginning of his signs in Cana of Galilee, and he manifested his glory and his disciples believed on him[2]"

This is very different from the notion of "belief" or "faith" that we might derive from many passages of the Synoptic Gospels, and, in particular, at this stage of the Gospel, from Luke. In the Synoptists, faith—a word that John never uses in its noun form[3]—seems mostly to represent faith in Christ's physical power of healing[4], and Luke represents the call of Peter as having been preceded by a miraculous draught of fishes[5]. In the Johannine narrative before us, Christ's recorded words are few and brief; and there are no acts of healing. But it is implied that His converse with the first disciples was prolonged and intimate And they in their turn brought to Him their brothers or close friends. A Person rises up, and around Him other persons shape themselves into a Church or Temple. It is a drama, or a picture, not a lecture, discourse, or even prophecy. Greeks might liken the opening

---

[1] Jn i 7, 12, 51   [2] Jn ii 11   [3] See *Joh Voc* **1467**.
[4] Comp. Mt ix 28 "Believe ye that I am able to do this?" Doubtless this "belief" in Christ's being "able" (which is not mentioned in the parallel narratives of Mk x, Mt xx, Lk. xviii) was of great importance for the purpose of the special act of healing But it was only one inferior aspect of "belief" in Christ Himself
[5] Lk v 4 foll

of the Johannine Gospel to Orpheus drawing stocks and stones after him, or to Amphion calling into their places with the spell of his lyre the stones that were to build up a great city.

This is certainly poetry, but it is also historical fact in this respect that the belief described by John is nearer than the belief of the crowds that are described by Mark as pressing round Christ's door at Capernaum—to that new, revolutionary, and divine belief, which Christ actually desired to produce and by which Christ's religion, wherever it has been successful, has achieved success. We shall presently find that Mark, alone among the Synoptists, has placed the precept to "believe"—however briefly—at the outset of Christ's preaching. Matthew and Luke have omitted it. John is historically correct in giving to such belief a prominence, from the beginning, if not in Christ's actual words, yet certainly in the atmosphere of His words and actions.

The Johannine "belief" was a personal trust in Christ as the infinitely lovable Lamb of God, as the Saviour whose very words were life[1], as one whose presence was as the very bosom of God. The Love of this Man, the Blood of this Lamb, the Spirit of this Son of God, John desires us to realise as having flowed into the souls of the disciples at Cana —not in its perfection, but in a kind of foretaste, through the affectionate and well-meaning intervention of the Lord's mother—when the new wine of the gospel was poured out for them, and when Jesus "manifested his glory and his disciples believed on him." How different, this—this "glory" of grace and truth manifested to this little knot of six, six among many guests at a bridegroom's table—from the glory of a popular "teacher," which Luke's readers might suppose to be meant, as having been attained by Jesus in Galilee, when "he taught in their synagogues, being glorified by all[2]"!

---

[1] Comp Jn vi 68 "Lord, to whom shall we go? Thou hast [the] words of eternal life"

[2] Lk. iv. 15 This is before the act of the Forgiveness of Sins

These considerations lead us to the conclusion that John —no less than Matthew, though he does not quote Isaiah as Matthew does—discerns in this visit of Jesus to Galilee a fulfilment of Isaiah's promise about the region "beyond Jordan," "Galilee of the nations," "the people that walked in darkness," "upon them hath the light shined." "Bethany beyond Jordan" is expressly mentioned as the place where John's baptizing came to pass, and, with it, the Epiphany or manifestation of Christ as the Light of the World by the descent of the Holy Spirit "Galilee" is also mentioned as the place to which Jesus "desired to go forth," before He "found"—and apparently in order to "find" and save—the soul of Philip, who (as we have seen above) is regarded as "walking in darkness" among the mingled races that inhabited the idol-worshipping city of Bethsaida. Thus, in answer to the question, "What was done in this visit?" we may say "the Light of the World came to lighten the darkness of the nations in accordance with the gospel, or good tidings, proclaimed by Isaiah"

In connection with this prophecy of Isaiah about Galilee and the Light, Jerome first quotes Matthew's version as representing the Hebrew rather than the LXX Then he says "And John the Evangelist relates that Jesus, with His disciples, in Cana of Galilee, being invited to a wedding, wrought His first sign there by turning water into wine — 'This did Jesus [as the] beginning of [His] signs in Cana of Galilee, and manifested His glory, and His disciples believed on Him.' Whence also, in the LXX, it is said, *Drink this first, do [it] quickly*[1], because 'the land of Zebulon' and 'the land of Naphtali' saw Christ's first miracles, so that [that land] first drank the draught of faith, which [land] had also

---

(Lk. v 20—6) Mark (11 12) raises the standard of "glorifying," by using it only once in the whole of his Gospel, and then in connection with the Forgiveness of Sins (although faith-healing also plays a prominent part in the narrative)

[1] Is ix. 1 (LXX) Τοῦτο πρῶτον πίε, ταχὺ ποίει, χώρα Ζαβουλών ..

first seen the Lord doing signs." Apparently Jerome means that the version of the LXX (which modern students would call an extraordinary error) was ordained to give a meaning different from the Hebrew, but conveying a truth of its own, and this, a prophecy of the first of Christ's miracles, the conversion of water into wine in Cana of Galilee.

It is unlikely that this error of the LXX has more than a very slight bearing—if any bearing—on the origination of the Johannine narrative; but it may have partially contributed to its prominence, and to the position given to it at the outset of the Gospel in connection with Galilee and the Jordan. Its origination might be explained from Hebrew and Jewish traditions, about the "wine" of the Law, taken up by Jesus and developed by Him in doctrine about the "new wine" of the Gospel Among parallelisms between the Giving of the Wine at Cana and the Giving of the Law at Sinai, there is one that should have been given in a previous treatise and may be conveniently placed here[1].

It relates to the threefold repetition of "on the morrow," followed by "on the third day[2]." From this readers are left to infer that, if "the third" means "the third" from the last mentioned "morrow," we are being prepared for a *sixth* day. Origen repeatedly assumes and mentions "six" in reference to what he calls the "economy" at Cana[3].

Now in the account of the Creation in Genesis there is nothing of this kind. The days are there enumerated, each in turn, from the first to the sixth, without any special mention of "the third day." But the account of the Giving of the Law in Exodus says " Be ready *against the third day*",

---

[1] It should have been inserted in *Son* **3583** (ix) *b*, or **3583** (xii) *d*, where it has been pointed out that the sign at Cana corresponds in some respects to the giving of the Law at Sinai, as well as to the six days of the Creation.

[2] Jn 1. 29, 35, 43; ii 1.

[3] E.g. *Comm. Joann* x. 2 (Lomm 1 277) μετὰ τὰς ἐξ τοῦ ὅτε (? leg. ἐξ ἐξότε) ἐβαπτίσθη ἡμέρας, τῇ ἕκτῃ γενομένης τῆς κατὰ τὸν ἐν Κανᾷ τῆς Γαλιλαίας γάμον οἰκονομίας (comp. *ib.* 6, Lomm. 1. 288).

and, about this, an ancient tradition says, "That is *the sixth day*[1]." The meaning is "*the sixth day* from the beginning of the month which was the beginning of the life of Israel as a free nation released from the bondage of Egypt[2]."

Summing up our conclusions as to the first Johannine visit to Galilee, we may say that it presents Christ to us as the irresistible Lamb of God and the beloved Bridegroom of Israel, destined to bring about the Wedding between divine and human nature All at present breathes peace. There are but faint suggestions of an impending cloud in the words "What have I to do with thee?" and "Mine hour is not yet come," and in the mention—unexpected, and, as it were, casual—of Christ's "brethren" as being distinct from His "disciples." John does not contradict expressly anything in the Synoptists, but he gives us a very different view, more poetic, more emotional, and more personal.

Truer, in a superficial or matter-of-fact sense, it is not. We are forced to believe that Christ's early popularity was largely due to those inferior powers which everyone could understand at once, acts of instantaneous healing and exorcism such as Mark has described at great length, and such as (doubtless) occurred in great numbers where crowd rivalled crowd in "belief"—of a certain kind. But if we admit that the "belief" that Jesus desired to inspire and ultimately did inspire was of a different kind, and was the real foundation and rock on which He built His church, then we shall probably

---

[1] *Mechilta* on Exod xix. 11 (Wu p 199)

[2] See Exod. xix. 1—16 where Targ. Jer I supplies numbers for the days as italicised in the following passage —"(1) On that day, *the first of the month*, came they to the desert. (3) And Moses *on the second day* went up to the top of the mountain. (9) And the Lord said to Moses *on the third day*, I will reveal myself [wrongly punctuated by Walton and Etheridge] .(10) And the Lord said to Moses *on the fourth day* (11) for on the third day the Lord will reveal himself...(16) And it came to pass on the third day, *the sixth of the month*"

admit that the poetic account of the first visit to Galilee in the Fourth Gospel gives us an insight not given by the Synoptic Gospels into the causes of Christ's success.

§ 8. *What happened in the second Johannine visit to Galilee?*

The second journey to Galilee is said to have been broken by a stay of two days in Samaria, where "many" believed in Jesus because of the testimony of the Samaritan woman, and "many more because of his [own] word." The narrative proceeds, with a paradoxical use of "*for*," which arrests attention —" After the two days he went forth from thence into Galilee, *for* Jesus himself testified that a prophet in his own country hath no honour. When therefore he came to Galilee the Galilaeans received him, having seen all things as many as he had done in Jerusalem at the feast, for they, too, had gone to the feast[1]."

Various attempts have been made to explain the "*for*" that thus introduces the reason why Jesus went into Galilee. But it does not become really intelligible unless we recognise that Jesus is deliberately passing from places where He *has* "honour" to places where He *has not* "honour." The Evangelist is repeating and emphasizing the reason given above, namely, that Jesus was regarded by many in Judaea as outstripping the Baptist in popularity, and that He did not desire this kind of reputation. He therefore departed from Judaea to Galilee. On His way, the Samaritans welcome Him and believe in Him, and He remains with them "two days." But He will remain no longer. He passes on, "after the two days," to Galilee, because there He would be "in his

---

[1] Jn iv 43—5 On the Johannine οὖν ("when *therefore* (οὖν) he came") see *Joh Voc* and *Joh Gr* (Indices, οὖν), and especially **2198— 200** and **2631—5**. The A V and the R V. differ greatly, *e.g.* vi 13—14 A.V. "*Therefore. then,*" R V "*So ..therefore*" A V. has "so" where R V. has "therefore" in iv 46, vi 19, R V has "so" where A.V. has "therefore" in vi 13 In all these passages the Greek has οὖν

own country," that is, in the place where He had lived with His family from a child[1], and where, proverbially, "a prophet hath no honour" John goes on to say, not without a touch of irony, that "therefore"—that is, in accordance with this proverb—the Galilaeans received Jesus, *not because of their experience of Him at home in Galilee but because of their experience of Him away from home in Jerusalem*, "having seen all the things as many as he had done in Jerusalem[2]." "All the things" apparently means works of healing mentioned above, concerning which Nicodemus had previously said "No one can do these signs, which thou art [daily] doing, except God be with him[3]."

What had happened among Christ's kindred and neighbours at Nazareth that had called forth this "testifying" of Jesus concerning "the prophet in his own country"? John has recorded nothing. Perhaps however John assumes an unrecorded visit to Nazareth between the miracle at Cana where Christ's brethren were absent, and the going down to Capernaum where they were present In that interval, Jesus may have been so contumeliously and roughly treated at Nazareth that the whole family went down with Him thence to Capernaum. Luke relates such a visit to Nazareth before his mention of the going down to Capernaum. But Luke's narrative includes an attempt on Christ's life not mentioned by Mark or Matthew and probably based on some misunderstanding[4].

---

[1] This, and not "the place of his birth," is the meaning of πατρίς in LXX and N.T. In canon. LXX, πατρίς, without var. r., occurs only 6 times—5 times for Heb. (Gesen 409 *b*) "kindred," "birth," or "offspring," and once for Heb. "land of kindred" (Jer. xlvi 16). Neither its Greek nor its Hebrew associations would favour the application of the word to the place where a child was born *in transitu*.

[2] Jn iv. 45

[3] Jn iii. 2, comp. ii. 23 "many believed on his name, beholding his signs, which he was [daily] doing"

[4] See Burkitt ii. 130 giving quotations of Lk. iv 29 "when they threw him from the hill he flew in the air," and comp. SS, which has "so that

JOURNEYING INTO GALILEE

Returning to the question "What happened during this second visit to Galilee?" we find, on the surface, a disappointing answer. For, if this second Johannine visit coincided with the first Mark-Matthew visit, placed by Mark and Matthew immediately after the Baptist's arrest, we ought to find it the beginning (practically) of the gospel in Galilee; there ought to be a great multitude of miracles of healing; Jesus, instead of being slighted and neglected, ought to be pestered with popularity. We appear, at first sight, to find nothing of all this in John.

Looking more closely, however, we shall find indeed traces of "all this," but we shall also find that John seems to think "all this" of very little importance, as being mostly fitful excitement or merely belief in faith-healing signifying very little. The Galilaeans "received" Jesus[1]. Yes, but it was because of what they had seen at Jerusalem. John seems to say to us, "Why should I repeat over again what Mark and Matthew have more than sufficiently reported, that the gospel of faith-healing at Capernaum was outwardly successful? It is better to make things even by emphasizing the Gospel of Cana—which, though it was not set forth with any mighty

---

they might hang him." But these are comparatively unimportant details. It is more important to note the parallelism between Lk iv. 30 "but he, passing through (διελθὼν διὰ) the midst of them, went his way," and Jn viii. 59 "but Jesus was hidden and came forth from the temple," and *ib.* x. 39 "he came forth out of their hand." It is possible that traditions about what happened to Jesus "in his Father's house" (see the first use of "father's house" in Gen xii. 1) may have been interpreted as meaning (1) at Nazareth in the house of Joseph, (2) in Jerusalem in the house of God. See *Joh. Gr.* **2543** on the "hiding" of Christ, probably regarded as supernatural.

[1] Jn iv. 45 ἐδέξαντο, "gave him a [hospitable] reception," the only Johannine use of the word, not so strong as ἔλαβον, and also weakened by the context ("having seen all things as many as he did in Jerusalem") Contrast Jn i. 12 "as many as received him [into themselves] (ἔλαβον), to them gave he authority to become God's children." On ἐδέξαντο see *Joh. Voc* **1721** *f*, and note Luke's use of δοχή, as "reception" or "entertainment," and πανδοχεῖον, "inn."

work or sign that was known to the world—was indeed a mighty work or sign to the Disciples[1]. Matthew and

---

[1] Comp Jn ii 11 "This beginning of his signs did Jesus and manifested his glory, and his disciples believed on him" This indicates that there was a "manifestation" to the disciples of (*ib*) "this beginning of his signs" Yet it is said above, "When the ruler of the feast tasted and *knew not whence it was .but the attendants knew—those who had drawn the water. .*" This seems to imply that—at that moment at all events—no one knew of the "sign" except "*the attendants*" And the "sign" is not said to have been divulged afterwards to the disciples, or to the master of the feast, or to the guests If it had been, should we not have expected the Evangelist to add "and *all that were there, both the disciples and the guests*, believed on him"? Yet, if it was not divulged to the disciples, why is it expressly said that now "they believed on him"? Surely something must have occurred to make them "believe" If so, what was it? Is there some latent confusion between literal and metaphorical tradition, which may be illustrated from Prov ix. 2—4 "She [*i e* Wisdom] hath mingled her wine. she hath sent forth her maidens," that is, to call "the simple" to the Feast?

The answer must be deferred till we come to Mark's story of the Feast in the House of the Publican, and doctrine about the "Calling" of Sinners, and the Children of the Bride-chamber, and the New Wine (Mk ii 14—22) At the close of it, Luke has (v 39) "*the old [wine] is good*" John here seems to add an apparently contradictory, but perhaps complementary, tradition, "*the new wine is good*" Both the Synoptic and the Johannine narrative must be studied in the light of the above-quoted poetic description of Wisdom "mingling" her "wine" for the "simple."

The Fourth Gospel suggests that the Logos gave two gifts of wine, one, rudimentary and preliminary, the "water" being kept distinct from the "wine", the other, complete and final, in which the "wine" is revealed as the "blood" of the Word, and the "water" and the "blood" are "mingled" In Proverbs, Wisdom sends forth her (Heb) "youthful [attendants]" (Heb fem., but LXX masc, δούλους) to call the guests. These "youths"—whom we may call "little-children," for παιδία is a frequent rendering of the masc Heb noun—may have been confused with the Johannine "attendants." If so, the original meaning may have been that the disciples, or attendants, who preached the Gospel of Wisdom—those whom Jerome (on Prov ix. 2 foll) calls "praedicatores infirmos ac despicabiles," the "little ones" whom the rulers of the Jews despised—these "*knew*" the Good Wine, and "*knew whence it was,*" but the rest did not Confusion of this kind may have been facilitated by the fact that the Hebrew word for "*attendants*" is often confused with

Luke have said that, when Jesus entered into Capernaum, a centurion humbly besought Him to speak the word of healing for son or servant[1], and to heal him from a distance because he, the centurion, was not worthy that the Lord should come to his house; they add that Jesus marvelled at the centurion's faith, as being beyond any that He had 'found in Israel' But did this mean that the centurion's belief was beyond that of the Lord's own disciples, such belief as I have recorded in the narrative of Cana? It was not so. But He meant that the man's faith, and his reverence for Christ, surpassed that of the multitudes of Jews in Capernaum."

If this is John's view, we may regard the Johannine sign of the healing of the nobleman's son as in some sense a complement and balance to the miracle of the healing of the centurion's son, as though John said, "To balance the narrative of the Centurion, I will set down another concerning a Nobleman He, too, had a son sick at Capernaum. When he heard that Jesus was at Cana, he came and begged Him to come down to heal the child. But Jesus said—speaking in rebuke of all the citizens of Capernaum—'Except ye see signs and wonders, ye will in no wise believe' The man replied, 'Sir, come down, ere my child die,' and Jesus said, 'Go thy way, thy son liveth.' And the man 'believed the word that

---

Hebrew words that resemble a form of "*know*," and is once actually confused with γνωστοί (Nehem v 10)

The "mingling" of water with "wine" is explained by Jerome as the "mingling" of the human with the divine in the Incarnation "Divinitatis suae arcana capere non valentibus, assumptae humanitatis sacramenta patefecit...in vino mixto conjuncta in unam Christi personam Deitatis et humanitatis ejus natura exprimitur vel certe in pane, corporis ipsius, in vino mixto, sanguinis Sacrosancti Mysterium, quo in altari (mensa videlicet ejus) satiamur, ostenditur." I have not found anything like this in the six or more passages where Origen quotes Prov ix 2—3

[1] Mt. viii 6 ὁ παῖς μου, "my boy," is ambiguous. The parall. Lk. vii. 2 δοῦλος is not. But "my boy" is abrupt if it means "my servant"—as if the centurion had only one servant Luke avoids this by "a servant who was very-dear (ἔντιμος) to him."

He spake,' and returned without repeating further the prayer 'Come down¹.' This is the only sign that shall be recorded in the account of this second journey to Galilee. Not that there were not others. But they were unimportant as compared with this. For this Nobleman was lifted up above the belief of those in Capernaum, who 'would not believe, except they saw signs and wonders' The belief that sprang from this sign seems to me to be a continuance, or resumption, in Galilee, of the belief that sprang from the sign at Cana, and it was performed near Cana. Therefore I call it the second after the return to Galilee:—'This is again the second sign done by Jesus after coming from Judaea into Galilee'."

---

¹ Jn iv 47—9 ἠρώτα ἵνα καταβῇ...κύριε, κατάβηθι. .invites comparison with Mt viii 7 λέγει αὐτῷ, Ἐγὼ ἐλθὼν θεραπεύσω αὐτόν, and with Lk vii 3 ἐρωτῶν αὐτὸν ὅπως ἐλθὼν διασώσῃ. It will be observed that in Luke, the elders say to Jesus, in effect, "come thyself," though Matthew represents Jesus as saying "I will come myself"

The original of Matthew-Luke was perhaps "The centurion sent," followed by "And he [*i e* the centurion] spake [*i e* through the messengers] that he [*i.e.* Jesus] should come and heal" The latter was understood wrongly by Matthew, as meaning "And he [*i e.* Jesus] said, himself, that he would come and heal" Luke understood it correctly and amplified it for clearness, stating who the messengers were and what they said.

CHAPTER VII

JESUS BEGINNING TO "PREACH"

THIS Chapter will cover less textual ground and more evangelic thought than is covered by any of the preceding Chapters, because it deals with the first utterance of the Gospel of Peace, and therefore with "peace" as conceived by Jews and as introduced by them to Gentiles. It will be shewn that "peace," or *Salem*, meaning also "perfection," "completeness," and implying the building up of parts into a perfect unity, conveyed to Jews a whole world of spiritual thoughts not patent to Gentiles. Of this we catch glimpses in the name "Salem" itself, and in Melchizedek, the King of Salem, or Peace; and in Jerusalem, supposed to mean the Vision of Peace; and especially perhaps in Solomon That king, in himself, does not stand high, either historically or spiritually; but his name meant the Completer or Perfecter, and early Jewish Christians would regard him as the type—though a faint and unworthy type—of a Second Son of David, who was to be the Prince of Peace indeed, and to build up the spiritual Temple of which it might be said in truth, "The Lord is there[1]."

Not without interest, though subordinate to these deeper considerations of spiritual thought, will be some textual considerations as to the several attitudes of the Synoptists toward the conception of peace. "The peace of God," being connected by Isaiah with the publishing of the gospel or good-tidings,

---

[1] Ezek xlviii 35

might have been expected to receive a prominent position at the outset of all the Christian Gospels. Yet this is not the case. Among other questions, we shall ask—and even if we cannot fully ascertain we shall hope to derive profit from asking and attempting to ascertain—why Mark and the Johannine Epistle never mention "peace" in the sense that we are considering; why Luke places it early in the introduction to his Gospel but not at the end, and why the Johannine Gospel, omitting it at the outset, inserts it at the end as a kind of legacy to be bequeathed to Christ's disciples when He departs from them, along with the gift of the Spirit which He breathes into them from Himself.

§ 1. *Christ's first words—in Mark and Matthew*

According to Mark, the first words uttered by Jesus in His preaching were "The [appointed] time is accomplished (*or*, fulfilled) and the kingdom of God hath drawn near; repent ye and believe in the gospel (*or*, good-tidings)," preceded by a statement that in these words He was "preaching (*or*, heralding) the gospel (*or*, good-tidings) of God[1]."

Neither in Hebrew nor in Greek is the noun "good-tidings" used in O.T. about "good-tidings" sent from God. But the verb "tell-good-tidings" is repeatedly thus used by Isaiah, meaning "tell the good tidings of the salvation of God[2]." This prepares us to believe that Mark regarded Jesus as referring to Isaiah's first use of the verb. "O thou that *tellest-good-tidings* to Zion, get thee up into the mountain...." This is all the more probable because Mark has just been representing the Baptist as quoting from the same chapter some

---

[1] Mk 1 14—15 (W.H.) κηρύσσων τὸ εὐαγγέλιον τοῦ θεοῦ [καὶ λέγων] ὅτι Πεπλήρωται ὁ καιρὸς... SS omits "and saying." It is probably an interpolation.

[2] Gesen. 142 *a*, Is xl. 9 (*bis*), xli. 27, lii 7 (*bis*), Nahum 1 15. All these except Is. xli. 27 have εὐαγγελίζομαι.

preceding words, "The voice of one that crieth, In the wilderness prepare ye a way. .[1]"

Accordingly, we find that what is practically the Marcan "[appointed] time," and the Marcan "accomplished (*or*, fulfilled)," are both in Isaiah's context, connected thus· " Speak ye comfortably to Jerusalem, and cry unto her that her *appointed-time-of-service* is *accomplished*; that her iniquity is pardoned .." This agrees with Mark in effect, so far as the "accomplishment" of the "time [of service]" is concerned, except for the difference between "*the*" and "*her*[2]". It should be added that the word used by Mark for "accomplish" is the same that Aquila regularly uses to represent the Hebrew word in Isaiah[3]. Also, whereas Mark adds that it is the good tidings "*of God*," this, too, is implied in Isaiah ("Comfort ye, comfort ye my people, *saith your God*[4]")

Yet in spite of all this evidence, patent to modern students comparing Mark with Isaiah, it is doubtful whether ordinary Gentile converts to Christianity in the first century would

---

[1] Mk 1. 3, Is xl. 3

[2] Is. xl. 2, R V. text "warfare," marg "time of service" See Gesen. 839 *a* Rashi gives (1) the Targum's interpretation ("a populo transmigratio," but Walton "populo transmigrationis [ejus])", (2) "*fore-ordained time* (as in Job vii 1)" Comp Dan x 1 R V "*warfare*," where Rashi has (as A V.) "*time-appointed*"—concerning the period of trial in store for Israel Rashi would give the same meaning to the word in Dan viii. 12 (R V and A.V. "*host*") i e he would take it as meaning, not a number of *men* collected for service, but a time appointed for trial and trouble, like the service of war Gesen 839 *a* limits the meaning "hard service of troubled life" to Job vii 1, xiv 14, Is xl 2, Dan x 1 Ibn Ezra, on Is. xl. 2, mentions the explanation "*host*," but prefers "*appointed time.*" This suits the parallelism of the context

[3] Πληρόω. It happens that here LXX has ἐπλήσθη (besides paraphrasing "period of [hard] service" as ταπείνωσις) This Heb. word for "fill" is also used in Jer. xxv 12, xxix. 10 about the "*accomplishing*" of the "seventy years" of the captivity (Gesen. 570)

[4] In writing to Gentiles this was a useful qualification. It is most freq. in the early Pauline epistles (Rom 1 1, xv. 16, 2 Cor. xi. 7, 1 Thess ii 2, 8, 9) comp. 1 Pet. iv 17, and Rev. xiv 6 εὐαγγέλιον αἰώνιον.

perceive the allusion to the "fulfilment" of the "appointed-time." And to some it may have seemed inconsistent with passages in the Gospels in which Jesus says "ye know not when *the appointed-time* is," or, "ye know not *the day nor the hour*[1]." Moreover, if we are to say "the appointed time of hard service *has now been fulfilled,*" ought we not to add "and the appointed time of consolation *has now begun*"? But Mark says merely "the kingdom of God *hath drawn near* (not, *begun*)"

Then follow precepts. These are not strictly parts of the "gospel," since imperatives are distinct from affirmatives. But they are consequences of the gospel. The first is "repent." The second is "believe in the gospel." Concerning "repenting," we have always to remember that the Hebrew word often conveys the thought of turning to the Lord God from false gods, and to the light from darkness. It is therefore not unfit to receive prominence in a new atmosphere of joy, since it means "Turn unto the Lord who hath graciously turned toward you."

Still, the precept "Believe in the gospel," coming at the end of the words assigned to Christ by Mark, does not seem equal, in the strength of its appeal and spiritual power, to corresponding precepts that might be derived from the context in Isaiah, which says, in effect:—"Why sayest thou, O Jacob, that thy way is hid from the Lord? He giveth power to the faint. Hope ye upon the Lord and He shall renew your strength[2]." To Jews, who knew what Isaiah's "good-tidings" or "gospel" meant—and who could see in it the promise of the return of the ransomed from the captivity of Babylon, of

---

[1] Mk xiii. 33, Mt xxv 13, comp Lk xii. 40. In Lk. xxi 8, false prophets or deceivers are introduced as saying "*the appointed-time* hath drawn near"

[2] Comp Is xl 27—31. On "repentance," see *Son* 3564 *a*, quoting Luther's saying "There is no true repentance that does not begin from the love of righteousness and of God."

any Babylon, political or spiritual, that might be at any time oppressing Israel—the precept "Believe in the gospel" would make a strong appeal. But on the ears of a Greek, ignorant of the prophets, the words would fall so abruptly, and with such a vernacular suggestion of believing in unexpectedness and good luck, that it is almost surprising that the clause has been allowed to remain in Mark unaltered, coming suddenly on the reader as the end and climax of Christ's earliest utterance[1].

Christ's first words, in Matthew[2], are a reproduction of a portion of those in Mark, only in a different order. Matthew omits "The time is accomplished" and "believe in the gospel." He puts the precept "repent" before the announcement of "the kingdom." Also, as usual, he alters "kingdom of God" into "kingdom of the heavens." The result is that the "preaching" of Jesus is represented as simply reproducing in identical words and order the "preaching" of John the Baptist when he came "*preaching* in the wilderness of Judaea, saying, *Repent, for the kingdom of the heavens hath drawn near*[3]." Moreover Matthew refrains, at this point, from following Mark by making any mention of "gospel" in his own person.

Why does Matthew thus apparently condense the already brief and obscure text of Mark? Was he dissatisfied with it as a representation of Christ's words? He does not describe Jesus as "preaching the gospel" till later on, "And Jesus went about in all Galilee, teaching in their synagogues, and *preaching the gospel of the kingdom*, and healing all manner of disease and all manner of sickness among the people[4]." Nor

---

[1] The *Diatessaron* alters the order thus, "Repent ye and believe in the gospel. The time is fulfilled and the kingdom of heaven hath come near."

[2] That is to say, the first words in Christ's public teaching (Mt. iv. 17)

[3] Mt. iii 2, rep iv. 17

[4] Mt. iv. 23, parall. to Mk i. 39 "and he went into their synagogues throughout all Galilee preaching and casting out devils," Lk. iv. 44 "and

does he mention the word "gospel" as used by Jesus till much later[1]. Does Matthew mean that "the preaching of the gospel," in the strict sense of the term, did not begin till the signs of the gospel appeared in acts of exorcism and healing? This might naturally be a popular view.—"The 'good tidings' of Isaiah," people might say, "included acts of healing[2]. John the Baptist's 'preaching' did not. But Christ's preaching did, after a short time Then the latter became *the preaching of the gospel*'." Some thought of this kind may have influenced the authors of the traditions followed by Matthew[3].

§ 2. *Christ's first words—in Luke*

It was not likely that Luke would accept from Matthew a version of Christ's first public utterance which described Him as repeating verbatim the preaching of John the Baptist.

---

he was preaching in the synagogues of Judaea" (see p 209 foll, above). "Kingdom" and "preach-the-gospel" occur in an immediately preceding saying of Christ (Lk. iv 43) "I must *preach-the-gospel-of* the kingdom of God" This Matthew omits But what Luke represents Jesus as *saying He must do*, Matthew represents Him as actually *doing*.

[1] Mt. xxiv 14, xxvi 13

[2] It is true that the *words* "preach good tidings," do not perhaps occur in Isaiah in connection with healing. There may however be an instance in Is. lxi 1 "*preach good tidings the opening [of the prison]* to them that are bound"—where, instead of "the opening [of the prison]," R V. marg. has "*the opening [of the eyes]*"; and the LXX, for "them that are bound," has "*the blind*," and, for "the opening," has "*the opening-of-the-eyes* (ἀνάβλεψιν)." But the *substance* of the "good tidings," namely, the Return of the Captives, is described long before; and that is definitely connected with the healing of the "*blind*," "*deaf*," "*lame*," and "*dumb*" (Is xxxv. 1 foll) "The wilderness...shall be glad...the eyes of the *blind* shall be opened ."

[3] It seems strange that the Synoptists do not contrast John the Preacher and Baptizer, who (Jn x 41) "worked no sign," with Jesus the Healer, who (Acts x 37—8) "after the *baptism* that John *preached*... went-about *benefiting and healing* all that were oppressed by the devil."

This might be all the more objectionable to Luke because he seems to have, so to speak, cleared out of the way all details about the Baptist, in order to prepare the way for an uninterrupted account of the acts and deeds of Christ. He has described in detail the Baptist's birth, appearance, doctrine—and his imprisonment, too, though out of chronological order—before describing his baptism of Jesus. His object is now to represent Jesus as introducing at last that new and great dispensation for which John came to prepare the way. John is the last of the prophets. Jesus is the Son. To represent the Son as opening His mission by repeating the same sentence as the Prophet might well seem strange. Jerome excuses it by saying that the Son repeats as a son what the Prophet proclaimed as a prophet. But the excuse is more ingenious than convincing.

On the other hand, how could Luke reproduce Mark's words " *The appointed-time is accomplished,*" when he has just written " Having completed every temptation the devil departed from him *until an appointed-time* "? Luke also had to face the difficulty—at least a difficulty for him—in the noun " evangel." This he never uses. But Mark uses it here twice in a single sentence.

A remedy, however, was open to a well-educated Greek, familiar, as Luke was, with the LXX, and aware that Mark was obscurely alluding to the " good-tidings " in Isaiah. The remedy was to quote instead of alluding. We can imagine Luke asking, " Why did not Mark make his meaning clear by this obvious method ? In Isaiah, ' *tell-good-tidings* ' is repeated in such a context as to give no offence, even to an educated Greek. Then Mark's readers would have understood the correspondence between the Old and the New Covenant or Testament. Isaiah prophesied the ' good-tidings ' of the return of Israel from the captivity of Babylon; Jesus, the Anointed of the Lord, was anointed to proclaim the 'good-tidings' of a return from the Captivity of the spiritual

Babylon. This is what Mark really meant. But he has not said it."

If that was Luke's view, he might naturally give at full length some prophecy about the "good-tidings" in Isaiah to which, as he conceived, Jesus was referring. Writing in his own person as an evangelist, Luke has already done this above, with reference to the prophecy concerning "the voice of one crying" There he not only made the meaning of the prophecy clear by quoting it fully, but also made it clear that the prophecy was not uttered by the Baptist but merely quoted by himself, Luke, evangelistically. In the present instance, Luke appears to have followed some tradition which alleged that Jesus, besides *alluding* to Isaiah, did actually *quote* from Isaiah. He may well have found what seemed to him sufficient evidence to shew that Jesus actually *read* from Isaiah a passage that adequately and briefly described Isaiah's "gospel" and the Messiah as being anointed to "preach" it.

Such a passage Luke alleges to have been read by Jesus (who afterwards applied it to Himself) in the course of His Galilaean teaching when He came to Nazareth, the place where He had been brought up, and when, according to His custom on the sabbath day, He entered into the synagogue: "The Spirit of the Lord is upon me, because he anointed me to publish-the-gospel to the poor; he hath sent me to proclaim release to captives and recovering of sight to the blind, to set at liberty them that are oppressed (*lit.* bruised), to proclaim the acceptable year of the Lord[1]." Luke also brings in Mark's word, "accomplished (*or*, fulfilled)," as part of Christ's comment on Isaiah; in the course of which He applies it, not to any "appointed-time," but to this "scripture" about the

---

[1] Lk. iv. 18, quoting Is lxi. 1—2. But "to set at liberty them that are oppressed (*lit* bruised)" is in Is. lviii. 6, not in Is. lxi. 1, where the clause following "anointed...meek (*or*, poor)" is "he hath sent me to bind up the broken-hearted." See *Son* **3584** *a*

JESUS BEGINNING TO PREACH

Anointed one, who was to "proclaim" such great things: "He began to say unto them, To-day hath *this scripture* been *fulfilled* in your ears"

§ 3. *Objections to the Lucan account of Christ's first words*

Mark and Matthew have not recorded any early visit of Jesus to Nazareth, nor have they related any attempt on Christ's life at Nazareth at any time. They have indeed recorded a visit, later on, to what they call "his own country," presumably meaning Nazareth, and their account of it resembles the account in Luke in two points. First, the Nazarenes say "Is not this the carpenter, or the carpenter's son, or Joseph's son?" as though this were inconsistent with His claims; secondly, Jesus observes, in reply, "A prophet is not without honour save in his own country" or "No prophet is acceptable in his own country."

But the sequel in Mark and Matthew exhibits nothing similar to the attempt at murder described in Luke, but merely says that Jesus "was not able there to do a single mighty work," or "did not do there many mighty works because of their unbelief[1]." There is no allusion in either Mark or Matthew to any pre-existing unbelief; and indeed Mark adds that He "marvelled" at their present unbelief. How could He "marvel," if, a short time ago, they had attempted to murder Him? It will be shewn hereafter that, besides these considerations, others also make it very difficult to believe that Mark and Matthew knew anything of the Nazarene outbreak described by Luke, and much more easy to believe that Luke's story is based on misunderstanding

Further, if we look closely into the words of Isaiah supposed to have been read and applied by Jesus to Himself, we

---

[1] Mk vi 1—6, Mt. xiii 53—8, Lk iv 16—30 Mark adds that Jesus healed a few infirm people and that He "marvelled because of their unbelief"

shall find that they represent a Person coming almost entirely as a Herald, Preacher, or Proclaimer, not as a Doer of deeds of healing or saving, nor as an actual Saviour[1] But heralding is rather the part of John the Baptist than the part of Jesus. It is as the Shepherd or Healer of Israel that Jesus should be represented. No doubt it would be a mistake on the other side, and it is a mistake from which Mark is not perhaps free, to lay so much stress on Christ's acts of exorcism and healing as to throw His spiritual healing into the shade But it seems also a mistake to lay so much stress on " the wonder " caused by Christ's teaching and by what Luke here calls " the words of grace which proceeded out of his mouth," and then to add that, almost in the moment when "all wondered" at these "words of grace," they asked " Is not this Joseph's son?" and promptly proceeded to attempt to take His life Luke does not seem to have ascertained all the circumstances of Christ's home. Where Mark tells us that Christ's "household," or "people at home," sought to restrain Him, saying that He was "beside himself," the parallel Luke differs and is probably less accurate[2]. John, in due course, states distinctly that the brothers of Jesus themselves "*did not believe*" *in Him*[3]. If Luke had known—what can hardly be doubted to have been a fact, for who would have invented it as a fiction?— that the Lord's own brethren did not believe, we might suppose that he would hardly have accepted a narrative which *holds up Christ's neighbours in Nazareth to censure for not believing at so early a date*, and even accuses them of an attempt to murder Him

---

[1] The only clause that expresses *doing*, as distinct from proclaiming, is, in Luke, "to set at liberty them that are bruised" But that is not in Isaiah lxi 1 (see above, p 240, n. 1) In Isaiah lxi 1 the only clause that expresses *doing* is "to bind up the broken-hearted"

[2] Mk iii 21, Mt. xii. 23, Lk. xi. 14—16. This must be discussed later on

[3] Jn vii. 5.

JESUS BEGINNING TO PREACH

Another objection to the Lucan narrative, from the Johannine point of view, is the obscurity of the concluding words—left unexplained—in the lesson from Isaiah: "to proclaim *the acceptable year of the Lord*" What was the "year"? Did it mean a literal "year" or not? We might have supposed that "year of acceptance" would be understood to be not literal, any more than "day of salvation", but, as a fact, the Valentinians took it in a literal sense, and, though bitterly attacked for it by Irenaeus, were abetted in this view by Clement of Alexandria and Tertullian[1]. So early a belief may very well have induced the author of the Fourth Gospel to emphasize a contradiction of a chronology that was based on the supposition that the period of the Lord's public work was no more than one "year of acceptance."

§ 4. *John on "appointed-time"*

The Marcan word "appointed-time," omitted here by Luke, a word fairly frequent in the Synoptists and capable of various meanings, is used by John in only one passage, but there thrice, perhaps with a play on the Hebrew word meaning both "*appointed-time*" and "*feast*" "Jesus therefore saith unto them, My *appointed-time* is not yet come, but your *appointed-time* is always ready, ..Go ye up unto the *feast* [i.e *appointed-time*]. I go not up [yet] unto this *feast* [i.e. *appointed-time*] because *my appointed-time hath not yet been*

---

[1] Clem Alex 407, Tertull *Adv Jud.* § 8, Iren ii. 22. 1—5 Origen on Lk iv 19 takes the words spiritually, but says, "Juxta simplicem intelligentiam aiunt uno anno Salvatorem in Judaea evangelium praedicasse, et hoc esse, quod dicitur 'praedicare annum Domini acceptum, et diem retributionis,' nisi forte quiddam sacramenti in praedicatione anni Domini divinus sermo significat" On Mt xxvi 2, after saying that the hour, the day, the month of the Crucifixion were defined, he adds "Ego autem puto etiam annum, de quo Propheta dicebat 'praedicare annum Domini acceptum et diem salutis'." "Retributio" and "salus" represent Heb. "vengeance," LXX ἀνταπόδοσις.

accomplished[1]" Having regard to the fact that the Greek "*appointed-time*" and the Greek "*feast*," in the LXX, are each represented about thirty times by one and the same Hebrew word, we may, without over-subtlety, regard these words as conveying a caution against imputing to Jesus definite doctrines about "times" and "seasons" of men, when His mind was set on the times and seasons of God. As in Philo, so here, "*appointed-time*" means God's appointed time bringing forth "the three fruits" of the spiritual Israel[2]

But this is not all. Besides this exceptional use of a Synoptic term, later on, John also at the outset expresses the same thought in his own language, using "*hour*" instead of "*appointed-time*." At Cana, during the feast, when Christ's mother says to Him "They have no wine," Jesus replies, "Woman, what have I to do with thee? *Mine hour is not yet come.*" As later from His brethren, so here, even from His mother, Jesus detaches Himself, when the thought of His "hour" places itself in apparent and momentary opposition to her suggestion. This saying stands up in plain opposition to any interpretation of the Marcan words in question that would make them mean "The appointed time for triumph is fulfilled." Before that could come, Israel must be able to say, "*My warfare is accomplished*" Christ's reply to His mother perhaps implies a thought of that kind, "*My warfare is not yet accomplished*; the wine of the Cross is not yet ready."

---

[1] Jn vii 6—8 See *Son* **3414** (ii) *c—d* In canon LXX (Tromm.), "appointed-time"=(30) καιρός, (31) ἑορτή. It is not probable that the appointed-time was regarded by John as "accomplished" even when Jesus cried "It is finished," or when He said "Receive the Holy Spirit" More probably it will not be "accomplished" (*Light* **3999** (iii) 15) till the final outpouring of the Spirit.

[2] Philo calls them Abraham, Isaac, and Jacob, by which he means faith, joy, and spiritual insight. Christians might call them faith, hope, and love See Philo i 277 and 455 quoted in *Light* **3781** *n*, and add his remarkable comment on man's making "time" into a false god, in opposition to the true God (*Quaest Gen.* on Gen vi. 13, where the Heb. "*end of all flesh*" has been rendered by LXX "*appointed-time* of every man").

§ 5. *John on "kingdom," "repentance," and "gospel"*

"Kingdom"—which, along with "appointed-time," is prominent in Mark's account of Christ's first words—John does not mention in the whole of his Gospel except negatively—first, to shew that the Kingdom of God can *not* be entered except under certain conditions, secondly, in the trial before Pilate, to shew that Christ's Kingdom is *not* "from this world[1]."

In both cases, Jesus is represented as contending against an ingrained misconception of what "kingdom" means. To Nicodemus Jesus says that none can "see," or "enter into," the Kingdom of God except by being "born from above." But Nicodemus has not mentioned either "kingdom of God," or "kingdom." He has merely said "We know that thou art a teacher come from God, for no man can do these signs that thou art doing except God be with him." Jesus says, in effect, "How do you know that I am 'come from God' and that God is 'with' me? Is it not because you think of God as the Great King in heaven, who does what He likes, and who sends His servants with power to do what they like, overruling the limits of mortal action, by what you call 'signs'? But God is not such a king. God is the Father in heaven, and you must be born from heaven if you are to 'see' what you call His 'kingdom'."

A similar thought, a negative one, pervades the second passage. And there, too, it is to be noted that "king" comes unexpectedly and abruptly from Pilate's mouth, no mention of the title having been made by Christ's accusers. "If this man," they say to Pilate, "were not an evil-doer, we should not have delivered him up unto thee." "Judge him yourselves," he replies. "No," they say, "it is a capital offence, and we have no power to inflict death." Then, for the first time questioning Jesus, Pilate says "Thou art [I think] the King of the Jews?" Jesus

---

[1] Jn iii 3—5, xviii 36

replies, in effect, "Is this your thought or theirs?" Pilate avoids, or perhaps evades, this question. "Am I a Jew? Am I to be supposed to understand all your Jewish bickerings? What hast thou done?" Then comes the reply of Jesus "My kingdom is not from this world," with an explanation of its non-worldly nature

Even those who are unable to believe that this dialogue is history must admit that it admirably represents what Pilate must have said if he said anything, and also that it is admirably adapted to supplement Synoptic and oriental expressions about "the Kingdom" and to shew that, in essence, the doctrine of Jesus about the true King was not unlike the doctrine of the best Greek philosophy.

As to the Marcan precepts, "repent," and "believe in the gospel," it has been pointed out that John never uses either the word "repent" or the word "gospel." Instead of "repent" he uses expressions that denote a new condition or attitude of the soul toward the light, or toward the truth, or toward the Father or the Son. Instead of "the gospel" he speaks of "the name of the Son" or "the Son." All "belief" is to be based on the Son

This last fact would also suffice to explain why John could not accept as adequate the words placed by Luke in Christ's reading at Nazareth, "The Spirit of the Lord is upon me, because he anointed me to publish-good-tidings to the poor." It was not to *publish* a gospel of peace, but to *be* a gospel of peace that Jesus came. Also what He was He was not only to "the poor," but to all the sons of man. To give such a prominence to "the poor," without regard to the question whether the meaning was "poor in spirit" or "poor in possessions[1]," would be, in the special circumstances of the Christian Church, a misleading course, especially as the Hebrew adjective was

---

[1] Comp Mt. v. 3 "poor in spirit," Lk vi. 20 "poor," on which see *Son* 3242 (iv) *a—c*

not adequately expressed by the Greek word meaning "poor[1]."
Not improbably John regarded the "publishing of the good
tidings" of peace to "the poor" as referring to the inclusion of
the Gentiles. He would certainly have said as the Epistle
to the Ephesians says, "For he [*i.e.* Christ] is *our peace*, who
made both [Jews and Gentiles] one and brake down the middle
wall of partition [between them][2]"

§ 6. *Christ's first words—in John*

So much for John's negative attitude to the Synoptists in
their accounts of Christ's first words. We have now a somewhat harder task before us For, in attempting to answer
the question positively "What were Christ's first words—that
is, His first public utterance—in John?" we find ourselves
obliged to ask "What are we to define as 'public?' How
many disciples must be present to constitute a 'teaching'?
Are two enough, according to Christ's saying about 'two or
three gathered together'? If they are, then Christ's first words[3]
are those addressed to two disciples of John the Baptist:
'John was standing, and two of his disciples. And he looked
stedfastly on Jesus as he was walking-about and saith, Behold,
the Lamb of God And the two disciples heard him speaking

---

[1] In Is lxi 1 R V has txt "*meek*," marg "*poor*"

[2] Eph ii 14, comp. Mic v. 5 "*And this [man] shall be [our] peace*,"
that is, the man from (Mic v 2) "Bethlehem Ephrathah" After Zech. ix 9,
"riding upon an ass," comes ix. 10 "he shall speak peace unto the
nations", and after the "riding upon an ass" in Jn xii 14 comes the
saying of the Greeks (xii. 21) "We would see Jesus"

[3] That is to say, those regarded as Christ's "first words" by John. It
may be asked, "What is the use of knowing this? If we did know it, we
should not be knowing *history* It would be merely Johannine *fiction*,
or—we will concede so much—*selection*" The answer is, that the
Johannine author is a man of such spiritual insight—not to speak of the
possibility that he had special information as to some facts—that we might
reasonably attach value even to his "fiction" (if it were fiction, which it
is not), and much more to his dramatic "selection," as throwing light on
the words and deeds of the historical Jesus

and followed Jesus But Jesus turned, and, having beheld them following, he saith unto them *What seek ye*[1]?'" This was the Teacher's first lesson

Nothing can well seem simpler than this. Yet it is a simplicity often ignored, or forgotten by clever people, who wish to teach too quickly, and try to fill a pupil's mind without first making him feel that it needs filling. In old days, says the Scripture, "a certain man" found Joseph "wandering in the field" and said "What seekest thou?" The Targum says the "man" was "Gabriel." Philo says it was "the convicting conscience[2]." Not improbably John is alluding to that ancient Hebrew story and to the Jewish traditions illustrating the first Biblical instance of that most searching question "What seekest thou?" But in any case, even if there were no such allusion, this selection of the first saying of Jesus—so flat and disappointing to minds that cannot recognise any beauty in the slow and unobtrusive methods of Nature—would claim attention as giving us a clue to the whole of the Johannine representation of Christ's method of teaching He came to make us little children And He began to teach us (as Nature teaches little children) by putting questions to us that we cannot fully answer He knows that we cannot answer, but He puts them to us in order that we may put them to ourselves, and then, failing to obtain the full answer from ourselves, obtain it from Him The first saying, then, is not "teaching" at all. It is merely a question that every one must answer for himself and yet cannot answer by himself.

The second saying is, "Come, and ye shall see[3]." It is in answer to the question "Rabbi, where abidest thou?" And this saying, again, is mystical. It is from the lips of the Son,

---

[1] Jn i 35—8. Note also the first utterance of the risen Saviour (Jn xx. 15) "Woman, why weepest thou? Whom seekest thou?" See above, p 191, n 5

[2] Philo i. 195—6 on Gen xxxvii. 15. See *Son* **3380**, comp **3620**.

[3] Jn i 39

who is always, even when on earth, "in the bosom of God."
By "coming" to Jesus, the two disciples were to "see"—what
even the Son could not put into human words—the glory as
of the Only begotten Son of God After many years of
waiting, the Son had seen the Spirit of Sonship descending
on Him, and felt it abiding in Him, sending Him forth to the
world that He might begin at once to open men's eyes at least
so far as this, that they, too, should "see" something of what
the Son "saw," the vision of the Fatherhood of God Here,
then, is something more than a question. It is a promise of
"seeing." And it might be said to imply mystically a promise
that they should "see" God's Fatherhood by entering into the
Circle of His Family, the Spirit of His Household, so that they
would become God's children But still there is nothing that
can be called—in the ordinary sense of the word—"doctrine"

The next saying is, to Peter, "Thou art Simon, son of
John, thou shalt be called Cephas[1]." Here, again, there is
a promise, preceded by something of the nature of a warning ·
"Thou shalt attain hereafter to be called 'rock,' but thou art
not 'rock' as yet Thou art simply Simon, son of John"
This takes us another step towards the doctrine of the
heavenly birth—since Peter was to be made akin to Him
whom the Scriptures repeatedly speak of as the Rock of
Israel, or the Rock of Salvation. At the same time this brief
narrative reveals Jesus as having power not only to attract
men—for by what means, if not by some special power, had
He attracted the two disciples?—but also to discern in man
both character and promise, and to call out or generate
strength in one who was at present weak in comparison
with his potential and future self.

The next saying is "Follow me[2]." It is addressed to
a convert named Philip, without a word of introduction, thus,
"On the morrow he resolved (*lit* desired) to go into Galilee,

---

[1] Jn 1 42   [2] Jn 1 43

and he findeth Philip" Not till afterwards comes the hinted explanation ("now Philip was from Bethsaida, of the city of Andrew and Peter") that Jesus knew Philip through talk with Andrew, and "resolved" to "find" this lost soul[1] Why did not the Evangelist put this explanation before the "finding"? It seems to be because he wishes to lead his readers on to see for themselves continuously—without an excess of didactic interruption on his part—how marvellously powerful is the personality of this "finder" of the souls of men, and how He not only has in Himself the Spirit that "finds" souls, but also can impart it to others by a kind of divine infection. Accordingly the next verse says, "Philip *findeth* Nathanael, and saith unto him, We have *found* him, of whom Moses in the law, and the prophets, did write, Jesus of Nazareth, the son of Joseph[2]." The "finding" in the second sentence is curiously —and we may almost say ironically—introduced. Philip has not really "*found*" the Messiah The Messiah has "*found*" him.

There is also something of irony but a great deal more of feeling that is far from irony, in the assignment of these particular words to Philip. By him, Jesus is assumed to be "the son of Joseph" For others (later on) as also in Luke, this is a stumbling-block[3] But it is not so to Philip. Again, for Philip, Jesus is "of Nazareth" (not "of Bethlehem"). That, in the very next sentence, is alleged by Philip's own friend as an obstacle to Messianic claims Philip does not repeat his implied argument by again appealing to "the law and the prophets" Having himself "seen," he invites Nathanael to do the same, "Come and *see*." Brief though

---

[1] See above, pp. 212, 213, 224   [2] Jn i 45
[3] Jesus is nowhere else called "the son of Joseph" except in Lk iv 22 and Jn vi 42. In these two passages the term is uttered in disparagement by unbelievers. Here (Jn i 45) it is uttered by an enthusiastic believer seeking to make a convert. Comp Lk. iii. 23 "*the son (as was supposed) of Joseph*"

the dialogue is—and unhistorical as it may be—it contains what even a sceptical historian might admit to be the secret of the success of the Church of Christ. The Church did not really base itself on "the law and the prophets" except so far as these were interpreted and personified by One superior to any Lawgiver and to any Prophet. And Philip's faith was really based on the personality of that divine Saviour who had come to Galilee to find and save him, as a shepherd might find a lost sheep, which he knows out of the whole of his flock, and can call by its separate name. Jesus, the Good Shepherd, had, as it were, called Philip by his name, and Philip at once "knew his voice." Or, to use the language of Isaiah, we may say that the Messiah had the power of "speaking to the heart of Jerusalem[1]," and that Philip had "the heart" that enabled him, or compelled him, to respond to the appeal.

§ 7   *The Dialogue with Nathanael*

Next comes Christ's dialogue with Nathanael. The context is noteworthy as containing the first instance of the making of a convert who has raised objections. In Nathanael faith is called out by Christ's supernatural and sympathetic knowledge ("when thou wast under the fig-tree I saw thee") Yet here again, as in the case of Philip, the faith is too great to be explained on intellectual grounds If Nathanael had been moved by nothing but Christ's power of "second sight," we can conceive that He would have gone so far as to say "Sir, I perceive that thou art a prophet," as the Samaritan woman says later on to Jesus when He tells her of her "five husbands"; but that he should say to the seer of the scene under the fig-tree "Thou art the Son of God, thou art King of Israel" is hardly explicable except on the supposition that the brain-evidence based on this power of "seeing" was merely an addition to a great mass of heart-evidence derived partly from

---

[1] Is xl 2 (R V. marg)

Philip's testimony but much more from the presence of Jesus Himself: "He 'saw me under the fig-tree'! Then all that has been said about Him by Philip, and all that my heart tells me about Him in His presence—all this, and more than all this, must be true!"

What follows may be divided into two parts. The first is a gentle half-reproach to Nathanael for building his belief on such slight grounds, and a promise, in the singular, that he shall have more solid grounds hereafter· "Because I said unto thee, I saw thee under the fig-tree, believest thou? Thou shalt see greater things than these." The second is a promise in the plural to all the converts present ("ye shall see") It seems to assume that the descent of the Holy Spirit at Christ's baptism had been accompanied with that momentary "rending" or "opening" of "the heaven" which the Three Gospels had described but which the Fourth has not described. And it assures the disciples that this "opening" shall henceforth be permanent, fulfilling the vision of Jacob's ladder in a new sense This new sense is introduced with a new term —new at least in this Gospel—"the Son of Man" It is used apparently with some allusion to Nathanael's exclamation "Thou art the Son of God." If so, it is adapted to startle the reader into an astonishment and perplexity that will not pass away but will set him thinking and questioning himself "What did the Lord Jesus mean when He apparently set aside Nathanael's confession 'Thou art *the Son of God*,' and, instead of praising him for it, directed his attention to what seems a lower title, saying to him, 'Ye shall see the heaven [always] open and the angels of God ascending and descending upon *the Son of Man*'?"

Taking the two parts of the utterance together we appear to find Jesus suggesting to Nathanael that, instead of beginning from "the Son of God" in his attempt to attain the supreme vision of the Truth, he would do better to begin from "the Son of Man", and instead of beginning from "the King of

Israel," a picture that calls up thoughts of courtiers and officers of state that come between the Sovereign and the subject, he would do better to aim at some conception of a closer communion When the "heaven" is once thrown "open," no messengers of heaven, no "angels," must be allowed to interpose themselves between God and the sons of man. The "angels" that minister to man's salvation are such as ascend to the Father from man's heart lifted up by the trustful and loving Spirit of Sonship, and descend, in the power of the same Spirit, with gifts of righteousness and peace. Jesus Himself, in His baptism, had "seen" this ascent and this descent, and He promised His disciples that they also should see it But if they were to "see" it they must begin, in some sense, from below. They must learn from the Son of Man to understand, and love, and spiritually "see," the other sons of man, their brethren and His. Then they will be able to ascend, from the Brother whom they have seen, to the Father whom no man can see but whom the Son of Man will "declare[1]"

§ 8   *Which of these accounts is the closest to history ?*

Roughly, we may answer the question at the head of this section by saying " Mark is closest as regards the preservation of words actually uttered by Jesus, such as ' appointed-time ' and ' gospel ', but John is closest as regards the representation of His thoughts, influence, and Spirit " If we accept Mark's phrase " there hath been fulfilled the appointed-time" as the closest approximation in the Four Gospels to Christ's earliest utterance, it will be subject to the proviso that Mark gives us here only a summary, inadequately expressed, of Christ's proclamations of the fulfilment of Isaiah's prophecy concerning the redemption of Israel from captivity. Mark was also probably right, we may say, in assigning to Jesus a word that the careful historian Luke and the spiritual

---

[1] Comp Jn i 18, xiv 9, 1 Jn iv 20

evangelist John never attribute to Him—*evangel*, or *gospel*. But then we should have to add that "gospel" was meaningless for all readers who could not supply an answer to the question "gospel *of what kind?*" "evangel *conveying what good tidings?*"

As to John, the combination of mysticism and history in his Gospel makes conclusions of a general kind very difficult We might be disposed to say that the preceding examination has shewn him to be a poet, not a historian. Writing an account of the creation of the Church, he certainly treats it as a six-days Genesis, followed by a Sabbath. " His chronology therefore," it might be said, " must not be regarded historically. The naming of Simon as Peter did not take place till long after the Johannine date John also places a visit to the Temple at the beginning, instead of at the end, of Christ's public career. Nothing, therefore, that he states as a fact, ought to be accepted as a fact, unless corroborated by some other Evangelist."

But every now and then come indications that John gives more heed to historical detail than we had supposed. Mostly, these relate to details in Mark omitted by Luke But the call of Philip is not mentioned by Mark, and in the Johannine account of it we found traces of allusion to a Matthew-Luke tradition Also the giving to Simon of the name of "Cephas" (a form of the name not found in any Synoptist) is corroborated by early Pauline Epistles. And the brief narrative of the naming gives the impression of fact, not of invention. Moreover the substitution of the Apostles for their Master, in the Johannine narratives of the Calling—so that Peter is not exactly "called" by Jesus but is brought to Jesus by Andrew, and Nathanael is brought to Jesus by Philip—does not seem at all likely to have been invented, or to have "sprung up" as an automatic tradition

The tendency of popular and erroneous tradition is to concentrate the action of a great man's agents or followers on the great man himself—as trial by jury used to be attributed to Alfred. But here we find actions that the Synoptists attribute to Jesus taken away from Him and attributed to disciples. What motive was there for this if Jesus did them? Was it to correct false inferences from the Synoptic accounts of the Call of Peter by shewing that he was, in two senses, second to Andrew, both as to the time, and as to the directness, of the calling? That would not explain the repetition of the indirectness in the calling of Nathanael. More probably the Evangelist is protecting his readers against taking Mark's condensations and summaries as literally exact. The calling of the four fishermen Apostles did not perhaps take place all at once, as an isolated action, in the manner described by Mark. And John is glad to emphasize the fact that, from the first, the influence of Jesus, when it passed into any disciple, could not be restrained from passing further. It was not like water in a cistern. It was a fountain It gushed forth from each converted soul, which, having now life in itself, could not but become a source of life to others.

At the same time it is possible to harmonize these Johannine accounts with those in the Synoptists, if we suppose that, after becoming the Lord's disciples, the Apostles returned to their homes and lived for the most part there until Jesus summoned them to go forth as missionaries. Such a reconciliation between the Three Gospels and the Fourth, adopted in the Diatessaron, is very much more easy than the task of reconciling the Mark-Matthew account, with the Lucan account, of the calling of Peter There the Diatessaron in consecutive narratives, first (following Mark-Matthew) represents Jesus as saying to Simon and Andrew, while casting their nets, "Follow me, and I will make you fishers of men" Then (following Luke) it represents Jesus as finding Simon again, washing his nets, and as repeating the call—after a miraculous draught of fishes—in similar words, "Fear not, henceforth thou shalt be a fisher of men unto life" Two such consecutive calls of Simon seem most improbable, especially when we find Mark and Matthew omitting the second, which is accompanied by something like a miracle, and Luke omitting the first, which has no claim to anything like a miracle. It may be said that the second call, like the second appearance to Hamlet of his father's ghost, was intended to "whet" Peter's "almost blunted purpose." But in that case, should we not have expected Luke, as an accurate historian, to have inserted the first calling in order to explain the meaning of the second? Luke gives us no hint of a first call. He leaves us under the impression that he is not supplementing the Mark-Matthew narrative but substituting for it one that he considers more accurate. It seems probable that there was actually current, in the days when Luke wrote his Gospel, a tradition, and a true one, connecting some kind of call of Peter—a second call—with a wonderful draught of fishes. And, so far, Luke was accurate. But he has been misled as to its date. According to John, it occurred much later on, after the Resurrection, when Peter, in penitence, returns to the service of his Lord.

For these reasons we can lay down no general rule as to the comparative accuracy of Johannine and Synoptic accounts, where they differ. True, we have ascertained that, where Luke deviates from or omits what is in Mark, John often steps in to explain what is obscure or harsh in Mark, and to explain it in a form differing from the form in Luke. But we have not ascertained that in all such cases John is superior in historical accuracy, though in many cases he appears to have been superior in spiritual insight.

As regards chronology, and especially the chronological question of the number of passovers included in Christ's public career, there is almost as much difficulty in Luke, who professes to write exactly and in chronological order[1], as in John,

---

[1] See the section entitled "Luke attempted to write in chronological 'order'" in *Introduction*, p. 108 foll.

JESUS BEGINNING TO PREACH

who makes no such profession. Luke says that the parents of Jesus went "*every year*" to the Passover, and, "when he was twelve years old, they went up *after the custom of the feast*[1]." The Law prescribed that every male Jew of age should go up to the three feasts. Luke, however, subsequently only once describes Jesus as going up to Jerusalem, and to only one feast, the Passover that closed His public life. It has been shewn in the Introductory Volume that if that public life included only one Passover, it is impossible to explain Mark's narrative about the cornfields in such a way as to reconcile it with the Synoptic chronology[2].

John, on the other hand, expressly describes Jesus as going up to the Feast of Tabernacles as well as to the Passover and possibly to the Feast of Weeks. That is at all events more consonant with what we might expect from a Jewish Messiah. There is also something scripturally and as it were dramatically satisfactory in the Johannine view that Jesus, immediately after the sign at Cana and a stay of "not many days" at Capernaum, went up to the Passover in Jerusalem to purify the Temple from defilement. Like the child Jesus, in Luke, so the man Jesus, in John, associates His entrance into public life with what He calls "my Father's house[3]." And by this speedy arrival Jesus also fulfils the prophecy in Malachi, "The Lord, whom ye seek, shall suddenly come to his temple[4]." We might suppose that in the next Passover (or Passovers) Jesus repeated this action, but that John omitted it (because he assumed that He repeated it). Hence he would omit it in his description of the last Passover, whereas the Synoptists inserted it in their descriptions of that Passover, because they

---

[1] Lk. ii. 42.
[2] See *Introduction*, p. 89 foll., referring to Mk ii. 23 foll.
[3] Jn ii. 16 "my Father's house," Lk. ii. 49 lit. "in the *things* of my father," but Syr. and Palest. have "*house*."
[4] Mal. iii. 1.

had no opportunity for inserting it before. This is what might be said in favour of the Johannine narrative[1].

"But is it possible," we may ask, "that Jesus, at the outset of His career, and unsupported as yet by any multitude of disciples, could have achieved, or would even have attempted, such a task as the expulsion of traders from the Temple— a task colossal, physically, and implying a deadly collision with the Jewish authorities? Surely it would have been premature!"

Perhaps it would have been premature, and, therefore, was not attempted. But perhaps it was premature, and, in spite of this, was actually attempted. As at Cana, the "hour was not yet come," but the action may have taken place, to be repeated afterwards. Moreover, as to our assumption that Jesus would have been "unsupported," are we safe in assuming it? Are there not indications that Jesus was more popular, early in His career, before He had, in effect, refused to make any attempt to release John the Baptist, than afterwards? The abuse of selling "doves" for "pence of gold" was rife at this time. "By this Temple," said Rabban Simeon Ben Gamaliel, "I will not lie down this night unless they be sold for pence of silver." Is it not conceivable that Jesus, too, a few years before Rabban Simeon, made the same protest, but in action as well as word, in the midst of a swarm of sympathizing Galilaean pilgrims—who did not much care about spiritual discourses, but did care a great deal about the inconvenience, as well as the religious and national disgrace, of such extortion in the rulers of God's Temple[2]?

---

[1] There remains, against the Johannine narrative, the difficulty of explaining why John the Baptist did not aid Jesus in the attempt to cleanse the Temple. On this, see *Introduction*, pp. 95—6.

[2] See *Son* **3585** *c—d* on the "pence of gold." Origen allegorizes all the accounts of the Cleansing of the Temple. Concerning the use of the "scourge of cords" in the Johannine account, he says (*Comm. Joann.* x. 16) "Let us consider the Son of God taking the cords...whether it does not imply, besides a self-willed audacity, the element of disorderliness (τὸ ἄτακτον) too." Westcott says "Jewish tradition (Sanhedr. 98 b, Wunsche)

Our conclusion is, that although Mark happens to have preserved Christ's original allusion to the "good-tidings," or "good-tidings of peace," mentioned in a certain passage of Isaiah—which Luke has expressed by referring to a different passage of the same prophet—yet all the Synoptists left much to be done in the way of expressing, first, the meaning of "the gospel," and, secondly, the precise part played by Jesus in "the gospel." The Fourth Evangelist, more clearly than the Three, sees and helps us to see, that Christ Himself *is* "the gospel." For He is, as Paul says, "our peace"—the essence of that Good Tidings of Peace which Isaiah and John the Baptist predicted, and which Jesus, by His personal and indefinable influence, brought into the hearts of His converts one by one, that they might bring it into the heart of the whole world.

§ 9 *Why is not the gospel, or "good-tidings," called "the good-tidings of peace" by Mark, as by Isaiah?*

This question all the more demands an answer because the Matthew-Luke account of the Instructions to the Apostles tells us that the first words of the missionary entering any house were to be " Peace be to this house[1] "; and Peter in the Acts describes God Himself as "preaching good-tidings of

---

figured Messiah as coming with a scourge for the chastisement of evildoers." But *Sanhedr.* 98 b neither mentions a scourge nor implies it (unless it is implied in the interpretation of Is. liii. 4 as meaning that the Messiah will be smitten with the scourge of leprosy) Wetstein, *Hor Heb*, and Schottgen, give no such reference to the Talmud. These facts indicate that evangelists had no reason for inventing the detail of the scourge but some reasons for omitting it

[1] Lk. x 5—6 "And into whatsoever dwelling ye enter, first say, Peace to this house. And if a son of peace be there, your peace shall rest upon him (*or*, it), but if not, it shall turn back to you," where the original appears to have been rendered more freely by Matthew (x 12) "And on entering into the dwelling salute it. And if the dwelling be worthy, let your peace come upon it. But if it be not worthy, let your peace return to you" See *Clue* **254** foll, *Son* **3371** *d*

peace through Jesus Christ[1]"; and almost all the Epistles open with a salutation mentioning "grace and peace." Yet Mark never mentions the noun "peace" except once, and that only in the phrase "Go in peace," uttered by Jesus to a woman whom He had healed. This last instance may throw light upon the answer to our question. The Three Gospels have severally:

Mk v. 34	Mt. ix. 22	Lk. viii. 48
Thy faith hath saved thee. Go-back in (*lit.* to) *peace,* and be (*lit.*) sound from thy plague (*lit.* stroke).	Thy faith hath saved thee. And the woman was made-whole (*lit.* saved) from that hour.	Thy faith hath saved thee. Go in (*lit.* to) *peace.*

It will be observed that the Three exactly agree in the words uttered by Jesus, "Thy faith hath saved thee," but differ as to what follows It is highly improbable that Matthew and Luke would have omitted what Mark has added if they had believed it to be His utterance. But the passage may be explained by others in LXX, where we find interchanges such as "go *in peace*" with "go *in health*[2]." The Hebrew "peace" means, or is confusable with, a great number of words signifying "health," "soundness," "completion," "making-up [a reward, or recompense]" &c. When it means "peace," it is capable of meaning not only peace as distinct from war, but also moral and spiritual peace, peace with one's own heart and peace with God. It may also mean the soundness of perfect physical health[3].

---

[1] Acts x. 36

[2] Exod. iv 18 βάδιζε ὑγιαίνων Οἱ λοιποί πορεύου εἰς εἰρήνην, Gen xxvi 31 μετὰ σωτηρίας: Οἱ λοιποί· μετ' εἰρήνης, Gen. xxxvii. 14 εἰ ὑγιαίνουσιν, Ἀ. Σ. τὴν εἰρήνην.

[3] Gesen. 1022 gives the noun as meaning "completeness, soundness, welfare, peace." In Prov xiii. 13 "he that feareth the commandment *shall be rewarded,*" A.V. marg gives "*shall be in peace*" (Aq. and Symm. εἰρηνεύει) and LXX has "*is in good health* (ὑγιαίνει)." For passages shewing that "and thou shalt become sound" might be confused with "and she became sound," see *Clue* **28, 84, 87, 240.**

JESUS BEGINNING TO PREACH

Now the "good-tidings of peace" in Isaiah apparently announces the return of captives to their home in Jerusalem through "a highway in the desert," along which the Lord, like a shepherd, leads His flock[1]. But in a preceding passage a similar return is described as that of "wayfaring men" (not sheep), whose leaders are bidden to "strengthen the weak hands" and "confirm the feeble knees," and to whom it is said, "Behold your God will come with vengeance, with the recompence of God, he will come and save you Then the eyes of the blind shall be opened and the ears of the deaf shall be unstopped. Then shall the lame man leap as an hart, and the tongue of the dumb shall sing; for in the wilderness shall waters break out, and streams in the desert[2]." Both passages appear to describe a journeying in the wilderness like that of the Exodus, when Israel was delivered not only from bondage but also from the danger of the diseases of Egypt[3] and from the danger of acquiescing in the idolatrous religion of their oppressors, and it is difficult to say where the spiritual or hyperbolical ends and the physical or miraculous (if intended) begins[4]

We have to try to put ourselves in a position where this difficulty would be greatly increased We have to try to imagine the unmeasured astonishment that would fall on pious and patriotic Jews, when, for the first time in Israel (Moses alone being excepted) there arose a great Prophet

---

[1] Is. xl 1—11   [2] Is xxxv 1—10.

[3] Comp Exod ix 14, and Deut vii. 15 "The Lord will take away from thee all sickness, and he will put none of the evil diseases of Egypt (which thou knowest) upon thee."

[4] The Jews differed (see Ibn Ezra on Is xxxv. 3) Most referred the prophecy to Messianic times, but R. Moses Hakkohen to the return of fugitives under Hezekiah On "the tongue of the dumb shall sing" Ibn Ezra's comment is "A figurative expression for 'they will find water everywhere' It is the reverse of Lam iv. 4" The Targum takes "blind," "deaf," &c, as "blind to the Law," " deaf to the words of the prophets," &c.

and Teacher, who not only taught with surpassing force and conviction, but also worked mighty works of healing on so vast a scale that even Elisha (so far as number of miracles was concerned) fell into insignificance beside Him. Was it not inevitable that such mighty works should assume a prominent, a too prominent, position in the popular conception of the "gospel" proclaimed by Jesus? Those who rejected Him would (doubtless) reject altogether the applications of prophecy to His works. But those who accepted Him as the Shepherd of Israel would also accept Him as the Shepherd predicted by Isaiah, and then, how could they fail to interpret these prophecies of Isaiah as literally predicting His mighty works? Especially would this be the case at a time when another prophet—and that a great one, like John the Baptist—was preparing the way for Jesus and working no mighty works at all. A contrast would inevitably be drawn, and exaggerations would be almost equally inevitable—"John worked no wonders, Jesus could work wonders at will."

Some apparently resulting exaggerations will come before us when we discuss Mark's Gospel in its order. For the present, in explanation of Mark's failure to mention, or at least to emphasize, "peace[1]," we may give, as one reason, the fact that he identified "the gospel of *peace*" with "the gospel of *healing*." More especially he dwells on that particular kind of "healing" which delivered a man from such internal wars and tumults of the soul as were attributed in those days to what was called demoniacal "possession."

This is but one of many instances where Mark, though often closely approaching the exact words uttered by Jesus, appears to have failed to express their meaning, sometimes

---

[1] It should be added however that Mark, alone of the Evangelists, uses the verb "be-at-peace." He alone inserts, in the doctrine about 'salt," the words (ix 50) "Have salt in yourselves and *be-at-peace* (εἰρηνεύετε) among one another."

perhaps through want of spiritual insight, but sometimes in consequence of some corruption in the tradition that he followed[1]

[1] In previous parts of Diatessarica so many instances have been given of errors caused by Hebrew corruption, and so few of errors caused by Greek corruption, that I venture to place here, out of its order, an apparent instance of the latter kind, in order to shew that such a possibility is not ignored (though, even here, Hebrew corruption also may not improbably have been at work)

It occurs in Mk x 21 "But Jesus (1) having looked stedfastly on him (ἐμβλέψας αὐτῷ) (2) *loved him* (ἠγάπησεν αὐτόν)." Matthew and Luke omit both clauses They might well omit "*loved him*" at all events. For why should Jesus have "*loved*" this wealthy "ruler," who said that he had fulfilled from his youth all the commandments including (according to Matthew) "thou shalt love thy neighbour as thyself," which Paul (Rom xiii. 8) describes as the "fulfilling" of the whole Law? Field suggests that ἠγάπησεν means "*caressed*," "*fondled*", *Hor. Heb.*, that חמד here meant "*pitied*," but was rendered "*loved*," as in LXX of Is lx. 10, Zech. x 6, Prov xxviii 13 This is perhaps the best solution. But another is given below

(1) The Hebrew original stated that Jesus looked stedfastly at the man and saw that "he *deceived* himself" In the earliest Greek tradition, this was rendered ΗΠΑΤΗϹΕΝ ΑΥΤΟΝ The writer of the extant Mark mistook this for ΗΓΑΠΗϹΕΝ ΑΥΤΟΝ—a confusion paralleled in 2 Pet ii. 13 R.V txt "*love-feasts*," marg "*deceivings*" (W H txt ἀπάταις, marg. ἀγάπαις), and freq in LXX (*e g* Sir xxx 23) The Johannine Epistle says (i 8) "If we say that we have no sin we *deceive* (πλανῶμεν) ourselves and the truth is not in us"

(2) But Hebrew confusion may also have been at work as follows. This rich ruler was one of the "rulers" about whom John (xii. 40) quotes Isaiah, "*he hath blinded*" (quoted by Matthew xiii. 14—15 (LXX) "*they have shut fast*") "their eyes" Isaiah's word, שעע (Gesen 1044) means (i) "*be blinded*," confusable (*ib.*) with (ii) "*look about*," and (iii) "*take delight in*," "*fondle*." Mark thrice repeats "*look*" or "*look about*," ἐμβλέπω or περιβλέπω, in this narrative (x 21, 23, 27) On the hypothesis of Hebrew corruption, he has based his narrative on the interpretations of שעע as (iii) "*fondle*," (ii) "*look about*," and dropped the right interpretation (i) "*blinded himself.*"

(3) As regards Mk x. 21 εἶπεν αὐτῷ Ἕν σε ὑστερεῖ, the original meaning probably was "*The one thing [needful]* is wanting to thee," namely, God, or the love of God, alluding to the preceding x. 18 εἰ μὴ εἷς ὁ θεός. Comp. Wetstein on Lk x. 41—2 quoting commentators who say that "the one thing needful" is either "the commandments," or the

§ 10. "*I came not to send peace but a sword*[1]"

The explanation given above of the non-mention of a "gospel of peace" in Mark does not apply so well to Matthew and Luke, who lay less stress on exorcism. Still less does it apply to John, who mentions no exorcism at all. In these Evangelists we must search for another reason. This investigation will be quite different from investigation of confusions between the words "peace," "safety" or "salvation," "healing," "life-giving," and the rest. It concerns the question, a purely spiritual one, "What is, in the highest sense, true peace?" What did Jesus say about "peace" in this sense? And in what way, if any, did He connect it with "gospel"?

The words placed at the head of this section are not the only indications that Jesus would not have called His gospel a gospel of *immediate* "peace." The context proceeds to say that one result of Christ's mission will be to produce division in families. Similar division is predicted by all the Synoptists, in the Discourse on the Last Days[2] When Philip (or whoever it was) was bidden to "leave the dead to bury their own

---

"love" that includes them all. After αὐτῷ (written as AYTO) TO may easily have dropped out before EN.

These facts suggest an entirely new view of the rich ruler. He "ran forth," but does not follow Jesus when He (Mk x. 17) "was going forth into the way." He thought he saw the truth, and said, in effect, "I see." But he blinded himself in his self-love, and hugged the wealth that blinded him when Jesus tried to open his eyes. This prepares the way for a contrast. The poor beggar Bartimaeus, conscious of blindness, beseeches Jesus to remove it. Throwing aside his cloak, the blind man leaps up and comes to Jesus. Then he receives his sight from Jesus, and (Mk x. 52) "followed him in the way."

[1] Mt. x. 34 (Instructions to the Twelve), "Think not that I came to bring peace on the earth. I came not to bring peace, but a sword," Lk xii. 51 "Suppose ye that I came-forward to give peace in the earth? No, I tell you, but only division."

[2] Mk xiii. 12, Mt. xxiv. 10, Lk xxi. 16. But Matthew repeats this prediction in Mt. x. 21 (Instructions to the Twelve) where it is much closer than Mt. xxiv. 10 (Last Days) to Mk xiii. 12.

dead," the "gospel" that came with such a bidding might naturally be declared by Philip's family to bring "not peace, but a sword"

How different from the gospel of Epictetus, who publishes a "good-tidings of peace" indeed. Well may he boast of its promises, if only they can be fulfilled. "You see," he says to his disciples, "the seeming greatness of the peace that Caesar provides for us—no more wars, no battles, not even brigandage of any importance or piracy worth mentioning" But (he goes on to ask) can he "provide us peace" from fever, shipwreck fire, earthquake or lightning? Can he from passionate love, from sorrow, or from envy? The answer is "Not from a single-one of these things But the Word (or Logos) of the philosophers promises even from these things to provide peace. And what saith it? 'If, O ye men, ye will give heed to me, then, wheresoever ye may be, and whatsoever ye may be doing, ye shall be neither vexed nor angered, neither constrained nor restrained. Untroubled and free from all bondage shall be your life.'

"Possessing such a 'peace,' not proclaimed by Caesar—for whence has Caesar power to proclaim this kind of peace?—but proclaimed by the [one] God through the Word (*or*, Logos), surely a man should find all he needs even when he is alone, looking at [facts] and thinking in himself, 'In my present state no evil can befall me For me a robber is not, earthquake has no existence The whole world teems with peace, teems with quietude Every road, every city—every fellow-traveller, neighbour, or companion—is deprived of the possibility of harming me[1].'"

Long before Arrian published his notes of the lectures of Epictetus, his teaching, and that of the earlier Stoics which he reproduced, must have been in circulation among many who did not profess to belong to the educated classes, and

---

[1] Epict iii 13 9 foll, on which see p. 453, n. 3

probably among many who, being slaves, had a fellow-feeling with the philosopher who had been a slave himself. Traces of his thought, if not of his language, appear in the Fourth Gospel[1]. But the chief interest of the passage above quoted lies in the fact that in the imperial world of the first century, there were some serious minds to whom the Pax Romana, even when it extended literally to every corner of the Empire, suggested the question, "What, after all, is true peace? One tyrant may devastate a city into a solitude and call that peace. That—we say in a chorus—is a false peace But is it not possible that another tyrant, by the constant pressure of his legal constraint, may convert cities of living men into cities of machine-like creatures, living in abundance of all material things, and enjoying what they call an unbroken peace because they have no right sense of evil within themselves, or outside themselves, against which they should make war? And is not that peace also false[2]?"

Such a feeling would correspond to the protest in Jeremiah against the false prophets, "They have healed the hurt of my people lightly, saying, Peace, peace, when there is no peace[3]." And Epictetus himself—can he be altogether acquitted of the charge of "healing the hurt of his people lightly"? He will have it that, for the philosopher, there are "no wars, no battles," all things "teem with peace" And yet elsewhere he deprecates marriage for the Stoic missionary, on the ground that the Stoic ought to be "free from distraction" during the present condition of things which is "as it were in line of battle[4]." Doubtless he would defend himself on the ground that the sole conflict is against a man's own vain

---

[1] See "Epictetus" in Indices to *Joh Gr*, *Son*, and *Light*.
[2] Comp Acts xxiv. 2 with *ib*. 26 about the "*peace*" that Tertullus professed to "enjoy" under Felix and the "money" that Felix hoped to extract from Paul. It is difficult to believe that Luke did not himself feel an ironical "enjoyment" in setting down this contrast.
[3] Jerem. vi 14, viii 11.　　　　　　[4] Epict. iii 22. 69

imaginations[1] But such a defence is based on his belief that no philosopher ought to call anything an evil, if he has not the power to remove it. The errors of his own disciples, the sorrows or sins of his own friends or children—these are things that the philosopher will rightly endeavour to remove. But if he fails, he will feel no sorrow, no trouble, no disquiet. Such feelings cannot enter into him. Such is the perfection of the Epictetian peace!

§ 11. *"Peace," in Mark and Matthew*

Such "peace" was, at all events, not for the disciples of Jesus. For them, there could be no peace till the Kingdom of God was established. Mark does not record the words in the Lord's Prayer acknowledging that this "Kingdom" is, as yet, to "come." But he does record, in Christ's first sentence, the statement that it has merely "*drawn near*"

What Christian "peace" meant, the Pauline Epistles shew, though they do not define it First, it included the certainty that all things work together for good for the children of God. Secondly, it included the recognition of the fact that the sins and evils against which the children of God are contending in the world are evils in fact—and not in mere word or fancy—evils that must needs pain, and sometimes even trouble, the souls of the righteous.

This peace, this combination of restfulness under conflict, joy beneath pain, confidence beneath trouble, this sense of daily victory underlying daily defeat, is expressed in various scenes of the Four Gospels, describing Jesus as bearing the sins and imperfections of friends as well as enemies, but especially in healing diseases. But the underlying strength is sometimes obscured by the superincumbent pain. The

---

[1] Epict. ii 18 29 ("call upon Him to be thy helper and ally ($\pi\alpha\rho\alpha\sigma\tau\acute{\alpha}\tau\eta\nu$)") suggests a warfare; but the metaphor passes to a storm—"as sailors call on the Dioscuri in a voyage" And as for "the storm," he says, "For the storm itself—what is it but a vain-imagination ($\phi\alpha\nu\tau\alpha\sigma\acute{\iota}\alpha$)?"

Evangelists speak of "virtue" as "going out of him," or of His "grief" or "anger" at men's "hardness of heart," or of His "sighing." Other expressions, such as "a soul exceeding sorrowful, even unto death," "troubled" or "troubling himself," and "Jesus wept"—will come before us in due course. For the present we are concerned with the much rarer forms in which the Evangelists severally express, in Christ's words or their own, the sense that the gospel was "A gospel of peace."

Mark does not express it. It has to be inferred from his representations of Jesus as a healer of diseases and a conqueror of "demons," or, as he prefers to call them, "unclean spirits[1]." The casting out of "an unclean spirit" appears to be, in Mark, the first announcement of what the amazed multitude call "new teaching," and the sign of "authority." Luke follows Mark closely, but alters "new teaching" into "what is this word?[2]" Matthew omits the whole story. He has previously used up (so to speak) the Synoptic tradition about the "amazement" caused by Christ's "authority" by appending it to his version of the Sermon on the Mount, whereas Mark and Luke use it twice—first as an introduction, and then as a conclusion, to an act of exorcism in a Synagogue. It should be noted below that Luke twice departs from Mark by adding "*word*" in connection with "*authority*." Perhaps Luke desired to express his dissent from Matthew's view. According to Matthew, "authority" referred to Christ's way of teaching: "Ye have heard that others say so-and-so, but *I* [*authoritatively*] *say this*." But Luke perhaps meant "It was not the

---

[1] See *Joh. Voc* **1695**. "Unclean" does not occur in John and only once (doubtfully) in Epictetus. But in Mark it occurs more frequently than in Matthew and Luke taken together, and always in the phrase "unclean spirit." Matthew (almost always) and Luke (generally) prefer "demon ($\delta\alpha\iota\mu\acute{o}\nu\iota\nu$)."

[2] Mk i. 27 "What is this? *A new teaching!* With authority he commandeth even the unclean spirits...," Lk iv 36 "What is *this word* —that with authority and power he commandeth the unclean spirits...?"

JESUS BEGINNING TO PREACH

Lord's *teaching* that was with authority. It was His *word*. He taught with knowledge. But He commanded with authority. He said authoritatively to a devil 'Go!' and it went, at His *word*[1]."

Later on, it cannot be said that Mark gives us many glimpses of a bright and joyful Gospel of Peace. In the discourse on the Last Days, communicated privately to four disciples, the promise of being "saved" is only for him that "endureth to the end," and the last word is "Watch." Also the last word of the genuine Marcan Gospel is "afraid." And the last saying attributed to Jesus in the Marcan Appendix—which does actually conclude on a note of triumph—refers to the "signs" of the Church as follows: "These signs shall follow them that believe, in my name shall they cast out

---

[1] In the following, Mark twice uses the verb "teach" and twice the noun "teaching." Luke once uses the verb "teach," and once the noun "teaching," but twice adds "word."

Mk i 21—2, 27	Mt vii 28—9	Lk iv. 31—2, 36
And they go into Capernaum, and straightway on the sabbath day he entered into the synagogue and taught(ἐδίδασκεν) And they were astonished at his *teaching*, for he was teaching (ἦν διδάσκων) them as having authority, and not as the scribes... And they were all amazed, insomuch that they questioned among themselves, saying, What is this? A new *teaching*! With authority he commandeth even the unclean spirits, and they obey him.	And it came to pass, when Jesus ended these words, the multitudes were astonished at his *teaching* for he was teaching (ἦν διδάσκων) them as [one] having authority, and not as their scribes	And he came down to Capernaum, a city of Galilee. And he was teaching (ἦν διδάσκων) them on the sabbath day and they were astonished at his *teaching*; for his *word* was with authority. And amazement came upon all, and they spake together, one with another, saying, What is this *word*, that with authority and power he commandeth the unclean spirits, and they come out?

devils, they shall speak with [new] tongues; they shall take up serpents, and if they drink any deadly thing, it shall in no wise hurt them; they shall lay hands on the sick, and they shall recover." Such is the end of the words of Jesus in the completed Gospel of Mark[1]. There is no word about love, concord, or harmony. A Greek, contrasting his Apollo with this Marcan Christ, might say that the latter was the God of Harmony and Light without his lyre and bow, an Apollo reduced to an Aesculapius.

Matthew ends on a higher note—though briefly and obscurely. He refers again to that "authority" which he had mentioned at the conclusion of the Sermon on the Mount, where he described the Lord as promulgating the new Law in the place of the Law of Mount Sinai. There Matthew had said that Jesus "was teaching as one having *authority*" Now he represents Jesus as saying "All *authority* hath been given unto me in heaven and on earth[2]"; and this followed by a precept to His disciples to "make disciples," and by a promise of His presence ("lo, I am with you always") What is this "authority"? Authority is to be looked for in the ideal Ruler, and Jesus Himself has described the true Ruler as one who makes himself least of all and minister of all[3] And this is implied in the nature of God the Father who is perpetually giving Himself to man, and who gives even His Son to die that man may live[4] Through His Son, the Prince of Peace[5], the Father, who is the eternal and ever-giving Love,

---

[1] The second Mark-Appendix closes thus "Jesus .sent forth by them [i e the Apostles] the holy and incorruptible preaching of eternal salvation"

[2] Mt xxviii 18

[3] Mk x 42 foll, Mt. xx 25 foll, Lk xxii 25 foll.

[4] Mk x 45, Mt xx 28

[5] Comp. Philo i. 103 "Let us therefore give to the tyrant the title of Archon of War, but to the [true] king the title of Emperor of Peace, Salem" He is referring to Melchizedek, king of Salem.

JESUS BEGINNING TO PREACH

radiating unity and concord, draws all His children into the perfect peace of "The Family that is above[1]"

The original point and spiritual force of the last words of Matthew's Gospel is perhaps a little weakened for many of us by controversies arising out of the precept to "make disciples" and "baptize," which makes mention of "the Father and the Son and the Holy Spirit." Some say, "Here we have the earliest reference to the doctrine of the Trinity, and in Christ's own words"; others allege that the clause about the Three Persons is an interpolation, others say that the text may be sound but that the words were not uttered by Christ, and that the passage is later than many portions of Matthew's Gospel. Amid these controversies we may forget perhaps to ask, "What meaning would a Jew, such as the author of what we may call the Jewish portions of Matthew's Gospel, attach to the whole passage—with or without the Trinitarian words—when he wrote it down as expressing the substance of the blessing pronounced on His disciples by Messiah, the Son of God, departing to heaven and sending them forth to continue His work on earth?"

The answer is reasonably to be looked for in the words that constitute the essence of the blessing, "*I am with you always*[2]" It is a repetition of the promise (mentioned by Matthew alone) that where the "*two or three*" of "the family that is below" are "*gathered together*" in the name of the Son, there the Son will be present[3]. The very word "*with*," when it means "*together with*" and is applied to persons, whether human or divine, often leads to a thought of "peace." Those whom "*God is with*," are also "*with*"—that is, "*at peace with*"—one another[4] In one of the Psalms, "the Lord of hosts [is]

---

[1] Comp *Son* 3342 *a* quoting *Berach* 17 *a* "that thou mightest make peace in *the family that is above* and in *the family that is below*"

[2] Mt. xxviii 20   [3] Mt xviii 20

[4] Compare the Pauline expressions "The God of *peace* be *together with you all*," and "The God of love and *peace* shall be *together with you*," in Rom xv. 33, 2 Cor xiii 11, Philipp iv. 9

with us" is repeated twice as a refrain of war; but between the two war-cries comes, "*He maketh wars to cease* unto the end of the earth[1]." Also in Isaiah, the name of the Child who is to be called "*God with us*"—which also is repeated as a war-cry against the "two kings" whom Israel abhors, and against the invader who is to "fill the breadth of thy land, O *God with us*," encouraging Israel to believe that the counsel of the enemy "shall not stand, for *God* [*is*] *with us*"—prepares the way for other names of the Child, of which the last is "Prince of Peace[2]."

The Child-name "*God with us*," or Immanuel, is mentioned by no Evangelist but Matthew[3], and the thought implied by it in his Gospel appears to be a Christian development of the thought in the above quoted psalm and in the prophecies. Matthew teaches us to ask, as Paul asks, "If God is for us, who is against us[4]?" But he also teaches something else, something more than a mere statement that God is "for" men. He suggests, in a mystical manner, that when men are "*together with*" one another, in the Spirit of the Son, they are also "*together with* God,"—and like God—the divine Personality being (so to speak) "*together with*" Itself. In other words, there is something in the unity of "the Family that is above" corresponding to that peace which binds together "the family that is below[5]."

Paul says that this peace, the peace of God, "passeth all understanding"—where critics are divided as to whether he means that it is like the love of Christ which "passeth knowledge," or that it surpasses all device and counsel of

---

[1] Ps xlvi. 7—11.   [2] Is. vii. 14, 16, viii. 8—10, ix 6.
[3] Mt 1 23.   [4] Rom viii 31
[5] Comp. Clem Alex. 956, who says, concerning God, τὸ μὲν ἄρρητον αὐτοῦ πατήρ, τὸ δὲ ἡμῖν συμπαθὲς γέγονε μήτηρ. This does not say, in so many words, "God is our Mother as well as our Father." But that appears to be the meaning for plain persons, who are not metaphysicians and yet not materialists.

men¹. Origen perhaps inclines to the former. But the latter is also true. This "peace" passes our intellect when we attempt to apprehend its power, and it surpasses all the wise devices of lawgivers and statesmen when they attempt to mould families into nations. Matthew, in words that recognise this power as "all authority," closes his Gospel thus · "*All authority* hath been given unto me in heaven and on earth Go ye therefore, and make disciples of all the nations, baptizing them into the name of the Father and of the Son and of the Holy Spirit², teaching them to observe all things whatsoever I commanded you. And lo, I am with you always even unto the consummation of the aeon."

§ 12. *"Peace," at the beginning of Luke but not at the end*

Luke's view seems to be that Jesus came to the House of Israel with the message "Peace be unto this house!" but that "no son of peace was there," so that the peace "returned back" to Him³ Peace is frequently mentioned at the outset of his Gospel but not at the end. In the Introduction, Zacharias says "the dayspring from on high" shall "visit us, to shine upon them that sit in darkness .to guide our feet into the way of peace⁴"; but that implies a promise that men

---

[1] Philipp iv. 7 Lightfoot prefers the latter The context in Origen's *Exhort. Mart.* § 4 and § 37 (Lomm xx. 235, 286) rather suggests that Origen, interpreting the word emotionally, preferred the former In no case does his context suggest the latter Comp Eph. iii 19

[2] Eusebius is said to quote Mt xxviii 19 about 25 times either with "baptizing them *in my name*," instead of the Trinitarian formula, or else stopping short at "*nations*," and only once (in a genuine work) with the usual text But no other authority is alleged as omitting the formula (except for brevity) If there had been variations in the Greek text, would they not have been appealed to in early times by controversialists? The quotations of the passage by Tertullian and Origen shew that writers might often stop short at "nations"—where the object was to shew that the Gospel included "the nations" as well as the Jews—while elsewhere (and less frequently) giving the sentence in full.

[3] See Lk x 5—6 quoted above, p 259, n 1.   [4] Lk 1 78—9

shall receive light to see "the way of peace," not that they shall accept its "guiding." A little later, the angels sing "Glory in the highest to God and on earth peace," but it is only "in men of well-pleasing[1]"—such as Simeon, to whom it is given to "depart in peace" because his prophetic eyes have "seen," in the Babe, Jesus, the "salvation" of God[2]. Passing over such expressions as "go in peace," "his possessions are in peace[3]," we come to the two above-quoted passages, first, the instructions to the Twelve about the conditional message "Peace be to this house," and secondly, the disclaimer "Think ye that I came hither to give peace in the earth[4]?" Thus we are being gradually prepared for the failure of the gospel of peace when it is at last brought to Jerusalem.

Here Luke deviates widely from Mark and Matthew by inserting a tradition about Christ's weeping, which indicates that there is no hope of peace for the City of Jerusalem. David wept as he ascended the Mount of Olives departing from the City But the City was soon to welcome him, returning in peace. Jesus, on the other hand, "near the descent of the Mount of Olives," wept when He drew near and saw the City, saying "If thou hadst known in this day, even thou, the things that pertain to peace[5]!"

As if to prepare the way for this prediction of (in effect) no-peace—at all events no-peace for Jerusalem on earth,

---

[1] Lk. ii 14 on which see Hort's note. For "men of well-pleasing," comp. Dan. x. 11, 19 "man of desirableness," Vulg. "vir desideriorum," R V. "man greatly beloved" In almost all Origen's quotations of this passage the context lays stress, not on the limitation of the "peace" to a particular class of men, but on Jesus as the Giver of the "peace," so as to suit a reading of "man" for "men," that is, "Peace on earth *in the Man in whom He is well pleased*," preparing the way for the utterance of the Voice from heaven in Lk. iii 22 "*in thee I am well pleased.*" Perhaps Origen regards the "men" as incorporated in the Man of well pleasing.

[2] Lk. ii 29—30.

[3] Lk. vii 50, viii 48, comp xi. 21. We may also pass, as irrelevant, xiv 32

[4] Lk x. 5—6, xii 51   [5] 2 S. xv. 30, Lk. xix. 37, 42

no-peace for the City made with hands—Luke previously inserts, as a parallel to the Hosanna clauses in Mark and Matthew, an utterance of "praise" that does not point to any future salvation "on earth" (as in the song of the angels at the beginning of the Gospel) but to things of the recent or immediate past· "for all the mighty works *that they had seen*[1]."

The appeal to Jerusalem, "if thou hadst known the things pertaining to *peace*," implies to a Jew a paradox of pathos not at once intelligible to a Gentile For the word Jerusalem is said by Philo to have meant "vision of *peace*," and certainly meant, in some form, "city of *peace*[2]." For a Jew, there was a special aptness in the repetitions of the Psalmist, "Pray for the *peace* of *Jerusalem*...*Peace* be within thy walls!...I will now say, *Peace* be within thee[3]!" And so for a Jew here, there would be something paradoxical as well as pathetic in the fact that "*the City of Peace*" did not know "the things pertaining to *peace*" To Hosea the Lord says, concerning his new-born son, "Call his name *Lo-ammi* (i e. *Not-my-people*), for ye are *not my people*, and I will not be your [God][4]" So here, the King of *Salem*[5], bringing the bread and wine of *peace* to His own beloved City who refuses it, hears the word of the Lord saying "Call her name *Lo-salem, Not-Peace*, because she knoweth *not* the things that pertain to *peace*."

"For the sake of the house of the Lord our God," says the Psalmist just quoted, "I will seek thy good[6]." Jesus is here described as feeling the bitterness of "seeking" to "do good" to Jerusalem and of inability to do it. The "peace" that He

---

[1] Mk xi. 9, Mt xxi 9 (comp. *ib.* 15), Lk xix. 37 "had seen" may mean "had been seeing." For Lk. xix. 38 "peace in heaven," see below, p. 276

[2] Comp *Light* **3809** *c*, quoting Philo i 691—2 The actual origin of the name is uncertain, but it is certain that Jews regarded "salem" as meaning "peace"

[3] Ps cxxii. 6—8   [4] Hos. i. 9.   [5] Heb. vii 2

[6] Ps cxxii 9. Comp. Jn ii. 17 "the zeal for thy house"

JESUS BEGINNING TO PREACH

has been "seeking" for Jerusalem on earth is not to be found. Hence, in Luke's narrative of the Riding into Jerusalem, the tone of angelic exultation over good tidings fulfilled below ("peace on earth") is exchanged for the tone of human aspiration to something that must be fulfilled above ("peace in heaven") And not until "peace in heaven" has been attained can "peace on earth" follow as its consequence[1].

It is perhaps in part because of this view of the "good tidings of peace"—as a promise that could not be fulfilled on earth—that Luke deliberately concludes his Gospel on a note of suspense —"Tarry ye in the city, until ye be clothed with power from on high." The rest is simply a silent blessing[2]. It is reserved for the Acts to relate what follows. Even in

---

[1] Later on, it will be shewn that Luke's "peace in heaven" may be connected with other passages bearing on the Entry into the Temple — (1) Jn xii 31 "Now is the judgment of this world, now shall the prince of this world be cast out," (2) Mt xxi 16 (Ps viii 2) "Out of the mouth of babes .that thou mightest still the enemy" Comp (3) Lk x 18 "I beheld Satan fallen as lightning" followed by Lk x 21 "reveal them unto babes" "That thou mightest still the enemy" refers (according to Jewish interpretation) to the adversaries, or Satans, of Israel, and Origen says (on Ps. viii 2) "Understand [by this] the genuine ($\dot{a}\lambda\eta\theta\iota\nu\grave{o}\nu$) Nebuchadnezzar", it is also "the devil" (*i e* the "slanderer," slandering men to God as in the case of Job, as well as God to men) and the babes are "the illiterates and fishermen through whom Jesus brought the devil down"

Uncertainties as to the particular meaning of "Hosanna" uttered at a Passover, and as to the best way of explaining it to Greeks, may have induced the later Evangelists to insert traditions of good (though not of threefold) authority, illustrative of the general and spiritual meaning. The remarks of Papias on Rev xii. 7 "war in heaven" (see Swete) with the early scholia on the passage, and Origen's remarks on Eph vi 12 "the spiritual [powers] of wickedness in the heavenly [places]," shew that "war in heaven" was a subject of early discussion, which necessarily led to the thought of "peace in heaven" See *Light* **3809** *b* foll. on *Odes of Solomon* viii 8 "And peace was prepared for you before ever your war was"

[2] "Silent" in this sense, that when Jesus (Lk. xxiv. 50) "lifted up his hands and blessed them," either He said nothing, or what He said has been passed over in silence by the Evangelist.

the Acts the Apostles are still to wait till they are "baptized with the Holy Spirit" and to "receive power when the Holy Spirit is come upon them." Nothing follows till the day of Pentecost Then the Spirit descends, but the descent suggests power rather than peace: "There came from heaven a sound as of the rushing of a mighty wind...and they were all filled with the Holy Spirit and began to speak with other tongues, as the Spirit gave them utterance[1]." Some indeed mocked and said, "They are filled with new wine." Peter successfully vindicates the disciples, and preaches the Resurrection of Jesus and the promise of remission of sins, and the gift of the Holy Spirit, to those who will repent and be baptized in the name of Jesus Christ.

This may be said to imply "peace." But the word is not mentioned. Our minds are led rather to the thought of a Spirit—active against evil—that creates a "*partnership*" or "*fellowship*" between man and man, as well as a sense of peace with God. Accordingly, when the first proclamation of the gospel by Peter on the day of Pentecost has brought three thousand converts into the Church, Luke says "They continued stedfastly in the teaching of the Apostles, and [in] the *fellowship*, the breaking of bread, and the prayers[2]"

As regards Jesus Himself, the last words recorded in the Acts are "Ye shall be my witnesses both in Jerusalem and in all Judaea and Samaria, and unto the uttermost part of the earth[3]" But He leaves behind Him, as it were, a second

---

[1] Acts II. 2—4
[2] Acts II 42 The different meanings of N T. κοινωνία ("*partnership*," "*fellowship*," "*communion*"—representing at least two Hebrew words) will come before us in the Call of the Fishermen, where Luke (alone) describes the sons of Zebedee (v 7—10) as both μέτοχοι and κοινωνοί with "Simon" (comp. Jn xxi 3 "We also come *with thee* [i e. *Simon*]," and Gal. II. 9 where the Apostles "to the Circumcision" make some kind of κοινωνία with the Apostles "to the Gentiles") The first N T. instance of κοινωνία is closely followed (Acts II 42—4) by "they had all things common (κοινά)."
[3] Acts I. 8

utterance, reminding the Apostles—when "a cloud received him out of their sight" and they stood "looking stedfastly into heaven"—that they are not to stand there gazing up as though to find their lost Master in one of the seven heavens· "Ye men of Galilee, why stand ye looking into heaven? This [same] Jesus that has been taken up from you into heaven shall in-the-same-way come [back] [in] the [same] manner [in] which ye beheld him going [away] into the heaven[1]."

Why are the Apostles bidden to be witnesses "in Jerusalem, Judaea, and Samaria," but not in Galilee[2]? And, though they are, of course, Galilaeans, why should they be addressed as "men of Galilee"? Is there not something that would strike an educated Greek as a little suggestive of narrowness, something as it were provincial, in the selection of these particular words as a final utterance, on the part of, or by the representatives of, the ascending Saviour?

Possibly Luke has a deliberate purpose in this emphasis on "Galilaean" Both in his Gospel and in the Acts he emphasizes it, as though he knew there was a prejudice in the Roman Empire against the name, but a prejudice that must be overcome In his Gospel alone is there a protest of Jesus that certain "Galilaeans" were not "sinners above all the Galilaeans" because they had "suffered these things," and a warning, to those who reported this calamity, that they, too,

---

[1] Acts 1 11

[2] Perhaps because the witnesses of the Ascension (Acts 1 11), the speakers with tongues (*ib.* 11 7), and the witnesses of the Resurrection (*ib.* xiii 31), are all said to be from "Galilee" Note that the only mention of spiritual peace in Acts is in x. 36—7 "The word that *he* [i e God] *sent.. preaching-the-gospel-of peace* through Jesus Christ... beginning from Galilee." This implies that *God* "preaches" Comp Mk 1 14 "Jesus came into Galilee preaching the *gospel of God*" Is Peter supposed to mean here that God "preaches-the-good-tidings of peace," in the sense of "peace after war"? Comp 2 Cor. v 20 "We are *ambassadors* on behalf of Christ, as though God were intreating by us, we beseech [you] on behalf of Christ, *Be ye reconciled to God*"

would perish, unless they repented[1]. Also, in the Acts, Judas the Galilaean is mentioned by Gamaliel as a ringleader of rebellion whose projects perished with him, but the mention is accompanied with the suggestion, in effect, that if the projects of Jesus the Galilaean do *not* perish with him, it will be a proof that heaven is on his side[2]. These and other facts[3] indicate that Luke may have regarded "Ye men of Galilee" as an exhortation from heaven at Christ's Ascension bidding the disciples not to be ashamed of belonging to a small and despised province of a small and despised people. It was to be a trumpet-call to them to go forth conquering and to conquer till the world should be forced to cry "Vicisti, Galilaee!"

Nevertheless, to the Christians of the Empire of the end

---

[1] Lk xiii 1—3   Luke also alone records (xxiii. 6) Pilate's inquiry "whether the man [*i e* Jesus] was a Galilaean," and the sequel

[2] Acts v. 37

[3] Epictetus iv 7 6 speaks of the endurance of the Galilaeans acquired by custom, as matching the endurance of madmen. Josephus erects the Galilaeans into a separate sect along with the Pharisees and Sadducees. They were somewhat despised by the Jews of Judaea (*Hor. Heb.* i 170—1) for their blunt ways and their rough dialect   Justin Martyr and Hegesippus both include "Galilaeans" in their lists of the "seven" pre-Christian Jewish sects (*Dict Christ Biogr*, "Genistae"). Justin says (*Tryph* 80) that Jews would not admit them to be really Jews. He also accuses Jews thus (*ib.* 108) "You have sent...men throughout all the world to proclaim that 'a godless and lawless heresy has sprung from one Jesus, a Galilaean deceiver, whom we crucified...'" These are the only two instances of the word in Justin.

John uses the word only in Jn iv 45 "When he [*i e* Jesus] came into Galilee *the Galilaeans* received him, having seen all the things that he did in Jerusalem at the feast, for they also went to the feast" This is equivalent to saying, "It is a mistake to suppose that the early signs of the Lord were mostly performed in Galilee, and, more particularly, in Capernaum (as we might infer from Luke (iv 23)) On the contrary, they were performed in Jerusalem. The Galilaeans themselves owed their knowledge of them mainly to the fact that they had come up to Jerusalem, when Jesus also came up, at the outset of His public work, to celebrate the Passover"

of the first century, still expecting—but not perhaps in many places expecting immediately—the Coming of the Lord Jesus, there must have been some sense of narrowness in the limitation suggested by "Ye men of Galilee." Also there may have been something a little unsettling in the prediction of a corporeal descent, which might occur at any moment, exactly corresponding to this corporeal ascent. To some, the words in the Acts might read almost as though the angels said "You must not expect Him," and yet, in the same utterance, "Wait for Him to come from heaven at any moment[1]." Looking at Luke's Gospel and Acts as setting forth the last utterances of Jesus about His "good tidings of peace," some might prefer the selection of words like those in Matthew, indicating that Christ, our Peace, though taken from us in the flesh, is still with us and will be with us for ever. For any later evangelist, the question might well arise whether it was not possible to find, among the many traditions about the last words of Jesus, some that might shew how He combined the promise of His Spirit with the promise also of His personal presence.

§ 13. *"Peace," at the end of John, promised*

"Peace" occurs for the first time in John when Jesus, just before His arrest, prepares the disciples for His departure. Then He mentions it thrice, first, with reiteration, at the beginning of this preparatory doctrine, and then at the conclusion of it, when He turns from discourse to prayer[2].

At the outset, the disciples have been questioning Him as to a substitute, a mysterious Other, or Paraclete, whom He has promised to give them during His own temporary absence: "I will make request of the Father and he shall give you Another, a Paraclete...the Spirit of truth, whom the world

---

[1] Compare a scholium in Cramer (on Acts i 11) οὐκέτι εἴασεν αὐτοὺς αὐτὸν προσδοκᾶν...οὕτως ἐλεύσεταί, φησι, καὶ ὡς ἐξ οὐρανοῦ αὐτὸν προσδέχεσθε.
[2] Jn xiv. 27 (*bis*), xvi 33

JESUS BEGINNING TO PREACH

cannot receive, for it beholdeth him not, and knoweth him not, ye know him, for he abideth with you and is [indeed] in you I will not leave you orphans, I come unto you. In that day ye shall know that I am in my Father, and ye in me, and I in you[1]." Then in answer to another perplexed disciple, Jesus explains that this "coming" of the Father and Himself, and (presumably) of the Other self, the Paraclete, is a coming into the heart of him who lovingly does the will of the Son " If a man love me, he will keep my word, and my Father will love him, and we will come unto him, and make our abode with him[2]." At this point comes the first mention of "peace," connected with a repetition of the promise of the Paraclete, " These things have I spoken unto you, while [yet] abiding with you. But the Paraclete, the Holy Spirit, whom the Father will send in my name, he shall teach you all things and remind you of all things that I have said unto you *Peace* I leave unto you, *the peace* that is mine own I give unto you. Not as the world giveth am I giving unto you. Let not your heart be troubled, neither let it be fearful[3]"

This passage, mentioning, as it does, "the Holy Spirit," and also twice mentioning "peace," resembles one in the Epistle to the Ephesians, "And he came and preached-the-gospel-of *peace* to you that were afar off, and *peace* to them that were nigh; for through him we both have our access, in one *Spirit*, unto the Father[4]." But that, again, seems based on a passage in Isaiah, which also contains a twofold mention of "peace," and which, though it does not mention "Spirit," contains the word "comfort," of which the Greek is a form of "Paraclete." " I have seen his ways and will heal him . and restore comforts unto him and his mourners. I create the fruit of the lips : *Peace, peace* to him that is far off, and to him that is near[5]."

---

[1] Jn xiv. 16—20 On "Another, a Paraclete," see *Son* **3618**. "Is [indeed]"=W H. txt ἐστίν, marg. ἔσται (R V "shall be").
[2] Jn xiv 23.   [3] Jn xiv. 25—7   [4] Eph. ii. 17—18.
[5] Is lvii. 18—19 (LXX) "I have seen his ways and healed him and

Jerome, on Isaiah, quotes both the Gospel and the Epistle as describing fulfilments of the prophecy, and both of them appear to refer to it. The repetition of "peace" is, in itself, unlikely to be a mere coincidence, and the unlikelihood will be increased by evidence that will be given later on

As for the meaning of the "near" and the "far off," Jewish opinion was divided about it, but according to the Ephesian Epistle they are the Jews and the Gentiles, between whom "peace" is made by bringing both into Christ, "for he is our peace, who made both one[1]." The Epistle implies—but does not express—that each soul individually also finds peace in Christ. The Gospel does more than imply, it expresses the fact that this peace is given to the disciples as a gift. In this "peace" there is no thought of being reconciled to an offended God It might be called (as Paul, above-quoted, calls it) a reconciling of our estranged, suspicious, and timorous hearts to a loving Father But John dwells on it rather as being freedom from vague fears and troubles as to our future fate. "Let not your heart be troubled, neither let it be fearful[2]." It is the power of the Father ("the Father is greater than I") —not His love—that the Son anxiously vindicates, as affording a firm foundation for that "peace" which He emphasizes by a twofold repetition, by the emphatic "*my-own*," and by changing "bequeathing" to "giving," so that the thought is of this kind, "Peace I leave you as a legacy. Nay, rather, peace I give you as an immediate and lasting gift, not like

---

comforted (παρεκάλεσα) him, and have given him the *true comfort* (παράκλησιν ἀληθινήν), *peace upon peace*, to those far off and to those near" This verbally resembles "the *Comforter*, the Spirit of *truth*" (Jn xiv. 16—17).

[1] Eph. ii 14 Comp Mic. v 5 "and this [man] shall *be peace* [for us, *i.e* for Israel]," and Zech ix 10 "he shall *speak peace* unto the Gentiles" As a rule, "*Peace be unto you*" would be a salutation to those *to whom one comes*. But Jesus in His farewell to the disciples (Jn xiv. 27—8) suggests that He will, as it were, leave "*peace*" with those *from whom He goes*, besides repeating "*peace*" (Jn xx 19, 21, 26) when He returns

[2] Jn xiv. 27.

the gifts of the world, transient and false, but true peace, *my own peace*. Troubles must needs pain your minds, but they must not penetrate them or make them timorous...I am still your Helper, and more your Helper than before. I go to the Father, and the Father is greater than I[1]."

Origen, quoting this passage, calls attention to the fact that the Hebrew " peace," expressed in the name of " Solomon," suggested the building up, or completion, of the Temple—a work not for David the type of war, but for Solomon the type of peace, and for Jesus as one Greater than Solomon[2] The conclusion of the Johannine version of Christ's Last Words implies the fulfilment of both types. War has preceded peace but is now over, consummated in victory. " These things have I said unto you that in me ye may have *peace*. In the world ye have tribulation, but be of good cheer, I *have-been-victorious-over* the world[3]"

§ 14 *"Peace" and "the Paraclete"*

The bestowal of the legacy of peace, described above, was preceded by a mention of some kind of Substitute for the Son, who was to take the Son's place as the Friend and Helper of the disciples when deprived of the visible presence of their Lord · " I will make request of the Father, and he shall give you Another, a Paraclete, that he may be with you for ever—the Spirit of

---

[1] Jn xiv 27—8. Some Latin versions transpose or confuse the two verbs "leave" and "give" They also repeat "my own" twice, or transpose it Chrysostom gives the impression of having a text that repeats "leave" twice (instead of "leave" and "give").

[2] *Comm Joann* vi 1

[3] Jn xvi. 33 "*have-been-victorious-over* (νενίκηκα)" See *Light* **3825—9**, on this passage and others such as 1 Jn v 4 "This is *the victory* that *hath-been-victorious-over* the world, even our faith" The advantage of rendering the verb "*be-victorious-over*" is that it retains the connection between it and the noun "*victory*" In illustration of victory and peace prepared before war, comp. *Odes of Solomon* viii 8 " Peace was prepared for you before ever your war was"

truth[1]" It is the presence of this Paraclete that is the guarantee for the legacy of peace "The Paraclete, the Holy Spirit, whom the Father will send in my name, he will teach you all things and quietly-remind you of all things that I said to you [on earth] Peace I leave you...the Father is greater than I[2]." Before proceeding to the last Johannine mention of "peace" on the occasion when Jesus said to the disciples "peace be unto you" and "receive the Holy Spirit," we have to ask what John means by "Paraclete," a term that he connects first with "the Spirit of truth" and then with the "Holy Spirit"

The word is from the Greek *paracaleo*, "call a person to," *advoco*, and was adopted into the Jewish language in the technical sense of an *advocate*—some one "called in" to speak or manage legal matters for a friend or client unable to speak for himself. In Greek, the etymological and the actual meaning of the word are often at variance, owing to the different meanings of *paracaleo* in LXX and other causes[3]. But these must not distract our attention from the undeniable fact that it is used by Philo in a doctrine that appears to be deliberately contradicted by John, as being diametrically opposed to right views both about Creation and about the right attitude of man toward God.

First, as to Creation, Philo says that God used no *paraclete* but only Himself in resolving to benefit Nature[4]. John states

---

[1] Jn xiv. 16, see *Joh. Gr* **2793**, *Son* **3618**. "Make-request-of" = ἐρωτήσω
[2] Jn xiv 26—8 "quietly-remind (ὑπομνήσει)."
[3] Παρακαλέω in LXX regularly represents the Heb "comfort," the root of *Nahum* and *Me-nahem* Menahem is given as one of the names of the Messiah in *J Berach* 11 4 (3) Outside LXX, παρακαλέω generally means "request," "invite," &c. Παράκλητος never occurs in LXX, but παρακλήτωρ once, Job xvi. 2 "comforter," where Aq and Theod have παράκλητος, taking it actively, although etymologically it should be passive. In Demosthenes, Barnabas, and Dio Cassius, παράκλητος is sometimes used in a bad sense, concerning a hired orator, or applauder, or supporter, coming not spontaneously but because he is "called in"
[4] Philo 1. 5 οὐδενὶ δὲ παρακλήτῳ—τίς γὰρ ἦν ἕτερος,—μόνῳ δὲ ἑαυτῷ

that in the beginning the Word was with God, and was God, and that "all things came into being through him." Next, as to the right attitude of man toward God, Philo indicates it by reference to the High Priest going into the presence of God in special vestments, which, he says, represent the four elements, "so that the whole of the world (Cosmos) may go in with him .. For it was necessary that he that is making [a] holy [offering] to the Father of the world (Cosmos) should *use as Paraclete [that Father's] Son* most perfect in excellence...[1]." That is to say the Cosmos, or World, is to be brought as man's Paraclete into the presence of God[2]. This is the very opposite of Johannine doctrine, In John, the Paraclete comes to "convict the world (Cosmos)" and convicts it "because the ruler of this world hath been judged", the

χρησάμενος ὁ θεὸς ἔγνω δεῖν εὐεργετεῖν τὴν ἄνευ δωρεᾶς θείας φύσιν ἐπιλαχεῖν ἐξ ἑαυτῆς οὐδενὸς ἀγαθοῦ δυναμένην (1) Possibly, as a judge may be said to "use" the services of the advocate on either side, stating the case of either client, so here the word may mean "advocate to state the case of Nature" (2) More probably it means "assistant" In either case, it puts aside the conception of God as "calling into counsel" His Word, or Son, when He made the world, and especially then when He said "Let *us* make man"

[1] Philo ii. 155 ἱερώμενον, "performing a holy service," is shewn to be the present participle of ἱεράομαι from the preceding context, where ἱερᾶται actually occurs.—δικαιῶν τὸν ἱερώμενον τῷ θεῷ, καθ' ὃν χρόνον ἱερᾶται, προφέρειν ἁπάντων. In both places Mangey (followed by others) accents the word ἱερωμένον, as the perf pass of ἱερόω, "*having been made holy*"—to the great detriment of the sense

Philo ii 520 contains unimportant instances of παράκλητος as "advocate." More important is the prediction (ii 436) that the scattered Jews will return to their country "destined to *use* (χρησόμενοι) *three Advocates* for their reconciliations to the Father (τρισὶ παρακλήτοις τῶν πρὸς τὸν Πατέρα καταλλαγῶν)" (1) the kindness of Him that is pleaded with (τοῦ παρακαλουμένου), (2) the holiness of the Patriarchs, (3) the "amelioration (βελτίωσις)" of those who are being thus "brought into a treaty" with God

[2] Comp. Philo i. 277 "For this world (ὁ μὲν γὰρ κόσμος οὗτος) is God's younger Son, as being perceived by sense (ἅτε αἰσθητὸς ὤν)," see *Light* 3717 *j*—*k*. On the Platonic doctrine of the Cosmos as "a living creature," and as μονογενής, see above, p. 28 foll

whole of the discourse about the Paraclete or the Spirit implies a warfare between the Paraclete and the world; and the discourse closes with the words "In the world ye have tribulation, but be of good cheer, I have been victorious over the world[1]."

It would be folly to infer that John, simply for the purpose of contradicting Philo, inserted in his Gospel a doctrine that he did not believe Jesus to have taught. Much more probably he found in the Christian Churches some traditions about a Paraclete or Advocate, or about the Holy Spirit regarded as a Paraclete, which were variously reported and liable to be misunderstood. Some, for example, might narrow down the office of the Holy Spirit to little more than that of a clever advocate helping Christians to plead their cause before magistrates, as in Luke —"Settle it therefore in your own hearts not to practise beforehand [your] defending yourselves, for I will give you a mouth and wisdom that all your adversaries shall not be able to withstand or gainsay[2]" In the Acts we see how this personal action of the "Holy Spirit," or "the Spirit of Jesus," might do much more than this—on one occasion "not suffering" an apostle to go to "Asia" or "Bithynia," and on another guiding him by a "vision" to Macedonia[3]. Again, the Corinthian Epistles shew how the action of the Spirit, when manifested in what was called "other tongues," or "kinds of tongues," or "speaking with tongues"—a manifestation of comparatively slight importance—might sometimes give rise to exaggerations, disorder, and foolish conceit[4]. These statements, outside the Gospels, point to some actual doctrine and promise of Jesus like that which is inside the Gospels. Jesus may or may not have used the term "Paraclete" on some of the occasions on which He promised the disciples the help of the Spirit; but whether He

---

[1] Jn xvi 8, 11, 33. "World" is κόσμος throughout this discourse
[2] Lk xxi. 14—15, Mk xiii 11, Mt x 19—20, Lk xii. 11—12 Mark and Matthew differ from Luke, see *Son* **3617**.
[3] Acts xvi. 6—10 [4] 1 Cor xiv. 2 foll

did or not, His actual doctrine appears to have implied the promise of spiritual helpfulness which is the essence of the term.

Whatever Jesus may have said about a Paraclete, or about anything equivalent to a Paraclete, might easily be corrupted by some of the earliest Christians, owing to the inveterate dread and distrust of God felt by man, and man's consequent desire to put up between himself and God what may be called veils of mediation. Jewish traditions, commenting on a passage in Job that mentions "an angel, an interpreter[1]," call this "angel" a Paraclete, and explain it as meaning that, in the day of judgment, one good deed, appearing as a man's Paraclete against nine hundred and ninety-nine evil accusing deeds, will save a man from condemnation.

Jesus, however, in a Lucan parable, is reported to have spoken, not about "works," but about "friends" who are to "receive into everlasting habitations[2]" the man that makes them "friends." The parable is obscure; and how its doctrine, from being spiritual, may degenerate into the mechanical, may be seen by comparing Clement of Alexandria with Jerome in their comments on it[3]. But it seems to mean that a man can do with his money what the good Samaritan did when he

---

[1] Job xxxiii 23—4 "If there be with him *an angel, an interpreter*, one among a thousand, to shew unto man what is right for him, then he is gracious unto him and saith, Deliver him from going down to the pit, I have found a ransom" Targ has "angelus unus, *paracletus*, de millibus (sic) *accusatoribus*" See Rashi, and Levy *Ch* ii. 300 *a*.

[2] Lk xvi. 9.

[3] Clem Alex 952—5 emphasizes the power of "those who have an everlasting habitation with the Father," those who are God's "little ones," and whose "angels" behold His face, to benefit their benefactors by receiving them into that habitation Jerome writes about the death-bed of the rich Fabiola (*Letters* lxxvii 11 ed Fremantle) "Having a presentiment of what would happen, she had written to several monks to come and release her from the burden under which she laboured," *i e* the remnant of her fortune, "for she wished to (Lk. xvi 9) '*make to herself friends of the mammon habitations*' They came to her, and she made them her friends..." On the disciples of Christ as being Christ's "friends," see *Joh Voc.* **1784—92**.

made himself a "neighbour," that is to say, a "friend," to the Jew whom he relieved. If that Jew was grateful, then the kindness was blessed to the Samaritan by making the Jew his "friend." If the Jew was ungrateful, still the kindness was blessed to the Samaritan, for it became and remained his "friend," lifting up his heart toward the Father of all kindness and preparing him to be "received into everlasting habitations." In the former case the kindness was "twice-blessed." In the latter, it was only "once-blessed." Still, it *was* "blessed," and became what might be called "an angel of introduction." Jesus always assumed that good works must be works of the heart. We can have no "treasure in heaven" unless our "heart" is there[1]. The angels that are to be our Paracletes cannot be ours unless we are as the "little ones" of God[2]. And these "angels" are not independent beings. They must be, as John teaches us, "ascending and descending on the Son of Man[3]."

Nevertheless, the doctrine of obtaining salvation by a substantial balance of good deeds over bad deeds has great attractions for the human mind, which, in religion more than in anything else, craves definiteness, safe routine, and absolutely certain assurances that if a man does this or that according to fixed rule, he will be saved. It is not therefore to be wondered at that John takes great pains, we must not perhaps say to make indefinite the doctrine of the Paraclete, but at all events to depict it in such different aspects that it may be impossible for the reader to explain away the Paraclete's help by any arithmetical theory of debit and credit.

Among these aspects must be mentioned the one in the Johannine Epistle where the Son Himself is called a Paraclete, with the epithet "*righteous*" attached to it, and with a mention of "*the whole world*." This epithet and this modifying phrase should shew us that we have to do with no ordinary advocate,

---

[1] Mt. vi 21, Lk. xii. 34.   [2] Mt. xviii. 10.   [3] Jn i 51.

pleading in our special favour, but with One who pleads for others as well as for ourselves—One who will by no means extenuate our particular offences even when He carries our sin-stained confessions, our imperfect sorrows, and our frail repentances, into the presence of the Father: "My little children, these things I write unto you that ye sin not. And, if any man sin, we have a Paraclete with the Father, Jesus Christ, a righteous [Paraclete], and he is the propitiation for our sins; and not for ours only but also for the whole world[1]."

§ 15. *"Peace," in John, how imparted*

The passage just quoted from the Johannine Epistle calling Jesus "a Paraclete," and "a righteous one," rather favours the view that the Epistle should be regarded not as an Epilogue, but as "calling out a welcome[2]" for the Gospel, which had been long orally preached and was now to be given to the world in writing. The writer seems here, as often elsewhere, to be reminding Christians of what they "know,"

---

[1] 1 Jn ii. 1—2.
[2] "Calling out a welcome." See Westcott's *The Epistles of St John*, (p. xxxix) "writes to call out a welcome for *what he knows to be the Gospel*," (p. xxxi) "the relative dates of the Epistle and of *the Gospel as written*," "It can only be said with confidence that the Epistle presupposes in those for whom it was composed a familiar acquaintance with *the characteristic truths* which are preserved for us in *the Gospel*." The words I have italicised appear to draw a distinction—which might easily be overlooked—between (1) 'the Gospel' meaning the fundamental truths of Christ's Gospel as a whole, and (2) "the Gospel" meaning the Fourth Gospel.

Those who had heard the Johannine doctrine preached year by year to them at Ephesus would need no Preface to it when at last it was committed to writing and published. But readers studying the new Gospel in other Churches might be greatly helped by an Introductory Epistle preparing them for its new expressions. For example, the Fourth Gospel mentions "life," ζωή, twice as often as all the Synoptists together, and for the first time thus. "in him [*i.e.* the Word] was life." For this we are prepared in the Epistle by (1 Jn i 1) "the Word of life." In the Gospel, Christ's doctrine draws towards its close with a mention of the Paraclete. The Epistle (1 Jn i. 1—ii. 1) prepares for it.

and thus to be preparing them for the reading of his Gospel, which will shew them, step by step, how Jesus led the Church to "know" it[1].

The Church had taught them to "know" the precepts of Christ. But something more might still be done by the writer to help them to "know" the Spirit of Christ, not as One seated in heaven[2] at the right hand of God, but as their continual Helper on earth, the source of their new life and joy, and of their fellowship with the Father and the Son. Years had passed away since many of the converts had been baptized; and they knew only too well that—though not sinning as before—they had not remained free from blemish and stain. Were they to remain thus stained, timorously awaiting the Coming of the Lord from heaven? Not so, they had the Paraclete already among them and in them on earth, Christ's Other Self, and the Disciple teaches them to say "He is the propitiation for our sins."

None of the Synoptic Gospels had mentioned the Paraclete by name. But the Johannine Epistle brings this new title before us at its outset in order to denote Christ's present Person or present Spirit, present with His disciples upon earth, and endowed with so blessed and divine a power of helping them, as almost to suggest that to send this Paraclete had been the end and object of the Saviour's Incarnation It seems as if the writer, assuming the fulfilment of the promise of the Paraclete at the beginning of his Epistle, thereby prepares his readers for the description of the actual promise of the Paraclete at the close of his Gospel.

But if this view of the relation between the Epistle and

---

[1] Comp 1 Jn ii 20—21 "Ye have an Anointing from the Holy One Ye all *know*. I have not written unto you because ye *know* not the truth, but because ye *know* it." There is no writing in N T. in which "know" (Eng Concordance) occurs proportionately so often as in the First Johannine Epistle

[2] The word "heaven" does not occur in the Johannine Epistle.

the Gospel holds good about the Paraclete, we are led to ask whether it holds good about other subjects, and, in particular, about the one we are considering. What does the Epistle say about "peace"? The answer is surprising. It says nothing. It does not even mention the word. There is not another writing in the New Testament about which we can say this—not even the short Epistle of Jude or the Epistle to Philemon or the shortest of the Johannine Epistles. How are we to explain this?

Possibly in this way. The Introductory Epistle *takes for granted all the deepest results* of the Life described in the Gospel. It tells believers *what they are to do in consequence of them*, but does not describe them over again. The opening of the Gospel is "In the beginning was the Word." The opening of the Epistle shews the object of going back to the beginning. "That which was from the beginning...that which we beheld and our hands handled...declare we, *that ye also may have fellowship*." The Epistle assumes that "*the peace of God*" *has been imparted by the Word to men, that they may have "fellowship* with the Father and with his Son Jesus Christ," that is to say, "the fellowship of the Holy Spirit."

"Peace," in Hebrew and Jewish thought, implied a great deal more than it does to us. The verb from which it is derived meant "complete." The noun meant "completeness," "soundness," "welfare" in every sense, as well as freedom from actual conflict or disturbance. One aspect of it might be described by the Greek word *parrhēsia*, "freedom of speech," such as exists between the members of a family, and such as ought to exist in man toward God, when man is truly the child of God, and this, too, is a favourite word in the Johannine Epistle[1]

---

[1] 1 Jn ii 28, iii 21, iv 17, v. 14. This use of παρρησία must be distinguished from its use in the adverbial clause ἐν π, that is, "in public," "openly." See Levy iv 103 *b* on the Hebraized *parrhesia*, "there is no *parrhēsia* under ten [persons]"

We return to the Gospel and to the description of Christ's bestowal of "peace" in it, prepared to believe that the gift will imply a responsibility resting on the recipient. On the evening of the day of Christ's Resurrection, "Jesus came, and stood in the midst, and saith unto them, *Peace [be] unto you*... the disciples rejoiced when they saw the Lord[1]." Then follows, without mention of any intervening word or action, a repetition "Jesus therefore said to them again, *Peace [be] unto you*: as the Father hath sent me, even so send I you. And when he had said this, he breathed into [them] and saith unto them, Receive ye the Holy Spirit, whosoever sins ye remit, they are remitted, whosoever [sins] ye retain, they are retained[2]." Referring the reader to a previous treatise for discussions on "remitting" and "retaining[3]," we may note here that, whereas the first of the two pronouncements of "peace" is followed simply by "rejoicing[4]," the second is followed by an action of Christ toward the disciples, and a precept enjoining on them action toward others. That is to say, the "peace" followed by the "in-breathing" is not to be the peace of a hermit or contemplative philosopher but that of a man moving among men. As the Son lives from the Father, and the disciples from the Father—through the Son, and the Spirit (or Paraclete)—so the world is to live from the same source, but through one more channel. The source is still the Father, but the Father's Gospel of Peace and Righteous Judgment,

---

[1] Jn xx 19—20 ἔστη εἰς τὸ μέσον (see *Joh. Gr.* 2307).

[2] Jn xx 21—3 On "breathing into," see *Son* 3086 *c—e*, 3623 *h—j*.

[3] *Son* 3414 (1), 3495 *e*, and *Joh Gr.* 2517 foll.

[4] Jn xx 20. Contrast Lk xxiv 36—7 "He stood in the midst of them [[and saith unto them, Peace [be] unto you]]. But they, *being terrified and affrighted*, supposed that they saw a spirit." "Joy" is repeatedly mentioned in Jn xv 11—xvi 24, in connection with the Spirit or Paraclete, and also in Christ's prayer for the disciples (xvii 13) "that they may have *the joy that is mine* fulfilled in themselves"—and nowhere else in Christ's words throughout the Gospel (but in the Baptist's words (iii 29) (twice) of the "joy" that comes from the Bridegroom's voice) This accords with Gal v 22 "the fruit of the Spirit is love, *joy*, peace...."

passing through the Son and the Holy Spirit to the disciples, is also to pass, through the disciples, to the world.

"Peace," here, perhaps suggests completion as well as restfulness. In the material Creation, God breathed the breath of life into the first-created man. In the spiritual Creation, the Son of God pronounces a twofold "peace" or "completion," and, at the second pronouncement, breathes into Man the life of the life-giving Spirit, an emanation from Himself imparted to those for whom He had given His life, and whom He has prepared to impart life to others.

§ 16. *The Johannine "peace" and the Epictetian "peace"*

Compared with this "peace," the peace above described as that of Epictetus[1] is a very mean, petty, and, we may almost say, selfish affair. Epictetus himself is much loftier—and his ideal hero and ideal philosopher are loftier—than the language that he occasionally uses to describe the blessings of his system. For his words amount sometimes to this, that if you have no care for anything that is not in your power to receive by an act of willing—no care for pleasure or comfort or wealth or power or fame or good repute, no care for neighbours or friends or family or native country, no care for the unphilosophic pains and distresses and agonies of the countless souls that cannot help caring about all these things—then you can look down on Paul's passionate sense of weaknesses, trials, and hindrances, and despise him for troubling himself about "the care of all the churches." "To me," you can say, "all things are harmless, all things are full of peace."

Paul, too, could have said "all things are harmless to me." But he could say more. He could recognise "the world" as being full of things harmful, swarming with harmful devices and hindrances of good, but he recognised also that he had power through the Spirit to surmount multitudes of such

---

[1] See p. 265 foll

obstacles, to pull down strongholds of evil, and to trample under foot the adders and scorpions of sin; "I can do all things," he said, "through Christ who maketh me strong." But this triumph was not to be effected without cost "We were well pleased," Paul says to the Thessalonians, "to impart unto you not the gospel of God only but also our own souls[1]" It was by this "giving of his own soul" that Paul conquered "the world" in the Roman empire, imitating his Master who had similarly taken Saul of Tarsus captive, converting him into Paul the servant of Christ This the Lord had done, not in the character of the Avenger, but avowedly in the character of the Persecuted, crying "Saul, Saul, why persecutest thou me?" And it was in this character that He "conquered the world," as the Fourth Gospel says "I came not to judge the world but to save the world," and "The bread that I will give is my flesh, for the life of the world[2]"

The important part assigned by John to the promise of the Paraclete, and to the fulfilment of that promise in the solemn imparting of peace and the Holy Spirit, is justified by many passages in the Epistles and the Acts, which describe Peter, Paul, and others, as receiving messages from Jesus or His Spirit, extending, in one instance, perhaps, even to an utterance about the Lord's acts and words "in the night on which he was delivered up[3]" That utterance has affected

---

[1] 1 Thess. ii. 8

[2] Jn xii. 47, vi 51, comp. Philipp iii 12, 2 Cor ii 14 Clement of Alexandria (960) says that the Apostle John pursuing an armed robber, who had once been a convert of his, and who now fled from him lest he should be reconverted, cried out to him "Why, my son, dost thou flee from me, thy father, unarmed, old? Son, pity me Fear not, thou hast still hope of life I will give account to Christ for thee. If need be, I will willingly endure thy death, as the Lord [endured] death for us For thee I will surrender my life Stand! Believe! Christ hath sent me' The sequel illustrates the power of the Spirit, in such an Apostle, to "conquer the world." The armed robber was disarmed and taken captive

[3] 1 Cor xi. 23, on which see *Paradosis* **1155, 1202, 1315**—**25** foll &c.,

JESUS BEGINNING TO PREACH

many millions of souls And who can doubt that the whole history of Christendom was powerfully influenced by the Voice that said to Peter " What God hath cleansed, that make not thou common[1] "? If Peter had been in the habit of writing letters, no doubt we should have heard of many more such visions and voices. They would not all, perhaps, have been of general or public import. Some might have been of a private character, like that which said to Paul, when he prayed to be delivered from his thorn in the flesh, " My grace is sufficient for thee" But even private directions might sometimes have far-reaching public effects, by determining an Apostle's action in particular cases, like those voices which said, in effect, " Go not into Mysia," " Obey the voice, that saith unto thee, Come over to Macedonia and help us," " Go not into Bithynia," " Stay here in Corinth, for I have much people in this city," " Bonds and afflictions await thee in Jerusalem," " Fear not, Paul, for thou must stand before Caesar[2] "

There is every reason, textual as well as historical, for supposing that this period of voice-intercourse between Jesus, and His disciples continued long after the " forty days'

---

and **1417** In *Paradosis* **1416—7** I took the view that, if Paul received this tradition from Ananias, as the Lord's messenger, sent specially to him, he " would naturally say 'I received from the Lord'" But the Greek commentators (of whom, unfortunately, Origen is not one) favour the view that it was received, directly, from the Lord Himself Chrysostom's commentary quotes <u>ἀπὸ</u> τοῦ κυρίου correctly, but proceeds to say πῶς δέ φησι <u>παρὰ</u> τοῦ κυρίου παρειληφέναι , and he applies παραδίδωμι to Christ thrice—as "delivering" (1) Himself, (2) "all things," (3) "the Supper"— in such a way as to suggest that he is combining, and perhaps confusing several interpretations

If the Pauline Eucharistic form—so much fuller than that of Mark and Matthew, and so satisfying to the Christian sense—was delivered by Ananias to Paul immediately on his conversion, must it not have been in use, presumably, much earlier? If so, how can we explain the fact that Mark and Matthew, writing much later, give such meagre equivalents?

[1] Acts x 15
[2] 2 Cor xii 9, Acts xvi 6—9, xviii 10, xx 23, xxvii. 24.

generally supposed to have limited Christ's personal intercourse with them after His resurrection[1], and, if this is so, we may reasonably say that John is substantially right in giving what some may call a non-historical prominence to the doctrine of the Paraclete, or Holy Spirit, who was to represent Christ to the Apostles after His departure and to guide them in their preaching of the gospel.

The Discourse of Jesus on the Paraclete seems to be, to some extent, the Johannine substitute for the Synoptic Discourse of Jesus on "the end of the world" and "the last days." Many will be found to assert that the Synoptic Eschatology was Christ's, while the Paraclete-doctrine was not. But this expression of preference is hazardous for three reasons.

First, Mark tells us that the Eschatological doctrine was given by Jesus to only four of the Apostles It was also given "privately." True, both these limitations are dropped by Luke, and the former by Matthew; but there is no reason why Mark should have inserted them if they were not of very early date. On the other hand, there is good reason why later writers might discard them as lessening the value of the revelation. Probably, therefore, these limitations belonged to the original •

Secondly, the authority of Mark and Matthew is lowered, as regards the Discourse on the Last Days, by the fact that Luke frequently and seriously differs from them, omitting, adding, and altering, in such a way as to indicate that he regarded Mark's text as below its usual standard of authority.

Thirdly, we must bear in mind that the special circumstances of the first century would combine with the general infirmities of human nature to make the mass of Christians much more interested about the approaching "end of the

---

[1] On Acts 1. 3 δι' ἡμερῶν τεσσεράκοντα, see *Joh Gr.* **2331** *c*, and *Notes* **2892** *a* foll on "The Interval between the Resurrection and the Ascension," and below, p. 298, n 2

age" than about Christ's doctrine concerning the Father in heaven and the spiritual reign of the Son of Man.

Taking these three considerations into account we shall not really be unreasonable if we venture to assert that, although the Synoptic Discourse on the Last Days may here and there contain phrases that actually proceeded from Christ's lips, along with others that were uttered through revelations received after the Resurrection, while the Johannine doctrine of the Paraclete does not include and does not aim at including half a dozen consecutive words actually uttered by Christ, yet the latter better represents Christ's own thought and attitude towards the future, and also the thought and attitude that He desired to enjoin on His disciples

§ 17. *The last Johannine mention of "peace"*

We pass now to the last Johannine mention of "peace." It occurs at the end of what may be called the body of the Gospel (as distinct from the Galilaean Appendix which describes the seven disciples "fishing" and receiving "bread" from Jesus). The last two verses of all—the verses preceding the Appendix—say "Many other signs therefore did Jesus in-the-sight-of the disciples which have not been written in this book; but these have been written that ye may believe that Jesus is the Christ the Son of God, and that, believing, ye may have life in his name[1]." "In-the-sight-of" occurs in John nowhere but here It would hardly have been inserted if it had not been intended to limit the "signs" to those *performed "in the sight of" the disciples alone, after the Resurrection.* Luke uses it to describe Jesus, after the Resurrection, as "eating *in the sight of" the disciples*[2]; and perhaps John is here referring to that Lucan tradition, in order to give point to the lesson, speedily to be taught, about

---

[1] Jn xx 30—31.
[2] See *Joh Gr* **2431**, and **2335** quoting Lk xxiv. 43.

the blessing on "those who have *not seen*" In any case, immediately before these words, comes a manifestation to Thomas, who has protested that he will not be convinced of the Lord's resurrection by mere sight without touch · "And after eight days, again, his disciples were within, and Thomas with them Jesus cometh, the doors being shut, and stood in the midst, and said *Peace [be] unto you*[1]."

Jesus bids Thomas not only "see" but touch "Reach [here] thy hand and put it into my side" But perhaps Thomas— in spite of his protest—ultimately believes without doing this For he is not recorded as doing it And afterwards Jesus mentions merely the proof of "seeing," saying to him, "Because *thou hast seen* me" (not, "because *thou hast touched* me"), "thou hast believed; blessed are they that have not seen and [yet] have believed." The Evangelist's selection of this "sign" in preference to "many other signs[2]" is explained by the

---

[1] Jn xx 26

[2] Paul's enumeration of the appearances of the risen Saviour omits all of the appearances to women, and may reasonably be supposed to omit others to the less authoritative disciples It does not even apparently include the manifestation to the seven disciples in Jn xxi 1 foll On the other hand it includes appearances not recorded in any Gospel That there were "many" appearances (many more than the five enumerated by Paul) would seem probable even if the period of them were limited by the phrase (Acts i 3) "*by the space of* forty days" Still more probable would it be if the original tradition from which the present Lucan text was derived described Jesus as "appearing [for the last time] *after an interval of* forty days"

See above, p 296, n 1, referring to *Notes* and *Joh. Gr*, to which add the following remarks on Acts xiii 31 "he appeared to them for (ἐπὶ) *several* (πλείους) *days*" (A V and R V "many days") The phrase is peculiar (in N T) to Acts xxi 10, xxv 14, xxvii 20, and not paralleled from Greek literature by Wetstein, Thayer, Steph *Thes* But it is fairly frequent in LXX, where it always represents Heb "*many days*" Gen r, followed by Rashi, makes the Hebrew phrase mean, in Gen xxi 34 (LXX ἡμ πολλάς), xxxvii 34 (LXX ἡμ τινάς, v r πολλάς), severally, "*twenty-six years*" and "*twenty-two years*" In O T it is mostly (though not always) applied to a period that would exceed forty days, *e g* Numb xx 15, Josh. xi 18, xxiii 1, xxiv 7.

obvious force of the lesson that it teaches, namely, that all generations of Christians may derive comfort—in their regret that it was not given to them to see Christ face to face—from the blessing pronounced on those who "have not seen and yet have believed."

For they are in the position of Thomas. He was absent, perhaps unavoidably far off, from the circle of disciples to whom Jesus first came, and on whom He twice invoked "peace." So were the Gentiles—unavoidably absent, or "far off." But the Epistle to the Ephesians says that Jesus came "preaching peace" to them —"peace to you [Gentiles] that were far off, and peace to them [*i.e* the Jews] that were nigh." We have seen that this quotation takes us back to Isaiah's prediction about "peace, peace, to him that is far off and to him that is near", which Jerome connected both with the Ephesian passage, and also with the promise of peace in John, "Peace I leave unto you, the peace that is my own I give unto you." In view of these scriptural traditions about peace to the "near" and the "far off," the present and the absent, it seems reasonable to suppose that John has here in view this prophecy of Isaiah, and this inclusion of the absent as well as the present in the Gospel of Peace.

It remains to point out that also in the verbal framework of this narrative there is an arrangement, characteristic of John and akin to Jewish mystical literature, which gives weight to this promise of peace made twice to the disciples, and then for the third time when Thomas is included in the circle. Several instances of an emphatic threefold repetition in John have been included in Johannine Grammar, and especially the statement that the last manifestation of Jesus was the "third," and the threefold repetition of the word "manifested[1]." But it should have been added that in a

---

[1] See *Joh Gr* **2589** quoting Philo i 243 "Now a holy matter is approved through *three witnesses*," and **2620** quoting Jn xxi. 1—14 "Jesus *manifested* himself again to the disciples on the sea of Tiberias."

noteworthy passage of *Berachoth* the passage from Isaiah about "*peace*" is quoted with another Biblical passage where "*peace*" is repeated three times, as instances of the well-omened significance of "*three*[1]."

This adherence to traditions of Biblical phrase and Jewish mysticism ought not to prevent us from seeing that in these Johannine poetic narratives of the promise of peace and its fulfilment, we have a clue to the explanation both of the rapid spread of Christianity through the Roman Empire, and also

---

Now he *manifested* himself thus . This is *the third time* that Jesus *manifested* himself to the disciples," where the remark naturally suggests itself, "How simple, in the first verse, to have written merely, 'Jesus *manifested* himself again thus. Tiberias,' using the verb but once!"

[1] See *Berach* 55 *b* quoting Is. lvii 19, along with 1 Chr xii 18 "and the spirit came upon Amasai, who was chief of the thirty [and he said] Thine are we, David, and on thy side, thou son of Jesse. *Peace, peace,* to thee, and *peace* to thine helpers, for thy God helpeth thee" (a passage also quoted in *Gittin* 62 *a* as shewing that the repetition is suitable for a royal salutation), 1 S xxv 6 "*Peace* be both unto thee, and *peace* be to thine house, and *peace* be to all that thou hast" (an instance where the "peace comes back" (see above, p 259, n. 1) to those who announce it, because "a son of peace" does not dwell in "the house" To these might have been added Ps. cxxii. 6—8 "O pray for the *peace* of Jerusalem.... *Peace* be within thy walls. I will now say, *Peace* be within thee For the sake of the house of the Lord our God I will seek thy good" This last passage may illustrate the transition of metaphor in Origen's mind when he passes from the thought of building the House on the Rock (*Comm. Joann.* vi 1) to the thought of "the peace that passeth all understanding," and then to the words (Jn xiv 27) " Peace I leave with you," and then asks us to consider "whether some similar lesson is not taught under the surface with regard to David and Solomon in the narrative about the temple" "Salim," "Jerusalem," "Solomon" are all associated in the Jewish mind not only with one another but also with the thoughts of "peace," "perfection," and the "completion" of the "perfect" Temple

Here it may be noted that Jerome, on Jn iii. 23 "Ænon near to *Salim,*" where "John was baptizing" (*Epist* 69), calls attention to "*Salim*" as meaning "*peace* or *perfection*" in connection with "the Lord's forerunner" Mystically interpreted, the meaning is that John was *on the way to* "*peace,*" but not actually there, being still (Jn iii 31) "of the earth"

of the subsequent successes and failures of the gospel. It was, so to speak, the "breathing" of peace—not the spoken words promising peace in the future or tendering it at a particular moment later on—that gave new life to the souls of men R. Jose the Galilaean said well that Messiah was named "Peace[1]." In breathing "peace" into the disciples, the Messiah breathed Himself into them. It was the possession, and carrying about in themselves, of this Personal Peace, that gave the early Christian Missionaries that success which distinguished them from the non-Christian philosophers.

There are many reasons why the Fourth Evangelist should desire to personify, or at least to connect with the Person of the Messiah, the thought of that "peace" which plays so prominent a part in Hebrew history and prophecy. Philo describes, in full, the nature of the threefold peace enjoyed by Abraham, peace of body, of soul, and of mind[2]. The same R. Jose that called attention to the Messiah's name of "Peace" said also "Great is peace, because even wars are waged for the sake of it[3]." Still more appropriately might it be pointed out that the first "war" mentioned in the Bible brings Abraham into the field, the rescuer of captives, and also introduces the first mention of the word "peace"—not indeed as peace, but as the name of the city of Salem, ruled over by Melchizedek, the King of Righteousness[4]. Peace pre-existed eternally in the mind of God before war came, according to the saying of the Odes of Solomon, "Peace was prepared for you before ever your war was[5]." But it could not be manifested to men

---

[1] *Derek Eretz* ad fin.

[2] Philo i. 514 foll. on Gen. xv. 15 "thou shalt go to thy fathers in peace."

[3] *Derek Eretz* ad fin. quoting Deut. xx. 10 foll. Philo ii. 372, quoting the same passage, says that "peace even though very costly ($\epsilon\pi\iota\zeta\eta\mu\iota\sigma s$) is more profitable than war." But the context in Deuteronomy describes aggressive war, not like that of Abraham rescuing Lot.

[4] Gen. xiv. 18.

[5] See *Light* 3809 b foll. quoting Ode viii. 8 as referring to Abraham.

apart from war, and the Fourth Gospel appears to aim at combining the two thoughts —1st, peace, from the beginning foreordained, through war; 2nd, peace, at the end, purchased by victory.

For this purpose, the Evangelist, in the very first sentence of his Gospel—though he does not mention the word "peace" —yet suggests a peace that passes understanding—the eternal concord of the divine unity between the Word and God, afterwards more clearly indicated by the phrase describing the Son as "in the bosom of the Father." Then—though again he does not mention the word "war"—he hints at the conflict through which this peace is to be obtained, by introducing the "light" as "shining in the darkness." Thus he takes back our thoughts to the beginning, when "darkness was on the face of the deep." "Darkness" and "light"! This, to some minds, may seem no more than an innocent contrariety But in others it may raise a suspicion of some evil opposition, some impending discord. On this "darkness" Philo remarks merely that the lower air was called thus because it was black. But Origen says that darkness means "first, the shadow cast by a body, and, secondly, a certain conception of the mind, that is, the devil[1]."

Not quite in this latter aspect, but in one somewhat like it, the Evangelist passes to an indication, first of a co-existence, and then of a hostile existence, as the relation between the Darkness and the Light, pointing to a conflict about the issue of which, until the Word shall have become flesh, the Gospel will pronounce nothing decided or positive. "The light shineth in the darkness, and the darkness *overcame it not.*" That

---

[1] Philo i 6, Origen on Gen i 2 (Lomm. viii. 106, n. 4) νοητόν τι, τουτέστιν ὁ διάβολος Comp. Justin Martyr *Apol* § 67 about "Sunday (τὴν τοῦ ἡλίου ἡμέραν)," as being the day on which God "made Cosmos, having *routed* darkness and matter (τὸ σκότος καὶ τὴν ὕλην τρέψας)" See Steph *Thes* vii 2384 quoting the Iliad xxi. 603 τρέψας v. r στρέψας, and comp Justin *Apol.* § 59 ὕλην ἄμορφον οὖσαν στρέψαντα

refers to the past It is merely negative. And it leaves us in suspense—hoping, yet questioning, or at least marvelling—as to the nature, and the outcome, and perhaps as to the possibility of the continuance, of this failure of the Darkness to "overcome" The hope grows as the drama of the Gospel proceeds, setting before us the seven acts of the victorious Word, revealing Himself in His seven characters, and with His seven signs[1], and shining forth at last as the conquering Light, not only not "overcome" but also Himself "overcoming." Thus we are led on to the evening before the Crucifixion, when Judas "goes out," the captive of Satan, from the presence of the Lord who had chosen him to be one of the Twelve Then it is "night" indeed[2] Then the hearts of the disciples are "troubled" and "fearful[3]" And that is the moment chosen for the first mention of "peace" in this Gospel—as the Lord's parting and permanent gift· "Peace I leave unto you, my own peace I give unto you." The Discourse closes with an exhortation to the disciples to make this "peace" that is in their hearts dominant over the "tribulation" that they will have "in the world," since "victory" has been purchased for them by the Lord of Light as a result of His death in the war against the Darkness of this world. "These things have I spoken unto you that in me ye may have peace In the world ye have tribulation, but be of good cheer, I have been victorious over the world[4]." Last of all comes the fulfilment and bestowal of that peace, after the Messiah has breathed His Spirit, His Peace, into the hearts of the disciples.

---

[1] "Seven." See *Joh Gr* Index "seven"
[2] Jn xiii 27, 30   [3] Jn xiv 1, 27.   [4] Jn xvi 33

CONCLUSION

§ 18. *Conclusion*

What lessons have we learned from the investigations in this volume—which deals, so far as consecutive study is concerned, with no more than fifteen verses of Mark's Gospel? Let us summarise our principal results.

(1) We have learned—what Mark's original must have shewn, but what Mark did not express—the meaning of the word "gospel" in our Lord's lips. It meant "the good-tidings of the peace of God."

(2) This "peace" meant unity between God and man, and hence between man and man. The doctrine of this "peace" was that God is the Father, Man is the Little Child, greatest when feeling himself to be least. Men cannot be at "peace" with the Father, unless they are at "peace" with His children.

(3) It was for the purpose of establishing this "peace" between God and man that Jesus believed Himself to have been sent into the world by God, and to have been baptized by the Holy Spirit descending from heaven. This Holy Spirit, felt by Him within Himself as the Spirit of Sonship, He was to impart to His disciples. They, in turn, were to transmit it to others, so as to bring all mankind into the Family of God.

(4) The fourth lesson is rather negative than positive. Jesus taught men to "repent." "Repent," in English, includes —and sometimes without including anything more—"be sorry." But, in the Prophets, and in the doctrine of Jesus, "repent" meant "turn toward God." Jesus taught that there was no real "turning toward God" except "becoming like God," and that no man could "become like God" by doing outward and (so to speak) artificial works, without the corresponding inward and natural work. As a fruit-tree cannot be made out of a stick by attaching to it leaves and fruit, but must be made by growth, so a son of man cannot be made

CONCLUSION

like God except by growing up as a son of God And he cannot become a son of God the Father unless he is born again in the Spirit of the Son.

(5) Here we must stop. For we must not anticipate what Mark has next to tell us about the Calling of the Fishermen, the teaching with "authority," the exorcism with "authority," and the acts of healing—all of which come to a sudden climax in the claim that "the Son of man hath power on earth to forgive sins."

With these and subsequent Marcan details—abrupt and obscure without Johannine interpretation—we shall be able to deal much more briefly as well as safely now that we have the clue afforded by the four above-mentioned lessons. For now we shall understand how simple and homelike—and yet how profoundly deep and mysterious, and how easy to be misunderstood by Pharisees and by Sophists and by all those whom Jesus called the children of this world—was the view that Jesus Himself took of His Mission and of His Person. He came into the world as the Son of Man, God's Little One, last-created according to the flesh, first-begotten according to the Spirit An ancient Jewish tradition on the Eighth Psalm represents contemptuous angels as looking down on God's helpless creature, outcome of the last day of the Creation, and as venturing to remonstrate with the Creator: "What is this feeble thing, man, that thou visitest him, what is this babe, the son of man, that thou regardest him?" But it was in this character, from first to last, that Jesus consistently claimed to heal, to forgive, to regenerate, and to rule, mankind The unity of Man with God, and of the Son of Man with the Son of God—that was His "gospel" And since He Himself was the expression of this unity we may say that He Himself was His own "gospel"

Receiving this Little One into our hearts, we do not exactly learn, say rather we experience, that God is Love—a proposition of portentous difficulty, or even impossibility, for

CONCLUSION

those who can receive no truth save through the senses and the intellect, but a certainty for the hearts of those who have been brought close to the heart of the invisible Father through the Spirit of His Son. This is the truth of truths which is impressed on us in the Fourth Gospel by "the disciple whom Jesus loved."

We may sum up the whole relation between the First Gospel and the Fourth by saying that, where Mark represents Jesus as saying "the Son of Man," and often supposes Him to mean a kind of royal Deputy at the right hand of God, the King, John represents Him as *saying* "I," but as always *meaning* "the Love of God in me." The Johannine meaning, though not the Johannine saying, seems historically correct. It was the Love of God, not the Sovereignty of God, that was really the pole-star of Christ's doctrine. And it is toward this star that the compass-needle of the Fourth Evangelist—amid all the labyrinthine windings through which he leads us—invariably points.

APPENDICES

CONTENTS OF APPENDICES

APPENDIX I
NAZARENE AND NAZORAEAN
ADDENDUM
NAZORAEAN AS A NAME FOR CHRISTIAN

		PAGE
§ 1	*Nêtzer and Tsemach*	326
§ 2	*Nazoraean and Christian*	329
§ 3	*Pliny on "Nazerini"*	332
§ 4	*Early misunderstandings of the terms "Christ" and "Christian"*	336
§ 5	*The term "Christ," how introduced or explained in the Gospels*	342

APPENDIX II
THE DISCIPLE THAT WAS "KNOWN UNTO THE HIGH PRIEST"

APPENDIX III
THE INTERPRETATION OF EARLY CHRISTIAN POETRY

§ 1	*"Without envy"*	373
§ 2	*"Thou shalt not acquire an alien the blood of thy soul"*	380
§ 3	*"And those that were silent became with speech"*	387
§ 4	*"I believed, therefore I was at rest"* . . .	389
§ 5	*"Unto thee have I fled, my God"* . . .	392
§ 6	*Why is the Greek word for "harp" always used in the Syriac version of the Odes?*	394
§ 7	*Alleged translation from Greek words with privative alpha*	396
§ 8	*The use of the Syriac relative after substantives to express possession*	400
§ 9	*"Until it was given in the midst"*	406
§ 10	*"He was known from before the (lit.) casting-down of the aeon"*	408
§ 11	*"The babe leaping"*	415
§ 12	*Evidence from the Anaphora of St James* . . .	420
§ 13	*"Without grudging"*	430
§ 14	*The detached possessive in Syriac*	432
§ 15	*"Danger," in Greek, corresponds to "strait," or "straitening," in Hebrew*	434
§ 16	*"Without danger," in Ode xxxix. 7* . . .	439
§ 17	*"No strait," in Isaiah lxiii 9*	442
§ 18	*The context in the Ode and the contexts in Isaiah* .	445
§ 19	*Conclusion*	451

APPENDIX I

NAZARENE AND NAZORAEAN

IN this Appendix it will be argued that (i) "*Nazarene*," meaning a man of Nazareth, and (ii) "*Nazoraean*," meaning the *Nêtzer* or Rod of Jesse mentioned by Isaiah, were probably interchanged by a play on the two words, so that the populace, acclaiming Jesus as the Lifegiver and Healer, altered "Jesus the Nazarene," into "Jesus the Nazoraean" To state the theory more exactly, we should say that they called Him Jesus the Nêtzer, or the Na(t)zoraean, partly because there was a pre-existing belief that the Messiah would be the Nêtzer, and partly because they vaguely felt what Matthew ventured definitely to express, that His residence from childhood onward in Nazareth had been ordained to fulfil the prophecy "He shall be called *Nazoraean* (i e. *Nêtzer*)[1]."

If this was the case, it would appear that "Nazarene[2]," a

---

[1] Mt 11. 23 R.V renders Ναζωραῖος sometimes "Nazarene" and sometimes "of Nazareth," but never by its exact form "Nazoraean."

[2] See Pliny v 81 "Coele habet Apameam Marsya amne divisam a *Nazerinorum* tetrarchia," which suggests a field that ought to be explored by anyone entering into the question of the origin of "*Nazarene*" But it seems to have attracted very little notice I am informed that nothing is known of these "*Nazerini*." Pliny is not referred to by *Encycl. Bib.* 3360 (where it is maintained that "'Nazareth' ought to mean 'Galilee'"), or by Hastings' *Dict* iii 496, or by Prof Burkitt in his *Syriac Forms of New Testament Proper Names*, on which see footnote on pp. 324—5. Strabo does not mention "*Nazerini*" Was Pliny misled by misunderstanding some reference to "Nazarenes" (see Schurer II ii 89) which had already reached his ears, coming from a Jewish source? See the Addendum on "Nazoraean as a name for Christian," where an attempt is made (§ 3) to answer this question, and also to give a general view of the uses of the term "Christ" in the several Gospels

NAZARENE AND NAZORAEAN

form used by Mark and Luke but not by Matthew and John, was an error, except in special contexts which may prove that the place-name, and not the Messianic title, was meant. It is proposed here to examine the Gospel uses of (i) "Nazarene," and (ii) "Nazoraean."

"Nazarene" occurs four times in Mark (1) "What have we to do with thee, Jesus, Nazarene?" (where Matthew omits the whole story, and Luke follows Mark[1]), (2) "having heard that it is Jesus the Nazarene[2]"; (3) "thou also wast with the Nazarene, [namely] Jesus[3]", (4) "Jesus ye seek, the Nazarene, the crucified[4]."

It will be observed from the notes below that only in the first of these four instances is Mark followed by any other Evangelist. That instance occurs in a case of exorcism. The demoniac exclaims "Jesus, Nazarene," and "I know thee who thou art, [thou] the Holy One of God." "Nazarene" might be formed from the noun-form "Nazara[5]" (used once by Matthew and once by Luke for the ordinary "Nazareth") a place not mentioned by Josephus or the Talmud and probably of small importance. It would appear to be a place-name that would suggest to many Jews, on first hearing it, the question "Where is it?" What are we to infer from its use here? Some such title as "Nazoraean," in a Messianic

---

[1] Mk 1 24 Ἰησοῦ Ναζαρηνέ (D Ναζαρηναι, d Nazorenae), Lk iv. 34 Ἰησοῦ Ναζαρηνέ (D Ναζορηναι, d Nazarenae). Mk and Lk agree *verbatim* in what follows "I know thee who thou art, the Holy One of God"

[2] Mk x 47 W H marg Ἰ ἐστὶν ὁ Ναζαρηνὸς ι e, perhaps,"Jesus [namely] the Nazarene," Mt xx 30 ὅτι Ἰησοῦς παράγει, Lk xviii. 37 ὅτι Ἰ ὁ Ναζωραῖος (D Ναζαρηνος, but d Nazoraeus) παρέρχεται.

[3] Mk xiv 67 καὶ σὺ μετὰ τοῦ Ναζαρηνοῦ ἦσθα τοῦ Ἰησοῦ (the MSS vary as to order, D and d Ναζορηνου), Mt. xxvi. 69 "Thou also wast with Jesus the Galilaean," Lk xxii 56 "This man, too, was with him."

[4] Mk xvi. 6 Ἰησοῦν ζητεῖτε τὸν Ναζαρηνὸν τὸν ἐσταυρωμένον (D om τὸν Ναζαρηνόν), Mt xxviii. 5 Ἰησοῦν τὸν ἐσταυρωμένον ζητεῖτε, Lk. xxiv 5 "Why seek ye the living with the *dead*?" For *nêtzer*=νεκρός, s p 325.

[5] Mt. iv 13, Lk iv. 16. Elsewhere (Mt. twice, Mk once, Lk. 4 times, Jn twice, Acts once) it is Ναζαρέτ, or Ναζαρέθ.

310

sense, would seem more appropriate. Can it be that, when Jesus rose to sudden fame in Galilee, people began at once to play on the words "Nazarene" and "Nazoraean," and that the demoniac followed the popular cry, which Mark has wrongly rendered? An affirmative answer is suggested by the very few instances in the *Aboth* where a Rabbi is introduced with a birthplace-name or something different from the ordinary "son of so-and-so[1]"

But before passing on to shew how the hypothesis of an original *Nêtzer* might suit the facts, we must recognise that the play on the two words, *Nazara* and *Nêtzer*, might be complicated, when passing into the first Greek Gospel, by a confusion with a third word, *Nazîr*, i e. "*Nazirite.*" This, in A.V., is always spelt with an *a*, incorrectly, "*Nazarite.*" The *Onomastica Sacra* shews that Eusebius confused the three terms, *Nazara*, *Nêtzer*, and *Nazîr*[2]. Jerome, as we shall see,

---

[1] In the *Aboth*, Rabbis are very rarely introduced by any title except *ben* "son of," or *ish* "man of" But there are at least the following exceptions (i 2) "Simeon *the Righteous*," (i. 7—8) "Matthai *the Arbeli*," i e. from a place called Arbela, (iii 17) "R Eliezer *the Modai*," i e from a place called Modai(m), (iii. 28) "R Eleazar *Chasmah*" (Levy ii 89 *b* "*Chisma*"), (iv. 16) "R Jochanan *the Sandalar*," i e. the maker (*or*, wearer) of sandals, (iv. 26) "Samuel *the Little*," (iv 30) "R. Eliezer *the Kappara*" (Levy iv 357 *a* "*the Cyprian*")

Some of these epithets or place-names are probably plays on words *Arbela* (Levy i 157 *b*) means "sieve", "sandal" suggests that the Rabbi, besides being a sandal-maker, obeyed the Marcan precept (Mk vi. 9) "be shod with *sandals*" (s *Corrections* 390 (ii) (ε) *a*); "*the Little*" might mean "the younger," but it is explained in *J. Sota* ix 13 "because he made himself little", "*the Cyprian*" (Levy iv. 357 *a*) may mean "the gum-seller" (in which I cannot see any allusive force), "*Modai*" (Levy iii 42—3) is a form of the word "know," and (*Sabb.* 55 *b*) R. Gamaliel said "We always need *Modai* (knowledge), for Eleazar the [man] of *Modai(m)* (knowledge) said " (Goldschm. "wir brauchen immer noch den *Modaer*," Levy "noch immer bedurfen wir des Ausspruches *des Modai*") ; lastly "*Chisma*" (Levy ii. 89 *b*) is expressly said to have been so called because he had once been a dumb and, as it were, *muzzled* teacher, and became "*unmuzzled*"

[2] (1) Νάζαρ (sic) is explained by Eusebius (see Index to *Onomastica*)

indicates that "*Nazirite*" was an early interpretation of Matthew's "*Nazoraean.*" Tertullian, after quoting from Luke the cry of the demoniac "What have we to do with thee, Jesus¹? Art thou come to destroy us? I know thee who thou art, the Holy One of God," and after saying that "a (or, the) prophet" had prophesied of "the Holy One of God²," and that "God's name of 'Jesus' was in the son of Nun," proceeds to explain "*Nazarene*" thus · "The Christ of the Creator had to be called *Nazaraeus* according to prophecy; whence the Jews also designate us by that very name (ipso nomine) *Nazaraeans*, after Him. For indeed we are those about whom it is written '*Nazaraeans* are made whiter than snow³'" Tertullian is quoting a passage in Lamentations rendered by A.V. "Her *Nazarites* were purer than snow⁴." He takes "*Nazarene*," in Luke, applied to Jesus, as meaning "*Nazirite*," and himself applies the term, in this sense, to the followers of Christ.

Obviously such an application could not long maintain itself against Jewish controversialists It is true that the

as ἄνθος, (2) Ναζαραῖοι (*v r* Ναζωραῖοι and Ναζαρινοί) as the ancient name of Christians, (3) Ναζαρέθ as (*a*) καθαριότης (*b*) ἄνθος ἀκραιφνὲς ἢ καθαρότης (*c*) the name from which Christ was called "Nazoraean," (4) Ναζαρέτ as ἀκρεμόνος (branch) αὐτοῦ ἢ καθαρός, (5) Ναζειραῖος as (*a*) ἅγιος (*b*) ἢ καθαρώτατος (*c*) ἢ ἐκ κοιλίας μητρὸς ἀφωρισμένος θεοῦ, (6) Ναζηραῖος (*v r*. Ναζοραῖος) as ἐξηνθισμένος, (7) Ναζωραῖος as (*a*) καθαρός (*b*) ἅγιος ἢ καθαρός (*c*) the name of Christ derived from Ναζαρέθ (adding καὶ Ναζαραῖοι (sic) (*v r* Ναζωραῖοι and Ναζαρινοί) τὸ παλαιὸν ἡμεῖς οἱ νῦν Χριστιανοί)

These details shew that whereas (1) the root of *Nêtzer* implies "flowering" or "growing," and (2) *Nazîr* implies "consecration," "purity," "separation (or, dedication) to God," &c., Eusebius oscillates between the two, with an additional occasional oscillation towards (3) "the town of Nazareth."

¹ Tertullian *Adv Marc.* iv 7 He omits "Nazarene" in the quotation, but proceeds to explain it in the next chapter, as though he had quoted it

² Clark's translation suggests, as the prophecy, Ps. xvi. 10 "thine holy one," and Dan. ix. 24 R.V. txt "the most holy"

³ Tertull. *Adv Marc.* iv. 8.

⁴ Lam iv. 7 R.V. "her *nobles* (marg., 'or, *Nazirites*')."

term "Nazirite" was used with some latitude, as is shewn by the Jewish discussion whether Samuel could be called "a Nazirite[1]"; and the Jewish and Syriac Versions of Ben Sira give Samuel this title[2]. But in the face of Christ's own statement that "the Son of Man came eating and drinking[3]," "Nazirite," applied to Christ, could hardly hold its ground. Nevertheless it is not only credible but even probable that Mark (whose Gospel does not contain the saying about "eating and drinking") is here recording unintelligently a tradition that called Jesus *Nazír* instead of *Nêtzer* and that took *Nazír* to mean "holy one." "*Nazirite* (i.e. *Nazir*) *of God*" is twice rendered in the LXX "*holy [one] of God*[4]." This does not indeed occur in any passage where "*the* Holy One" is used in its highest sense. It refers merely to Samson. But it might easily combine with other causes to lead the earliest of the Evangelists into an error as to this difficult title. While explaining "thou *Nêtzer*" as "thou *Nazarene*," Mark might naturally add—in accordance with his frequent habit of combining two interpretations[5]—"thou *Nazirite of God*" in the sense of "thou *holy one of God*."

It will be shewn hereafter that the influence of a familiar term like "*Nazirite*" (spelt with a *z*) might go even further than the influence of the name of an insignificant place like *Nazara*, to cause a substitution of *z* for *tz* in early Greek transliterations of *Nêtzer*. But we now pass to the consideration of other passages in the Gospels testing the *Nêtzer* hypothesis, beginning with the denials of Peter. In the first denial, where Mark has "Thou also wast with the Nazarene [namely] Jesus," Matthew has "Thou also wast with Jesus *the Galilaean*[6]"

---

[1] See the Talmudic *Nazir* ix 5 (Mishna).
[2] Sir xlvi 13 *c* "a Nazirite of the Lord in prophecy" (not in LXX), Syr "a Nazirite in prophecy" (om. "of the Lord").
[3] Mt xi. 19, Lk vii 34.
[4] Judg xiii. 7 LXX ἅγιον θεοῦ, al exempl Ναζιραῖον θεοῦ, rep. xvi. 17.
[5] See *Clue* passim, and especially **128** foll.
[6] Mk xiv 67, Mt xxvi. 69

In the second denial, where Mark has "This [man] is [*one*] *of them*," Matthew has "This [man] was with Jesus *the Nazoraean*[1]" If "Nazoraean," meaning *Nêtzer*, was regularly used about Jesus by His Galilaean followers in Jerusalem, it would naturally be repeated by the Roman soldiers, and afterwards by Gentiles in general, as a mere place-name—"Nazoraean" being regarded by Mark and other Greek writers as an inaccurate form of "Nazarene."

"Nazoraean" occurs in all the Gospels except Mark, and still more frequently in the Acts[2]. But it does not occur in the LXX nor in Greek literature apart from Christian influence Matthew says (1) that "Nazoraean" was connected with residence in "Nazareth," but also (2) that the residence was ordained in order to fulfil a prophecy about "Nazoraean"—which is not a form of "Nazareth." His words give us the impression of an early play on words by which Christ's disciples converted some form of "Nazareth" or "Nazara" into some word used in prophecy to denote the Messiah: "He [*i.e.* Joseph] came and dwelt in a city called Nazareth; that it might be fulfilled which was spoken by the prophets, that 'he shall be called *Nazoraean*[3]'."

Jerome, in his commentary on Matthew, gives two explanations of this One is, that "Nazaraeus" means "holy," and that all the Scriptures declare that the Lord will be holy. Another is, that there is a reference to Isaiah's mention of "Jesse" and "a *branch* out of his roots[4]" In his commentary on Isaiah he goes further · "That expression [as to] which, in the Gospel of Matthew, *all ecclesiastical writers seek, and cannot find* where it is written 'that he shall be called (?) *Nazoraean*

---

[1] Mk xiv 69, Mt xxvi 71 Lk xxii. 58 has "Thou also art [one] of them" R.V nowhere renders "Nazoraean" literally, see p 309, n 1.

[2] Mt ii 23, xxvi 71, Lk xviii. 37, Jn xviii 5—7, xix 19 (Acts 7 times, including xxii 8 "I am Jesus *the Nazoraean*")

[3] Mt ii 23 ὅπως πληρωθῇ τὸ ῥηθὲν διὰ τῶν προφητῶν ὅτι Ναζωραῖος κληθήσεται.

[4] Is xi. 1.

(Lat text *Nazaraeus*),' *learned men among the Hebrews think to be taken from this passage.*" He goes on to say that the peculiar sound of the Hebrew צ, (*tz*) in *ntzr*, " branch," being between *s* and *z*, cannot be expressed in Latin

The hypothesis of this allusion gives us a reasonable explanation of the term " Nazoraean," if it was a Messianic name, derived from Isaiah, " And there shall come forth a shoot out of the stock of Jesse, and a *branch* (*nêtzer*) out of his roots shall bear fruit." The Targum paraphrases "*branch*" as Messiah thus : " And there shall go forth a king from the sons of Jesse and a *Messiah* from his sons' sons shall be anointed [as prince]" It ought not to surprise us if, among many Messianic names in the first century, that of the Branch of the Tree of Jesse, the Prince of the House of David, the symbol of the Kingdom of Peace, became familiar and popular, so that the Messiah might be hailed as *Nêtzer*, along with the more prosaic and ordinary title " Son of David."

The name "Jesse" is associated with old age ; and there was a picturesque paradox in the history of the old man's youngest son, a mere stripling, overlooked at first among his elder brethren—all of whom were " rejected "—and coming unexpectedly to the rescue of Israel[1]. No wonder that the story suggested to the poets and prophets of his people the thought of a branch springing out of the root of a tree decaying and almost dead In later times, when the tree of the house of David had suffered grievously from foreign conquerors, it was natural that Isaiah, after predicting that the Lord would " lop the boughs with terror," should refer to the "branch" from "Jesse" in his comforting prophecy, " And there shall come forth a shoot out of the stock of Jesse, and a branch out of his roots shall bear fruit, and the Spirit of the Lord shall rest upon him[2] "

---

[1] See 1 S xvii. 12 (R V.) "the man was an old man stricken [in years] among men," and *ib.* xvi 7 " I have rejected him [*i e* Eliab] "
[2] Is xi 1—2

Philo appears to refer to this passage when he says, not long after quoting Isaiah about Israel as being once childless and desolate, but now a mother of many children[1], that "when the trunk is cut down, but the roots not taken away, *new shoots spring up* by which the old decrepit tree is surpassed[2]." It may be the same, he says, in mankind. Wherever a small seed of virtue is left, it may become a source of all that is best and most glorious, through which desolate cities are once more inhabited, and nations advance in population. This is his philosophic and impersonal and abstract way of saying what Galilaeans would express by avowing their faith in the "Branch" from the aged Jesse, who would "assemble the outcasts of Israel, and gather together the dispersed of Judah," and stand for "an ensign of the peoples, unto whom the nations shall seek[3]."

That "Jesse" was the subject of Jewish mystical thought at an early time appears from Chronicles, where his name is spelt so as to make it identical with "man"—"vir, potens robore," says Rashi[4]. *Sota* goes further. It fastens on the warlike meaning of "man" and ignores "Jesse." Instead of saying that "David son of [a] man [that was an] Ephrathite[5]" might have two meanings, 1st, son of Jesse who was called "man" (*vir*), and 2nd, "son of God," since God is "a man of war[6]," it gives the second meaning alone. Probably there were in the first century very many legends about Jesse of which only a few survive[7]

---

[1] Philo ii. 434—5 quoting Is. liv 1.
[2] *Ib* ii 437 alluding to Is. xi 1.   [3] Is. xi. 12, 10.
[4] 1 Chr ii 13 The passage also spells "David" "plene cum *yod* propter honorem Davidis," and omits "Elihu," so as to make David the seventh son instead of the eighth
[5] 1 S xvii. 12. R V omits "man."
[6] *Sota* 42 *b* quoting Exod xv. 3
[7] See *Berach* 58 *a* about Jesse as being one who always moved "with *a multitude*," a legend arising from 1 S xvii 12 (*lit.*) "went among *men*," Rashi "numerabatur in coetu *virorum honoratorum*," Targ. (Walton) "*juvenibus*," LXX "*men*" but *v.r* "*years*"

The early evidence from Chronicles bearing on the spelling of Jesse's name gives somewhat more importance than might be otherwise attached to the curious statement of Epiphanius about "Jessaeans," as an early name for Christians. It deserves mention here as it bears on the meaning and spelling of "Nazoraean."

Epiphanius says that all Christians (before they were called Christians at Antioch) were called "Nazoraeans," and indeed, "for a short time, Jessaeans." The Jessaeans he there regards as deriving their name from Jesse[1]. But, later on, he suggests that the Jessaeans may have derived their name either from Jesse, or from Jesus as meaning Healer or Saviour[2]. He identifies them with those whom Philo calls Essaeans (known to us as Essenes) some of whom accepted Jesus as Messiah, from whom—as being conceived in the womb at Nazareth, and hence called "Jesus the Nazoraean," they called themselves *Nazoraeans*[3]. Finally, he says, "But it was a different sect that called themselves *Nasaraeans*, for the sect of the *Nasaraeans* was before Christ and did not know Christ[4]."

We cannot depend on the judgment of Epiphanius or on his knowledge of Hebrew. He neither quotes Isaiah nor indicates a belief that any of these sect-names might be derived from the prophet's combination of "Nêtzer" and "Jesse." But his silence at all events shews that he is not inventing facts, or adapting facts to a theory of his own derived from the text of Isaiah. He is merely enumerating and describing (what he believes to have been) Jewish and Christian sects. Among the most ancient of these he finds (1) "*Nazoraeans*," connected with "Jesse," and (2) a still earlier sect "before Christ," called "*Nasaraeans*." If there were such sects, or early traditions

---

[1] *Haer.* xxix p 116 foll   [2] *Ib* p. 120   [3] *Ib.* pp. 120—1.
[4] *Ib* p 121 *Ἄλλοι δὲ Νασαραίους ἑαυτοὺς ἐκάλεσαν* The ἄλλοι appears to be emphatic "it was others."

NAZARENE AND NAZORAEAN

mentioning such names, it must occur to every one that the names had some connection with Isaiah's mention of the *Nêtzer* of *Jesse*.

Against these views it may be urged that the Talmud knows nothing of such a Jewish sect, or of such a Messianic name. But the Talmudic silence, under the circumstances, would prove little. The Talmudists would naturally be silent about a Jewish sect, or a Messianic title in Scripture, that had originated a term fraught with such sinister associations to their nation, as "Nazoraean" and the kindred "Nazarene."

There is a trace, however, of allusion to "Nazoraean," if connected with *nêtzer*, in a Talmudic story about one of five disciples of Jesus, called Nêtzer, put to death by the Sanhedrin. He pleaded for his life, on the ground of the favourable mention of "the branch" ("*branch* of Jesse") in Isaiah. But he was answered by another text of Isaiah mentioning "an abominable *branch*," where LXX has "corpse" for "*branch*." He was told that he was the latter, and must be killed[1].

So far as it goes, the evidence of the Talmud favours the derivation from "branch" rather than from *Nazara*. For it calls Jesus (or His followers) *Nôtzri*. This does not resemble *Nazara*. But it closely resembles a form of "branch" (*Nôtzer*) extant in the text of Ben Sira, "*The branch* of violence shall not be unpunished[2]." And it is easy to believe that the Jews parodied a form of *Nêtzer*, to distinguish the Branch of the

---

[1] See Levy iii 431 *b* quoting *Sanhedr* 43 *a* which plays on Is xi. 1, xiv 19. To the Jewish mind, regarding Israel as the Vine of the Lord, the Messiah might seem to be not only a Branch from the roots of Jesse but also a Branch from the roots of the Vine. To Christians the Messiah seemed the Vine itself. Yet the thought of "David" as the Branch seems merged with the thought of David, and David's Son the Messiah, as the Vine, in *Didach* § 9 "We give thee thanks, our Father, for the *holy vine of David*." On "corpse" for "branch" see p 325.

[2] Sir xl 15, Gesen. 666 *a*. The margin drops the *ô*. It is also dropped in *Ben Nêtzer* (referring to Dan vii 8 "a little horn" (*Gen r* on Gen xxxii 11, Wu p 374)).

Christians from that true *Nêtzer* of Jesse which God might call "the *branch* of my planting[1]."

According to this view, "the Nazoraean," in the mouths of the peasants and fishermen of Galilee, meant the Prince of the House of Jesse, or David, who was to "judge the poor with righteousness," and to bring about a reign of universal peace; and hence, whenever we find in a Gospel an appeal to the "Son of David" or a mention of "Son of David," we ought not to be surprised if some parallel Gospel has "Nazoraean." Jesus came, literally, from Nazareth or Nazara. But the people that acclaimed Him would say in their hearts "Not Nazarene, but Nazoraean," and their tongues would repeat only the latter. A literalistic Evangelist like Mark might feel bound to give the place-name literally, but he would not express the popular feeling

Conveying, as it does, the notion of a "shoot," growing up from the root of Jesse into life and vigour, "Nazoraean," if meaning *nêtzer*, would suggest to all Jews thoughts of strengthening, healing, revivification, and resurrection Peter's first proclamation of the gospel begins with it "Ye men of Israel, hear these words · *Jesus the Nazoraean*"—going on to describe His resurrection from death as predicted by David His ancestor, and His establishment as "both Lord and

---

[1] Is lx 21   On *ha-Nôtzri* applied to Jesus, see *Christianity in Talmud and Midrash* (R T Herford) p 52 n   "It is well known that the name of Nazareth does not occur in the Talmud, and indeed first appears in Jewish writings so late as the hymns of Qalır (A D 900 *circa*), in the form Nātzerath. This is probably the correct Hebrew form; but there must have been another form, Nōtzerath, or Nōtzerah, to account for the adjective Nōtzrı "

Since this form "Nōtzerath," which "must have been" in existence, if we are "to account for the adjective Nōtzrı," cannot be found, it is natural to look in some other direction for an origin of *Nôtzri*, as being "the Branch" in a bad sense, like "the abominable branch," or "the branch of violence."

For an illustrative parallel, see Schurer I. II. 298 on the late Jewish interpretation of Bar-Cosıba, whom Akiba had called "*star*," as "*deceiver*."

Messiah[1]" Peter's first act of healing is also introduced with it, "In the name of *Jesus Christ, the Nazoraean*, walk" This is followed by a proclamation of Jesus as "the Prince of life whom God raised from the dead," and, later on, by the declaration, "In the name of *Jesus Christ, the Nazoraean*, whom ye crucified, whom God raised from the dead, doth this man stand here before you whole[2]." In all these passages, and still more perhaps in one of the accounts of Paul's conversion containing the words "I am Jesus *the Nazoraean*, whom thou persecutest," most readers—if they approach these stirring announcements with a desire to realise them as if hearing them for the first time—will feel (I think) that there would be something flat in the mention of "the Nazoraean" if it only meant "born at Nazara"—a name suggesting "Where is it?"—but that it would sound an inspiriting and stirring note if it also alluded to "the ever living Prince of Life, the Nêtzer, the Branch of the Lord's Planting[3]."

As regards the Gospels, most of the instances in the Synoptic tradition have been mentioned above[4], and it

---

[1] Acts ii 22—36 Acts ii 1—21 introduces, but does not proclaim the gospel. [2] Acts iii 6—15, iv 10

[3] Acts xxii 8 Between this and the Petrine instances comes Acts vi 14 "We have heard him [*i e* Stephen] say that this Jesus, the *Nazoraean* [as these heretics call him] (ὅτι Ἰησοῦς ὁ Ναζωραῖος οὗτος) will destroy this place." The other instances in the Acts are xxiv 5 "a ringleader of the sect of the *Nazoraeans*," and xxvi 9 "contrary to the name of Jesus the *Nazoraean*" "Nazarene" does not occur in the Greek of the Acts (in spite of xxiv. 5 R.V "Nazarenes," as to which see p 309, n 1)

[4] No mention has been made of an instance peculiar to Luke, in the story of Emmaus (xxiv. 19), "the things concerning Jesus *the Nazarene*" It is the only instance of "Nazarene" in Luke (apart from Lk iv. 34 where he closely follows Mark) Possibly Luke simply retains the form used in a narrative that he incorporates in his Gospel But it would have a distinctive meaning if it implied that the two disciples had, for the moment, given up their Messianic hopes, and that Jesus, whom they would but recently have called "*the Nazoraean*, the Branch of the Lord's planting," had, for the moment, become to them simply "*the Nazarene*," beloved and longed for, but only as "Jesus *of Nazareth*."

should be added that an insertion peculiar to Matthew, immediately after the Riding into Jerusalem, mentions "prophet" and "from Nazareth," whereas the other three Gospels mention "king" or "kingdom" in the preceding welcome of Jesus, but Matthew does not[1]. In John, "Jesus the Nazoraean" is the reply twice made by the cohort and the servants of the chief priests to the question asked by Jesus, "Whom seek ye[2]?" Jesus makes, and confirms, the avowal that He *is* "Jesus the Nazoraean" ("I am he"). A little afterwards Pilate writes on the Cross "Jesus *the Nazoraean*, the King of the Jews," and confirms it with "What I have written I have written" The Fourth Gospel gives us the impression that the whole of the inscription was written by Pilate as God's instrument. The Synoptists do not insert in it "Jesus *the Nazoraean*." Mark has simply "the King of the Jews." Matthew and Luke add "this" or "this is Jesus[3]." What Pilate understood by "Nazoraean" we are not told Whatever it meant, the accused had been arrested under that appellation, and would be consistently tried and executed under it, whether it meant to Romans "of the town of Nazara" (as it probably did) or "commonly called Nazoraean." But John, by making Pilate write on the Cross "Jesus *the Nazoraean*," along with "King of the Jews," certainly succeeds in conveying the impression that Providence was giving a royal glory to the former title.

From this, the last Johannine instance of "Nazoraean," let us return to the Johannine introduction of "Nazareth" in the dialogue between Philip and Nathanael, in which the latter objects to Nazareth as the Messiah's birthplace and yet

---

[1] Mt. xxi. 11, comp Mk xi 10, Lk. xix 38, Jn xii. 13 "king" (or "kingdom"), Mt xxi. 9 om "king."

[2] Jn xviii. 5, 7.

[3] Mk xv. 26, Mt. xxvii. 37 οὗτός ἐστιν Ἰ ὁ β. τῶν Ἰουδαίων; Lk. xxiii 38 ὁ β τῶν Ἰουδαίων οὗτος

accepts Jesus in spite of the objection. In the case of Philip it might well be said that the objection to "Nazareth," as the Messianic home, appeared to be not met but overridden. Are we to suppose that it was "overridden" in the case of Nathanael also? The context suggests that there may be another explanation.

It is liable to the charge of being "subtle." But it is at all events in accordance with all the facts enumerated above. In particular, it accords with the Matthaean tradition (as interpreted from Isaiah) that the residence in Nazareth was ordained in order that Jesus "might be called *the Branch*," *i.e.* the Prince of the House of David, and the Branch of God's planting. It is this—that Nathanael, an "Israelite without guile" and also learned in the Scriptures, being forced by the power of Christ's personality to receive Him as the Messiah, and yet being at the same time told that He is "from *Nazareth*," is driven at once to the same conclusion as that set forth by Matthew, namely, that the connection of the Messiah with the village of *Nazareth* was ordained "in order that He might be called *Nêtzer*"

Historically and logically Nathanael's exclamation is unjustifiable. He ought (we may say) to have waited for fuller information. Then he would have ascertained that Jesus was born in Bethlehem—which was either (as Matthew implies) the home, or (as Luke says) the lodging-place, of Joseph and Mary at the time of the birth. But the Synoptic Gospels give us no hint that the birth at Bethlehem was publicly known during Christ's life. The Fourth Gospel goes further. It gives us reasons for confidently asserting that it was *not* publicly known. It represents objections—raised by some of "the multitude," and also by "the Pharisees," that the Christ or "the Prophet[1]" could not come "out of Galilee"—as being

---

[1] Jn vii 52. On the necessity of this interpretation see *Johannine Grammar* **2492**

allowed to pass uncontradicted. In both cases, supporters of Jesus are present Some of them had said before "This is the Christ" But they have nothing to say now. Nicodemus pleads for Christ, but when they fling in his face "Art thou also of Galilee?" he leaves the gibe unanswered[1].

Putting ourselves in the position of Nathanael, convinced that Jesus must be the Messiah, and also that He was "from Nazareth," and knowing nothing of the alleged birth at Bethlehem, could we, as Jews, with Jewish ways of interpreting Scripture, find a much better refuge—for the moment at all events—than the assumption that, if Jesus was indeed "from Nazareth," it was divinely ordained, in order that He might be "called Nazoraean," that is to say, the Branch, who was at once the Son of God and the Son of Israel?

In concluding our consideration of this very difficult question we shall do well to remember that in the transition of Christian tradition from the language of the East to that of the West, it would be natural to introduce into the thought a definiteness that was not part of the original. Birthplace-names such as "the Stagirite" would not suggest to a Greek a metaphorical or mystical interpretation, or anything but plain "Aristotle." But Abram *the Hebrew*—the first mention of "Hebrew" in the Bible—is rendered by LXX as meaning that "Hebrew" was "the Crosser, or Passer, Over." R. Jehuda, commenting on this passage, implies that the Patriarch "*passed over*" from the world of falsehood to the world of truth, and Philo takes the same view[2]. Also "Elijah *the Tishbite*" is taken by the author of Horae Hebraicae as alluding to the mission of Elijah to be "the Converter[3]"

---

[1] Jn vii. 41—2, 52

[2] *Light on the Gospel* **3948** foll

[3] See *Hor Heb.* iii 21 (on Lk 1 17). He adds that "the Targum and other Rabbins would have it from the city *Toshab*." But it is difficult to believe that there was not found in "*Toshab*" some allusion to the Prophet's task

Even those who took Tishbite to mean "from Toshab" might admit that the prophet's birthplace-name was, as it were, a prophecy of the "conversion" that was to be the prophet's work. And that thoughts of this kind extended to the use of birthplace-names in the earliest traditions of the Talmud is indicated by the instances given above from *Aboth* This general consideration should go a long way toward convincing us that Jesus was called "the Nazoraean," not "the Nazarene," by His disciples, and that Mark, in substituting the latter for the former, has committed a natural but a serious error[1].

---

[1] Professor Burkitt in the course of some valuable remarks about Nazareth &c in *Syriac Forms of New Testament Proper Names* (published for the British Academy, 1912) says (p. 18) "It seems to me most probable that the word is really connected with נזיר and the vow of the Nazirites," adding "It is a desperate conjecture, and I would not make it, were it not that *the ordinary view of Nazareth seems to me wholly unproved and unsatisfactory.*" With the words that I have italicised I heartily agree, but he adds "And the most unproved and least satisfactory part of the ordinary view is that part of it which is attested by the Syriac Versions, whereby the *z* is made to represent a Semitic צ." From this I venture to differ for the reasons given above, maintaining that the Syriac has preserved the original "Semitic צ" which belonged to *Nêtzer*.

No doubt, Professor Burkitt is right in saying (p. 28 foll.) that the Semitic צ is rarely represented by the Greek ζ. Yet he himself points out that "Zoar" (the name of the city near the Dead Sea, where Lot took refuge) is an exception, and he indicates the reasons (1) It was a well-known place and spelt Ζοάρα or Ζωάρα by Ptolemy. (2) It was supposed to mean "Little-borough" Now "little" is spelt in Hebrew with צ (*tz*) but in Aramaic with *z* He adds that "though ז and צ do not indiscriminately or regularly interchange, yet one or two roots containing these letters do interchange, and זער—צער is one."

Here he does not go so far as Levy in recognising the likelihood of interchange of צ and ז Levy *Ch.* I. 209 says that the Aramaic ז is "*often*" interchanged with similar sibilants, "*especially*" *s* and *tz* ("ס und צ"), and gives an instance a little later (*ib.* 214 *b*) where the Hebrew צידה "viaticum," has passed into the Aramaic זודא (see also Levy III 213 *b* מצר and מזר). If Levy is right, it becomes much more easy to understand how the Hebrew *nêtzer* might pass into the early Christian Church in a form that substituted *z* for *tz* That Jewish Christians ever called

Christ "a Nazirite" seems to me in the highest degree improbable, both because Christ's manner of life was alien from such a title, and because the title had no Messianic traditions, but that the term "Nazirite"—interpreted as "the consecrated one" or "holy one of God"—was one of several causes that led Gentile Christians to misunderstand a Jewish play on the titles "Jesus *the Nêtzer*" and "Jesus *of Nazara*," seems very probable indeed. Comp. *Ezr-Apoc* xiii. 45 "Arzareth," where *z* is Heb *tz*

In particular, there are the following grounds for believing that "Jesus the *Nêtzer*" would be a controversial phrase, in the first half of the first century, between Jews and Christians in disputes concerning the Resurrection of Christ. (1) According to Matthew (xxviii. 15), the Jews persistently accused the Christians of stealing the body of Jesus from the sepulchre [According to John (xx 2), the women for a short time believed that it had been "taken away" by others ("they")] (2) The Jewish accusers would probably apply to such a Christian theft, even though they somewhat strained the verbal prophecy, the words of Isaiah (xiv. 19) "cast forth from thy sepulchre like an abominable *nêtzer*, as the raiment of those that are slain, that are thrust through with the sword" (3) Here the LXX has "dead ($\nu\epsilon\kappa\rho\acute{o}s$)" for *nêtzer*, and Aquila and Symmachus have $\grave{\iota}\chi\acute{\omega}\rho$ and $\check{\epsilon}\kappa\tau\rho\omega\mu\alpha$, implying that the body was a mangled mass of flesh and blood. (4) We have seen above (p 318) that, according to the Talmud, the Jews used Isaiah's words to justify them in killing a certain Nêtzer, a Christian heretic (5) Isaiah's preceding context (xiv. 13) "I will ascend ($\grave{\alpha}\nu\alpha\beta\acute{\eta}\sigma o\mu\alpha\iota$) into heaven" was applied ironically to Jesus Himself (*Notes on New Testament Criticism* **2998** (xviii) *a*) by Rabbi Abbahu (about 280 A.D.). (6) Both passages of Isaiah were referred by the Jews primarily to Nebuchadnezzar, whose pride made him boast of "ascending" to heaven, and whose apprehended resurrection from the dead caused his enemies to "thrust-through" his corpse "with the sword" From the Jewish point of view, a secondary application to Jesus was very natural (7) On the other hand, concerning the true *nêtzer*, the *nêtzer* from the root of Jesse, the LXX—calling it "a flower"—said (Is. xi 1) "a flower from the root shall ascend ($\grave{\alpha}\nu\alpha\beta\acute{\eta}\sigma\epsilon\tau\alpha\iota$, but Heb *lit* 'bear-fruit')" (8) Where Mark (xvi 6) has "*ye seek* Jesus *the Nazarene, the crucified*," the parallel Luke (xxiv. 5) has "why *seek ye the living with the dead* ($\nu\epsilon\kappa\rho\hat{\omega}\nu$)?"

The facts suggest that the tradition on which Mark was based contained some contrast between the true and the false "*nêtzer*" to this effect. "Ye are seeking the [living and growing] *nêtzer* as [if He were the *nêtzer*] *thrust-through* [and helpless among the dead]" If so, Mark has retained *nêtzer* as "Nazarene" and "*thrust-through*" as "crucified" Luke has retained neither word, but has given something approaching to the sense of both

ADDENDUM

NAZORAEAN AS A NAME FOR CHRISTIAN

AGAINST the thesis that Nazoraean represents an original Nêtzer it has been urged by a friend (1) that the word Tsemach, Branch, mentioned by Jeremiah in the prophecy " I will raise-up unto David a righteous Branch[1]," is recognised in Jewish literature as referring to the Messiah, whereas Nêtzer is not so recognised. It has also been suggested to me (2) that Aramaic-speaking people would not at once catch the meaning of Nêtzer

§ 1 *Nêtzer and Tsemach*

To deal, first, with the second objection. I admit that Nêtzer, as a common noun, meaning "shoot [of a tree]," is very rare indeed in Aramaic[2]. But the Targum on Isaiah renders "*a shoot (nêtzer)* from his roots" by "*Messiah* from his son's sons," *i e* as a proper name[3]. We may fairly suppose that many Jews in the first century were accustomed to hear the Hebrew Nêtzer thus interpreted as the Aramaic Messiah, or Anointed, when this passage of Isaiah was read to them in the synagogue, and that they accepted Nêtzer as a proper name, with a feeling—not perhaps always very definite but

---

[1] Jerem xxiii. 5 "raise-up," not "raise" (Gesen 879 *a*), comp *ib* xxxiii 15, Zech iii. 8, vi 12. It is unfortunate that our English Bible renders both Tsemach and Nêtzer by "branch"

[2] See Levy *Ch* ii. 126 *a*.   [3] Is xi 1

still a feeling—that besides being a Messianic name, it conveyed a notion of "growth" or "shooting up into life."

Next, to meet the objection that in Jewish literature Tsemach is recognised, whereas Nêtzer is not recognised, as meaning Messiah. A reason for this (so far as it is true) may perhaps be found in the Talmudic treatise entitled Sanhedrin— which omits both Nêtzer and Tsemach from its list of Messianic titles[1]. It is the only Talmudic treatise that contains an anti-Christian story about a heretic Nêtzer, who pleaded for his life, saying that he was the "nêtzer" in the eleventh chapter of Isaiah, and who received the reply that he was the "nêtzer" in Isaiah's fourteenth chapter ("an abominable *branch*[2]"). Anti-Christian allusions are also found based on passages in Daniel where "nêtzer" occurs, and, under the title Ben Nêtzer, there are probably hostile references to Jesus[3]. Such a feeling of hostility may afford an explanation of the comparative rarity of Jewish references to Nêtzer in a Messianic sense[4].

It is not so easy to explain why Sanhedrin omits Tsemach. Rashi commenting on "the Branch," Tsemach, in two passages of Zechariah, says (1) "The name is given to the growing greatness of Zerubbabel," who "was Nehemiah, as it

---

[1] Levy IV 197 *b* calls attention to this omission in *Sanhedr.* 98 *b*.

[2] See p 318 above

[3] So Levy 1 240 *a* referring to *Gen r.* (on Gen xxxii 11) quoting Dan. vii 8 (comp xi 7) And comp *Cetuboth* 51 *b* (quoted in *Hor Heb.* 1 337) where a distinction is drawn between "the kingdom of Ahasuerus" and "the kingdom of *Ben Nêtzer*" These traditions are late But they point back to a very early use indeed of "Nêtzer," in a hostile sense, such as may have been acutely felt by Paul when he heard the words "I am Jesus *the Nazoraean*, whom thou art persecuting."

[4] See, however, *Echa* (on Lam 1 16, Wu. pp 87—8) which gives a list of Messianic titles, quoting first Zech vi 12 in support of *Tsemach*, and then, at some interval, Is xi 1 including *Nêtzer* On the other hand *Jer. Berach.* 11 4 (3), after giving *Tsemach* and other titles, quotes only the first half of Is. xi 1 "a rod. stem of Jesse," stopping short before *Nêtzer*

is said in Sanhedrin", (2) "This is Zerubbabel...some explain it about Messiah; but the whole of the context bears on the second temple[1]." This reference to Sanhedrin is remarkable because that treatise, when quoting the first of the passages in Zechariah mentioning the Branch, makes no mention of Zerubbabel, and stops short, omitting "behold, ..Branch[2]" Also Ibn Ezra, commenting on Isaiah's saying "In that day shall *the Branch* (*tsemach*) of the Lord be beautiful and glorious," says, "Some refer this to Hezekiah; I think that it signifies the righteous portions of the inhabitants of Jerusalem that will be saved[3]." This view accords with the collective meaning of *tsemach* in the passage describing the destruction of "the *leafage* (or, *growth*) (*tsemach*) of the ground" in Sodom[4], and it also supports Aquila in rendering *tsemach* in Zechariah not by "*branch*," but by a word not recognised as existing elsewhere in Greek literature, meaning "*upgrowth*[5]." These facts seem to shew that *tsemach* was not so well fitted as *nêtzer* to express "a scion," in such a personal sense that Christians might apply it to Jesus as the "Branch from the root of Jesse," while Jewish persecutors of Christians might apply it to Him as "the abominable branch." Thus the effect of the alleged preponderance of *tsemach* over *nêtzer* in a Messianic sense decreases when closely examined, and it becomes of still less weight when

---

[1] Rashi, on Zech. III. 8, VI 12. He is silent about the interpretation of Tsemach in Isaiah and Jeremiah.

[2] *Sanhedr.* 93 a, when quoting Zech. III 8, makes no mention of the Branch nor of Zerubbabel, but specifies Hananiah, Mishael, and Azariah (Dan. I. 7, III. 13—30) as the (Walton) "viri portenti" mentioned by Zechariah. *Sanhedr.* nowhere quotes Zech. VI. 12

[3] Is IV. 2 Rashi's note, on "Erit germen Domini," is simply "Vobis decori"

[4] Gen XIX 25

[5] Zech VI. 12, LXX ἀνατολή, Aq ἀναφυή, Sym. βλάστημα Steph *Thes* quotes no other instance of ἀναφυή except "inc Zech. III. 8" (not recognised by Field)

we perceive that, toward the end of the first century, the Messianic *nêtzer* might pass out of frequent Jewish use except in a few traditions that preserved the record of Jewish hatred of the false Nêtzer's followers, variously called the Nazoraeans or Nazarenes.

§ 2. *Nazor-aean and Christ-ian*

We have been hitherto working forward from the Old Testament word Nêtzer, and finding, as we think, that it leads us to the very common New Testament word "Nazoraean." Let us now work back from the very rare New Testament word "Christian," and see whether that leads us to the same term "Nazoraean."

"The disciples," it is said, "were first called Christians in Antioch[1]." The termination in "Christ-ian," as also in the Mark-Matthew "Herod-ian[2]," implies a *sect* or *faction*. Cicero in this sense uses the words "Sullan" and "Marian"; Caesar called the followers of Pompey "Pompeians"; the Emperor Augustus gently reproached the historian Livy with being a "Pompeian"; and under the shortlived Emperor Galba the contending factions are called by Tacitus "Othonians" and "Vitellians," whereas the imperial forces are not called "Galbans[3]."

The next step is to shew that it was the Jews who prejudiced the Gentile world against the disciples of Jesus by

---

[1] Acts xi 26

[2] On Mt. xxii 16, Jerome explains "Herodians" as (1) "militibus Herodis," (2) "seu quos illudentes Pharisaei ..'Herodianos' vocabant, et (? ut) non divino cultui deditos." The second explanation (doubtless) gives the meaning correctly Chrys, however, assumes the first, "Herod's soldiers," and perhaps some interpretation of this kind resulted in a tradition peculiar to Luke (xxiii 11 "Herod's soldiers"). "Herodians" means the "party," or "clique," of Herod, in a bad sense, as opposed to "the observers of the Law"

[3] See these words in Lewis and Short's Lexicon, and see Tacitus, *Ann* iv 34 for the epithet applied to Livy.

NAZARENE AND NAZORAEAN

circulating reports that they belonged to what the disciples themselves would call a "way," but the Jews a "faction," or "sect". Paul was sent northward to Damascus "that, if he found any that were of *the Way*," he might bring them bound to Jerusalem[1] Thus Luke phrases it But the Jews, we may be sure, would call the "way" a "heresy," as Justin Martyr says to the Jew Trypho, "After you had crucified Him...you selected and sent out from Jerusalem chosen men through all the land saying that *the godless heresy of the Christians* had sprung up...[2]." This is the first mention of "*Christian*" in the Dialogue with Trypho, and we must note that, according to Justin, *the name originated from the Jews*, who created what Justin calls in the preceding sentence "the wicked *prejudice against the Righteous One*" The Gentiles in the North—in Damascus, for example, and Antioch, and Edessa—would probably know very little, and trouble themselves still less, about the disciples of Jesus, until Jews came to give them a bad name: "You have in Damascus, or Antioch, or Edessa, *a mischievous and disaffected party of Jews who are both atheists* in the sight of heaven and rebels against Caesar on earth."

But by what name would the Jews call these "heretics"? They could not have called them by the name literally corresponding to "*Christianoi*", for that would have been "*Messianoi*," and they would never have told the Gentiles that the leader of this detested sect was "Messiah." But they might have said to the Gentiles at Antioch about them something like what Tertullus, the spokesman of the Jews against Paul, said before Felix later on: "We have found this man [*i.e.* Paul] a pestilent fellow, and a mover of insurrections among all the Jews throughout the world, and a ringleader of *the sect of the Nazoraeans*[3]." Not till afterwards

---

[1] Acts ix. 2   [2] *Tryph* § 17
[3] Acts xxiv 5

would it be necessary to explain that the "Nazor" from whom these "Nazoraeans" derived their name was so called by his followers, partly because he happened to be born at a village called Nazara, but mainly because they believed him to be the royal Nêtzer, or "scion," of the House of David, that is to say the "Messiah," or "Anointed," or, in Greek, "Christos"—though, in fact, he was a mere Pretender, a false "Christos[1]." It was not likely that Greek-speaking Antiochians would trouble themselves about such outlandish and uncouth terms as "Nêtzer" and "Messiah." But they would be very likely to seize on the personal and pronounceable name of "Christos," as being the originator of this novel blend of atheism with sedition—stigmatized in very early times as a deadly superstition[2]. Then, as an almost inevitable consequence, according to the analogy of such terms as the Mariani, the Sullani, and the Pompeiani, the citizens of Antioch would construct the new name, "Christiani"

This personal, and Hebrew, and non-geographical origin of the term "Nazoraean" may explain, perhaps, why Luke in the Acts, giving three widely different accounts of Paul's conversion, records, in the first and the third, the description given by Jesus of Himself, without any addition, simply as "I am *Jesus*, whom thou art persecuting"; but in the second, as "I am *Jesus the Nazoraean*, whom thou art persecuting[3]." In

---

[1] For the representation of Nêtzer in Aramaic as "Messiah," see the Targum on Is xi 1 For the addition of -*aîos* comp Josephus *Ant* xii 6, 1 Macc ii 4—5 where "Caddis, Thassi, Maccab-*eus*, Avaran, and Apphus" are given as the surnames of five brothers, and only the most famous of the names receives the Greek termination -*aîos*

[2] Tacitus *Ann.* xv 44 "Reos...quos, per flagitia invisos, vulgus *Christianos* appellabat Auctor nominis eius *Christus* repressaque in praesens *exitiabilis superstitio* rursum erumpebat" Suetonius (*Nero* 16—19) enumerates, among the "blameless or praiseworthy acts" of Nero, his punishment of "*Christiani, genus hominum superstitionis novae ac maleficae*" See p 340, n. 1

[3] Acts ix. 5, xxvi 15, xxii 8

the first and the third of these narratives Luke is writing in his own name, or is describing Paul as pleading before a Gentile tribunal. But in the second narrative he describes Paul as pleading before a multitude of *Jews in Jerusalem, and expressly says that Paul spoke* "*in Hebrew*[1]." In Jerusalem, and uttered "in Hebrew," an allusion to "Jesus *the Nêtzer*," whose followers Paul had often tried to compel to "blaspheme" in the synagogues of the City[2], would be both intelligible and effective. And how effective, too, if Paul actually heard that word in the moment of his conversion! For then it would imply "I am Jesus, not 'the abominable branch'—as you have been ignorantly calling me and striving to make my followers call me—but the Holy Branch, the Branch of David, the Redeemer of Israel[3]!"

§ 3. *Pliny on "Nazerini"*

The passage quoted above from the speech of Tertullus is the only instance of the plural "Nazoraeans"—or any form of Nazar, such as "Nazarenes"—in the New Testament. Neither Nazareth, nor Nazoraean, nor any form akin to either of these words, occurs in all the works of the Apostolic Fathers and the Apologists, except in a single passage where Justin Martyr says that Joseph, the spouse of Mary, "went up from Nazareth where he lived, to Bethlehem[4]." The word

---

[1] Acts xxi. 36, xxii 2

[2] Acts xxvi 11, comp xxii 4

[3] Chrysostom says on "Nazoraean" in Acts xxii 8 (Cramer) that "the city is appropriately added for the purpose of recognition (καλῶς ἡ πόλις πρόσκειται ὥστε ἐπιγνῶναι αὐτούς)" Does Chrysostom mean that Paul *added* "Nazoraean" before the Jews, that they might understand who was meant? If so, does he suppose that Paul did not "add" the term "Nazoraean" before Festus because Festus would understand without it? He does not make it clear that he assumes that *Jesus Himself did not utter the word* "*Nazoraean*," but he gives the impression of assuming this.

[4] *Tryph.* § 78. The *Onomastica*, however, testifies to its ancient use, 143 (comp 285) "Sed et nos *apud veteres quasi pro opprobrio* Nazaraei dicebamur, quos nunc Christianos vocant"

is not given in fairly copious Indices to Irenaeus and Clement of Alexandria; and it has been shewn that Tertullian confuses the word with Nazirites[1]. These indications of the rarity of the word in early Christian writings make Pliny's mention of " Nazerini "—along with a name given in Teubner's text as " Mabog "—all the more worthy of investigation. " Coele habet Apameam, Marsya amne divisam a *Nazerinorum* tetrarchia, Bambycen quae alio nomine Hierapolis vocatur, Syris vero *Mabog*—ibi prodigiosa Atargatis, Graecis autem Derceto dicta, colitur[2]." Apart from " Nazerini," Lewis and Short's Lexicon contains all these names except "*Mabog*," for which Teubner's notes give as variations " Mabo " and " Magog." Horae Hebraicae, quoting the passage, gives " *Magog*," and Breithaupt's notes to Rashi, on Ezekiel's mention of " Gog of the land of *Magog*[3]," refer to the quotation without noting it as an error or as a various reading.

To obtain some information about Mabog and its rival readings we turn to the earlier parallel account in Strabo. It mentions three of Pliny's names, all rare—" Bambyce," " Atargatis," and " Hierapolis"; but instead of " Mabog," as the third name for " Bambyce " or " Hierapolis," it substitutes " Edessa " thus : "*Bambyce*—which they call both *Edessa* and *Hierapolis*—wherein they honour the Syrian goddess Atargatis[4]." Now Pliny, too, mentions "Edessa" a little later on, but he says that it was " formerly called *Antioch*[5]." If we assumed this to be right, and if we combined Pliny and Strabo, we should have to suppose that the ancient Bambyce—which,

---

[1] The Indices mentioned are those of Grabe and Klotz. On Tertullian's " Nazaraeans," *i.e.* (R V. marg) " Nazirites," see above, p 312, n 4.

[2] Pliny *Nat. Hist.* v 81 (ed. Teubner) "Atargatis" and "Derceto" are supposed to be equivalents to Astarte or Aphrodite.

[3] Ezek xxxviii. 2. See *Hor Heb*. i. 338.

[4] Strabo 748.

[5] Pliny *Nat. Hist.* v. 86, Pliny's only mention of the eastern Edessa. The Index gives a second reference (VI 216), but that refers to " Edesus " in Europe. The Index to Pliny shews that "Antiochs" were numerous.

Plutarch tells us[1], was the old name of Hierapolis—was also called by two other names, namely, Edessa and Mabog (or, Magog)

But assuming "Antioch" to be in all probability an error (as will presently be shewn) let us consider how Pliny may have been led into the error by stories that came to him from Jewish sources.

Both Antioch and Edessa were strongholds of Christianity from a very early date. As to Antioch, we have the authority of the Acts, above quoted. As to Edessa—besides the evidence afforded by a persecution of Christians in Edessa under Trajan —Eusebius has preserved copies of letters, believed by him to be genuine, which passed between Jesus and Abgarus, the Toparch of Edessa; and Thomas was believed to have been sent by Jesus to heal the Toparch of leprosy after the Ascension; whence, says Eusebius, "the whole of the city of the Edessenes is to this day devoted to the appellation of Christ[2]"

Until geographers, or other critics, can give us some other explanation of "Mabog," the *prima facie* explanation seems to be that it was a mistake for "*Magog*," and that it was a Jewish name to describe the stronghold of idolatry in the North. But, if that is so, then it would seem probable that Pliny's "*Nazerinorum* tetrarchia," or "the tetrarchy of the Christians," is a mistake for Edessa, the toparchy of Abgarus and stronghold of Christianity. Both names may thus be consistently explained. The country of the heretics in the North the Jews called "the land of *Magog*"; the heretics

---

[1] Plut *Vit. Anton.* 37.

[2] Euseb 1 13, 11. 1 ἡ πᾶσα τῶν Ἐδεσσηνῶν πόλις τῇ Χριστοῦ προσανάκειται προσηγορίᾳ See Steph. *Thes* VI. 1919. Perhaps the meaning is that it was proud of being preeminently the City of Christ as King. See Suicer p 1552 quoting Greg Nyss ἡ τοῦ Χριστοῦ προσηγορία τὴν βασιλείαν ἐνδείκνυται. Under Trajan (*Dict Christ Biog.* 11 41) "a fierce persecution was carried on at Edessa"

themselves they called "the followers of the *Nêtzer*" or "*Nazoraeans.*" Luke, in the Acts, has given this latter word accurately Pliny, in a form approaching that of Mark, has given it inaccurately as "*Nazerini.*"

We return to Pliny's statement that "*Edessa* used to be called *Antioch.*" This is not stated in the parallel passages of Strabo. Nor is it borne out by anything that Strabo says. He mentions indeed elsewhere several cities named Antioch. But he mentions only one in Syria, namely, that on the Orontes[1] Supposing Pliny to be wrong, we can again explain this error, too, as arising from Jewish sources, if he had heard from them that (1) "the *Nazoraeans* (or, *Nazerini*) had their stronghold in *Edessa*," and, at the same time, that (2) "they began first to be called *Christiani* (the Greek name for *Nazoraeans*) in *Antioch*"

We may conclude this section by noting that the above mentioned facts accord better with the hypothesis of an original Nêtzer, meaning a person, than with that of an original Nazara, meaning a town, as the source of the names "Nazoraeans" mentioned in the Acts, and "Nazerines" mentioned by Pliny. For both these sectarian names may be explained with little difficulty as meaning the followers of the Nazor (or, Nazer) But if Jesus Himself is to be called the "Nazarene," or "Nazarine," as being born at Nazara, then His followers would (strictly speaking) be called "Nazarenaeans" or Nazarinaeans, or by some other form that would separate the followers of "the Nazarene" from "the Nazarene" Himself

It is easier to imagine the Jews cursing followers of the hateful Ben Nêtzer, or Nêtzer, than to imagine them cursing followers of the native of an insignificant village called Nazara And analogy deserves some consideration. Sects and great

---

[1] Strabo 751 says that "Bambyce," which he has previously called (748) "another name for *Edessa* and Hierapolis," is (751) "to *the east of Antioch*" There he might have been expected to add, if he had believed it to be true, that "*Edessa* itself used to be called *Antioch*"

religious communities may, no doubt, derive their names from places as well as from persons. But instances of the former are comparatively rare; and the places are not insignificant villages, but districts or countries, as, for example, the Moravians. The followers of Judas of Gamala were not called Gamalites but Galilaeans, and Judas himself was called Judas the Galilaean. Buddhism, Zoroastrianism, Mohammedanism, are not named in this way; nor (as far as I know) is there any evidence that Mohammedanism was ever introduced to the world as "Meccanism," or Mohammedans known as "Meccans."

§ 4. *Early misunderstandings of the terms "Christ" and "Christian"*

Justin Martyr's first mention of "Christian" in his First Apology contains a play on *Christos*, "Christ," and *chrēstos*, "good," thus: "We are accused of being *Christians*; now that what is good (*chrēston*) should be hated is not right[1]" No attempt is made in the First Apology to explain the real meaning of "Christos"; and an apparent attempt to do so in the Second Apology is probably a corrupt restatement of the view that the name is connected with the root of "*chrēstos*[2]." We must try to realise the fact that "christos" does not occur in pre-Christian Greek (apart from the LXX) except to mean

---

[1] *Apol* § 4. Justin makes no attempt to explain "Christos," either here, or *ib.* § 12, Ἰησοῦς Χριστός, ἀφ' οὗ καὶ τὸ Χριστιανοὶ ἐπονομάζεσθαι ἐσχήκαμεν It will be convenient to differentiate, by a long ē, the Greek Χρηστός (*Chrēstos*) when anglicised, from the Latin *Chrestus*, sometimes used as a proper name.

[2] In 2 *Apol.* § 6, κεχρῖσθαι is perhaps a corruption of κεχρῆσθαι in a statement that the Father and Creator "used" the Son in the Creation (δι' αὐτοῦ πάντα ἔκτισε). The text is generally recognised as corrupt Compare the *Preaching of Irenaeus* § 53, which combines a statement (1) that the Father "*anointed and set-in-order*" everything through the Son, with another (2) that the Son "*was anointed*" at His coming into the world (Is. lxi. 1) The first two mentions of χρηστός in the LXX Concordance (1 S. xxiv. 11, 2 S. i. 14) are various readings for χριστός "anointed."

a "lotion" as distinct from "potion¹." On the other hand "Chrēstos" was in frequent use as a name throughout the empire before Christian times². It would hardly fail to be frequent in Latin also, like Onēsimus, being a kindly and convenient name for a slave Cicero rebukes Coelius for sending him, instead of personally interesting news, "accounts of adjourned cases and *Chrestus' compilation*"—perhaps meaning a Miscellany published by some "Chrestus" who was, in those days of Cicero, as well known (though not so favourably) as the bookselling firm of "the brothers Sosius" a little later in the days of Horace³

It was a common custom to use the vocative, masculine or feminine, on tombstones, in such phrases as "Farewell, *Chrēste*, or, (fem) *Chrēstē*!" When the name of the departed happened itself to be *Chrēstos* or *Chrēstē*, the similarity might suggest some allusion to the meaning of "*chrēstos*," "good," which, when applied to food, often means "delightful" or "sweet⁴",

---

¹ See Steph *Thes* (which gives instances of χριστός, in this sense, corrupted to χρηστός) In the Lexicons or Concordances to Plato, Aristotle, Demosthenes, Aristophanes and Lucian, χριστός is non existent Was it partly for this reason that Aquila substituted (Lactantius IV 7 "badly interpreted from the Hebrew") ἠλειμμένος, "oiled"?

² See Boeckh's Inscriptions (Index) and especially those from Latium, Etruria, and Umbria The *Berlin Urkunde* 1139 gives δοῦλο[ν] Χρῆτο[υ] with a query "nicht Χρηστου," dated 26th year of Augustus, from Egypt

³ Cicero *Ad Fam* II 8 1 "Quid? Tu me hoc tibi mandasse existimas, ut mihi gladiatorum compositiones, ut vadimonia dilata, et Chresti compilationem mitteres, et ea, quae nobis, quum Romae sumus, narrare nemo audeat?" The Index to Cicero does not mention "Chrestus" elsewhere. Lewis and Short say he was "a slave or freedman of Cicero," but mention no passage that supports this view Without support, it seems improbable that Cicero should thus contemptuously describe the news sent him by one of his own slaves or freedmen not mentioned elsewhere in his voluminous correspondence

⁴ So did the Hebrew "good" (Gesen. 373 *b*) being applied absolutely to honey, wine, fruit. Comp. Jerem. xxiv 2—5 "*good* figs (LXX χρηστός)," Gen III 6 "when the woman saw that the tree was *good* for food" (LXX καλός) Lk v 39 applies χρηστός to "wine."

and hence in two cases a "beautiful *Chrēstē*," or a "*Chrēstos*," is called "sweetest child[1]," in language recalling that of the Petrine Epistle, which bids Christians come to the milk of the Word, and "taste that the Lord is *good* (*chrēstos*)"—where something between "good" and "sweet" would perhaps best express the sense[2].

A Latin confusion between "Christus" and "Chrestus" may help to explain a difficult passage in Suetonius, which says that the Emperor Claudius, among a number of acts of favour or repression, mostly unimportant, "expelled Jews (*or*, the Jews) from Rome making constant disturbances at the

---

[1] Boeckh 6490 (χρῆστος (sic) being restored for χρησωος) where the little Chrēstos is called φίλτατον καὶ γλυκύτατον παιδίον, and 6489, where καλὴ Χρήστη is called τέκνον γλυκύτατον

[2] Clem Alex 124, as the text stands, quotes 1 Pet ii 1—3 as χριστὸς (for χρηστὸς) ὁ Κύριος But probably he quoted it correctly, only with a sense of the play on the word, and the scribe of Clem. Alex (like some scribes of the Epistle) has changed χρηστός to χριστός Compare Clem Alex 438 οἱ εἰς τὸν Χριστὸν πεπιστευκότες χρηστοί τε εἰσι καὶ λέγονται ...καὶ οἱ Χριστοῦ Χριστιανοί The conception of the Word of the Lord as the fruit of the Tree of Life, and distinct from the fruit of the Tree of the Knowledge of Good and Evil, might be illustrated from Ps xxxiv. 8 "*Taste and see* that *the Lord* is good.." The Psalm might be called the Psalm of Experience, and might be interpreted as meaning "Do not '*see*' first, and then '*taste*,' like Eve, who '*saw* that the tree was good for food.' Taste first. Learn by experiences, not by appearances" Rashi, after quoting "Taste.. good," simply adds "Taste His Word" Comp. Heb vi 5 "*having tasted the word of God* that it is good (καλὸν γευσαμένους θεοῦ ῥῆμα)", and Clem *Cor.* 36 "that through Him [*i e.* Jesus] we should *taste the knowledge that dieth not* (τῆς ἀθανάτου γνώσεως)," quoted by Clem. Alex 613 shortly after several verses from the Psalm of Experience.

The Fourth Gospel is permeated with this belief in "learning by experience," which it expresses dramatically in "Come and ye shall see" or "Come and see," uttered in various circumstances (Jn i 39, 46, iv 29) but, in all cases, resulting in conversion caused not by mere "seeing" but by "coming" and experiencing "Tasting" is implied from the beginning of the Fourth Gospel in the "sign" of "the good wine" at Cana, and in the doctrine of Christ's flesh and blood given to be the food of the world.

instigation of Chrestus[1]." No expulsion of Jews from Rome by Claudius is mentioned by Josephus, who, on the contrary, records several edicts issued by him in their favour[2]. No doubt, the Acts mentions such an expulsion, but in such a form that, when Suetonius and the Acts are compared, we may perceive a source of misunderstanding. The Acts says that when Paul came to Corinth "he found a certain Jew named Aquila, a man of Pontus by race, lately come from Italy with his wife Priscilla, because Claudius had commanded *all the Jews* to depart from Rome, and he came unto them...[3]." Now Jews from Pontus were present at the first Christian Pentecost[4]. Christians in Pontus are among those to whom the Petrine Epistle was addressed[5]. The Epistle to the Romans places "Prisca and Aquila" at the head of the saluted Christians, and even before "Epaenetus the firstfruits of Asia" and others who, Paul says, were "in Christ, before me[6]." These facts favour the supposition, which the words in the Acts also favour, that Paul "*came*" *to Aquila and Priscilla, as soon as he "found" them, and that they were already Christians, and not converted by Paul.*

If this is correct, we may suppose that Luke has inserted "all the" before "Jews" owing to some misunderstanding. Claudius had not really expelled "*all the* Jews," nor even "*the*

---

[1] Suet *Claud* 25 "Judaeos impulsore Chresto assidue tumultuantes Roma expulit" The preceding act is a remission of tribute to the citizens of Ilium; the following act is a permission to the ambassadors of the Germans "to sit in the orchestra" It is quite possible that Suetonius knew so little about "Chrestus" that he supposed him to be still alive, but the meaning of "impulsor" might be "[still, as of old, their] instigator."

[2] Joseph. *Ant* XIX 5 and 6

[3] Acts xviii. 2. It is added (*ib.* 3) "And, because he was of the same trade, he abode with them." But that is not given as the reason why "he came unto them" If they were already Christians, that would be a cogent reason. It is expressly said (*ib* 8) about "Crispus, the ruler of the synagogue," that he was converted. It is not said about Aquila, presumably because he was already a Christian.

[4] Acts ii. 9   [5] 1 Pet. i. 1.   [6] Rom. xvi. 3—7

Jews"—a nation that he favoured as a rule—but only "*Jews constantly making a disturbance*"—so it was alleged by their enemies—"*at the instigation of Chrestus*[1]" Some of the Christian Jews in Rome may have abused the right of speech at first allowed them in Jewish synagogues. Or the Christian Jews may have been entirely guiltless, and the "disturbance" entirely due to the persecuting and orthodox Jews But in any case many difficulties disappear if we suppose that Suetonius is giving an unimportant place to what he regarded as a very unimportant act, the expulsion of some Jews, alleged to be "tumultuous," whom, being called "Christiani" or "Chrestiani," he inferred to be making tumults at the instigation of their leader "Chrestus." On this hypothesis, Luke was led into error by taking "*Jews*" to mean "*all the Jews*," which he substituted for the sake of clearness[2].

These very early misunderstandings of the name "Christos" go some way toward justifying Justin Martyr in making no attempt to explain the meaning of the word in his Apologies. And he had other reasons for refraining. It was difficult to explain to the Greeks that "Christos" was, so to speak, a Hebrew official title, meaning one anointed for the office of priest, prophet, or king It was also difficult to explain when, and where, and by whom, Jesus was thus anointed, so that He came to be called "Jesus the Anointed, or Christ."

Justin, in his Dialogue, takes an entirely different line from that taken in his Apology. In the Apology, presenting a petition in behalf of "unjustly hated men," he demands that the charges

---

[1] In Tac. *Ann* xv. 44, it is said (*Rev of Theol and Phil.* 1914, p 358) that the best MSS read "Chrestianos," as the error of the "vulgus," followed by "Christus" as a corrective.

[2] See Hastings *Dict* ("Claudius") "Dio (LX vi 6), perhaps correcting Suet., asserts that the Jews, whose numbers were so great as to make expulsion difficult, were not indeed expelled, but only forbidden to assemble together." This approaches the truth, if it is taken to mean that Claudius effectually "forbade" the Christian Jews to "assemble" with the rest, in synagogues, by banishing them from Rome

against them shall be investigated, and then says that the charge is simply that they are called "Christianoi" Not till after mentioning and referring to "Christianoi" does he say that they had "Christos" as their Teacher[1]. But in the Dialogue, Trypho, the Jew, when he makes his first mention of "Christos," at once connects the name with "anointing," thus : "But *Christos*, if indeed He has come into being and exists somewhere, is unknown, and is not even aware of Himself or possessed of any power, until Elias come and *anoint* Him and make Him manifest to all[2]." Later on Justin himself grapples with this objection and endeavours to shew that Jesus was "anointed[3]" Thus the word "anoint," which is absent from the Apology, recurs repeatedly in the Dialogue. And the Dialogue nowhere plays on the similarity between "Christos" and "Chrēstos"

The importance attached, in the Dialogue with Trypho the Jew, to the "anointing" of Jesus, necessarily reflects also some importance on Elias, without whom, according to Trypho, the Messiah cannot be revealed. Hence the Dialogue repeatedly mentions Elias, and attempts to shew that the "spirit" that was in Elias was also the "spirit" that was in John the Baptist[4]. But the Apology nowhere mentions Elias, except along with Abraham and the three Children in the Furnace, as being Christians before Christ[5].

---

[1] *Apol* § 1 "this petition in behalf of those who are . unjustly hated and ill-treated," §§ 3—4 "that the charges be investigated,.. accused of being *Christianoi*,. to hate what is *good (chrēston)* is unjust...if any of the accused say that he is not [a *Christian*] if anyone acknowledge that he is [a *Christian*] some *having received* [*teaching*] *from the*[*ir*] *Teacher*, *Christos* (παραλαβόντες τινὲς παρὰ τοῦ διδασκάλου Χριστοῦ) ."

[2] See *Tryph* § 8 The term is introduced, a little before, by Justin, quoting his Christian teacher, *ib.* § 7 τὸν παρ' αὐτοῦ (i e *the Creator*) Χριστὸν υἱὸν αὐτοῦ

[3] See *Tryph* §§ 38, 49, 56, 63, 86   [4] *Tryph*. § 49.

[5] *Apol.* § 46. Elias is not mentioned by the other Apologists, nor by the Apostolic Fathers, except in Clem. *Cor.* § 17, where Elijah, Elisha, and Ezekiel are mentioned as "going about" in the skins of goats and

§ 5. *The term "Christ," how introduced or explained in the Gospels*

These facts may help us hereafter to understand the very different ways in which the Four Evangelists introduce and explain the term "Christ." This subject will come before us again when we discuss Peter's Confession. But here we may briefly compare their methods of introducing the title and add a few words on their several uses of it.

Mark, in his opening sentence, "the beginning of the Gospel of Jesus Christ," makes no attempt to explain the name "Jesus" or the appellation "Christos." But by the abrupt haste with which he passes on to "John baptizing in the wilderness"—and to the baptism of Jesus by John, whom his Gospel regards as Elias—he appears to share the above stated belief of Trypho the Jew that it was essential that Elias should "anoint" the future Deliverer in order that He should be manifested as "the Anointed," *i.e.* "the Christ[1]." In the Marcan version of the Petrine Confession, "the Christ" is uttered without addition[2]. It is only during the Trial and

---

sheep, preaching the coming of Christ. Clem Alex 610, quoting Clem Cor. by name, adds "John [the Baptist]" to the three prophets, and "folds of camel's hair" to the clothing. Gen r, on Gen iii 21, includes "goatskins" and "camel's wool" in the clothing made by God for Adam and Eve; and the passage was variously allegorized by Origen and earlier writers (see Iren. i 5 5). These curious details may have some bearing on the Mark-Matthew details (omitted by Luke) about the Baptist's clothing.

[1] A Petrine discourse in Acts appears to explain (x 36) "Jesus Christ" by a contextual mention of "anointing" (x 38) "*anointed* (ἔχρισεν) him [*i.e.* Jesus] with the Holy Spirit." Also compare iv 26 "were gathered together against his *Christ*" with *ib.* 27 "Jesus whom thou didst *anoint*." Both passages appear to refer to the baptism of Jesus by John. In N T, χρίω occurs elsewhere only in Lk iv 18 (quoting Is. lxi 1), 2 Cor i 21 χρίσας ἡμᾶς, and Heb i 9 (quoting Ps xlv 7).

[2] Mk viii 29 "Thou art *the Christ*," Mt xvi 16 "Thou art *the Christ, the Son of the living God*," Lk ix 20 "*The Christ of God*." Comp Jn vi. 69 "*The Holy One of God*."

the Crucifixion that additions are made, and these apparently by the enemies of Jesus, "Art thou *the Christ, the Son of the Blessed?*" "Let *the Christ, the King of Israel,* come down now from the Cross¹."

In Matthew, as in Mark, the Gospel opens with the words "Jesus Christ," subsequently referred to as "Jesus who is called Christ," without attempt to explain either term² But when the birth in Bethlehem is related, the name "Jesus" is described as supernaturally dictated and explained, "*for he shall save* his people from their sins³" A little later—but indirectly, not expressly—the meaning of "Christ" is explained by the fact that, when the Magi come saying "Where is he that is born *king of the Jews?*" "Herod the king" was "troubled" and "inquired where *the Christ* should be born⁴" There are no later explanations of the term, except in Peter's Confession "Thou art the Christ, the Son of the living God⁵." Before, and during, the Trial, the term is used as one of ridicule, applied to a Pretender, pretending to be either prophet or king, and Pilate twice repeats it, as if it had been—though it has not been—previously mentioned by the accusers of Jesus⁶

Luke mentions the name "Jesus" for the first time in the utterance of Gabriel "Thou shalt call his name Jesus⁷" But

---

¹ Mk xiv 61, xv 32   ² Mt i 1, 16   ³ Mt. i 18—21
⁴ Mt ii 2—4 This, and the subsequent massacre of the children in Bethlehem, would be regarded by Christians as the first of the attempts of "the kings of the earth" to "set themselves (Ps ii 2, Acts iv 26) against the Lord and against his *Christ.*"
⁵ Mt xvi 16 But note also Mt xxvi 63 "*the Christ, the Son of God,*" parall to Mk xiv. 61 "*the Christ, the Son of the Blessed*"
⁶ Mt. xxvi 68 "Prophesy to us, O Christ!" xxvii 17, 22 "Jesus, *who is called Christ*" (not in Mark)
⁷ Lk i 31—3 "And thou shalt call his name Jesus He shall be great and shall be called the Son of the Most High, and the Lord God shall give unto him the throne of his father David and he shall be king over the house of Jacob for ever; and of his kingdom there shall be no end"

the angel's utterance, though prolonged, gives no explanation of the name, which might just as well have been Solomon or Hezekiah, for aught that occurs in the context. The angel goes on to mention "Son of the Most High," "the throne of his father David," "kingdom," and "being king"· but all these are to be the gifts of God or the achievements of "Jesus." There is no mention here of Christ, i e Anointed—such as we found in Matthew in connection with "King of the Jews."

But Luke mentions "Saviour." And perhaps he preferred, as it were, to insinuate the name of "Jesus," in its Greek form, as *Sōtēr*, "Saviour," and also to imply it in the early repetition of the word *Sōtēria*, "*saving* (or, *salvation*)": "My spirit hath exulted in God my *Saviour*", "He hath raised up a horn of *salvation* for us," "*salvation* from our enemies," "to give knowledge of *salvation* to his people[1]." Then, on the night of the Saviour's birth, the word "Christ" is for the first time mentioned by the Angel to the shepherds, "There is born to you today a Saviour, *who is Christ, Lord,* in the city of David[2]." This, as in the only other Lucan passage where the

---

[1] Lk i. 47, 69, 71, 77. "*Salvation*" does not occur in the Gospels elsewhere, except Lk xix 9, Jn iv 22 Σωτηρία in LXX represents (1) Heb. corresponding to *Salem*, meaning "peace," "completeness," "health," (2) Heb. corresponding to *Jesus*, meaning "*salvation*" The first instance of the latter is Gen. xlix 18 "I have waited for thy *salvation*, O Lord," which Jer Targ paraphrases thus, "I expect not the *salvation* of Gideon, nor look I for the *salvation* of Samson, for their *salvation* will be the *salvation* of an hour; but thy *salvation* I have waited for, and will look for, O Lord, for thy *salvation* is the *salvation* of eternity"

[2] Lk. ii. 11 σωτὴρ ὅς ἐστιν χριστὸς κύριος R V txt "a Saviour, which is Christ, the Lord," marg "*or*, Anointed Lord." Χριστός occurs twelve times in Luke, but always with the article except here and xxiii. 2 λέγοντα ἑαυτὸν χριστὸν βασιλέα εἶναι, where R.V. marg. recognises the same ambiguity as here. Krauss p 374 gives *sôtar* as the name of a Rabbi from σωτήρ But Levy iii 502 a calls the Rabbi R Samuel bar Sutar, and says that the meaning is the same as when the word is spelt with *z* for *s* (Levy i 522 a), i e. "*little*," Lat "*paulus*" Spelt thus, it is frequent as a proper name, *e g* Mar Sutra, R. Sutra bar Tobia

article is omitted before "*Christ*," appears to mean "*anointed*" as king. So, too, does the next instance, where it is said that Simeon was not to die till he should see "*the Lord's Anointed*" —a frequent phrase in Scripture to denote lawfully appointed kings of the Chosen People[1].

Later on, but before the baptism of Jesus, Luke says that all men were "reasoning in their hearts" about John the Baptist "whether he might be *the Christ*," and that John, while disclaiming the title, added that a successor would come, mightier than himself, who would baptize with the Holy Spirit and with fire[2]. This implies—or favours the implication—that "the Christ" would thus "baptize." The next mention of the word refers to the exclamation of "devils," which "came out" exclaiming to Jesus "Thou art the Son of God," on which Luke remarks that Jesus "suffered them not to speak, because they knew that he was *the Christ*[3]." These passages indicate the popular acceptance of the word "*Christ*" as meaning something more than an ordinary king. But at the trial before Pilate, Luke represents the chief priests as charging Jesus with "calling himself *Christ, a king*[4]"; and, although there is no parallel to this in Mark and Matthew, the context implies that Pilate must have assumed this to be the meaning.

In a very remarkable addition to the Mark-Matthew tradition about the mockers round the Cross—who, in effect, twice told the "Christ," or the "King," to "save himself"— Luke adds a third utterance, coming from one of those crucified with Him: "Art thou not *the Christ*? *Save thyself* and us[5]." And after the Resurrection, as though taking up this taunt about the paradox of the Saviour's inability to "save himself," Jesus Himself says—in two passages containing the last

---

[1] Lk ii 26, comp. 1 S xvi. 6, xxiv. 6 &c
[2] Lk iii. 15—16   [3] Lk. iv. 41   [4] Lk. xxiii 2.
[5] Mk xv 30—2, Mt xxvii 40—4, Lk. xxiii 35—43 Mk-Mt mention those crucified as simply "reviling" or "reviling in the same way"

mentions of the title—"Was it not needful that *the Christ* should suffer these things?" "Thus it is written that *the Christ* should suffer[1]."

It will be observed that Luke, in his Gospel, never mentions "Jesus Christ" or "Jesus that is called Christ." The reason probably is that he tries to write as a historian in chronological order, and believes that "Jesus" could not be accepted as "Christ," in the full sense of the term, till the Holy Spirit had been sent down by Him, after His resurrection, because "No man can say 'Jesus is Lord,' save in the Holy Spirit[2]" Hence it was not till the day of the first Christian Pentecost that Peter, addressing himself to all "Israelites," and beginning from the title of "Jesus the Nazoraean"—which we have seen reason to interpret as Jesus the Nêtzer, the Branch from the root of Jesse or David—passes at once to His death and resurrection, as being predicted by His ancestor and prototype David in the words "Thou wilt not leave *my soul* in Hades, neither wilt thou give *thy Holy One* to see corruption[3]" Commenting on this prediction of David concerning "the fruit of his loins," Peter declares that David "spake of the resurrection of *the Christ*" Then, returning to the name of Jesus, and saying "*This Jesus* did God raise up," he adds "Being, therefore, by the right hand of God exalted, and having received of the Father the promise of the Holy Spirit, he hath poured forth this"—*i e* the Spirit—"which ye see and hear[4]" Finally, asserting that David spoke about his descendant as "*my Lord*," he concludes with these words: "Let all the house of Israel therefore know assuredly that God hath made him both (1) '*Lord*' and (2) '*Christ*,' this (3) *Jesus* whom ye crucified[5]." In this threefold combination we have the essence of the Lucan Gospel It calls on us to believe the "good tidings" that God the Father has revealed Himself through "*the Lord Jesus Christ*."

---

[1] Lk xxiv 26, 46 [2] 1 Cor xii 3
[3] Acts ii 22—7 [4] Acts ii. 33 [5] Acts ii. 36.

NAZARENE AND NAZORAEAN

The Johannine Gospel, apart from its Prologue and its Appendix, may be almost said to begin and end with a combination of the name Jesus and the title Christ· "The law was given through Moses. the grace and the truth [of God] came through *Jesus Christ*," "Many other signs, therefore, did Jesus...but these are written that ye may believe that *Jesus* is *the Christ*, the Son of God[1]." But the proof that "Jesus" is "the Christ" is not quite like the Petrine proofs above described in which "David" played a large part. The proofs in the Lucan Gospel and Acts are largely prophecies and mighty works, the proof in the Fourth Gospel is largely "the grace and the truth" that issued from Jesus[2].

As to the meaning of the name Jesus the Fourth Gospel is silent. Readers of the LXX would naturally connect the name with the "Jesus," *i.e.* Joshua, first mentioned as "choosing men" to "fight with Amalek[3]", and there are, perhaps, indications that the Evangelist regarded Jesus as a kind of second Joshua, beginning, like the first, "beyond Jordan," and "choosing out men" for the great conflict in which He was to "gain the victory," not over Amalek, but over "the world[4]."

But this is doubtful, and unimportant as compared with

---

[1] Jn i. 17, xx 30—31.

[2] In previous parts of Diatessarica attention was not drawn to the connection between (1) the Johannine "*grace*," "*truth*," and "*anointed*" (implied in "Christ") and (2) the Psalm on the Anointed, quoted in the Epistle to the Hebrews (1. 8—9) as referring to Christ, and mentioning "*grace*" and "*truth*" as attributes of the Bridegroom, whom God has "*anointed*" (Ps xlv 2, 4, 7) Also Jn i 18 "only-begotten, *God*" appears to correspond to Ps xlv 6 "Thy throne, *O God*" This Psalm is frequently quoted by early Christian writers (*e g* Justin Martyr repeatedly) with special reference to Χριστός and χρίω The Johannine allusion confirms the view (*Johannine Grammar* **2371**) that ἀνήρ in Jn 1 30 is used allusively so as to include the meaning of "husband"

[3] Exod. xvii 9 "And Moses said unto *Joshua* (LXX *Jesus*) Choose us (LXX for thyself) men, and go out, fight with Amalek" John alone represents Jesus as using ἐκλέγομαι about His choice of the Twelve (vi. 70, xiii. 18, xv 16—19).

[4] Jn xvi 33.

the Evangelist's early, definite and prominent explanations of the term "Christ" The first mentions of it (after the Prologue) are "I am not *the Christ*," "Why baptizest thou, then, if thou art not *the Christ*?" "We have found *the Messiah (which is, being interpreted, Christ)*," "I know that *Messiah* cometh (*he that is called Christ*)," "Can it be that this man is *the Christ*[1]?" In the first of these, where the Baptist says "I am not *the Christ*"—in answer to the simple question "Who art thou?" —we are taught that thoughts and expectations of "the Christ" were in the air[2], and in the second we find that "the Christ" (along with Elias and "the Prophet") was assumed to have authority to baptize. From the third, uttered by Andrew, we learn that "Messias"—the Hebrew and Aramaic for "Anointed"—was the word in use among the people, from the fourth, repeating this Aramaic word, we see that even a Samaritan woman shared in the Messianic expectations of the Jews, and regarded "the Messiah" as one who was to settle all disputed questions.

To this Samaritan woman alone does Jesus reveal Himself ("I that speak unto thee am he[3]") And why? The question is thrust on us because—after many more questionings of the Jews among themselves, as to whether "the rulers" knew that Jesus was really "the Christ," and as to the "signs" that "the Christ" was to work, and as to the place whence "the Christ" was to "come[4]"—the Jews at last say to Him "How long dost thou hold us in suspense? If thou art *the Christ*,

---

[1] Jn i 20, 25, 41, iii 28 (as i 20), iv 25, 29

[2] Comp. Lk. iii. 15 "all men reasoned whether he were the Christ"

[3] Jn iv 26 She then says to the Samaritans (*ib* 29) "Can it be that this is the Christ?" The narrative describes an ascent of faith from a stage somewhat like that of Nathanael (comp. Jn i 50). The woman had believed because Jesus had "told" her "all things that ever" she "did", and the Samaritans had, at first, believed on her evidence. But finally, the Samaritans say to her "Now we believe, not because of thy speaking, for we have heard for ourselves and know that this is indeed *the Saviour of the world*"

[4] Jn vii. 26—7, 31, 41—2

tell us plainly[1]." Jesus does *not* "tell them plainly." He replies "I told you, and ye believe not The works that I do in my Father's name, these bear witness of me"

This answer, difficult in itself, must not be made more difficult by supposing that "the works" here mentioned were restricted to Christ's acts of healing "The works" (doubtless) included "the words"—those words about which Peter had said, "Lord to whom should we go? Thou hast [the] words of eternal life[2]" And the real reason why the Jews did not believe in *this* "Christ," *this* "Shepherd of Israel," was because they had formed for themselves a different ideal, an official Christ, an official Shepherd, so that, if Jesus had said to them "I am your Christ," He would have said what was not true This the next words explain · "But ye believe not, because ye are not of my sheep My sheep hear my voice, and I know them, and they follow me, and I give unto them eternal life[3]"

This doctrine seems at first sight to lead to the conclusion that, for the purposes of "the Gospel," the human race may be divided into two classes, "sheep" and "not-sheep", the "sheep" will "hear" at once, the "not-sheep" will never hear, therefore it is useless to preach But the Evangelist means, on the contrary, that all men are, in their higher nature, sheep of the true Shepherd, or children of the Father in heaven, in whose image they were created, and that, if they will put away their false notions of an official non-human Shepherd, and an official non-human Father, and recognise

---

[1] Jn x 24
[2] Jn vi. 68
[3] Jn x. 26—8 Against this view may be urged Mk xiv 61—2 "Art thou *the Christ*, the Son of the Blessed? And Jesus said, *I am* (Mt *Thou hast said*) " But the parallel in Luke differs in a very remarkable manner both from Mark and from Matthew, and, when the three come before us in their order, they will be found (I believe) to confirm the view taken above as to the reasons for the general (but not invariable) unwillingness of Jesus to call Himself, or to be called, "Christ"

that *God and Man must be known together, and not the One without the other*, they will be drawing near to that eternal life which consists in knowing the only true God. Thus perhaps, if the text is not corrupt, we may explain the final Johannine mention of "Jesus Christ," in which the Evangelist ventures to represent Jesus as calling Himself by His own name: "And this is eternal life—that they should know thee, the only true God, and him whom thou hast sent, *Jesus Christ*[1]." Apparently it does not mean that we are to "know" two distinct Persons. It means that we are to know the First "*and*" the Second, that is, *not without* the Second. This agrees with the saying in the Prologue, that no man has seen God, but the Only-begotten who is in the bosom of the Father has declared Him[2]. It agrees also with the saying in the Epistle, that whosoever does not love the brother whom he has seen cannot love God whom he has not seen[3]. By "the brother" who is "seen," is meant Man, as "seen" through Jesus Christ, "seen" to be divine in spite of all his imperfections and sins. "Seen" otherwise—seen without the mediation of some such ideal as that which we call "Jesus Christ"—man cannot be sincerely "loved," or honestly called "brother."

---

[1] Jn xvii 3   [2] Jn i 18   [3] 1 Jn iv 20

APPENDIX II

THE DISCIPLE THAT WAS (R.V) "KNOWN UNTO THE HIGH PRIEST[1]"

THE Fourth Gospel differs from the Three in representing Peter's denial as being the result, in part at all events, of an action proceeding not from himself, but from another—an unnamed person[2] According to this Gospel, though Peter followed Jesus to the High Priest's palace, he remained standing at the door outside[3]. It was natural that he should desire to learn the issue of the trial of Jesus as soon as possible, and this he could do by waiting—probably with others who had not the right of entry—outside the palace. Inside, he could do Jesus no good, and his presence there (as he must have well known) would expose him to great peril It would also, if he

---

[1] See Addendum on p 371 referring to criticisms by the Rev J B. Mayor, Litt D , and to my reply, in the *Expositor* for Jan and Feb 1914

[2] Jn xviii 15—16 (R V) "And Simon Peter followed Jesus, and [so did] another disciple Now that disciple was known unto the high priest, and entered in with Jesus into the court of the high priest , but Peter was standing at the door without So the other disciple, which was known unto the high priest, went out and spake unto her that kept the door, and brought in Peter." R V is not quite accurate See below, pp 357—8, n. 6 (*ad fin*), and p 360, n. 1.

[3] The Evangelist apparently assumes that there was one and the same αὐλὴ τοῦ ἀρχιερέως, "courtyard of the High Priest," for Caiaphas and Annas—the latter having separate chambers from the official chambers of Caiaphas, but no separate "courtyard" He also makes it clear at the outset that the proceedings of the trial were irregular, by saying that the prisoner was taken "first" to "Annas", who had no official position Some early authorities have transposed the text, *e.g* SS arranges consecutively Jn xviii 13, 24, 14, 15, 19—23, 16—18, 25 &c

THE DISCIPLE KNOWN UNTO THE HIGH PRIEST

was arrested, prevent him from carrying word to the rest of the disciples and to the anxious women about the fate of their Master.

But some one came out of the palace and, in effect, brought Peter in. Nonnus, one of our earliest authorities for the interpretation of this passage, says that he *"took" Peter "by the hand,"* and *"brought him in."* But the present text of the Gospel says, ambiguously, either that he spoke to the portress and *also* brought Peter in, or that he spoke to the portress, and *she* brought Peter in. Our Revised Version prefers the former, Chrysostom the latter. In either case one can see that Peter could hardly refuse the invitation. Doubtless, to accept it involved a tremendous future risk, but to refuse it involved an immediate cowardice. The unnamed disciple said, in effect, to Peter, "Do you not want to know, as I do, what they will do to the Master? You must want it. Then come in." This almost amounted to *"taking Peter by the hand and leading him in"*[1]

The question for us is, "Who thus, in effect, drew Peter into the net of temptation?" It is generally taken for granted that it was John the son of Zebedee. Chrysostom assumes this. So does Jerome. But Chrysostom, as we shall see, slightly alters the text of the Gospel so as to favour his view, and Jerome does not represent the Greek exactly. The reason for assuming it appears to be mainly this, that, later on, in connection with Peter, *"the other disciple whom Jesus loved"* undoubtedly means John, and here, in connection with Peter, the text mentions *"another disciple,"* afterwards referred to as *"the other disciple."* It is perhaps natural, at first sight, to infer that *"other disciple"* when mentioned with "Peter" means John in the earlier instance because it certainly means John in the later

---

[1] See below, p 358, n 3. Nonnus perhaps meant "taking by the hand" to imply a guarantee that the "other disciple" knew Peter. But Peter might feel the action to be, in effect, coercive.

THE DISCIPLE KNOWN UNTO THE HIGH PRIEST

But does it not make a difference that whereas, later on, the "*other disciple*" is called the one "*whom Jesus loved*," here the "*other disciple*" is described as (R V. twice) "*known unto the high priest*"? Will it not make a still greater difference if we presently find (as we shall) that the phrase rendered by R V in the second instance "*known unto the high priest*" really means "*intimate friend*," and implies "*the friend that was in his counsels*"? For the Gospel says, in the very verse that precedes, "Now Caiaphas was *he that gave counsel to the Jews that it was expedient that one man should die for the people.*" Is it likely that a Gospel written in the name of "the disciple whom Jesus loved" should say, in effect, that that disciple was "in the counsels of" the High Priest who was plotting the death of Jesus—and this on the very eve of His crucifixion?

And are there not also some *a priori* grounds for doubting whether the action assigned to the unnamed disciple is quite suitable to John? We generally think of him as thoughtful, retiring, and less impulsive than Peter. On the shore of Gennesaret, John does not swim to Jesus. He merely says to Peter "It is the Lord." It is Peter who plunges in But here what are we to say about the conduct of this unnamed disciple in the palace of Caiaphas? To bring Peter—we may almost say with Nonnus, to "take Peter by the hand and draw him "—into a crowd of the High Priest's guards and servants[1], where he, the single one of the Twelve who had been bold enough to strike a blow for his Master, could not possibly escape notice, followed by suspicious questioning, and ultimately by detection! It may have been well intended, but was it wise and thoughtful? And when it was done, when Peter was inside, left like a hunted creature at bay amid his enemies,

---

[1] It has been suggested that others, attracted by curiosity, may have pressed into the courtyard, among whom Peter might have, for a time, escaped notice That may be granted as not improbable And it would diminish the immediate risk But even so, the risk would be so great as to make Peter's entry explicable only by very special circumstances

THE DISCIPLE KNOWN UNTO THE HIGH PRIEST

was it thoughtful or kind to desert him without a word or act of recorded helpfulness?

It may be said, "John was engaged in a higher duty He was in the upper room, watching the trial of his Lord" But would his Lord have preferred this? Are we quite sure that He would have called it a "higher duty"? Even if John had spoken in the Lord's defence, Jesus might perhaps have preferred that he should be defending his brother disciple in his struggles with Satan who was "sifting him like wheat" But to be above and to do nothing, when he might have been below, helping the brother Apostle, whom, by his own impulsive conduct, he had plunged into temptation—was this the kind of conduct that we should expect in the disciple whom Jesus specially loved?

These considerations, it is hoped, may bespeak a patient hearing for the suggestion—not, I believe, quite novel[1], but,

---

[1] Alford *ad loc* says "There is no reason to doubt the universal persuasion that by this name John intends *himself*...The idea that it was *Judas Iscariot* (Heumann), is surely too absurd to need confutation The [ὁ] ἄλλος, συνεισ τῷ Ἰησ, ἦν γνωστὸς τῷ ἀρχ (as a matter of individual notice), and the whole character of the incident, will prevent any real student of St John's style and manner from entertaining such a supposition for a moment"

Keim (*Jesus of Nazara* VI 58) says "Foolish explanations of the 'other disciple' as an unknown person (Aug, Calov, Gurlitt), as a citizen of Jerusalem (Grotius), even as Iscariot (Heum)" The sentence finishes here I am informed that Meyer's *Gospel of John* Vol II p 311, adds "Calovius and Calvin" to Augustine and Grotius, as givers of what Keim calls "foolish explanations," and as exceptions to what Alford calls "the universal persuasion"

Westcott, after remarking that the text has *another disciple*, not *the other*, says "The reader cannot fail to identify the disciple with St John" This may give to some readers, who do not "fail," a sense of their own superiority to Augustine, Grotius, and Calvin But others, who do "fail," may be consoled by feeling that they fail with eminent men

These three quotations appear to shew that the Judas-hypothesis has not yet received attention from "any real student of St John's style and manner" in this country

See *Son of Man* **3460** *c* for an attempt to explain "*the High Priest*" (in

THE DISCIPLE KNOWN UNTO THE HIGH PRIEST

as far as I know, not hitherto presented for serious consideration in this country—that the unnamed disciple was not John but Judas Iscariot, and that this subtle, perhaps we must say this over subtle, Evangelist intended us to distinguish "*another disciple who was the friend of the High Priest*" from one whom he will describe later on as the "*other disciple whom Jesus loved.*" Both disciples are connected in a peculiar way with Peter. But the former, whatever may have been his motives, acted as Peter's enemy The latter acted as Peter's friend. The first Johannine mention of Judas Iscariot followed a confession of Simon Peter, and was accompanied by the word "devil", and the context implied that Judas was then acting like an instrument of Satan and endeavouring to lead Peter and the rest of the disciples astray, following after Satan[1]. Now, in the High Priest's palace, consistently with his previous attempt to mislead Peter, Judas attempts again, and on this occasion succeeds. He actually leads the foremost of the Apostles to deny his Lord. This is the work of *the "other" disciple who was the friend of the High Priest*

How different the influence on Peter of *the "other" disciple whom Jesus loved*! He accompanies Peter to the tomb of the Lord, and outstrips him in the race. Judas drew Peter into the hall of Caiaphas, the House of Temptation. John indirectly, by emulation, stimulated Peter to go before him into the tomb of Jesus, which was the preparatory House of Faith. Later on, again, it was "that disciple whom Jesus loved" who "saith unto Peter, It is the Lord," and Peter "girt his coat about him—for he was naked—and cast himself into the sea." It seems to be implied that Peter reached Jesus before the rest of the disciples reached Him. If he did, it was thanks to "that disciple whom Jesus loved."

"known to *the High Priest*") as a name given m Christian tradition to Jesus

[1] Jn vi 68—71, on which see in *Introduction* p 146, the section entitled "Attraction and recoil, Peter and Judas"

THE DISCIPLE KNOWN UNTO THE HIGH PRIEST

Reviewing all these facts, can we not imagine that the Fourth Evangelist may have meant antithesis where we have taken him to mean identity? "How could you suppose"— he might perhaps say to us, complaining of our dulness of comprehension—"that I intended you to identify *another disciple who was the bosom friend of Caiaphas, the murderer of Jesus*, with *the other disciple whom Jesus loved?*" And this, at least, might be said in support of such a complaint, that the Johannine narrative does make the action of the unnamed disciple responsible for what followed. If the friend of the High Priest had not taken Peter into the High Priest's hall, Peter—humanly speaking—would not have denied his Master.

Passing now to an examination of the Johannine context mentioning the disciple that was a friend of the High Priest, we must be prepared to find the text varying a great deal and possibly corrupt. The points of main interest in it are emphasized in the early poetic commentary of Nonnus. For example, he repeats the thought of being "well known," *in three different meanings*, in one line thus —(1) "[intimately] known," (2) "renowned," (3) "accustomed"[1]. A literal translation of his paraphrase of the passage may perhaps usefully prepare the reader for the difficulties of the Gospel text. Usually Nonnus agrees with Chrysostom, but in this passage they differ widely. The extract covers the ground from Peter's entrance up to the question that elicits the first of the three denials[2] —

---

[1] For instances of such repetition called "conflation," see *Clue* 113—27.
[2] Jn xviii 15—17, paraphrased by Nonnus xviii 69—80. The Greek is as follows

Ἰησοῦν δὲ φέροντες ἐπέρρεον ἀσπιδιῶται
καὶ οἱ ὀπισθοκέλευθος ὁμάρτεε τηλόθι Σίμων
καὶ νέος ἄλλος ἑταῖρος, ὃς ἰχθυβόλου παρὰ τέχνης
γνωτὸς ἐὼν ἀρίδηλος ἐθήμονος ἀρχιερῆος
Χριστῷ σύνδρομος ἦλθεν ἔσω θεοδέγμονος αὐλῆς
καὶ βραδὺς αὐτόθι Πέτρος ἐλείπετο νόσφι θυράων

THE DISCIPLE KNOWN UNTO THE HIGH PRIEST

So, bearing Jesus [with them] the spearmen flowed on,
And on His track went with them afar off Simon
And a young [man][1] another companion [of Christ]—who, from his trade of fishing[2],
Being a friend[3], renowned, of the (?) accustomed[4] high priest,
Running-with Christ, came within the God-receiving courtyard,
And, tardy[5], there where he was, Peter was left, away from the portals.
But another [? the other][6] companion of Christ, moving rapidly in the covered building,

---

Χριστοῦ δ' ἄλλος ἑταῖρος ὑπωρόφιον γόνυ πάλλων
ἄνθορεν ἐκ μεγάροιο καὶ ἀμφιπόλῳ πυλαωρῷ
εἶπε καὶ ἤγαγε Πέτρον ἔσω πολυχανδέος αὐλῆς
χειρὸς ἔχων καὶ δμωὶς ἐπεσβόλος ὄμματι λοξῷ
δερκομένη πυλαωρὸς ἀνίαχε γείτονι Πέτρῳ
τοῖον ἔπος μὴ καὶ σὺ πέλεις Χριστοῖο μαθητής,

[1] "Young" Νέος, in this context, might conceivably mean "newly converted" But if it means "young," Nonnus may allude to the youthfulness traditionally attributed to John the son of Zebedee. "Another companion" is repeated below, with "of Christ," so that we seem obliged to supply "of Christ" here, and cannot well take the words as meaning, "and another young man, [his] companion "

[2] "Fishing" This apparently refers to the occupation of John the son of Zebedee But how Nonnus supposed that this could make him a "friend of the High Priest" I cannot even suggest Perhaps, however, Nonnus is here erroneously applying to John the son of Zebedee literally a tradition that was applied to Judas Iscariot metaphorically Judas had planned, along with the High Priest, the arrest of Jesus It might be said, therefore, that Judas and Caiaphas were united in spreading for Jesus (Eccles ix 12) "*the evil net*" (comp Hab 1 13—15 concerning "the wicked " who "catcheth" men in "his net" since they are "as the fishes of the sea")

[3] "A friend" (see below, p 363) *lit* "intimately known." The Greek word might also mean " renowned," and Nonnus adds the latter.

[4] "Accustomed" occurs in Nonnus (Jn xxi 4) "he asked the seafaring *accustomed* fishermen (ἐθήμονας ἰχθυβολῆας)" Nonnus uses it very frequently, *e g* of "customary" gifts, home, couch, food &c Perhaps he means that the High Priest was "familiar" to him like his own home

[5] "Tardy" presumably implies either fear, or the knowledge that he would be refused admission, so that haste was needless All he could do was to wait at the door to learn the issue as soon as possible

[6] "Another" seems to make no sense, and ἄλλος "the other" would

THE DISCIPLE KNOWN UNTO THE HIGH PRIEST

Leapt-back[1] from the palace, and to the attendant porter[2]
Spake, and led Peter inside the spacious courtyard,
Holding him by the hand[3]. And a maid, jeering at him, with suspicious eye,
Beholding him, she [I say] that kept the gate called aloud to
[? her or his] neighbour[4] Peter
Such saying [as this]—"Can it be that thou, too[5], art a disciple of Christ?"

---

make good sense I can find no instance of the latter in Greek But comp Jn xx 3 (Nonnus) ὡμάρτησε μαθητὴς *Ἄλλος ὁμῶς ἐπὶ σῆμα*, where the meaning must be "*the other*" Nonnus does not repeat here, as the Gospel does, "friend" and "High Priest" Here we may note that R V is not quite right in rendering identically, by "known *unto*," both xviii 15 γνωστὸς τῷ (*dative*) and xviii 16 ὁ γνωστὸς τοῦ (*genitive*) The first need not, the second must, imply intimacy

[1] "Leapt-back," a rarer meaning than "leapt-up," but required by the sense, and allowable (Steph *Thes*) It implies emotion or distraction in the Disciple

[2] "Porter" (not "*portress*" which the Gospel text has). This is also the reading of SS (see below, p 360, n 3) The Disciple speaks to the Porter, and, to make Peter's admission sure, takes him in, as it were, under his wing If we may suppose an interval, the Porter's maidservant—though saying nothing at the moment, in the presence of the Porter and the Disciple—flouts Peter afterwards Chrysostom expressly dissents from this view "*Why did not the Disciple himself bring Peter in?* He was keeping-close to Christ and following close on Him. For this cause he bade the woman bring Peter in"

[3] "Taking him by the hand" *i e* as guarantee of personal knowledge This is perhaps more probable than the view that Peter hesitated, as though saying "I can be of no service, inside the Palace, either to my Lord or to the rest But I would fain wait outside to learn the issue as soon as may be and let the others know of it," and as though the Disciple replied "But come in you must, for I know you wish (as I do) to see as well as to hear"

[4] "Neighbour" Does this mean that she came close to Peter and sat down near him, so that he was, for the time, her "neighbour"? Or does it mean that Peter was the "neighbour" of the other Disciple at the time of entering?

[5] "Thou, too," that is, "thou as well as thy companion" Nonnus takes this as a jibe (s ἐπεσβόλος) Chrysostom does not , he explains "thou, too" thus "Because John was inside"—that is, because Peter had, as his companion, inside the palace, a friend of her Master, the High Priest—and he adds "*So mildly* did she accost him"

THE DISCIPLE KNOWN UNTO THE HIGH PRIEST

In the Gospel narrative there are some variations in the MSS and Versions, and some also in one part of the (apparently) genuine text as compared with another part. They necessitate not only a close examination of this passage speaking of "*another* disciple" but also a comparison of it with the passage that later on speaks of "*the other* disciple[1]." The former is said to have been "known to," and "the intimate-friend of," the High Priest. The latter is said to be the one "whom Jesus was wont to love." Some inferior MSS and authorities have altered "*another*," here, into "*the other*," conforming the former to the latter—naturally, but possibly with the result of completely changing the sense Also the Syro-Sinaitic Version, consistently, in both passages, either omits "*other*" or alters it into "*one*" or "*that*." The similarity between the Hebrew "*one*" (sometimes meaning "*a certain person*") and "*other*" is so great as to cause many errors in the LXX[2] These facts must be remembered in studying the Johannine text, which runs thus[3] " Now there was following Jesus Simon Peter and another[4] disciple[5] Now that

---

[1] Jn xx 2 foll   [2] See *Indices to Diatessarica* p 22
[3] Jn xviii 15—17 Ἠκολούθει δὲ τῷ Ἰησοῦ Σίμων Πέτρος καὶ ἄλλος μαθητής ὁ δὲ μαθητὴς ἐκεῖνος ἦν γνωστὸς (marg γνωστὸς ἦν) τῷ ἀρχιερεῖ, καὶ συνεισῆλθεν τῷ Ἰησοῦ εἰς τὴν αὐλὴν τοῦ ἀρχιερέως, ὁ δὲ Πέτρος ἱστήκει πρὸς τῇ θύρᾳ ἔξω ἐξῆλθεν οὖν ὁ μαθητὴς ο ἄλλος ὁ γνωστὸς τοῦ ἀρχιερέως καὶ εἶπεν τῇ θυρωρῷ καὶ εἰσήγαγεν τὸν Πέτρον λέγει οὖν τῷ Πέτρῳ ἡ παιδίσκη ἡ θυρωρός Μὴ καὶ σὺ ἐκ τῶν μαθητῶν εἶ τοῦ ἀνθρώπου τούτου ,
[4] Chrys , and some inferior authorities, have "the other" Comp Jn xxi 2 "and *others* of [*lit* from] his disciples *two*" Why does not John name the "two"? Is it because he was ignorant? There are reasons for conjecturing that Andrew and Philip are meant Nonnus expressly mentions "Andrew" after "Peter," making eight instead of seven Pseudo-Peter breaks off thus, § 14 "But I, Simon Peter, and Andrew my brother, having taken our nets went to the sea And there was with us Levi, the son of Alpheus, whom the Lord ." Chrys. has, freely, καὶ ἦσαν Σίμων ὁμοῦ καὶ Θωμᾶς καὶ Ναθαναὴλ ὁ ὑπὸ τοῦ Φιλίππου κληθεὶς καὶ οἱ υἱοὶ Ζεβεδαίου, καὶ ἄλλοι δύο
[5] Blass prints xviii 15 [ἠκολούθει δὲ τῷ Ἰησοῦ Σίμων Πέτρος] καὶ εἷς ἐκ τῶν μαθητῶν γνωστὸς ἦν τῷ ἀρχιερεί καὶ συγεισῆλθεν τῷ Ἰησοῦ εἰς τὴν αὐλήν

THE DISCIPLE KNOWN UNTO THE HIGH PRIEST

disciple was *friend* (lit. *known*) *to*[1] the high priest and entered in with Jesus into the court of the high priest, but Peter was standing at the door outside. There came out therefore the other disciple that was *the friend* (lit. *the known*) *of*[2] the high priest, and spoke to the portress[3] and brought in (*or*, she brought in[4]) Peter. There saith therefore to Peter the maid-servant[5] [that was] the portress, Can it be that thou also art [one] of the disciples of this man?"

---

[1] Γνωστὸς τῷ here, but ὁ γνωστὸς τοῦ in the next verse, so that the text leads us perhaps from a possibility of the meaning "acquaintance," to a certainty of the meaning "intimate friend." The reading γνωστὸς ἦν τῷ ἁ was probably intended to separate γνωστός from ἁ and to suggest that it did not mean "friend of," but only "known to"

[2] See below, pp. 362—3 for the proof that γνωστός in this sentence means "intimate friend"

[3] "Portress," but Nonnus and SS "porter" masc.

[4] "She brought in." So Chrys., but it is less probable than "(he) brought in." Εἰσάγω is used in the parall Lk xxii 54 of bringing Jesus as a prisoner into the palace, and sim in Acts xxi 37, xxii 24, and of the "leading in" of the feeble and helpless, in Lk ii. 27, xiv. 21, Acts ix 8. So there is something to be said for Nonnus' rendering "led, taking by the hand." But in a few NT instances the word means simply "introduce" (Acts xxi 28—9, Heb i 6). The only other NT. use of the word is in Acts vii 45, of "bringing in" the tabernacle

[5] "The maidservant." There were discussions about the Attic and the Hellenic meanings of παιδίσκη (see Steph *Thes*.) but there can be no question about the NT use of the word, as always denoting a servant not free. Comp Gal. iv 22 foll "one by the *handmaid* (A V *bondmaid*) the other by the freewoman." In Acts xvi 16, it means a slave possessed with a spirit of divination, who brings her masters "much gain." Also note Lk xii 45 τοὺς παῖδας καὶ τὰς παιδίσκας (parall Mt. xxiv 49 συνδούλους) where A V. has "maidens," but R V "*maidservants*." So in Acts xii 13 A V. "damsel," R V "maid," but probably "*maidservant*" employed as portress, not necessarily young (comp Lk xxii 57 "*Woman*, I know him not") All the Evangelists use παιδίσκη in this passage. But whereas they call her (Mk xiv 66) μία τῶν παιδισκῶν, (Mt xxvi 69) μία παιδίσκη, (Lk. xxii. 56) παιδίσκη τις, John explains that she was "the maidservant that was the portress (ἡ παιδίσκη ἡ θυρωρός)"

But, if so, why did not John call her thus at once —"he spake to *the maidservant that was portress*.. then saith to Peter *the portress*"? Why write "the portress (τῇ θυρωρῷ)" first, and "the maidservant that was

We pass to the Synoptic narrative, which describes Peter's entrance as being without any intervention

Mk xiv. 54	Mt. xxvi. 58	Lk xxii. 54—5
And Peter had followed him afar off, even within, into the court of the high priest, and he was sitting with the officers.	But Peter followed him afar off, unto the court of the high priest, and entered in, and sat with the officers	But Peter followed afar off. And when they had Peter sat in the midst of them

It will be observed that Luke (and Luke alone) describes Peter as being "*in the midst of*[1]" those whom Mark and Matthew describe as "the officers" Also John (and John alone) connects Peter's entrance with a "*portress.*" Compare:

2 S iv. 6 (Heb.)	2 S. iv. 6 (LXX)
And thither *they entered even-into the midst of* the house.	And behold *the portress* of the house

Here LXX has the same word as John (θυρωρός), and Gesenius prefers such a reading of the Hebrew text as is implied by the LXX[2]. In Hebrew, "*porter,*" or

---

portress (ἡ παιδίσκη ἡ θυρωρὸς)" second? The order is hardly explicable, and it suggests that τῇ θ is an error for τῷ θ, and that (as Nonnus and SS say) the disciple first "spake to *the porter,*" and then there followed the action of "*the maidservant that was portress,*" that is to say, a subordinate of the "porter" She overheard what had been said to the "porter" by the disciple of Jesus, and presently came and jested at Peter about it.

An interval may be supposed to have elapsed after the disciple has brought Peter in The disciple leaves Peter, and departs to the upper chamber Peter comes into the throng of servants and guards Then the maidservant comes and asks him whether he, too—like his influential companion the friend of the High Priest—is a disciple of Jesus

[1] Lk xxii 55 μέσος Lk. has used ἐν μέσῳ in the same verse, "and when they had (*lit*) kindled-around (περιαψάντων) (*Son of Man* **3369** *a*) a fire *in the midst of* (ἐν μέσῳ) the court."

[2] Gesen 1045 *a* The interchange of "*into the midst*" and "*porter*" would be easier in Aramaic than in Hebrew (Levy *Ch* ii 561 *b*)

THE DISCIPLE KNOWN UNTO THE HIGH PRIEST

"*gate-keeper*," is identical in consonants with "*gate.*" Hence there appears to be a similarity between this confusion of "*gate-keeper*" and "*in the midst*" in Samuel, with a confusion of "*gate-way*" or "*porch*" with "*in the midst*" in Isaiah, where the Hebrew "*in the midst*" is rendered by LXX "*in the porch*[1]." This is all the more to the point because Mark alone, a little later, mentions as the scene of the second denial, "*fore-court*," and the parallel Matthew alone mentions "*porch*[2]," and the confusion between these words and "*porter*," in the LXX, is very frequent[3] Since therefore "*in the midst*" is confused by the LXX twice with "*portress*" or "*porch*," and since "*porter*" and "*porch*" are still more frequently confused, the question arises whether this (at first sight) insignificant phrase of Luke, "*in the midst*," may not be of crucial importance in guiding us through the mazes of the narrative of the Denial as told in the Four Gospels, and also in leading us to some satisfactory explanation of the personality and action of the disciple who, as our Revised Version says, "*was known to the high priest*"

But here we must stop to ask whether "known" is an adequate rendering The Greek word, as applied to persons, is extremely rare. It occurs in N.T only here and in two passages where the parents of Jesus are described as searching for Him among their kindred and "acquaintance," and where "all his *acquaintance* .stood *afar off*" round His Cross[4]. The margin of the latter passage refers us to the Psalms, where the same Greek word is repeated, "Thou hast put mine *acquaintance* far from me," repeated thus, "Lover and friend hast thou put far from me, and mine *acquaintance* into darkness[5]." But even our Revisers have rightly shrunk from rendering it by "*acquaintance*," and have retained "*familiar-friend*," in the

---

[1] Is lxvi 17, LXX ἐν τοῖς προθύροις.

[2] Mk xiv 68 προαύλιον (not elsewhere in N T), Mt xxvi 71 πυλών

[3] The same Heb word means (Tromm Index p. 127 *b*) πυλών (6), πυλωρός (3) and in another form πυλωρός (28), θυρωρός (2), πύλη (6)

[4] Lk 11 44, xxiii 49, γνωστός

[5] Ps lxxxviii 8, 18

complaint "It was thou, a man mine equal, my companion, and my *familiar-friend*[1]" In Greek literature it is almost non-occurrent in this sense, but in the Greek Bible, when applied to persons and used as a noun, it appears to mean this and nothing else—"intimate-friend," "a person in one's bosom" or "in one's counsels[2]." Hesychius places it as parallel to "brother[3]."

If the Greek noun is to have the signification that it has elsewhere in the Greek Bible, it ought here to mean Judas Iscariot, described first, preparatively, as "known to the high priest," and then as the "intimate partaker of the high priest's counsels." Judas had made a covenant with the chief priests to betray Jesus, and had arranged with them a plan by which the arrest might be effected without disturbance. His comings and goings during these negotiations might naturally give him an entry to the High Priest's palace, and lay him open to the Christian reproach that he, who should have been the "familiar friend" of Jesus, had made himself the "familiar friend" of Caiaphas. That was the way in which Christians might apply the words in the Psalm "It was thou, *my familiar friend*." Concerning this utterance Jerome says "It was the saying of Christ about *Judas*"; and Origen assumes it[4]

---

[1] Ps lv 13. Γνωστός occurs also in 2 K x 11 RV "*familiar friends*," AV txt "*kinsfolks*," marg "*acquaintance*," Ps xxxi 11 "I am become a fear to mine *acquaintance*." These are the only instances where γνωστός represents "intimately-known [friend]." In Ps lxxvi 1 γνωστὸς...ὁ θεός, and Is xix 21 "known to the Egyptians," it means "renowned," "known as a conqueror." In Prov xxxi 23 "her husband is *known* in the gates," LXX περίβλεπτος, Sym has γνωστός. In Nehem v. 10 "likewise my brethren and my *servants* (Heb lit *youths, lads*)" LXX has γνωστοί which makes better sense. The Heb for "known" and for "youths" might be somewhat similar.

[2] Used absolutely it might mean "noble" or "renowned." Nonnus has (1) γνωτὸς, (2) ἀρίδηλος, (3) ἐθήμονος, as quoted above, p 356, n 2, also see Jerome *Epist* 127 § 5, "John was *of noble birth and known to the high priest*."

[3] Steph *Thes* also refers to Cyrill Lex Ms γνωστοὺς, ἀδελφούς.

[4] Ps lv 13 (Gesen 394 b) Vulg "*notus*," on which however Jerome

If Judas brought Peter into the court of the High Priest's palace, that will explain a difficulty in the following

Mk xiv 66—7	Mt xxvi 69	Lk xxii. 56
And as Peter was beneath[1] in the court, there cometh one of the maids of the high priest, and seeing Peter warming himself, she looked (*lit* looking - attentively) upon him and saith, Thou also wast with the Nazarene, [even] Jesus	Now Peter was sitting without in the court and a (*lit.* one) maid came unto him saying, Thou also wast with Jesus the Galilaean.	And a certain maid seeing him as he sat in the light [of the fire] and looking stedfastly upon him, said, This man also was with him

What reason had the maid for bringing this charge? None is given by the Synoptists Mark and Luke suggest one by the words "looking-attentively" and "looking-stedfastly upon him," as though she had seen him before. But they have not told us when or how she had seen him before.

(*inter alia*) says, in the person of Christ, " Quia me, pei legis mysterium, *cognoveras esse venturum,*" as though it meant "*knowing*," and on "dux" he says "*dux* dicit, propter quod Christum tradidit, *dux mortis fuit*" It is quoted by Origen (Lomm ii 440—1) to shew that Judas once loved Jesus (comp *ib* iv 403)

[1] "Beneath," κάτω Comp 1 K vi 8 R V. txt "*middle*," but R V. marg "Sept and Targ. have *lowest*" Trommius' Index p 131 gives consecutively (1) a word frequently meaning κάτω, κάτωθεν &c, (2) a word regularly rendered "*middle*," μέσος (7 times) but περίστυλον, "portico," once, and ὑποκάτωθεν, "below," once (as in 1 K vi 8) Κάτω occurs only 9 times in N T (setting aside Jn viii 6—8) Its use by Mark alone here affords an additional proof of a Hebrew original Probably the Marcan "*below*," like the Lucan "*midst*," originated in a poetic thought Simon was not only in *the midst of* temptation, but also *sunk* or *sinking* in it, *beneath* the waters of Sheol, comp Sir li 2 foll, where the writer praises God for deliverance "from flames of a fire not blown," "from cunning lips," and from temptations in which, he says, "my soul drew near unto death and my life to Sheol *beneath* (κάτω)" Κάτω, in N T, is not used metaphorically except in Jn viii 23, "ye are from *beneath* (κάτω)"

THE DISCIPLE KNOWN UNTO THE HIGH PRIEST

On the other hand, if this (RV) "*maid*" was really "*the portress*," and if she had often admitted Judas before to the palace while he was arranging his plans with Caiaphas, and if she now admitted Peter along with Judas, and as a companion introduced by Judas, then the "maid's" reason is easily explained, even without Mark's and Luke's "looking-attentively" and "looking-stedfastly[1]." The "friend" being a disciple of Jesus, it was natural that the maid should think Peter, too, a disciple, and perhaps, like Judas, a traitor in the High Priest's pay. And she says, either when she lets him in, or, more probably, a little afterwards, "Can it be that thou, also, (like thy companion) art one of this man's disciples?"

Here we must note that all the four Evangelists have the significant "also" ("Thou *also*" or "This man *also*") although the Fourth Evangelist alone gives us something to explain its insertion. It means "thou also *like thy companion*." Without mention of a companion-disciple, "also" is not capable of any natural explanation[2]. This favours the Johannine narrative. But it also favours the view that the companion was Judas—whose comings and goings of late had made him familiar to

---

[1] "Looking attentively (ἐμβλέψασα)" and "looking stedfastly," however, may not be superfluous if they refer to the action of the portress, when seeing Peter *for the second time*. At first, while admitting Peter under the protection of "the high priest's friend," she may have simply noted his face, but said nothing. Later on, coming near Peter, she recognises his face by the light of the fire and addresses him.

[2] That is to say, if the portress had not known of the presence of *another follower of Jesus* in the palace, she would have said to Peter simply "*Thou art one* of the man's followers." But having just admitted Judas, she naturally says to Peter "*thou, also*." Origen says, mystically (on Mt xxvi 69) "Forsitan autem et quicunque est in atrio Caiaphae principis sacerdotum, non potest confiteri Dominum Jesum, nisi fuerit egressus ex atrio ejus." Most unfortunately, Origen's commentary on "the disciple that was the friend of the high priest" is lost. But we may infer from these words that, in Origen's opinion, "the disciple"—whoever he may have been—"could not confess Jesus" as long as he was in the palace. Is this easily reconcilable with the view that it was "the beloved disciple"?

THE DISCIPLE KNOWN UNTO THE HIGH PRIEST

the "portress"—and not John, whom we can hardly suppose to have been recently cultivating the acquaintance of Caiaphas with special assiduity.

In a previous treatise an explanation has been given of the prominence given by Luke to the phrase "*into the midst*," and of the phrase "*lighting the fire around.*" Luke thinks of Peter as one "*in the midst*" of a fiery trial, a "burning" appointed "to try" the soul[1].

Historically, it is possible to combine an original "*into the midst*," or "*in the midst*," with an original in which Judas, not being deemed worthy of any other title, was called "*that one of the disciples who was the high priest's bosom friend*[2]." It is conceivable that Judas, distracted by contending emotions, after first leaving Peter at the door of the palace and going up to watch the trial, rushed back again and brought Peter in —perhaps even, as Nonnus says, taking him by the hand[3]— and there left him, in the midst of the guards and servants, to take his chance. Meantime, Judas hurried back again into

---

[1] See *Son of Man* 3369 *a—e*, quoting 1 Pet iv 12—14, and *Acta Petri* § 7, where Peter says he was "driven mad by 'the devil'" Comp Nonnus (on Jn xviii 25) ἀλύων

[2] Comp. the curious phrase in Mk xiv. 10 "Judas Iscariot *the one* of the Twelve." Here ὁ εἷς τῶν δώδεκα seems to mean "the member of the Twelve that was unique in betraying Jesus" There is also perhaps an allusion to Christ's prediction (Mk xiv. 18, Mt xxvi 21) "*One of you* shall betray me" (comp Jn vi. 70 "*One of you* is a devil")—so that it might mean "*the one* of the Twelve that was pointed out by the Lord" The parall Mt xxvi 14 drops "*the*" before "one" The parall. Lk xxii. 3, "Judas, who was called Iscariot, *being of the number of the Twelve*," is perhaps a paraphrase, meaning that he was that single exception who though "*of the number of the Twelve*," was not really to be called thus, but only "Iscariot" Compare the following parallels (1) Mk xiii. 1 "*one of his disciples*," Mt xxiv. 1 "*his disciples*," Lk. xxi. 5 "*some*"—where "*one*" might denote Judas Iscariot—impressed by the splendour of the Temple, (2) Mk xiv 4 "*some*," Mt xxvi 8 "*the disciples*," Jn xii 4 "Judas Iscariot, *one of his disciples*, he that was to deliver him up"

[3] But see *Indices to Diatessarica* pp 21—2, shewing that the confusions between "grasp-with-the-hand (אחז)," "one (אחד)," "another (אחר)" &c. are very frequent

the judgment-chamber to witness the result of the trial—perhaps still not without some faint and sudden hope that, after all, Jesus would be forced to resort to His miraculous powers, or would, at all events, somehow escape death. Matthew places the suicide of Judas as happening "when he saw that Jesus was condemned," so that his remorse and death (in Matthew) closely follow Peter's penitence. According to Matthew, therefore, the two Apostles—if Judas was "the high priest's friend"—were together almost up to the last moment of the life of the betrayer The motives of Judas in leading Peter into a position of sore temptation may not have been malignant. They may even have been friendly. But, friendly or not, they turned out badly for Peter.

The same thing must be said, so far as concerns the result, if the unnamed disciple was not Judas, but that one of the Twelve whom Jesus specially loved. His action "turned out badly for Peter" And does that seem an event likely in itself, or likely to be picked out for record by the author of the Fourth Gospel though passed over by the Three? The more we reflect on the consistent conception of the quiet, thoughtful, and retiring character of the beloved disciple in the Fourth Gospel, the more difficult shall we find it to believe that he was an intimate friend of Caiaphas, or that he was made the instrument of plunging Peter into temptation by his impulsive conduct, or that the author of the Fourth Gospel intends us to believe this. Perhaps Origen's instinct led him right when he said, in his mystical fashion, that it was "impossible for a disciple of Christ to confess Jesus while he was in the palace of Caiaphas[1]." If Origen really meant this—even mystically—would he have accepted our modern view, that, at the very moment when Peter was in that palace, the beloved disciple was also there, and not only there, but there in the character of "the friend of the

---

[1] See p. 365, n 2.

high priest" who had been, for days past, plotting his Master's death?

On the other side it may be urged that if Origen had believed the "other disciple" to be Judas, some record of his belief would have been preserved by other early commentators. But why? The belief of Augustine, that the "other disciple" was not John, but some unknown person, does not seem to have been preserved by other early commentators. Jerome's view—that John was "of noble birth and known to the High Priest"—indicates an early and desperate conjecture to explain an obscure passage that may well have received many early explanations not all of which have survived[1]. Such as have survived teem with inconsistencies. Chrysostom first says that it was "*a great moral triumph*" that the disciple followed Jesus when the others deserted, but then he adds that the Evangelist said that he was an acquaintance of the High Priest, "so that *no one should wonder at his following, or proclaim his praise for his bravery*[2]" Ammonius the Elder says "John went in with Jesus, along with the multitude *in the character of one unknown* [*to the High Priest*], and then *in the character of one known* [*to the High Priest*], spoke to the portress and brought in Peter[3]." The whole of Jerome's laboured explanation, quoted above, shews that kind of

---

[1] According to Jerome (*Letters* cxxvii 5, ed Wace and Schaff, p 255) it was because John "had renounced both rank and wealth" that Jesus "loved the evangelist more than the other disciples. For John was of noble birth and known to the high priest, *yet* was so little appalled by the plottings of the Jews that he introduced Peter into his court..." Would not one have supposed that instead of "*yet*"—which I have italicised—Jerome would have written "*and consequently*"? And had not John's elder brother, James, also "renounced both rank and wealth," so that, according to Jerome's view, Jesus should have loved James "more than the other disciples"?

[2] "*A great moral triumph*," μέγα κατόρθωμα, but Cramer "*a very great wonder*," μέγιστον θαῦμα

[3] Cramer *ad loc* Συνεισῆλθεν ὁ Ἰωάννης τῷ Ἰησοῦ μετὰ τοῦ ὄχλου ἀγνώστως, καὶ τότε ὡς γνωστὸς εἶπε τῇ θυρωρῷ, καὶ εἰσήνεγκε τὸν Πέτρον

incoherence and inconsistency which vacillates between a "nevertheless" and a "therefore."

I have not been able to find any references to this passage in Irenaeus, Clement of Alexandria, and Tertullian If none can be found, there is little basis for inference as to what Alford calls the "universal opinion," so far as concerns the Ante-Nicene Fathers But Augustine's dissent from that "universal opinion," when combined with Origen's remark on the impossibility for a disciple of Christ to confess Jesus while he was "in the palace of Caiaphas," appears to me to go some way toward demonstrating that in the first three centuries the modern view was by no means "universal," and that Origen as well as Augustine, dissented from it.

In concluding these remarks on the Johannine account of Peter's Denial it may be well to add that, although the evidence rather favours John against the Synoptists, it must not be inferred that this favourable judgment extends to all the details and still less to the context As regards the Johannine "*portress*," we are able to point out, not only that her introduction illuminates the whole of the Synoptic narrative, but also that there are verbal grounds for preferring it to the parallel Lucan insistence on the trial of Peter "*in the midst*" of his enemies For we have seen that, in Samuel, modern scholars prefer the LXX "*portress*" to the actual reading of the Hebrew text "*in the midst*" Yet in the preceding Johannine context there occurs a detail to which attention will be called in due course, where John seems to have mistaken the "going backward" and "falling away" of the *disciples*, at the moment of Christ's arrest, for the "going backward" and "falling to the ground" of *the Roman cohort*

In view of the palpable sources of the misunderstanding

THE DISCIPLE KNOWN UNTO THE HIGH PRIEST

noted below[1], comment on this "going backward" is needless. John appears to have made a great mistake. But it is nothing more than a mistake It is a misinterpretation of two or three words, every one of which can be shewn to have been ambiguous There is no solid ground for basing on his error the charge of indifference to fact. But there is ground, here as elsewhere, for concluding that no tradition, of any Evangelist, should be accepted on the authority of that Evangelist alone, without examining its relation to Evangelistic traditions as a whole These, as being Greek writings or translations, must of course be criticized as Greek But this is only a secondary aspect. Primarily they are to be interpreted as the product of Hebrew and Jewish thought, and in the light of that "scripture" to which Jesus constantly refers

---

[1] Mk xiv 50
And *they* (i e the disciples) all left him and fled.

Mt xxvi 56
Then *the disciples all left him and fled*

Lk xxii 53—4
Omits

Jn xviii 6
They (i e the soldiers) *went away backward and fell to the ground*

(1) Mark's words seem clear enough to us But Matthew, by adding "disciples," faintly suggests that, in his opinion, some might take the original of Mark's ἀφέντες αὐτόν as "[the soldiers] letting go their prisoner" Luke, by omitting the whole, confirms the view that there was *some* obscurity

(2) "Left him," ἀφέντες αὐτόν, is ambiguous, since it might mean "[the soldiers] letting him go [for the time]," comp 2 Chr. xxviii 14, 1 Macc xiii 16, 19

(3) "Went backward," ἀπῆλθαν εἰς τὰ ὀπίσω, is ambiguous, since it might mean that Christ's disciples went backward in the sense of falling away, or deserting Him It is actually so used in Jn vi 66 ἀπῆλθον εἰς τὰ ὀπίσω Delitzsch has in both places the same Heb (for ὀπίσω) and it is connected (Gesen. 30 *b*) with (1) revolt as well as (2) repulse

(4) "Fell," ἔπεσαν, is ambiguous, since the Hebrew regularly rendered πίπτω may mean "fall away," "desert," as in 1 S xxix 3 Jer xxxix. 9. No doubt Mark's "*fled,*" ἔφυγον, is clear enough. But see Jer xxxvii. 13 "fall-away," lit "fall," LXX here, and later on, φεύγω, Aq. πίπτω, Sym αὐτομολέω

(5) "To the ground," χαμαί, is added by John to πίπτω as it is by

370

THE DISCIPLE KNOWN UNTO THE HIGH PRIEST

the LXX in Dan. ii. 46. The LXX adds it merely for emphasis. Here, in an obscure tradition, John had also motives of clearness.

John, as has been said above, appears to have made a great mistake. But we shall make a still greater mistake if we suppose that so great a writer has erred through mere love of such hyperbole as originated the fanciful legend in the Acta Pilati of the Roman standards bowing before Jesus. John *did his best to interpret what Luke had omitted and what some early traditions had probably obscured and variously reported.* Biassed by idealism, he nevertheless did not invent, but interpreted a Hebrew original in a new way. Historically he was not justified. But he was justified by grammar as well as by conscience. And that is the great point—to shew that this extraordinary and most spiritual Evangelist did not soar above earthly considerations of fact so far as he could ascertain it.

Addendum

A criticism of this Appendix (as Chapter II of *Miscellanea Evangelica* (*I*)) by the Rev. J. B. Mayor, Litt.D., which reached me too late for discussion in the body of this work, will be found, followed by my reply, in the *Expositor* for Jan. and Feb. 1914.

Some of Dr Mayor's remarks appear to me to be based on a misunderstanding of my view, as though I maintained that Judas *really* was—or was *really* supposed by the Evangelist to be—the "familiar friend" of Caiaphas. I had never intended to maintain this. My view— perhaps not expressed with sufficient fulness to be quite clear—was that Judas, at once the tool of Caiaphas and the partner of his plots, was *ironically called* "the High Priest's *familiar friend*," with a bitter and reproachful allusion to the treacherous " *familiar friend*" in the Psalms. The Johannine thought seemed to me to be this. "Judas, who was chosen to be *familiar friend* of the true High Priest, himself chose to be the *familiar friend* of the false one."

Dr Mayor translates ἐθήμων (see p. 357) "*customer*" thus. "being, from his trade of fishing, a well-known acquaintance of his customer, the high priest (literally, 'the customary high priest')." The Greek *Thesaurus*, Hesychius, and Nonnus himself, afford no instance of this meaning. Hesychius explains it by συνήθης. and συνήθης, "companion," is used by Symmachus in Ps. lv. 13 "But it was thou.. my *companion* and my familiar friend"—the passage where LXX renders "*familiar friend*" by γνωστός.

APPENDIX III

THE INTERPRETATION OF EARLY CHRISTIAN POETRY

IN previous volumes of Diatessarica it has been shewn that Hebrew poetic expressions, passing into Greek prose and interpreted prosaically, might give rise to serious misunderstandings. Recently the discovery of the Syriac poems commonly known as Odes of Solomon, but perhaps better called Songs of Solomon, has brought before Biblical students two questions. The first is, "Are we to interpret these particular poems as originally written in Syriac, or as coming to us from a Syriac version of Hebrew, or from a Syriac version of Greek?" The second is of a general character, "Will the different hypotheses of origin, in this and other similar discoveries, make any great difference in the interpretation?"

In the Ninth Part of Diatessarica, a volume entitled Light on the Gospel from an Ancient Poet, I gave reasons for thinking that the Odes came to us from Hebrew. A contrary view has been recently set forth by Dom Connolly with great ability, and fortified by definite quotations of Syriac expressions that appeared to him to correspond exactly to expressions in original Greek[1]. Although I am unable to agree with its conclusions, I am heartily grateful to Dom Connolly who, in response to an appeal of mine for

---

[1] *The Journal of Theological Studies*, July, 1913, pp. 530—8. *Greek the Original Language of the Odes of Solomon*. By the Rev R. H. Connolly, O.S.B.

facts, has adduced eight passages, besides repeating one previously adduced, that seem to him to present "cogent reasons for concluding not merely that the Syriac is a translation from Greek, but also that the Odes were composed in Greek." It appears to me that the discussion of these passages may be used to throw light on many obscurities that await us in the interpretation of passages in the Gospels, when we doubtfully ask ourselves, "Is this or that to be interpreted, as Greek thought, logically and literally, or as Jewish thought, poetically and metaphorically?"

If my readers learn from Dom Connolly as much as I have learned, they will be grateful to me for presenting his arguments to them I proceed to take first Dom Connolly's eight new quotations, placing after them (§ 9) the one previously adduced, and (§ 10) a tenth, previously alleged by Dom Connolly, but only briefly touched on in his last article.

§ 1 "*Without envy*"

The argument from this phrase, for a Greek original, is stated by Dom Connolly thus.—"In Ode vii 4 we read. 'He caused me to know Himself without envy in (*or*, by) His simplicity....' Dr Harris notes that the Syriac expression 'without envy' stands for ἀφθόνως, and to me it appears that it evidently does so"

Later on[1] Dom Connolly quotes Dr Harris as saying "An interesting example" of the Syriac phrase as a rendering of ἀφθόνως "will be found in Ode 11 *v* 6, where we read 'speaking waters touched my lips from the fountain of God without grudging' (*i e.* abundantly[2])" It will be observed that

---

[1] *Journ Theol Stud* p 536.

[2] Dom Connolly is quoting from Dr Harris' introduction to the second edition, p 47. In his textual rendering (second ed p 105) Dr Harris has "plenteously" "Fountain of God" should be "fountain of the Lord," see p 398, n. 1

Dr Harris gets rid of the negation "without," and of the moral thought of "grudging," by paraphrasing the two words as one, "abundantly." Dom Connolly adopts this positive paraphrase by adding, in words that I italicise, "*Here the context requires the really positive idea which* ἀφθόνως *expresses, but which the Syriac does not express*" Now I admit that ἀφθόνως—unless used in special contexts which we shall consider later on—would naturally mean "abundantly" and nothing more. Thucydides and Polybius use it of darts showered "abundantly" on the enemy, and Athenaeus of cakes "abundantly" soaked in honey[1]. That being the case, if I believed that the Poet himself wrote in Greek using ἀφθόνως in its ordinary Greek sense, I should say that "abundantly" (with a footnote attached) was the best translation, and that "without grudging," though a literal rendering of the Syriac, misled the English reader.

But if the Poet wrote in Hebrew then the aspect of the phrase is completely changed. For then we shall have to ask whether this is not one of many instances of Hebrew negative thought about the gifts of God. They are given "*with-not* (i.e. *without*) money and *with-not* (i.e. *without*) price"; they are "*without* repentance"; they are given by One who "upbraideth *not*[2]." Ben Sira also says "Buy her [*i.e.* the truth] for yourselves *without* money[3]." It is as a climax of this Hebrew negative contrast that Jesus says "*Not* as the world giveth give I unto you[4]." Philo writes in Greek but thinks in Hebrew when he says "God is *not* a tradesman selling his goods at a profit but a Being that would fain give all things, pouring-up (*sic*) the everflowing streams of graces, *not* craving an exchange[5]."

When Paul bids the Corinthians give "*not grudgingly* or of necessity," he is but carrying on the Hebrew doctrine that

---

[1] See Steph. *Thes* 1 (2) 2651
[2] Is. lv. 1, Rom. xi 29 ἀμεταμέλητα, Jas 1. 5.
[3] Sir li 25 *lit* "with-not money." [4] Jn xiv. 27
[5] Philo 1. 161 "pouring up"=ἀναχέων.

God said to the Israelite "Beware that there be *not a base thought in thine heart...and thine eye be evil* against thy poor brother . Thou shalt surely give him, and thine heart *shall not be grieved* (lit *shall not be made evil*) when thou givest him[1]." And all Christians know how Jesus emphasized this ancient Hebrew warning that the "eye" of the true Israelite must *not* be "evil[2]."

We shall shew, later on, that Philo and the earliest of the Christian Fathers connect the thought of "*grudging*" or "*envy*" with the thought of the Tree of Life in Paradise, protesting that God *did not* "*grudge*" *His best gifts to Man*. Passing over that for the present, we may here note that "*pouring-up streams*" refers to the "stream" that "*went up*" in Paradise (according to LXX and Philo) to water the earth[3]. This (said Philo) was the Mind, the Controlling Power in man, the source through which God dispenses to him His gifts and graces.

Now a reference to the other uses of "without *envy*"— which I will venture to render " without *grudging*[4]"—throughout the Odes, suggests that it is used in connection with a Tree of Life or a Fountain of Life which the Poet regards as being in the midst of Paradise. This Tree of Life is also the Tree of Knowledge, the Knowledge of God Himself. As regards the Tree of the Knowledge of good and evil, God might be said by sceptics like Celsus to have broken His own rule against "muzzling" the ox that "treadeth out the corn[5],"

---

[1] 2 Cor ix 7 μὴ ἐκ λύπης, Deut xv 10 (LXX) οὐ λυπηθήσῃ τῇ καρδίᾳ σου

[2] Mk vii 22, Mt vi 23, Lk xi. 34

[3] Philo i 249, 573, quoting Gen. ii 6 R V. "mist," but LXX and Philo πηγή, Aq. ἐπιβλυσμός

[4] A different Syriac word is used in Ode vii. 23 "And hatred shall be thrown from the earth, and together-with *envy* shall it be drowned (*or*, sunk)"

[5] Deut. xxv 4   The Heb. verb for "muzzle" which occurs only there (see Gesen 340 *b*, which rejects Ezek. xxxix. 11) is identical with the Syr.

THE INTERPRETATION

and to have "muzzled" Man For He placed it in the midst of Eden and yet forbade him to eat of it But as regards the Tree of that higher Knowledge which is Life and which is also God's Love, there is, for the disciples of the Messiah, "*no muzzling*," or "*no grudging*." "Walk ye," says the Poet, "in the knowledge of the Most High [*that is*] *without grudging*." This—the last instance of the phrase—is to be explained by the preceding one, "Put on [thyself] the good-grace of the Lord [*that is*] *without grudging*, and come into Paradise, and make thee a crown from His tree, and put it on thy head[1]." This is typical of Abraham (who abandoned the worship of idols and of the stars and was "justified by grace"); and so, too, is a preceding instance "I have left the way of error and have come to Him and have received from Him redemption [*that is*] *without grudging*[2]." The same thought is expressed thus under the metaphor of a fountain, probably regarded as being in the midst of Paradise, " And speaking water touched my lips from the fountain of the Lord [*that is poured forth*] *without grudging*[3]." Passing from these instances to the earliest one of all, we find in them grounds for believing that in this, too, the metaphor is somewhat, though not quite, similar. The Poet seems to begin his poems with a conception of a Tree of Life or Love which is the Lord Himself and in which human souls, the "members" of the Tree, "hang" as branches. Ode i and Ode iii say "The Lord is on my head like a crown, nor shall I be apart from Him...Thou livest upon my head, and thou hast blossomed upon my head. Thy fruits are full and perfect, full of thy salvation..[4]. I put on And His

---

"envy" or "grudge" The noun-form occurs in Ps xxxix 1 R V "a bridle," or, "a muzzle."   [1] Odes xxiii 4, xx 7

[2] Ode xv 6 On "[that is]," see p 430 foll. In xvii. 12 "I gave my knowledge without grudging," "without grudging" modifies "gave"

[3] Ode xi. 6. Comp Rev. xxii 1—2 "And he shewed me a river of water of life *in the midst of the street thereof*"

[4] Here Ode i ends, probably incomplete. Ode ii and the first words of Ode iii are missing. But we may infer from Ode xx. 7, quoted above,

members are with Him and in them do I hang. .And I shall not be a stranger[1] because there is *no grudging* with the Lord...."

Dom Connolly then passes to consider the phrase "*in His simplicity,*" which follows "*without grudging.*" "Why," he asks, "is the expression used? If we translate it literally into Greek we seem clearly to have the answer. (ἐν) τῇ ἁπλότητι αὐτοῦ is 'in His bounty' (2 Cor. viii 2, ix. 11, 13, and ἁπλῶς Jas 1 5), and this is precisely what the context requires" Similarly he would render the same Syriac word by "generous" in Ode xxxiv. 1 where Dr Harris has "No way is hard where there is a *simple* heart"

But even if we accept the hypothesis of an original Greek ἁπλότης, we must not forget that it always implies "singleness" as opposed to doubleness or duplicity. Dom Connolly refers to 2 Cor. viii 2 for the meaning of "bounty," but the context shews that τὸ πλοῦτος τῆς ἁπλότητος αὐτῶν must be explained from *ib.* 5 "*they gave themselves first to the Lord, and to us through the will of God*" Origen explains Rom. xii. 8 ὁ μεταδιδοὺς ἐν ἁπλότητι by saying (*ad loc*) that a man must not seem to be benefiting the needy while in his heart he is seeking praise from men—must not "*seem to be doing one thing* with his hands, while he is *really doing another thing* in his heart." That is to say, he must not be guilty of duplicity. He must be singlehearted And so elsewhere. In NT, ἁπλότης never means "bounty" or "liberality," in the popular sense of either word—apart from "singleheartedness"

---

that the object of "put on" is, or corresponds to, a branch, or garland, from the Tree There is room, however, for more than one view It may be (as in the Pauline Epistles) "putting on" Christ, the New Man &c, or it may be "putting on" the grace of Christ And the "branches" may be the fruits, gifts, or graces of Christ. See *Light on the Gospel* **3670** foll.

[1] Comp Eph ii. 19 "no more strangers," where, as here, there is the thought of "one body" on "the cross" But the Epistle passes on to liken the body to a building, the Poem likens it to a tree

THE INTERPRETATION

I have given reasons elsewhere for preferring to render the Syriac (a form of *psht*) by some form of "*single*," meaning "*singleness*" in the sense of "*singlehearted kindness to man or love to God*[1]," without that latent streak of self-interestedness which often makes a man "doubleminded." In this sense, the Syriac *psht* occurs in Christ's phrase about the "*single* eye[2]," where Delitzsch has a form of the Hebrew *tôm* (literally *completeness, soundness*). The adjective *tâm*, applied to Jacob in Genesis, is rendered by Aquila ἁπλοῦς[3]. The longer form of the root *tôm* used by Delitzsch—identical, when unpointed, with what is called in R.V *Thummim*—is used in God's precept to Abraham, "Be thou *perfect*," and is rendered by Aquila τέλειος[4] Onkelos renders *tôm* and *tâmîm* by a form of *shalem* This, both in Hebrew and Aramaic, often implies "soundness"—in the sense of freedom from such blemish or unsoundness as makes a thing not really what it professes to be In the precept, "Be ye therefore *perfect*[5]," Delitzsch has a form of *shalem*[6] In the two instances in which ἁπλότης represents a Hebrew word in O T. it does not mean liberality, but "*singlemindedness*[7]"

---

[1] See *Light on the Gospel* **3760** *d*, and *Test XII Patr* ed. Charles pp 103—5, on "singleness of heart."
[2] Mt vi 22   [3] Gen xxv 27
[4] Gen. xvii 1, LXX ἄμεμπτος
[5] Mt v. 48, see *Son of Man* **3482** *a*
[6] So ed 1878   I am informed that in ed 1877 Delitzsch has *tâmîm*
[7] In 2 S xv. 11, it means that the followers of Absalom were honestly deceived, and had no dishonest purpose   In 1 Chr xxix 17, the LXX means "*in singleness of heart [and without desire to bribe the Lord or receive reward] I willingly-gave* all these things .." The Heb has "*uprightness* of heart." The first part of the verse says "Thou *triest the heart* and hast pleasure in *uprightness*" Not the "abundance" of the offering but the "singlemindedness" is emphasized   Comp the use of "*perfect*" (a form of *shalem*) in *ib* 9 "with a *perfect* heart they *offered-willingly* to the Lord," where Rashi says "*With one heart* they gave, with a well-wishing mind, *not with two hearts*; for there is a giver that gives unwillingly (not a well-wisher) or because he is ashamed of others   And such a man is called by the name of '*two-hearted*'"

In support of his view Dom Connolly alleges Jas. i 5. This is rendered by R V "Let him ask of God, who giveth to all *liberally* (ἁπλῶς) and upbraideth not." Delitzsch renders ἁπλῶς by a form of the Hebrew word (*nâdab*, "incite" or "impel") used by David in Chronicles, as above quoted, when he says, about his preparations for the Temple, "I *willingly-gave* (lit. *followed my own impulse in giving*) all these things[1]." The Hebrew *nâdab* is applied to those who "volunteer" *Nâdîb* is a name for a "prince," because the profession of a prince is to be a "volunteer" and take the lead for the service of his subjects Accordingly Delitzsch has "He giveth to all *with willingness and with [there-is] no rebuking*" The Hebrew used here by Delitzsch, for "*rebuking*," occurs—among several instances of rebuking encroachments of various kinds—in Ruth, where Boaz says to his reapers "Pull out some [wheat] for her from the bundles, and leave it, and let her glean, and *rebuke* her not[2]." The picture of Ruth, the stranger, amid the reapers of her future husband, treated as a friend or native, and allowed to do something more than ordinary "gleaning," and this *without* "*rebuking*," may illustrate the thought of a passage in the Odes where "*no grudging*" occurs for the first time: "Dearly-love I the Beloved, and [indeed] my soul loveth Him. And where His rest [is], there also am I And I *shall not be a stranger*, because there is *no grudging* with the Lord [Most] High and [Most] Compassionate[3]."

In concluding these remarks on the phrases "no grudging" and "singleheartedness," I by no means go so far as to assert that the considerations urged above prove that the poet wrote in Hebrew; but I do venture to assert that they effectually meet the arguments alleged from these phrases to shew that he wrote in Greek And I think many will feel that the

---

[1] 1 Chr xxix 17, quoted above.
[2] Ruth ii. 16, comp. Gesen 172 a
[3] Ode iii 5—7.

hypothesis of a Hebrew original, or at all events of what may be called an undercurrent of Hebrew allusion, helps us to do justice to the Odes as poetry. It is a poor thing to say that God gives "abundantly," as compared with the saying that He gives like a Father who "grudges nothing" that is for the good of His children, in spite of their frequent ingratitude. And to speak of God as "liberal," or as giving "liberally," is less beautiful (as well as less Hebraic) than to speak of His "heart" as being "single" in its love for man[1].

We shall return to this subject later on, when we deal with "Alleged translation from Greek words with privative alpha," shewing that Philo certainly, and the Book of Wisdom probably, connected God's giving of the highest knowledge with the thought of "freedom from grudging," in a very definite sense, meaning a great deal more than that He gave "abundantly."

§ 2. "*Thou shalt not acquire an alien the blood of thy soul*[2]"

[Codex N inserts "*by*" before the noun interpreted "blood" (or, by some, "price"). But, as Dom Connolly does not adopt that reading, I pass it by. I have ascertained, however, that the facsimile of Dr Harris' MS agrees with Codex N in inserting "by." Dom Connolly was under the erroneous impression that they agree in rejecting "by," and four of his arguments—those specified below as from *a* to *d*—are based on that error.

After this Section was in type, I heard from Dom Connolly, to whom I had written on the subject, that his mistake was caused, in part, by a somewhat obscure footnote in Dr Harris' second edition. But still, as his allegations

---

[1] See *Light on the Gospel* **3718** foll. on "God's 'heart' and Man's 'faith,'" and **3999** *b—d* where it is contended that "The 'way' of 'the simple heart'" lays an "emphasis on singleness of heart" which "illustrates other passages in the Odes mentioning the 'heart' of God."

[2] Ode xx. 5 as quoted by Dom Connolly.

under the four headings are of general interest as bearing on the relation between Greek and Hebrew thought, I have not cancelled my observations on them]

It is alleged by Dom Connolly that (*a*) "the blood of thy soul" is merely the Syriac way of saying "thine own blood", that (*b*) "acquire.. soul" is a Syriac "translation of the Greek οὐχ ἕξεις (or the like) ἀλλότριον τὸ ἴδιον αἷμα", that (*c*) the Greek ἕξεις meant "regard", that (*d*) the Greek αἷμα meant "flesh and blood"—so that the meaning was "thou shalt not regard as an alien thine own (flesh and) blood", that (*e*) the passage, with its context, alludes to one in Isaiah "When thou seest the naked, that thou cover him, and that thou hide not thyself from thine own flesh" (R.V.), where "for the second clause the LXX has καὶ ἀπὸ τῶν οἰκείων τοῦ σπέρματός σου οὐχ ὑπερόψῃ", that (*f*) a later verse in the Ode alludes to the same passage in Isaiah, that (*g*) the Ode and the LXX of Isaiah both mention "fatness," where the Hebrew of Isaiah and the Syriac of Isaiah have a different word. The conclusion is, "If then the Odist is dependent on Isaiah here, he must have used the LXX in other words, this Ode was composed in Greek."

These arguments deserve careful and separate examination. If they were sound, they would seem to me to establish the conclusion that "the Ode was composed in Greek" But most or all of them appear to me to be unsound.

(*a*) "Thy blood" occurs, in Hebrew, thrice, in the phrase "thy blood be upon thy head," and "the dogs shall lick thy blood," and several times (in different contexts) in Ezekiel. In not a single one of these instances is it rendered in Walton's Syriac by "the blood of thy soul[1]" It is therefore,

---

[1] 2 S. 1 16, 1 K 11. 37, xxi. 19, Ezek xvi 22, xix. 10 &c See Mandelkern p 298. According to my view, the Syriac of the Odes is a very early and pre-literary rendering of Hebrew, so that the Syriac of O T is peculiarly well adapted to illustrate the Syriac of the Odes.

THE INTERPRETATION

to say the least, unsafe to say that the Syriac phrase here is "merely the Syriac way of saying 'thine own blood'."

(*b*) The Syriac "acquire" is said to be a translation of the Greek ἕξεις which meant "have" in the sense of "regard" but was wrongly taken to mean "have" in the sense of "acquire." But the Syriac Thesaurus, though it gives multitudes of instances of "acquire" as a rendering of ἔχω, gives none, as far as I can find, where the Greek means "regard."

(*c*) In the few instances in N.T. where ἔχω means "regard," the Syriac does not use the word "acquire[1]." Moreover a later Ode, using a different word for "regard," has "I was *regarded by them as a stranger*," as though to shew that, if the meaning had been "*regard as a stranger*," the translator knew other words to express it[2]

(*d*) The Greek αἷμα may be used in various *adverbial phrases* to denote blood-relationship, but the use of *the noun to signify a blood-relation* would seem to be rare and highly poetical. Indeed we should have to pronounce it nonexistent, if we trusted in Stephens' Thesaurus It quotes no Greek instance at all, but only Virgil's "projice tela manu, *sanguis meus*[3]"

---

[1] See Mk xi 32 and parallels, also Lk. xiv 18, Philipp ii 29, Philem 17 The sentence "[Thou] that possessest things impossible [as] possible" quoted by Dom Connolly from the Syriac 'Anaphora of St James' seems to me—having regard to the Hebrew use of "possess" or "purchase" in a sense approaching to "create," "bring into being"—intelligible as it stands, "Thou that dost call into being things [that men would have called] impossible" No doubt "create" would be a more usual and obvious word than "purchase", but "purchase" has associations (Gesen. 889*a*) with God's victorious redemption that would make the word appropriate here

[2] Ode xvii 6 The word there used for "stranger" is a form of ξένος, different from the word in the passage under consideration

[3] The *Thesaurus* wrongly says "Sed tamen et pater filium vocat *sanguinem* suum, ut Od π 300 εἰ ἐτεόν γ᾽ ἐμός ἐσσι καὶ αἵματος ἡμετέροιο." It adds, however, the correct translation "*e* meo *sanguine*," and then quotes Virgil *Aeneid* vi 836, and vernacular Italian, "*Sangue mio*"

It is asked, "Does not this phrase in itself involve a Grecism? Is there any Hebrew authority for the use of 'blood,' like 'flesh,' in the sense of kith and kin?" To both these questions the answer is negative. First, it does not involve a Grecism; secondly, there is no Hebrew authority for the use of blood to mean kith and kin. But the conclusion should be "*Therefore we must render 'the blood of thy soul' here as having nothing to do with 'kith and kin'.*" It might allude to some phrase where the shedding of blood is implied—such as that in Genesis, where both the Hebrew and the Syriac insert "souls," "Your blood, [*the blood belonging*, or, *according*] *to your souls*, will I require¹"

(*e*) "A general parallelism" is said to be indicated between Isaiah lviii and Ode xx. "The unacceptable fast" and the conditions for an "acceptable fast," in the Prophecy, are placed as parallel to "the acceptable sacrifice" and the conditions for it in the Ode. Then it is said that "there is a good deal more than this general parallelism," and the texts are put side by side to shew it :—

Isaiah lviii. 7	Ode xx 5, 6
"When thou seest the naked, that thou cover him, and that thou hide not thyself from thine own flesh" (R.V.).	5 "Thou shalt not regard as an alien thine own blood, neither shalt thou seek to devour thy neighbour, 6 neither shalt thou deprive him of the covering of his nakedness."

Then it is inferred, first, that the Odist is borrowing from Isaiah, and subsequently (from the context in the Ode and the context in Isaiah) that he is borrowing from the rendering of Isaiah as given by the LXX which differs from the Hebrew.

Now of course a very important part of this "general parallelism" and of these apparent coincidences—namely, that between "*thine own flesh*" and "*thine own blood*"—altogether

---

¹ Gen. ix. 5. The Syr. omits "to" and has "your blood that [is] of your souls."

disappears when we adopt the correct reading in the Ode as above described, "*acquire with the blood of thy soul*" Nevertheless it appears to me that Dom Connolly would have been safe in inferring that the Poet had Isaiah in view. But I do not think he is right in making Isaiah alone responsible for what he calls "a momentary outburst of realism, in *vv.* 5 and 6, which is quite unlike the Odist's usual manner"

Because the Poet had Isaiah in view, does it follow that he had Isaiah alone in view? There is a passage in Exodus which Isaiah himself may well have had in view. It forbids the Israelite to deprive his neighbour of his garment at night, "for it is his only *covering*[1]" And the context in that passage implies a prohibition to "devour" one's "neighbour" by usury[2]. I should add therefore that the Poet is probably looking back to both passages, to the Law as well as to the Prophet The Law, in two respects, agrees more closely than the Prophet with the text of the Ode For the Law, like the Ode, mentions sacrifice, and the Law, like the Ode, is negative, not positive. It begins by prohibiting sacrifice to strange gods[3], and goes on to prohibit the affliction of strangers, widows, and the poor. Isaiah makes no mention of sacrifice. But the first four verses of the Ode ("I am a priest of the Lord . nor thy soul do violence to soul") imply that it is on righteous sacrifice that the Poet bases his prohibitions of unrighteousness.

(*f*) It is suggested that the words of the Ode "and glory [cod. N. His glory] shall go before thee[4]" allude to words in the Prophecy "and *thy righteousness* shall go before thee." But the thought is different. Whatever reading we may

---

[1] Exod xxii 26—7 "If thou at all take thy neighbour's garment to pledge, thou shalt restore it ..for that is his only *covering*," where the Syr for "*covering*" is the same as in the Ode

[2] Comp. Exod xxii. 22 "ye shall not afflict any widow," and Mk xii 40 &c "devour widows' houses"

[3] Exod xxii. 20 "He that sacrificeth unto any god, save unto the Lord only, shall be utterly destroyed"

[4] Ode xx 8

adopt, the "glory" is presumably God's. And "God's glory" is not man's "righteousness." The Poet seems to me to have in view many passages where the Lord, or the glory of the Lord, sometimes manifested in a pillar of fire or cloud, is regarded as going before His people, *e.g.* "The Lord hath made bare His holy arm...*the Lord will go before you*," and "*the glory of the Lord* shall be revealed[1]."

(*g*) A further allusion to the LXX of Is lviii is alleged in the Ode's context, "come into His Paradise...and thou shalt *be fat* in [the?] truth in the praise of His name[2]," corresponding to Is. lviii. 11 LXX "and thy bones *shall be made fat* (πιανθήσεται) and shall be as a garden well-watered (μεθύων)" where the Hebrew has "and the Lord *shall make-strong* thy bones." From this agreement with the LXX it is argued, and with great apparent cogency, "If then the Odist is dependent on Isaiah here, he must have used the LXX. In other words, this Ode was composed in Greek."

But it should have been added that Walton's *literal rendering of the Hebrew in Isaiah* is "impinguabit," "*will fatten.*" And this is the first of three interpretations of the word mentioned in Ibn Ezra's commentary on the passage Aquila, Theodotion, and Symmachus give three distinct renderings. The LXX "*fatten*" is a fourth. The R.V. "make strong" is a fifth Why should not the Odist—even supposing that he was alluding to this passage in Isaiah alone, and to no other similar passage in Scripture—have adopted that interpretation of the Hebrew which is placed first by Ibn Ezra and (I am informed) by Kimchi? Surely, in the face of these facts, it is unsafe to say "he must have used the LXX."

---

[1] Is. lii 10—12 and xl. 5. I should be disposed to add Is. lviii. 8 "the glory of the Lord shall be thy rearward."

[2] Ode xx 7 "His Paradise". so Dr Harris' English text, but his Syriac, and Harnack's German, have "Paradise." Also "His *name*" is an error for "His *holiness.*"

I do not, however, believe that the Odist is alluding to Isaiah alone. If that had been the case, I think he would have given Isaiah's phrase in full, "he shall *make fat thy bones*" or "*thy bones shall be made fat*"—expressions found in Proverbs and Ben Sira[1]—instead of "*thou shalt be fat.*" Moreover, what is the meaning of "*fat...in the praise of His holiness*"? It seems to need some explanation not to be gleaned from the context of Isaiah.

Now there are only two places in Scripture where the adjective "fat" is applied to man—one, in a neutral sense, "the fat ones of the earth," but the other in a good sense applied to the righteous man who is as it were "*fat," and flourishing, to the glory of God*. "They shall still bring forth fruit in old age; *fat and green shall they be, to proclaim that Jehovah is righteous*[2]." The latter is applied by several Jewish traditions to Abraham. His "*fatness*" was to the glory of God, and his connection with Paradise is recognised in Luke's Parable of Dives and Lazarus, as well as in Jewish literature in general and the Odes in particular[3]. The Psalmist, then, and not the LXX of Isaiah, may very well have been in the Poet's mind when he says to the soul, typified by Abraham, "Thou shalt receive of His kindness and of His grace[4], and *thou shalt be fat* in [the?] truth in the praise of His holiness." In any case the language does not necessitate, or even indicate, a Greek original[5].

---

[1] Prov xv 30 (xvi 2), Sir. xxvi 13.

[2] Gesen 206 *b*, referring to Ps xxii 29, xcii. 14—15

[3] See *Light on the Gospel* **3873** *c*, **3875** *e*. Comp. Ps. xxxvi. 8 "They shall be abundantly satisfied with the *fatness* of thy house; and thou shalt make them drink of the river of thy pleasures"—apparently alluding to Paradise as well as to the Temple (*Light* **3853—5**).

[4] See *Light on the Gospel* **3822** It is in connection with Abraham that God's "kindness and truth" are first mentioned, and his name is also closely connected with "grace."

[5] Space does not admit of an attempt to shew how the words rendered above "thou shalt not acquire an alien the blood of thy soul" might be

OF EARLY CHRISTIAN POETRY

§ 3. "*And those that were silent became with speech*[1]"

This is Dom Connolly's rendering of a sentence (in Ode xii) rendered by Dr Harris "And in the word [*mellĕthā* here] were those that were silent." The Ode treats of the Word A previous verse called it *pethgāmā*, saying "the swiftness of *the Word* (*pethgāmā*) is indescribable" The present verse says "And by it [i.e. *the pethgāmā*] the worlds spoke one to another, and"—according to Dom Connolly's rendering—"those that were silent *became with*[2] *speech* (*mellĕthā*)" The words that I have italicised he explains as meaning "acquired the power of speech, became vocal," adding "I am now confident that this is the true meaning,

---

interpreted on the hypothesis of a Hebrew original. I believe, but cannot at present prove, that the text is corrupt, and that, if it could be restored, it would imply a prohibition of the worship of "a strange god" (*lit* "provoking with a stranger")

The following facts seem to me to point in that direction. (1) The word used here for "*stranger*" is found (*Thes* 2380) masc in Deut. xxxii 16, meaning "*strange* [*gods*]," and fem in Lev xx 2—5, meaning "*Molech*" (2) In Deut xxxii 16 "they *provoked* him with strange [gods]," the Heb for "*provoke*," or "*make-jealous*," is the causative of קנא. This is confused with "*acquire*" (קנה) in Ezek viii 3 by Theod. "the image of the jealousy of *the acquirer*" (Heb "the image of jealousy *which-maketh-jealous*"), and in Prov iii 31 by LXX "*acquire* not" (Heb. "*envy* not") (3) Conversely, in Is. xl. 11 Heb "*acquire* (i e redeem)" is rendered by LXX ζηλοῦν "*be jealous for*" (4) Levy Ch ii 372 a gives קנא (as well as קני) as meaning "acquire" &c , and in Deut xxxii 6 "He that possessed thee," where Onk paraphrases with "thou art *His* (דיליה),'' Jer I and Jer II have forms of קנא (5) The causative of Heb. קנא occurs (Gesen 888 b) only in four passages (Deut. xxxii 16, 21, Ps lxxviii 58 and Ezek viii. 3), and is, in each of the four, associated with the thought of "strange [gods]," "no-god," "idols" &c (6) A prohibition of idolatry would accord with the parallelism noted above between the Ode and Exod xxii 20 foll , which prohibits sacrifice to "any god save unto the Lord only."

[1] Ode xii. 8

[2] Dom Connolly adds, in a note, "The Syriac preposition 'in' may also be translated 'by' or 'with,' as the context requires"

and I believe that the Syriac of v. 8ᵇ is merely an attempt at translating literally καὶ τὰ ἄφωνα ἔμφωνα ἐγένετο"

We must carefully distinguish this conclusion from one that would accept the rendering "those that were silent *became in discourse,* or *converse,*" i.e discoursed or conversed together—taking *mellĕthā* to mean Logos, in a somewhat different sense (it is true) from *pethgāmā,* but still Logos. Dom Connolly (*a*) pins himself to φωνή as the ground for (*b*) an assonance between ἔμφωνα and ἄφωνα. " Similar assonances," he adds, "emerge in the most obvious way," namely (*c*) Ode xxi. 3 " grace and joy," which he would trace to an original χάριν καὶ χαράν, and (*d*) Ode xxx. 6 " And it (the fountain of living water) came *undefined and unseen...,*" where, he says, " the italicized words are quite literally ἀόριστος καὶ ἀόρατος..."

(*a*) If *mellĕthā* were the rendering of φωνή, should we not expect to find instances of this correspondence in the Thesaurus? But in the vast space devoted (coll. 2110—3) to the noun, it is said to represent λόγος, ῥῆμα, φθέγματα, λαλιά, and λέξις, but not once φωνή. Now φωνή is to be sharply distinguished from λόγος The Fourth Gospel says that John the Baptist is a φωνή, intending us to distinguish that φωνή from the Λόγος. Ignatius makes the same distinction. As a martyr, in Christ, he will be (he tells us) a *logos*; outside martyrdom, he will be a mere " cry " or φωνή[1]. Except in very special contexts, φωνή would not mean " speech " in the sense of " converse " or " discourse."

What the Poet means is that those aeons which were once silent, now at last, in the sphere of the redemptive Word, or Logos, became themselves λογικοί, or ἐν λόγῳ. The Fourth Gospel says " Whatever is called into existence in Him," *i e.* in the Logos, "was life" This Ode, distinguishing between the creative Logos and the redemptive Logos, says that the silent aeons "*became in the Logos*" in a new sense,

---

[1] See *Son of Man* **3628** *d.*

namely, "*in a harmonious concord or converse*,"—something very different from a mere φωνή or "cry[1]."

(*b*) As to the alleged assonance between ἔμφωνα and ἄφωνα, it is disposed of, if the preceding paragraph is correct, because the *thought* is not concerned with φωνή. But we may add that ἔμφωνος, according to the Greek Thesaurus, is not found in the sound text of any author earlier than Ælian (c 250 A D.).

(*c*) Ode xxi. 3 "grace and joy" is commented on as being "exactly χάριν καὶ χαράν." But are such assonances characteristic of the best Greek religious poetry? The LXX, at all events (which Dom Connolly believes to have been used by the Odist) though it contains many beautiful combinations of χάρις and of χαρά with other words, never combines the two[2].

§ 4. "*I believed, therefore I was at rest*[3]"

On this passage Dom Connolly says "I find it hard to believe that we have here a purely accidental coincidence with the LXX" His argument is as follows: "The Ode says, 'I believed, *therefore*,' in the same Syriac words which translate ἐπίστευσα διό in 2 Cor iv 13 (= Ps. cxv. 1[4]); while in the Psalm neither the Hebrew nor the Syriac version of it expresses 'therefore'"

---

[1] See *Johannine Grammar* **2596** And note Rom xii. 1 and 1 Pet. ii 2 λογικός, and Justin Martyr's frequent assumption that God, through the Logos, has made men λογικοί (*e g Apol* § 10) with a view to their redemption

[2] Another assonance is suggested, ἀόριστος καὶ ἀόρατος, as the original of Ode xxx 6 "[the fountain of living water] came *undefined and unseen*." Ἀόριστος is not among the score of epithets of the Spirit in Wisd. viii. 22—3, and it does not occur in the LXX, the N.T., the Apostolic Fathers or the Apologists. It is also often used in a bad sense. But I have found it in Clem Alex 857 applied to the love of God as being "unlimited" *Thes Syr* 2550 gives the Syriac word, with neg, as ἄπειρος and perhaps ἀπέραντος, but not as ἀόριστος.

[3] Ode xxviii. 4.   [4] Ps cxvi 10 in Heb and R.V

THE INTERPRETATION

But there are special circumstances to be considered. The Syriac of the Psalm has "I-believed *and* I spoke." Aquila has "*because* I shall speak." Field renders the Hebrew "*etiamsi* dicerem.*" Rashi has "*when* I spoke" (as also has R V. marg). R.V. text has "I believe, *for* I will speak" These facts suggest that the writer may be alluding to the quotation, not as being in the LXX, but as being *in an interpretation of the Psalm— one among many interpretations—familiar to Christians through the second Epistle to the Corinthians*, as though the writer said to himself, "The Apostle says that he believed *and therefore he burst forth into speaking*, but 'speaking' must be under the control of the Holy Spirit which must rest on the speaker, so that one might also say 'I believed *and therefore I attained rest*[1]'."

It may be argued that a Christian poet, writing in Hebrew, would not be likely to follow Paul in misquoting Hebrew Scripture. But he is not "misquoting", he is alluding and deliberately varying. We must try to understand the Jewish traditions about "believing" and "resting." They are worth noting here as they bear on other passages in the Odes which connect "belief" with "a song-of-glorifying," and in which we find, latent or expressed, the thought of crossing "great rivers" or passing along a "way" that is "levelled" for "believers" by the Lord—in other words, allusion to the crossing of the Red Sea and the Jordan[2]. The two acts of "crossing" were emblematic of a typical "entering into rest,"

---

[1] For an allusion in Ode vi. 17 to a phrase used in 1 Thess v. 12 see *Light on the Gospel* **3747** *h*

[2] Comp Ode xvi 5 "I am strong in His song-of-glorifying, and there is to-me *belief* in Him" with xli. 1 "A song-of-glorifying to the Lord [will be uttered by] all His offspring, and they will (?) pour-out-to-the-utmost (*or*, collect) the truth of His *belief*" Also comp xxii 7 "Thy hand hath levelled the way for them that *are-believing* in thee" with xxxix 4—11 "those who cross them [*i e* great rivers] in *belief* are not shaken .and a way has been appointed . for those who agree with (Harnack, *zustimmen*) the Way of His *belief*."

partially accomplished by Moses, but completely by Joshua (the first Jesus)

The Epistle to the Hebrews, after quoting—from the Psalms—"that they should not *enter into his rest*," says "We see that *they were not able to 'enter in' because of unbelief.*" Substitute "*I*" for "*they*," and take away the negatives, and we have exactly our Poet's thought —"*I was able to enter in because of belief*," or "*I believed, therefore I attained-rest*¹." Many thoughts like these are collected in the early commentary, called *Mechiltha*, on the words that precede the Song of the Red Sea —" And Israel saw...and they believed in the Lord and in his servant Moses. Then sang Moses and the children of Israel this song unto the Lord²." The Hebrew "believe" means radically "make firm," "make stedfast," and the commentary collects instances where this connection is indicated, as in Chronicles, "*Believe* (i e. make strong) and ye shall be *believable* (i.e. *made-strong*, R.V. *established*³)" There is the same play in the Ode here: "I *believed*, therefore (*lit.* because of that), I *attained-rest*: because *believable* is he in whom *I have believed.*" This "belief" implies stability, or "*rest*", and *Mechiltha* says that, as a reward for "*belief*," Abraham "inherited this world and the world to come," and "the Holy Spirit *rested* on Israel and they sang unto the Lord."

These thoughts appear to me to have been in the Poet's mind, when he wrote the words under discussion, "I believed, therefore I attained-rest" He was not thinking merely of the perplexing and disputed passage in the Psalm above quoted, nor merely of Paul's quotation of it, but partly also of those

---

¹ See Heb. III 11—IV 10, which deals with "*rest*" and "*unbelief.*" Note, too, the Christian allusion to the first "Jesus" in IV 8 "For if *Jesus* [*i e.* Joshua] had given them *rest.*"

² Exod XIV. 31—XV. 1

³ 2 Chr. xx 20. R V. finds the same play in Is. VII. 9 "If ye will not *believe*, surely ye shall not be *established*"

deep consequences of "belief" which were suggested by the Jewish traditions concerning the belief of Abraham before the birth of Isaac, and the belief of Israel at the Red Sea. "Israel burst out into song," the Poet might say, "Yes, but what followed? The Psalmist says, '*Then believed they his words, they sang his praise, they soon forgat his works*[1].' Let me rather think of Abraham, who '*believed*,' but did not '*forget*,' and who, as a reward, entered into the rest of Paradise, '*I believed, therefore also I entered-into-rest*[2].'"

It may be objected that this is far-fetched· "The Poet ought not to be supposed to have been *consciously* thinking of the Jewish traditions concerning the belief of Abraham. He was expressing his own inner experience, though naturally reminiscences of tradition &c. might accompany the sense of his own experience. To suppose more than this is to suppose what is not natural" My reply would be· "True, it *is* not 'natural' for *us now*. But it *was* 'natural' *then* for a poet in the first century, who not only called himself a son of Abraham but also still, even in the light of the Messiah, looked back on Abraham as the Rock of the Old Church, and as the first of the Fathers through whose name God revealed Himself to mankind, calling Himself 'the God of Abraham[3].'"

§ 5. "*Unto thee have I fled, my God*[4]"

It is alleged by Dom Connolly that the Hebrew words for "flee," and their Syriac equivalent, the word here used, are not, so far as he knows, "used metaphorically of fleeing for refuge to, taking refuge in, God, they regularly denote a real

---

[1] Ps. cvi 12—13.
[2] If it were asserted that, in this world, Abraham did *not* "enter into rest," the spiritual Jew would certainly deny this, as he does in *Mechiltha* See *Light on the Gospel* **3867** "he was at home with God," even when wandering in Palestine
[3] Gen. xxvi 24.
[4] Ode xxv 1.

local flight"; and he therefore asks "Is not this a translation of πρὸς σὲ κατέφυγον (cf Ps. cxlii 9)¹?"

But the Syriac word is used in the Hexapla as a rendering of "Many nations shall *flee* (καταφεύξονται) *unto the Lord*²." It does not mean merely "flee," but "flee-away," and is appropriately used of "fleeing-away" from the prison of a cruel Master to the House of Freedom³.

On the supposition that the Odist is quoting from the Psalm, we have to remember that the Hebrew "*I have hidden*" is quite exceptionally used with "unto thee." The Targum paraphrases the clause, the Syriac omits it The LXX κατέφυγον indicates that LXX read בסתי as נסתי "I *fled*" The root of the latter (נוס) is given by Trommius as meaning φεύγω 119 times and καταφεύγω 7 times⁴. If this is accepted, then the Hebrew *does here exceptionally use flee* "*metaphorically of fleeing for refuge to, taking refuge in, God,*" and Dom Connolly's objection falls to the ground⁵.

---

¹ Ps cxliii. 9, R.V. txt "I flee unto thee to hide me," marg "*Heb.* Unto thee have I hidden." Walton's Syriac omits the clause.

² Zech. ii 15 (11)

³ The Heb (Gesen 530—1) is simply used of strangers "attaching themselves" to the Lord in Is. lvi 3, Zech ii. 15, Jerem. l 5. The Syriac word used in the Ode, and in Zech. Hexapl , pulls out the notion of *deserting* from heathendom   See *Thes* 2997 quoting " ethnicos mores aufugiemus," Jo Eph ccxxiv 19

⁴ This reading is preferable to חסה "seek refuge" Gesen. 492 *a* says "בסתי. is error for חסיתי acc to LXX κατέφυγον SS." It adds "but חסה not constr wi אל־" It might have added "and חסה is never rendered φεύγω or καταφεύγω "

⁵ Comp Prov xviii. 10 "The name of the Lord is a strong tower; the righteous *runneth into it* and is safe." To me there seems much condensed beauty in the Masoretic reading "I hid unto thee," but translators would naturally paraphrase it.

THE INTERPRETATION

§ 6. *Why is the Greek word for "harp" always used in the Syriac version of the Odes?*

This question is asked by Dom Connolly in order to suggest the answer, "Because the Odes were written in Greek." But the facts do not suggest that answer, if we do not bind ourselves to a hypothesis that the Odist adhered to some rule about the rendering of the two Hebrew words for stringed instruments, *nebhel* and *kinnōr*, in the Syriac version of the Psalms, a rule that varies according as the two words stand singly, or, as often, coupled[1]. The Odist never couples such words He uses but one word for harp, and this four times, namely, a Syriac transliteration of the Greek κιθάρα

This Syriac *kithra* is found in eight instances (or practically five) in O T.[2] In the first instance it represents the Heb. *kinnōr*, occurring in the passage describing Jubal's invention of the "*harp*" and "pipe[3]" There it seems to represent stringed instruments as "pipe" represents wind instruments. In Samuel, mentioning "*psaltery (nebhel)*, timbrel (*tōph*), pipe, and harp (*kinnōr*)," Syr has *kithra* for *nebhel*[4] So it has in the next instance, "Rejoice in the Lord, O ye righteous Give thanks unto the Lord with the harp· sing praises unto him with

---

[1] It may be added that Aquila and the rest differ both from the LXX and from one another in their renderings of these words. Trommius gives *nebhel* (in the musical sense) as κιθάρα (1), νάβλη (13), ναύλη (1), νέβελ (2), ὄργανον (2), ψαλμός (1), ψαλτήριον (7) In Ben Sira xxxix 15 (? corrupt) "songs of nebhel and instruments of strings (?)," LXX has ἐν ᾠδαῖς χειλέων καὶ ἐν κινύραις, Syr. "cum laudibus, gratiarum actione, et elata voce," in *ib* xl. 21 "nebhel," LXX has ψαλτήριον, Syr. *epōdos* from the Greek ἐπῳδός (*Thes.* 331)

[2] *Thes* gives Gen iv 21, 1 S. x. 5, Ps xxxiii 2, lxxxi. 2, Dan iii 5, 7. Walton gives it also in Dan iii. 10, 15 Dan iii 5—15 contains *verbatim* repetitions, so as to be practically one passage.

[3] Gen iv 21 The Pesh Syr renders "pipe" by *kinnōr*, either misrendering the text, or having a different text

[4] 1 S. x 5 Syr. also has *kinnōr* to represent *tōph*, "timbrel"

the *psaltery* (*nebhel*) of ten strings[1]," and in the next, "Take ye up the psalm, and give [forth the sound of] the timbrel, the pleasant harp (*kinnōr*) with the *psaltery* (*nebhel*)[2]" On this passage, the Midrash on *Tehillim* quotes a tradition of R Asi, quoted by Rashi as from R Simeon: "Why is it called *nebhel*? Because it *makes-foolish* (i.e *stultifies*, or *puts to shame*, a form of *nbl*) all [other] kinds of music" Rashi quotes this in a context that indicates a belief that the *nebhel* represented a fuller and grander music than that of the *kinnōr*. In both of these Psalms, the music is not that of an individual worshipper, but that of the nation. They are songs of Israel full of allusions to the Exodus and to the passage of the Red Sea—latent for Gentiles but manifest to the most degenerate Jew[3].

I can see no reason why the author of the Odes should not have used the Hebrew *nebhel* and the Syriac translator rendered it as *kithra* The Thesaurus (3613) gives a picture of this *kithra* as an instrument with ten strings, and this suits the general thought of the Odes, though we must not suppose that the Odist alludes to it literally when he speaks of "a harp of many voices[4]."

---

[1] Ps xxxiii. 1—2   A V. "the psaltery [and] an instrument of ten strings"

[2] Ps lxxxi 2

[3] Comp Ps xxxiii 7 "He gathereth the waters of the sea as an *heap*" (on which see Rashi) with Exod xv 8 "as an *heap*," and Ps xxxiii. 17 "a *horse* is a vain thing" with Exod xv 1 "the *horse* and his rider" (on which see *Light on the Gospel* **3795** *a*)   Also note the reference to the Exodus in Ps lxxxi 5 "He appointed it in Joseph for a testimony when he went out over the land of Egypt"   See Philo (i. 374—5) who after quoting Exod xv. 1 "the horse and his rider," enters into the allegory of the "lyre" as denoting the harmony of the righteous soul   And Clement of Alexandria (784) says that "the people that is in the act of being saved" may be called a "harp," when "under the inspiration (ἐπίπνοιαν) of the Word and the recognition of God, it glorifies [God]."

[4] See *Light on the Gospel* **3792** *c*   I have said little about the transliteration of κιθάρα in the Aramaic of Daniel iii. 5—15 because Levy gives

THE INTERPRETATION

§ 7. *Alleged translation from Greek words with privative alpha*

(*a*) The first of these is Ode xii. 5 "for the swiftness of the Word is *indescribable*," lit. "without recounting". This Dom Connolly identifies with ἀνεκδιήγητος. But the Syriac for "without" is really a form of the negative preceded by the relative ("that not"), a form also frequent in New Hebrew. The Syriac may sometimes be used, as will be seen below, to express a Hebrew original like Ps. cxlvii 5 "To His [*i.e.* God's] understanding *there-is-not number*"—though in that particular passage the Syriac follows the Hebrew. The instances of "*there-was-not* (or, *there-is-not*) *number*" are very frequent in Hebrew. In very few of these does the LXX use ἀναρίθμητος[1]. So frequent is the Hebraic phrase "there is no number" that in the present passage we may regard it as pointing to a Hebrew, as against a Greek, original. And if it should be urged that "*number*" is not the same thing as "*recounting*," we may reply that the Hebrew verb whence "number" is derived means "count," "recount," "relate," and that the noun itself is recognised by Gesenius as capable of meaning "*recounting*," or "*relation*[2]"

no reason to suppose that it could be used in Hebrew. Nor is there space to discuss Joseph *Ant* vii 12 3 ἡ μὲν κινύρα δέκα χορδαῖς ἐξημμένη τύπτεται πλήκτρῳ, ἡ δὲ νάβλα δώδεκα φθόγγους ἔχουσα τοῖς δακτύλοις κρούεται Is there any difference between χορδαί and φθόγγοι? The Psalms speak of "ten strings," where does Josephus find "twelve"? "Twelve strings" would favour Clement's view that the "lyre" meant the "twelve" tribes of Israel, the whole harmonious "people (λαός)." But I have found no such allusion

[1] This may be seen by comparing the numerous instances of "no number" in Gesen. 708—9 with ἀναρίθμητος and ἀριθμός in the LXX Concordance Sometimes the Heb is preceded by "until" or "to," *e.g.* 1 Chr xxii. 4 "and cedar trees *to* there was no number," καὶ ξύλα κέδρινα, οὐκ ἦν ἀριθμός, where the LXX makes no attempt to render the preposition.

[2] Gesen. 707—9, quoting Judg. vii. 15 R.V. "telling," but Gesen. "recounting," where the LXX has ἐξήγησιν, Luc. διήγησιν. This resembles ἀνεκδιήγητος, when stripped of its negative On Ps xix. 1 "the

Note the following instances of the Hebrew "there-is-not":—Deut. xxxii 4 "a God of faithfulness *and there-is-not iniquity*," LXX καὶ οὐκ ἔστιν ἀδικία, with v.r. additional ἐν αὐτῷ, Syr *et non est* iniquus, Jerem v 21 "hear ye this, people foolish and (lit.) *there-is-no heart*," LXX ἀκάρδιος, Targ and Syr. as Heb., but *Syr. substitutes the relative for "and"*, Ps. civ 25 "creeping things *and there-is-no number*," LXX ὧν οὐκ ἔστιν ἀριθμός, Targ as Heb, but Syr., *without* ἔστιν, "*that-not*"—*the form* ("dlâ'") *being the same as in Ode* xii 5, Exod xxi. 11 "she shall go out free *there-is-no money*," LXX ἄνευ ἀργυρίου, Onk "*with-not* money," Jer. Targ and Syr "*that-not* money", Jerem. ii 32 "days *there-is-no number*," LXX ὧν οὐκ ἔστιν ἀριθμός, Targ. *dlâ'*, but Syr. rel ("*d*") with negative verb, Hos. iii. 4 (rep. five times) "The children of Israel shall abide many days, *there-is-no* prince, and *there-is-no* sacrifice..." LXX rep. οὐκ ὄντος, Targ. as Heb, but Syr. *dlâ'* ("*that-not*") as in Ode xii 5.

These facts shew that the Syriac *dlâ'*, though it may often represent the Greek privative *alpha* in later Syriac literature, cannot be relied on as representing *alpha* in any earlier literature that may reasonably be supposed to be affected by the Hebrew Bible The weight of the Greek *alpha* is altogether overbalanced by the weight of the Hebrew "*there-is-not*."

Nor does the case for the Hebrew stop here. Less than half of it has been represented. Gesenius (pp 519—20)[1]

heavens are *recounting* the glory of God," LXX διηγοῦνται, the Midrash (Wu. p. 171) implies that it *cannot* be "recounted," quoting Ps. lxv. 1 in the form "To thee silence is praise" Comp. Ps. lxxi. 15 "My mouth shall recount thy righteousness...for I *know not the recountings*," i e. the numbers thereof (Gesen. 708 *b*).

[1] See also Gesen p. 115 for instances of a preposition connected with *bal*, "not," and with the thought of defect or failure, as in Ps. lxiii. 1 "a dry land *without* water." This word is accountable (Trommius, Heb Index, p. 19) for the *alpha* privative in ἀγνωσία (1), ἀκουσίως (1), ἀδίκως (1), ἄνυδρος (1). In such cases, a detachable Syriac negative is naturally to be explained as from Hebrew, not from Greek.

gives a multitude of instances where the Hebrew "not"—either as "*lo'*" or as *blo'* ("in-not" or "with-not")—is represented in phrases that have gone far beyond the limits of the Greek *alpha*, e.g "they made me jealous with *a not-God*," "with *a not-people*," "rejoice in a *not-thing*" (i.e a thing of naught), "a morning *not-clouds*" (i.e. cloudless), "a waste *not-path*" (i.e. pathless). In these cases LXX seldom has *alpha* privative and often has a confused rendering. The Hebrew use is especially frequent when the negative is preceded by the preposition meaning "in" or "with," "*in-not* righteousness," "*in-not* justice," "*with-not* price," *i.e.* gratuitously

(*b*) Dom Connolly lays special stress on the phrase "*without* (lit. *that-not*) grudging" in Ode xi. 6 translated by Dr Harris (in the Introduction to his second edition, p. 47) "Speaking waters touched my lips from the fountain of God *without grudging* (i e *abundantly*)[1]" Here, and in Ode vii 3 "He caused me to know Himself *without grudging*," and xx 7 "Put on the grace of the Lord *without grudging*," Dom Connolly maintains that the Syriac is "quite inadequate to express 'liberally,' 'freely,'" *which he infers to be the real meaning* "from the requirements of the context and from the literal correspondence of the Syriac phrase to ἀφθόνως." The Syriac expression, he adds, "is found as a translation of ἄφθονος, ἀφθόνως, in 4 Macc. iii. 10 (ἀφθόνους πηγάς), and Wisd. vii. 13; and the crudeness of the Syriac in the former case is paralleled by the passages in the Odes"

This argument appears to ignore the following facts. (1) In special contexts, the Greek ἄφθονος, applied to things, may mean "without grudging." (2) There is probably such a special context in Wisdom, but not in Maccabees. (3) Philo, as has been pointed out above, uses ἄφθονος with allusion to sayings of Plato about God's freedom from envy.

---

[1] Dr Harris has "plenteously" in his text of the second edition (p. 105), which also has (correctly) "fountain of the Lord" (not "fountain of God").

(4) Philo, in connection with the Tree of Life mentioned in Gen. iii. 22 "And now lest he [*i.e.* man] put forth his hand, and take also of the tree of life, and eat, and live for ever," defends God from the charge of "*envy*" or "*grudging*." (5) In Wisd vii. 13 "I learned without guile and impart her [*i.e.* Wisdom] *without grudging* (ἀφθόνως)," the English version, while giving in its text "*liberally*," has in its margin, "or, *without envy*, as in ch. vi. 23." The reference is to "I will bring the knowledge of her [*i.e.* of Wisdom] into light, and will not pass by the truth, neither will I go along with wasting *envy*." (6) Irenaeus, replying to the question "Was not God able to bring forth Man from the beginning perfect?" says that He bestows what is good "*ungrudgingly*[1]." (7) Tertullian—apparently following the thought noted above in Philo—describes the devil, in connection with the prohibition to eat of the Tree, as representing that God "*envied* men the property of divinity[2]." (8) Clement of Alexandria contrasts the Lord, whom "*envy* does not touch," with "another," whom he describes as "*the envier*," in allusion to God and the devil, and to the eating of the tree[3].

These facts should be combined with those in the Odes where "*no grudging*," or "*no envying*," is connected with "*knowing the Lord*," with "*the speaking water from the fountain of the Lord*," with "putting on [oneself] the grace of the Lord. and coming into Paradise, and making a crown from His tree," and with "*the knowledge* of the Most High." Thus combined, they seem to me to go beyond indication and to approach demonstration For the conclusion as to *thought*, in this paragraph, must be distinguished from the conclusion as to *word*, *i.e.* the verbal origin, whether Greek or

---

[1] Iren iv 38. 1—3
[2] *Adv. Marcion* ii. 10
[3] See Clem Alex. 832, on which see Mayor quoting Theoph. *Aut* ii 25 "not as though *grudging* (φθονῶν)—as some suppose—did God command him not to eat of knowledge."

399

THE INTERPRETATION

Hebrew, of the Syriac negations above enumerated. As to the latter, the verbal question, I do not assert that Hebrew origin is proved, but I do venture to assert that Greek origin is not proved nor even made probable. As to the former—the thought—no doubt whatever is left on my mind that the Poet is not thinking of an "*abundant*" or "*plentiful*" fruit of knowledge, or water of knowledge. Like Philo and the author of Wisdom, and the early Christian Fathers—and like Plato too—he is exulting in the revelation that the All-sufficing Father not only gives but also gives "*without grudging.*"

§ 8. *The use of the Syriac relative after substantives to express possession* [*See also* § 14]

(*a*) It is alleged that "in original compositions by the best Syriac writers," a suffix would suffice to represent possession, *e.g.* "my-right-hand" in one word But the Odes have, in at least one passage, "the right-hand *that-is-to-me*[1]." This is a form that "should not be used (in cases where a possessive suffix is grammatically possible) except to give some sort of prominence to the possessor or to emphasize the fact of possession."

(*b*) It is alleged that "there is no obvious reason for emphasis— 'my own'—here." This "indiscriminate employment after a noun, and equivalent to μου, αὐτοῦ, in the same position, is frequent in translations from Greek (though not in the earliest) but is hardly met with in native Syriac works."

(*c*) It is then alleged that this usage in the Odes cannot be explained from Hebrew. "I cannot think that a Syriac translation from Hebrew of, say, the third or fourth century, would have contained these anomalous constructions; for Hebrew has no detachable possessive particle and relies entirely upon suffixes"

(*d*) Eight examples of this "unidiomatic use" in the Odes are given by Dom Connolly.

---

[1] Ode viii. 21, on which see pp. 401—2, n. 2, and below, § 14.

(*a*) First, as to the style of the Odes, no one, I think, maintains—certainly I do not—that their Syriac resembles that of "original compositions by the best Syriac writers." My view—which I held subject to correction from further evidence—was that it is early Syriac of an uncouth and rudimentary character, and not an "original composition" in Syriac, but translated from Hebrew. The language of the Syriac Odes appeared to me to present more resemblance to the pre-literary Syriac Versions of O T than to literary Syriac, but on this point the reader is referred to § 14 below.

(*b*) Secondly, as to "no obvious emphasis" in the particular passage quoted above, I should be disposed to say that the emphasis is as obvious and as characteristic as in many passages of the Fourth Gospel where Jesus speaks of "my sheep," "my peace," "my love," "my kingdom[1]." The context breathes of God's Fatherly appropriation of men as His own —

"For I do not turn my face from *my own*. Because I know them, and before they came into being I observed them (*or*, reviewed them) and their faces [too] [Yea] I (*emph*) sealed them (*emph*) I (*emph*) framed their members, and *my own* breasts did I prepare for them, that they might drink *my own* holy milk, that they might live thereby I was well pleased in them, and am not ashamed of them For *my own* work are they and the strength of my designs Who therefore will rise up against my work, or who will there be that is not compliant with them? [It was] I [that] willed by my good pleasure and [thereby] formed and fashioned the understanding and the heart, and they are verily *my own*, and *on my own right hand* have I set my elect[2]."

---

[1] Jn x 26, xiv 27, xv 9, xviii 36 In O T comp Cant. i. 6 "*Mine own* vineyard," better rendered in viii 12 "*Mine own* vineyard, [the vineyard] *that is mine*" It is appropriate in Songs of Solomon.

[2] Ode viii. 15—21, as translated in *Light on the Gospel* 3797—817

(c) In the next place, the statement that "Hebrew has no detachable possessive particle and relies entirely upon suffixes," though true, is liable to mislead if it causes us to ignore the influence likely to be exerted on translations from Hebrew by the Hebrew use of the relative with the dative pronoun to denote possession. The Hebrew "qui [erat *or* est]" with dative ("*'asher-l'*") is represented in New Hebrew by *shel*, which corresponds in some respects to the Aramaic and Syriac forms in which the relative *d* corresponds to the relative *sh*. The full Hebrew phrase is very widely used. The instances given by Gesenius under the heading of the Hebrew datival preposition all refer to sacred things appropriated to Jehovah, or to Aaron His priest, or to His altar, or to Jehovah's people for whom a sacrifice is to be offered[1]. Hence it might well be used in Hebrew Songs to express

"*My own* right hand" is capable of meaning "*my own* right hand which is not like that of an earthly king." Somewhat similarly a distinction of royalty is indicated by this construction of the relative in Hebrew, Targum, and Syriac, but not in LXX, in the instructions given by David for the coronation of Solomon (1 K 1 33) "Set him upon the mule *that is mine* (lit *that is to me*)." Here the LXX has (as one might expect) the reduplicated article, not the relative. But the Syriac follows the Hebrew, as also does the Targum, only substituting for the Heb *'asher-l* respectively the Syriac and Aramaic equivalents.

[1] See Gesen 513 *b* referring to Exod xxix 29, xxxix 1, 39, Lev vii. 20, 21, xvi 6, 15. In these cases, however, the ordinary possessive suffix could not be used, so that the relative phrase was necessary. For others see Gesen 83 *a*, noting the correspondence of the Biblical *'asher-l* to *shel* which is "in habitual use" in New Hebrew, "as a mark of the genitive."

Schlatter, on Jn 1 41, τὸν ἀδελφὸν τὸν ἴδιον, calls attention to the emphatic use of *shel* ("*his own* son and not another's") in *Mechilt*. (Wu p 277, on Exod xxi 31 (Schl. by error xxi 28)) In *Aboth* (ii 2) "Rabban Gamliel (lit.) his son [*the son*] *that* [*belongs*] *to* R Jehudah ha-Nasi" is perhaps unique (instead of the usual *ben* followed by the name of the father) Has it anything to do with the fact that R Jehudah (Taylor) "is said (*Kethuboth* 103 *b*)" to have nominated *his own* son to succeed him as Nasi? See below (§ 12) for further details on *shel*, also Gesen 979 on the relative *sh-*, as being probably not an abbreviation but "an original demonstrative particle," but "in usage, limited to late Hebrew" (not used in the Prophets, exc Jonah and Lamentations)

divine appropriation or possession as above mentioned, and, if so used in Hebrew, it would naturally be retained in an early literal Syriac translation[1] *Shel*, with various suffixes, occurs no less than thrice (*e g. shellî*, "quod [est] mihi") in the short Song of Solomon, and probably once in the Song of Jacob[2] There is also an instance elsewhere of *shel* with 1st pers. pl. suffix, meaning "[eorum] qui [sunt] nobis[3]" It is true that the use of *shel* in Solomon's Song is not an exact parallel. For it supplements, and is not a substitute for, the possessive suffix Nevertheless it may prepare us for finding in a first-century Hebrew original of the Odes of Solomon somewhat strange combinations of Old and New Hebrew with Aramaic idiom. But in any case the evidence of the LXX, so far as it goes, points to the conclusion that in the Syriac version, the use of the detachable possessive particle would be in accordance with a development of Hebrew precedent and not derivable from anything correspondent in Greek[4]

(*d*) I pass to Dom Connolly's eight instances of the unidiomatic expression

(1) Ode viii 21 "and at my right hand" This has been shewn above to mean "my own right hand," and therefore to be in accordance with Syriac idiom [But see p 432 foll]

---

[1] Besides 1 K 1 33 quoted above, note 2 K xvi 13 "the peace offerings that were his own," *i e* his own idolatrous invention, where the Targ and the Syr follow the Hebrew, but the LXX has the reduplicated article So, too, in Cant 1 6, viii 12 "my vineyard, *that which is mine*" (where the Hebrew has the shorter form *shel*) the Syr also has the relative and dative, but the LXX has (1) ἐμός, (2) μου ἐμός

[2] Cant 1 6, iii 7, viii 12, Gen xlix 10 (on which see p. 428)

[3] 2 K vi 11 "Who of [those] that [belong] to us [is] on-the-side-of (*lit* toward) the king of Israel?" (Gesen 513 *b*)

[4] Gesen 980 *a*, comparing Heb *shel* with the corresponding Syriac, quotes Lk vi 42 "*my* words," as having the emphatic possessive "my words that are to me" This must be an error for Lk ix 26 But there Walton gives only the ordinary suffix, and Burkitt gives "ashamed of me, before men, and of *them that are mine.*" In the parall Mk viii 38 Burkitt gives the ordinary suffix In Jn x 26, xiv. 27 &c. SS has the detachable suffix, but omits it in other places where the emphasis would justify it.

THE INTERPRETATION

(ii) Ode xi 18 "in thy land." The right rendering is "in *the land that is thine own*." There is a contrast, throughout the Ode, between "the folly that is diffused *over the earth*," man's abode, and the fruitfulness of the abode prepared above by God, God's *own* abode, or "Paradise"—called "*thy* Paradise," "*His* Paradise." This contrast finds expression here. It is said of the evil and corrupt, "They have changed *from darkness into light…from wickedness to the pleasantness that is thine own*; and they turned away the bitterness of the trees from themselves as soon as they were planted in *the land that is thine own*[1]."

(iii) Ode xii 4 "of thy beauty." "Thy" is an error for "his," and Dr Harris's rendering "His own beauty" appears to me to express the Poet's emphasis on the contrast between the beauty above and the beauty below, and also the feeling that all true beauty comes as God's "own" gift.

(iv) and (v) Ode xvii. 12—13 "in my love" and "my blessing." The Messiah is here speaking describing Himself as "the door of everything," and as going to "loose" the "bondmen" whom He calls "His" ("my bondmen"). In such a context, both of the alleged phrases appear to be parallel in their emphasis to Johannine emphatic phrases, such as "the peace that is mine" and "the love that is mine," which might be rendered by the emphatic Syriac form in question[2]. Ought not these parallelisms to lead us to reflect that perhaps the same reason that makes the emphatic ἐμός

---

[1] In Jn xvii 17 "*thy word* (ὁ λόγος ὁ σός) is truth," Syr Walton (but not SS) has "thy word [the word] that [is] thine."

[2] Jn xiv 27 εἰρήνην τὴν ἐμήν, SS and Walton "peace [the peace] that [is] mine." So Jn xviii 36 (Walton) "my kingdom [the one] that [is] mine" (SS missing). But in Jn xv. 9 (Walton) "my love [the love] that [is] mine," SS has "my love." Jn uses ἐμός in these passages with the article. But it is without the article in Jn iv 34 ἐμὸν βρῶμα, where SS and Walton have "my food [the food] that [is] mine." Ἐμός occurs but twice in the whole of the Epistle to the Romans, whereas it occurs thrice in the brief Epistle to Philemon.

so frequent in John, who uses it nearly four times as often as all the Synoptists taken together, may also make the emphatic possessives frequent in the Odes? The Odes, like the Fourth Gospel, are pervaded with the thought of personality—the close personal relations between Man and his Redeemer The Lord is regarded as saying to those whom He has redeemed "Ye are *my own*," and each redeemed soul as echoing back to the Redeemer "*my own*—yes, thou, too, art my own[1]"

(vi) Ode xxv. 2 "and my helper." The context appears to justify us in finding emphasis here: "I was rescued from my bonds and unto thee, O God, did I flee; for thou art the right hand of my Salvation and *the Helper* (lit.) *that is mine own*," i e. the Helper that will never desert me, but will be mine for ever It has been pointed out above[2] that the words may imply that the redeemed soul is closely united with the Redeemer.

(vii) Ode xxvi 2 "His holy song." The context implies that the mouth of the Poet can sing the song that belongs to God because the Poet himself is God's · " I poured out praise unto the Lord, *because I am His own*, and I will speak the holy psalm *that is His* because my *heart is toward Him*" Moreover the passage resembles passages like those that speak of "*the holy garments of Aaron*," where Hebrew, Targum, LXX and Syriac, might all naturally have the relative[3]. Either of these causes would suffice to defend the relative here on the supposition that the passage is translated from Hebrew.

(viii) Ode xxviii. 9 "but my [suffering of] wrong." This instance differs from all the rest and admits perhaps of

---

[1] Compare the first verse of the first Ode, "The Lord is on my head like a crown, nor shall I be apart from Him," with the last of the last Ode, "They are free men, and they are mine."

[2] See § 5 above.

[3] Comp Exod xxix. 29 where all have the relative, see above, p 402, n 1.

THE INTERPRETATION

a different explanation. The Thesaurus alleges no instance where the word is used with a genitive or possessive suffix, but gives the impression that "*my wrong,*" *if expressed by the mere possessive suffix,* would mean "*my wrong-doing*" (like ἀδικία μου in Greek)[1] For this reason the Poet may write exceptionally "the wrong that [is] to me," meaning "the wrong done to me[2]"

These instances do not necessarily point to a New Hebrew original, although the Syriac idiom is more like New Hebrew than Greek, but on the other hand they do not indicate that the original was Greek. Other instances may perhaps be alleged in future studies of the Odes proving Dom Connolly's conclusion. But these, in my opinion, do not prove it[3].

§ 9 "*Until it was given in the midst*[4]"

Dom Connolly argues that these words "could not be a translation from Hebrew, since they contain an unsemitic

---

[1] See *Thes.* 1478. It gives a feminine form of the word, with a 3rd pers pl possess suffix, as meaning "eorum fraudes," *i.e* the wrongs they had *done*

[2] For a similar Hebrew use of *shel* to denote the objective genitive, see *Jebam.* xi 7 (Mishna) (lit) "For *his-striking* and for *his-cursing that* [*belongs*] *to* (*shel*) this [man] and *that* [*belongs*] *to* that [man]," meaning "For striking and for cursing this man or that" The "his" refers not to the striker but to the stricken (see *Jewish Qu Rev* July 1908, p 728).

[3] I have confined myself to Dom Connolly's instances, and am far from asserting that all the detachable possessives in the Odes can be explained on the ground of emphasis But many can, that do not at first seem emphatic, *e g* Ode xvii 13 "and I sowed *my fruits* in hearts, and transformed them in myself"—(see *Light on the Gospel* **3874** *b*)—"and they received *the blessing that is mine* and lived" Here it may be said that there is no more emphasis on "*my* blessing" than on "*my* fruits." I differ There appears to me to be climax as regards emphasis on personality In the first clause there is some emphasis on "fruits," which (*Light* **3874** *b*) means "my *fruitful seed*" The meaning is "I first sowed my fruitful seed in hearts Thus I transformed them—in myself—into my own nature And thus they received *the blessing that belongs to my nature*, and passed into life eternal." [See p. 432 foll.]

[4] Ode xxx 6

idiom, viz, εἰς τὸ μέσον τιθέναι, *in medio ponere,*" and he adds "Dr Abbott adduces from Numb. xxx 5 the phrase 'in the middle', but there a real local 'middle,' of a carefully specified area, is in question¹" But besides Numb. xxxv. 5, there are other instances of the Hebrew "*in the midst*" (which corresponds to the Syriac²) used absolutely, in such a way as to indicate that it could be employed in New Hebrew absolutely, in a context where a locality is not expressed but only implied³ And the Ode does imply locality. It begins with the words "Fill ye waters for yourselves from the living fountain of the Lord . and come.. and rest by the fountain of the Lord...it gives rest to the soul." Now "rest," in the Odes, implies Paradise—that place of beauty and fruitfulness about which it is said in Revelation that "*in the midst* of the open-place thereof (πλατείας)...there was a river of water of life⁴" Unfortunately the text in Isaiah about idolaters, and "gardens," and "*in the midst,*" is disputed ; but in any case it is an instance of the absolute use of "*in the midst*⁵." Rashi takes it as meaning "*in the midst* of the garden," and Ibn Ezra either thus or as "*in the midst* of the idolaters." Either interpretation would, by antithesis, illustrate the present passage In New Hebrew, this word for "midst" may mean "the inner" as distinct from "the outer" nature⁶, so that there may also be an undercurrent of meaning Not only is the

---

¹ *Journ. Theol Stud* p 531. I adduced Numb xxxv. 5 (not xxx 5)
² The Syriac word is derived from μέσος, which also exists as a form of New Hebrew as well as Aramaic
³ *In the midst*" is used absolutely in Gen. xv 10, Numb. xxxv 5, Josh viii 22 (*lit.* "to Israel *in the midst*"), Judg. xv 4, Is lxvi 17. Of these, only Numb. xxxv 5 and Is lxvi. 17 point to locality. But they are sufficient to shew that the absolute use of the phrase in New Hebrew must have been very early Delitzsch uses it absolutely in Mt xiv 6, Mk iii 3, Mk xiv 60, Lk. vi. 8, for ἐν τῷ μέσῳ and εἰς τὸ μέσον and εἰς μέσον.
⁴ Rev. xxii 1—2 For the connection between "*rest*" and "*Paradise*" in the Odes, see *Light on the Gospel* 3847—83, and especially 3859—64.
⁵ Is lxvi. 17.
⁶ Levy iv 631 *b*, 641 *b*, and i 256 *b*.

THE INTERPRETATION

"fountain" set as God's gift, "in the midst[1]" of Paradise so that it flows forth to all therein, but it also flows "undefined and unseen," like the Spirit in the "heart," "midst," or "inward" man—so that "until it was given *in the midst* [of the heart] they did not know it[2]"

This is perhaps too subtle. But an interpretation without any play on words and simply taking "in the midst" to mean "in the midst of Paradise," seems to me far more likely than one that bases itself on an original εἰς τὸ μέσον τιθέναι of which the usual meaning would be "set a prize before all, for all to contest," "propose," "bring forward in public," "make a public contribution." And the use of "give" for "*ponere*" would in itself favour Hebraic origin.

§ 10 "*He was known from before the* (*lit.*) *casting-down of the aeon*"

I pass to a tenth instance, previously alleged by Dom Connolly from Ode xli. 16, which he renders "*from before the constitution of the world*[3]." The words are, he assumes, a Syriac translation of πρὸ καταβολῆς κόσμου used by the Odist writing in Greek. Καταβολὴ κόσμου occurs ten times in N T. In seven out of ten cases the Peshitta renders it by the phrase used in the Ode here, "*the casting-down of the aeon.*" It is not a phrase used in Hebrew Hebrew prefers "*founding*, or *establishing*, or *creating*, the earth, or the habitable-world." Nor is the phrase used by *Syr. vet* "Syriac," we are told, "has other words, corresponding to the Hebrew ones, to express

---

[1] Comp Jerem xxxi 33 "I will give [*i e* set as a gift] my law in their inward parts," where the LXX also has "give," but the Syr has not.

[2] See *Son of Man* 3362 (1) *a—c* for ambiguities and plays of words on "*midst*," and comp Origen (*Comm* Joann vi 15 on Jn 1. 26) "there standeth one *in the midst of* you whom ye know not," that is, "*invisible* in His divine nature (ἀόρατος τῇ θειότητι αὐτοῦ), being present with every human being and coextensive with the whole universe in its every part" Also note the saying in the Oxyrhynchian Logia "I stood *in the midst* of the world"

[3] *The Journal of Theological Studies*, Vol XIV, p 315.

'foundation'." The conclusion is thus put: "How then does it come into the Odes? Obviously as a Syriac translation of πρὸ καταβολῆς κόσμου by one who was familiar with the usual Peshitta version of this phrase."

This seemed to me, at the first reading, irresistible. And it still seems to me stronger than any of Dom Connolly's other instances But in view of the fact that those other instances (in my opinion) point to a Hebrew rather than to a Greek original, and that they include no other alleged instance of allusion to the Peshitta, I was led to examine the subject more thoroughly, and to ask whether we could find any passage in Scripture that represents or suggests a picture of the Creator as preparing for the foundation of the world by some kind of "casting-down." If we could, it appeared to me that we should be justified in concluding that this alleged single instance affords no proof of a Greek original, or of a translation taken from the Peshitta.

A fallacy seems to me to lie in the assumption that a Christian writer in Hebrew at the end of the first century could not be aware of the Christian use of a remarkable phrase like καταβολὴ κόσμου, which, as we shall see, was variously interpreted in early times The Greek might be rendered literally, "casting-down"—in connection with God's "*casting-down,*" or "*laying-down,*" of the ground-plan of Creation or "the aeon." That is what καταβολή means here. But καταβολή may mean "casting-down" in the sense of "destruction," and it is so rendered, in the only instance in which Justin Martyr uses it, in T. & T. Clark's translation ("destruction of the Tower"). There was therefore a temptation to paraphrase it. Latin translators called it *constitutio*. Early Syriac translators paraphrased it in various ways, and conformed the phrase to the thought of Biblical Hebrew. But the Greek phrase might be taken in a poetic and allusive sense, and our Poet (I contend) took it thus, and used it literally, poetically, and allusively. Some centuries afterwards

THE INTERPRETATION

the translators of the Peshitta took it literally, and (probably) not poetically. That is to say, they resorted to this Syriac word merely as a safe and literal translation of a term that they knew to be variously interpreted (as it was for example by Origen and others) Perhaps they regarded it as meaning "established" or "founded" But our Poet apparently does not This appears from the fact that, when he means "established" or "founded," he uses other words[1]

The following facts shew that the phrase probably attracted attention in early times:

(1) There is no passage in the Gospels where two Evangelists agree in assigning this phrase to Jesus

(2) Where Matthew quotes it as part of a Psalm, Matthew has "*from the casting-down,*" and some readings of Matthew have "*from the casting-down of the world* (cosmos)"; but the Psalm, in the Hebrew, has "*from beforetime,*" and, in the Greek, "*from the beginning*[2]."

(3) Where Luke speaks of blood "*shed from the casting-down of the cosmos,*" Matthew has "*shed upon the earth,*" which suggests that an original "*from the casting-down*" was misunderstood by Matthew as meaning "from the casting-down [on the earth] of Abel's blood" and expanded by Luke by adding "of the cosmos" so as to make the meaning clear[3].

---

[1] Odes xxii 12 (Harnack) "Grundlage," xxxv 5 "Fundament," xxxviii. 17 "Fundament," use a word (*Thes* 4348) that has no connection with the word we are considering, viz "casting-down" Our word is used also of (*Thes* 3928) "casting' or "depositing" seed in the earth (and also in Heb xi 11 VHh)

[2] Mt xiii 35, quoting Ps lxxviii 2 Why did Matthew use this paraphrase? Perhaps because, in view of various renderings of the Hebrew, he wished to express the thought of what Jerome calls, not "fundamentum" but "initium fundamenti" Horace might think of it as the rubble, so to speak, cast into the depth of the waters, to prepare a basis for a foundation (comp Hor *Carm.* iii 1 34—5 "jactis in altum molibus, huc frequens caementa demittit redemptor")

[3] Lk. xi 50, Mt. xxiii 35 ἐπὶ τῆς γῆς. Matthew would no doubt be influenced by the repeated mention of γῆ in Gen iv. 10—12.

(4) The Hebrew *kedem* which means "*beforetime*" is rendered in LXX once "*before the aeons*", and, when "from" is added, "from beforetime" is once rendered "*before* [*the*] *aeon* (*sing*)"[1].

(5) Epictetus bids us regard man as our brother, "who has Zeus for his ancestor, and is, as it were, son from the same *seed* and from the same *casting-down* from above[2]" There is a similar connection certainly in the Epistle to the Hebrews (καταβολὴ σπέρματος), and perhaps in Clement of Rome[3].

(6) Origen and Chrysostom take καταβολή as "*casting-down*[4]." Jerome[5] explains it from the phrase "cast (jaciunt) foundations," and points out that *the Latin "constitutio" does not exactly express the meaning*, which is (he says) not "fundamentum," but "initium fundamenti" This is a very different thing from "constitutio."

(7) Before the first century καταβολή seems to have been used to mean the "putting down" of ready money, the "casting" of seed, the "descent" of fever, disease &c., but not "foundation," except (1) in the phrase "from the bottom," i e. *de novo*, (2) in special contexts implying foundation[6]. The Thesaurus gives no instance (apart from N.T) of "before *the casting-down*," in the sense of "before the *foundation* of the world."

---

[1] Ps lv 19, Ps lxxiv 12

[2] Epict i 13. 3, where the Latin has "Coelesti *satu* editus"

[3] Heb xi. 11, Clem § 57 οἱ τὴν καταβολὴν (but Lightf *foundation*) τῆς στάσεως ποιήσαντες (the only instance in the Apostolic Fathers (exc. Barn v. 5 quoting Gen 1 26 as uttered by God to "the Lord" "from *the casting-down* of the world")) In Justin Martyr *Tryph* § 102 ἐν τῇ ἐπὶ τοῦ πύργου καταβολῇ, it prob means God's "*descent*" (and not, as in T & T Clark's translation, "destruction"). Comp. Gen xi 7 "let us go *down*"

[4] Origen on Jn xvii. 24, and Chrys. on Eph 1 4 They are thereby led into strange interpretations

[5] Jerome on Eph 1 4.

[6] See Steph. *Thes.* quoting (1) phrases with ἐκ and (2) Polyb. xiii 6 2, καταβολὴν ἐποιεῖτο καὶ θεμέλιον ὑπεβάλλετο πολυχρονίου τυραννίδος

THE INTERPRETATION

(8) An earlier Ode connects God's „ design" of Redemption with "'casting-down" under the term "shooting." It is described as being like an arrow that is "*shot*," and also as "like a letter", and this letter, which has a divine "seal" upon it, is "a great tablet" "wholly written by the finger of God[1]" This "seal" is apparently "Truth[2]," and the vision is connected with the revelation of "the Son of Truth from the Father, the Most High," who "inherited and took possession of everything."

(9) Of the two scriptural passages that describe in poetic detail the creation of the world, one, in Job, expressly mentions God as "*casting-down* (or *throwing*, or *shooting*) the corner-stone," just before He "shut up the sea with doors[3]." The other, in Proverbs, mentions "the sea" first, and says "When he gave to the sea its bound...when he marked out the foundations of the earth[4]" The former passage suggests the thought of God as "casting down" into the waters a living and growing Stone, the Stone of Truth and Order, which might be regarded by a poet as an "earnest" or "instalment (καταβολή)" of the ultimately developed Cosmos, or Harmony of the universe.

(10) According to a tradition in *Joma*, "The Holy One, blessed be He, *threw a stone* into the sea, and from this the world was *founded*[5]" Such a tradition accords with the

---

[1] Ode xxiii, see *Light on the Gospel* **3887—91**

[2] See *Light on the Gospel* **3891** *b* quoting Bab. Talm. on a "paper" or "tablet" *falling from heaven*, with "Truth" inscribed on it, whence the inference is drawn "Truth is God's seal"

[3] Job xxxviii. 6 R V "*laid*," but Heb "*shot*" or "*threw*" The Hebrew for "*shoot*" in Job is rendered in Targ and Syr by the word used in Ode xxiii 5 "violently-shot." The Hebrew has, as derivatives (Gesen. 435 foll) the well-known *Tôrah*, "teaching" or "law," as well as fertilising "rain"—so that its associations are far more exalted than we might suppose Jerome *ad loc* interprets the "corner-stone" as the Son and the "*shooting*" as referring to the Incarnation. [4] Prov. viii. 29.

[5] *Joma* 54 *b*, quoting Job xxxviii. 6 The thought of God the Redeemer "casting down" the substratum for a foundation is quaintly illustrated by

thought of Job, and of the Odes, especially if we add, from the Ode about the Arrow, the sign of a "seal," and, from the Talmud, that "Truth is God's seal," and, from the Ode again, "He was known from before the *casting-down of the aeon* that He might save souls for ever by *the truth of His name*[1]."

(11) It may be worth adding that the Greek word καταβολή occurs abundantly in New Hebrew. Its meaning is said to be generally, "mattress," or "covering on which something rests." No instance is alleged (so far as I know) of a metaphorical use[2]. But it may have influenced the use of the term in the earliest Christian literature.

(12) "*The foundation of the world*"—that is to say, the Greek phrase thus rendered in our Authorised Version of Matthew—is rendered very variously in various English Versions of the Gospels. And the variations have a direct bearing on our investigation. For they indicate a danger in such a conclusion as we are now considering, which is, in effect, "*Since the Poet here uses a phrase that occurs in the later Syriac version of N.T., and not in the earlier Syriac versions known to us, meaning 'the foundation of the world,' it follows that he wrote after that later Syriac version.*"

In Mt xiii. 35, for example, we might infer, that an English author quoting "*from the foundation of the world*" (as A.V. A.D. 1611) and not "from the begynning(e) of the world(e)" (as Tyndale, Cranmer, and Geneva, A.D. 1534—57) wrote after A.D. 1611. But he might be quoting from the Rheims Version (A.D. 1582).

Again, in Mt. xxv. 34, if we inferred from a mention of "*foundations*" that he was quoting, with a slight variation, the

---

the above-quoted Horatian "caementa demittit redemptor," *i.e.* the contractor.

[1] It must be admitted, however, that the "*shooting*" of the "stone" or the "arrow" is not the same word as the "*casting-down*" in the Ode.

[2] See Levy iv. 279 *a*. Krauss (pp. 523 and 566) gives more than a dozen instances. He adds (p. 524) one instance of Heb καταβλητόν as meaning "payment of a fine."

Rheims Version (A.D. 1582), we might be wrong again, for "*foundations*" in the plural occurs in the Geneva Version (A.D. 1557)

Lastly, if we inferred from an author quoting Luke xi. 50, "*from the making of the world*" (as in the Rheims Version) that he wrote after 1582, we might be once more wrong For he might be quoting from Wiclif (A.D. 1380)[1]

In view of these facts it appears to me quite reasonable, as well as charitable to our Poet, to suppose that when he spoke of "*the casting-down of the aeon*," he did not mean what he speaks of elsewhere as "*foundation*," "*founding*," or "*establishing*" The conclusion that the expression is to be taken "obviously as a Syriac translation of $\pi\rho\grave{o}$ $\kappa\alpha\tau\alpha\beta o\lambda\tilde{\eta}\varsigma$ $\kappa\acute{o}\sigma\mu o\upsilon$ by one who was familiar with the usual Peshitta version of this phrase" is also open to this objection, that not one more instance of such "translation" is even alleged in the very able paper to which this Section calls attention The other nine alleged instances of Greek influence appear to me to point either to Hebrew, or at all events not to Greek And though this, the tenth, points to Greek, it is perfectly compatible with the belief that our Poet wrote in Hebrew. Writing in Hebrew did not preclude him from borrowing thoughts from the Greek of the Gospels any more than from the Greek of Philo[2].

---

[1] Compare also Jn xvii 24, where "before the making of the world" is not only in Wiclif (using "making," as he always does in the Gospels) but also in Tyndale and Cranmer

The argument in the text is this, that in early times there may have been other renderings of the Scriptures beside those that have come down to us, and that the author of the Odes may have followed one of these, which anticipated the Peshitta in using the phrase under consideration, though not quite in the sense in which the Peshitta uses it

[2] See *Light on the Gospel* (Index "Philo") It may be added that a poet writing in Hebrew, but versed in Greek, might be influenced in word, as well as in thought, by the flexibilities of the Greek language, so as to strain Hebrew to the utmost in order to express them, *e g* in the matter of emphasis and emphatic possessives discussed above in § 8

§ 11 "*The babe leaping*"

After writing as above, I received from Dom Connolly, in the course of an interesting correspondence, the following observation, which he has authorised me to quote. "I wish some one would deal with the N.T echoes in the Odes. There seem to me to be a number. Perhaps the most striking is that in Ode xxviii 3 'as a babe that exults in the womb of its mother' (see the Syriac versions of Lk. i. 40)" This alleged "echo" well deserves investigation I also believe that it is an "echo"—but not an "echo" of anything that is peculiar to the New Testament.

Let us first do justice to the similarity. It is enhanced by the contexts Luke says "When Elisabeth heard the salutation of Mary, the babe *leaped in her womb*; and Elisabeth was filled with the Holy Spirit, and she lifted up her voice with a loud cry and said "Blessed art thou.. [1]" The Ode in question says " As the wings of the doves over their nestlings, and the mouth of their nestlings toward their mouths, so also are the wings of the Spirit over my heart My heart is delighted and *leaps* [for joy], like the babe that *leaps in the womb* of his mother[2]"

I admit that this is very "striking." The obvious inference —obvious at all events to those who assume a Greek original for the Odes—is that the Odist wrote in Greek, and copied from Luke, who says that John the Baptist, as an unborn babe, "*leapt in the womb*" at the approach of the Redeemer who was in the womb of Mary.

But—what about the source of Luke's narrative itself? Grant that it is historical, and that every word of it is exactly true Still, we may fairly say, " If this experience of Elisabeth is found to be in accordance with something in Jewish traditions about other mothers of Israel, we ought first of all to

---

[1] Lk 1. 41—2   [2] Ode xxviii. 1—3.

examine those traditions We are all the more bound to do this because the Greek phrase '*leap in the womb*' occurs nowhere in the Bible except as an obvious misrendering of '*push-against-one-another* in the womb,' applied to Jacob and Esau[1] If this 'leaping' or 'exulting'—which really implies an 'exulting' to the glory of God—can be found in fairly early Jewish tradition, applied to unborn babes, glorifying the Lord their Redeemer in return for a special act of His redeeming power, then we ought not to commit ourselves to Luke, or at all events to Luke alone, as the source of our Poet's utterance"

Now we do find language of this kind in very early and widespread Jewish tradition It is extant in (*inter alia*) the commentary of *Mechiltha* on the Redemption of Israel at the Red Sea. *Mechiltha* was mentioned above (§ 4) to shew that the very next words in the Ode to those we are now considering ("I believed, therefore I was at rest") probably implied an allusion to the connection between "rest," "stability," and "belief" According to *Mechiltha* it was as a reward of "belief" that "the Holy Spirit rested on Israel and they sang unto the Lord." Now we can go still further in the illustration of our Ode with the aid of *Mechiltha*, applying it to the "exultation" or "leaping" of the unborn child. For *Mechiltha*, on Exod xv. 1 (Wu p 116) "I will sing unto Jehovah," quotes Rabbi Meir (whom Schurer places among the Rabbis of "the Third Generation," about 130—60 A.D) thus —

---

[1] Gen. xxv 22 The LXX has mistaken רצץ, "crush," for a reduplicated form of רוץ (found as a v r in Levy *Ch* 1 165 *b*) The Heb רוץ occurs only in Job xli 22 (14) where the LXX has mistaken it for רוץ, and consequently rendered it "run," instead of "dance" On Gen xxv 22, Rashi says " Rabbini nostri exponunt .ut significet ריצה i e. *cursum*," because whenever Rebecca passed by a Schoolhouse of Shem, Jacob "ran" (i e "*currebat* ut egrederetur"), and Esau did the same when she passed a place of idol-worship But the Talmuds and Midrashim are not alleged for this view *Tehillim* (Wu 1 327) adopts the usual interpretation "crushed," which Rashi gives as an alternative

"R. Meir says, *Even the babes unborn* (die Embryonen), which were in the wombs of their mothers, *opened their mouths and uttered the song* before God." This is not the eccentric and unsupported suggestion of a single Rabbi. It is repeated in both the Talmuds, and Rashi assumes it[1].

It may be urged that "opened their mouths and uttered the song" is not the same thing as "*exulted*" or "*leapt*." But we find the Targum on the Psalms using this word "*leap*" as a rendering of the Hebrew for "psallere[2]," and it was a very natural way of paraphrasing a word that might raise objection, if taken literally. Indeed, objection is actually raised and answered in the Babylonian *Sota* ("How could the babe see?")[3] It is worth noting how Origen combines the "*leaping*" of the unborn babe in Luke with an utterance of praise by his mother: "The voice of the salutation of Mary coming-to-pass in the ears of Elisabeth filled John with itself. Therefore John '*leaps*,' and his mother *becomes as it were her son's mouth, and also a prophetess*. [4]"

I cannot recall anything in Greek profane literature that would induce an early Christian poet writing in Greek to liken his soul to "a babe leaping in his mother's womb," because it "exults" in the motherly love of the Holy Spirit. The poetic tradition attributed to Rabbi Meir about the mothers of Israel at the Passage of the Red Sea sounds genuinely Jewish. It is difficult—I should call it impossible—to believe that R. Meir borrowed "the exultant song of the unborn babes" from Luke, but it is quite intelligible as part of a whole series of what would in English be called ballads, but would be better called, among the Jews, school-poetry—unwritten poetic amplifications of the poetry of the Old Testament, current in the first century and

---

[1] See *b Sota* 31 *a*, *j Sota* v 4 (Schwab vii 287), *Berach* 50 *a*, and Rashi on Ps lxviii 26 (as also *Tehillim* ad loc.)

[2] Ps xxi 13

[3] Also see Wagenseil on *Sota*, pp. 617—9

[4] Origen, *Comm. Joann* vi 30 (Lomm. i 254).

later concerning that notable Deliverance which was stamped on the Jewish mind by the institution of the Passover. There are other passages in this Ode, that seem to allude to the Exodus or the Wandering in the Wilderness, such as "I have been set on His incorruptible pinions[1]" and "I was persecuted and they supposed that I was swallowed up, for I seemed to them as one of the lost[2]" Others shew us how a Jewish Poet might merge the thought of Israel in the thought of Moses or the Messiah, just as Matthew applies to Jesus part of the saying of Hosea concerning Israel, "Out of Egypt have I called my son....I taught Ephraim to walk," "he took them in his arms[3]." Into these we cannot enter[4], but they combine to convince us that we have in the composer of the Odes a man saturated with Jewish tradition, Christianized but not Hellenized, and much more likely to borrow the phrase we are discussing from prevalent first-century Jewish tradition, represented for us in the second century by Rabbi Meir, than from a single Greek instance in Luke of an apparently non-Greek phrase[5].

---

[1] Ode xxviii. 6   Comp Exod xix 4 "I bare you on eagles' wings."
[2] Ode xxviii. 8   Comp Exod xiv 3, xv 9 "they are entangled...," "my hand shall destroy them"
[3] Hos xi. 1—3, Mt. ii. 15
[4] One of them is Ode xxviii 13 "But I was carrying water in my right hand, and their bitterness I endured by my sweetness." This looks like a Christian view of the much discussed "*tree*," which God (Exod xv. 25) "*taught*" Moses—not "*shewed*" but "*taught*," says *Mechiltha*, in effect, *ad loc.* Wu "lehrte ihn"—near the waters of Marah. See *Indices to Diatessarica* p xxxv foll on the various Jewish and Christian traditions as to this "*tree*"—which Origen interprets as the Cross

By "apparently non-Greek," I mean that the Thesaurus, under σκιρτάω, not only gives no other instance of ἐσκίρτησε βρέφος except Lk i. 44, but also gives another word (ἀσκαρίζω) as the word used by Hippocrates in this sense As for σκιρτάω, it has been shewn above that, as applied by the LXX to Jacob and Esau, it had a meaning alien from Luke's purpose.

I have only space for a few words on another similarity, to which Dom Connolly called my attention—between Ode VIII. 3 "to bring fruits to the Lord, living, holy," and Rom XII 1 "to present your bodies, a living sacrifice, holy, acceptable to God." He added that "*bring*," not "*bring forth*," was the meaning of the Syriac.

If we could be certain that the Syr "*bring*" (the causative of *ĕtha*, familiar to us in *Maran-atha*) did not mean "*bring forth*," but "*bring as an offering*," I should then suggest that the Poet had in view a contrast between (Gen. iv. 3—5) the first two sacrifices—the "*bringing*" of "*the fruit of the ground*" (by Cain) and the "*bringing*" of living animals (by Abel). The Syriac "bring" is the same there as here. Cain's act is traditionally regarded as what one might call "a dead work"; Abel's, as an act of faith by which—as Philo (i. 200) says—"though dead he still *lives*." The hypothesis of an allusion to Genesis would enable us to paraphrase the passage in the Ode with its preceding context thus "Let your worship spring from your heart and from the leaping up of love from the heart to the lips, so as to bring unto the Lord an offering, not of selfish and dead works (like Cain's) but one that is holy and lives for ever (like Abel's)."

But the Thesaurus 416—7 gives many instances where Syriac Versions use the causative of *ĕtha* with "fruit," to mean "*bring forth*." Among these are (in Pesh., Palest., and SS) Jn xv 8, 16, where the "bringing forth" of "fruit" by the disciples is described as tending to the "glorifying" of "the Father," and Jesus says (SS and Pesh.) "I have chosen you and set you that ye should be going [on] *bringing forth fruit, and your fruit should remain*[1]" "Remain" implies that their "fruit" will be "living." Also it must needs be "holy," for they (Jn xv. 4—6) "*remain*" in "the Vine", and the Vine is (*Didach* IX 2) "the *Holy Vine* of David," the Vine of the Spiritual Israel

---

[1] Jn xv 16 The Palest Syr does not include this verse

THE INTERPRETATION

There is no reason, however, why a true Israelite should not be regarded by a Jewish poet as a fruitful tree in two aspects. He not only "*brings forth*" fruit, but also "*brings*" fruit to the Lord *as an offering* For these reasons, instead of saying that the Poet is echoing the Apostle, I should be disposed to say that both the Poet and the Apostle are going back in thought to Abel's sacrifice, with Cain's in the background Cain was the type of those who tithed mint, anise, and cummin. Abel was the type of those whose hearts cried out—and whose hands expressed—(Ps. xl. 8) " I delight to do thy will, O my God." Concerning this heartfelt sacrifice of penitence and praise Isaiah represents God as saying " I create the fruit of the lips," and Hosea represents penitent Israel as saying " we will duly-offer *bullocks*, [*namely*] *our lips* "—thoughts echoed in the Epistle to the Hebrews (which speaks of " the fruit of lips that make confession " to God's name) and also in the present Ode[1].

§ 12. *Evidence from the Anaphora of St James*

Dom Connolly's inference from what appeared to him the indiscriminate use of the Syriac detachable possessive in the Odes led me to investigate the matter, in the following circumstances, after most of the preceding paragraphs were in type. In a letter, full of suggestive observations—which I would most gladly discuss did space allow—he asked me to look at some proof sheets of the Syriac Liturgy (Anaphora) of " St James," which he was kind enough to enclose for my inspection. In these, he had underlined passages where the detachable possessive occurs. He pointed out how, in this Syriac, " translated from the Greek (mostly extant) probably in the second half of the 5th century," this detachable possessive " came to be employed almost to the exclusion of possessive

---

[1] Is lvii. 19 "fruit," Theod καρπόν, but not the usual Heb for "fruit", Hos. xiv. 2 (on which see Jerome and *Joma* 86 *b*), Heb xiii 15.

suffixes," illustrating his remark by a comparison of such a translation with the Peshitta version of the Psalms where the detachable possessive could hardly be found. He added that even the Peshitta version of the Gospels would shew nothing to parallel the use of the possessive in the document he enclosed, so that the facts confirmed his conclusion that "the Syr. text of the Odes is a relatively late one"

These remarks appeared to me to deserve the most careful consideration, and I have endeavoured to do justice to them. They may lead my readers, as they have led me, to a quite new appreciation of the variations of Christian hymnology in the earliest times, if they will have the patience to go back as far as possible to the original authorities, and the courage to face detailed fact For of course the first step was to go back to the Greek of the Anaphora If the Greek contained nothing but unemphatic possessive expressions where the Syriac contained the detachable possessive, then Dom Connolly had proved his point. I therefore turned to Swainson's *The Greek Liturgies*, where the Greek of the Anaphora is printed in four parallel columns, and compared the Greek with the Syriac[1].

I found that the instances underlined by Dom Connolly began a little before the words "This is my body" and were very numerous indeed Moreover, as to the sacred formula itself, Dom Connolly pointed out that, whereas the Peshitta uses the unemphatic suffix "*my-body,*" the Syriac Anaphora has "*the body that-is-mine*" (as also "*the blood that-is-mine*"). Here, however, we have to note that the Greek does not follow the tradition of the Three Synoptists, τὸ σῶμά μου, but that of Paul, τοῦτό μού ἐστιν τὸ σῶμα[2] Now although the possessive μου, *when placed before its noun and the article, ought to be unemphatic* and to throw the emphasis on the noun, yet

---

[1] *The Greek Liturgies*, by C A Swainson, D D. (Cambridge At the University Press, 1884), to be hereafter referred to as *Liturg.*

[2] 1 Cor xi 24 adds τὸ ὑπὲρ ὑμῶν Anaph. adds τὸ ὑπὲρ ὑμῶν κλώμενον καὶ διαδιδόμενον εἰς ἄφεσιν ἁμαρτιῶν.

THE INTERPRETATION

there appeared reasons for thinking that the author of the Anaphora—or at all events the writers of some texts of it—might regard it as *emphatic*[1]

One reason was this, that all through the Anaphora, where there is an antithesis (as there often is) between the goodness and kindness of God and the imperfections and necessities of Man, the Greek writer rarely, if ever, uses the unemphatic expression to signify "His" or "Thy" Even where there was no such antithesis, I have failed (so far) to find *the unemphatic form, in Greek, to signify divine possession*. In the Pauline tradition there was a reason for the unemphatic "my" applied to "body," because Paul meant to emphasize "[body] *that is for you,*" reserving the personal emphasis for "*my own* commemoration" and "*my own* blood" in the following context[2]. But the Greek writer of the Anaphora, who blends

---

[1] See *Johannine Grammar* 2776—84 on "The Possessive Genitive." When the genitive pronoun comes *between* the article and its noun, it is emphatically reverential, *Liturg.* p. 260 τῶν ἀχράντων σου μυστηρίων, *ib* τὸ ἅγιόν σου θυσιαστήριον But see below for variations in the texts indicating that the Greek possessive, even when preceding the article, may have been regarded by the scribes of the Anaphora as emphatic.

In Dom Connolly's Syriac text of the Anaphora, the order of the words is " This *that-which-is-mine* is the body," representing exactly the order of the Pauline formula, Τοῦτό μού ἐστιν τὸ σῶμα I am informed by Rev G. Margoliouth that this is the order of the Syriac in the Liturgy of St John the Evangelist (*e g* Brit Mus MSS Or. 2293 and 2295), but that in the Anaphora of St James the Brother of the Lord, the reading in the MSS referred to is "This [is] my-body that-is-for-you," and that, in the printed texts (Rome, 1592 and 1843) a unified form of the words has been employed, the reading in every Anaphora being "This is the-body [*the body*] *that-is-mine*" (apparently influenced by the Harklensian version, in which the Syriac "*that-which-is-mine*" comes last)—not only in the Gospels, where μου comes last, but also in the Epistle to the Corinthians, where μου does not come last.

[2] 1 Cor xi 24—5 may be paraphrased as meaning "This is the body that-I-give-you (τοῦτό μού ἐστιν τὸ σῶμα) which [is offered] in your behalf (τὸ ὑπὲρ ὑμῶν) do this with-a-view-to (εἰς) the commemoration of me (emph.) (τὴν ἐμὴν ἀνάμνησιν) ..This cup is the new testament (*or*, covenant) in my-own (emph.) blood (ἐν τῷ ἐμῷ αἵματι)"

the Pauline with the Synoptic tradition, has not "*my own* (τὸ ἐμὸν) blood," but τοῦτό μου ἐστὶ τὸ αἷμα[1] It is not improbable that the Greek writer in both cases regarded the μου as emphatic It is at all events highly probable, if not certain, that the Syriac translator would regard it as emphatic, and would represent it by the Syriac detachable possessive which represents our reverential "Thy," "His," and (in modern hymnology) "My."

There is all the more excuse for the Syriac translator (if he is wrong) because, even as regards the sacred formula, the different MSS of the same Liturgy sometimes vary. For example, in the Liturgy of Alexandria, one Codex has τοῦτό ἐστι τὸ σῶμά μου (with the Synoptists), but two others τοῦτό μού ἐστιν τὸ σῶμα (with Paul)[2] A Liturgy of Saint Basil also has the Synoptic form[3]. Both these Liturgies, in all the MSS, add some version of the clause τὸ ὑπὲρ ὑμῶν, which is not in the Synoptists. Both also have the same possessive form, in their various MSS, for "the body" and "the blood" But the Liturgy of Saint Chrysostom has the Pauline form for "the body" and the Synoptic form for "the blood[4]."

The unemphatic Greek possessive in the Anaphora occurs in such expressions as "Purify my lips and heart" and "Sanctify our souls and bodies and spirits[5]"; but a cursory glance at several pages of Swainson's edition has revealed no other instances For the most part, even when the Greek writer is using "our" or "my" about men, he uses the emphatic form where there is contrast (as there often is)

---

[1] *Liturg* pp 274—5
[2] *Liturg* pp. 52—3 They also vary as to αἷμα similarly.
[3] *Liturg* p 82.
[4] *Liturg.* p 129 So also has a "Liturgy of Saint Basil" on p 160
[5] *Liturg* pp. 256, 262. That is because there is an emphasis on the nouns as distinct from the possessive In the former sentence, ἐξάλειψόν μου τὰ παραπτώματα is the reading of two MSS, but a third omits μου and a fourth has it at the end of the clause.

THE INTERPRETATION

between Man and God, or else the neutral form[1] In Eucharistic Liturgies there must needs be a pervasive emphasis of pronouns in contrasts between God's kindness and helpfulness and Man's unworthiness and helplessness[2].

It is quite true that in the Syriac Version of the Old Testament the detachable Syriac possessive is extremely rare. But there is good reason for the rarity. The Hebrew Scripture, even where it emphasizes the contrast between what is God's and what is Man's, does not use *shel*, which might have enabled the Psalmist to express emphasis The Biblical Hebrew, therefore, leaves it unexpressed. The LXX follows the Hebrew. The Syriac follows the Hebrew or the LXX. The result is that in the Old Testament and its most ancient versions the contrast of thought is left unexpressed by grammatical inflexion

But when the first century brought into Jewish literature the thoughts that gathered round the belief in the Incarnation, then the contrast between the love and kindness that came down from God to Man, and the helplessness and sinfulness that went up in appeal from Man to God, would require altogether new forms of expression And these would naturally spring into greatest prominence in Christian Liturgies. We have above noted one phase of this development,

---

[1] *Liturg* pp. 262 and 265 τὰς νοερὰς ἡμῶν ὄψεις τοῦ ἀπεριλήπτου φωτὸς πλήρωσον may at first sight be regarded as emphatic without contrast. But that contrast is *implied* may be seen by comparing p 264, where the same expression occurs, only with σου inserted before φωτὸς ἀποπλήρωσον There is a contrast in all the passages—expressed or implied—between "our" and "Thy."

[2] Comp *Liturg* p. 256, "Reject not *my* (τὴν ἐμὴν) unworthiness. according to *thy* great mercy (τὸ μέγα ἔλεός σου, Paris MS 476 τὸ μέγα σου ἔλεος)," *ib.* p 258 "Not in *our* righteousness (ταῖς δικαιοσύναις ἡμῶν) do we trust but in *thy* good mercy (ἐπὶ τῷ ἐλέει σου τῷ ἀγαθῷ)," *ib.* p 264 "having deemed me, *thy* sinful servant, worthy to stand at *thy* holy altar," where Rot. Mess. has τὸν. .σου δοῦλον, but Paris MS 476 τὸν...δοῦλόν σου, *ib.* p 276 "Requite us not according to *our* iniquities (τὰς ἀνομίας ἡμῶν) but according to *thy* kindness (κατὰ τὴν σὴν ἐπιείκειαν)."

when comparing the brief and original form—neither emphatically personal nor yet unemphatic—of the sacramental words of Institution, as recorded by the Synoptists, with the newer and amplified form given in the Pauline tradition. The latter, we found, emphasizes, first, the sacrificial nature of the gift of "the body," and then the personal nature of the "commemoration" The Greek Anaphora carries further this development. We may take, as a verbal test of Eucharistic emphasis—as a kind of Eucharistometer—the use of the emphatic personal "Thy" ($\sigma\acute{o}\varsigma$) applied to the Lord. It occurs less than a dozen times in the LXX version of the Psalms[1]. But it occurs twice or thrice in the first few lines of most MSS of the Anaphora[2]. This confirms the conclusion that, in the Anaphora, the Syriac emphatic rendering springs, not from an indiscriminate use of the detachable possessive, but from a desire to render literally the original Eucharistic thought.

With such thought—the thought of Eucharistic contrast—the Odes of Solomon are from first to last imbued We are therefore safe in saying that in a very great number of cases the Syriac detachable suffix is no more indiscriminate in the Odes than in the Anaphora. But can we go further and conclude that the Syriac Translator of the Odes, when using these possessives, may be literally translating from Hebrew? On that point more evidence is necessary, not only as to the usage of what is generally called Mishnaic Hebrew[3], but also

---

[1] This includes all uses in the Psalms.

[2] *Liturg.* pp. 256—7 The texts vary slightly (One MS has πολλὴν for σήν) It occurs also once or twice on pp. 258—9 (where again the texts vary), thrice on pp. 270—1 &c In the Apostolic Fathers—apart from Hermas (who uses it in precepts about "one's own wife" &c.)—σός occurs (as an adjective with noun) only in Clem. Rom. § 60 τῆς σῆς ἀληθείας (a quasi-Eucharistic prayer), and *Didach.* ix 4, x 5 (rep) εἰς τὴν σὴν βασιλείαν (in the actual Eucharist).

[3] We have to bear in mind that, even after the exile, Biblical Psalms —and some of the most beautiful of them—were still composed in

as to the kind of Hebrew that would be written in the first century by a Jewish poet writing in the name of Solomon, and in a tone very different indeed from that of the extant Psalms of Solomon, and resembling in some respects the tone of Solomon's Song in the Bible

If we were to trust merely to the evidence of the Prayers of ancient post-Christian Rabbis recorded in the Talmud, it would appear that even in contrasts between God's kindness and Man's need, the Rabbis contented themselves with the ordinary Hebrew suffix without using the detachable particle[1].

But in the Jewish Thanksgiving after Meals—which (I am informed) is of very great antiquity—the divine "His" is expressed by a form of *shel* thus. "we have eaten of *that-which-is-His*[2]." And Levy quotes, from the Jerusalem as

---

Hebrew, not in Aramaic. What is called "Mishnaic Hebrew" was not invented by those who uttered the earliest of the sayings known to us as Mishna It was merely one form of literary Hebrew—namely, that form which had come into use, by the second century, among Rabbis teaching in the schools. Even in the Talmuds there are great differences of style The prose of legal discussion may be found intermixed with the poetry of a soaring imagination or extravagant fancy. The Hebrew of the Odes of Solomon (if they were composed in Hebrew) may have been as different from the Hebrew of the more prosaic parts of the Mishna as the English of Marlowe from the English of Bishop Burnet

[1] See the Prayers in *Berach* 16 *b* foll They contain (as far as I have seen) no instance of a reverential "Thy" &c represented by anything more than the possessive suffix Several of them begin with "May there be *a will* (or, *good-pleasure*) *from-before-thy-face*" (Goldschmidt and Schwab "*thy will*") In the prayer of "Rabh" for "a life *of* peace, a life *of* good, a life *of* blessing ..," "of" is represented in each case by *shel*.

[2] *Jewish Prayer Book*, ed Singer, p. 279 " Blessed be (our God) He of whose bounty we have partaken," but *lit*. "Blessed be He [as to] whom (שׁ) we have eaten *from-that-which-is-His* (מִשֶּׁלּוֹ)" The form in the Mishna of *Berach* vii 3, repeating the grace several times—with variations adapted to the numbers present—does not contain the italicised words, except partially at the last two repetitions, where it has "for that which we have eaten."

On the use of *shel* with suffix as a possessive pronoun, a few remarks

well as from the Babylonian Talmud, words ascribed to God as follows " Slay [the sacrifices, or beasts] *that-are-mine* in *that-which-is-mine* [i e in my Temple] and *that-which-is-thine*

may be found in Albrecht's *Neuhebraische Grammatik*, 1913 (pp. 56—7), but the subject is much more fully treated in an Article in the *Jewish Quarterly Review*, 1908, Vol XX, No 80, pp 647—737 on Mishnaic Hebrew, by the Rev Moses H Segal. He gives abundant instances of Hebrew "circumlocution of the genitive," with and without "anticipation," and speaks (p 724) of the use of *shel* as very ancient Of Mishnaic "circumlocution with anticipation" he says (p 728) "generally the construction has an emphatic force", but (p 731) "gradually the idiom began to be used more frequently, and then regularly whenever any stress was to be laid upon a noun, and, in the course of time, even where no emphasis was intended "

"In about forty passages in the Mishna," he adds (p 732), "and frequently in the Midrashim, circumlocution by של with the appropriate suffix is found in the place of the possessive suffix attached immediately to the noun itself This construction is used (*a*) on grounds of grammar, where, namely, the noun cannot take the suffix through being indeclinable or consisting of a compound expression, and (*b*) on grounds of style, where it is desirable to leave the noun unchanged for the sake of lucidity or emphasis "

Almost all Mr Segal's instances are taken from the Mishna, where we cannot expect poetic expression The impression left by his laborious research is that if it had extended to the poetic and mystical portions of the Midrashim, it might have given us instances like that in *Sabbath* 104 *a* (Goldschmidt) " *He, Vay*, das ist der Name des Heiligen ," where the literal Hebrew has " *He, Vaw*, this is His name [*the name*] *that* [*belongs*] *to* (*shel*) the Holy One ' In *Gen r* (on Gen xxviii 11, as quoted in Levy iii 219 *b*)—where reasons are given for calling God PLACE—*shel* is used with "the Holy One," and with " His world " "Why do they form [as they do] His Name [the Name] *that* [*appertains*] *to* the Holy One and call Him PLACE ? Because He is its-place [the place] *that* [*appertains*] *to* His world " That is, the world is included in Him , He, though in His world, is not included in it But *shel* is not used with " Him " in what follows "We should not know whether the Holy One [is the] place of His world, or whether His world [is] His place, but, from that which is written (Exod. xxxiii 21) 'See, [there is] place with me,' it follows that the Holy One [is] its-place [the place] *that* [*appertains*] *to* [the] world, and not [that] His world [is] *His place*" The antithesis, to be exact, would require at the close—instead of "*His place*"—"*His place* [*the place*] *that* [*appertains*] *to Him*" But, either as being too lengthy, or for some other reason, it is avoided in *that-which-is-thine* [i e in thine own house][1]." We have seen above that *shel* occurs thrice in the short Song of Solomon which is written in Hebrew. Moreover in the Song of Jacob—instead of "until *Shiloh* come"—most ancient authorities agree in reading some form of *shel*, meaning "*that* [*kingdom*] *which* [*is reserved*] *for Him*," or "*He for whom* [*the kingdom &c is reserved*][2]." Is it unreasonable that, in attempting to account for the very numerous emphatic pronominal contrasts in the Odes of Solomon, expressed by the Syriac relative, those who are taking a Hebrew original as their working hypothesis should say that an explanation may be first sought—at all events in some instances—in the Hebrew *shel*?

It must be admitted, however, that as to some phrases, hallowed by old Hebraic usage, it is difficult to believe that a poet writing in later Hebrew would resort to the form *shel*, as for example in the phrase "*Thy* right hand"—even when it was emphatically contrasted with the feebleness of "the right hand" of Man But what follows? Grant that the Poet, in a phrase of contrast, wrote, in Hebrew, "thy right hand" with the simple Hebrew suffix. Would not a translator, whether into Greek or Syriac, feel that the emphasis on "thy," though manifest to Jews, required to be brought out distinctly in a translation for Gentiles? Some of them, being idolaters, might even think of "thy right hand" as being distinct from "thy left hand" or "thy foot" or some other member of their God. Even by the more intelligent the full

---

[1] Levy iv. 556 *b* quoting *j Abod sar.* V, 45 *b* and *Kidd* 57 *b* It is interesting to note that in the Prayer of Jesus—represented differently in Mark xiv 36 οὐ τί ἐγὼ θέλω ., Mt. xxvi. 39 οὐχ ὡς ἐγὼ θέλω..., Lk. xxii 42 μὴ τὸ θέλημά μου —SS has "Not *my will, that-which-*[*is*]*-mine*...but *that-which-*[*is*]*-thine*," in all three Gospels

[2] Gen. xlix 10, LXX and Theod τὰ ἀποκείμενα αὐτῷ But *al. exempl* ᾧ ἀπόκειται, as Onk "the Messiah *whose is the kingdom*," and the Peshitta "*He whose it is*"

force of the Hebrew suffix would probably not be felt. A Syriac translator, faithful even to baldness in other respects, might well deviate in this one respect from a Hebrew original, expressing faithfully with his pen what the writer of the Hebrew would expect his readers to express with their voice[1].

When the preceding sections of this Appendix first appeared, as Chapter III of Miscellanea Evangelica (I), Dom Connolly sent me some valuable comments on them, all of which I should have liked to quote here in full, had space allowed. But as some of them entered into minute details of Syriac idiom, and as I trust he will himself publish the substance of them hereafter, I will deal merely with one or two, the full consideration of which seems to me to lead to two conclusions. The first is (in accordance with Dom Connolly's view), that the Syriac text of the Odes is a translation later than the early Syriac translations of the Gospels The second is (contrary to Dom Connolly's view), that the composer of the Odes, whatever may have been the language in which he composed, did not use the LXX version of the Scriptures.

No apology need be made to students of the Odes of Solomon for quoting authorities and facts fully as well as numerously For facts, and not opinions—facts supported by full quotations in which the context as well as the text has been verified—are what is most wanted in the present stage of the study of these profoundly interesting but difficult poems.

---

[1] On this point, however, see Dom Connolly's remarks below, which indicate that an indiscriminate use of the detachable possessive in a Syriac translation—though leaving the original language an open question—would prove the translation to be late

THE INTERPRETATION

§ 13. "*Without grudging*"

In Ode xxiii 4, which I rendered "Walk ye in the knowledge of the Most High *that is without* grudging," the literal Syriac for "*that is without*" may be expressed by "*quod-non*," meaning "*as-to-which* [*there is*] *not*," e g "a land *as-to-which* [*there is*] *no*[*t*] inhabitant." But, in effect, this "*quod-non*" has come to mean "*sine*," "without" Hence Dom Connolly maintains that "*without grudging*," and not "*that is without grudging*," would have been the correct rendering

This would have been, no doubt, strictly and grammatically correct. But would it not have been misleading ? Take such an instance as Job xxxviii 26 (Syr) "that the rain may fall on a land *without* (*quod-non*) man[1]" Is it not obvious that in this passage, even if, according to strict Syriac idiom, "without man" is adverbial and ought to be connected with "fall," it would make nonsense to connect it thus ? It is, in effect, adjectival and connected with "land[2]" The sense determines

---

[1] Walton "ut cadat pluvia super terram *absque* homine" The Heb lit is (Walton) "pluere. *super terram non vir*, desertum non homo *in eo*" "In eo," which may apply to both Heb clauses, is not rendered in the Syriac The Syriac appears to be influenced by, but not identified with, the Hebrew.

[2] We might illustrate the point from English use in (1) "He gave me a book (*or*, the book) *without a cover*," and (2) "He gave me a book (*or*, the book) *without hesitation*" The sense determines the connection. A precise writer might write (1) fully, thus, "*He gave me a book that was without a cover*," or "*the book that he gave me was without a cover*" But it would not be terse And the author of the Odes is very terse. So far as I have noted, he *never uses, after a noun, the full Syriac form* ("quod-quod-non") *which would correspond to the full English form* "*that-is-without*", and Rev. G Margoliouth, who has examined the whole of the Odes, informs me that he has been unable to find an instance in any of them It might often conduce to clearness, after pronouns (e g "they *that are without sin* do this," as distinct from "*they, without sin*, do this"), and it occurs once somewhat similarly in Ode xxviii 11 ("those that *ignorantly* attack," where "*that ignorantly*" is lit "*qui-in-quod-non (ddlâ) scientia*").

the connection. And if we appeal to the sense in the Ode under consideration, and ask who is supposed to be the person that is "without grudging," the answer seems fairly clear. There is no thought of the recipients of God's gift, as being warned "not" to "grudge" the extension of the gift to others. The Poet is thinking of the Giver's ungrudgingness and is urging us to respond to it: "Walk in the knowledge of the Most High—[His gift] *as-to-which [there is] no grudging*"

This will appear still more clearly if we follow the reading of Codex N, which inserts a clause about "grace" in the above quoted Ode (xxiii 4) "Walk ye in the knowledge of the Lord, *and ye shall know the grace of the Lord without grudging.*" "Grace," in such a context, implies a gracious gift, and a gracious gift implies that there is "*no grudging*" *in the giver*

This is a very different thought from that of "*no lack*" *in the receiver*, and we shall miss the Poet's meaning in several of his poems if we confuse the two. For example, in "Put on [thyself] the good-grace of the Lord *without grudging*, and come into Paradise[1]," the Poet seems to use "*without grudging*" for "*as-to-which [there is] no [question of] grudging*," or "[*given*] *without grudging*" For this he has prepared the way, a little before, by connecting the adverbial "without grudging" with God's "giving": "I *gave* my knowledge *without grudging*[2]." And for the *thought* of God as the Giver without grudging he has prepared the way at the very outset of his poems, "Thou hast blossomed on my head . there is *no grudging with the Lord*...[3]." The same thought extends to such expressions as "I have received from Him redemption *without grudging*," and "Speaking water touched my lips from the fountain of the Lord *without grudging*[4]."

When the Poet wishes to say merely that a gift of God has been given "*abundantly*," so that the recipients have "*no lack*"

---

[1] Ode xx 7. [2] Ode xvii 12
[3] Odes i 3, iii. 7   Ode ii is missing
[4] Odes xv 6, xi 6

of it, there is another scriptural phrase for it, identical in Hebrew and Syriac. And this he actually uses on at least one occasion, "Life.. hath been given *without lack* to all that trust in Him[1]." But the thought connected with "*not grudging*" in the Odes is of quite a different character. It goes back to old traditions about the tree of knowledge in Paradise, and back to old questions about the purpose of the Creator in saying to Adam "Thou shalt not eat of it." Did He "*grudge*"? Or did He "*not grudge*"? Man's "*not lacking*" is the effect of God's "*not grudging*." But the effect must not be confused with the cause.

§ 14. *The detached possessive in Syriac*

I now pass to a point on which the evidence adduced by Dom Connolly has compelled me to change my views—namely, the use, and the inferences from the use, of the Syriac detached possessive instead of the possessive suffix Contending against the inference that the Syriac translation was late, I have endeavoured to shew (in § 8 of this Appendix) that in all the instances alleged by Dom Connolly, there is an emphasis that would justify the detached possessive, even in early Syriac And, so far as concerns the instances there alleged, I retain my opinion, that they might be explained by emphasis. But my investigation did not cover the text of all the Odes And even in those that had come under my notice, I had been obliged to confess that such an instance as "the right hand that is thine own" could not be satisfactorily accounted for on my hypothesis of literal translation into early and rudimentary Syriac from an original Hebrew composition

Moreover, against my hypothesis of early Syriac, Dom Connolly informed me that the style of the Odes as a whole—about which I am not competent to speak—is "particularly

---

[1] Ode xv 11. Comp Exod xvi 18 (concerning the manna) "He that gathered little *had no lack*," where the same word as that in the Ode is used in the Hebrew, the Targums, and the Syriac.

poor in distinctive Syriac idioms that so frequently occur in the Old Syriac of the Gospels," and that it "has no archaic forms" In particular, as to the use of the detachable possessive, he called my attention to the contrast between its rare use in early Syriac translations of the Gospels, and its indiscriminate use in the Syriac translation of Revelation, which is comparatively late[1]. I accordingly proceeded to examine that translation, rendering the detachable possessive experimentally, by "*that-is-my-own, thine own* &c.," as I have rendered it in the Odes[2]. Here are some of the results, taken all from the first chapter· "The Revelation of Jesus Christ, which God gave to him, that he should shew to the servants *that-were-his-own.* sending through the angel *that-was-his-own* to the servant *that-was-his-own* [namely] John," " Who loveth us and loosed us from the sins *that-are-our-own* through the blood *that-is-his-own*," "I, John, your brother, and the partner *that-is-your-own*," " The mystery of the seven stars which thou sawest in the right hand *that-is-my-own*[3]"

There is nothing in the Odes that comes up to this indiscriminate use of the detachable possessive. In the whole of the poems, there are probably *no more than sixteen instances of it*[4], *while there are fourteen in the first chapter of Revelation alone*. Nevertheless my impression is that in the Odes, taken as a whole, there is at all events a somewhat super-abundant use—such as cannot be explained completely by what I have above ventured to call the emphasis of

---

[1] I am informed that the Syriac rendering of Revelation (Walton) is to be dated A D. 616

[2] It would have been safer to have omitted "*own*" in the Odes But having inserted "*own*" in the Odes, in the belief that emphasis was intended, I insert it here in Revelation, for consistency (though no emphasis can be intended) to shew that perhaps I may have been wrong in some of my renderings in the Odes As to many of them, I retain the belief that "own" was justified because emphasis was intended.

[3] Rev. I. 1, 5, 9, 20 I have not given all the instances, but only specimens of its use with 1st, 2nd, and 3rd person.

[4] For this information I am indebted to Rev. G. Margoliouth.

A. B.

THE INTERPRETATION

"eucharistic contrast." Although that still seems to me a partial cause, I now think we must add to it another cause, namely, the lateness of the Syriac. And, if the Syriac of the Odes is admitted to be of late date, as compared with the date of the Old Syriac of the Gospels, another inference follows. It becomes increasingly probable that the Syriac is a translation, not from Hebrew—even though the poems were written originally in Hebrew—but from a Greek version of the Hebrew. For it is not likely that early Hebrew poems of such beauty, perhaps composed (as I have endeavoured to shew[1]) about the beginning of the second century, would remain for two or three centuries untranslated into Greek, the common language of the Empire, and yet be remembered and valued enough to be translated into Syriac at the end of that period.

§ 15. *"Danger," in Greek, corresponds to " strait," or " straitening," in Hebrew*

We pass now to a more important question, namely, whether the composer of the Odes did, or did not, use the LXX in referring to the Scriptures. The evidence, at first sight, seems too frail to justify a voyage of discovery. But even if the object of the voyage remains undiscovered, there are discoveries to be made on the way. Moreover a careful examination of the evidence, viewed in its environment, will shew that there is much more substance in it than a brief glance could shew.

Taken by itself, however, the evidence consists of a single brief phrase to which—among other facts that seemed to point to a translation from Greek—Dom Connolly called my attention. The phrase contains the Greek *kindūnos*, "danger," in Syriac letters. *Kindūnos* is not among the very long list of Greek words, such as *nomos*, "law," adopted from Greek

---

[1] See *Light on the Gospel* 3923—37.

into late Hebrew, or Aramaic, or both. It is in Syriac alone[1]. Occurring in one of the Odes not translated in my volume, it had escaped my notice; and Dom Connolly asked me how I explained it on the hypothesis of a Hebrew original, and what I regarded as the Hebrew equivalent.

Acknowledging the fairness of this challenge I proceeded to investigate, first, the uses of the Syriac *kindūnos*, and especially its uses in versions of the Scriptures; then the uses of the Greek noun *kindūnos* and the corresponding verb in the Scriptures, and the Hebrew words or thoughts to which they corresponded. Lastly, I analysed the context of the Ode, and the thoughts in it, and compared them with thoughts and contexts suggested by the Hebrew equivalent in its various Hebrew forms The investigation led me to two conclusions:—1st, that Dom Connolly was certainly right in suggesting that the word was a sign of late Syriac, and not improbably right also in suggesting that it was a sign of translation from Greek, 2nd, that I had been right in suggesting that *the composer of the Odes composed in Hebrew*, because, in this particular phrase, there were indications that, although alluding to Scripture, he did not allude to the LXX but to the Hebrew, where the LXX and the Hebrew exhibited a remarkable divergence from each other. I now proceed to give the detailed facts through which these conclusions were reached.

In the first place it can speedily be shewn that neither the Syriac nor the Greek *kindūnos* exactly expresses any Hebrew thought. When Luke, using the Greek corresponding verb (*kindūneuein*), says that the disciples, during the storm on Gennesaret, "*were-in-danger* [*of perishing*]," one Syriac version, it is true, has *kindūnos*, but the earlier versions have "*they were* (or, *the ship was*) *near to sink*"—very much as in the Hebrew and Greek of the corresponding passage in Jonah[2].

---

[1] Dom Connolly subsequently informed me that it is the only word of the kind that he has found in the Odes.

[2] Lk. viii. 23 (SS, Curet., and Walton) "near to sink." Comp. Jon. i. 4

THE INTERPRETATION

It is true that Delitzsch translates Luke literally "they were *in hazard*"; but he uses a noun of which the corresponding verb, though frequent in New Hebrew and Aramaic, occurs only once in Scripture[1]. The other two instances of the verb, *kindūneuein*, in canonical LXX, confirm the view that the meaning of risk or hazard, often connected with *kindūnos*, is not exactly expressed by any single word in Hebrew[2]. The Syriac Thesaurus confirms the inference suggested by the non-adoption of the word into Aramaic, and shews that, although frequently used independently in later Syriac, and as a rendering of the Greek *kindūnos* in N.T., it does not occur as a faithful rendering of any one Hebrew word in O T., but is used loosely to express danger of being drowned, snared, condemned to death, &c.[3]

We now pass to the only instance where the Greek noun *kindūnos* represents a Hebrew word: "The cords of death compassed me and the *kindūnoi* of Sheol gat hold upon me[4]." The Hebrew root in various forms implies "[extreme and painful] *pressure*," "pressing [almost to death]" It may be "pressure" from surrounding enemies, or from anxieties, but it

---

R V. "the ship *was like to be broken*," Heb. lit. "navis *putabat conteri*," Syr "navis in illa *volutabatur ad fracturam patiendam*," Targ. "adeo ut navis *quaereret* conteri." But *Thes* 3605 quotes VHh Lk viii 23, and Hex. Jon. i. 4 as using masc. and fem. forms of Syr. *kindūnos*.

[1] Eccles. x 9 "he that cleaveth [logs of] wood *hazards himself* by them." Delitzsch (1878) uses the corresponding noun, "*hazard*" But I am informed that Delitzsch (1877) had במצוקה *i e*. (Gesen. 848 *a*) "in straitness"

[2] Is xxviii. 13 (Heb) "and be *snared*," Dan. i. 10 (Heb.) "so should ye *inculpate* my head," Theod καταδικάσητε (Gesen. 295 *a*). "Danger" in R V. is mostly *legal* "danger," *i e* liability, as in *Merch of Venice* iv. 1 180.

[3] See *Thes* 3605 There is no Syr. verb corresponding to κινδυνεύω In Sir xxxi (xxxiv) 13, LXX ἕως θανάτου ἐκινδύνευσα, Hex. Syr has "I incurred *kindūnos*," to express ἐκινδύνευσα, where Walton's Syr has "ad mortem usque *perveni*."

[4] Ps cxvi. 3 (R.V.) "the *pains* of Sheol."

may also express the "anguish" or "straitening" of "travail[1]."
The form used here occurs only twice elsewhere.—(1) "All
those that pursued her [*i.e.* the Chosen People] overtook her in
the straits," (2) "Out of *my straits* I called upon the Lord, the
Lord answered me [and set me] in a large place[2]." The last
of these passages, with its threefold reference in the context to
"all nations" that "compassed" Israel "around," illustrates
well the general Hebrew conception of the "pressure," or
"hemming in," that constitutes Israel's "danger[3]." And the
preceding one, with its mention of "*pursuing*" and "*over-
taking*," may contain a particular reference to that danger—
above all other dangers—which befell Israel at the Red Sea,
when Pharaoh said of Israel "*The wilderness hath shut them
in*" and "I will *pursue*, I will *overtake*[4]." If it does, there is a
play on the word "*straits*," and the meaning is that, whereas
in "*the straits*" of old, between the mountains and the sea, the
Lord had frustrated the boast of Egypt, He had not done
the same in the case of Assyria. By Assyria, though not by
Egypt, Israel had been "*overtaken* in *the straits*[5]."

---

[1] See Gesen 865 *a* on צרה, "specif of travail, Jer. xlix. 24 (simile), cf.
iv 31" on which see below, p. 438, n 2 In Jerem xlix 24, LXX om.
"anguish travail" The root is צרר (I) "bind," from which comes מצר,
the participial form used in Ps cxvi 3 The adjective, or noun, צר, is far
more common, meaning "strait," "straits," "distress" The noun צר,
from צרר (II) "be-hostile," means "adversary" Hence ambiguity

[2] Lam. i 3, Ps cxviii 5

[3] For the threefold repetition of "compassed me about," see Ps. cxviii
10—12, where the context implies the pressing nature of the peril, and
the imminence of death, but for the Lord's intervention (*ib.* 17—18)
"I shall not die.. he hath not given me over to death"

[4] See Exod xiv 3, and also xv 9 "The enemy said I will *pursue*,
I will *overtake*," where the Heb. is identical with that of Lam. i. 3.
Rashi, on Lam 1 3, gives as his first explanation, the literal one of a
defile ("hinc atque illinc altitudo (montium)") from which there is no
escape, and, as a third, one that makes "straits" refer to times of
affliction The LXX has "in the midst of those who put [her] to
tribulation (τῶν θλιβόντων)."

[5] See Exod xiv. 2—3 "Speak unto the children of Israel that they .

It remains to add that the Greek *kindūnos*—besides an unimportant and erroneous use of it by Symmachus in Genesis to mean "disaster" or "mischief[1]"—is used (to represent a form of the above mentioned Hebrew *tsrr*) by Aquila in Jeremiah, "*the anguish* (R.V.) of her that bringeth forth her first child[2]." The rendering ascribed to Aquila is "danger (*kindūnos*) [and tribulation (*thlipsis*)]" This reminds us of a Johannine saying, using the metaphor of "travail," and conveying the assurance to Christ's disciples that although, "in the world," there is in store for them *thlipsis* (i e tribulation), as for a "woman in travail," yet they may be "of good cheer" because Jesus has been "victorious over the world[3]." This means, in effect, "There is in store for you *pressure but not pressure to death, tribulation but no real 'danger*[4]'."

Now if we ask how this "pressure of tribulation" is expressed in Hebrew we find that by far the most frequent equivalent is a short form, *tsar*, or *tsarah*, of the Hebrew root above mentioned; and *tsarah* is the word in Jeremiah rendered

---

encamp *before Pi-hahiroth, between Migdol and the sea, before Baal-zephon* .," where Jer. Targ. and *Mechilt*. ad loc. imply, or declare, that Israel was surrounded by hostile idols, and mountains, and the sea, and the Egyptians (Jer Targ "the idol hath shut them in close upon (*or*, before) the desert," *Mechilt*. p. 81 " R. Joshua says 'Hachiroth was on this side, Migdol on that side, the sea before them, the Egyptians behind them'"). Also Josephus (*Ant* ii 15 3 foll , and ii. 16. 1) repeatedly mentions the "*small space*" into which the fugitives were forced, being surrounded by the "mountains," the sea and the Egyptians (as also does Philo ii 108, only that he omits "mountains," perhaps not seeing much meaning in "Pi-hahiroth," for which LXX has ἐπαύλεως, but Ἄλλος has ἀκροτ[άτου] τῆς Χερόθ).

[1] Gen. xlii. 4.
[2] Jerem. iv 31 צָרָה, Aq κίνδυνον [καὶ θλίψιν], Symm. θλίψιν, LXX τοῦ στεγναμοῦ σου.
[3] Jn xvi. 21 Ἡ γυνὴ λύπην ἔχει...οὐκέτι μνημονεύει τῆς θλίψεως (R V. *anguish*)..., *ib*. 33 Ἐν τῷ κόσμῳ θλίψιν (R V. *tribulation*) ἔχετε, ἀλλὰ θαρσεῖτε, ἐγὼ νενίκηκα τὸν κόσμον.
[4] Comp 2 Cor. iv. 8 θλιβόμενοι ἀλλ' οὐ στενοχωρούμενοι.

kindūnos by Aquila¹. Having therefore the authority of Aquila, as well as that of the LXX, for supposing that, in the rare event of the occurrence of the Greek *kindūnos* in a translation from Hebrew, it might represent the Hebrew *tsar* or *tsarah*, and might represent, literally or metaphorically, the "straits" of Israel, encompassed by enemies, we now turn back to the phrase with which we started, "*without danger*" in Ode xxxix. 7, in order to consider its context.

§ 16. "*Without danger*," *in Ode xxxix.* 7

The Ode might be entitled "On the Crossing of Mighty Rivers." It begins thus, "Mighty² rivers are the power of the Lord, and they carry away, head downwards³, those who despise Him⁴." In the poetry of Israel, celebrating the deliverances of the nation by Jehovah, the Euphrates would be one of the "mighty rivers," and the Nile, or the Red Sea, would be the other. Strictly described, the Red Sea is not

---

¹ Its frequency is disguised by the fact that our English versions render it by many different words, "anguish," "distress," "sorrow," "strait," "tribulation." Comp 1 S. xxviii. 15 with 2 S xxiv. 14 (rep. 1 Chr. xxi 13), where Saul is made to say "I am sore distressed," but David "I am in a great strait." Yet, in the Hebrew, both use precisely the same words, and in the same order.

² The Syr. "mighty," as verb or adj (*Thes.* 3003) is used of the "*overpowering*" waters of the Deluge in Gen. vii. 18 (and Wisd. x. 18), and then of the cry of Sodom, of famine, and of crushing task-work, in Gen xviii 20, xliii. 1, Exod v. 9, &c. It is used of the waters of the Euphrates in Is. viii. 7, and of "*mighty* rivers" in Ps lxxiv. 15. See below, p 440, n. 3.

³ "Head downwards" is a phrase used (*Thes* 626) to describe the crucifixion of St Peter Here it seems to mean sunk deep, and past helping.

⁴ Ode xxxix 1—2. Comp. Rom. ix 22, "Willing to shew his *wrath*, and to *make his power known*," with the refrain in Exodus about Pharaoh's being forced to "*know*" the Lord It begins in Exod vii 5 "the Egyptians *shall know* that I am the Lord," rep vii 17, viii. 10, &c. Pharaoh had "despised" the Lord and said (*ib.* v. 2) "I *know not* the Lord" The "mighty river" was "the power of the Lord" upon him, in return for his "despising," and it "carried him away."

THE INTERPRETATION

a "river"; but, being "the tongue of the Egyptian sea," it may be treated poetically as one with the hostile Dragon of Egypt, the Nile, and it is so treated in Scripture[1]. Moreover the same passage of Isaiah that describes the Nile as "the tongue of the Egyptian sea," also speaks of the Euphrates, as being preeminently "*the River*[2]"—the mightiest of "mighty rivers"—the crossing of which was the emblem of Israel's return from captivity in Babylon, as the crossing of the Egyptian Sea was the emblem of Israel's release from bondage in Egypt. In an earlier passage Isaiah contrasts this "mighty river" of God's wrath and judgment with His own gentle waters: "Forasmuch as this people hath refused the waters of Shiloah that go softly...therefore, behold, the Lord bringeth up upon them the waters of *the River*, strong and *many* (Syr. *mighty*) [even] the king of Assyria[3]"

The Ode proceeds to shew how these "mighty rivers" are to be crossed. There is to be a "*sign* (or, *ensign*[4])" in them,

---

[1] See Is xi 15—16 "The Lord shall utterly destroy *the tongue of the Egyptian sea* [i.e. the Red Sea] and shall shake his hand over the River ...and there shall be an high way. .from Assyria, like as there was for Israel in the day that he came out of the land of Egypt." Also comp Is xix 5 "the waters shall fail from *the sea*," where Field has "de *mari* [*Nilo*]," and where R V marg refers to Ezek xxxii 2 "Thou [*i e.* Pharaoh] art as a dragon in the *seas* and thou brakest forth in thy *rivers* .."

There appears to be an allusion to the Dragon of Egypt, sending forth a pursuing stream after Israel, in Rev. xii. 15 "*The serpent* cast out of his mouth, after the woman, *water as a river*" "*The earth*" saves Israel, (ib) "*The earth* opened her mouth and *swallowed up the river*" So in Exodus (xv. 12) "Thou stretchedst out thy right hand; *the earth swallowed them* [i e. *the Egyptians*]"

[2] So the Targum and Rashi And so R V. marg. which refers to Is. vii 20 "with a razor...in the parts beyond *the River*, [even] with the king of Assyria" On "the River" meaning Euphrates see Gesen 625 *b*

[3] Is. viii. 7. Comp Wisd x. 18 "*much* (πολλοῦ) water" (of the Red Sea which drowned the Egyptians) Syr. *mighty*

[4] The Syriac for "ensign" corresponds to Heb. "banner" or "ensign" (*Thes* 413) in Is. v. 26, xxx. 17, Jerem. iv. 6, Ezek. xxvii. 7, to which add Ps. lx 4 "thou hast given an *ensign* to them that fear thee" The radical meaning of the Heb. is (Gesen. 651) "raised-up-as-a-signal."

and it is said, "*The ensign* in them is the Lord, and *the ensign* is the way of those who cross in the name of the Lord. Put on, therefore, the name of the Most High, and know Him" And now come the words for the discussion of which we have been so long preparing ourselves —"And ye shall cross *without danger*, for the rivers will be subject to you[1]." And the question arises, Are we to infer from the context in the Ode, and from the illustrative passages adduced from Exodus and Isaiah, that this phrase, unique in the Odes, alludes to some phrase contained in the Hebrew poetry that describes the Crossing of the Sea by Israel, or does it simply mean—as it almost certainly would, if the Poet thought in Greek, and probably would if he composed in Greek—"in safety," "without the slightest risk[2]"?

The answer appears to be that a *prima facie* case has been made out for supposing that the Poet *thought*, even if he did not write, in Hebrew—because the conception of "mighty rivers" as God's chastising instruments is much more prominent in Hebrew than in Greek—but that he may very well have regarded the Red Sea as being passed over by Israel, as Isaiah says, "dry shod[3]," *i.e.* without the slightest risk, so that the Greek *kindūnos*, with a negative, would suit his meaning. It is true that Aquila renders the Hebrew "strait" by *kindūnos*. But where (it may be asked) can we find in Scripture the Hebrew "strait" used in a negative phrase? It occurs abundantly in positive phrases, such as David's "I am in a great strait," but nowhere do we find in Scripture such a phrase as "*no strait*" meaning "*no extreme peril*"

This is true, so far as concerns the text of our English versions of Scripture And, if it were also true of Hebrew Scripture, we could go no further in our attempt to explain

---

[1] Ode xxxix. 7.
[2] That would be the natural meaning of ἀκίνδυνος, see Steph. *Thes.* quoting Eurip. *Iph. A.* 17 where the word goes with ἀγνώς and ἀκλεής
[3] Is. xi 15

THE INTERPRETATION

"no danger" in the Syriac before us from a similar phrase in Hebrew. But we shall now shew that the Hebrew "*no strait*" occurs in the following circumstances. (1) It is used in the written Hebrew text (as distinct from the Hebrew oral version) of a passage in Isaiah (2) Although this rendering is rejected by the text of our Revised Version, it is retained (in some form) by the Targum, the Syriac, and Theodotion, and is supported by Rashi. (3) It is connected in Isaiah's context with the name of "Moses," and with the crossing of the Red Sea. (4) The context in the Ode mentions an "ensign" for those who cross, and also a "way" made for them through the deep; and Isaiah, in a previously quoted passage, where he describes the two rivers—namely, "the tongue of the Egyptian Sea" and "the River [Euphrates]"—also mentions an "ensign" of "the peoples" and for "the nations," and a "high way for the remnant of his people[1]." (5) "*No strait*" does not occur anywhere in the Bible except in the passage of Isaiah above mentioned and now to be commented on[2].

§ 17. "*No*[*t*] *strait*," *in Isaiah* (lxiii. 9, *Heb*)

This passage—according to the tradition called Masora, which (in, or about, the eighth century) aimed at fixing the correct reading of the Scriptures[3]—was one of fifteen where "*not* is written by error for *to him*[4]" The word for "*strait*" is the above-mentioned *tsar*, and the feminine *tsarah* occurs in the context thus· "In all their *straitening* (*tsarah*) [there was] *no*[*t*] *strait* (*tsar*)[5]" This may be interpreted as meaning

---

[1] Ode xxxix. 6 "*ensign*" (twice), *ib* 6, 11 "*way*", Is. xi. 10 "*ensign* of the peoples," *ib*. 12 "*ensign* for the nations," *ib*. 16 "*a high way*"

[2] This appears from Mandelkern, p. 1005.

[3] Gratz, Eng. transl. iii. 114 Etymologically, "Masora" means "tradition." But it has come to mean the peculiar "tradition" described above

[4] Gesen. 520 *b*. "By error" represents the view of the Masora, not the fact (see Gesen.).

[5] So Walton "In omni angustia eorum non angustia."

442

"In all the *straitening* of Israel there was *no* [*real*] *strait*"— that is, no cause for despair, "because God, while allowing them to suffer tribulation, could not allow them to be destroyed[1]." But this interpretation, it must be admitted, assumes a bold, brief, and obscure paradox, which might well deter some from accepting the negative, and the Targum and Rashi, who retain the negative, dilute the poetic paradox into prosaic and unsatisfactory paraphrases[2].

The result has been that in Rabbinical and in modern times the alteration of "*no*[*t*]" into "*to him*" has prevailed, "In all their straitening [there was] *to him straitening*," or, as in R.V text, "In all their affliction *he was afflicted*[3]." This rendering expresses a very beautiful thought, beautifully expressed in several Jewish traditions[4]. Jerome, calling attention to the

---

[1] Comp. 2 Cor. iv. 8 ἀπορούμενοι ἀλλ' οὐκ ἐξαπορούμενοι, i e "resourceless yet *not quite* (or, *not really*) *resourceless*," οὐκ ὄντως ἀπορούμενοι.

[2] Targ. (Walton). "In omni tempore quo peccaverunt coram eo ut adduceret super eos tribulationem, non tribulavit eos," i e "in all the time wherein they tempted Him by their sins to straiten them, He did not straiten them" (perhaps using Aram "straiten" (Levy *Ch* ii. 213—4) as "bring to destruction"); Rashi "In omni angustia eorum quam induxit super illos, non affecit angustia illos juxta eorundem opera," i.e "in all the straitening that He brought upon them, He did not straiten them in proportion to their [evil] works"

Jerome has, in his text, "In omni tribulatione eorum *non est tribulatus*" which he explains by adding "ut parumper eos desereret, et nudatos auxilio suo cogeret ad rogandum," i.e. (seemingly) "God did not share their straitening, but departed from them that they might miss and seek Him." But he adds with a "vel certe" denoting preference— "Nequaquam tribulavit eos, sed contrario, caeteris persequentibus, adjutor fuit," i.e. "He did not [*really*] straiten them, but on the contrary was [really] helping them" In all these passages "tribulare" is not the right word It should have been "angustiare," which is distinguished from the former in 2 Cor. iv. 8 (Vulg.) "*tribulationem* patimur sed non *angustiamur.*"

The Syriac has the negative, thus · "In cunctis calamitatibus eorum non afflixerit eos"

[3] But R V. marg. has the negative, thus. "In all their adversity he was *no adversary*"

[4] See *Son of Man* 3518*f*, 3550 *a* foll , to which add *Mechilt.* on Exod.

THE INTERPRETATION

twofold reading of the Hebrew, either as negative or as pronoun, illustrates the latter from Isaiah's description of the Suffering Servant[1], and the similarity would naturally predispose Christians after Jerome's time to accept the pronominal reading.

But we are dealing with an Ode of Solomon, a poem supposed (according to our working hypothesis) to have been written about as early as the end of the first century, and we do not find the LXX, or Theodotion, or the Syriac Version, or the Targum—greatly though they diverge from one another—supporting the alteration of the written Hebrew negative. Theodotion ("*no besieger*") is somewhat like our R V. margin, "*no adversary*[2]." The LXX has "From all their tribulation *no ambassador*[3]"—which needs special note, for two reasons. First, it comes as a climax to the evidence upholding the early date of the negative reading. Secondly, it shews that the author of the Odes, if he was alluding to this passage of Isaiah, *did not allude to the LXX, which has "no ambassador," but to the Hebrew, which has "no strait."*

That he was alluding to this passage of Isaiah appears to be made additionally probable by the notoriety attaching to its various interpretations in early times. And that he would prefer the terse paradoxical negative reading is consistent with his characteristic brevity. The paradox was

---

xvii 15, xix. 2 (Wu. pp. 178, 193), and *Exod. r.* on Exod. iii. 2 (Wu. pp 33—4) quoting Ps xci 15 "I am with him in straitness," as well as Is. lxiii. 9, and implying that God spoke "in the thorn-bush" as being "in straits" But *Sota* 31 *a* leaves the reading in Isaiah an open question.

[1] Jerome (on Is lxiii. 9) "in omni tribulatione eorum ipse est tribulatus, id est, Deus, ut non solum 'peccata' sed et 'tribulationes' nostras ipse portaret. Ipse enim 'infirmitates nostras portat et pro nobis dolet'"—a combination of Is. liii 4, Heb. "languores nostros ipse tulit, et dolores nostros ipse portavit," LXX "iste peccata nostra portat, et pro nobis dolet"

[2] Theod. οὐ πολιορκητής, i e "no one pressing them to extremity."

[3] This is explicable on the supposition that LXX read *tsir* (Gesen 851 *b*) for *tsar*, comp Is xxi 2 R V. "*besiege*," LXX "*ambassadors*."

illustrated above by the Pauline expression "resourceless, yet not utterly resourceless", but it is still more like "as deceivers and [yet] true, as unknown and [yet] well known, as dying and behold we live...as sorrowful but always rejoicing...as having nothing and [yet] possessing all things[1]."

§ 18. *The context in the Ode and the contexts in Isaiah*

Parallelisms between the Ode and Isaiah have been pointed out above, all illustrating the picture of Crossing the Deep. In the West, this metaphor did not spring out of the national history of the Greeks or Romans. But it was widely known in connection with the conveyance of the souls of the dead to the banks of the Styx under the guidance of Hermes with his magic wand. With Israel, the Crossing was not only national —being nationalised at the Red Sea and the Jordan—but also ancestral, since "Abraham the Hebrew" meant "Abraham the Crosser of the Euphrates[2]." The Christian Church accepted the Jewish Messiah as being all, and more than all, that was implied in the wand-bearing Hermes of the West, conveying the dead to the abodes of judgment. They also accepted Him as being all, and more than all, that was implied in the rod-bearing Moses of the East, parting the waters of the Red Sea, and leading his people from slavery into the Land of Promise and of Freedom. What, therefore, to Christians, would the Messiah's "wand" or "rod" naturally become? Above, we noted that both the Ode and Isaiah speak not only of "mighty rivers" and of a "way" across them, but also of an "ensign" in connection with the Crossing. And here the question arises as to the nature of this "ensign."

In the passage where Isaiah connects the Crossing with the name of Moses, he makes no mention of "*ensign*," but only of

---

[1] 2 Cor iv 8, vi 8—10

[2] See *Light on the Gospel* **3948**, quoting Philo on Abraham the Perātēs, and also on the Nile and the Euphrates in connection with Abraham

the "*spirit*," or "*arm*," as representing God's presence: "Where is he that put *his holy spirit* in the midst of them? that caused his glorious *arm* to go at the right hand of Moses? that divided the water before them...¹?" Elsewhere, as interpreted by Aquila, Isaiah says "He shall come as a river [that is] straitening, *the spirit of the Lord is an ensign in it*²." With this we must compare the Song of Moses which says, according to the Hebrew, "Thou didst *blow with thy spirit* (or, *wind*), the sea covered them," but according to Onkelos, "Thou didst *speak by thy Word*, the sea covered them³." Here it seems that the invisible "*spirit*," acting through the invisible "wind⁴" for the deliverance of Israel, and clearing a way for them through the waters, might be regarded as being the "spirit" and the "arm" at the right hand of Moses. But the visible representative of "the spirit" would naturally be that "rod" of which God said to Moses "Lift thou up thy *rod*, and stretch out thine hand over the sea and divide it⁵."

It may be objected, however, that the Ode makes no mention of a "rod." And further, against the hypothesis of allusion to the Crossing of the Red Sea, it may be urged that there is an apparent incompatibility between the picture in the Ode and the picture in Exodus, as to the nature of the "way" across the deep. Alluding to Exodus, the Psalmist says, "Thy way [was] in the sea, and *thy footsteps were not known*⁶." But the Ode says "And His footprints *stand [firm] in the water, and are not destroyed*; but *they are like a tree* (or, *beam*) *that is firm-set in truth*"—a thought repeated, though

---

¹ Is lxiii. 11—12. For the earlier context mentioning "ensign," see p. 442, n. 1.

² Is. lix. 19 (Aq.) ἐλεύσεται ὡς ποταμὸς στενὸς (*tsar*), πνεῦμα κυρίου σύσσημον ἐν αὐτῷ, R V. txt "He shall come as a rushing stream, which the breath of the Lord driveth," marg. "when the adversary...standard against him." ³ Exod. xv. 10.

⁴ Comp Ps civ 4 (R V. marg) "Who maketh his angels winds."

⁵ Exod xiv. 16.

⁶ Ps lxxvii 19 A V. "are not known," R.V. "were not known."

varied, in the next verse, which says that, in spite of the waves, "*The footprints of our Lord the Messiah remain firm and are not effaced and not destroyed, and a way has been appointed for those who cross after Him*[1]."

But in truth there is no incompatibility; there is only development. The Poet does not deny that, in the old days, the "footsteps" were "not known" But he asserts that now, in the new days, the "footsteps" remain "firm-set," and constitute a permanent "way" for those who will follow the Lord. We may illustrate the difference by the difference of the language of Mark—about the momentary "rending" of the heavens on the occasion of Christ's baptism—from the language imputed afterwards to Jesus by the Fourth Gospel, "Ye shall see the heaven opened [once for all] and the angels of God ascending and descending upon the Son of Man[2]."

No doubt, the metaphor of planting implied in "firm-set as a tree" seems very far away from anything in the picture of Israel's passage through the waters. But it would be better to say "seems *to us*." For it happens that a Jewish tradition on the Levitical precepts as to "planting," quotes in connection with them this very verse from the Psalms about the "foot-prints" of the Lord. "How can we possibly '*follow*' God," asks the Rabbi, "as Scripture bids us? For '*His way was in the sea*[3].'" The reply given is, in effect, that we can "*follow*" Him spiritually, by imitating His "*planting*" in Eden[4], that is, by cultivating a life that brings forth good fruit Nor is this so far-fetched as it seems. It is only a superficial or childish view of the Path through the Waters to regard it as merely "the great work which the Lord did upon the Egyptians[5]." That was

---

[1] Ode xxxix. 9—11.

[2] Jn 1. 51 ἀνεῳγότα, on which see *Son of Man* **3376**, comp. **3136** Comp Mk 1 10 σχιζομένους.

[3] *Lev. r.* (on Lev. xix. 23, Wu p. 167) quoting Deut. xiii. 4 and Ps. lxxvii. 19

[4] Gen 11 8   [5] Exod xiv 31

THE INTERPRETATION

but the means to an end. The fuller and maturer view regards the end, and is positive, not negative: "Till the people pass over which thou hast purchased; thou shalt *bring them in and plant them in the mountain of thine inheritance*[1]." The "great work" of "swallowing up[2]" or eradicating the evil is but a small part of the infinitely greater work of "planting" the good.

Why does not the Ode mention the Messiah's "rod" as dividing the waters of Sheol, and as the "sign" in the new Exodus corresponding to the "rod" of Moses in the old one? Perhaps because—having regard to the aspect of "the rod of God" as "a rod of iron"—the Poet preferred the metaphor of the "tree." He has previously mentioned the "*rod*" in connection with the Lord's "*sign*[3]." But he appears not to mention it again in the whole of the Odes. And there, it is as an emblem of "*power*," an inferior attribute: "He led me in His light and gave me *the rod of His power*." This is the western and perhaps the cosmopolitan view of the "rod" or "sceptre" of kings. But the story about Aaron's rod, which brought forth leaves, flowers, and fruit, might naturally help to establish in the minds of devout Jews a connection between "a rod of God," or "sceptre of God," and a "tree," not prominent—and perhaps not existent—in western literature[4].

To add to the multiplicity of metaphors, open to a Jewish poet of the first century singing of the Rod of Moses as the type of the Cross of Christ, Isaiah, in one and the same

---

[1] Exod. xv. 16—17
[2] Exod. xv. 12, see p 440, n. 1
[3] Ode xxix 7. See *Light on the Gospel* 3958 as to the reading, and the allusion, and the traditions about "the rod of God" Harnack's Index gives no other instance of "rod" in the Odes. The context mentions "subduing" and "overthrowing." Comp *Light* 3913 "It was characteristic of Hebrew thought to assume that WORD or NAME had more power over the forces of evil than the rod, mace, or sceptre, of a king If rod was to be used, it must be as Isaiah says (xi. 4) 'the rod of his mouth'"
[4] Numb xvii. 8 (Heb. 25).

passage that predicts a Messianic "rod," uses two words, the first of which might suggest, at least to readers of the Greek versions of the Scriptures, the thought of the "wand" of Hermes, the Conductor of departed souls. "There shall come," he says, "a *rod* (or, *shoot*) out of the stock of Jesse, and a branch out of his roots shall bear fruit," and then "he shall smite the earth with the *rod* (or, *sceptre*, or, *club*) of his mouth," and later on, concerning "the root of Jesse," that it "standeth for an *ensign* of the peoples," and, "unto him shall the nations seek[1]." Now here both Rashi and Ibn Ezra take the rare Hebrew word meaning "*rod* (or, *shoot*)" as "sceptre" or "rod" (not, as "shoot"); and Aquila renders it by the diminutive "wand-ling" (*rabdion*) This, though it might mean "twig," is applied both by Epictetus and by Babrius to the wand of Hermes by which he "calls forth souls from Orcus[2]," and is applied by them in such a way as to indicate a customary or proverbial application[3]

---

[1] Is xi 1, 4, 10 "*Rod* (or, *shoot*)" is חטר (LXX ῥάβδος), which occurs only here and Prov xiv. 3 (LXX βακτηρία), "*rod* (or, *sceptre*, or, *club*)" is שׁבט, rendered by LXX ῥάβδος (24), σκῆπτρον (15), but here, because of the metaphor ("rod of his mouth") λόγος A third word, מטה, "*rod* (or, *staff*)" is rendered by LXX ῥάβδος (48), σκῆπτρον (2), and this is used of Aaron's "rod" A fourth word, מקל, "*rod* (or, *stick*)" is rendered by LXX βακτηρία (4), ῥάβδος (14), and is used of the traveller's "staff" with which Jacob (Gen. xxxii. 10) "passed over Jordan"

[2] Virgil *Aeneid* iv 242

[3] ‛Ραβδίον does not occur in LXX, nor again in translations of the Bible exc Prov xiv 3 (Theod) Gesen 310 *b* gives the Heb word as occurring elsewhere only in Prov xiv 3 (R V. txt) "*rod*," marg. "*shoot*" Steph *Thes* quotes Babr. 117, 9. Epictet iii. 20 12 says "This is *the* [*true*] *wand* (*rabdion*) *of Hermes*" It is not an outside "wand," he adds, that turns dross to gold, it is an inside "wand" by which we can turn calamities to blessings, "all these things will be made profitable by the [true] *wand of Hermes.*" Cicero *De Off.* 1 44 158 "*virgula* divina, *ut aiunt*" indicates that the diminutive was used in Latin also, proverbially, to mean "magic wand"

Since Hermes is called χρυσόρραπις, there may be an allusion to his "golden wand" in the saying of Epictetus about turning anything, at pleasure, to gold But the epithet also invites illustration from the

THE INTERPRETATION

Thus, by Christians, one and the same emblem, the Cross of Christ[1], might be regarded as a Wand of Power dividing the waters of Sheol, and also a Sign or Standard for Christ's saints following in His footsteps, and also as a Bridge or Way from death to life appointed for future ages, and lastly as a Tree of Life set up in the very depth of the sea of sin. This last is indeed a bold metaphor. Israel was "baptized" (Paul says) in the Red Sea, and Barnabas speaks of the "*tree* planted *by the courses of waters*" as meaning the Cross and Baptism[2]. But the Ode seems to mean more than this. Perhaps it looks forward to a time when the waters of Sheol are to be dried up, and, as Revelation says, "The sea is no more[3]" It prepares the way for the picture brought before us in one of the versions of the Descensus ad Inferos: "And the Lord *set His Cross in the midst of Hades,* which is the sign of victory, and which will remain even to eternity[4]."

Golden Bough, which was a passport across the Styx (*Aeneid* vi 140—4, where perhaps "*virga,*" "branch," is used allusively in "...aureus, et simili frondescit *virga* metallo") The Caduceus of heralds is said to have been (Lewis and Short) "orig. an olive-stick with στέμματα"

[1] See *From Letter to Spirit* 928 (1)—(x) on "taking up the cross," where the conclusion is that "it was not a Roman custom to bear the cross "— *i e* the massive vertical post fixed in the earth and "at least 13 ft. long"— "but only to bear the *patibulum, furca*, or '*yoke*'" The Jewish phrase "take the yoke upon thee" would prepare the way for the interpretation "take the cross upon thee" Thus the old Roman word "furcifer" would prepare the way for the new Christian word "crucifer" It is obvious that the upright part, and the transverse part, of the Cross would lend themselves to different metaphors The former would suggest (among other things) a standard or tree, the latter, a way-mark.

[2] 1 Cor x 2   Barn § 11 (quoting Ps 1 3)   He says that the Psalm means "Blessed are they who, placing their trust in the Cross, have gone down into the water"

[3] Rev xxi. 1 "And I saw a new heaven and a new earth...and the sea is no more."

[4] *Descens ad Inf* (Lat 2nd Vers.) § 10 (26). The Greek Version represents Jesus as apparently bringing the Cross into Hades, when Jesus says § 8 (24) "For I, behold, am again raising you all up through the tree (ξύλου) of the Cross"

§ 19. *Conclusion*

These details have led us away from the merely verbal question as to the explanation of the Syro-Greek *kindūnos* in one of the Odes. But they have led us back to the subject of this Appendix, which is the Interpretation of Early Christian Poetry And on that subject they will have thrown light if they have helped us to discern, in the Odes as a whole, a transition of Jewish thought passing from a pre-Christian into a Christian atmosphere. We may see something like it in Justin Martyr's view of the "rod[1]." But Justin piles type on type, not always accurately, and never with any sense of poetic symbolism, proportion, or development[2]. The author

---

[1] See *Tryph* § 86, where the text, unaltered, can be explained as follows. Justin says he will shew that, "*after Christ was crucified*, He had with Him the symbol of the Tree of Life," *i e* the Cross, "and [the symbol] of those things that should come to pass for all the righteous," *i e* for their redemption This might refer to Jesus, after death, carrying His Cross into Hades Then Justin mentions the "rod" of Moses, and the "tree" that Moses cast into the waters of Marah, and the "rods" that Jacob put into water-troughs, and the "rod" with which Jacob "boasted that he had crossed the river," and Aaron's "rod" which blossomed, and the "rod" that (according to Isaiah) was to "come forth from the root of Jesse."

[2] After mentioning the "rod from the root of Jesse," Justin (*Tryph* § 86) passes to (Ps i. 3) the "tree planted by the courses of waters," and to God's appearance "from a tree to Abraham" in Mamre, and to "seventy willows and twelve springs" found by Israel "after crossing *the Jordan*" Here "Jordan" is an error for "Red Sea" He goes on to quote, as types, not only the "rod and staff" with which "David affirms that God comforted him," but also the "*tree*" or "*stick*" (2 K vi. 6, ξύλον) which Elisha cast into the river Jordan, in order to recover the axe-head, "even as our Christ, by being crucified on the *tree*, and by purifying [us] through water, redeemed us, though sunk (βεβαπτισμένους) in the most grievous sins ."

Justin's substitution of "Jordan" for "Red Sea" raises the question of the similarity, and the dissimilarity, of the two narratives of Crossing, regarded symbolically. Comp *Light on the Gospel* **3965** "It [*i e* the rod] is a sign-post, or way-mark, that not only points out the way, but also is 'the Way'—the way across the waters of temptation and death, *our Red*

of the Odes, on the other hand, here as elsewhere, in dealing with the Christian "sign" or "ensign," appears to be poetically developing the two ancient types (1) of Moses "*stretching forth*" his hand or his rod, and (2) of Moses "*spreading forth*" his hands[1] The former may be regarded as an attack on sin, the latter as an intercession for sinners. By a slight alteration of the former[2], the Poet includes both in the Cross of Christ, where the hands may be regarded as "stretched forth" in victory and "spread forth" in prayer. As compared with the thoughts of Justin concerning the Cross, the thoughts of the author of the Odes appear not only more poetic and more consistent, but also closer to what would probably be the transitional Jewish-Christian conceptions of the first century.

It is peculiarly important for those students whose pasture in ancient literature has been mostly "classical" to recognise that every thought in the New Testament, and every verbal association, for which no parallel or illustration has been alleged from the Greek and Latin authors with whom they are familiar, should be examined with the *prima facie* assump-

---

Sea and our Jordan" I am now disposed to believe that the thought of the passage of the Jordan is overshadowed in the Odes by the thought of the Red Sea Origen (*Lib Jesu Nave Hom* 1. 4) draws a striking contrast between the two But a Christian development of the Passage of the Red Sea might borrow from the Passage of the Jordan the setting up of the twelve stones (Josh iv 5—21) as a permanent memorial, and might apply it to "the sign," "the rod," or "the tree"

[1] Exod ix 22—33 In ix 33 "*spread forth* his hands," the LXX has "*stretched forth* the hands," erroneously. See *Notes on N T Criticism* 2926—34, on the Christian use of ἐκτείνω χεῖρας (as compared with the Hebrew use of ἐκτείνω χεῖρα) and its bearing on Jn xxi 18 "thou shalt *stretch forth thy hands*" Also see *Light on the Gospel* 3951—82, on "sign" in the Odes, and on "sign" and "spreading out" In Odes xxvii 1—3, xlii 1—3, the "spreading-out" and the "stretching-out" are mentioned close together, with the apparent purpose of distinguishing them.

[2] *I.e* substituting "hands" for "hand" In LXX, "stretch out the hands," plural, is very rare (*Notes on N T Criticism* 2928) and never a legitimate rendering of Hebrew

tion that the thought or verbal association is derived from Hebrew or Aramaic literature with which they are unfamiliar. They may not succeed in tracing such a derivation. But they are bound to make the attempt Common sense, as well as common modesty, demands this

Take, for example, the first clause in that Pauline list of the "dangers" of a Christian Missionary. It follows the statement that he is "in journeyings often"—a word used twice out of four times in LXX concerning the Exodus of Israel[1]. Then the "dangers" are enumerated, and it will be seen that the first of them bears on the subjects—the "mighty rivers" and the "danger"—that have been brought before us in the Odes of Solomon: "*Dangers from* (lit. *of*) *rivers*, dangers from (lit *of*) robbers, dangers from [my own] nation, dangers from Gentiles, dangers within city [walls], dangers in wilderness[es] [outside], dangers at sea, dangers among falsebrethren...[2]." Origen twice quotes clauses from this passage including the first clause, but on neither occasion does he place it in the Pauline order; Heliodorus, apparently imitating the Pauline passage, omits the first clause, and Wetstein, while illustrating from Plutarch "dangers at sea" and "in wilderness[es]," gives no ancient illustration of "dangers from rivers"[3]. The Greek Thesaurus gives no instance of the

---

[1] Wisd. xviii 3, xix. 5 (the other instances are Wisd. xiii. 18, 1 Mac. vi. 41). In N.T, it occurs elsewhere only in Jn iv. 6 "wearied by his *journeying*" [2] 2 Cor xi 26

[3] *Comm. Rom* i 3 (Lomm vi 18) " in frigore et nuditate, periculis latronum, *periculis fluminum*, periculis maris," *ib* iv 8 (Lomm vi 289—90) " qui in periculis saepe versetur, periculis maris, *periculis fluminum*, periculis latronum, periculis in falsis fratribus "

Wetstein illustrates from Plutarch's *De Exilio*, p 603 E, "going-astray (πλάνας) in wilderness[es] (ἐρημίᾳ) and dangers at sea (ἐν θαλάσσῃ)," and from Heliodorus ii 4 κινδύνοις θαλασσῶν, κινδύνοις πειρατερίων .λῃσταῖς— where note that Heliodorus, if he is imitating Paul, drops "dangers from rivers." Comp Epict. iii. 13 13 ἐμοὶ σεισμὸς οὐκ ἔστιν...πᾶσα ὁδός, πᾶσα πόλις...ἀβλαβής—where there is no mention of "rivers" in the long list of things from which most people anticipate harm

phrase. Why does Paul not only use it but also place it first in the list of all his "dangers"?

The answer is probably this. Paul is thinking not only of himself as the recently appointed apostle, or missionary, to the Gentiles, but also of Israel, the spiritual Israel, as the Missionary appointed from of old—represented by the Messiah, but also bound to serve the Lord nationally and individually as His missionaries—receiving the promise of divine protection "Fear not, for I have redeemed thee... *When thou passest through the waters*, I will be with thee; and *through the rivers*, they shall not overflow thee, when thou walkest through the fire, thou shalt not be burned, neither shall the flame kindle upon thee[1]." He is thinking also of Abraham, the "Hebrew," or Perātēs, or Crosser, and of Jacob, and of Moses, all of whom received, in various ways, the protection of the divine Presence when they "passed through the waters," or "through rivers"[2]. Hence, with a Jewish instinct, he places "dangers from rivers" first. No Gentile writer would have naturally written thus, and the phrase does not come to Gentile readers without some sense of strangeness.

It is futile to urge, against these arguments from Hebrew history and literature, that Paul was referring to literal fact, and to say "he had been actually endangered in his missionary journeying, by swollen streams and floods." Who denies it? So had Gentiles, many a time, been similarly endangered, when journeying under pressure. But no Gentile in the whole of the vast region of extant Gentile literature, is alleged to have given to such a "danger" the Pauline prominence. Until such instances or at least one instance is alleged, we

---

[1] Is. xliii 2. Rashi explains "waters" as "Red Sea" ("quando transivisti per mare Suph, tecum fui") and "rivers" as the nations among which Israel sojourned and yet was not destroyed ("commoratus es inter Ægyptios atque populos [alienigenas] qui multitudine similes fuerunt aquis fluminis, nec tamen te consumere potuerunt")
[2] See *Light on the Gospel* **3948**

ought in fairness to say: "Paul appears to be thinking as a Jew. The Jews were given to proselytizing. They compassed sea and land—so we read in Matthew—to make one proselyte When their preachers went forth, trusting in the divine protection, and came to any obstacle or danger, literal or metaphorical, that checked their advance, it was natural for them to think of it as a river. Sometimes it might be an actual river or a sea, but whether it was or was not, it was natural for them to think of their prospective proselytes as calling to them and saying, not '*Come*,' but '*Come across*, and help us'[1]"

The study of this Pauline passage supports the conclusion that the language of the version of the Odes from which the present Syriac was translated is less important than the character of the Scriptures, and the traditions about the Scriptures, from which the author derived his knowledge of Hebrew literature Even supposing the Odes to have been composed in Hebrew, the present Syriac may have been translated, not from the original Hebrew, but from a Greek translation of it. This would be analogous to the now generally accepted explanation of II Esdras (4 Ezra). That work dates from about the same period as I have ventured to assign to the Odes, namely, 100 A D. or a little later. That the Latin text of 4 Ezra is a translation from Greek is (I believe) now regarded as certain, and that the Greek was a translation from an original Hebrew text is made probable if not certain by recent

---

[1] Comp Acts xvi. 9. The phrase "pass through (*or*, across) rivers" is used by Rabbi Jochanan about a zealous and audacious teacher of what the Rabbi regarded as heretical doctrine, imported into Jerusalem from Babylon "O Babylonian, *thou hast passed through three rivers* and spoken fiction," (Levy 1. 193) "du reistest durch drei Strome und sagtest Erdichtetes," referring to *j. Jeb. VIII.* 3. 9 *c*, and *j. Schabb. VII.* 1 9 *a*. Schwab iv 81, vii. 121, translates somewhat differently ("tu as su passer à pied sur trois fleuves," "tu as eu le courage de venir jusqu'ici, en traversant trois fleuves").

investigations¹. It is, of course, possible that the author of the Odes, while composing them in Greek, followed a Greek translation of the Scriptures that deviated from that of the LXX; but on the whole it appears to me probable that the author wrote in Hebrew, and certain that he *thought* in Hebrew, that is to say, like a poet saturated with the Hebrew Scriptures, as interpreted and amplified by Jewish traditions.

---

¹ See *The Ezra-Apocalypse*, by G. H Box, M A., London, 1912, pp. 1—xxxiii

www.ingramcontent.com/pod-product-compliance
Lightning Source LLC
Chambersburg PA
CBHW071233300426
44116CB00008B/1013